The
Canadian
Legal System

Fourth Edition

by

Gerald L. Gall
B.A., LL.B.

Member of the Ontario Bar
Professor of Law
The University of Alberta

With Chapter 8
The Legal System in Quebec
by F. Pearl Eliadis, B.C.L., LL.B., B.C.L. (Oxon.)

 CARSWELL

Canadian Cataloguing in Publication Data

Gall, Gerald L.
    The Canadian legal system

4th ed.
Includes bibliographical references and index.
ISBN 0-459-55376-3 (bound). – ISBN 0-459-55398-4 (pbk.)

1. Law – Canada.   I. Title.

KE444.G35 1995   349.71   C95-932670-7
KF385.G35 1995

 The paper used in this publication meets the minimum requirements of American National Standard for Information Sciences — Permanence of Paper for Printed Library Materials, ANSI Z39.48-1984.

Thomson Professional Publishing

One Corporate Plaza, 2075 Kennedy Road, Scarborough, Ontario M1T 3V4
Customer Service:
Toronto 1-416-609-3800
Elsewhere in Canada/U.S. 1-800-387-5164
Fax 1-416-298-5094

DEDICATED

To the memory of my father and mother
ROBERT GALL and ROSE GALL

To my wife
KAREN

and to my children
MELANIE, WENDY and ANDREW

FOREWORD TO THE FOURTH EDITION

The Canadian legal system has increasingly become the subject of debate in Canadian society. There have been recent calls for reform in several areas of the law — from demands for change in the criminal justice system to insistence on recognition of the rights of previously marginalized groups. Of great concern to all Canadians has been the continuing debate over whether there should be constitutional change, and if so, what form that change should take.

Perhaps now more than ever, then, it is incumbent on Canadians to develop a better understanding of their legal system and its role in Canadian society as a whole. In order to participate in a meaningful way in the debate about change, Canadians must have an appreciation of the law and the system within which it is administered.

Professor Gall's text, *The Canadian Legal System*, now in its fourth edition, continues to provide comprehensive instruction on the fundamental principles of the legal system, and its relationship to the larger society it serves.

The text is accessible and useful to laypersons and legal specialists alike. It begins with a general exploration of the nature of law itself, including its sources, traditions and functions, and then goes on to discuss the unique form the legal system has taken in Canada. It canvasses the history, and explains the doctrinal underpinnings of the common and civil law traditions which form the core of the Canadian system. An all-new chapter provides an in-depth discussion of the Quebec legal system, and its relationship with the system found in the rest of Canada. The book outlines the fundamental divisions, and their constitutional bases, of power and responsibility in both the Canadian government and judiciary. The final chapter provides a projection of the direction in which changes in the legal system are developing.

Professor Gall recognizes that any true understanding of the law requires an understanding of the complex interrelationship between it and the various component parts of society as a whole; his text endeavours to provide the information essential to that understanding in an accessible and instructive form. He deserves our thanks for this further invaluable contribution to an understanding of the law.

December, 1995   The Honourable Chief Justice Allan McEachern
                        Chief Justice of British Columbia

FOREWORD TO THE THIRD EDITION

For a work on the Canadian legal system to be in its third edition is the best evidence of its usefulness and its reception by the public. The reader will find the same qualities of clarity, conciseness and comprehensiveness in the additional sections and notes covering the many developments which have occurred over the seven years since the second edition. The approach remains the same and covers the same broad scope ranging from legal philosophy to the workings of the courts and the new technology for legal research.

It will be found most helpful in many respects but particularly as an excellent introduction to the law for a broad public, as a primer for students of the law and as a starting point and guide to further research.

Two major chapters dealing respectively with "The Constitutional Basis of Legislative and Judicial Authority" and "The Role of Judges and Lawyers" are particularly important as they gather together considerable material which is widely dispersed and deal with subjects on which very little has been written dealing in a comprehensive fashion with the Canadian scene.

The third edition includes some additions for a more complete coverage, such as the paragraphs dealing with the Critical Legal Theory of Jurisprudence and an extensive bibliography of American writings on legal interpretation. More important is the updating to cover the many new developments including recent and even current events. Of special note are the sections related to the *Charter of Rights*, administrative law, the proposals for constitutional amendment, the independence of the judiciary and the appointment, removal and immunity of judges, Ontario court reform, alternative dispute resolution and a number of topics related to the practice of law, including specialization, legal ethics and technology.

These several additions are also reflected in the major revisions to the bibliographies which conclude the relevant chapters. Indeed, one is struck by the quantity and scope of legal writing in Canada in recent years. This in itself underscores the importance of works such as Professor Gall's both as an introduction and a guide. In fact, the length of these bibliographies may in the future call for some further guidance as to the areas of special interest of the various writings.

Having myself been trained in the civil law, I take this opportunity of commending Professor Gall for including a chapter on "The Quebec Legal System", written by Mr. Justice Paul Reeves of the Quebec Superior Court, as well as several comparative law references. At a time of great challenge to society and the law, there is every need for the creativity and the thinking of the best legal minds from all legal backgrounds. In Canada, we have the advantage of having direct access and indeed belonging to the two great legal traditions and systems in the world. With the advent of the *Charter* and international convenants on human rights, an approach to legal problems rooted in principle in the civilian tradition is of increasing importance in the evolution of law in Canada. One must beware that the great wealth of legal writing in each of these two systems not be an impediment to interest in and awareness of thinking and developments in the other traditions and that there is a need for writings that serve as introductions and links between them. Professor Gall is to be commended for his initiative in this and the encouragement it may be to others.

We owe our thanks and appreciation to Professor Gall for his continuing dedication and contribution to legal education and the understanding of the law by an ever broadening public.

The Honourable Charles D. Gonthier
Justice of the Supreme Court of Canada

May, 1990

FOREWORD TO THE SECOND EDITION

There is a story in the life of Martin Buber, the eminent philosopher, which appears to me to have relevance in the present context.

In the middle 1930's, when Hitlerism was bringing an ethical blackout to Germany and other countries, Martin Buber left Germany and came to live in Palestine, as it was then called. The Hebrew University of Jerusalem, sensing its good fortune in having this distinguished scholar within its midst, quickly arranged to add him to its faculty. One difficulty presented itself. The language of instruction of the Hebrew University was Hebrew. It was a language which Professor Buber, for all his awesome talents, did not speak. But exceptional situations give rise to exceptional remedies. The University authorities permitted Buber to give his lectures in German, with a translator present who rendered the subject matter into Hebrew. This was to be only a temporary arrangement, while Professor Buber immediately began the study of Hebrew to equip himself for the day when he would be able to teach in the University's official language.

That day did indeed come. One day a friend asked the great Professor how he was getting along with his lectures in Hebrew. Professor Buber replied, "I can lecture well enough in Hebrew to be underdstood. But I can't lecture well enough in Hebrew *not* to be understood."

That answer may have been given tongue in cheek. But it does draw attention to a frailty sometimes found in academic persons, namely, the deliberate desire to express themselves in language not readily comprehensible at a first reading. Such persons have elevated obscurity to the level of a principle.

When I read the work of an academic, I address myself to the question of whether the author belongs to the "obscurity" school or not. I addressed myself to that question in reading the present work. The verdict was one easy to reach and pleasant to announce. Professor Gerald Gall belongs to the "lucidity" school, not the "obscurity" school. Every page is written in clear, simple, translucent prose.

My joy with regard to the style of this book is exceeded only by my pleasure with its content. If, when I had put down the final page of The Canadian Legal System, I had been asked to state in one word what I liked best about this book, my answer would have been its *comprehen-*

siveness. For it deals with virtually every aspect of our legal system. With an economy of words the author has highlighed the essential features of the legal system of our country. Everything is there — the common law and statute law, the origin and development of equity, Canada's relationship to English law, our courts and the media, the adversarial system and its search for truth, the role of lawyers and judges in making the legal system work, the allegiance of bench and bar to codes of ethics, the doctrine of stare decisis and the role of decided cases as precedents, the problems involved in the interpretation of statutes, the function of administrative tribunals and their obligation to adhere to natural justice and rules of fairness, law in the computer age and the emergence of "jurimetrics", the function of legal aid in making possible greater access to the courts, and the recurring obligation of judges and lawyers to participate in programs of continuing legal education. These are only some of the topics in the book.

Do you ask about the civil law of Quebec? It's there, and Professor Gall acknowledges his gratitude to Mr. Justice Paul Reeves of the Quebec Superior Court for contributing that chapter. And the new Canadian Constitution, and its Charter of Rights and Freedoms, proclaimed by the Queen in Ottawa on April 17, 1982? It's there too. Indeed the author's chapter on this subject is one of the high points of the book. Any reader seeking enlightenment on the Constitution or the Charter could well make this chapter the starting point of his endeavours.

This brings me to a point that should be stated. Not all the topics in the book are explored in depth. The author probably had to make a choice. Should he deal more fully with the subjects before him, and thus end up with a book two or three times its present size? Or should he excise a number of those subjects, perhaps half, and give himself room to treat the remaining half in greater detail? Both of such courses have their obvious disadvantages. Instead, Professor Gall elected in favour of comprehensiveness, covering many topics, all of them adequately even if not completely. I think readers will agree that he made the wisest choice.

In his concluding chapter, dealing with new directions that law must take to meet the challenge of this technological age, Professor Gall says:

> In short, to borrow the words of s. 1 of our new Charter of Rights and Freedoms, we must preserve and protect the 'free and democratic society' that Canadians cherish. By the pursuit of innovative new directions, we can ensure that the Canadian legal system will continue to endure as a cornerstone of liberty and democracy in Canada.

Professor Gall's book is itself a significant step towards the attainment of that high objective.

The Honourable Samuel Freedman
Former Chief Justice of Manitoba

June, 1983

PREFACE TO THE FOURTH EDITION

It has now been 21 years since I was first approached by Carswell to write a treatise on the Canadian legal system and 18 years since the first edition was published. Indeed, at the time, I would not have believed that the project would have evolved into second, third and fourth editions. Now, on the occasion of the publication of the 4th edition, I am particularly excited by the fact that this is one of the few Canadian legal treatises that has resulted in a 4th edition.

The Canadian Legal System's international profile is also very satisfying. I have been told that the book has been seen in China, Israel, Australia, England, the United States, and elsewhere. Moreover, it is one of the few Canadian books (fiction or non-fiction) that is being published in Chinese in China. It has been translated by Professor Liu Yigong of Lanzhou University and published by the China Social Sciences Publishing House in Beijing. As well, *The Canadian Legal System* is also being translated (and published) into Japanese in Japan by Professor Ken Kuwahara, a professor of law at Aichi Gakuin University, a scholar who has studied and taught extensively in Canada and Japan.

Change is endemic to our legal system. In fact, over the past two decades, our legal system has experienced significant modification. For example, the practice of law has changed with the tremendous growth in the size of the practising bar. Large firms have become larger and these larger firms have, in turn, merged with other large firms. As a result, some major law firms are now national and international with branch offices around the world.

The courts are being restructured throughout Canada. Some courts are merging with others, which, in some jurisdictions, new courts are being created. The method of appointing our judges has undergone alteration. We now have a National Judicial Institute. This Institute, together with other agencies, is engaged in continuing education programs for judges, a phenomenon that was unheard of at the beginning of the 1970s, and which now constitutes a permanent feature of our judicial system.

New areas of the law have emerged (for example, entertainment law) and there have been substantive changes in existing areas of the law. We have seen, over the past thirteen years, the emergence of the Canadian Charter of Rights and Freedoms as probably the most important constitutional document in the nation's history. This has had the effect of transforming the Supreme Court of Canada into, essentially, a public law court with a Charter emphasis.

There continue to be many new directions in the Canadian legal system. Most notably, the marriage of law and technology has solidified in recent years.

But some things never change. It has been said that the greatest impediments to access to justice are the twin problems of cost and delay. It is still an unfortunate fact of life that for the average citizen to engage in litigation is still an extensive enterprise often marked by great delays.

This volume endeavours to capture all of the above changes as they relate to the essential features of our legal system.

I am always impressed by the competence and enthusiasm of law students in conducting various projects, and this project is no exception. May I thank those students who have assisted me on this project; namely, Cheryl-Ann Murray, Ken Armstrong, Lynn Moran, Karen Fleming, Mike Walker, Jacqueline Cullen and Patricia Strangeway. I also wish to thank the University of Alberta's Small Faculties Committee for the Advancement of Scholarship for providing funds for some of the above research assistance.

The Weir Memorial Library of the University of Alberta has always been supportive of each of the four editions of this book. In this case, may I acknowledge the support of Wanda Quoika-Stanka and Caron Rollins and others in the library system who have helped to find obscure references on a moment's notice.

I would also like to acknowledge the inspiration provided by the late William Henkel, Q.C., a former Assistant Deputy Attorney General of Alberta, in the continuing achievement of this project. In the third edition, I paid tribute to the late Honourable R.J. Matas of the Manitoba Court of Appeal. Both Mr. Henkel and the Honourable R.J. Matas were guiding lights and friends in the pursuit of my professional endeavours.

I am grateful to the Honourable Allan McEachern, the Chief Justice of British Columbia, for preparing the Foreword to the fourth edition. Chief Justice McEachern is a highly respected jurist. I have always enjoyed working with him on various projects in the past and I was delighted when he unhesitantly/readily agreed to prepare the Foreword.

I also wish to thank Pearl Eliadis, the Past-President of the Canadian Human Rights Foundation, who wrote the excellent chapter on The Legal System in Quebec. Ms Eliadis holds a civil law degree (together with common law and graduate common law degrees) and practised for a number of years in Quebec. She is presently the Director of Public Policy and Public Education at the Ontario Human Rights Commission.

I wish to gratefully acknowledge the staff of Carswell, including Bernie Aron, Catherine Campbell, and my production editor, Elizabeth Gillen. Ms Gillen is a highly competent and pleasant individual who brings a great deal of enthusiasm to her work.

My greatest debt of appreciation is owed to my wife, Karen, whose understanding and support are legion. More than that, however, she was invaluable in providing concrete help in the preparation of this work. Not only did she provide stenographic and computer assistance, but also she was always there to test a word, phrase and more importantly, an idea. As well, Karen prepared the index to all four editions of *The Canadian Legal System*. This book is dedicated to Karen, a tribute which she justly deserves.

Finally, I would like to acknowledge the continuing support and encouragement of my reading audience. I have had considerable feedback over the years and the message that emerges from my readers is that *The Canadian Legal System*, the book, has served to allow readers a comprehensible but understandable appreciation of the Canadian legal system, itself. In writing all four editions of this treatise, that has been my objective.

To those embarking upon a study of law, either in a formalized law school setting, or in pursuit of a casual but concerned interest, may I wish you every success in your endeavours. I hope this volume, in at least some measure, makes your journey more pleasant and, at the very least, more understandable.

December, 1995.   Gerald L. Gall
Edmonton, Alberta

TABLE OF CONTENTS

TABLE OF CASES

INTRODUCTION

Law essentially serves two functions in modern, western, industrial society. First, it serves to order and regulate the affairs of all "persons", be they individuals, corporations or governments. Secondly, law acts as a standard of conduct and morality, variously directed at individuals and groups, businesses and governments. In short, through both of these functions, the law seeks to promote and achieve a broad range of social objectives.

But law is not merley an abstract phenomenon. It can and does take many forms. Most important, our lives are ordered through a vast number of legislative enactments as well as an even far greater number of regulations passed thereunder. But, apart from this, much of the law may be found in the vast body of judicial pronouncements enunciated, most often by judges at appeal levels, in the decisions of our courts. This case law arises out of disputes in interpreting the complex and sometimes ambiguous language contained in statutory enactments or perhaps disputes as to the meaning or applicability of a particular rule of common law. The common law is that great body of law borne out of British legal tradition and built up and developed over centuries of judicial pronouncements.

Students of the law discover early that law is even more complex and flows from an even greater number of sources than depicted above. They also discover that, whatever the source, men must transmute this somewhat abstract notion of law into a breathing, living entity, with meaning and availability to all persons. This translating process has taken the form of creating intricately styled societal institutions. These institutions, in turn, must then function in the context of a complex and highly interwoven judicial system. The institutions must be manned by appropriately trained persons. And the entire machinery of interconnected institutions as part of a single, functioning system must operate in an orderly, efficient manner.

To do this, various customs, usages and conventions have been developed throughout the history of our British legal tradition. These include the notions of fairness and natural justice which are so vitally enshrined in the judicial administrative process. But our institutions have also been guided, not only by specific, technical procedural rules, but also by what might be described as prevailing judicial attitudes. These attitudes, somewhat akin in nature to historically derived customs and usages, are the basis of our common law system and include such notions as precedent and stare decisis, as well as the rules and principles of statutory interpretation. Indeed, the very process of construing statutes and documents consumes much of the time and energy expended by judges and practitioners of the law.

Nonetheless, however perfect the foregoing model appears, perfection must ultimately depend upon the acceptance of the system by those it governs in order to achieve its desired objectives. A legal system must command the support of the members of society, for without general social acceptance it simply cannot function, at least not in the context of liberal, democratic society.

Finally, the law must be regarded, as Lon Fuller once wrote, "as a dimension of human life".[1] As such, it can compel society to take one of many possible directions, the two extremes of which are set out by Professor Fuller in his treatise *Anatomy of the Law*:

> [Law] can appear as the highest achievement of civilization, liberating for creative use human resources otherwise dedicated to destruction. It can be seen as the foundation of human dignity and freedom, our best hope for a peaceful world. In man's capacity to perceive and legislate against his own defects we can discern his chief claim to stand clearly above the animal level. Philosophers of former ages have, indeed, not hestitated to see some kinship with the divine in man's ability to reorder his own faulty nature and in effect, to recreate himself by the rule of reason.
>
> A shift in mood and all this bright glitter surrounding the law can collapse into dust. Law then becomes man's badge of infamy, his confession of ineradicable perfidy.[2]

In Canada most people would agree that our legal system must strive to achieve the former direction of the two set out above. Indeed, presumably, that is the very motivation underlying any movement for law reform. Moreover, to regard law "as the foundation of human dignity and freedom" is philosophically and ideologically consistent with the basic, underlying values reflected in the Canadian Charter of Rights and Freedoms. However, for Professor Fuller's former direction to be successfully achieved it is necessary that all person working within the legal system possess a responsible awareness of the nature of the system, of the institutions within the system, of the roles expected of those persons manning these institutions, and of the judicial attitudes which bind all of the foregoing together into a simple, complex, functioning entity. That entity is the legal process in Canada. And it is the essential task of students of the law to examine, understand and critically appraise this process.

---

[1] Fuller, *Anatomy of the Law* (Mentor, 1969), p. 9.
[2] *Ibid.*

Chapter 1

THE NATURE OF LAW

Professor Philip S. James defines law as "a body of rules for the guidance of human conduct which are imposed upon and enforced among the members of a given state".[1] In offering that definition, the English legal scholar distinguished between the immutable laws of natural science and man-made law. He regards the latter as "a collection of rules of human conduct, prescribed by human beings for the obedience of human beings".[2] In further writings, he states that law "is a set of rules which form the pattern of behaviour of a given society"[3] and that law is "a set of rules which are generally obeyed and enforced within a politically organized society."[4] Professor James also discusses the somewhat vaguer distinction between man-made law and moral precepts. While it is indeed convenient for the student, upon embarking on a study of the Canadian legal system, to have a working definition of law such as that offered by Professor James, it is also a somewhat artificial starting point.

What is more important than a basic definition of law is the fundamental realization that law — be it in the nature of statutory law, judicial pronouncement, or otherwise — is merely one part of an overall functioning legal system. The positive law of a given state is but a single component of that overall system. As a result, the law must be studied in terms of its interrelationships with the various other components of the legal system. In short, it is far more important to begin a study of our legal system with a definition of the system as the sum of its constituent parts. In turn, it is of even more fundamental importance to provide a definitional framework to the very process by which that sum operates as a working and meaningful entity. An understanding of this process provides the clearest appreciation of the nature of the Canadian legal system and its

---

[1] *Introduction to English Law* (London: Butterworths, 1962), p. 5.

[2] *Ibid.*, p. 4.

[3] P. James, *Introduction to English Law* 12th ed. (London: Butterworths, 1989), p. 3.

[4] *Ibid.*, p. 5.

constituent elements. Accordingly, an examination of the nature of law more appropriately becomes an examination as to the nature of the legal process itself.

The legal process may thus be considered as the vehicle by which our legal system operates in order to govern and enforce the conduct of the people of Canada and in order to promote the best interests of the people as a whole. As well, the legal process is the vehicle by which we resolve disputes in a just, orderly and peaceful fashion when they arise.

It is also important to realize that the legal process is part of an overall complex of interacting processes that form the lifeblood of modern, western, industrial society. It is fundamental, but absolutely essential to appreciate this basic notion. Our society functions through the interaction of a complex matrix of highly interrelated processes. Our society can be looked at in terms of our economic system and the economic processes inherent within that system, or it can be examined in terms of our political system, including the political processes which define the nature of our political system. Even our individual interactions as well as our group and social interactions, according to the conventional wisdom espoused in the disciplines of psychology and sociology, are also part of this overall complex matrix that we call our society. In short, the legal process is but one of the many ongoing processes that make society function. In addition, it cannot be separated from the other processes in that all of the processes which define our society are highly interrelated and impinge on each other with assured regularity.

R. I. Cheffins and R. N. Tucker define law having regard to the foregoing notion. As they stated in their treatise entitled *The Constitutional Process in Canada*:

> Law, in our view, is that part of the over-all process of political decision-making which has achieved somewhat more technical, more obvious and more clearly defined ground rules than other aspects of politics. It is still, however, an integral subdivision of the over-all political process. The student of politics, law and legal philosophy is concerned, among other things, with the question of allocation of all types of resources, and with questions of the relationships between individual citizens and the state, as well as the relationships between states. The study of the legal and political process in any nation is a study of how decisions are made, who makes them, what the decisions are, how they influence subsequent events, and how alterative decisions might have led to different results.

> One of the chief problems in any constitutional system is to decide when decisions should be made within formal legal channels, and when matters should be left to other more informal and usually more flexible arenas. This is one of the things a formal constitutional document attempts to determine. A constitution usually serves a variety of needs. First, it is a badge of nationhood, an indication that the nation has arrived on the national scene fully clothed with the appropriate legal garb. In addition, as already indicated, constitutions set up certain structures and assign them different authority. These structures are usually given such titles as Parliament, Congress, Courts, Executive Officers,

Administration. Each of these various types of bodies irrespective of its title, is usually assigned some rather nebulous area of power.[5]

The authors make further reference to this fundamental but important notion as to the nature of the legal system when they define what they regard as the purpose of a constitution. As they stated:

> A constitution is more than a mechanical set of ground rules. It is a mirror reflecting the national soul. It reflects those values the country regards as important, and shows how these values will be protected. It is for the constitutional student to try to correlate and explain the extent to which the national idea is implemented within the day-to-day framework of political processes.[6]

It is obvious from the foregoing that when one reads, for example, a reported decision of a court of law, one is reading not only the judgment rendered by the court with respect to the facts presented by the opposing litigants, but also a judgment that must be regarded, realistically, as reflecting the judge's notion as to what constitutes public policy, the existing state of morality and the political and economic conditions of the day. The latter considerations, namely, prevailing political and economic conditions, often form a substructure or foundation upon which many decisions are based. Moreover, with the Canadian Charter of Rights and Freedoms now entrenched in the Constitution,[7] there is a new dynamic in the process of judicial decision-making. As R. I. Cheffins and P. A. Johnson state, the inclusion of the Charter in the Constitution is:

> bound to place the courts much more in the forefront of the political process. In addition to having to determine legality based on the dividing lines of the federal system, they will now have to add another perspective of consideration, namely, whether the legislation also violates the Charter of Rights. True, commentators can argue that this is purely a legal process to be determined by legal reasoning. The difficulty, however, is that the Charter of Rights is couched in very general terms, including such phrases as "freedom of expression," which leave the judiciary considerable latitude in defining the restraints to be placed on a legislature with respect to the limitation of freedom of expression.[8]

Consider, for example, the obscenity provisions in the Criminal Code of Canada and the cases decided pursuant to those provisions. The state of the law appears to be that a publication will be regarded as obscene if it involves an undue exploitation of sex, with such "undue exploitation" measured against national community standards. With the somewhat restrictive rules as to the admissibility of evidence, how can a judge

---

[5] *The Constitutional Process in Canada*, 2nd ed. (Toronto: McGraw-Hill Ryerson, 1976), P. 3. See also R.I. Cheffins and P.A. Johnson, *The Revised Canadian Constitution: Politics as Law* (Toronto: McGraw-Hill Ryerson, 1986).

[6] *Ibid.* p. 4.

[7] See Chapter 5 for a detailed discussion.

[8] *The Revised Canadian Constitution: Politics as Law* (Toronto: McGraw-Hill Ryerson, 1986), p. 9.

from Edmonton, for example, who might never have been outside of his province throughout his lifetime, determine national community standards? In effect, that judge, under the guise of applying national community standards, is applying local standards with which he is familiar. Yet the judge must make this determination and it would be folly to believe that his own concept of the existing or prevailing state of morality did not enter his decision.[9]

A more important example relates to constitutional cases. These vital national policy decisions have affected the very fabric of our constitutional order in Canada by defining the scope of the respective federal and provincial legislative jurisdictions. Indeed, questions as to federal and provincial relations on a given issue often end up in a court where prior settlement cannot be effected by negotiation and compromise. The decisions of the Supreme Court of Canada and the Judicial Committee of the Privy Council prior to 1949 certainly reflect or in some way relate to the prevailing political and economic conditions of the day. A conclusion of this sort is somewhat in accordance with a realist school of judicial philosophy. To adopt any other view, and to ignore other factors which enter into a judicial decision, would probably be somewhat misleading and would create a highly artificial impression.

Even if a novice, in embarking upon an examination of the legal process in Canada, subscribes to the basic notion that the law is systematic

---

[9] *R. v. Towne Cinema Theatres Ltd.*, [1985] 1 S.C.R. 494, [1985] 4 W.W.R. 1, 37 Alta. L.R. (2d) 289, 45 C.R. (3d) 1, 18 C.C.C. (3d) 193, 18 D.L.R. (4th) 1, 59 N.R. 101, 61 A.R. 35; and *R. v. Video World Ltd.*, [1987] 1 S.C.R. 1255, 35 C.C.C. (3d) 191, 48 Man. R. (2d) 240, 77 N.R. 77, affirming [1986] 1 W.W.R. 413, 22 C.C.C. (3d) 331, 36 Man. R. (2d) 68 (C.A.).

See also *R. v. Ramsingh* (1984), 14 C.C.C. (3d) 230, 29 Man. R. (2d) 110 (Q.B.); *R. v. Wagner* (1985), 43 C.R. (3d) 318, 36 Alta. L.R. (2d) 301 (Q.B.), affirmed (1986), 50 C.R. (3d) 175, 43 Alta. L.R. (2d) 204, 26 C.C.C. (2d) 242, 69 A.R. 78 (C.A.), leave to appeal to S.C.C. refused (1986), 50 C.R. (3d) 175n, 26 C.C.C. (3d) 242n; *R. v. Pereira-Vasquez* (1988), 26 B.C.L.R. (2d) 273, 43 C.C.C. (3d) 82 (C.A.); *R. v. Neil's Ventures Ltd.* (1985), 61 N.B.R. (2d) 42, 158 A.P.R. 42 (Prov. Ct.); *R. v. Germain.*, [1985] 2 S.C.R. 241, 21 C.C.C. (3d) 289, 21 D.L.R. (4th) 296, 62 N.R. 87; *R. v. Householders Television & Appliances Ltd.* (1984), 20 C.C.C. (3d) 561 (Ont. Co. Ct.), affirmed (1985) 20 C.C.C. (3d) 561 at 571 (Ont. C.A.); *R. v. Saint John News Co.* (1982), 47 N.B.R. (2d) 91, 124 A.P.R. 91 (Q.B.); *R. v. Doug Rankine Co.* (1983), 36 C.R. (3d) 154, 9 C.C.C. (3d) 53 (Ont. Co. Ct.); *R. v. Sudbury News Service Ltd.* (1978), 18 O.R. (2d) 428, 39 C.C.C. (2d) 1 (C.A.); and *R. v. P.* (1980), 51 C.C.C. (2d) 485 (Ont. Co. Ct.), affirmed (1981), (sub nom. *Pink Triangle Press*) 19 C.R. (3d) 393, 58 C.C.C. (2d) 505 (C.A.), leave to appeal to S.C.C. refused (1981), 40 N.R. 6n (S.C.C.).

See most recently, *R. v. Butler*, [1992] 1 S.C.R. 452, 89 D.L.R. (4th) 449, 134 N.R. 81, [1992] 2 W.W.R. 577, 78 Man. R. (2d) 1, 11 C.R. (4th) 137, 8 C.R.R. (2d) 1, 16 W.A.C. 1, 70 C.C.C. (3d) 129; *R. v. Hawkins*(1993), 15 O.R. (3d) 549, 26 C.R. (4th) 75, 66 O.A.C. 46, 86 C.C.C. (3d) 246, 20 C.R.R. (2d) 362, (sub nom. *R. v. Ronish*) 26 C.R. (4th) 75 (C.A.), leave to appeal to S.C.C. refused (1994), 17 O.R. (3d) xvi (note), 87 C.C.C. (3d) vi (note), 20 C.R.R. (2d) 362n, 72 O.A.C. 239n, 175 N.R. 158n (S.C.C.).

in nature, functioning as a continual process in the context of many inter-acting societal processes, this, in itself, does not render a totally accurate appreciation of the legal process in Canada. Aside from an understand-ing of the various roles of the persons in the legal system, of the institu-tions which form the basic structural components of that system, and of the various judicial attitudes which, through convention, essentially make the whole process operational, there is, however, one basic component, the absence of which will not allow a thorough understanding of the nature of the legal process. The roles of the persons who man the legal system, the various institutions within the system and the judicial attitudes which, through convention, make operational that system, will all be discussed in subsequent chapters. Before those discussions, it is essential for the new student of law to appreciate this additional entity within the process, the judicial philosophy or jurisprudence which, depending upon the particu-lar school of thought adopted by an individual, undoubtedly affects the way in which a judge judges, a prosecutor prosecutes, a lawyer defends or advocates, and the way in which every citizen views the law and the legal system.

One perceives the issues and appreciates the consequences depending upon the particular philosophy that one espouses. An appreciation of the nature and function of the law is not an absolute. One must realize that nature and function are variables that depend upon which particular school of judicial philosophy or jurisprudence one holds. With that in mind, let us now consider some of the major schools of jurisprudence.

Probably the best illustration of the various schools of judicial thought is set out in the now classic fictitious case of the *Speluncean Explorers*.[10] The case was written by a noted legal scholar and proponent of the natu-ral law school of thought, Professor Lon Fuller of Harvard University. Professor Fuller, using contrived facts,[11] modelled various judges' deci-sions arising out of those facts as a mirror of the various schools of jurisprudence. The case of the *Speluncean Explorers* is now a classical model of how particular facts in a particular dispute or matter are resolved in accordance with the way in which a judge perceives the nature and func-tion of the law. As indicated, each judge resolves the questions before the court in terms of his own view of the appropriate judicial philosophy which ought to govern decision-making by a court. Aside from providing an excellent initial exposure to the science of jurisprudence, the case of the *Speluncean Explorers* drives home the fundamental notion that, given

---

[10] (1949), 62 Harvard L. Rev. 616.
[11] The fictitious case was, however, somewhat modelled after the real case of *R. v. Dudley and Stephens* (1884), 14 Q.B.D. 273.

a constant set of facts, different judges may resolve the same problem in different ways, in accordance with different philosophies of law.

In short, an examination of judicial philosophy is not merely an abstract, academic, and purely theoretical endeavour, but rather it is vital to an honest and full appreciation of the legal process as it operates in a real-life context.

The Speluncean Explorers case is not only illustrative of the various schools of jurisprudence reflected in the various judgments rendered by the members of the court, but it also serves to exemplify: (1) how judges participate in the legal process in accordance with their perception of the nature and purpose of law and the legal system; and (2) the ways in which judges resolve the great dilemmas they must face, in order to effect just results.

Part of a later chapter will be devoted to an examination of the role of judges in our legal system. But, for the present discussion, consider the above two matters in the context of the case of *The Speluncean Explorers*.

Briefly, the facts of that fictional case are as follows. Four men were trapped beneath the ground as the result of a cave-in. In order to survive until rescued it was necessary for them to choose, by lottery, and to eat one of their number. Although the original proponent of this technique of survival subsequently reversed his position, a scheme of chance was devised and the original proponent himself was the hapless victim. The surviving three men were later charged with murder and the "case" is a report of the decision of a final court of appeal considering an appeal against conviction (and the consequential sentence of execution).

One judge, adopting a positivist approach to law, simply interprets the written language of the governing statute literally and upholds the conviction. Another judge, obviously a proponent of natural law thinking, looks to a "state of nature" in which the men found themselves and rejects the notion that the men were bound by the regular, positive law of the land. Moreover, he argues against a literal interpretation of the governing statute. That judgment, incidentally, raises the broader (and currently relevant) question of the role, if any, of judges, in interpreting statutes, of "legislating". By that it is meant that some judges may interpret a statute in such a way as to subvert or twist the literal language of that statute to such an extent that they have, in fact, usurped the role of Parliament. (This approach is particularly noteworthy in view of the new role of Canadian judges under the Charter of Rights and Freedoms.) Further reference will be made to this concern in the subsequent chapter on statutory interpretation.

Another judge in the *Speluncean Explorers* case wishes to ignore the substantive issues, uphold the conviction, and exhort the Chief Executive to exercise his prerogative and grant executive clemency. Another judge, perplexed by the difficult issues he must face, simply withdraws from the case.

Finally, the remaining judge, in reflecting a variant of the philosophy of legal realism, based upon gossip that comes to his attention, urges his colleagues not to resort to an appeal to the Chief Executive for clemency, in that it has come to his attention that this would have the opposite effect on the Chief Executive.

The important point to appreciate in the present context is as follows. Five judges, viewing the same facts and considering the same body of law, have taken different approaches. Why? First, some judges have perceived the nature and purpose, and the role and function of law and the legal system in accordance with a particular school of legal philosophy to which they subscribe. Secondly, judges want to effect just results (although that notion will obviously differ from judge to judge), but the rigidities of the law often do not allow those results to ensue. This, historically, is the basis of the development of the law of equity. At any rate, in order to effect just results, when faced with onerous circumstances, judges might very well resort to exhorting the Chief Executive to offer the prerogative of clemency, as was done by Chief Justice Truepenny in the *Speluncean Explorers* case. But in real life, judges utilize all sorts of available techniques, such as distinguishing cases, ignoring precedent, and a variety of other devices. These techniques, too, will be discussed in the subsequent chapter on the rules and principles of statutory interpretation.

Many scholars and philosophers have laboured over thousands of years in order to categorize and define distinct schools of judicial thought. It is perhaps simplistic and preliminary to summarize, in this initial chapter, the major schools of jurisprudence. However, a student of the legal process in Canada should appreciate the major divisions of judicial thought and the difficulty faced by judicial philosophers over thousands of years in defining the theoretical parameters of the various schools of judicial philosophy. At the outset, it is important to recognize that:

> In jurisprudence we are not concerned to derive rules from authority and apply them to problems; we are concerned rather to reflect on the nature of legal rules, on the underlying meaning of legal concepts and on the essential features of legal systems.[12]

---

[12] *Salmond on Jurisprudence*, 12th ed. (London: Sweet & Maxwell, 1966), p. 1.

Basically, the three major schools of jurisprudence are the positive law school, the natural law school and the realist school of law. Again, it is important to realize that, first, there are many other schools of jurisprudence which provide an equally legitimate perception of legal systems and the legal process and, moreover, all of the foregoing schools have many variants (there is, for instance, no one absolute school of natural law). Furthermore, for example, one might classify the various schools of jurisprudence in terms of the following subdivisions: natural law, German transcendental idealism, analytical positivism, sociological jurisprudence, American realism, Scandinavian realism, Marxian theory of law, and others. Accordingly, it is somewhat artificial to compartmentalize the many schools of jurisprudence into three major divisions; yet, at the same time, this compartmentalization does provide at least a fundamental understanding of the various divisions of legal thought.[13]

POSITIVISM

Basically, positivism, expressed in its simplest terms, regards valid law as the command of the sovereign law-giver, enforced through a system of sanctions imposed by the sovereign. But there is not, however, a single, universally accepted view of analytical positivism. Rather, there are many schools of positivist thought characterized by a common thread running through them. This common thread is a scientific attitude which, as Bodenheimer states, "rejects a priori speculations and seeks to confine itself to the data of experience".[14]

Generally, positivists such as Austin hold the view that there must be a strict separation between law and morality. Or, restated, the positivists emphasize what "is" the law, over considerations as to what "ought to be" the law. A positivist might ask whether a given law is a good law or a bad law, but it is purely a secondary consideration. In other words, legal validity depends only upon legal criteria and not upon moral criteria. A positivist will regard a bad law in the same way in which he will regard a good law.

As Bodenheimer put it, "it is characteristic of legal positivism that it

---

[13] Some, but certainly not all, of the major treatises on judicial philosophy are as follows: *Salmond on Jurisprudence, ibid.*; W. Friedmann, *Legal Theory*, 5th ed. (London: Stevens and Sons, 1967); R. W. Dias, *Jurisprudence*, 5th ed. (London: Butterworths, 1985); D. Lloyd and M. D. A. Freeman, *Introduction to Jurisprudence*, 5th ed. (London: Stevens, 1985); E. Bodenheimer, *Jurisprudence* (Cambridge: Harvard University Press, 1974); H. L. A. Hart, *The Concept of Law*, 2nd ed. (Oxford: Clarendon Press, 1994); H. L. A. Hart and T. Honoré, *Causation in the Law* (Oxford: Clarendon Press, 1985).

[14] *Jurisprudence, ibid.*, p. 92.

contemplates the form and structure of the law rather than its moral and social content".[15]

The early positivists, particularly Bentham and Austin, should be contrasted with the more modern view of H. L. A. Hart. In *The Concept of Law*, he is critical of the older Austinian view and presents an alternative perspective of positivist thinking. Hans Kelsen,[16] too, offers yet another view of positivism by constructing a theory under which the law is a system of norms which can be traced back to a fundamental source, Kelsen's *Grundnorm*.

Positivism probably represents the most widely held view of law, although obviously there is no one view of positivism that is satisfactory to all proponents who subscribe to this school of jurisprudence.

NATURAL LAW

In their treatise *Introduction to Jurisprudence*, D. Lloyd and M. D. A. Freeman categorize natural law theorists as those "jurists who believe in some higher system to which mere positive law should conform".[17] Moreover, as Lloyd stated elsewhere, "We have a feeling of discontent with justice based on positive law alone, and strenuously desire to demonstrate that there are objective moral values which can be given a positive content."[18]

The problem, of course, with natural law is defining the particular nature of the natural law to which the positive law must conform. The danger is that anyone can invoke his version of the natural law in order to suit his purposes.

Historically, natural law thought can be traced to the ancient Greek and Roman philosophers, including Plato, Socrates and Aristotle. Many years later, St. Thomas Aquinas, inspired by Aristotle, developed a natural law theory based upon Christian theology. In short, Aquinas believed that there existed God-given objective moral values.

Essentially, the main characteristic of natural law is that a "natural law" is the law, and a "positive" contrary to the law of nature is not the law. For example, St. Thomas Aquinas stated in *Summa Theologica*

---

[15] *Ibid.*, p. 104. See also H. L. A. Hart, "Positivism and the Separation of Law and Morals" (1958), 71 Harvard L. Rev. 595.

[16] Hans Kelsen, "Reine Rechtslehre" (Pure Theory of Law) (Berkeley: University of California Press, 1967).

[17] D. Lloyd and M. D. A. Freeman, *Introduction to Jurisprudence*, 5th ed. (London: Stevens, 1985).

[18] D. Lloyd, *The Idea of Law*, (Middlesex: Penguin Books Ltd., 1973).

that "an unjust and unreasonable law and one which is repugnant to the law of nature, is not law but a perversion of law".[19] The opposite, of course, is believed by a positivist, namely, that the valid law is the positive law of the land, regardless of the invocation of a natural law.

To inquire as to the content of the natural is essentially to investigate the written philosophy of the various theorists. The writings often (but not always) reflect the historical period in which a particular philosopher wrote. For example, after the Reformation, philosophers such as Hobbes, Locke, Spinoza, Montesquieu, Grotius and Rousseau emphasized reason as the source of the natural law and placed less reliance on a theological content in the natural law.

The American Constitution (which was influenced by the philosophies of Locke and Montesquieu) is an example where the natural law is set out in statutory form and becomes the central component of the positive law of the land, to which all other positive laws must conform. Similar examples in Canada are the new Canadian Charter of Rights and Freedoms, as well as the Canadian Bill of Rights, although it should be remembered that both contain opting out provisions, by way of a *non obstante*, or notwithstanding clause, and the latter can be repealed by simple statutory enactment. A similar example, on the international level, of incorporating the natural law as a central component of the international positive law to which all other international laws must conform, is the Universal Declaration of Human Rights, enacted by the United Nations. The natural law may also be incorporated into a custom or usage, or prevailing attitude, such as the common law notion of natural justice. The particular conception of the natural law in all of the foregoing examples relates to a value-oriented perception of the natural law. In this model, law and morality should be mutually inclusive. The actual state of the law must conform to the ideal state of the law. The leading contemporary thinker in this school of jurisprudence is Professor Lon L. Fuller, the author of many works, including the fictional case of the *Speluncean Explorers*, discussed earlier.

Perhaps the best definition of natural law judicial philosophy is stated in *Salmond on Jurisprudence*,[20] where the author states that the essence of natural law is as follows:

> The central notion is that there exist objective moral principles which depend on the essential nature of the universe and which can be discovered by natural reason, and that ordinary human law is only truly law insofar as it conforms to these principles.

---

[19] Pt. II, 1st part, Q. 95, art. 2, at p. 25, footnote 6.

[20] Salmond, *supra,* note 12, at p. 15. See also Paul Jackson, *Natural Justice*, 2nd ed. (London: Sweet & Maxwell, 1979), and John Finnis, *Natural Law and Natural Rights* (Oxford: Clarendon Press, 1980).

REALISM

There are many schools of judicial realism, but essentially all of these schools have one theme in common. In analyzing the judicial process, it is not sufficient merely to conclude that a judge is deciding the cases of individual litigants having regard only to the particular facts adduced in evidence, as such facts are applied to cold, hard, legal rules, be they statutory in nature or in the nature of precedent cases at common law. There are, in short, other components to judicial decision-making. For example, the following elements have been suggested as constituting relevant input in judicial decision-making: the personality of the judge, the ability of the judge to distinguish, ignore and re-interpret precedent, the political or policy-making role of judges based upon a subjective perception of justice and equity by a particular judge, and the political, social and economic substructure that defines the context of a given case.

Some twentieth century proponents of judicial realism in the United States include Oliver Wendell Holmes, Roscoe Pound, Benjamin Nathan Cardozo and Jerome Frank. Legal realism, including the sociological school of law, subscribes to the view that the legal process is not an objective exercise in fact-finding, nor is it an objective exercise in applying the facts to the particular rules of law. While one might say that the realists are basically skeptics, one might also say that they appreciate the psychological or human element in judicial decision-making, and, to that extent, they appreciate the legal process as it in fact operates, not only as it should operate in theory.

THE HOHFELDIAN SCHEME

The denotation of legal relationships in terms of the "rights" of one party vis-à-vis those of another is often misleading. That is so because the term "rights", in ordinary and commonplace usage, has given rise to a variety of meanings. Legally, however, the term has a more precise meaning. Indeed, in Canada, the term "civil rights" has a particular meaning constitutionally (see s. 92(13) of the Constitution Act, 1867). Nonetheless, confusion in terminology does exist. Jurisprudential theoreticians have directed themselves to this problem and have produced clever, novel and interesting results. For example, as R. W. Dias points out,[21] Jeremy Bentham was the first to distinguish between a right and a liberty. Following this, Bernhard Windscheid distinguished between a right and a power,

---

[21] *Jurisprudence* (London: Butterworths, 1970), p. 249. In a later edition of this work, the author, however, only states that "[i]t is apparent from a work of Bentham, published only in 1945, that he too distinguished, clearly and convincingly, between claim and liberty". See Dias, *Jurisprudence*, 5th ed. (London: Butterworths, 1985), p. 24.

The Canadian Legal System

while Bierling distinguished between a right, a liberty and a power. However, in 1902 Salmond analyzed right, liberty and power as well as duty, disability and liability, and, in essence, set the stage for the remarkable analysis of Wesley Newcombe Hohfeld.[22] In 1913, Hohfeld logically and brilliantly set out his scheme of jural relations (jural correlatives, jural opposites and jural contradictories).[23]

The Hohfeldian analysis has gained much respect for its brilliance and clarity although it has not been without criticism. Professor Arthur L. Corbin, writing in a foreword to Hohfeld's treatise on *Fundamental Legal Conceptions*,[24] suggests why the Hohfeldian scheme has encountered some criticisms:

> Hohfeld's articles disturbed the mental complacency of professors of law as well as of students. This was due not only to the fact that mastery of his work is a severe disciplinary process, but also to the fact that they got the erroneous impression that his analysis of concepts and terms was offered as a method of determining social and legal policy — not only for the purpose of distinguishing between a right and a privilege, between a right and a power or an immunity, but also as a method of determining whether any of these jural relations existed or should exist.[25]

There is, moreover, a significant practical value in the mastery of the Hohfeldian analysis. Generally speaking, as Professor Corbin reminds us:

> One whose own mind is cloudy and confused is certain to convey only cloudy and confused thoughts to others, but the identification of a specific word that will convey an exact thought and no other is an almost necessary process in the clarification of one's own mind.[26]

Discussing the importance of an Hohfeldian analysis, Professor Corbin places it in its proper perspective:

> Hohfeld's analysis of concepts and his arrangement of terms does indeed give great aid to the analysis of legal problems and in breaking down our complex and variable terms.

---

[22] See K.N. Llewellyn, *Jurisprudence (Realism in Theory and Practice)* (Chicago: University of Chicago Press, 1962), p. 491.

[23] This scheme first appeared in 1919 as two essays in pamphlet form and then subsequently published in 1923 by Yale University Press It was then set out in Hohfeld, *Fundamental Legal Conceptions (As Applied in Judicial Reasoning)* (New Haven: Yale University Press, 1946), and was subsequently represented geometrically in a table prepared by Professor G. L. Williams. Most recently it appeared in W.N.Hohfield, *Fundamental Legal Concepts (To Be Applied in Judicial Reasoning)* (Westport: Greenwood Press, 1978). For an excellent discussion and explanation of the Hohfeldian scheme, see the following treatises:

(i) Dias, *supra.* note 21, at p. 40;

(ii) Stone, *The Province and Function of Law* (Buffalo: William S. Hein and Co. Inc., 1968), p. 115;

(iii) Pound, *Jurisprudence*, Vol. IV (St. Paul: West Publishing Company, 1959), p. 77.

Interestingly, Pound, in the above treatise, refers to Hohfeld's work as "an elaborate scheme . . . after the manner of Hegelian logic."

[24] W.N. Hohfield, *Fundamental Legal Concepts* (Westport: Greenwood Press, 1978)

[25] *Ibid*, p. xi.

[26] *Ibid*,. p. viii.

It solves no problem of social or juristic policy, but it does much to define and clarify the issue that is in dispute and this enables the mind to concentrate on the interests and policies that are involved, and increases the probability of an informed and sound conclusion.[27]

Despite some criticism, Hohfeld's work has gained a significant measure of acceptance and approval. The Hohfeldian vocabulary has been utilized regularly in the American Restatements,[28] and, along similar lines, Dias suggests that although the courts may not be using the exact Hohfeldian language, they are thinking it. That is,

what is important is not the words, but the ideas which they represent. One may think Hohfeld without talking Hohfeld. One can utilize the analysis to keep one's mind clear when grappling with problems, and may then state the result in any other terms.[29]

On the following page is a schematic representation of the Hohfeldian analysis incorporating, inter alia, the work of Sir John Salmond and Wesley Newcombe Hohfeld. The particular form of schematic representation, as set out on the following page, was originally devised in this geometric form by Professor G. L. Williams.

Consider, for example, the person who has fulfilled all the statutory requirements for the annual renewal of his driver's licence. Assume that upon the tendering of the appropriate fee, the government clerk has no discretion to refuse the granting of the renewal. Applying the Hohfeldian scheme, the presence of the right to have the licence renewed in the citizen implies the duty to renew in the clerk. In addition, the presence of the right to have the licence renewed in the citizen implies the absence of a privilege in the clerk not to renew. Finally, the presence of the duty in the clerk to renew implies an absence of a privilege in the clerk not to renew.

It can therefore be seen from the above that fundamental notions, such as "rights" and "duties", possess precise interrelationships in accordance with the Hohfeldian analysis. In examining the various legal sources of law, it is important to regard the legal rights and obligations and the related notions set out in those various sources of law with equal precision. Otherwise, we might fall prey to serious disorder. As Professor Ronald M. Dworkin of Yale University wrote, in an essay on positivism:

Lawyers lean heavily on the connected concepts of legal right and legal obligation. We say that someone has a legal right or duty, and we take that statement as a sound basis for making claims and demands, and for criticizing the lack of public officials. But our understanding of these concepts is remarkably fragile, and we fall into trouble when we try to say what legal rights and obligations are.[30]

---

[27] *Ibid*. p. x-xi.

[28] A series of volumes authored by the American Law Institute which summarize the state of the law in given general areas and how it is changing.

[29] Dias, *supra*, note 21, at p. 41.

[30] "The Model of Rules" in Law, Reason and Justice (Essays in Legal Philosophy), Graham Hughes (ed.) (New York: New York University Press, 1969), p. 3.

THE HOHFELDIAN SCHEME

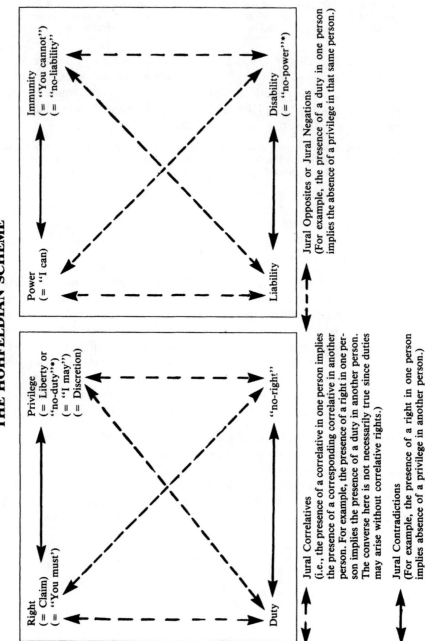

Right (= Claim) (= "You must")

Privilege (= Liberty or "no-duty"*) (= "I may") (= Discretion)

"no-right"

Duty

Power (= "I can")

Immunity (= "You cannot") (= "no-liability")

Disability (= "no-power"**)

Liability

Jural Correlatives
(i.e., the presence of a correlative in one person implies the presence of a corresponding correlative in another person. For example, the presence of a right in one person implies the presence of a duty in another person. The converse here is not necessarily true since duties may arise without correlative rights.)

Jural Contradictions
(For example, the presence of a right in one person implies absence of a privilege in another person.)

Jural Opposites or Jural Negations
(For example, the presence of a duty in one person implies the absence of a privilege in that same person.)

* This particular terminology was suggested in *Salmond on Jurisprudence.*

CRITICAL LEGAL THEORY

During the past decade and a half, a new theory of jurisprudence has emerged in North America. Spawned in Europe and the United States, critical legal thought is a theory of jurisprudence that is essentially an amalgam of traditional legal realism and modern cynicism. Whereas a realist will identify extra-legal factors that impact upon the judicial decision-making process, the critical theorist will go much further. He will identify what he believes are dysfunctional aspects of the legal system, having regard to the underlying purposes, values and assumptions that serve as the underpinning of the legal system. Moreover, he will challenge those same purposes, values and assumptions in terms of their contemporary relevance, their rationale and, indeed, their validity. That determination, of course, will reflect the critical theorist's world view and those personal and political values that contribute to the formation of his world view.

For example, in the constitutional realm, many critical theorists regard the Canadian Charter of Rights and Freedoms somewhat negatively. They might argue that the purpose of the Charter is to protect the rights of minorities and the disadvantaged. Instead, they would argue, what has happened is that the Charter has been used in the courts most effectively by the rich and powerful, including large corporations which can afford high-priced lawyers. Some would even argue that the real purpose of the Charter is to placate minorities and the disadvantaged without really assisting them.

Most lawyers and scholars are unconvinced by the views of the critical theorists. Many regard critical theorists as extremists and reject their view of law and the legal system. For the reader interested in critical legal theory, the following is a selected bibliography:

Hutchinson, A. *Dwelling on the Threshold*. Toronto: Carswell, 1987.

Hutchinson, A. and P. Monahan. "Politics and the Critical Legal Scholars: The Unfolding Drama of American Legal Thought". (1984), 36 Stan. L. Rev. 199.

Kelman, M. "Trashing". (1984), 36 Stan. L. Rev. 293.

Unger, R. M. "The Critical Legal Studies Movement". (1983), 96 Harvard L. Rev. 563.

Unger, R. M. *Knowledge and Politics*. New York: Free Press, 1975.

Unger, R. M. *Law in Modern Society: Towards A Criticism of Social Theory*. New York: Free Press, 1976.

CONCLUSION

Clearly, then, there is no comprehensive philosophy of law acceptable to all persons, just as there is no comprehensive philosophy of life with universal acceptance. At the very least, the formulation of a philosophy of law is a function of a particular appreciation of the nature and purpose of law. A given appreciation of the nature and purpose of law must, in turn, depend not only upon a keen intellectual insight, but also upon the philosopher's perception of the world in which he lives and his judgment of the values that ought to be promoted.

A detailed study of jurisprudence is beyond the scope of this book, but it is nonetheless important to realize that there is no one view as to the nature and purpose of law. Indeed, Maher and Waller, in their treatise, *Derham, Maher and Waller: An Introduction to Law*, state several definitions of law which have been offered throughout history:

(a) Law is the will of God Expressed in His commands revealed to man through His chosen instruments. Obedience to God's will is the supreme command.

(b) Law is in two great parts: Divine law, and human law. They may conflict. Differing theories were developed to explain man's duty if faced with a conflict between the dictates of the two.

(c) Law is the product of man's capacity to reason, and it consists of all those principles and rules which, by the use of reason, can be seen to be necessary for, or which can be seen to promote man's peaceful and happy life in a society of men.

(d) Law is in two great parts: Natural law and positive law. Natural law is the product of reason (as in (c) above) whereas positive law is made up of all the rules in force in actual legal systems. The two may sometimes conflict. Differing theories have been developed to explain man's duly when faced with a conflict between the two.

(e) Law is the command of the sovereign. The sovereign is that person, or group of persons, in any independent human society who, owing no obedience to any outside body or person, enjoys the habitual obedience of all persons in his society.

(f) Law is the instrument man uses in his attempt to achieve justice in society.

(g) Law is an instrument of social engineering.

(h) Law is an instrument by which capitalist society ensures the suppression of the proletariat with the establishment of communism, law will wither away.

(i) Law is what the courts declare to be the law.[31]

As suggested earlier, the perfect definition of law is elusive, but perhaps the most realistic approach is to avoid attempts at defining law at all. Rather, the law should be regarded as the core matter which those persons and those institutions in any legal system utilize in order to effect an ongoing process in regulating the affairs and conduct of persons in

[31] Maher and Waller, *Derham, Maher and Waller: An Introduction to Law*, 6th ed. (Sydney: The Law Book Co., 1991), p.178.

society. With this fundamental notion, it is probably unnecessary to search for an all-encompassing definition of law. Law is more than the setting for a great drama played by lawyers and judges. More accurately, it is the foundation for the infinite number of dramas played by all persons in society, every day of their lives.

The nature of law is not unlike the nature of the evolution of life. It had a beginning, it has many times changed throughout its long history, and it responds to changing needs and circumstances.

Even its destiny is analogous, for humankind has the power to adapt the law to the needs of a modern, mass, technocratic society, just as it has the technology to avoid environmental hazards which place its future in jeopardy. But law is more than this, for it is possible that people, through law, can control their destiny and improve the quality of life. More than anything else, an organized system of law represents this opportunity. From this somewhat lofty perspective, one, however, can easily retreat to an equally appropriate notion of law. For example, law may simply be regarded as the means of ensuring that criminals go to jail or that dogs, while outdoors, are kept on leashes. However one views the law, ultimately there is but one certain notion. Since virtually all aspects of life are affected by the omnipresent influence of the law, the law simply defies a single all-encompassing definition. And that, in itself, is a significant comment on the expansive and pervasive nature of law.

SELECTED BIBLIOGRAPHY OF TREATISES ON AN INTRODUCTION TO LAW

Allen, C. K. *Law in the Making*. 7th ed. Oxford: Clarendon Press, 1964.

Baker, J. *An Introduction to English Legal History*. London: Butterworths, 1971.

Boyd, N. *Canadian Law, And Introduction*. Toronto: Harcourt Brace, 1995.

Brand, P. *The Making of the Common Law*. London: Hambledon Press, 1992.

Brandon, S., I. Duncanson, and G. Samuel. *English Legal History*. London: Sweet & Maxwell, 1979.

Cairns, Huntington. *Legal Philosophy from Plato to Hegel*. Baltimore: Johns Hopkins Press, 1949.

Claydon, J., and D. Galloway. *Law and Legality*. Toronto: Butterworths, 1979.

Cohen, M. (ed.). *Ronald Dworkin and Contemporary Jurisprudence*. Totowa, N.J.: Rowman & Allanheld, 1983.

Cohen, Morris Raphael. *Cohen and Cohen's Readings in Jurisprudence and Legal Philosophy.* 2nd ed. Boston: Little, Brown, 1979.

Coval, S. C., and J. C. Smith. *Law and its Presuppositions: Actions, Agents and Rules.* Boston: Routledge and K. Paul, 1986.

D'Amato, A. *Jurisprudence: A Descriptive and Normative Analysis of Law.* Dordrecht: Martinus Nijhoff, 1984.

Darbyshire, P. *Eddey on the English Legal System.* 5th ed. London: Sweet & Maxwell, 1992.

Derrett, J. D. M. *An Introduction to Legal Systems.* New York: F.A.Praeger, 1968.

Deschenes, J. *The Sword and the Scales.* Toronto: Butterworths, 1979.

Dworkin, R. M. *Law's Empire.* Cambridge, Mass.: Belknap Press of Harvard University Press, 1986.

Dworkin, R. M. *A Matter of Principle.* Cambridge: Harvard University Press, 1985.

Eddey, K. J. *An Introduction to Public Law.* London: Butterworths, 1967.

Finch, J. D. *Introduction to Legal Theory.* 3rd ed. London: Sweet & Maxwell, 1979.

Fitzgerald, P. and K. McShane. *Looking at Law: Canada's Legal System.* Ottawa: Bybooks, 1979.

Gibson, D.L. *All About Law — Exploring the Canadian Legal System.* Toronto: J.Wiley, 1990.

Golding, Martin P. *Philosophy of Law.* Englewood Cliffs, N.J.: Prentice Hall, 1975.

Harris, P. *An Introduction to Law.* 4th ed. London: Weidenfeld, 1993.

Hart, H. L. A. *Causation in the Law.* 2nd ed. Oxford: Clarendon Press, 1985.

Hart, H. L. A. *The Concept of Law.* 2nd ed. Oxford: Clarendon Press, 1994.

James, P. S. *Introduction to English Law.* 11th ed. London: Butterworths, 1985.

Kiralfy, A. K. R. *The English Legal System.* 8th ed. London: Sweet & Maxwell, 1990.

Lloyd, Dennis. *The Idea of Law,* Middlesex: Penguin, 1973. Reprinted with revisions in 1976.

Lloyd, Dennis and M. D. A. Freeman. *Introduction to Jurisprudence.* 5th ed. London: Stevens, 1985.

Lyons, David. *Ethics and the Rule of Law.* New York: Cambridge University Press, 1984.

Maher, F. and L. Waller. *Derham, Maher and Waller: An Introduction to Law*. 6th ed. Sydney: Law Book Co., 1991.

Martin, Rex. *Rawls and Rights*. Lawrence, Kansas: University Press of Kansas, 1985.

McLeod, I. *Legal Method*. Hampshire: MacMillan, 1993.

Morris, Clarence. *The Great Legal Philosophers: Selected Readings in Jurisprudence*. Philadelphia: University of Pennsylvania Press, 1971.

Newton, C. R. *General Principles of Law*. 3rd ed. London: Sweet & Maxwell, 1983.

Olivecrona, Karl. *Law as Fact*. 2nd ed. London: Stevens, 1971.

Osborne, C. (ed.) *Introduction to Legal Practice* 3rd ed. London: Sweet & Maxwell, 1991.

Phillips, O. H. *A First Book of English Law*. 8th ed. London: Sweet & Maxwell, 1988.

Plucknett, T. F. T. *Studies in English Legal History*. London: Hambleton, 1983.

Posner, R.A. *The Problems of Jurisprudence*. Cambridge: Harvard University Press, 1990.

Radcliffe, G. R. and G. N. Cross. *The English Legal System*. 6th ed. London: Butterworths, 1977.

Rawls, John. *A Theory of Justice*. Cambridge, Mass.: Belknap Press of Harvard University Press, 1971.

Raz, J. *The Authority of Law*. Oxford: Clarendon Press, 1979.

Raz, Joseph. *The Concept of a Legal System: An Introduction to the Theory of Legal System*. 2nd ed. Oxford: Clarendon Press/New York: Oxford University Press, 1980.

Salmond, John William, Sir. *Salmond on Jurisprudence*. 12th ed. London: Sweet & Maxwell, 1966.

Sargent, N. (ed.) *Introduction to Legal Studies*. North York: Captus Press, 1991.

Schauer, F. *Playing by the Rules: A Philosophical Examination of Rule-Based Decision-Making in Law and in Life*. Oxford: Clarendon Press, 1991.

Sim, R.S., and D. M. Scott. *"A" Level English Law*. 3rd ed. London: Butterworths, 1970.

Simmonds, N. E. *Central Issues in Jurisprudence: Justice, Law and Rights*. London: Sweet & Maxwell, 1986.

Smith, P.F. *Smithe & Bailey on the Modern English Legal System*. London: Sweet & Maxwell, 1991.

Talos, W.S. *Understanding the Law.* Toronto: McGraw-Hill Ryerson, 1990.

Thorne, Samuel Edmond. *Essays in English Legal History.* London and Ronceverte, West Virginia: Hambledon Press, 1985.

Troller, A. *The Law and Order — An Introduction to Thinking About the Nature of Law.* Leyden: A. J. Sithoff, 1969.

Twining, W. L. *Legal Theory and Common Law.* New York: B. Blackwell, 1986.

Unger, Roberto Mangabeira. *The Critical Legal Studies Movement.* Cambridge, Mass.: Harvard University Press, 1986.

Waddams, S. M. *Introduction to the Study of Law.* 4th ed. Toronto: Carswell, 1992.

Walker, R. J., and M. G. Walker. *Walker & Walker's English Legal System.* 7th ed. London: Butterworths, 1994.

White, R. *The Administration of Justice.* 2nd 3d. Oxford: Blackwell, 1991.

Wilson, G. *Cases and Materials on the English Legal System.* London: Sweet & Maxwell, 1973.

Chapter 2

THE DIVISIONS OF LAW

THE MAIN DIVISIONS OF LAW

The various sources of law will be discussed in the next chapter, but emerging from the various legal sources of law is not a single, homogeneous entity to which we can refer as "the law". Rather, what emerges is a complex paradigm, containing many divisions and subdivisions, each characterized in terms of its interrelationship with all other components of a complicated and integrated system. This conception of our legal system cannot, however, be defined in terms of a single, representative model. Rather it must be examined by reference to various degrees of abstraction.

From the most fundamental and general abstraction, "the law" may be broken down as follows:

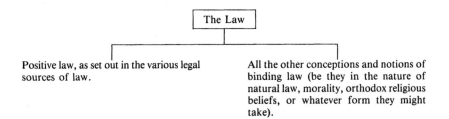

Given that the student of the law is primarily concerned with the positive law, it is necessary to become more specific and define "the law" in terms of a more meaningful and less general abstraction. As such, the positive law may be subdivided as follows:

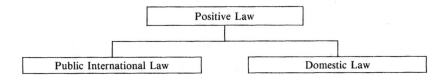

Public international law is concerned with the affairs of nations as members of the international community and the affairs of men within nations from the perspective of internationally recognized customs and conventions, rules and principles, and treaties and other obligations.

Domestic law, in this sense, refers to the positive law which governs the affairs of all persons within a sovereign, independent nation.

It should be noted that the respective spheres of international law and domestic law are not unrelated. For example, a principle of international law may be relevant in resolving a dispute in a Canadian court under the domestic law of Canada.[1] This is particularly important in the new era of the Canadian Charter of Rights and Freedoms. Since part of the Charter is drafted from international instruments as models, it is not surprising that the courts have been receptive to international cases as precedents (for example, cases decided by the European Court of Human Rights). Moreover, s. 1 of the Charter, the so-called "limitations clause", specifies that rights in the Charter are subject to "reasonable limits as can be demonstrably justified in a free and democratic society". This explicitly invites the courts to look at limits in other jurisdictions, provided they are free and democratic societies.[2] And finally, in human rights cases an aggrieved person may resort to an international agency to resolve an otherwise domestic complaint. More specifically, one may turn to the United Nations Human Rights Committee established under the Optional Protocol of the International Covenant on Civil and Political Rights, of which Canada is a ratified signatory.[3] So, although there is a logical division

---

[1] See, for example, *Re Wren*, [1945] O.R. 778, [1945] O.W.N. 795, [1945] 4 D.L.R. 674 (H.C.). For a more recent illustration, see *Canada Trust Co. v. Ontario (Human Rights Commission)* (1990), 74 O.R. (2d) 481, 38 E.T.R. 1, 12 C.H.R.R. D/184, 69 D.L.R. (4th) 321, (*sub nom. Leonard Foundation Trust, Re*) 37 O.A.C. 191 (Ont.C.A.).

[2] See *R. v. Keegstra* (1984), 19 C.C.C. (3d) 254 (Alta. Q.B.), where the court looked at hate propaganda laws in several jurisdictions. The case at trial in its first instance, provides the best illustration of a court examining laws in other free and democratic societies. However, the case has a checkered history. The trial decision was appealed to the Alberta Court of Appeal and then to the Supreme Court of Canada. On matters related to criminal procedure it was then reconsidered by the Alberta Court of Appeal, the result of which a new trial was ordered. The decision at the new trial was then subsequently further appealed to the Alberta Court of Appeal. See 60 Alta. L.R. (2d) 1, [1988] 5 W.W.R. 211, 65 C.R. (3d) 289, 43 C.C.C. (3d) 150, 87 A.R. 177, 39 C.R.R. 5 (C.A.), additional reasons at 79 Alta. L.R. (2d) 97, [1991] 4 W.W.R. 136, 3 C.R. (4th) 153, 63 C.C.C. (3d) 110, 114 A.R. 288 (C.A.), reversed 77 Alta. L.R. (2d) 193, [1991] 2 W.W.R. 1, 1 C.R. (4th) 129, 61 C.C.C. (3d) 1, 117 N.R. 1, 114 A.R. 81, 3 C.R.R. (2d) 193. However, it was the initial trial court that mainly looked at other jurisdictions in the s. 1 determination. This case is later discussed in Chapter 5.

[3] *Lovelace v. Can.*,[1983] Can. Hum. Rts. Y.B. 305, R. 6/24, Report of the Human Rights Committee (1981), 36 U.N.G.A.O. R. Supp. (No. 40) 166. More recently, see also *Bhinder v. Canada*, [1989] Can. Hum. Rts. Y.B. 305, Communication No. 208/1986 and *Lubicon Lake Band v. Canada*, [1991] Can. Hum. Rts. Y.B. 221, Communication No 167/1984.

between international and domestic law, there is also an interrelationship between the two.

Owing to interjurisdictional variations in the substantive law, a body of rules has been developed in order to resolve those variations. These rules are sometimes referred to as "private international law" or, alternatively, "conflicts of law".

The positive, domestic law of Canada can now be subdivided in terms of two basic components. The first is concerned with the substantive legal principles set out in the various legal sources of law. The second is concerned with the mechanism by which the substantive law is brought into operation. That is:

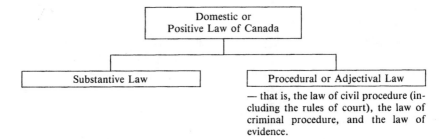

— that is, the law of civil procedure (including the rules of court), the law of criminal procedure, and the law of evidence.

The positive, domestic, substantive law of Canada is subdivided further in terms of yet a more specific abstraction:

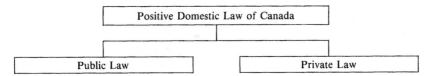

The public law is defined, essentially, as those areas of the law in which the public interest is primarily involved. There are, basically, four areas of public law:

1. *Constitutional law* — Intrinsically, the public interest is involved in that, essentially, the fundamental questions of Canadian constitutional law relate to the relationship between the various components of a federal state. Constitutional law now also includes considerations relating to the Canadian Charter of Rights and Freedoms and the protection of the fundamental freedoms guaranteed therein.

2. *Administrative law* — Here, the public interest is involved in that although a private interest may be the subject of an administrative deci-

sion, that decision is based upon certain guidelines which promote and advance the public interest. For example, if a private interest, such as a radio station, applies to the administrative tribunal regulating that industry for a renewal of the station's licence, the tribunal will render its decision in accordance with the guidelines or terms of reference as set out in the tribunal's enabling legislation. Presumably, those terms of reference will provide the basis under which the private application for licence renewal will be decided. Of more importance, however, those terms of reference and the tribunal's exercise of authority under them will reflect what constitutes a benefit to the public interest at large.

3. *Criminal law* — Here, the public interest is involved in the sense that crime is regarded as an offence against the state, against the people and against the public interest. That is why the police, as agents of the executive branch of government, conduct an investigation of an alleged crime. That is why a Crown attorney, as the agent of the provincial (or, on occasion, the federal) Attorney General, will prosecute a crime. That is why, in the event of a conviction, federal and provincial authorities will seek to rehabilitate, segregate, deter and punish the convicted person (and deter others, by way of example). And that is why various provincial criminal injuries compensation boards will render awards to innocent victims of crimes of violence, in part for reason of the state's failure to protect its subjects from the injuries arising out of criminal conduct.

4. *Taxation law* — Here, the public interest is served by the collection of moneys needed to finance the operations of government and the conduct of public programmes.

The private law is defined, essentially, as those areas of the law in which the private interest is primarily involved. Of course, the public interest does enter into a court's consideration of essentially private matters. This occurs, for example, whenever a court entertains notions of "public policy".

Likewise, there may be private law considerations that are relevant in public law matters. Moreover, a single human act can lead to both private law and public law consequences. For example, if one person hits another person, that act could lead to public law consequences (i.e., a criminal prosecution arising out of what is essentially regarded as an act against the state) and private law consequences (i.e., a civil suit by the victim against the perpetrator for the tort of battery). So, private law and public law are not mutually exclusive. Therefore, public law relates to those areas where the public interest is primarily involved and private law relates to those areas where the private interest is primarily involved. Because of this interrelationship, a key part of the definition is the phrase "primarily involved".

However, the above notwithstanding, private law encompasses those areas of the law where our legal system must resolve essentially private disputes. Most of the workload faced by our courts occurs in the area of private law. Indeed, if one examines a typical Canadian law school curriculum, one will readily observe that the curriculum, and probably necessarily so, is heavily weighted towards a private law emphasis.

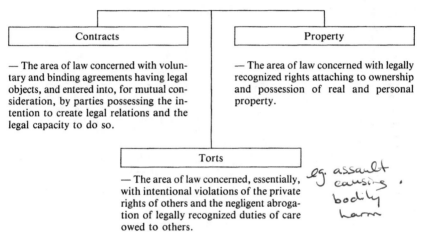

PRIVATE LAW

Contracts

— The area of law concerned with voluntary and binding agreements having legal objects, and entered into, for mutual consideration, by parties possessing the intention to create legal relations and the legal capacity to do so.

Property

— The area of law concerned with legally recognized rights attaching to ownership and possession of real and personal property.

Torts

— The area of law concerned, essentially, with intentional violations of the private rights of others and the negligent abrogation of legally recognized duties of care owed to others.

eg. assault causing bodily harm

It is difficult to precisely subdivide the private law into all of its various components; however, in order to complete the picture, the above represents a more specific and detailed abstraction of the main divisions of law emerging out of and encompassing the various legal sources of law.

More specifically, the private law is also concerned with the following subdivisions. (See diagram "Private Law", *infra.*)

Given that the Supreme Court of Canada picks and chooses the cases it wishes to hear under our "leave" system (to be described at a later point) and given that in our new era of having an entrenched Canadian Charter of Rights and Freedoms as part of our Constitution, it is not surprising that the Supreme Court of Canada has, in fact, chosen to emphasize in its docket public law cases (mainly criminal law and Charter cases). The result is that most private law cases are decided by provincial courts of appeal as the courts of last resort, whereas in the past many of those cases would have gone to the Supreme Court of Canada.

Synthesizing all of the foregoing, the following diagram sets out a complete representation of the main divisions of law. (See diagram "The Law", *infra.*)

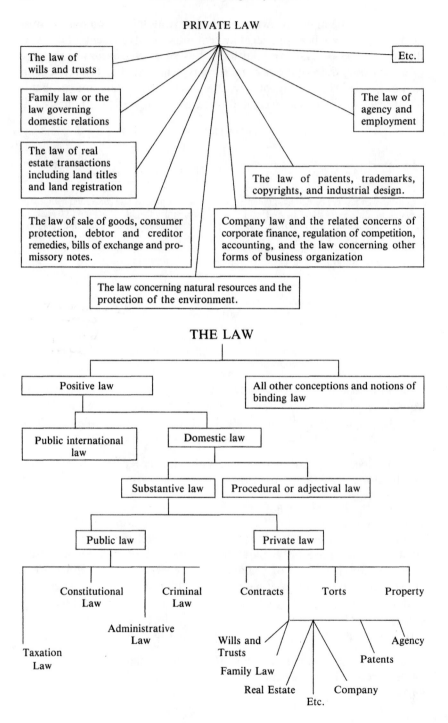

PRIVATE LAW

The law of wills and trusts

Family law or the law governing domestic relations

The law of real estate transactions including land titles and land registration

The law of sale of goods, consumer protection, debtor and creditor remedies, bills of exchange and promissory notes.

The law concerning natural resources and the protection of the environment.

Etc.

The law of agency and employment

The law of patents, trademarks, copyrights, and industrial design.

Company law and the related concerns of corporate finance, regulation of competition, accounting, and the law concerning other forms of business organization

THE LAW

Positive law

All other conceptions and notions of binding law

Public international law

Domestic law

Substantive law

Procedural or adjectival law

Public law

Private law

Constitutional Law

Criminal Law

Administrative Law

Taxation Law

Contracts

Torts

Property

Wills and Trusts

Family Law

Real Estate

Company

Etc.

Patents

Agency

Having regard to all of the foregoing, the reader can appreciate that the various legal sources of law manifest themselves in terms of various categories. These categories may then, in turn, be classified in terms of various divisions and subdivisions. However, in attempting to achieve precision in defining the main divisions of the law, it is important not to lose sight of the reality that law is, as many perceptive persons have observed, a "seamless web" where a reverberation in one place is reflected by motion elsewhere. In short, however precise the attempt to define the main divisions of the law, one must appreciate the integrated nature of the law and the legal system and thus not fall prey to an element of artificiality which befalls an attempt at categorization. That intellectual danger notwithstanding, the foregoing representation of the main divisions of law, at various levels of abstraction, is representative of our legal system, as a complex entity, encompassing regulation over virtually all of the affairs of man in modern, industrial society. Those affairs are complex, and so must be the legal system which governs the orderly conduct and regulation of those affairs. That is why, in essence, there are, at all levels of abstraction, so many (and a growing number of) divisions of law. In short, out of the two fundamental legal sources of law, statutes and cases, emerges a complicated system, characterized by many divisions and subdivisions and directed at resolving the great problems and complexities that define modern society.

OTHER DISTINCTIONS

1. THE COMMON LAW

The reader should appreciate that the same words in different contexts possess different meanings. For example, the body of the case law is referred to as the common law. As such, the reliance upon the "common law" in a search for precedents in order to resolve new cases is a principal feature of the "common law system" of law. The reader should also be aware that there are two major sources of law: cases and statutes (and many cases, of course, also arise out of the interpretation of statutes). In defining the nature of the common law system, it would be misleading to ignore the importance of the statutes. Consider, for example, the following distinction between common law and statute law in the common law system.

> The common law has its foundation in those general and immutable principles of justice which should regulate the intercourse of men with men, wherever they may reside. The statute law emanates from the wisdom of the legislature of the day, varies with varying circumstances, and consists of enactment which may be beneficial at one time and injurious at another.[4]

---

[4] *Uniacke v. Dickson* (1848), 2 N.S.R. 287 at 289-90 (S.C.), per Justice Halliburton Peace.

2. THE DIFFERENCES BETWEEN THE COMMON LAW AND CIVIL LAW SYSTEMS

Nine provinces in Canada are said to be common law provinces; that is, the private law of those provinces is administered in accordance with principles associated with "common law" systems of law. On the other hand, Quebec's private law is administered in accordance with principles associated with "civil law" systems of law.

The common law and civil law systems have developed similarities, but their fundamental approaches to the law are substantially different. The civil law system begins with an accepted set of principles. These principles are set out in the civil code. Individual cases are then decided in accordance with these basic tenets. In contrast, the common law approach is to scrutinize the judgments of previous cases and extract general principles to be applied to particular problems at hand. This difference in approach helps to explain the different manner in which the two systems regard the doctrine of stare decisis. Owing to the doctrine of stare decisis, judges in a common law system are bound to follow precedent cases, decided by judges of higher courts, given a similar fact situation in the precedent case and the case at hand. In contrast, however, in the civil law system, the codified principles, and not the cases, are supreme. As a result, theoretically at least, judges are not bound by previous decisions and may differ in their interpretation of the civil code. In deciding cases, a civil law judge is essentially applying the various codified principles to the cases at hand. In doing so, he must, of course, interpret those principles. But he need not rely on prior interpretation in a "precedent" case. Instead, he can choose to conduct his interpretation in accordance with the dictates of justice. He may even consider that an instant case is an exception to a particular codified principle.

Practically speaking, however, civil law judges do not ignore previous cases. There are several reasons for this. First, once a given principle, as set out in the civil code, has been given the same interpretation a number of times, a civil law judge would be risking reversal on appeal if he entertained a new analysis in interpreting the same principle. Secondly, judges do, in fact, follow previously decided cases because of the necessity of providing an element of predictability in the law. As will be seen at a later point in the book, the interests of certainty and predictability play an important role as rationales for the doctrines of precedent and stare decisis in the common law provinces.

It has been said that another major distinction between the two systems is that the civil law system is codified while the common law system is not. However, with the tremendous increase in the amount of legislation (both primary and subordinate legislation) in common law jurisdictions, that observation is no longer valid. The true difference between the common law and civil law systems may be found in the approach described above. Notwithstanding this, legislation in common law jurisdictions is not intended to be self-contained. In contrast, codified civil law is expected to replace all that has gone before and is intended to be a conclusive statement of the law. This attitude was demonstrated in the very beginnings of the civil law.

Fundamentally, the difference between the civil law system and the common system relates not only to the importance of precedent in the common law system and the relative lack of importance of precedent in the civil law system, but also to the general approach taken by the courts in the two systems. In a common law system, the courts extract existing principles of law from decisions of previous cases, while in the civil law system, the courts look to the civil code to determine a given principle and they then apply the facts of an instant case to that principle. If the code is silent in respect of a given matter, a judge will then attempt to apply general principles contained in the code to the specific fact situation before him.

3. TERMINOLOGY

It is also important for the reader to realize, in initially confronting the Canadian legal system, that in the formal legal terminology, the same words have different meanings in different contexts. For example, we have referred extensively to the term "common law". The term "common law" means different things in different contexts. The common law system is often contrasted with the civil law system. On the other hand, we have referred to the common law in contrast with statute law as the two major legal sources of law in Canada. Moreover, civil law is often referred to not as a system, but as, essentially, private law. In this sense, civil law is often contrasted with criminal law. In the latter context, the civil law refers to, for example, rights and remedies in connection with the law of contracts, torts and real property. In other words, here, the civil law is concerned with rights and duties in connection with one's fellow citizens in a private capacity. This is contrasted with criminal law, which is concerned with the rights and duties enjoyed by the subject in connection with the state. As well, there are other connotations of the term common law. For example, its original meaning was the law common to all of England as opposed to merely local law. Also, the common law is often contrasted with the law of equity. Equity is, essentially, the branch of law which grew and developed in the old Courts of Chancery. The reader should appreciate the main connotations set out above, as well as possess an awareness that these fundamental words and phrases have different meanings in different contexts, although the same words and phrases are used.

4. CONCLUSION

From the above, it becomes obvious that our system of law is truly multi-faceted. A typical Canadian law school curriculum has some thirty or more available subjects taught. The vast number of areas of the law, including new, emerging areas, such as environmental and consumer law, makes it almost impossible for a lawyer to become an expert in all areas of the law. Indeed, the growing number of areas of the law is one reason why officially accredited specialization is a development that has recently occurred.[5] At the same time, all areas of the law remain interrelated. It has, for good reason, been said that the law is a "seamless web" — when it makes an impact in one of its areas, it causes reverberations elsewhere. Accordingly, although there are truly many divisions of law, they are in fact moulded together in the context of a single, multi-dimensional legal system.

---

[5] For a detailed discussion of this development, see Chapter 13.

Chapter 3

THE SOURCES OF LAW

INTRODUCTION

The natural laws of physics require, in defining the concept of sound, that there be a source, a medium and a recipient. The positive laws which govern the affairs of man in society, like sound, also require a source, a medium and a recipient, in order to be real in more than a philosophical way.

The law, be it biblical or contemporary, requires a law-giver. Because law is not a single, homogeneous entity, but rather an amalgam of all kinds of entities of various natures, then it follows that each type of commandment or law that governs our behaviour may be traced to its own unique source or law-giver. In other words, just as there are many categorizations of law, there are many sources of law, each possessing its own unique nature.

As indicated above, the law, as a medium, requires a law-giver. Throughout history, there have been many renowned law-givers. Consider, for example, the following list of the great law-givers whose contributions to the development of law span many centuries and contribute to the growth of law in many nations.[1]

1. Hammurabi, 1950 B.C., Babylon
2. Moses, 13th century B.C., Egypt
3. Confucius, 551-479 B.C., China
4. Justinian, 483-565, Roman Empire
5. Mohammed, 570-632, Arabia
6. Grotius, 1583-1645, Holland
7. Napoleon, 1769-1821, France

---

[1] World Peace Through Law Center, "Renowned Law Givers and Great Law Documents of Humankind" (Washington, 1975). See also Alan Watson, "The Evolution of Law: Continued" (1987), 5 Law and History Rev. 537.

  8. Menes, 3100 B.C., Egypt
  9. Solomon, 973-933 B.C., Israel
 10. Lycurgus, 9th century B.C., Greece
 11. Draco, 7th century B.C., Greece
 12. Solon, 600 B.C., Greece
 13. Augustus, 63 B.C.-14 A.D., Roman Empire
 14. Charlemagne, 742-814, Roman Empire
 15. St. Louis, 1214-1270, France
 16. Blackstone, 1723-1780, England
 17. John Marshall, 1755-1835, U.S.A.

The foregoing list of law-givers most certainly contains some of the greatest contributors in the development of law throughout history. In addition, however, there have also been, throughout history, great bench marks of legal documentation. Some of these documents are as follows:[2]

  1. Ten Commandments, 13th century B.C.
  2. Koran, 652, Arabia
  3. Magna Carta, 1215, England
  4. Declaration of Independence, 1776, U.S.A.
  5. U.S. Constitution, 1787, U.S.A.
  6. Bill of Rights, 1791, U.S.A.
  7. Declaration of the Rights of Man and of the Citizen, 1791, France
  8. Universal Declaration of Human Rights, 1948.

To define the sources of law in Canada, one must assume, first, that what constitutes the law is merely the positive law of the land, without regard to any form or system of natural law, and, secondly, that the sources of that positive law represent the traditional law-givers in an Anglo-Canadian constitutional system. Specifically, those traditional sources will be discussed in detail in Chapter 4 in connection with the discussion on the Canadian constitutional system.

For the time being, however, it is important to consider, on a more general level, the various sources of law. The problem is, however, one of proper characterization and categorization. Since the sources of law are often set out in different ways, the result is that those sources are often difficult to define with precision. For example, consider the diagrammatical representations of the sources of law, as set out on the following pages by the leading authors of introductory texts in English law.

---

[2] *Ibid.*

SOURCES

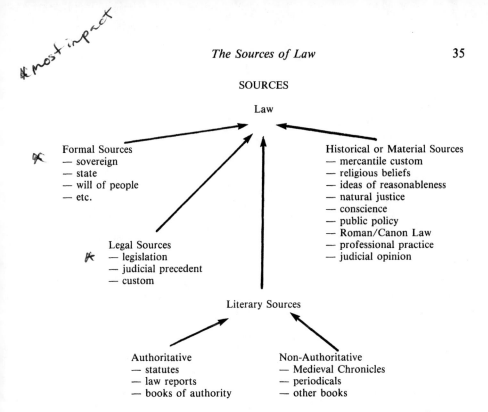

O.H. Phillips, *A First Book of English Law*, 8th ed. (London: Sweet & Maxwell, 1988), pp. 119-20.

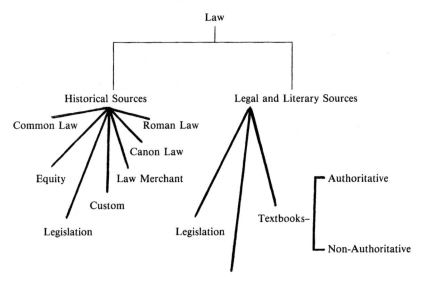

R. Walker and R. Wade, *Walker & Walker English Legal System*, 7th ed. (London: Butterworths, 1994), Part I, pp. 3-90.

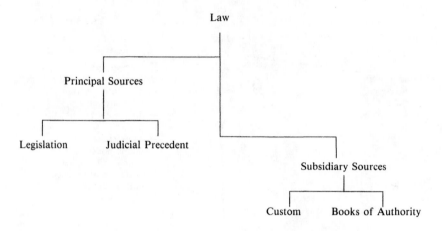

P.S. James, *Introduction to English Law*, 12th ed. (London: Butterworths, 1985), pp. 7-23.

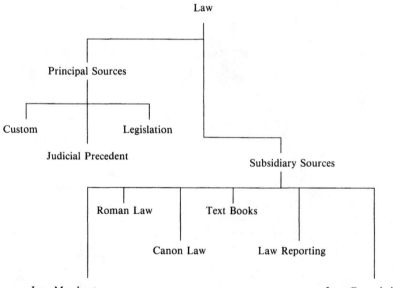

R.S. Sim and D.M. Scott, *"A" Leval English Law*, 3rd ed. (London: Butterworths, 1970), p. 33.

From these diagrams it is obvious that there exist not one, but many models of the various sources of law. Also, it is important to define what is meant by "source of law". One could be referring, of course, to the historical sources of law. In doing so, we would be looking to "the factors that have influenced the development of the law and to which the content of the law may be traced . . . for example, mercantile custom, religious beliefs, ideas of reasonableness, natural justice, conscience, public policy, borrowings from Roman civil law and Canon law, professional practice and juristic opinion."[3]

By inquiring into the sources of law, we could also be entertaining an examination as to what constitutes the "formal" sources of law. "A Formal Source of Law is that from which a system of law derives its validity, whether that be, for example, the general will or the will of a dictator".[4] This question of validity, as we saw in the first chapter, may be answered, in part, by reference to a particular school of jurisprudence to which one subscribes.

More likely, and this concerns us the most, by inquiring into "sources of law", one is conducting an examination into the various "legal" and "literary" sources. Essentially, the "authority for any proposition of law is the *legal* source of that proposition; the legal sources have been defined as the gates through which new principles can find entrance into the law. *Literary* sources are simply the materials in which the *legal* sources are recorded".[5]

The foregoing represents the various connotations of an inquiry into the "sources of law". Our inquiry, in this chapter, is primarily directed at an examination into the various legal sources of law. An examination of literary sources of law is, in effect, closely related to an examination of the techniques of legal research. Essentially, the process of legal research is the process by which, through an examination of the various literary sources of law, the legal sources of law are discovered. And through an examination of the legal sources of law, we are able to discover the various rights, duties, powers and privileges which define the nature of control that the law exerts over human affairs. However, in order to appreciate that "nature of control", it is important first to appreciate what constitutes, in a somewhat philosophical but nonetheless useful way, the con-

---

[3] O. H. Phillips, *A First Book of English Law*, 8th ed. (London: Sweet & Maxwell, 1988), p. 36.

[4] R. J. Walker and M. G. Walker, *The English Legal System*, 6th ed. (London: Butterworths, 1985) p. 88. See also, R. Walker and R. Wade, *Walker & Walker English Legal System*, 7th ed. (London: Butterworths, 1994).

[5] *Ibid.*

cepts of "rights", "duties", "powers", "privileges", and other related notions.

THE LEGAL SOURCES OF LAW

What are the various legal sources of law? To the extent that public policy and prevailing morality are part of our judicial system, one could perhaps conclude that the legal sources of law have no specific bounds.

Indeed, prevailing morality might be a source of law. For example, in the obscenity sections under the Criminal Code, a judge must look at the prevailing Canadian community standards in order to determine whether a particular matter under adjudication constitutes an undue exploitation of sex. Moreover, a judge often takes judicial notice of many factors not contained in any specific formal source, in order to adjudicate a particular problem. And moreover, notions of public policy often underlie a given decision. Accordingly, one might, at the outset, feel that the legal sources of law have no specific bounds. But, in reality, that is not the case, for there are very specific sources which one should turn to and rely upon in determining the legal sources of law.

Basically, the two main sources of law are statutory enactments and cases adjudicated by courts. However, there are other legal sources of law as well. For example, at a later point in this chapter, brief mention will be made of the royal prerogative, custom and convention, and morality, as legal sources of law. For the time being, however, the two main sources of law are statutory enactments and cases adjudicated by judges in courts of law.

1. STATUTES

Statutes are the most important legal source of law. Under the major written component of the Canadian constitution, namely, the Constitution Act of 1982 (incorporating, among other things, the former British North America Act of 1867), there are eleven sovereign legislative bodies in Canada. One is the Parliament of Canada, and the others are the ten provincial legislatures. By the provisions of the Constitution Act, each is granted legislative authority to enact statutes, but the legislative competence of each is, however, specifically limited to certain classes of matters. It is important to realize that a sovereign legislative body can enact statutes pursuant only to its legislative competence. Such legislation is referred to as primary legislation, in that it is passed by the sovereign legislative body itself. However, there is another category of legislation in Canada, and this is referred to as subordinate legislation.

Subordinate legislation is legislation enacted by a person, body or tribunal subordinate to a sovereign legislative body. Subordinate legislation takes many forms: by-laws, ordinances, statutory instruments, orders in council, rules and regulations. The body enacting subordinate legislation must do so only in accordance with the authority granted it under the enabling or governing legislation passed by the sovereign legislative body.[6] In short, a sovereign legislative body enacts governing legislation, and pursuant to that governing legislation, authority is granted to a delegate or a subordinate body to pass regulations, orders in council, by-laws, ordinances, rules, statutory instruments, and otherwise. A good example of a delegated authority is a municipal council. Pursuant to enabling provincial legislation, municipalities are created and municipal councils are granted authority to enact by-laws in accordance with the limitations set out in the enabling provincial legislation.

2. CASE LAW

The second major legal source of law is the decisions of courts in adjudicating particular matters. In deciding cases, judges, especially at the appellate levels, often set out in writing the material facts of the particular case, the issues of law involved and the reasons for decision, among other things. The reasons for decision, or ratio decidendi, may serve as a precedent for future courts to follow in the event that a similar fact situation is adjudicated again. The courts are bound to follow precedent cases in accordance with the doctrine of stare decisis. Accordingly, as a result of the operation of the doctrines of precedent and stare decisis, a body of case law has developed which acts as a guide for judges in deciding future cases. This body of case law is referred to as the common law. Because the common law is such a major legal source of law in the Canadian legal system, with the exception of the province of Quebec, the Canadian legal system is characterized as a common law system of law.[7] Essentially, the common law contains a set of principles enunciated through the decisions of courts over the past six hundred years. In other words, as new fact situations arise and as judges decide new cases, the existing principles are broadened, exceptions are developed, and the body of case law is expanded. In short, all of the case law and all of the principles and exceptions enunciated as part of that case law for the past six hundred years, initially in Great Britain, and subsequently in Canada, form the basis of the common law, the second major legal source of law in Canada.

---

[6] There are some restrictions on subordinate or delegated legislation and these restrictions are set out in Chapter 11 in connection with the discussion of statutes, and in Chapter 12 in dealing with an introduction to administrative law.

[7] The doctrines of precedent and stare decisis are discussed in detail in Chapter 10.

Consider the following commentaries on the historical evolution of the common law:

> This term, common law, which we have been using, needs some explanation. I think that it comes into use in or shortly after the reign of Edward the First. The word "common" of course is not opposed to "uncommon": rather it means "general", and the contrast to common law is special law. Common law is in the first place unenacted law; thus it is distinguished from statutes and ordinances. In the second place, it is common to the whole land; thus it is distinguished from local customs. In the third place, it is the law of the temporal courts; thus it is distinguished from ecclesiastical law, the law of the Courts Christian, courts which throughout the Middle Ages take cognisance of many matters which we should consider temporal matters — in particular marriages and testaments. Common law is in theory traditional law — that which has always been law and still is law, in so far as it has not been over-ridden by statute or ordinance. In older ages, while the local courts were still powerful, law was really preserved by oral tradition among the free men who sat as judges in these courts. In the twelfth and thirteenth century as the king's court throws open its doors wider and wider for more and more business, the knowledge of the law becomes more and more the possession of a learned class of professional lawyers, in particular of the king's justices. Already in John's reign they claim to be juris periti. More and more common law is gradually evolved as ever new cases arise; but the judges are not conceived as making new law — they have no right or power to do that — rather they are but declaring what has always been law.[8]

More recently, this evolutionary process has been described as follows:

> The starting point, therefore, is an assumption, or a theory, or a fiction if you will, that the common law of England is a comprehensive body of rules by reference to which every conceivable problem can be determined. Only a small portion of that body of rules has at any particular time been "found" and set forth in judicial decisions for our guidance. The rest remains to be found and applied from time to time as circumstances require. It follows that, in theory at least, the common law never changes. When a rule of the common law is found and enunciated for the first time, that is not a new law. It has always been the law but is now found for the first time. When the ultimate court of appeal overrules a line of cases in the lower courts and enunciates a rule that was never enunciated before, that is not a change in the law. The law was always as it is now revealed to us and we were in error, prior to the new decision, in thinking that it was something else.
>
>   . . .
>
> As a practical fact, whenever the ultimate court of appeal enunciates a rule which was never enunciated before, something new has been created; in fact, a new rule of law has been added to the body of rules that previously existed or one of the old rules that existed in fact has been altered or abrogated. However it is the theory of our system of law that the ultimate court of appeal is finding and expounding the true rule of the common law as it has always been.[9]

On the other hand, as indicated in the previous chapter, in the province of Quebec, the legal system is based not on the British tradition of common law but rather on the French and Roman tradition of codification of law. The Quebec Civil Code is essentially a domestic adaptation

---

[8] F. W. Maitland, *Constitutional History of England* (Cambridge: Cambridge University Press, 1908), pp. 22-23.

[9] W. R. Jackett, "Foundations of Canadian Law in History and Theory", in O.E. Lang (ed.), *Contemporary Problems of Public Law in Canada* (Toronto: University of Toronto Press, 1986), pp. 27-28.

of the Napoleonic or French Civil Code and, to some extent, also reflects the earlier Roman Code. This is not to say that the common law does not share those influences. Indeed, many statutes are a codification derived from some of the same historical sources. However, in the province of Quebec, codification represents the essential embodiment of the law, in that a judge need not abide by a precedent. He might, instead, rely on his own interpretation of a provision in the Quebec Civil Code.

The role of precedent and stare decisis in developing and evolving the common law and, in particular, in providing a mechanism by which the common law can respond to changing social conditions, is discussed in some detail in Chapter 10. In addition, reference should be made to a further discussion of the civil law system set out in the next chapter. But, for the time being, the reader ought to appreciate the importance of case law or the common law as a major legal source of law in Canada.

3. PARLIAMENTARY SOVEREIGNTY AND THE RELATION OF CASES TO STATUTES

Under the British doctrine of parliamentary sovereignty, Parliament can make or unmake any laws provided, in the Canadian context, that Parliament or a provincial legislature does so in accordance with the constitutional limitations set out in the Constitution Act of 1867. The doctrine of parliamentary sovereignty and some restrictions on the Canadian application of that doctrine are discussed in detail in Chapter 5. However, for the purposes of the present discussion, it is important to appreciate the sovereign power of Parliament or a provincial legislature to enact law. We have thus far defined the two major sources of law — statutory enactment and case law. The question then becomes: What is the relationship between the two? By virtue of the operation of the doctrine of parliamentary sovereignty, Parliament has the authority to repeal or modify any principles set out in the case law. Accordingly, in the event that a particular common law rule is antiquated or somehow in need of reform, the sovereign legislative body can enact legislation in effect to repeal, modify or alter (or perhaps codify) that common law rule. The various interpretation statutes do, however, contain provisions to the effect that a statute is remedial (rather than confirmatory) of an existing common law rule. Even if a common law rule is modified by statute, that statute, however, must conform to the standards required under the Charter of Rights and Freedoms. These constitutional standards are discussed in the next chapter.

There is a second aspect to the relationship between statutes and cases. Much of the common law is developed, not solely through an adjudication of new fact situations with reference to past and settled principles of common law, but also out of an interpretation of existing statutory provisions. Statutory interpretation represents a major portion of the role and function of the judge. As such, there have been many rules and principles developed in order to assist the court in interpreting ambiguous statutory provisions. These rules and principles are discussed in detail in Chapter 11.

4. MISCELLANEOUS LEGAL SOURCES OF LAW

As indicated earlier, there are other legal sources of law, although they do not assume the importance that the foregoing sources of law possess. The first of these is the royal prerogative. Although, generally, the royal prerogative is not exercised without the advice and consent of the executive branch of government, it does, nonetheless, legally and constitutionally, represent another legal source of law. Actually, many powers are constitutionally vested in the Crown. In the Canadian context, these powers are vested in the Crown in right of the Dominion and in the Crown in right of the provinces. The powers of the Crown in right of the Dominion are vested in the Governor General of Canada, and the powers of the Crown in right of a province are vested in the Lieutenant Governor of a province. The powers vested in the Governor General of Canada have historically been set out in letters patent and letters of instruction issued by Westminster to the Governor General. The last letters patent issued to the Governor General were issued in 1947. In addition, there is case authority in Canada to the effect that the Crown in right of a province possesses the same power as the Crown in right of the Dominion. At any rate, there are certain prerogatives of the Crown which are historically derived and which presently exist. Most Crown prerogatives, however, have been abolished by virtue of statutory enactment. Moreover, once a statute repeals a Crown prerogative, it can never again be revived as a Crown prerogative. It may subsequently be revived in statutory form, but as a Crown prerogative it is lost forever.

Consider the following examples of Crown prerogatives. Before the abolition of the death penalty in Canada, there existed a Crown prerogative to commute the execution of a sentence of death to life imprisonment. Also, the Crown presently has the prerogative to pardon persons convicted of crimes. Thirdly, certain provinces possess a tortious immunity for the Crown; that is, by virtue of the Crown prerogative, the Crown may not be sued in tort. However, most provinces have either repealed or modified this Crown prerogative by statute, so that the Crown may be sued in tort, provided that certain notice requirements are satisfied and, in some provinces, provided that permission is obtained from the Crown to be sued in tort.

The Crown prerogative is probably best described as an historical vestige of colonial times. Notwithstanding this, the Crown prerogative does provide that certain powers reside in the Crown. But, as indicated earlier, more of these powers would not be exercised without the advice and consent of the executive. There might, exist some exceptions to this, and, as such, the Crown prerogative represents another legal source of law of which the reader should be aware.

Another miscellaneous legal source of law is that of custom and convention. Essentially, custom and convention is a legally recognized and legally enshrined practice or usage. It is, of course, difficult to determine at what point in time a practice or usage hardens or crystallizes into a custom or convention and, as such, becomes a legal source of law. Also, the occasions when this occurs are few. That notwithstanding, the English rule is that for a custom to be regarded as a legal source of law in a particular case, "the the judges had to be satisfied as to the validity of the custom on seven grounds".[10] The various grounds upon which a practice or usage will be considered to have crystallized into a custom or convention are as follows: continuous operation; open exercise; exercise conducted peaceably and as of right; reasonable, certain and obligatory in nature; consistency with other customs and compatibility with statutes.[11]

Note that continuous operation has come to mean that the custom must be traced back to at least 1189. As a result, it is fair to conclude that custom is rarely a legal source of law of significant import today. The major exception to this, however, is Canadian constitutional law, where custom or convention plays a very significant role.

---

[10] Sim and Powell-Smith, *Questions and Answers on General Principles of English Law* (London: Butterworths, 1969), p. 41.

[11] The nature of convention in our legal system was considered at some length in *Manitoba (A.G.) v. Canada (A.G.)*, [1981] 1 S.C.R. 753, [1981] 6 W.W.R. 1, 125 D.L.R. (3d) 1 (*sub nom. Reference re Questions Concerning Amendment of the Constitution of Canada as Set out in O.C. 1020/80*), 34 Nfld. & P.E.I.R. 1, 95 A.P.R. 1, 39 N.R. 1, 11 Man. R. (2d) 1. This matter is also discussed in Chapter 5 on the constitutional basis of legislative and judicial authority in Canada.

See *Reference re Language Rights under s. 23 of the Manitoba Act, 1870 & s. 133 of the Constitution Act, 1867*, [1985] 1 S.C.R. 721, [1985] 4 W.W.R. 385, 19 D.L.R. (4th) 1, 35 Man.R. (2d) 83, 59 N.R. 321 (*sub nom. Reference re Manitoba Language Rights*).

In other words, in the process of Constitutional adjudication, the court may have regard to unwritten postulates which form the very foundation of the Constitution of Canada. In the case of the *Patriation Reference* this unwritten postulate was the principle of federalism. In the present case it is the principle of rule of law.

See also *O.P.S.E.U. v. Ontario (A.G.)*, [1987] 2 S.C.R. 2 at 38, 59 O.R. (2d) 671 (headnote), 28 Admin. L.R. 141, 41 D.L.R. (4th) 1, 87 C.L.L.C. 14,037, 23 O.A.C. 161, 77 N.R. 321, in which the Supreme Court of Canada later stated:

In addition, the constitution of Ontario comprises rules of a different nature but of great importance called conventions of the constitution. The most fundamental of these is probably the principle of responsible government which is largely unwritten . . .

Another legal source of law, to whatever extent courts will rely upon it, is juristic writings of notable scholars. However, to possess that status (and not be regarded as merely another literary source of law) the writing must be authoritative and the author distinguished. Even then, as a legal source of law, juristic writings might fall prey to the concern that they do no more than offer opinion as to the state of the law.

The final legal source of law is that of morality. Assume that a judge, in the conduct of an adjudication, is not able to find a particular piece of legislation upon which to rely. And assume further that he is not able to find a case or judicial precedent which relates to the fact situation before him, nor is he able to find a custom or convention which is applicable. Then, the question arises as to the principles upon which a judge must rely in deciding that case. "It is the judge's duty to decide every case brought before him and he cannot refuse to do so on the pretext that there is no relevant statutory text [or other legal source of law] applicable to the fact.[12] In that situation, the judge "must find out for himself, he must determine what the law ought to be, he must have recourse to the principles of morality.[13] It should be obvious, however, that only rarely will a circumstance arise in which a judge will not have recourse to a more specific legal source of law.

5. CONSTITUTIONAL SOURCES OF LAW

In defining the various sources of the Canadian constitution, one identifies the various legal sources of law in a somewhat different manner than that outlined above. In doing so, one points to the major legal sources of law and isolates them in terms of more specific, but generically described, categories. For example, statutes, as a legal source of law, may be subdivided, constitutionally, in terms of the following categories: British statutes, especially the Canada Act of 1982 with its constituent components, including the Constitution Acts of 1982 (containing the Canadian Charter of Rights and Freedoms), and 1867 (the old B.N.A. Act); pre-Confederation colonial statutes; post-Confederation Canadian statutes; and quasi-constitutional Canadian statutes. Also, there are additional legal sources of law which have unique constitutional significance, such as letters of instruction to Governors General and letters patent. These constitutional/legal sources of law are discussed in Chapter 5; however, those readers who are interested in pursuing these matters further may consult the following source: R. M. Dawson, *Dawson's Government of Canada*, 6th ed., rev. by N. Ward (Toronto: University of Toronto Press, 1987).

---

[12] A.K.R. Kiralfy, *The English Legal System*, 8th ed. (London: Sweet & Maxwell, 1990), p. 75.
[13] J. C. Gray, *The Nature and Sources of Law*, 2nd ed. (Boston: Beacon Press, 1963), p. 302.

THE LEGISLATIVE PROCESS

This chapter has dealt essentially with statutes as the most important legal source of law. The enactment of legislation is the main task of our elected representatives at all levels. Accordingly, those persons who have not had occasion to engage in a study of political science should appreciate at least the very basic elements of the legislative process. Essentially, a bill is passed into law in accordance with the following procedures. The government introduces a proposed bill into the particular legislative body, at which time the bill is given a routine first reading, that is, it is introduced and then passed without debate. Then, at a future time, the bill is re-introduced by the minister responsible for the subject matter contained in the bill for a second reading. At this stage in the legislative process, the bill is made the subject of a full debate. In introducing the bill at second reading, the responsible minister usually sets out the rationale behind the proposed enactment. If the bill passes second reading, the effect of the successful vote is that the legislative body has approved the bill in principle. Then the bill is usually forwarded to the appropriate standing committee of the legislative body for any hearings and/or further considerations that the standing committee may wish to entertain. (In some cases, however, it is referred instead to a committee of the whole.) The bill is then re-introduced into the legislative body, at the so-called report stage of the legislative process, containing any amendments arising out of the recommendations of the standing committee.

At the third reading, any amendments arising out of committee are debated and the bill is then usually passed, with the principle enunciated at second reading intact, subject only to any detailed amendments made as a result of considerations by the standing committee. Provincially, at this point, the bill has now been enacted into law, subject to formal approval by the Lieutenant Governor. Federally, the whole process repeats itself in the Senate, after which the bill then goes to the Governor General for formal approval. In respect of the latter, it is possible that the bill emerging from the House of Commons might differ, to some extent, from the bill subsequently emerging from the Senate. If that is the case, any amendments passed in the Senate must be referred back to the House of Commons for approval. Also it is possible that a bill might originally be initiated in the Senate and then proceed through the House of Commons in accordance with the above procedure.

In addition to the foregoing, legislation may be introduced by private members of the House of Commons and-or Senate (by private members I am referring to members of the opposition and to backbenchers of the governing party). These bills, however, virtually always meet with failure and do not represent a significant component of the legislative process.

Complex modern society

THE GROWTH OF PRIMARY AND SUBORDINATE LEGISLATION

In recent years there has been a major proliferation of legislative enactments at all levels of government. Because Parliament and the various provincial legislatures cannot possibly deal with every matter, and indeed lack the requisite expertise to do so, a common legislative practice is for the sovereign legislative body, be it Parliament or a provincial legislature, to enact governing or enabling legislation. Under that enabling legislation, the power to make statutory instruments — orders in council, regulations, by-laws, etc. — is delegated to an inferior body. That inferior body may be the cabinet, a minister of the cabinet, an administrative tribunal, a municipal council, or one of many other forms of inferior legislative authority. That inferior body may then enact subordinate legislation, in accordance with its terms of reference as set out in the enabling statute. In doing so, it may not, of course, exceed its jurisdiction as provided in the enabling statute.

There are certain additional constraints placed upon the delegated authority, including the rule of construction that the delegate may not re-delegate (as expressed in the Latin maxim *delegatus non potest delegare*). Even this rule of construction is subject to two exceptions — the first relating to an express provision in the enabling statute permitting a re-delegation, and the second to an implied delegation, the absence of which would prevent the operation of the intended legislative scheme.

The vast increase in both primary and delegated legislation represents a significant phenomenon in recent years. Probably it can best be understood in light of two possible explanations. First, as modern technology increases and as social problems become more complex, it follows that there must be, not only a legislative response, but often a complex legislative response. Often, such a response must be couched in technical language and must cover a wide range of activities in order to effect the desired regulation. Perhaps no better example can be found than the enactment of regulations under the Anti-Inflation Act.[14] The Anti-Inflation Act was enacted to deal with severe inflation and recession during the mid-1970's. Secondly, it has been said that no aspect of human life and human affairs is not covered by law. Indeed, when a new problem arises, the modern tendency, on the part of the public at large and of our legislators, is to immediately demand legislation in order to resolve the problem. For example, one can cite many recent legislative enactments which regulate the affairs of business, in previously little or unregulated areas. One might point to the Canadian Environmental Protection Act,

---

[14] S.C. 1974-75-76, c. 75 [since repealed 1988, c. 2, s. 68 (Sched. IV, item 33)].

R.S.C. 1985, c. 16 (4th Supp.) (providing government with sweeping powers to regulate substances deemed dangerous to the environment), the Competition Act (replacing the old Combines Investigation Act), R.S.C. 1985, c. C-34 and the major amendments thereto enacted in R.S.C. 1985, c. 19 (2nd Supp.), s. 45 (addressing concerns related to the concentration of market power in business), major revisions to the Income Tax Act (S.C. 1988, c. 55, ss. 1-203), the basic enabling statute and consequential amendments to other statutes enacted in order to implement the Canada — U.S. Free Trade Agreement, consumer protection legislation at all levels of government, and many others. On the other hand, one might argue that government intervention has decreased in terms of the regulation of private life and morality. For example, one can point to such recent examples as the liberalization of laws respecting abortion, homosexuality, divorce, attempted suicide, and others. The one exception to this latter notion, however, relates to the prevention of and protection against discrimination. This is an area where the state has interceded to an increasing extent in regulating private conduct.

In any event, there can be no doubt that the proliferation of statutory enactments can give rise to problems. In the province of Alberta, at the beginning of 1974, there existed some 7,000 regulations contained in 25,000 pages (see the Report of the Select Committee of the Legislative Assembly on Regulations in the Province of Alberta, November 1974). According to the Alberta Legislative Counsel's Office, in 1982 there were 2,024 regulations in force. As of 30th June 1989, there are now 1,638 regulations in force contained in approximately 20,000 pages. Only 424 of these regulations are pre-1978 in origin. The figures are interesting. While the number of regulations has drastically decreased and many older regulations have been cleaned up, they still occupy in excess of a staggering 20,000 pages. A similar situation exists in every province. Generally speaking, the problem arising out of the vast number of regulations resolves itself into four specific concerns: the need for advance consultation by all regulation-making authorities; the important requirement that the regulations be made accessible both to government personnel and members of the general public; the need for a continuing consolidation and revision of all regulations presently in force; and finally, the need to scrutinize all regulations in order to ensure that they have been enacted in accordance with the terms of reference contained in the enabling statute and that they have not violated any rule of law or any provision contained under a bill of rights.[15]

---

[15] See J.M. Keyes, *Executive Legislation: Delegated Law Making by the Executive Branch* (Toronto, Butterworths, 1992).

These concerns were articulated in the Report of the House of Commons Special Committee on Statutory Instruments under the chairmanship of Mark MacGuigan, M.P. As a result of that report, the Statutory Instruments Act was enacted by Parliament in 1971.[16] Under s. 26 of that Act, provision was made that statutory instruments were to be referred to any committee of one or both Houses of Parliament established for the purpose of reviewing delegated legislation. Subsequently, a standing Joint Committee of the House of Commons and Senate on Regulations and other Statutory Instruments was established. It tabled its first major report in the House of Commons and Senate on 4th February 1977. In that report, the Committee "accused the government . . . of using its sweeping decision-making power to trample citizens' basic civil rights". It pointed to the 14,000 federal regulations in force.[17] During the year ending 31st March 1989 there were in force 2,867 federal regulations, statutory instruments other than regulations and other documents made under statutory or other authority that are required to be published.[18] As at December 31, 1994, there were in force 3007 federal regulations, statutory instruments other than regulations and other documents.[19] There are also an unknown number of regulations that are not required to be published as they were made under the authority of the Canadian Wheat Board Act, the National Defence Act and the Royal Canadian Mounted Police Act.[20] When these thousands of federal regulations are added, for example, to the thousands of provincial regulations in Alberta, the amount of regulatory control, not to mention primary legislation, is clearly overwhelming. On the provincial level, these same concerns were articulated in the Report of the Select Committee of the Legislative Assembly on Regulations in the Province of Alberta. In addition, this whole question has been made the subject of research conducted by the Law Reform Commission of Canada.[21]

In connection with the question of advance consultation and scrutiny of regulatory enactments, all of the reports recommend that a standing committee of the various legislative bodies be established to conduct that

---

[16] S.C. 1970-71-72, c. 38 [now R.S.C. 1985, c. S-22].

[17] See the Edmonton Journal, 4th February 1977 (including editorial comment on 7th February 1977) and editorial comment in the Toronto Star, 5th February 1977.

[18] Table I, Canada Gazette, Pt. II. Note the decrease in actual number of regulations. This parallels the decrease in provincial regulations (in Alberta, for example) described above. However, some of the decrease in the number of regulations may be attributed to a consolidation of existing regulations.

[19] See Table I, Canada Gazette, Pt. II.

[20] Table III, Canada Gazette, Pt. II.

[21] See *Access to the Law* (Toronto: Carswell/Methuen, 1975), by Dean Martin Friedland of the University of Toronto.

function. Indeed, such a committee has been established federally as a result of the recommendations contained in the MacGuigan Report.

Accessibility is probably the most important concern arising out of regulatory proliferation. There is, of course, the problem that arises in connection with the existence of secret regulations. However, that problem aside, even in respect of public regulations, lawyers as well as members of the general public face difficulties due to the lack of consolidation of the thousands of regulations in force. In order to research a given point of law contained in a regulation, a lawyer often has to engage in a substantial time-consuming research project. One solution is, of course, to provide for a continual or at the very least periodic consolidation of existing regulations in force. However, a better solution, which appears likely to be implemented at some time in the future, relates to the development of computer technology. Computerized information retrieval systems would revolutionize the process of legal research. Indeed, there has been considerable research in Canada in recent years exploring these possibilities.

We live in an age in which society has imposed certain demands. It might be regarded as the maturation of the consumer age, in which society has come to recognize the legitimate demands of consumers in ensuring protection at the market place and the preservation of the environment. Accordingly society has come to recognize that the law can no longer be regarded as falling within the monopolistic preserve of the legal profession. The law belongs to all people in contemporary society and every person has the right to know how the law affects him.[22]

This is not, of course, to say that lawyers do not now serve a useful function. Indeed, the opposite is true, for it is a function of the lawyer, in serving his clients, to translate the language of the law to an understandable form. But persons in modern society, as consumers in our legal system, want more than a mere translation. They want, first, the ability to understand the law themselves and this, essentially, is in the nature of an invocation to more precise draftsmanship. Secondly, the consumer in the legal system wants the law to be accessible to him. And clearly, to refer again to the Alberta example, with 1,638 regulations contained in 20,000 pages, not to mention the problem arising out of a lack of consolidation, the average citizen has little, if any, access to the law. Moreover,

---

[22] Interest groups (both public advocacy interest groups and private lobbyists) play a significant role in the legislative process. Recently at the Federal level there has been some regulation of their activities. See the Lobbyist Registration Act, R.S.C. 1985, c. 44 (4th Supp.). The influence of public advocacy groups, however, has been somewhat diminished recently as government has reduced their public funding. See the Globe & Mail, April 1, 1995. For a discussion of the role of lawyers in this lobbying function, see G. Gall, "The Lawyer as Lobbyist" (1977) 25 Alta. L.R. 400.

in spite of the consolidation of regulations and the consequential reduction in their numbers over the past 15 years, accessibility to the law still remains a pressing concern.

Perhaps the answer lies in computer technology. Perhaps it lies in fewer and simpler statutes. Perhaps we are simply "over-judicialized". Indeed, there are over 10,000 crimes contained in federal statutes and regulations. Probably, the best answer lies in a more responsive legal professional disseminating legal information to all segments of the public and in servicing previously underserviced areas of the public. The answer also lies in ensuring that members of the legal profession, as educators, reformers and practitioners, maintain a continuous scrutiny of new and existing legislation. In order to serve the consumers of the legal system, the law must possess, at the very least, the fundamental characteristics of clarity and accessibility.

Chapter 4

THE BRITISH LEGAL TRADITION

INTRODUCTION

The influence of the British legal tradition is felt by many of the institutions within our system; it is the British tradition that underlies many of the processes and attitudes which make our system operational. No stronger comment on the influence of the British legal tradition in the Canadian legal system can be made than that by the late Chief Justice of Canada, Bora Laskin,[1] referring to a letter written over one hundred and twenty-five years ago:

> What a Toronto correspondent wrote in 1856 in a letter to the Law Times (28 L.T. 85) about England and Upper Canada has a familiar ring even today in respect of England and common law Canada; he said:
>
> > The laws of the two countries are almost identical. The practice or administration of the law is the same in each country . . . I do not invite an emigration of English lawyers, for in Upper Canada the profession is well supplied from native sources. But it will be a consolation to such members of the English Bar as may resolve to enter into competition in the colonies to know that they will labour under no disadvantage.[2]

There can be no doubt that the British influence on the Canadian legal system is very significant. However, it is also important to realize that the Canadian legal system, as a whole, consists of two major components. As indicated in an earlier chapter, the private law in nine of the provinces of Canada is governed by the common law system, while, in the province of Quebec, private law is governed by a civil law system. While the system of law in Quebec is not derived from the British legal system, it does possess an element of British influence. Unfortunately, most lawyers in the common law provinces do not possess more than a fundamental understanding of the civil law tradition in Quebec. Canada is a unique nation in that her citizens can experience the two major systems of law prevailing

---

[1] When he delivered the 21st series of Hamlyn Lectures on "The British Tradition in Canadian Law", in December 1969.

[2] *Ibid.*, p. xiii.

throughout the world.[3] It was rarely mentioned in the referendum debate of the 1970's nor in the now renewed debate and controversy concerning the role of Quebec in Confederation that within Confederation, as it presently exists, Canada is indeed fortunate in having both of the major systems of law in the world operate within her boundaries. In the late 1980's the debate has focussed on the uniqueness of Quebec. That debate has centred around the Meech Lake Accord, its distinct society clause and the use of the English and French languages. But again, little is mentioned of the richness of Canada in being able to experience the world's two greatest legal systems. Accordingly, a later chapter will be directed at a major discussion of the Quebec legal system.

THE RECEPTION OF ENGLISH LAW IN CANADA

1. THE ORIGIN OF THE COMMON LAW

The common law system of law originated in feudal England at about the time of the Norman conquest. It became a practice at that time that the King, in the course of travelling throughout England, would listen to complaints of his subjects and resolve disputes in accordance with the particular customs of that local area of the country. Customs which were not local, but rather were known throughout the land, were called "common customs".

Eventually, responsibility for this adjudication fell to the King's body of advisors, who established three types of courts. First, there was the Court of Common Pleas, for the adjudication of private disputes, one individual against another. Secondly, there was the Court of King's Bench, for criminal matters. Finally, there was the Exchequer Court, in which monetary matters were resolved. The decisions of these courts subsequently became known and were regarded as the "common customs" or "common law" of the land. Eventually, they began to take on a formal aspect and the judges of the various courts held themselves bound by past decisions, and therein lay the origin of the common law as a body of jurisprudence or past decisions upon which judges rely in deciding the cases before them.

The common law of England subsequently spread to the colonies of the British Empire, including the British colonies in North America. Of the two major systems of law in the world, the common law system is not as extensively followed as the civil law system. However, the

---

[3] The State of Louisiana in the United States is, to a minor extent, in a situation similar to that of Quebec. Louisiana also has a civil law tradition. However, there is not the duality of language that parallels the duality of legal systems in the Canadian context.

common law system governs the law in most of the English speaking world except Scotland) and in many parts of the non-English speaking world, encompassing those nations that are presently or were formerly part of the British Commonwealth. The common tradition linking the common law world is this reliance on a body of case law that developed over centuries of judicial decision-making in solving current problems before the courts.

The mechanism by which the British colonies in North America adopted the common law system in general and the English law, as it existed at the time, specifically, is somewhat complicated. Generally speaking, the method by which English law was received in a British colony depended upon how that colony was acquired by Great Britain. If it had been acquired by settlement, one set of rules would apply. And if it had been acquired by treaty or cession, yet another set of rules would apply. In Canada, the reception of English law in the territories and in each of the provinces differed. No attempt will be made in this text to consider the complicated history of the reception of English law in detail. However, set out below is a brief and summary review of that history. In addition, interested readers may consult various writings which consider the history of the reception of English law in Canada in considerable detail.[4]

2. CONFEDERATION

Under the provisions of the British North America Act of 1867 (since renamed the Constitution Act of 1867), the Dominion of Canada was created. The original B.N.A. Act provided for a union of the then existing provinces of Canada, Nova Scotia and New Brunswick. Upon union, the province of Canada was divided into the province of Ontario (formerly called the province of Upper Canada) and the province of Quebec (formerly the province of Lower Canada), and these two provinces were united with Nova Scotia and New Brunswick. In addition, the original B.N.A. Act provided for the possibility of future admission of the provinces of Newfoundland, Prince Edward Island and British Columbia, as well as Rupert's Land and the North-Western Territory.

3. WESTERN PROVINCES

English law was first brought to the Canadian west by the Hudson's Bay Company under its Charter of 3rd May 1670. When British subjects settled a colony, they brought with them the existing English common law and statutory law.

---

[4] In particular, see B. Laskin, *supra*, note 1, at p. 3; and J.E. Cole, "Reception of English Law" (1977), 15 Alta. L.Rev. 29, among others.

Under the combined operation of the Rupert's Land Act, 1868 (U.K.), c. 105, the Manitoba Act, S.C. 1870, c. 3, and the Order in Council of 23rd June 1870, the Hudson's Bay Company surrendered its land to the new Dominion, Rupert's Land and the North-Western Territory were admitted into the Dominion, and the province of Manitoba was created. The admision into the Dominion of Rupert's Land and the North-Western Territory and the creation of the province of Manitoba all became effective on 15th July 1870. That date is significant, moreover, for reason that it is the date when the province of Manitoba and the North-Western Territory received English law, as it existed at that time.

By virtue of an 1871 amendment to the Constitution Act of 1867, the Parliament of Canada had legislative authority to create new provinces out of the existing territories. Pursuant to that authority the Alberta Act, S.C. 1905, c. 3, created the province of Alberta and the Saskatchewan Act, S.C. 1905, c. 42, established the province of Saskatchewan. Under those statutes, there was provision for the continuance of the law as it existed in the territories, and the reader will recall that in the territories, English law was received as it existed on 15th July 1870. As a result the effective date of the reception of English law in the provinces of Alberta and Saskatchewan as also 15th July 1870.

Generally speaking, the date of reception of English law for those colonies acquired by settlement is the date at which the colonial legislature, once established, enacted its first statute. The province of British Columbia acquired English law by settlement. The Law and Equity Act, R.S.B.C. 1979, c. 224, expressly provides for a reception of English law as it existed on 19th November 1858.

4. MARITIME PROVINCES

The Maritime provinces were also acquired by settlement and, therefore, the date for reception of English law is the date at which each of the colonial legislatures was instituted. For the provinces of New Brunswick[5] and Nova Scotia, this occurred in 1758; for the province of Newfoundland, in 1832. In Prince Edward Island, the colonial legislature was instituted in 1773; however, English law was actually received in 1763 pursuant to a royal proclamation.

---

[5] Arguably, in New Brunswick, the reception date is 1660. Lawyer Eric Teed, in correspondence dated May 1980, wrote:

> New Brunswick has English law by virtue of the discovery of John Cabot in 1947 who claimed down to Virginia. There have been several cases which ruled 1660 was the date of reception of English law. The Maritimes have English law by virtue of English discovery of settlement prior to the French settlement, not by virtue of conquest.

5. CENTRAL CANADA

Although the province of Quebec is presently a civil law jurisdiction, for a short time it was ruled by English law. After Quebec fell to the British, English civil law and criminal law were introduced by the Royal Proclamation of 1763. Subsequently, although English criminal law remained, French civil law was reinstated by virtue of the Quebec Act, S.C. 1774, c. 83.

Under the Constitutional Act, S.C. 1791, c. 31, the provinces of Upper Canada and Lower Canada were created. In Ontario (Upper Canada), following the above enactment, a legislature was created and it enacted its first statute in 1792, under which the English civil law was made applicable to the new province. That Act was assented to on 15th October 1792, and that date is generally regarded as the date for the reception of English law in the province of Ontario.

6. OTHER SIGNIFICANT DATES

After the reception of English law in the "colonies" English legislation affected the "colonies" only if it was applicable to and intended to apply to the colony. Conversely, no colonial statute could be repugnant to any British statute or common law, and it would be inoperative to the extent of any repugnancy. However, upon the enactment of the Colonial Laws Validity Act, 1865 (28 & 29 Vict., c. 63), the above doctrine of repugnancy applied only to colonial statutes which were repugnant to British statutes specifically directed at the colonies.

Significantly, following the enactment of the Statute of Westminster, 1931 (22 & 23 Geo. 5, c. 4), the British Parliament had no further capacity to legislate for Canada, unless Canada so requested. The English common law, however, still had a significant impact so long as Canadian courts considered themselves bound by decisions of the higher English courts under the doctrine of stare decisis. This was particularly so until the Supreme Court of Canada became the final court of appeal in respect to all criminal and civil matters in 1949.[6]

THE LAW OF EQUITY

With the reception of English law, Canada inherited not only the English common law but also the law of equity. Historically, the various courts

---

[6] For a more detailed examination of significant developments throughout the history of Canadian law, see W.R. Jackett, "Foundations of Canadian Law in History and Theory" in O.E. Lang (ed.), *Contemporary Problems of Public Law in Canada* (University of Toronto Press, 1968.

established by the King's advisors, referred to earlier in this chapter, became very formal and rigid in applying the law and in providing the appropriate remedies in the course of adjudicating particular disputes. As a result many subjects would petition the King for extraordinary remedies, as the King was regarded as the fountainhead of justice. The King, in response to these petitions, would provide these extraordinary remedies in the appropriate circumstances. However, as this responsibility became increasingly burdensome, he transferred this jurisdiction for providing extraordinary remedies to his Chancellor. The Chancellor would then receive the various petitions and would dispense these remedies in the appropriate circumstances. By reference to "appropriate circumstances", one means, first, that owing to the rigidity of the rules under which the regular courts operated, they could not provide a remedy in a particular circumstance. Secondly, the petitioners had to fulfill certain preconditions. Eventually, the Chancellor, too, found this responsibility burdensome, and accordingly he transferred jurisdiction to special courts established for the sole purpose of granting those extraordinary remedies. These courts became known as the courts of chancery. After a period of time, these courts, like the King's courts, became somewhat formalized and operated under a regime of rigid rules to which subjects had to adhere before the granting of these extraordinary remedies would be permitted.

In essence, what developed then were two systems of courts in England: the King's regular courts or courts of common law, and the courts of chancery or, alternatively expressed, the courts of equity. The reader will recall the various connotations given to the term "common law". This is yet another connotation, for here the term "common law" means a system of courts of common law providing common law remedies, as opposed to a system of courts of equity providing what are known as equitable remedies.

Parallel with the development of the two systems of courts was the development of two systems of law. The common law courts concerned themselves with the common law, while the courts of chancery concerned themselves with what became known as the law of equity. The extraordinary remedies dispensed by the latter system of courts became known as equitable remedies and the preconditions that had to be fulfilled before the courts of chancery would entertain a petition for an equitable remedy became known as the rules of equity. Probably the most important rule of equity is that a petitioner will not receive an equitable remedy unless he comes to the court "with clean hands". This means, essentially, that he must not taint his case by any wrongdoing whatsoever on his part. Examples of the more important of the equitable remedies are those of rescission and specific performance in the law of contract, but there are several others as well.

In the latter part of the last century, by virtue of the enactment of the Judicature Acts by the Parliament of Great Britain and by the legislative assemblies of the provinces of Canada, the courts of common law and the courts of equity emerged, with the result that we now have only one system of courts dispensing both common law and equitable remedies. However, since a court will not now entertain an application for an equitable remedy unless the applicant has satisfied the various rules of equity referred to above, the distinction between law and equity is still important.

THE CANADIAN CONSTITUTIONAL SYSTEM

The Canadian constitutional system is the subject of a major discussion in Chapter 5; however, for our present purposes, we will examine that system in the context of the British legal tradition.

The major written portions of the Canadian constitution are the Constitution Acts of 1867 (the old B.N.A. Act) and 1982 (including the new Canadian Charter of Rights and Freedoms).[7] The significance and content of the major constitutional changes of 1982 are discussed in the next chapter; however, in the preamble to the original B.N.A. Act, the drafters of our constitution included a provision to the effect that the various provinces, upon union, desired that Canada possess a constitution "similar in principle to that of the United Kingdom". Those operative words "similar in principle to that of the United Kingdom", have been known as the "Implied Bill of Rights" in the Canadian constitution.

The effect of the "Implied Bill of Rights" has been to import into our constitutional order various doctrines of British constitutional law.[8] Generally speaking, those words, contained in the preamble, incorporate into the Canadian constitutional system notions of fair play and fundamental freedoms (i.e., freedom of association and assembly, freedom of the press and freedom of speech). More specifically, however, those words import into our constitutional system three fundamental doctrines of British constitutional law. In particular, those fundamental doctrines are the doctrine of responsible government, the doctrine of rule of law and the doctrine of all parliamentary sovereignty. The importance and effect of the latter two doctrines are discussed in detail in Chapter 5.

---

[7] The third major written portion of the Canadian constitution would have been the Meech Lake Constitutional Accord of 1987 or the Charlottetown Accord of 1993. Neither of these were enacted into law. See the discussion in Chapter 5.

[8] See *A.G. Can. v. Dupond*, [1978] 2 S.C.R. 770 at 772 (headnote), 5 M.P.L.R. 4, 84 D.L.R. (3d) 420, 19 N.R. 478 (*sub nom. Dupond v. Montreal*).

Per Beetz J. (For the majority — Martland, Judson, Ritchie, Pigeon and de Grandpre JJ. concurring):

In addition to the above, under the Canadian constitution, executive power vests in the Crown in Great Britain. However, the Queen now acts only through her representatives in Canada. As a result, in particular, executive authority at the federal level vests in the Governor General of Canada. Provincially, executive power vests in the various Lieutenant Governors of the respective provinces. In addition, there is case authority to the effect that the Crown in right of a province has the same executive authority as the Crown in right of the Dominion. Many of the executive powers vested in the Governor General and the Lieutenant Governors are set out specifically in the Constitution Act of 1867. In addition, traditionally the Queen's representatives in Canada have had their authority defined and communicated to them by way of letters of instruction and letters patent issued in 1947, with the result, essentially, that the Queen's representatives in Canada now have plenary executive authority, as the Queen does herself in the United Kingdom.

Notwithstanding the fundamental nature of the link between the exercise of executive authority in Canada and the Crown in Great Britain, the above is not a truly representative description of the constitutional and de facto exercise of executive power in Canada. This is so for reason of the conventional rules of Canadian constitutional law. In particular, although there are in the Constitution Act of 1867 various specific powers

---

In reply to the submission made by appellants that s. 5 and the Ordinance are in relation to and in conflict with the fundamental freedoms of speech, of assembly and association, of the press and of religion which were inherited from the United Kingdom and made part of the Constitution by the premable of the *B.N.A. Act* or protected by the *Canadian Bill of Rights*, it should be remembered that:

(1) none of the freedoms referred to is placed above the reach of all legislation by the Constitution;

(2) none of these freedoms is a single matter coming within exclusive federal or provincial jurisdiction;

(3) these freedoms are distinct and independent of the faculty of holding assemblies, parades, gatherings, demonstrations or processions on the public domain of a city;

(4) the right to hold public meetings on a highway or in a park is unknown to English law; consequently it cannot have become part of the preamble of the B.N.A. Act;

(5) the holding of assemblies, parades or gatherings on the public domain is a matter which, depending on the aspect, comes under federal or provincial competence;

(6) the *Canadian Bill of Rights* does not apply to provincial and municipal legislation.

Laskin C.J.C. and Dickson and Spence JJ. dissented on other grounds.

See also D.A. Schmeiser, "The Entrenchment of a Bill of Rights" (1981), 19 Alta. L. Rev. 375 at 379:

[v]arious judges have also suggested the existence of an implied bill of rights in our constitution, at least until the recent rejection of that doctrine by the Supreme Court of Canada in Attorney General for Canada and Dupond.

which are vested in the Governor General (such as, for example, the power to summon Parliament), in reality, under the conventional rules of Canadian constitutional law, the Governor General acts only upon the advice and consent of the Prime Minister and his cabinet. Also, for example, under the Constitution Act of 1867, the Crown has a legislative role, namely, to assent to legislation (or, alternatively, to refuse to assent to or to reserve assent of legislation). However, under the conventional rules of constitutionl law, the power to refuse to assent or to reserve assent will, most likely, no longer be exercised. In short, executive power in Canada, with some limited exceptions, lies in the hands of the Prime Minister and his cabinet and, provincially, with the various premiers and their cabinets.

In addition to the foregoing, in Canada the Crown serves another function of considerable importance. Specifically, the Crown symbolically represents, to use the words of the late Chief Justice Bora Laskin, the "personification of the State".[9]

OTHER COMPONENTS OF THE BRITISH LEGAL TRADITION IN CANADA

The late Chief Justice, in the published version of the 1968 Hamlyn Trust Lectures referred to earlier, discusses other components of the Canadian legal system which share a British legal tradition; the historical evolution of Canadian courts along British lines, including, inter alia, the independence of the judiciary and the use of the jury trial in Canada; the British influence on the development of the legal profession in Canada, including legal education, the admission to practice, and legal scholarship and research. In connection with the legal profession, it is important to appreciate that the practice of law in the United Kingdom differs somewhat from that in Canada. In the United Kingdom, persons are trained and admitted to the bar to practise as either a barrister or a solicitor, but not both. In contrast, however, in Canada a person is admitted to the bar of his or her respective province to practise as both a barrister and a solicitor.

In addition to all of the foregoing, there is one other matter of great significance in defining the British influence on Canadian law. Specifically, Canada has inherited through the operation of the doctrine of stare decisis a rich body of jurisprudence containing centuries of often brilliant reasoning in the decisions of English courts.[10]

---

[9] B. Laskin, *supra*, note 1, at p. 119.

[10] For a discussion of the modern English barrister, see the Guardian, 30th July 1979.

Under the doctrine of stare decisis, Canadian courts, at least prior to 1949,[11] when the Supreme Court of Canada became the final court of appeal in all criminal and civil matter, were bound to follow decisions of high English courts. In particular, the Supreme Court of Canada (nd, by implication, all inferior courts) felt themselves bound to follow all decisions of the House of Lords and the Judicial Committee of the Privy Council. In 1949, however, the Supreme Court of Canada became the final court of appeal and thereafter there existed no resort to appeal to any English court. As a result, decisions of the House of Lords and the Judicial Committee of the Privy Council are no longer binding on Canadian courts. However, even to the present day, decisions of these courts, under the doctrine of stare decisis, remain highly persuasive. A fuller discussion of this is set out in detail in Chapter 10.

CONCLUSION

In summary, there can be no doubt that historically, and, to a lesser extent, presently, the British legal tradition plays a vital role in defining the nature of the Canadian legal system. Given that patriation of the Canadian constitution has occurred, as the Supreme Court of Canada continues to evolve and develop as the highest court in the nation and the final court of appeal,[12] and as Parliament and the provincial legislatures provide fresh and innovative solutions to present and future problems, it is reasonable to expect that the reliance on the British legal tradition will diminish in time. That prediction notwithstanding, the British tradition in the Canadian legal system is considerably more than a mere historical vestige. When one examines the Canadian legal system as a whole, as an organic, viable and operational structure, one will never be able to divorce that structure from its British origins.

Indeed, as the late Chief Justice Laskin stated:[13]

More than two hundred years have passes since English law and English legal institutions were rooted in a yet unborn Canada. Sustained at first by remote control from Westminster and by domestic control of colonial governors, the English tradition has survived Canadian legislative and judicial independence, and remains a vital and omnipresent force in Canadian law.

This chapter has reviewed the extent to which the British legal tradition pervades the Canadian legal system. As we expand our examination

---

[11] Interestingly, it wasn't until 1986 that Australia abolished appeals to the Judicial Committee of the Privy Council.

[12] This process of development will, no doubt, be aided by the 1975 amendment to the Supreme Court Act, under which the court may pick and choose those cases of national or legal importance it wishes to decide.

[13] Hamlyn Lectures, *supra*, note 1, at p. 1.

of that system, the truth of the foregoing will become evident. Indeed, as we shall see in the next chapter, the constitutional basis for the legislative and judicial authority in Canada is, to a significant extent, set out in a statute of the United Kingdom. Before 1982, that constitutional basis was set out in the old B.N.A. Act. In 1982, the enactment of the Canada Act by the U.K. Parliament provided Canadians with the so-called "new" constitution. The new constitution contains, among other things, the Canadian Charter of Rights and Freedoms[14] and a domestic amending formula. These major developments are discussed in the next chapter. The Canada Act, which incorporates both the old B.N.A. Act of 1867 and the new instrument (including the Charter and the amending formula), states:[15]

> No Act of the Parliament of the United Kingdom passed after the Constitution Act, 1982, comes into force shall extend to Canada as part of its law.

Notwithstanding the above provision, the Canadian constitution, is still technically embodied in a British statute, the Canada Act of 1982. That in itself is a commentary on the importance of the British legal tradition in Canadian law and in the Canadian legal system.

---

[14] Great Britain does not have a written constitution per se. It also lacks a modern constitutional bill of rights similar to our Charter (and is unlikely to acquire one in the foreseeable future). As a result, given the importance of our Charter as a cornerstone of constitutional jurisprudence, it follows that the influence of British courts, at least insofar as constitutional jurisprudence is concerned, will predictably diminish.

[15] 1982 (Eng.), c. 11, s. 2.

Chapter 5

THE CONSTITUTIONAL BASIS OF LEGISLATIVE AND JUDICIAL AUTHORITY

INTRODUCTION

Professor R. I. Cheffins and lawyer R. N. Tucker discuss the purpose of a constitution in their treatise *The Constitutional Process in Canada* as follows:

> One of the chief problems in any constitutional system is to decide when decisions should be made within formal legal channels and when matters should be left to other more informal and usually more flexible arenas. This is one of the things a formal constitutional document attempts to do. A constitution usually serves a variety of needs. First, it is a badge of nationhood, an indication that the nation has arrived on the national scene fully clothed with the appropriate legal garb. In addition, as already indicated, constitutions set up certain structures and assign them different authority. These structures are usually given such titles as Parliament, Congress, Courts, Executive Officers, Administration. Each of these various types of bodies, irrespective of its title, is usually assigned some rather nebulous area of power . . .

> A constitution is more than a mechanical set of ground rules. It is a mirror reflecting the national soul. It reflects those values the country regards as important, and also shows how these values will be protected. It is for the constitutional student to try to correlate and explain the extent to which the national idea is implemented within the day-to-day framework of political processes. Every nation's approach to these legal and political problems has much in common with that of every other nation, and much that is peculiarly the nation's own. Every nation draws, to a considerable extent, on the experience of other nations. Similarly, no state can function legally and politically without some internal recognition that it is, in at least some ways, part of a world community. Thus there have developed between states narrow legal, and wider customary, methods of communication and organization, which affect the domestic political order.[1]

Moreover, in a subsequent work, Professor Cheffins and lawyer P.A. Johnson state that:

---

[1] 2nd ed. (Toronto: McGraw-Hill. 1975).

A constitution must first provide for the creation of the basic organs and institutions of public authority. Second, it must define the powers possessed by each of the public institutions and in some respects define the relationships between these various institutions. Third, a constitution must provide for the processes by which law is created, and at the same time provide for the limitations on the power exercised by the officials of public institutions. Thus a constitution assigns legal responsibility, defines the limits of authority, and establishes the processes which must be followed before this authority can be exercised. Furthermore, a constitutional document must provide for a method of change, both of political leadership and of the basic constitutional framework, the latter by way of amendment to the constitution.

In Canada it is necessary to look at a whole series of statutes and other legal documents to ascertain how, at least to some extent, power is allocated in the Canadian system. However, as will be demonstrated later, many of the rules with respect to the functioning of authority in a constitutional system are not defined in authoritative legal documents but rather are the result of consensus among the actors in a political and constitutional system. It must always be remembered that the legal rules of the constitution are inextricably linked with the informal functioning of the political process. It is impossible to detach the legal rules of the constitutional game from the political process which gives the entire polity vitality and life. It must also be remembered that quite often the legal rules are very misleading when examined without reference to the historical and political context of the country.[2]

Essentially, Professor Cheffins, Mr. Tucker and Mr. Johnson are maintaining that a constitution should be regarded as an integral part of the polity of a given nation. As such, a study of constitutional law ought to be conducted in the context of the Canadian political system. But also, that study ought to be conducted in the context of the social and economic underpinnings upon which Canadian society is founded.

THE CONSTITUTIONAL BASIS

Generally, the Canadian constitution is very complex and is derived from numerous sources. Prior to 17th April 1982, in terms of the most fundamental consideration, the Canadian constitution could be reduced to two major components — a written component and an unwritten component. The written component consisted primarily of three British statutes enacted by the Parliament of Great Britain. In order of enactment, those statutes were the Colonial Laws Validity Act of 1865, the British North America Act of 1867, and the Statute of Westminster of 1931. When taken together these three statutes provided the basic framework of the Canadian constitution and enshrined in our constitutional system the doctrine of ultra vires. Under the doctrine of ultra vires, the B.N.A. Act possessed a supremacy over all statutes enacted by the Parliament of Canada and by the legislatures of the ten provinces. The result of this was that any Act passed by Parliament or a legislature had to conform to the jurisdictional constraints set out in ss. 91 and 92 of the B.N.A. Act.

---

[2] R.I. Cheffins and P.A. Johnson, *The Revised Canadian Constitution: Politics as Law* (Toronto: McGraw-Hill Ryerson, 1986), p. 3.

However, even then (i.e., prior to 17th April 1982) it was, simplistic and incorrect to regard the B.N.A. Act as the total embodiment of the Canadian constitution. It was far more accurate to regard it instead as the main element of the written component of the constitution. In addition to the above, there were (and are) other elements of the written component of the Canadian constitution. For example, existing laws at Confederation are also elements of the written component in that they continue in force by virtue of s. 129 of the B.N.A. Act. Furthermore, legislation creating the provinces of Alberta, Saskatchewan and Manitoba must necessarily be regarded as an important element in the constitution. In addition, one usually regards letters patent and letters of instruction from Westminster to the colonial Governor before Confederation and to the Governor General since Confederation as part of the written constitution. Indeed, the creation of the office of the Governor General in Canada and the delegation of all Crown prerogative power to that office was effected by the issuance of the last letters patent in 1947. In addition, every statute and every regulation of Parliament and of the provincial legislatures is also regarded as a part of the written constitution.

Some persons argue that some regular statutes possess, by their very nature, a special status. These so-called quasi-constitutional statutes include the Canadian Bill of Rights, R.S.C. 1985, App. III, the Supreme Court Act,[3] R.S.C. 1985, c. S-26, provincial bills of rights and like statutes. Although these statutes are not entrenched in the constitution and could strictly be repealed at any time, they intrinsically occupy a special status for reason that their subject matters fall within the constitutional realm. Some statutes, like the Canadian Bill of Rights, contain primacy provisions which, in effect, require that all other statutes of the same legislative jurisdiction must conform to the substantive provisions contained in the statute possessing primacy, unless those other statutes specifically state that they shall operate notwithstanding the statute containing the primacy provision.

However, notwithstanding all of the foregoing, the B.N.A. Act was the most important component of the written constitution.

Reference was made above to 17th April 1982. That is the date Canada received a so-called "new" constitution. This major event in Canadian history followed a somewhat tumultuous series of events that have trans-

---

[3] The Supreme Court of Canada is, to some extent, given constitutional status in the Constitution Act of 1982. This process was to be completed through the Meech Lake Constitutional Accord of 1987. Under the Accord, the Supreme Court of Canada would have become fully entrenched, with the result that any changes to the composition or any other aspects of the Court require the unanimous consent of the Parliament of Canada and the legislatures of all the provinces. See the discussion, *infra*.

pired over the past few years. Those events have been described in some detail in several publications, including E. McWhinney, *Canada and the Constitution 1979-1982: Patriation and the Charter of Rights* (Toronto: University of Toronto Press, 1982); R. Sheppard and M. Valpy, *The National Deal: The Fight for a Canadian Constitution* (Toronto: Fleet Books, 1982); G. Stevenson, *Unfulfilled Union: Canadian Federalism and National Unity*, Revised Edition (Toronto: Gage Publishing Limited, 1982); and D. Milne, *The New Canadian Constitution* (Toronto: James Lorimer & Company, 1982).

Essentially these events followed a decade of constitutional negotiations between the provinces and the federal government to restructure and modernize the Canadian constitution. However, after the failure, in September 1980, of the federal government and the ten provinces to reach an accord on a revised constitution, the federal government unilaterally proceeded with the placing before the Parliament of Canada of a new constitutional package. That package, of course, included a Canadian Charter of Rights and Freedoms. That Charter, among other things, attracted considerable debate. Hundreds of submissions were made to the Special Joint Committee of the Senate and House of Commons, a committee created to consider changes to the resolution then before Parliament containing the constitutional package. At the same time, there was much debate as to the wisdom of entrenching a bill of rights in the constitution and as to the quality of the proposed Charter of Rights and Freedoms. The debate embraced both sides of the Atlantic, as the British Government and Members of Parliament were strongly lobbied by Canadian politicians hoping to influence the manner in which Britain would deal with the Canadian request to enact the Charter. Much of the discussion centred on the unilateral nature of the federal action, and questioned whether the enactment by the Canadian Parliament of a resolution authorizing the Parliament of the United Kingdom to include a Charter of Rights and Freedoms in the new Canadian constitution infringed on provincial legislative powers under the B.N.A. Act. If so, the discussion then centred on whether a convention existed that the consent of the affected provinces was needed before the Parliament of Canada could make such a request. This issue was to some extent jurisprudential in nature, as the question whether such a convention existed directly led to the question of the status of convention in our legal system.

In any event, these issues were canvassed in three separate constitutional references made to the Courts of Appeal in the provinces of Manitoba, Newfoundland, and Quebec with an appeal therefrom to the

Supreme Court of Canada.[4] During this process, Parliament dealt with the resolution before it, making some significant changes in the Charter of Rights and Freedoms, largely as a result of submissions made to and recommendations made by the Special Joint Committee referred to earlier.

Subsequently, the Supreme Court of Canada upheld the legality, though not the constitutionality (in the conventional sense) of the unilateral federal move to patriate the constitution with its entrenched Canadian Charter of Rights and Freedoms. Subsequent to this decision, the federal and provincial governments convened in a final effort to reach an agreement. This led to a breakthrough in which the federal government and all provinces except Quebec agreed to patriation of a somewhat revised package, the revisions including a new amending formula and some changes in the Charter of Rights and Freedoms. Further changes to the Charter, arising from a lobbying effort by native and women's groups, were later agreed to. The entire package was finally approved by the Parliament of Canada in December 1981 and then enacted by the Parliament of the United Kingdom, following which the patriation was effected by the signature of Her Majesty the Queen on the instrument of Proclamation on 17th April 1982. More specifically, a Joint Resolution of the House of Commons and the Senate was enacted in December 1981, after the consent of nine provinces was obtained. That Joint Resolution requested Her Majesty the Queen to place before the Parliament of the United Kingdom an Act called the Canada Act of 1982 (technically cited as 31 Elizabeth II). The Canada Act was passed by the United Kingdom Parliament and proclaimed in Ottawa on 17th April 1982 by Her Majesty the Queen.

Quebec's failure to accept the patriation package made it feel like the "odd man out" in the Canadian "constitutional family". This led to renewed constitutional discussions, starting around 1985, where the government of Quebec made a series of proposals that, if accepted by all, would lead to Quebec's return to the "constitutional family".

In the interim, of course, Quebec is as legally bound as all of the provinces by the provisions of the Canada Act of 1982 and of its Schedule B, the Constitution Act of 1982. So, the Quebec proposals, although full of substance, also assumed a great symbolic significance.

Essentially, the Quebec proposals can be divided into two components. The first deals with the distinctiveness of Quebec in the Canadian federation, and the second, although not entirely unrelated to the first, deals

---

[4] See *Manitoba (Attorney General) v. Canada (Attorney General)*, [1981] 1 S.C.R. 753, [1981] 6 W.W.R. 1, 125 D.L.R. (3d) 1 (*sub nom. Reference Re Resolution to Amend the Constitution*), 11 Man. R. (2d) 1, 34 Nfld. & P.E.I.R. 1, 95 A.P.R. 1, 39 N.R. 1; and *The Supreme Court Decisions on the Canadian Constitution* (Toronto: Jarnes Lorimer & Co., 1981).

with a potpourri of other matters. These other matters arguably tend to enhance the role of the provinces in their relationship with the federal government. Not surprisingly, then, when Quebec proposed this package, including the latter portion which enhances the role of the provinces, at the time all of the provinces initially agreed to the package under a principle of so-called 'juridical equality'. This package became known as the Meech Lake Constitutional Accord.

The Accord recognized the province of Quebec as constituting a distinct society within Canada. At the same time, it recognized, as a fundamental characteristic of Canada, that there is an Anglophone minority in Quebec and a Francophone minority elsewhere in Canada.

The provinces were, for the first time, given a formal role in nominating persons to sit on certain federal institutions (namely, the Senate and the Supreme Court of Canada).

For some time, social programs falling within provincial legislative jurisdiction (health care, for example) had been largely financed by the federal government. This was so because the federal government had a greater spending ability than the provinces due to its greater taxing power. The provincial concerns with this arrangement related to the fact that the federal government often attached conditions to this financing. Under the Accord, a province was able to opt out of one of these programs provided it established one of its own and provided its own program had objectives compatible with the national objectives of the program from which it opted out. If that was the case, the federal government would continue to finance the new provincial program with reasonable compensation.

Under the Constitution Act of 1867, the provinces and the federal governments were given joint or parallel jurisdiction over immigration. That led to a series of agreements relating to the settlement of new immigrants in Canada. In essence, the Accord constitutionalized those agreements.

The Accord also constitutionalized the federal-provincial consultative process by requiring that at least one First Ministers' meeting be held annually and by requiring that the issues of Senate reform and the fisheries be discussed at those meetings.

Finally, the Accord slightly changed the existing formula for constitutional amendment. Before the Accord, there were two formulae for amendment. The general formula required the consent of the Senate and House of Commons and of the legislatures of two-thirds of the provinces, provided those provinces comprised 50 per cent of the population of

Canada. For some specialized listed matters, the formula required the consent of Parliament and the legislatures of all of the provinces. There actually was a third section listing other specialized matters but these matters required only the general amending formula. The Accord took this latter list of specialized matters, added some more and moved them over to the first list of specialized matters. As a result, all of the listed specialized matters (such as changes to the Senate and the creation of any new provinces)[5] required the unanimous consent of Parliament and the legislatures of the provinces.

To become law, the Accord had to be ratified by Parliament and the legislatures of all the provinces in accordance with s. 41 of the Constitution Act of 1982. As Quebec's legislative assembly was the first to pass the required resolution of approval on 23rd June 1987, the Accord had to receive unanimous ratification on or before 23rd June 1990. In early June of 1990, all first ministers finally agreed to ratify the Accord subject to guarantees that there would be further constitutional discussion after the Accord on such issues as an elected Senate, the amending formula and equality and aboriginal issues. Notwithstanding this, on the final date for ratification, the Accord unravelled. Although all parties in Manitoba finally agreed to the Accord, it required public hearings unless there was unanimous consent of the legislature to dispense with such hearings. One member of the legislature, Elijah Harper, withheld his consent and ultimately the Accord never came to a vote in Manitoba. On the same day, wishing to allow Manitoba more time, the federal minister responsible for federal-provincial relations suggested that the ratification date be extended three months, on the third anniversary of Saskatchewan's ratification, necessitating a re-ratification in Quebec. This upset the premier of Newfoundland, who then decided not to bring the Accord to a vote in the legislature on that day. The Meech Lake Accord at that point had died.

Following these events, a series of deliberations took place on the future of Confederation both within and outside of Quebec. In fact, there were four bodies empanelled to engage in these discussions — a parliamentary and an extra-parliamentary body within Quebec and a parliamentary and an extra-parliamentary body nationally. Specifically, within Quebec, there were the Allaire Committee and the Belanger-Campeau Committee; and nationally, there were Beaudoin-Edwards Committee and the Spicer Commission. These studies lead to various reports including the federal document, *Shaping Canada's Future Together*. Subsequently, the federal

---

[5] This provision has already been challenged. See *Penikett v. R.*, [1988] N.W.T.R. 18, [1988] 2 W.W.R. 481, 21 B.C.L.R. (2d) 1, (*sub nom. Penikett v. Can.*) 45 D.L.R. (4th) 108, (*sub nom. Yukon Territory (Commissioner.) v. Can.*) 2 Y.R. 314 (Y.T. C.A.), leave to appeal to S.C.C. refused [1988] N.W.T.R. xliv (note), [1988] 6 W.W.R. lxix (note), 27 B.C.L.R. (2d) xxxv (note), 46 D.L.R. (4th) vi (note), 3 Y.R. 159n, 88 N.R. 320n (S.C.C.).

government convened a series of five national conferences discussing various aspects of the proposal contained in the aforementioned document. This, in turn, lead to a federal report, *A Renewed Canada*. All of the foregoing finally culminated in negotiations among the federal government, the provincial governments (including Quebec in the latter stages of negotiations), the territorial governments and representatives from the Assembly of First Nations, the Native Council of Canada, the Inuit Tapirisat of Canada and the Metis National Council. These negotiations resulted in the so-called Charlottetown Accord.[6]

The Accord dealt with a number of constitutional issues. For example, with respect to the division of legislative powers, it provided for exclusive provincial jurisdiction over forestry, mining, and some other areas. It also requred the federal government to conduct negotiations with the provinces in order to 'harmonize' policy in such areas as telecommunications, labour development and training, regional development and immigration. The provinces were given exclusive jurisdiction in respect of cultural affairs. The federal government would however retain jurisdiction over national cultural institutions such as the Canadian Broadcasting Corporation and the National Film Board. Two centralizing features in the constitution are the federal power of reservation and disallowance and the declaratory power in s. 92(10)(c) of the Constitution Act of 1867. The Accord would have abolished the former and allowed the latter subject only to provincial consent. One important feature of the Accord related to the use of the federal spending power. Because Parliament has far greater taxation authority than the provinces, it also has the greater spending authority. Over the years, this has lead to financing arrangements under which the federal government finances, through transfer payments and other fiscal devices, all or part of programs that otherwise would fall within provincial legislative authority, such as medicare, social services, advanced education, etc. In so doing, the federal government has typically attached conditions on this financing arrangement. One such example is the prohibition of extra-billing by doctors contained in the Canada Health Act. Again, typically, any province which authorizes a program or activity in contravention of these conditions would have to pay a financial penalty. The Charlottetown Accord allowed the provinces to establish their own programs in these areas with guarantees of federal compensation provided the provincial programs conformed to national standards.

The Accord also provided for an enhancement of Canada's social and economic union. In respect of the former, it envisaged a 'social charter'

---

[6] For greater detail, see Russell, P., *Constitutional Odyssey*. Toronto: University of Toronto Press, 1993 and Jeffrey, B., *Strange Bedfellows, Trying Times: October 1992 and the Defeat of the Powerbrokers*. Toronto: Key Porter Books, 1993.

to seek and promote such objectives as health care, welfare, education, environmental protection and collective bargaining. In respect of the latter, it envisaged objectives such as internal free trade among the provinces with the elimination of barriers in respect of goods, services, labour and capital, and other provisions related to employment, standard of living and development.

The Accord addressed the issue of aboriginal self-government but provided for a hiatus of three years before the concept would be juridicially recognized. It also dealt with aboriginal representation in the Parliament of Canada.

The Charlottetown Accord also contained the so-called 'Canada Clause' which set out the values that define the nature of the Canadian character. One of those values was the recognition that Quebec is a distinct society within Canada. Other values included egalitarianism, diversity and other qualities of Canadian society. This provision, like the present s. 27 of the Canadian Charter of Rights and Freedoms relating to multiculturalism, is an interpretive section, directing our courts to construe the Constitution having regard to the existence of these constitutionally entrenched values.

The Accord also sought to make various institutional changes in the Canadian polity. For example, the Supreme Court of Canada, its composition and the appointment process were to be constitutionally entrenched. The Senate would have been changed in the following ways, reflecting the demands of many that Canada adopt a so-called 'Triple E Senate' — an equal, elected, and efficient Senate. Each province would have an equal number of senators, and the senators would be elected either by the legislature of each province or, at large, within each province. The Accord reduced the powers of the Senate and, on some matters, required a so-called 'double majority'; that is, a majority of the senators generally and a majority of francophone senators. Changes were also made to the House of Commons. Following a redistribution, the number of seats in the House would be increased. In addition, any redistribution would require that a province could not have fewer seats than any other province with a smaller population. However, the province of Quebec would never be allotted less than one quarter of all the seats in the House.

The Accord formally institutionalized the federal/provincial/territorial consolitative process, allowing for aboriginal inclusion in the process in appropriate circumstances. The Accord increased the number of matters in the existing amending formula that require unanimous consent for amendment.

Unlike the Meech Lake Accord, the ratification process here would be different. The parties to the Charlottetown Accord provided for a national referendum. In fact, three provinces had referendum legislation — British Columbia, Alberta and Quebec. As it turned out, British Columbia and Alberta decided to participate in the federal referendum, with the result that two referenda, asking the same question were held on the same day, October 26, 1992.[7]

Nationally, 54% of the votes cast opposed the Accord. It did, however, receive approval in New Brunswick, Newfoundland, Prince Edward Island, the Northwest Territories and, by the narrowest of margins, Ontario. After the failure of the Meech Lake Accord, Canadians again could not reach a national consensus during the Charlottetown debate and referenda. As a result, there remained considerable uncertainty as to what might follow, given especially the possibily of Quebec separation looming in the background. This uncertainty was exacerbated by two political events in the intervening years since the failure of the Charlottetown Accord. Federally, there was a dramatic alteration of the political landscape of the House of Commons after the 1993 federal election. Not only was there a change of government but the Official Opposition was the separatist Bloc Quebecois. Provincially, in Quebec, there was also a change of government and the separtist Parti Quebecois assumed power. In so doing, the new Quebec government promised that a referendum on Quebec separation would be held some time during 1995. In preparation for the referendum, draft legislation was prepared and a series of public consultations were held. The referendum was originally scheduled for the spring of 1995 but delayed until the fall of 1995. As it turns out, the Referendum was scheduled to be held on October 30, 1995.[8] The question posed in the Referendum was as follows:

Do you agree that Quebec should become sovereign, after having made a formal offer to Canada for a new economic and political partnership, within the scope of the Bill respecting the future of Quebec and of the agreement signed on June 12, 1995?

The Bill referred to in this question is Bill 1, An Act respecting the future of Quebec (including its Declaration of Sovereignty in its Preamble)[9] and

---

[7] The question posed in the referenda was simply as follows: Do you agree that the Constitution of Canada should be renewed on the basis of the agreement reached on August 28, 1992?

[8] The Referendum attracted vast media coverage during the fall of 1995. For detailed coverage of the Referendum campaign, see The Globe & Mail, daily, from September 12, 1995 to November 2, 1995. See also the following selection of some of the media coverage: "The Choice: The issues and the stakes in Quebec's sovereignty referendum", A Southam Newspaper Group Special Section, The Montreal Gazette, October, 1995; "The Choice: Referendum Special", Maclean's, October 30, 1995; P. Wells, "Be Vewy, Vewy Quiet", Saturday Night, September 1995; The Toronto Star, September 16, 1995; The Edmonton Journal, October 31, 1995; and C. Denis and D. Schneiderman, "Towards the Referendum: Campaign Contradictions", (1995) 6:4 Constitutional Forum 126.

[9] Bill 1, National Assembly, 35th Legislature, 1995.

the agreement of June 12, 1995 referred to in the question is the *Text of the Agreement Between The Parti Québécois, the Bloc Québécois and the Action démocratique du Québec* ratified by Messrs, Jacques Parizeau, Lucien Bouchard and Mario Dumont.[10]

The Referendum, itself, was conducted pursuant to the provisions of the Quebec Referendum Act.[11]

At the beginning of the Referendum campaign, the so-called "No" side (opposed to separation) had a substantial lead in the polls. But as the campaign progressed, and particularly with the assumption of the leadership of the "Yes" side by M. Bouchard, the leader of the Bloc Québécois, from M. Parizeau, the Premier of Quebec, during the final three weeks of the campaign, the "Yes" side gained momentum. Ultimately, after an emotional and somewhat controversial campaign, the "No" side achieved victory by a narrow margin of 50.56%.

Following the vote, there was considerable controversy relating to the counting of the ballots (i.e. the large number of 'spoiled' ballots), the enumeration of eligible voters and other concerns.[12] The Premier of Quebec, Jacques Parizeau, then resigned from office and the leader of the Bloc Québécois, Lucien Bouchard, announced his intention to assume the leadership of the Parti Québécois and become Premier of Quebec. He further announced an intention to conduct another referendum on separation in 1997.[13]

During the final days and shortly after the campaign, federal politicians announced their intention of meeting some Quebec concerns. For example, Prime Minister Jean Chrétien said that he would take measures toward recognizing Quebec's 'distinct society' and guaranteeing Quebec a de facto veto over constitutional changes.[14] However, in the course of political developments in the month following the referendum, M. Bouchard indicated he would not entertain any federal initiative

---

[10] M. Parizeau, at the time, was the Premier and Leader of the Parti Québécois. M. Bouchard was the Leader of the Opposition in Parliament and the Leader of the Bloc Québécois and M. Dumont was the Leader of the Action démocratique du Québec.

[11] S.Q. 1993, C-64.1, as amended.

[12] One concern that attracted considerable attention was the allegedly xenophobic remarks by the leaders of the "Yes" campaign, including the comment by Premier Parizeau blaming the result, in part, on "the ethnic vote". See, for example, The Globe & Mail, November 1, 1995.

[13] See The Globe & Mail, November 22, 1995. Before then, there will likely be a provincial election in Quebec. Moreover, Quebec law provides that only one such referendum may be held during an electoral term, although this could be easily amended. Also likely before another referendum there will be a mandatory federal/provincial conference required under the provisions of the Constitution Act of 1982.

[14] See The Globe & Mail, November 1, 1995.

relating to the Constitution and the Prime Minister countered that, given this attitude, no such initiative would be forthcoming in the near future.[15]

In the meantime, after the Referendum, the Prime Minister created a special Cabinet committee to formulate a new constitutional proposal. The proposal that emerged, primarily designed to address Quebec's long-standing concerns, provided for three non-constitutional initiatives to be enacted by the House of Commons. The first initiative, in the form of a motion[16] of the House of Commons, would recognize Quebec as a distinct society within Canada (i.e., a society characterized by the French language, its unique culture and a civil law system[17]). A second initiative[18] would grant a veto to the Western region, the Atlantic region, Ontario and Quebec with respect to all future constitutional changes to national institutions such as the Senate, creation of new provinces and any amendments regarding the distribution of powers.[19] That is, for a constitutional change to be effected, the consent would be required of any two of the four western provinces provided those two constituted 50% of the population of the west, any two of the Atlantic provinces provided those two provinces constituted 50% of the population of the Atlantic region, Ontario and Quebec.[20] Under the third initiative,[21] the federal government would give up any role it plays in respect of labour/market training, apprenticeship programs, co-operative education programs and workplace-based training, thus allowing the provinces to fully assume this respon-

---

[15] See The Globe & Mail, November 23, 1995. As the Prime Minister stated:

"I never said that we would change the Constitution," Mr. Chrétien said. . . "I said that we would make changes to the federation — constitutional changes if necessary — but I never said they were going to be constitutional.

[16] Notice of Motion was tabled in the House of Commons on November 27, 1995.

[17] See Chapter 8 of this book for a detailed discussion of the legal system in Quebec.

[18] This part of the package was introduced as a bill in the House of Commons on November 29, 1995. See Bill C-110, An Act Respecting Constitutional Amendments.

[19] See Release, Office of the Prime Minister, November 27, 1995 and see The Globe & Mail, November 28, 1995.

[20] This provision, although not identical, is very similar to the amending formula agreed to at the Victoria Conference of 1971. It should be noted that in the existing constitutional amending formula, in addition to the provincial consent requirement, the consent of the House of Commons is always required for any amendment. According to Bill C-110, a constitutional amendment could not be tabled unless the above veto/consent provision is adhered to. Essentially, this initiative is a 'manner and form' requirement or a 'condition precedent' to any federal consent to a future constitutional amendment. Thus, when the consent of the House of Commons does occur, the requisite number of provinces, under the Constitution, must also consent to the proposed amendment (i.e., for some amendments, this would require the consent of two-thirds of the provinces constituting 50% of the population of Canada).

[21] This initiative formed part of a larger employment insurance program introduced into the House of Commons on December 1, 1995. See The Globe & Mail, December 2, 1995.

sibility. According to the Prime Minister, it is possible that these initiatives "could [eventually] be incorporated into the Constitution".[22]

It is likely, in the foreseeable future, that political posturing/sparring/strategizing will dominate the political agenda in connection with the relationship between Quebec and the rest of Canada. Utimately, there is the long-term uncertainty as to the future status of Quebec within Confederation. This uncertainty includes the question as to whether concrete initiatives, such as those described above, will be successful with respect to addressing Quebec concerns, and, at the same time, be acceptable to the other provinces.[23] With a possibility of another referendum, there is also uncertainty as to the relationship of an independent Quebec to Canada and there is uncertainty as to the juridical status of an independent Quebec in the international community. In short, the possible separation of Quebec has become, over the past quarter century, a defining feature of the Canadian legal system.[24]

In any event, the Canada Act of 1982 contains just four sections. The first section makes reference to Schedule B of the Canada Act. The second section provides that no Act of the Parliament of the United Kingdom shall extend to Canada from this point forward. The third section states that the English and French texts of the Canada Act are equally authoritative, and the fourth section merely provides that the name of the Act is the Canada Act. As a result, when looking at the substance of the so-called "new constitution", one must focus on Schedule B to the Canada Act, which is itself styled and cited as the Constitution Act of 1982. The Constitution Act of 1982 contains numerous parts. Part 1 is the Canadian Charter of Rights and Freedoms. Part 2 is concerned with the rights of the aboriginal peoples of Canada. Part 3 deals with equalization and regional disparities. Part 4 is more or less a transitional provision dealing with a constitutional conference. Part 5 contains the new domestic procedure for amending the Constitution of Canada. Part 6 provides for a

---

[22] Release, Office of the Prime Minister, November 27, 1995.

[23] For some early commentary on and reaction to these initiatives, see The Globe & Mail, November 28, 1995, November 29, 1995 and November 30, 1995.

[24] For some recent books dealing with the issue of separation see Clark, Rt. Hon. J., *A Nation Too Good to Lose: Renewing the Purpose of Canada*. Toronto: Ken Porter Books Ltd., 1994; Cook, R., *Canada, Quebec and the Uses of Nationalism*, 2nd ed. Toronto: McLelland & Stewart, Inc., 1995; Côté, M., & Johnson, D., *If Quebec Goes ...: The Real Cost of Separation* Toronto: Stoddart Books, 1995; Freeman, A. and Grady, P., *Dividing the House: Planning for a Canada Without Quebec*. Toronto: Harper Collins Publihers Ltd., 1995; *If You Love this Country: 15 Voices in a United Canada*. Toronto: Penguin Books, 1995; Johnson, W., *A Canadian Myth: Quebec, Between Canada and the Illusion of Utopia*. Montreal, Toronto: Robert Davies Publishing, 1994; Lamont, L., *Breakup: The Coming End of Canada and the Stakes in America*. Toronto: Ken Porter Books Ltd., 1995. For further details relating to the separation debate, see, for example, the following sources:

specific amendment to the B.N.A. Act of 1867, now cited as the Constitution Act of 1867. Part 7 contains some important general provisions. Finally, the Constitution Act contains a Schedule, which is by virtue of s. 52(2) an integral part of the Act.

More specifically, s. 52(1) provides that the Constitution of Canada is the supreme law of Canada. Section 52(2) goes on to specify what constitutes the Constitution of Canada. It points out that the Constitution includes the Canada Act and its Schedule (namely, the Constitution Act of 1982 in its English and French texts and its Schedule) and any amendments to any of those instruments. The Schedule to the Constitution Act is therefore an integral part of the Constitution. It contains all of the British North America Acts passed since 1867. They have, however, been renamed as the various "Constitution Acts". The B.N.A. Act of 1867 is therefore brought forward as part of the Constitution as Item 1 in the Schedule to the Constitution Act of 1982. Accordingly, all the jurisprudence to date dealing with the division of legislative powers in ss. 91 and 92, as well as the other sections of the B.N.A. Act, is brought forward and remains as relevant now as it always has been.

This raises the question as to what is, in fact and in law, "new" about the so-called new Constitution. Since all the old provisions are brought forward as well as all the attendant jurisprudence, what is new is, essentially, the Charter of Rights and Freedoms. It is now an entrenched instrument forming an integral part of the Constitution and occupying a constitutional status amendable only by formal constitutional amendment. The second major "new" aspect of the Constitution is the domestic amending formula. There are some other "new" matters but they are not quite as important.

In addition, since the coming into effect of the Constitution Act of 1982, there have been some minor subsequent amendments. The first occurred in 1983[25] and involved a slight change to the aboriginal rights section of the Charter and a more substantial change to the separate aboriginal rights Part of the Constitution Act. Another amendment occurred in 1987[26] and applied only to the province of Newfoundland. Two further amendments occurred in 1993.[27] Other quasi-constitutional legislation has been enacted since 1982.[28] On September 5, 1995, the province of Newfoundland

---

[25] Constitution Amendment Proclamation, 1983 (Can.).

[26] Constitution Amendment, 1987 (Newfoundland Act).

[27] Constitution Amendment, 1993 (New Brunswick) and Constitution Amendment, 1993 (Prince Edward Island).

[28] Northwest Territories Act (Can.), 1985; Parliament of Canada Act (Can.), 1985; Yukon Act (Can.), 1985; and Nunavut Act (Can), 1993.

conducted a referendum in respect of the future of denominational schools. Under the Terms of Union of Newfoundland with Canada, a Schedule to the Newfoundland Act (item 21 to the Schedule to the Constitution Act, 1982), the new province of Newfoundland was required to establish nominational schools that existed at the time of the Union. As a result, there exist in Newfoundland, several denominational schools. The object of the referendum was to determine whether this system of denominational schools should remain or whether it should be replaced by a public school system. In the referendum the latter option was chosen and now requires a constitutional amendment for its implementation.

It should be emphasized that the B.N.A. Act and all the law dealing with the division of powers are brought forward and continue in force. However, there have been some minor changes. Sections 20, 50, 91 (1) and 92 (1) have been repealed and re-enacted as part of the Canadian Charter of Rights and Freedoms.

Essentially, the structure of the Charter follows a categorization scheme of civil liberties that has been widely accepted. Professors Trudeau and Laskin (as they then were) and later Professor Tarnopolsky (as he then was) and even later Professor MacGuigan (as he then was) have all had a part in the development of this categorization scheme, which is essentially a rationalization of the various cases concerning civil liberties. Those cases usually were decided on the basis of the division of powers, the courts using what has been described as the 'power allocation' technique of protecting civil liberties. It is a rationalization in the sense that once a particular type of civil liberty is identified, it can then be categorized as to whether that type of civil liberty can be legislated federally or provincially. This rationalization arose out of an analysis of the jurisprudence in respect of the traditional categories of civil liberties. The four basic categories are the egalitarian civil liberties (which deal with equality under the law), the legal civil liberties (which deal with protections contained in the Criminal Code and other statutes), the political civil liberties (which deal with the fundamental freedoms, namely freedom of the press, freedom of speech, freedom of assembly and association and freedom of religion), and finally the economic civil liberties (which deal with the right to freely enter into contracts, the right to own property and the right to sue for damages in the event of a breach of a duty owed to a plaintiff, etc). These traditional categories have been followed in the drafting of the Charter, although the economic civil liberties were eventually taken out (an omission which created quite a political controversy at the time). In addition, new categories of civil liberties, including mobility rights, linguistic rights, multicultural rights, and aboriginal rights have been included in the Charter. Nonetheless, the Charter essentially reflects the various traditional categories which are now preserved within it.

1. THE PROVISIONS OF THE CHARTER

1. The Canadian Charter of Rights and Freedoms guarantees the rights and freedoms set out in its subject only to such reasonable limits prescribed by law as can be demonstrably justified in a free and democratic society.

Structurally, the Charter begins in section 1, with the so-called 'limitations clause' to which most other sections are referable. The theory behind having a limitations clause is that no right is absolute, and therefore the clause provides a court with a basis for placing limits on the exercise of particular rights. It is interesting to note that in the international spectrum, the one right which is recognized as immune from any forms of limitation is the protection against cruel treatment or punishment. In Canada, however, that provision in the Charter is still referable to s. 1 and the limitation imposed by it.

The meaning of the words of s. 1 was the subject of several early cases under the Charter (for example the *Protestant Separate School Board* and *Rauco* cases).[29] However, the issue was fully and definitively explored by the Supreme Court of Canada in *R. v. Oakes*, [1986] 1 S.C.R. 103, 53 O.R. (2d) 719 (headnote only), 50 C.R. (3d) 1, 19 C.R.R. 308, 24 C.C.C. (3d) 321, 26 D.L.R. (4th) 200, 14 O.A.C. 335, 65 N.R. 87. The so-called '*Oakes* test' consists of a two-part analysis in determining what constitutes a "reasonable limit" under s. 1. This test was recently re-affirmed by the Supreme Court of Canada in *R. v. Videoflicks Ltd.*,[30] where Chief Justice Dickson stated:

Two requirements must be satisfied to establish that a limit is reasonable and demonstrably justified in a free and democratic society. First, the legislative objective which the limitation is designed to promote must be of sufficient importance to warrant overriding a constitutional right. It must bear on a "pressing and substantial concern". Second, the means chosen to attain those objectives must be proportional or appropriate to the ends. The proportionality requirement, in turn, normally has three aspects: the limiting measures must be carefully designed, or rationally connected, to the objective; they must impair the right as little as possible; and their effects must not so severely trench on individual or group rights that the legislative objective, albeit important, is nevertheless outweighed by the abridgment of rights.[31]

In other words, a limit is reasonable and demonstrably justified in a free and democratic society if the limit is a rational, non-disproportionate,

---

[29] *Que. Assn. of Protestant Sch. Bds. v. A.G. Que.*, [1984] 2 S.C.R. 66, 9 C.R.R. 133, 10 D.L.R. (4th) 321, 54 N.R. 196; and *Germany v. Rauca* (1983), 41 O.R. (2d) 225, 34 C.R. (3d) 97 (*sub nom. R. v. Rauca*), 4 C.C.C. (3d) 385, 4 C.R.R. 42, 145 D.L.R. (3d) 638 (C.A.).

[30] [1986] 2 S.C.R. 713, (*sub nom. R. v. Edwards Books & Art Ltd.*), 58 O.R. (2d) 442n, 55 C.R. (3d) 193, 87 C.L.L.C. 14,001 (*sub nom. Edwards Books & Art Ltd. v.R.*), 28 C.R.R.I, 19 O.A.C. 239, 71 N.R. 161, 30 C.C.C. (3d) 385 (*sub nom. Edwards Books & Art Ltd. v. R., R. v Nortown Foods Ltd.*), 35 D.L.R. (4th) 1.

[31] 28 C.R.R. 1 at 40-41. For a recent discussion of the *Oakes* test, see S. Fine, "When the law comes to a head". The Globe & Mail, March 11, 1995.

minimally intrusive means of achieving a pressing and substantial state objective. In *Andrews v. Law Society of British Columbia,* [1989] 1 S.C.R. 143, 34 B.C.L.R. (2d) 273, 25 C.C.E.L. 255, [1989] 2 W.W.R. 289, 36 C.R.R. 193, 10 C.H.R.R. D/5719, 56 D.L.R. (4th) 1, 91 N.R. 255, the Supreme Court slightly altered this test by suggesting that a court could look at whether the means a legislature chooses to achieve its objective is the lesser intrusive means, as opposed to the least among possible alternatives; and in *R. v. Whyte,* [1988] 2 S.C.R. 3, 29 B.C.L.R. (2d) 273, 64 C.R. (3d) 123, 6 M.V.R. (2d) 138, [1988] 5 W.W.R. 26, 42 C.C.C. (3d) 97, 35 C.R.R.1, 51 D.L.R. (4th) 481, 86 N.R. 328, the Court discussed the importance of balancing in applying the proportionality test. In *R. v. Swain,* [1991] 1 S.C.R. 933, 5 C.R. (4th) 253, 63 C.C.C. (3d) 481, 3 C.R.R. (2d) 1, 125 N.R.1, 47 O.A.C. 81 the Supreme Court indicated the test can also be applied to a common law rule.[12]

> 2. Everyone has the following fundamental freedoms:
>   (a) freedom of conscience and religion;
>   (b) freedom of thought, belief, opinion and expression, including freedom of the press and other media of communication;
>   (c) freedom of peaceful assembly; and
>   (d) freedom of association.

Section 2 of the Charter, which is broken down into four subsections, is concerned with the fundamental freedoms. It is interesting to note that while freedom of conscience is included in s. 2 to protect persons who hold agnostic or atheistic views, its inclusion may be inconsistent with the Preamble, which is part of the Charter, and which recognizes "the supremacy of God".

Some of the leading cases under this section are: *RJR–MacDonald Inc. v. Canada (Attorney General),* [1994] 1 S.C.R. 311, 111 D.L.R. (4th) 385, 54 C.P.R. (3d) 114, 164 N.R. 1, 60 Q.A.C. 241 (freedom of expression and tobacco advertising); *Adler v. Ontario* (1994), 19 O.R. (3d) 1, 116 D.L.R. (4th) 1, 22 C.R.R. (2d) 205, 73 O.A.C. 81 (Ont. C.A.), leave to appeal to S.C.C. granted (1995), 21 O.R. (3d) xvi (note), 25 C.R.R. (2d) 188 (note), 119 D.L.R. (4th) vi (note) (S.C.C.); *Canadian Civil Liberties*

---

[32] See also *R. v. Robson* (1985), 45 C.R. (3d) 68, 31 M.V.R. 220, 19 C.C.C. (3d) 137, 15 C.R.R. 236, 28 B.C.L.R. (2d) 8, [1988] 6 W.W.R. 519, 19 D.L.R. (4th) 112 (C.A.); *R. v. Southam Inc.* (1983), 41 O.R. (2d) 113, 34 C.R. (3d) 27, 33 R.F.L. (2d) 279 (*sub nom. R. v. Southam Inc.*), affirming 38 O.R. (2d) 748 (*sub nom. Ref. re s. 12(1) of Juvenile Delinquents Act Canada*), 30 C.R. (3d) 72 (*sub nom. Re S. 12 of Juvenile Delinquents Act*), 29 R.F.L. (2d) 1, 70 C.C.C. (2d) 257, 2 C.R.R. 84, 141 D.L.R. (3d) 341 (C.A.); *R. v. Ladouceur* (1987), 59 O.R. (2d) 688, 57 C.R. (3d) 45, 46 M.V.R. 1, 35 C.C.C. (3d) 240, 41 D.L.R. (4th) 682, 20 O.A.C. 1 (C.A.), affirmed [1990] 1 S.C.R. 1257, 73 O.R. (2d) 736n, 21 M.V.R. (2d) 165, 77 C.R. (3d) 110, 108 N.R. 171, 4 O.A.C. 1, 48 C.R.R. 112, 56 C.C.C. (3d) 22; *Reference re Public Service Employee Relations Act (Alberta).* 51 Alta. L.R. (2d) 97, [1987] 3 W.W.R. 577, 78 A.R.1, 87 C.L.L.C. 14,021, (*sub nom. A.U.P.E. v. Alberta (A.G.)*) 28 C.R.R. 305.

v. Ontario (Education Minister) (1990), 71 O.R. (2d) 341, 46 C.R.R. 316, 65 D.L.R. (4th) 1, 37 O.A.C. 93 (Ont. C.A.) (freedom of religion, religious studies and school curriculum); *R.B. v. Children's Aid Society of Toronto*, [1995] 1 S.C.R. 315, (1994) 21 O.R. (3d) 479n, 26 C.R.R. (2d) 202, 122 D.L.R. (4th) 1, *(sub nom. Sheena B., Re)* 176 N.R. 161, 78 O.A.C. 1 (freedom of religion and the right of parents to raise children according to their faith); *Dolphin Delivery Ltd. v. R.W.D.S.U., Loc. 580,* [1986] 2 S.C.R. 573 *(sub nom. R.W.D.S.U. v. Dolphin Delivery Ltd.)*, 9 B.C.L.R. (2d) 273, 38 C.C.L.T. 184, [1987] 1 W.W.R. 577, 87 C.L.L.C. 14, 002 *(sub nom. R.W.D.S.U., Loc. 580 v. Dolphin Delivery Ltd.)*, 25 C.R.R. 321, 71 N.R.83 (S.C.C.) (freedom of expression and picketing); *Re ss. 193 & 195.1 of Criminal Code*, [1990] 1 S.C.R. 1123 (freedom of expression and communicating for the purpose of prostitution); *Slaight Communications Inc. v. Davidson,* [1989] 1 S.C.R. 1038, 26 C.C.E.L. 85, 89 C.L.L.C. 14,031, 40 C.R.R. 100, 59 D.L.R. (4th) 416, *(sub nom. Davidson v. Slaight Communications Inc.)* 93 N.R. 183; *R. v. Butler,* [1992] 1 S.C.R. 452, 11 C.R. (4th) 137, [1992] 2 W.W.R. 577, 70 C.C.C. (3d) 129, 8 C.R.R. (2d) 1, 89 D.L.R. (4th) 449, 78 Man. R. (2d) 1, 134 N.R. 81, 16 W.A.C. 1, application for re-hearing refused [1993] 2 W.W.R. 1xi (note) (S.C.C.) (freedom of expression and pornography); *R. v. Zundel*, [1992] 2 S.C.R. 731 (freedom of expression and communicating false news); *Dagenais v. Canadian Broadcasting Corp.*, [1994] 3 S.C.R. 835, *(sub nom. Canadian Broadcasting Corp. v. Dagenais)* 20 O.R. (3d) 816n, 34 C.R. (4th) 269, 94 C.C.C. (3d) 289, 25 C.R.R. (2d) 1, 120 D.L.R. (4th) 12, 175 N.R. 1, 76 O.A.C. 81 (freedom of expression and publication bans); *Committee for the Commonwealth of Canada v. Canada,* [1991] 1 S.C.R. 139, 4 C.R.R. (2d) 60, 77 D.L.R. (4th) 385, 120 N.R. 241, 40 F.T.R. 240n application for re-hearing refused (May 8, 1991), Doc. 20334 (S.C.C.) (freedom of expression on public property); *Edmonton Journal v. Alberta (A.G.)*, [1989] 2 S.C.R. 1326, 71 Alta. L.R. (2d) 273, 41 C.P.C. (2d) 109, [1990] 1 W.W.R. 577, 103 A.R. 321, 45 C.R.R. 1, 64 D.L.R. (4th) 577, 102 N.R. 321 (freedom of the press and accessibility to courts); *Re Public Service Employees Relation Act,* [1987] 1 S.C.R. 313, 51 Alta. L.R. (2d) 97, [1987] 3 W.W.R. 577, 78 A.R.I, 87 C.L.L.C. 14,021, *(sub nom. A.U.P.E. v. Alberta (A.G.))* 28 C.R.R. 305, 38 D.L.R. (4th) 161, *(sub nom. Reference re Compulsory Arbitration)* 74 N.R. 99; *P.S.A.C. v. Canada*, [1987] 1 S.C.R. 424, 87 C.L.L.C. 14,022, 32 C.R.R. 114, 38 D.L.R. (4th) 249, 75 N.R. 161, *(sub nom. A.F.P.C. c. Canada)* [1987] D.L.Q. 230n and *R.W.D.S.U. v. Saskatchewan*, 1 S.C.R. 469 (freedom of association and the right to strike); *Professional Institute of the Public Service of Canada v. NorthWest Territories* (commissioner), [1990] 2 S.C.R. 367; [1990] N.W.T.R. 289, [1990] 5 W.W.R. 385, 90 C.L.L.C. 14,031, 49 C.R.R. 193, 72 D.L.R. (4th) 1, 112 N.R. 269; *Lavigne v. O.P.S.E.U.*, [1991] 2 S.C.R. 211, 3 O.R. (3d) 511n, 91 C.L.L.C. 14,029,

4 C.R.R. (2d) 193, 81 D.L.R. (4th) 545, 126 N.R. 161, 48 O.A.C. 241 (application for re-hearing refused); (1991), 4 O.R. (3d) xii (note) (S.C.C.) (freedom of association and the 'right' not to associate); *R. v. Big M Drug Mart*, [1985] 1 S.C.R. 295, [1985] 3 W.W.R. 481, 37 Alta. L.R. (2d) 97, 13 C.R.R. 64, 18 C.C.C. (3d) 385, 18 D.L.R. (4th) 321, 85 C.L.L.C. 14,023, 58 N.R. 81, 60 A.R. 161, and *R. v. Videoflicks Ltd.,* [1986] 2 S.C.R. 713, (*sub nom. R. v. Edwards Books & Art Ltd.*), 580 R. (2d) 442n, 55 C.R. (3d) 193, 87 C.L.L.C. 14,001 (*sub nom. Edwards Books & Art Ltd. v. R.*) 28 C.R.R. 1, 30 C.C.C. (3d) 385 (*sub nom. R. v. Nortown Foods Ltd.*), 35 D.L.R. (4th) 1, 87 C.L.L.C. 14,001, 19 O.A.C. 239, 71 N.R. 161, 30 C.C.C. (3d) 385 (*sub nom. Edwards Books & Art Ltd. v. R.; R. v. Nortown Foods Ltd.*), 35 D.L.R. (4th) 1 (Sunday closing and freedom of religion); *Zylberberg v. Sudbury (Bd. of Education)* (1988), 65 O.R. (2d) 641, 34 C.R.R. 1, 52 D.L.R. (4th) 577, 29 O.A.C. 23 (C.A.) (freedom of religion and school prayers); *R. v. Jones*, [1986] 2 S.C.R. 284, 47 Atla. L.R. (2d) 97, [1986] 6 W.W.R. 577, 25 C.R.R. 63, (*sub nom. Jones v. R.*) 28 C.C.C. (3d) 513, 31 D.L.R. (4th) 569, 69 N.R. 241, 73 A.R. 133, (freedom of religion and private schools); *R. v. Kopyto* (1987), 62 O.R. (2d) 449, 61 C.R. (3d) 209, 39 C.C.C. (3d) 1, 47 D.L.R. (4th) 213, 24 O.A.C. 81 (C.A.) (freedom of expression and contempt of court); *R. v. Red Hot Video* (1985), 45 C.R. (3d) 36, 15 C.R.R. 206, 18 C.C.C. (3d) 1 (B.C. C.A.), leave to appeal to S.C.C. refused (1985), 46 C.R. (3d) xxv (note) (S.C.C.), and *Information Retailers Assn. of Metro. Toronto v. Metro. Toronto (Mun.)*; (1985), 52 O.R. (2d) 449, 32 M.P.L.R. 49, 22 D.L.R. (4th) 161, 10 O.A.C. 140 (C.A.) (freedom of expression and obscenity); *R. v. Keegstra*, [1988] 5 W.W.R. 211, 60 Alta. L.R. (2d) 1, 65 C.R. (3d) 289, 43 C.C.C. (3d) 150, 39 C.R.R. 5, 87 A.R. 177, additional reasons at 79 Alta. L.R. (2d) 97, [1991] 4 W.W.R. 136, 3 C.R. (4th) 153, 63 C.C.C. (3d) 110, 114 A.R. 288 (C.A.), reversed [1990] 3 S.C.R. 697, 77 Alta. L.R. (2d) 193, [1991] 2 W.W.R. 1, 61 C.C.C. (3d) 1, 117 N.R. 1, 114 A.R. 81, 3 C.R.R. (2d) 193 and *R. v. Andrews* (1988), 65 O.R. (2d) 161, 65 C.R. (3d) 320, 43 C.C.C. (3d) 193, 39 C.R.R. 36, 28 O.A.C. 161 (C.A.), affirmed [1990] 3 S.C.R. 870, 75 O.R. (2d) 481n, 1 C.R. (4th) 266, 61 C.C.C. (3d) 490, 77 D.L.R. (4th) 128, 3 C.R.R. (2d) 176, 47 O.A.C. 293 (freedom of expression and hate propaganda); *Irwin Toy Ltd. v. Québec (A.G.)* [1989] 1 S.C.R. 927, 25 C.P.R. (3d) 417, 39 C.R.R. 193, 58 D.L.R. (4th) 577, 24 Q.A.C. 2, 94 N.R. 167, and *Ford v. Québec (A.G.),* [1988] 2 S.C.R. 712, 36 C.R.R. 1, 54 D.L.R. (4th) 577, 10 C.H.R.R. D/5559, 19 Q.A.C. 69 (*sub nom. Chaussure Brown's Inc. v. Québec* (P.G.)), 90 N.R. 84 (freedom of expression and commercial advertising); and *Reference re Public Service Employee Relations Act (Alta.),* [1987] 1 S.C.R. 313, [1987] 3 W.W.R. 577, 51 Alta. L.R. (2d) 97, 38 D.L.R. (4th) 161, 87 C.L.L.C. 14,021, [1987] D.L.Q. 225, 78 A.R. 1 , 74 N.R. 99, 78 A.R. 1, 28 C.R.R. 305 (*sub nom. Reference re*

Compulsory Arbitration) (freedom of association and the right to strike).

3. Every citizen of Canada has the right to vote in an election of members of the House of Commons or of a legislative assembly and to be qualified for membership therein.

4. (1) No House of Commons and no legislative assembly shall continue for longer than five years from the date fixed for the return of the writs at a general election of its members.

(2) In time of real or apprehended war, invasion or insurrection, a House of Commons may be continued by Parliament and a legislative assembly may be continued by the legislature beyond five years if such continuation is not opposed by the votes of more than one-third of the members of the House of Commons or the legislative assembly, as the case may be.

5. There shall be a sitting of Parliament and of each legislature at least once every twelve months.

Sections 3 to 5 deal with the so-called democratic rights and those rights are concerned with the matters previously contained in ss. 91(1) and 92(1) of the former B.N.A. Act of 1867. The leading cases under s. 3 are: *Can. Disability Rights Council v. R.*, 21 F.T.R. 288 [1988] 3 F.C. 622, 38 C.R.R. 53 (T.D.) (the right to vote and the mentally incompetent); *Muldoon v. R. (sub nom. Muldoon v. Canada)* 21 F.T.R. 154, [1988] 3 F.C. 628 (T.D.) (the right to vote and members of the judiciary); *Sauve v. Canada*, [1993] 2 S.C.R. 438, *(sub nom. Belczowski v. Canada)* 15 C.R.R. (2d) 1, 153 N.R. 242, 64 O.A.C. (the right to vote and persons in custody); and *Re Provincial Electoral Boundaries*, [1991] 2 S.C.R. 158, [1991] 5 W.W.R. 1, *(sub nom. Carter v. Saskatchewan (Attorney General))* 5 C.R.R. (2d) 1, *(sub nom. Reference re Electoral Boundaries Commission Act, ss. 14, 20 (Saskatchewan))* 81 D.L.R. (4th) 16, 127 N.R.I, 94 Sask. R. 161.

6. (1) Every citizen of Canada has the right to enter, remain in and leave Canada.

(2) Every citizen of Canada and every person who has the status of a permanent resident of Canada has the right

(*a*) to move to and take up residence in any province; and

(*b*) to pursue the gaining of a livelihood in any province.

(3) The rights specified in subsection (2) are subject to

(*a*) any laws or practices of general application in force in a province other than those that discriminate among persons primarily on the basis or province of present or previous residence; and

(*b*) any laws providing for reasonable residency requirements as a qualification for the receipt of publicly provided social services.

(4) Subsections (2) and (3) do not preclude any law, program or activity that has as its object the amelioration in a province of conditions of individuals in that province who are socially or economically disadvantaged if the rate of employment in that province is below the rate of employment in Canada.

Section 6 deals with a relatively new category of civil liberties, namely mobility rights. The leading cases under this section are: *Skapinker v. Law Society of Upper Canada*, [1984] 1 S.C.R. 357, 8 C.R.R. 193, 20 Admin. L.R.I, 11 C.C.C. (3d) 481, 9 D.L.R. (4th) 161, 3 O.A.C. 321, 53 N.R. 169; and *Black v. Law Society (Alta.)*, [1989] 1 S.C.R. 591, [1989] 4 W.W.R. 1, 66 Alta. L.R. (2d) 97, 37 Admin. L.R. 161, 38 C.R.R. 193, 58 D.L.R. (4th) 317, 96 A.R. 352, 93 N.R. 266.

7. Everyone has the right to life, liberty and security of the person and the right not to be deprived thereof except in accordance with the principles of fundamental justice.

8. Everyone has the right to be secure against unreasonable search or seizure.

9. Everyone has the right not to be arbitrarily detained or imprisoned.

10. Everyone has the right on arrest or detention
    (a) to be informed promptly of the reasons therefor;
    (b) to retain and instruct counsel without delay and to be informed of that right; and
    (c) to have the validity of the detention determined by way of habeas corpus and to be released if the detention is not lawful.

11. Any person charged with an offence has the right
    (a) to be informed without reasonable delay of the specific offence;
    (b) to be tried within a reasonable time;
    (c) not to be compelled to be a witness in proceedings against that person in respect of the offence;
    (d) to be presumed innocent until proven guilty according to law in a fair and public hearing by an independent and impartial tribunal;
    (e) not to be denied reasonable bail without just cause;
    (f) except in the case of an offence under military law tried before a military tribunal, to the benefit of trial by jury where the maximum punishment for the offence is imprisonment for five years or a more severe punishment;
    (g) not to be found guilty on account of any act or omission unless, at the time of the act or omission, it constituted an offence under Canadian or international law or was criminal according to the general principles of law recognized by the community of nations;
    (h) if finally acquitted of the offence, not to be tried for it again and, if finally found guilty and punished for the offence, not to be tried or punished for it again; and
    (i) if found guilty of the offence and if the punishment for the offence has been varied between the time of commission and the time of sentencing, to the benefit of the lesser punishment.

12. Everyone has the right not to be subjected to any cruel and unusual treatment or punishment.

13. A witness who testifies in any proceedings has the right not to have any incriminating evidence so given used to incriminate that witness in any other proceedings, except in a prosecution for perjury or for the giving of contradictory evidence.

14. A party or witness in any proceedings who does not understand or speak the language in which the proceedings are conducted or who is deaf has the right to the assistance of an interpreter.

Sections 7 to 14 are concerned with the legal rights or the various protections afforded to those persons in contact with our criminal justice system. These legal rights constitute probably one of the most important parts of the Charter and are deserving of significant attention. Section 7, however, has proven to be extremely important in and of itself. The term "fundamental justice" in s. 7 has both procedural and substantive significance. The leading cases under this section are: *R. v. Wholesale Travel Group Inc.,* [1991] 3 S.C.R. 154; 4 O.R. (3d) 799n, 8 C.R. (4th) 145, 67 C.C.C. (3d) 193, 38 C.P.R. (3d) 451, 7 C.R.R. (2d) 36, 84 D.L.R. (4th) 161, 130 N.R. 1, 49 O.A.C. 161; *Re ss. 193 & 195.1 (1) (c) of the Criminal Code (Canada),* [1990] 1 S.C.R. 1123, 77 C.R. (3d) 1, [1990] 4 W.W.R. 481, 56 C.C.C. (3d) 65, 48 C.R.R. 1, 68 Man. R. (2d) 1, 109 N.R. 81; *R. v. Martineau,* [1990] 2 S.C.R. 633, 76 Alta. L.R. (2d) 1, 79 C.R. (3d) 129, [1990] 6 W.W.R. 97, 109 A.R. 321, 58 C.C.C. (3d) 353, 50 C.R.R.

110, 112 N.R. 83; *R. v. Logan*, [1990] 2 S.C.R. 731, 74 O.R. (2d) 644n, 79 C.R. (3d) 169, 58 C.C.C. (3d) 391, 50 C.R.R. 152, 112 N.R. 144, 41 O.A.C. 330; *United Nurses of Alberta v. Alberta (Atorney General)* (1992), [1992] 1 S.C.R. 901, 1 Alta. L.R. (3d) 120, 13 C.R. (4th) 1, [1992] 3 W.W.R. 481, 125 A.R. 241, 71 C.C.C. (3d) 225, 92 C.L.L.C. 14,023, 9 C.R.R. (2d) 29, 89 D.L.R. (4th) 609, 135 N.R. 321, 14 W.A.C. 241; *R. v. Hebert*, [1990] 2 S.C.R. 151, 47 B.C.L.R. (2d) 1, 77 C.R. (3d) 145, [1990] 5 W.W.R. 1, 57 C.C.C. (3d) 1, 49 C.R.R. 114, 110 N.R. 1; *R. v. Broyles*, [1991] 3 S.C.R. 595, 84 Alta. L.R. (2d) 1, 9 C.R. (4th) 1, [1992] 1 W.W.R. 289, 120 A.R. 189, 68 C.C.C. (2d) 308, 8 C.R.R. (2d) 274, 131 N.R. 118, 8 W.A.C. 189; *R. v. Seaboyer*, [1991] 2 S.C.R. 577, 4 O.R. (3d) 383n, 7 C.R. (4th) 117, 66 C.C.C. (3d) 321, 6 C.R.R. (2d) 35, 83 D.L.R. (4th) 193, 128 N.R. 81, 48 O.A.C. 81; *R. v. Stinchcombe*, [1991] 3 S.C.R. 326, 83 Alta. L.R. (2d) 193, 8 C.R. (4th) 277, [1992] 1 W.W.R. 97, 120 A.R. 161, 68 C.C.C. (3d) 1, 18 C.R.R. (2d) 210, 130 N.R. 277, 8 W.A.C. 161; *Rodriguez v. British Columbia (Attorney General)*, [1993] 3 S.C.R. 519, 82 B.C.L.R. (2d) 273, 24 C.R. (4th) 281, [1993] 7 W.W.R. 641, 85 C.C.C. (3d) 15, 17 C.R.R. (2d) 193, 107 D.L.R. (4th) 342, 158 N.R. 1, 56 A.C. 1; *R. v. Daviault*, [1994] 3 S.C.R. 63, 33 C.R. (4th) 165, 93 C.C.C. (3d) 21, 24 C.R.R. (2d) 1, 118 D.L.R. (4th) 469, 173 N.R. 1; *Reference re s. 94(2) of the Motor Vehicle Act (B.C.)*, [1985] 2 S.C.R. 486, [1986] 1 W.W.R. 481, 36 M.V.R. 240, 69 B.C.L.R. 145, 48 C.R. (3d) 289, 65 C.C.C. (3d) 289, 63 N.R. 266, 24 D.L.R. (4th) 536, 24 D.L.R. (4th) 536, 18 C.R.R. 30, [1986] D.L.Q. 90 (headnote) (*sub nom. Constitutional Question Act, R.S.B.C. 1979, Chap. 63*) (S.C.C.); *Singh v. Canada (Minister of Employment & Immigration)*, [1985] 1 S.C.R. 177, *R. v. Morgentaler*, [1988] 1 S.C.R. 30, 63 O.R. (2d) 281n, 62 C.R. (3d) 1, 82 N.R. 1, 26 O.A.C. 1, 44 D.L.R. (4th) 385, 31 C.R.R. 1, 37 C.C.C. (3d) 449 (*sub nom. Morgentaler v. R.*) (S.C.C.) and *R. v. Vaillancourt*, [1987] 2 S.C.R. 636, 60 C.R. (3d) 289, (*sub nom. Vaillancourt v. R.*) 32 C.R.R. 18, 39 C.C.C. (3d) 118, 47 D.L.R. (4th) 399, 10 Q.A.C. 161 , 68 Nfld. & P.E.I.R. 281, 209 A.P.R. 281, 81 A.R. 115.

Some of the important cases under ss. 8 to 14 are as follows: *R. v. Dyment*, [1988] 2 S.C.R. 417, 66 C.R. (3d) 348, 10 M.V.R. (2d) 1, 229 A.P.R. 13, 45 C.C.C. (3d) 244, 38 C.R.R. 301, 55 D.L.R. (4th) 503, 73 Nfld. & P.E.I.R. 13, 89 N.R. 249; *R. v. Sanelli, (sub nom. R. v. Duarte)* [1990] 1 S.C.R. 30, 71 O.R. (2d) 575, 74 C.R. (3d) 281, 53 C.C.C. (3d) 1, 45 C.R.R. 278, 65 D.L.R. (4th) 240, 103 N.R. 86, 37 O.A.C. 322; *R. v. Wiggins*, [1990] 1 S.C.R. 62, 42 B.C.L.R. (2d) 1, 74 C.R. (3d) 311, 53 C.C.C. (3d) 476, 103 N.R. 118; *R. v. Thompson*, [1990] 2 S.C.R. 1111, 49 B.C.L.R. (2d) 321, 80 C.R. (3d) 129, [1990] 6 W.W.R. 481, 59 C.C.C. (3d) 225, 50 C.R.R. 1, 73 D.L.R. (4th) 596, 114 N.R. 1; *R. v. Hufsky*, [1988] 1 S.C.R. 621, 63 C.R. (3d) 14, 4 M.V.R. (2d) 170, 40 C.C.C. (3d)

398, 32 C.R.R. 193, 84 N.R. 365, 27 O.A.C. 103; *Thomson Newspapers Ltd. v. Canada (Director of Investigation & Research)*, [1990] 1 S.C.R. 425, 72 O.R. (2d) 415n, 76 C.R. (3d) 19, 54 C.C.C. (3d) 417, 29 C.P.R. (3d) 97, 47 C.R.R. 1, 67 D.L.R. (4th) 161, 106 N.R. 161, 39 O.A.C. 161; *R. v. McKinlay Transport Ltd*, [1990] 1 S.C.R. 627, 72 O.R. (2d) 798n, 76 C.R. (3d) 283, 55 C.C.C. (3d) 530, 47 C.R.R. 151, *(sub nom. Canada v. McKinlay Transport Ltd.)* [1990] 2 C.T.C. 103, 68 D.L.R. (4th) 568, 106 N.R. 385, 39 O.A.C. 385; *R. v. Simmons*, [1988] 2 S.C.R. 495, 67 O.R. (2d) 63, 66 C.R. (3d) 297, 45 C.C.C. (3d) 296, 18 C.E.R. 227, 38 C.R.R. 252, 55 D.L.R. (4th) 673, 89 N.R. 1, 30 O.A.C. 241; *R. v. L. (T.P.)*, [1987] 2 S.C.R. 309, 82 N.S.R. (2d) 271, 61 C.R. (3d) 1, 207 A.P.R. 271, *(sub nom. L. v. R.)* 37 C.C.C. (3d) 1, 32 C.R.R. 41, 44 D.L.R. (4th) 193, 80 N.R. 161; *R. v. Manninen*, [1987] 1 S.C.R. 1233, 61 O.R. (2d) 736n, 58 C.R. (3d) 97, 34 C.C.C. (3d) 385, 38 C.R.R. 37, 41 D.L.R. (4th) 301, 76 N.R. 198, 21 O.A.C. 192; *R. v. Brydges*, [1990] 1 S.C.R. 190, 71 Alta. L.R. (2d) 145, 74 C.R. (3d) 129, [1990] 2 W.W.R. 220, 104 A.R. 124, 53 C.C.C. (3d) 330, 46 C.R.R. 236, 103 N.R. 282; *R. v. Kalanj*, [1989] 1 S.C.R. 1594, 70 C.R. (3d) 260, [1989] 6 W.W.R. 577, 48 C.C.C. (3d) 459, 40 C.R.R. 50, 96 N.R. 191; *R. v. Wigglesworth*, [1987] 2 S.C.R. 541, 28 Admin. L.R. 294, 60 C.R. (3d) 193, [1988] 1 W.W.R. 193, *(sub nom. Wigglesworth v. R.)* 37 C.C.C. (3d) 385, 32 C.R.R. 219, 45 D.L.R. (4th) 235, 81 N.R. 161, 61 Sask. R. 105; *R. v. Généreux*, [1992] 1 S.C.R. 259, 70 C.C.C. (3d) 1, 88 D.L.R. (4th) 110, 8 C.R.R. (2d) 89, 133 N.R. 241; *R. v. Oakes*, 1 S.C.R. 103, 53 O.R. (2d) 719 (headnote only), 50 C.R. (3d) 1, 24 C.C.C. (3d) 321, 19 C.R.R. 308, 65 N.R. 87, 14 O.A.C. 335; *R. v. Whyte*, [1988] 2 S.C.R. 3, 29 B.C.L.R. (2d) 273, 64 C.R. (3d) 123, 6 M.V.R. (2d) 138, [1988] 5 W.W.R. 26, 42 C.C.C. (3d) 97, 35 C.R.R. 1, 51 D.L.R. (4th) 481, 86 N.R. 328; *R. v. Smith*, [1989] 2 S.C.R. 1120, 73 C.R. (3d) 1, 52 C.C.C. (3d) 97, 45 C.R.R. 314, 63 Man. R. (2d) 81, 102 N.R. 205; *R. v. Askov*, [1990] 2 S.C.R. 1199, 75 O.R. (2d) 673, 79 C.R. (3d) 273, 59 C.C.C. (3d) 449, 49 C.R.R. 1, 74 D.L.R. (4th) 355, 113 N.R. 241, 42 O.A.C. 81; *R. v. Morin*, [1992] 1 S.C.R. 771, 12 C.R. (4th) 1, 71 C.C.C. (3d) 1, 8 C.R.R. (2d) 193, 134 N.R. 321, 53 O.A.C. 241; *R. v. Smith*, [1987] 1 S.C.R. 1045, 15 B.C.L.R. (2d) 273, 58 C.R. (3d) 193, [1987] 5 W.W.R. 1, 34 C.C.C. (3d) 97, 31 C.R.R. 193, 40 D.L.R. (4th) 435, 75 N.R. 321; *Dagenais v. C.B.C.*, [1994] S.C.R. 104; *R. v. Smith*, [1987] 1 S.C.R. 1045, 15 B.C.L.R. (2d) 273, 58 C.R. (3d) 193, [1987] 5 W.W.R. 1, 34 C.C.C. (3d) 97, 31 C.R.R. 193, 40 D.L.R. (4th) 435, 75 N.R. 321; *Dubois v. R.*, [1985] 2 S.C.R. 350, 41 Alta. L.R. (2d) 97, 48 C.R. (3d) 193, [1986] 1 W.W.R. 193, 66 A.R. 202, 22 C.C.C. (3d) 513, 18 C.R.R. 1, 23 D.L.R. (4th) 503, 62 N.R. 50; *R. v. Mannion*, [1986] 2 S.C.R. 272, 47 Alta. L.R. (2d) 177, 53 C.R. (3d) 193, [1986] 6 W.W.R. 525, 75 A.R. 16, 28 C.C.C. (3d) 544, 25 C.R.R. 182, 31 D.L.R. (4th) 712, 69 N.R. (3d) 193; *R. v. Kuldip*, [1990] 3 S.C.R. 618, 1 C.R. (4th) 285,

61 C.C.C. (2d) 385, 1 C.R.R. (2d) 110, 114 N.R. 284, 43 O.A.C. 340; *Director of Investigation & Research, Combines Investigation Branch v. Southam Inc.*, [1984] 2 S.C.R. 145, [1984] 6 W.W.R. 577, 33 Alta. L.R. (2d) 193, 41 C.R. (3d) 97 (*sub nom. Director of Investigation & Research, Combines Investigation Branch v. Southam Inc.*), 27 B.L.R. 297, 2 C.P.R. (3d) 1, 9 C.R.R. 355, 14 C.C.C. (3d) 97 (*sub nom. Hunter v. Southam Inc.*), 11 D.L.R. (4th) 641, 84 D.T.C. 6467, 55 A.R. 291, 55 N.R. 241; *R. v. Collins*, [1987] 1 S.C.R. 265, [1987] 3 W.W.R. 699, 13 B.C.L.R. (2d) 1, 56 C.R. (3d) 193, 28 C.R.R. 122, 33 C.C.C. (3d) 1, 38 D.L.R. (4th) 508, 74 N.R. 276; *R. v. Therens*, [1985] 1 S.C.R. 613, [1985] 4 W.W.R. 286, 38 Alta. L.R. (2d) 99, 45 C.R. (3d) 97, 32 M.V.R. 153, 13 C.R.R. 193, 18 C.C.C. (3d) 481, 18 D.L.R. (4th) 655, 40 Sask. R. 122, 59 N.R. 122; *Dedman v. R.*, [1985] 2 S.C.R. 2, 46 C.R. (3d) 193, 34 M.V.R. 1, 20 C.C.C. (3d) 97, 11 O.A.C. 241, 60 N.R. 34; *R. v. WIS Development Corp.*, [1984] 1 S.C.R. 485, 31 Alta. L.R. (2d) 289, 40 C.R. (3d) 97, 12 C.C.C. (3d) 129, 53 A.R. 58; *R. v. Mills*, [1986] 1 S.C.R. 863, 58 O.R. (2d) 544n, 52 C.R. (3d) 1, 21 C.R.R. 76, 26 C.C.C. (3d) 481, 29 D.L.R. (4th) 161, 16 O.A.C. 81 (*sub nom Mills v. R.*), 67 N.R. 241; *R. v. Rahey*, [1987] 1 S.C.R. 588, 57 C.R. (3d) 289, 33 C.C.C. (3d) 289, 39 D.L.R. (4th) 481, 78 N.S.R. (2d) 183, 193 A.P.R. 183, 75 N.R. 81; *R. v. Stanger*, [1983] 5 W.W.R. 331, 26 Alta. L.R. (2d) 193, 7 C.C.C. (3d) 337, 2 D.L.R. (4th) 121, 46 A.R. 242 (*sub nom. R. v. Bramwell; R. v. Kerr; R. v. Leskosek*) 6 C.R.R. 257, 10 W.C.B. 237 (C.A.).

15. (1) Every individual is equal before and under the law and has the right to the equal protection and equal benefit of the law without discrimination and, in particular, without discrimination based on race, national or ethnic origin, colour, religion, sex, age or mental or physical disability.

(2) Subsection (1) does not preclude any law, program or activity that has as its object amelioration of conditions of disadvantaged individuals or groups including those that are disadvantaged because of race, national or ethnic origin, colour, religion, sex, age or mental or physical disability.

. . .

28. Notwithstanding anything in this Charter, the rights and freedoms referred to in it are guaranteed equally to male and female persons.

Section 15 deals with equality rights and probably should be read together with s. 28. Section 15(1) provides for equal protection and equal benefit of the law and equality before and under the law, while s. 15(2) provides for the legality of affirmative action programmes. Section 28 provides that, notwithstanding anything in the Charter, the rights and freedoms referred to in it are guaranteed equally to male and female persons.

Two of the leading cases on s. 15 are: *Andrews v. Law Society (B.C.)*, [1989] 1 S.C.R. 143, [1989] 2 W.W.R. 289, 34 B.C.L.R. (2d) 273, 25 C.C.E.L. 255, 36 C.R.R. 193, 56 D.L.R. (4th) 1, 10 C.H.R.R. D/5719,

91 N.R. 255; and *R. v. Turpin*, [1989] 1 S.C.R. 1296, 69 C.R. (3d) 97, 39 C.R.R. 306, 48 C.C.C. (3d) 8, 34 O.A.C. 115, 96 N.R. 115.

One of the important issues in connection with this section is the definition of "discrimination". Mr. Justice McIntyre, in *Andrews*, describes "discrimination" as follows:

> I would say then that discrimination may be described as a distinction, whether intentional or not but based on grounds relating to personal characteristics of the individual or group, which has the effect of imposing burdens, obligations, or disadvantages on such individual or group not imposed upon others, or which withholds or limits access to opportunities, benefits and advantages available to other members of society. Distinctions based on personal characteristics attributed to an individual solely on the basis of association with a group will rarely escape the charge of discrimination, while those based on an individual's merits and capacities will rarely be so classed.[13]

In *Turpin*, the Supreme Court of Canada reaffirmed the rationale employed in the *Andrews* case and commented upon the different approach to equality to be taken under the Charter as opposed to the Canadian Bill of Rights:

> In defining the scope of the four basic equality rights it is important to ensure that each right be given in full independent content, divorced from any justificatory factors applicable under s. 1 of the Charter. This is particularly important in the context of the right to equality before the law which was protected in a very different form in s. 1(b) of the Canadian Bill of Rights. Justificatory factors are of course relevant to the determination of whether a valid federal objective justifies a departure from the principle of equality before the law under the Canadian Bill of Rights. However, as in the case of the jurisprudence of other countries, great care must be taken not to import concepts and analytical processes derived from documents different in structure and content from the Charter: see *Re B.C. Motor Vehicles Act, supra*, at p. 498; *Que. (A.G.) v. Chaussure Brown's Inc., supra*, at pp. 57-58. I would emphasize in this connection the following passage from the judgment of McIntyre J. in *Andrews, supra*, at p. 22 [p. 294 (B.C.L.R.)]:
>
> > Any justification of an infringement which is found to have occurred must be made, if at all, under the broad provisions of s. 1.
>
> . . .
>
> The guarantee of equality before the law must be interpreted in its Charter context which may involve entirely different considerations from the comparable provision in the Canadian Bill of Rights.

As for the definition of discrimination, the court held:

> The internal qualification in s. 15 that the differential treatment be "without discrimination" is determinative of whether or not there has been a violation of the section.
>
> . . .
>
> McIntyre J. recognized in *Andrews* [at p. 297 (B.C.L.R.)] that "The . . . 'enumerated and analogous grounds' approach most closely accords with the purposes of s. 15 and the definition of discrimination outlined above", and suggested that the alleged victims of discrimination in *Andrews*, i.e., non-citizens permanently resident in Canada were "a good example of a 'discrete and insular minority' who came within the protection of s. 15" [p. 298 (B.C.L.R.)]. Similarly, I suggested in my reasons in *Andrews* that the determination of whether a group falls into an analogous category to those specifically enumerated in s. 15 is "not to be made only in the context of the law which is subject to challenge but rather in the context of the place of the group in the entire social, politi-

cal and legal fabric of our society" [p. 306 (B.C.L.R.)]. If the larger context is not examined, the s. 15 analysis may become a mechanical and sterile categorization process conducted entirely within the four corners of the impugned legislation. A determination as to whether or not discrimination is taking place, if based exclusively on an analysis of the law under challenge, is likely, in my view, to result in the same kind of circularity which characterized the "similarly situated similarly treated" test clearly rejected by this court in *Andrews.*

. . .

A search for indicia of discrimination such as stereotyping, historical disadvantage or vulnerability to political and social prejudice would be fruitless in this case, because what we are comparing is the position of those accused of the offences listed in s. 427 in Alberta. To recognize the claims of the appellants under s. 15 of the Charter would, in my respectful view, "overshoot the actual purpose of the right or freedom in question": see *R. v. Big M Drug Mart* at p. 344 [S.C.R.].[34]

In *Egan v. Canada,* [1995] 2 S.C.R. 513, 95 C.L.L.C. 210-025, 12 R.F.L. (4th) 201, C.E.B. & P.G.R. 8216, 124 D.L.R. (4th) 609, 182 N.R. 161, 29 C.R.R. (2d) 79, it was held that there are three steps in determining what constitutes discrimination. They are:

1. The first step looks to whether the law has drawn a distinction between the claimant and others.

2. Questions whether that distinction results in disadvantage, and examines whether the impugned legislation imposes a burden, obligation or disadvantage on the group persons to which the claimant belongs which is not imposed on others or does not provide them with a benefit which it grants others.

3. Assesses whether the distinction is based on an irrelevant personal characteristic which is either enumerated in s. 15(1) or one analogous there too.

In assessing relevancy for this purpose one must look at the nature of the personal characteristic and its relevancy to the functional values underlying the law.

Other recent cases that dealt with s. 15 include: *Vriend v. Alberta,* 18 Alta. L.R. (3d) 286, [1994] 6 W.W.R. 414, 152 A.R. 1, 20 C.H.R.R. D/358, (*sub nom. Vriend v. Alberta (Attorney General)*) 94 C.L.L.C. 17,025 (Q.B.); *Thibaudeau v. R.,* [1995] 2 S.C.R. 627, 12 R.F.L. (4th) 1, (*sub nom. R. v. Thibaudeau*) 95 D.T.C. 5273, (*sub nom. Thibaudeau v. Canada*) [1995] 1 C.T.C. 382, 124 D.L.R. (4th) 449, 29 C.R.R. 1, (*sub nom. Thibaudeau v. Minister of National Revenue*) 182 N.R. 1; *Haig v. Canada,* 9 O.R. (3d) 495, 10 C.R.R. (2d) 287, 16 C.H.R.R. D/226, (*sub nom. Haig v. R.*) 92 C.L.L.C. 17,034, 94 D.L.R. (4th) 1, 57 O.A.C. 272

---

[33] [1989] 2 W.W.R. 289 at 308.

[34] 69 C.R. (3d) 97 at 121, 125, 126, 127.

(C.A.); *McKinney v. University of Guelph*, [1990] 3 S.C.R. 229, 2 O.R. (3d) 319n, 2 C.R.R. (2d) 1, 91 C.L.L.C. 17,004 13 C.H.R.R. D/171, 76 D.L.R. (4th) 545, 118 N.R. 1, 45 O.A.C. 1; *Harrison v. University of British Columbia*, [1990] 3 S.C.R. 451, 52 B.C.L.R. (2d) 105, [1991] 1 W.W.R. 681, 2 C.R.R. (2d) 193, *(sub nom. Connell v. University of British Columbia)* 91 C.L.L.C. 17,001, 13 C.H.R.R. D/317, 77 D.L.R. (4th) 55, 120 N.R. 1; *Stoffman v. Vancouver General Hospital*, [1990] 3 S.C.R. 483, 52 B.C.L.R. (2d) 1, [1991] 1 W.W.R. 577, 2 C.R.R. (2d) 215, *(sub nom. Vancouver General Hospital v. Stoffman)* 91 C.L.L.C. 17,003, 13 C.H.R.R. D/337, 76 D.L.R. (4th) 700, 118 N.R. 241; *Douglas/Kwantlen Faculty Assn. v. Douglas College*, [1990] 3 S.C.R. 570, 52 B.C.L.R. (2d) 68, 50 Admin. L.R. 69, [1991] 1 W.W.R. 643, 2 C.R.R. (2d) 157, 13 C.H.R.R. D/403, *(sub nom. Douglas College v. Douglas/Kwantlen Faculty Assn.)* 91 C.L.L.C. 17,002, 77 D.L.R. (4th) 94, 118 N.R. 340; *Symes v. R. (sub nom. Symes v. Canada)*, [1993] 4 S.C.R. 695, 19 C.R.R. (2d) 1, [1994] 1 C.T.C. 40, 110 D.L.R. (4th) 470, 94 D.T.C. 6001, *(sub nom. Symes v. Minister of National Revenue)* 161 N.R. 243; *Schachter v. Canada*, [1992] 2 S.C.R. 679, 53 F.T.R. 240n, 10 C.R.R. (2d) 1, 92 C.L.L.C. 14,036, 93 D.L.R. (4th) 1, 139 N.R. 1; *Whitbread v. Walley*, [1990] 3 S.C.R. 1273, 52 B.C.L.R. (2d) 187, [1991] 2 W.W.R. 195, 77 D.L.R. (4th) 25, 120 N.R. 109, *Dywidag Systems International Canada Ltd. v. Zutphen Brothers Construction Ltd.*, [1990] 1 S.C.R. 705, 97 N.S.R. (2d) 181, 40 C.L.R. 1, 41 C.P.C. (2d) 18, 258 A.P.R. 181, 46 C.R.R. 259, 106 N.R. 11; *Rudolph Wolff & Co. v. Canada*, [1990] 1 S.C.R. 695, 43 Admin. L.R. 1, 41 C.P.C. (2d) 1, 46 C.R.R. 263, 69 D.L.R. (4th) 392, 106 N.R. 1, 39 O.A.C. 1. The *Schachter* case stands for the proposition that a court may 'read in' language to a statutory provision as a means to remedy a so-called 'underinclusive' category contained in that statute. That is, in *Haig v. Birch*, the Ontario Court of Appeal read in sexual orientation as a prohibited ground of discrimination in the Canadian Human Rights Act so that that Act conformed to the requirements of s. 15 of the Charter. Similarly, in *Vriend*, the Alberta Court of Queen's Bench read in sexual orientation as a prohibited ground of discrimination in the Alberta Individual's Rights Protection Act so that that Act also conformed to s. 15 of the Charter.[35] Neither the Canadian Human Rights Act nor the Individual's Rights Protection Act contains an explicit prohibition with respect to discrimination on the basis of sexual orientation. But the courts, in applying *Schacter*, have, in effect, filled a gap in the legislation which, historically, would have had to be done by legislative bodies. It demonstrates the bold, new remedial authority vested in

---

[35] *Vriend v. Alberta*, 18 Alta. L.R. (3d) 286, [1994] 6 W.W.R. 414, 152 A.R.I, *(sub nom. Vriend v. Alberta (Attorney General))* 94 C.L.L.C. 17,025, 20 C.H.R.R. D/358 (Q.B.) The *Vriend* decision is presently under appeal in the Alberta Court of Appeal.

the courts by the Charter. Interestingly, after *Andrews*, the court could only do this if sexual orientation would be considered analgous to an enumerated prohibited ground of dicrimination in s. 15. In the recent *Egan* case, the Supreme Court of Canada expressly found that it was.

There is a detailed discussion of the Canadian Bill of Rights in a later section of this chapter. Also, for a further discussion of the relationship between the Canadian Bill of Rights and the Charter, see *R. v. Therens*, [1985] 1 S.C.R. 613, [1985] 4 W.W.R. 286, 38 Alta. L.R. (2d) 99, 45 C.R. (3d) 97, 32 M.V.R. 153, 13 C.R.R. 193, 18 C.C.C. (3d) 481, 18 D.L.R. (4th) 655, 40 Sask. R. 122, 59 N.R. 122.

16. (1) English and French are the official languages of Canada and have equality of status and equal rights and privileges as to their use in all institutions of the Parliament and government of Canada.

(2) English and French are the official languages of New Brunswick and have equality of status and equal rights and privileges as to their use in all institutions of the legislature and government of New Brunswick.

(3) Nothing in this Charter limits the authority of Parliament or a legislature to advance the equality of status or use of English and French.

17. (1) Everyone has the right to use English or French in any debates and other proceedings of Parliament.

(2) Everyone has the right to use English or French in any debates and other proceedings of the legislature of New Brunswick.

18. (1) The statutes, records and journals of Parliament shall be printed and published in English and French and both language versions are equally authoritative.

(2) The statutes, records and journals of the legislature of New Brunswick shall be printed and published in English and French and both language versions are equally authoritative.

19. (1) Either English or French may be used by any person in, or in any pleading in or process issuing from any court established by Parliament.

(2) Either English or French may be used by any person in, or in any pleading in or process issuing from, any court of New Brunswick.

20. (1) Any member of the public in Canada has the right to communicate with, and to receive available services from, any head or central office of an institution of the Parliament or government of Canada in English or French, and has the same right with respect to any other office of any such institution where

    (*a*) there is a significant demand for communications with and services from that office in such language; and

    (*b*) due to the nature of the office, it is reasonable that communications with and services from that office be available in both English and French.

(2) Any member of the public in New Brunswick has the right to communicate with, and to receive available services from, any office of an institution of the legislature or government of New Brunswick in English or French.

21. Nothing in sections 16 to 20 abrogates or derogates from any right, privilege or obligation with respect to the English and French languages, or either of them, that exists or is contained by virtue of any other provision of the Constitution of Canada.

22. Nothing in sections 16 to 20 abrogates or derogates from any legal or customary right or privilege acquired or enjoyed either before or after the coming into force of this Charter with respect to any language that is not English or French.

    23. (1) Citizens of Canada

    (*a*) whose first language learned and still understood is that of the English or French linguistic minority population of the province in which they reside, or (*b*) who have received their primary school instruction in Canada in English or French and reside in a province where the language in which they received that instruction is the language of the English or French linguistic minority population of the province, have the right to have their children receive primary and secondary school instruction in the same language.

(2) Citizens of Canada of whom any child has received or is receiving primary or secondary school instruction in English or French in Canada, have the right to have all their children receive primary and secondary school instruction in the same language.

Linguistic rights are contained in two separate categories. The first category, dealing with the official languages of Canada and New Brunswick[36] is contained in ss. 16 to 22,[37] while the second category, dealing with the controversial issue of minority language education rights, is contained in s. 23. Two major cases in connection with s. 23 are as follows: *Quebec Assn. of Protestant School Boards v. Quebec (Attorney General) (No.2)*, [1984] 2 S.C.R. 66, 9 C.R.R. 133, 10 D.L.R. (4th) 321, 54 N.R. 196 and, *Mahe v. Alberta*, [1990] 1 S.C.R. 342, 3 Alta. L.R. (2d) 257, [1990] 3 W.W.R. 97, 106 A.R. 321, 46 C.R.R. 193, 68 D.L.R. (4th) 69, 105 N.R. 321

Two of the three kinds of applications that may be made under the charter are set out in s. 24.

24. (1) Anyone whose rights or freedoms, as guaranteed by this Charter, have been infringed or denied may apply to a court of competent jurisdiction to obtain such remedy as the court considers appropriate and just in the circumstances.

(2) Where, in proceedings under subsection (1), a court concludes that evidence was obtained in a manner that infringed or denied any rights or freedoms guaranteed by this Charter, the evidence shall be excluded if it is established that, having regard to all the

[36] The Government of Manitoba announced shortly after the Charter came into force that it wished to propose an amendment to the Constitution making English and French the official languages of that province. However, the government of the day, in the face of significant opposition, did not proceed with the proposal.

In 1890 the Manitoba legislature passed the Manitoba Language Act, making English the official language of the province. This law remained unchallenged until 1979, when the Supreme Court of Canada, in *Manitoba (A.G.) v. Forest*, [1979] 2 S.C.R. 1032, [1980] 2 W.W.R. 758, 49 C.C.C. (3d) 353, 101 D.L.R. (3d) 385, 2 Man. R. (2d) 109, 30 N.R. 213, held that the law was unconstitutional and that both English and French rights defined in s. 23 must be protected. In *Reference re Language Rights Under s. 23 of the Manitoba Act, 1870*, [1985] 1 S.C.R. 721, [1985] 4 W.W.R. 385, 19 D.L.R. (4th) 1, 35 Man. R. (2d) 83, 59 N.R. 321 (*sub nom. Reference re Manitoba Language Rights*), it was held s. 23 of the Manitoba Act 1870, was constitutionally entrenched. As a result, all laws passed in only one language were held to be invalid. The Supreme Court of Canada ordered their re-enactment in both English and French but declared their validity pending their re-enactment. The Supreme Court of Canada also dictated the date by which the laws had to be re-enacted. It was in this case that the Supreme Court of Canada invoked the so-called 'state necessity doctrine'.

[37] See, for example: *Assn. of Parents for Fairness in Education, Grand Falls Dist. 50 Branch v. Société des Acadiens du Nouveau-Brunswick Inc.*, [1986] 1 S.C.R. 549, 19 Admin. L.R. 211, 69 N.B.R. (2d) 271, 177 A.P.R. 271, 23 C.R.R. 119, 27 D.L.R. (4th) 40 (*sub nom. Sociéte des Acadiens du Nouveau-Brunswick Inc. v. Assn. of Parents for Fairness in Education, Grand Falls Dist., 50 Branch*) (S.C.C.).

circumstances, the admission of it in the proceedings would bring the administration of justice into disrepute.

Section 24 deals with enforcement, inasmuch as s. 24(1) provides a mechanism for an application to a court for a remedy in the event of a breach of a substantive right, while s. 24(2) deals with the exclusion of evidence obtained through a breach of a substantive right.[38] The other procedural section that is of considerable importance is s. 52(1),[39] about which more will be said later.

After s. 24, the substantive protections of the Charter are more or less completed and the balance of the Charter is concerned with applicability and procedural matters.

25. The guarantee in this Charter of certain rights and freedoms shall not be construed so as to abrogate or derogate from any aboriginal, treaty or other rights or freedoms that pertain to the aboriginal peoples of Canada including

(a) any rights or freedoms that have been recognized by the Royal Proclamation of October 7, 1763; and

---

[38] For a discussion of s. 24(1), see D. Gibson and S. Gibson, "Enforcement of the Canadian Charter of Rights and Freedoms: section 24" in E. Beaudion and G. Ratushny, eds, *The Canadian Charter of Rights and Freedoms (2d ed.) Toronto: Carswell, 1989. See also R. v. Boyle,* [1990] 2 S.C.R. 906, 79 C.R. (3d) 332, *(sub nom. R. v. Hess; R. v. Nguyen)* [1990] 6 W.W.R. 289, *(sub nom. R. v. Nguyen; R.v. Hess)* 59 C.C.C. (3d) 161, 50 C.R.R. 71, 73 Man. R. (2d) 1, 119 N.R. 353, 46 O.A.C. 13; *R. v. Swain,* [1991] 1 S.C.R. 933, 5 C.R. (4th) 253, 63 C.C.C. (3d) 481, 3 C.R.R. (2d) 1, 125 N.R. 1, 47 O.A.C. 81; *Re Language Rights under s.23 of the Manitoba Act, 1870,* [1985] 1 S.C.R. 721, [1985] 4 W.W.R. 385, 19 D.L.R. (4th) 1, 35 Man. R. (2d) 83, 59 N.R. 321; *R. v. Seaboyer,* [1991] 2 S.C.R. 577, 4 O.R. (3d) 383 (note), 7 C.R. (4th) 117, 66 C.C.C. (3d) 321, 6 C.R.R. (2d) 35, 83 D.L.R. (4th) 193, 128 N.R. 81, 48 O.A.C. 81; *R. v. Schachter,* [1992] 2 S.C.R. 679, 92 C.L.L.C. 14,036, 10 C.R.R. (2d) 1, 93 D.L.R. (4th) 1, 139 N.R.I. 53 F.T.R. 240 (note); *R. v. Rahey,* [1987] 1 S.C.R. 588, *(sub nom. Rahey v. R.)* 57 C.R. (3d) 289, 33 C.C.C. (3d) 289, 39 D.L.R. (4th) 481, 33 C.R.R. 275, 78 N.S.R. (2d) 183, 193 A.P.R. 183, 75 N.R. 81.

For a discussion of s. 24(2), see *R. v. Strachan,* [1988] 2 S.C.R. 980, 67 C.R. (3d) 87, [1989] 1 W.W.R. 385, 46 C.C.C. (3d) 479, 37 C.R.R. 335, 56 D.L.R. (4th) 673, 90 N.R. 273; *R. v. Collins,* [1987] 1 S.C.R. 265, [1987] 3 W.W.R. 699, 13 B.C.L.R. (2d) 1, 56 C.R. (3d) 193, 28 C.R.R. 122, 33 C.C.C. (3d) 1, 34 D.L.R. (4th) 508, 74 N.R. 276; *R. v. Amato,* [1982] 2 S.C.R. 418, [1983] 1 W.W.R. 1, 29 C.R. (3d) 1, 69 C.C.C. (2d) 31, 140 D.L.R. (3d) 405, 42 N.R. 487; and *R. v. Mack,* [1988] 2 S.C.R. 903, [1989] 1 W.W.R. 577, 67 C.R. (3d) 1, 44 C.C.C. (3d) 513, 37 C.R.R. 277, 90 N.R. 173. In the *Collins* case, the test used to define the scope of s. 24(2) was that suggested by Professor Yves-Marie Morissette in "The Exclusion of Evidence under the Canadian Charter of Rights and Freedoms: What to Do and What Not to Do" (1984), 29 McGill L.J. 521. The test was as follows:

Would the admission of the evidence bring the administration of justice into disrepute in the eyes of a reasonable man, dispassionate and fully apprised of the circumstances of the case?

[39] See *R. v. Big M Drug Mart,* [1985] 1 S.C.R. 295, [1985] 3 W.W.R. 481, 37 Alta. L.R. (2d) 97, 13 C.R.R. 64, 18 C.C.C. (3d) 385, 18 D.L.R. (4th) 321, 85 C.L.L.C. 14,023, 58 N.R. 81 60 A.R. 161.

(*b*) any rights or freedoms that now exist by way of land claims agreements or may be so acquired.[40]

27. This Charter shall be interpreted in a manner consistent with the preservation and enhancement of the multicultural heritage of Canadians.

There are, however, other sections, interpretative in nature, which deal with such matters as aboriginal rights in s. 25 and multicultural rights in s. 27, but the main human rights package is contained in ss. 2 through 23 inclusive.

2. THE SIGNIFICANCE OF ENTRENCHMENT

52. (1) The Constitution of Canada is the supreme law of Canada, and any law that is inconsistent with the provisions of the Constitution is, to the extent of the inconsistency, of no force or effect

(2) The Constitution of Canada includes

(*a*) the Canada Act, including this Act;

(*b*) the Act and orders referred to in Schedule I; and

(*c*) any amendment to any Act or order referred to in paragraph (*a*) or (*b*).

(3) Amendments to the Constitution of Canada shall be made only in accordance with the authority contained in the Constitution of Canada.

. . .

32. (1) This Charter applies

(*a*) to the Parliament and government of Canada in respect of all matters within the authority of Parliament including all matters relating to the Yukon Territory and Northwest Territories; and

(*b*) to the legislature and government of each province in respect of all matters within the authority of the legislature of each province.[41]

---

[40] Constitution Amendment Proclamation, 1983. Aboriginal rights are also the subject of Part II of the Constitution Act of 1982. In addition, the move toward Aboriginal Self-government has been the subject of substantial constitutional debate for several years, including discussions in relation to the Charlottetown Constitution Accord. In some recent commentary on this issue, see The Globe & Mail, August 11, 1995; The Globe & Mail, August 12, 1995; and The Edmonton Journal, August 12, 1995.

[41] One of the major determinations of the first few years of Charter litigation was that the Charter applies only to the public sector and not the private sector. See *Dolphin Delivery v. R.W.D.S.U., Loc. 580,* [1986] 2 S.C.R. 573, (*sub nom. R.W.D.S.U., Loc. 580 v. Dolphin Delivery Ltd.*) [1987] 1 W.W.R. 577, 9 B.C.L.R. (2d) 273, 38 C.C.L.T. 184, 33 D.L.R. (4th) 174, 25 C.R.R. 321, 87 C.L.L.C. 14,002, 71 N.R. 83. More recently, see also *Committee for the Commonwealth of Canada v. Canada,* [1991] 1 S.C.R. 139; *Comité pour la République du Canada-Committee for the Commonwealth of Canada v. Canada,* [1991] 1 S.C.R. 139, 4 C.R.R. (2d) 60, 77 D.L.R. (4th) 385, (*sub nom. Committee for the Commonwealth of Canada v. Canada*) 120 N.R. 241, 40 F.T.R. 240 (note), application for re-hearing refused (May 8, 1991), Doc. 20334 (S.C.C.); *McKinney v. University of Guelph,* [1990] 3 S.C.R. 229, 2 O.R (3d) 319n, 2 C.R.R. (2d) 1, 13 C.H.R.R. D/173, 91 C.L.L.C. 17,004, 76 D.L.R. (4th) 545, 118 N.R. 1, 45 O.A.C. 1; *Harrison v. University of British Columbia,* [1990] 3 S.C.R. 451, 52 B.C.L.R. (2d) 105, [1991] 1 W.W.R. 681, (*sub nom. Connell v. University of British Columbia*) 91 C.L.L.C. 17,001, 13 C.H.R.R. D/317, 2 C.R.R. (2d) 193, 77 D.L.R. (4th) 55, 120 N.R. 1; *Stoffman v. Vancouver General Hospital,* [1990] 3 S.C.R. 483, 52 B.C.L.R. (2d) 1, [1991] 1 W.W.R. 577, (*sub nom. Vancouver General Hospital v. Stoffman*) 91 C.L.L.C. 17,003, 13 C.H.R.R. D/337, 2 C.R.R. (2d) 215, 76 D.L.R. (4th) 700, 118 N.R. 241 and *Douglas/Kwantlen Faculty Assn. v. Douglas Collage,* [1990] 3 S.C.R. 570, 50 Admin. L.R. 69, 52 B.C.L.R. (2d) 68, [1991] 1 W.W.R. 643, (*sub nom. Douglas*

(2) Notwithstanding subsection (1), section 15 shall not have effect until three years after this section comes into force.

33. (1) Parliament or the legislature of a province may expressly declare in an Act of Parliament or of the legislature, as the case may be, that the Act or a provision thereof shall operate notwithstanding a provision included in section 2 or sections 7 to 15 of this Charter.[42]

(2) An Act or a provision of an Act in respect of which a declaration made under this section is in effect shall have such operation as it would have but for the provision of this Charter referred to in the declaration.

(3) A declaration made under subsection (1) shall cease to have effect five years after it comes into force or on such earlier date as may be specified in the declaration.

(4) Parliament or a legislature of a province may re-enact a declaration made under subsection (1).

(5) Subsection (3) applies in respect of a re-enactment made under subsection (4).

The entrenchment of various provisions in a constitution is significant because of the legal status those provisions occupy after entrenchment. Section 52(1) states that the Constitution of Canada is the supreme law of Canada and that any law that is inconsistent with the provisions of the Constitution is, to the extent of the inconsistency, of no force or effect. The result of this is that a constitutional challenge can now be based not only on whether a legislative body has exceeded its power under ss. 91 and 92, but also on whether it has violated substantive rights. This changes our constitutional orientation in Canada to one somewhat akin to that of the United States. In Canada, to date, we have only been concerned, by and large, with jurisdictional questions, namely, who has jurisdiction to pass what laws. However, we are now also concerned with the issue of whether those laws, in terms of their content or substance, conform to the Charter of Rights and Freedoms, which now forms an integral part

---

College v. Douglas/Kwantlen Faculty Assn.) 91 C.L.L.C. 17,002, 13 C.H.R.R. D/403, 2 C.R.R. (2d) 157, 77 D.L.R. (4th) 94, 118 N.R. 340

But other issues regarding the application of the Charter were also determined. See *B.C.G.E.U., Re,* [1988] 2 S.C.R. 214, *(sub nom. B.C.G.E.U. v. British Columbia (A.G.))* [1988] 6 W.W.R. 577, 31 B.C.L.R. (2d) 273, 30 C.P.C. (2d) 221, 44 C.C.C. (3d) 289, 53 D.L.R. (4th) 1, 88 C.L.L.C. 14,047, 71 Nfld. & P.E.I.R. 93, 220 A.P.R. 93, 87 N.R. 241; *Operation Dismantle v. R.,* [1985] 1 S.C.R. 441, 12 Admin. L.R. 16, 13 C.R.R. 287, 18 D.L.R. (4th) 481, 59 N.R. 1; *Blainey v. Ont. Hockey Assn.* (1986), 54 O.R. (2d) 513, 10 C.P.R. (3d) 450, 21 C.R.R. 44, 7 C.H.R.R. D/3529, 26 D.L.R. (4th) 728, 14 O.A.C. 194 (C.A.) leave to appeal to S.C.C. refused (1986), 58 O.R. (2d) 274, (headnote), 17 O.A.C. 399n *(sub nom. Ont Hockey Assn. v. Blainey),* 10 C.P.R. (3d) 450n, 21 C.R.R. 44n, 7 C.H.R.R. D/ 3529n, 72 N.R. 76n (S.C.C.); *McKinney v. University of Guelph* (1986), 57 O.R. (2d) 1, 14 C.C.E.L. 1, 22 Admin. L.R. 29, 32 D.L.R. (4th) 65, 9 C.H.R.R. D/4685, 87 C.L.L.C. 17,009 (H.C.), affirmed 63 O.R. (2d) 1, 29 Admin. L.R. 227, 46 D.L.R. (4th) 193, 9 C.H.R.R. D/4573, 24 O.A.C. 241, affirmed [1990] 3 S.C.R. 229, 91 C.L.L.C. 17,004, 2 O.R. (3d) 319n, 13 C.H.R.R. D/171, 450 A.C. 1, 2 C.R.R. (2d) 1, 76 D.L.R. (4th) 545, 118 N.R.1; *Slaight Communications Inc. v. Davidson,* [1989] 1 S.C.R. 1038, 26 C.C.E.L. 85, 59 D.L.R. (4th) 416, 89 C.L.L.C. 14,031, 93 N.R. 183.

[42] See *Ford v. Quebec (A.G.),* [1988] 2 S.C.R. 712, 36 C.R.R 1, 54 D.L.R. (4th) 577, 10 C.H.R.R. D/5559, 19 Q.A.C. 69 *(sub nom. Chaussure Brown's Inc. v. Qué. (P.G.)),* 90 N.R. 84.

of the Constitution. Thus, our orientation has changed from one of jurisdiction to one of jurisdiction and content. At the same time, the doctrine
of parliamentary sovereignty has been preserved by virtue of the non
obstante provision contained in s. 33 of the Charter, which provides that
Parliament or a legislature may expressly declare that an Act of Parliament or the legislature shall operate notwithstanding the Charter of Rights
and Freedoms. Two things ought to be said about this provision. First,
the notwithstanding clause applies only to certain sections of the Charter, namely, s. 2 and ss. 7 to 15, and to no other sections. Secondly, the
political experience in Canada today indicates that it is not politically expe-
dient to exercise this override option. For example, the human rights legislation of Alberta and Saskatchewan has contained similar such opting out
provisions which have never been used in either of those two provinces.
Federally, a similar provision exists in the Canadian Bill of Rights, but
it has been used only once (and this was in respect of the federal statute
passed in 1971 replacing the application of the War Measures Act by temporary measures legislation imposed at the time). It is true that an opting
out provision has been used a number of times in Quebec with respect
to Quebec's human rights legislation. But Quebec ranks as an exception
to the general experience elsewhere which strongly suggests that it is politically inexpedient to use an opting out provision.

Under the Charter itself, there have been four instances where the notwithstanding clause has either been invoked or has been threatened to be
invoked. First, shortly after the Charter came into force, the Quebec
National Assembly enacted a law[43] which provided that all Quebec laws
"shall operate notwithstanding the provisions of sections 2 and 7 to 15
of the Constitution Act, 1982". The Quebec Court of Appeal, however,
held that the law was invalid for reason that it was an omnibus attempt
to make those sections of the Charter inapplicable to all Quebec laws.
In other words, the court held that a legislature must be more specific
in identifying the particular sections of the Charter that are to be overrid-
den with respect to particular pieces of legislation.[44] This notion, however, was subsequently overturned in *Ford v. A.G. Que.*[45]

Secondly, the Government of Alberta threatened to invoke the notwithstanding clause when its law prohibiting strikes for public servants engaged
in essential services was challenged. The Government stated that if it lost

---

[43] An Act Respecting the Constitution Act, 1982, c. 21.

[44] See *Alliance des Professeurs de Montreal v. Quebec (A.G.),* 21 C.C.C. (3d) 273, 21 D.L.R.
(4th) 354, [1985] C.A. 376, [1985] R.D.J. 439, 18 C.R.R. 195 (C.A.), leave to appeal to
S.C.C. granted [1985] R.D.J. 439n, 21 C.C.C. (3d) 273n, 21 D.L.R. (4th) 354n, 18 C.R.P.
195n (S.C.C.)

[45] *Supra*, note 18.

the case it would invoke the notwithstanding clause. As it turned out, it won the case.[46] However, pending this decision, the Government of Saskatchewan feared that its own comparable labour laws would, in effect, be struck down by an adverse decision in the Alberta case. As a result, it invoked the notwithstanding clause to make its labour laws affecting public servants immune from the application of s. 2 of the Charter. Finally, following the *Ford* decision, the Government of Quebec recently invoked the notwithstanding clause. In the *Ford* case, the Quebec language law, as it pertains to commercial signs, was struck down as being in violation of s. 2 of the Charter. To circumvent the decision and to restore the integrity of its language law, the Government invoked s. 33 of the Charter.

> 26. The guarantee in this Charter of certain rights and Freedoms shall not be construed as denying the existence of any other rights or freedoms that exist in Canada.

Notwithstanding the entrenchment of the Charter of Rights and Freedoms in the Constitution, there are rights that continue to exist under various federal and provincial laws. Indeed, this is anticipated in s. 26 of the Charter, which provides that rights and freedoms guaranteed in the Charter shall not be construed as denying the existence of any other rights and freedoms that exist in Canada. Accordingly, federally, the Canadian Bill of Rights continues in force, at least to the extent that any of the provisions of the Canadian Bill of Rights do not conflict with the rights contained in the Charter. The same is true of the various provincial bills of rights. For example, in Alberta the Individual's Rights Protection Act and the Alberta Bill of Rights also continue in force. This is significant in that there are some rights contained in these various provincial and federal enactments which are not contained in the Charter, and there are some rights which are contained in the Charter which are not contained in the various other human rights enactments.

In addition, it is important to realize that the Charter is drafted so as to avoid what Professor Tarnopolsky (as he then was) refers to as the "frozen concepts" interpretation of the Canadian Bill of Rights, which limits its applicability to rights which existed at the time of its enactment. The Charter is applicable to all rights — existing and newly-acquired.

It is also important to realize that other significant statutes do remain in force subject to their conformity to the Charter, and one of these is the federal Emergencies Act.

---

[46] See *Reference re Pub. Service Employee Relations Act (Alta.),* [1987] 1 S.C.R. 313, [1987] 3 W.W.R. 577, 51 Alta. L.R. (2d) 97, 38 D.L.R. (4th) 161, 87 C.L.L.C. 14,021, [1987] D.L.Q. 225, 78 A.R. 1, 74 N.R. 99 (*sub nom. Reference re Compulsory Arbitrations*), 28 C.R.R. 305 (*sub nom. A.U.P.E. v. Alberta (A.G.).*

3. THE PROCESS OF CHARTER ADJUDICATION/INTERPRETATION

Essentially, there are three types of applications that can be made under the Charter. The first is an application under s. 24(1) for a remedy by an aggrieved party whose rights have been infringed. While the charging words differ from section to section (for example, the fundamental freedoms apply to "everyone", the democratic rights apply to "every citizen", the mobility rights apply, in one section, to "every citizen", and, in another section, to "every citizen of Canada and every person who has the status of a permanent resident of Canada", some of the legal rights sections apply to "everyone", while others apply to "every person", and the equality rights section applies to yet another formulation, that is, "every individual"), the enforcement section, namely s. 24-(1), applies to "anyone whose rights or freedoms have been infringed or denied".

The second type of application that may be made under the Charter is an application to exclude evidence under s. 24(2). The test that is applied is whether the use of such evidence (which was obtained in a manner that infringed or denied any rights or freedoms guaranteed by the Charter) "would bring the administration of justice into disrepute". That wording had been interpreted by the Supreme Court of Canada in the Rothman[47] decision. In applying the test, the courts have considered such key factors as the nature of the evidence, the nature of the conduct and the effect of the evidentiary exclusion.[48]

The third type of application is provided for in s. 52(1), which provides that the Constitution of Canada is the supreme law of Canada and that any law that is inconsistent with the provisions of the Constitution is, to the extent of the inconsistency, of no force or effect. This invites our courts, upon application, to overturn legislation on the basis of the position of primacy occupied by the Constitution of Canada in our legal system. A question arises as to who may make an application under s. 52(1). Clearly, only persons whose rights have been infringed can make applications under ss. 24(1) and 24(2), but what is the scope of the locus standi requirements in order to apply under s. 52(1)? As a result of the decisions in *Thorson*,[49] *McNeil*[50] and *Borowski*,[51]

---

[47] *Rothman v. R.*, [1981] 1 S.C.R. 640, 20 C.R. (3d) 97, 59 C.C.C. (2d) 30, 121 D.L.R. (3d) 578, 35 N.R. 485.

[48] *R. v. Collins*, [1987] 1 S.C.R. 265, 13 B.C.L.R. (2d) 1, 56 C.R. (3d) 193, [1987] 3 W.W.R. 699, 33 C.C.C. (3d) 1, (*sub nom. Collins v. R.*), 28 C.R.R. 122, 74 N.R. 276

[49] *Thorson v. A.G. Can.*, [1975] 1 S.C.R. 138, 43 D.L.R. (3d) 1, 1 N.R. 225.

[50] *McNeil v. N.S. Bd. of Censors*, [1978] 2 S.C.R. 662, 84 D.L.R. (3d) 1 , 25 N.S.R. (2d) 128, 36 A.P.R. 128, 19 N.R. 570.

[51] *Borowski v. Canada (Minister of Justice)*, [1981] 2 S.C.R. 575, [1982] 1 W.W.R. 97, 24

it appears that almost any person can make an application to strike down legislation under s. 52. It should be pointed out that, while s. 24 provides a statutory right of standing to aggrieved persons, s. 52, as a result of the *Borowski* decision, seems to suggest that standing to challenge impugned legislation is discretionary.

An interesting issue arises as to whether notice is required under the appropriate provincial statutes before an Act can be declared unconstitutional. The conventional view is that notice is not required with respect to a s. 24(1) application, nor with respect to a s. 24(2) application for the exclusion of evidence. However, it is likely that notice will be required under the various provincial statutes with respect to any application under s. 52. However, the view has also been expressed that since the Constitution is supreme and since there is no notice provision contained therein, even provincial notice requirements are invalid as they do not conform to the Constitution. The prudent barrister probably would be wiser to give the requisite notice with respect to a s. 52 application before challenging a particular law, unless of course there are very special circumstances.

One of the more important issues relates to the evidentiary considerations in constitutional decision-making. Dr. Barry Strayer's (now Mr. Justice Strayer's) view of the process of constitutional adjudication, as he uses that phrase in his book *Judicial Review of Legislation in Canada*,[52] is that in addition to the application of normal rules of statutory interpretation, there are special rules in respect of the process of constitutional adjudication. He makes a distinction between evidence adduced to prove

---

C.R. (3d) 352, 24 C.P.C. 62, 64 C.C.C. (2d) 97, 130 D.L.R. (3d) 558, 12 Sask. R. 420, 39 N.R. 331. See, more recently, *Finlay v. Can. (Min. of Fin.)*, discussed later in this chapter. See also S. Blake, "Minister of Justice v. Borowski: The Inapplicability of the Standing Rules in Constitutional Litigation" (1982), 28 McGill L.J. 126, and H. Kushner. "Case Comment on Minister of Justice et al. v. Borowski" (1983), 17 U.B.C. L. Rev. 143; D.J. Mullan and A.I. Roman, "Minister of Justice of Canada v. Borowski: The Extent of the Citizen's Right to Litigate the Lawfulness of Government Action" (1984), 4 Windsor Yearbook of Access to Justice 303; J. Tokar, "Administrative Law: Locus Standi in Judicial Review Proceedings" (1984), 14 Man. L.J. 209; D. Gibson, *The Law of the Charter: General Principles* (Calgary: Carswell, 1986); T.A. Cromwell, *Locus Standi* (Toronto: Carswell, 1986). With respect to the standing of public interest groups, see *Canadian Council of Churches v. R.*, [1992] 1 S.C.R. 236, 2 Admin. L.R. (2d) 229, 16 Imm. L.R. (2d) 161, 5 C.P.C (3d) 20, (*sub nom. Canada Council of Churches v. Canada Minister of Employment & Immigration)* 8 C.R.R. (2d) 145, 88 D.L.R. (4th) 93, (*sub nom. Canadian Council of Churches v. Canada)* 132 N.R. 241, 49 F.T.R. 160 (note) and *Hy and Zels Inc. v. Ontario (Attorney General)*, [1993] 3 S.C.R. 675, 18 C.R.R. (2d) 99, 107 D.L.R. (4th) 634, (*sub nom. Magder (Paul) Furs Ltd. v. Ontario (Attorney General)* 160 N.R. 161, 67 O.A.C. 81 and see P. Bowal & M. Cranwell, "Persona Non Grata: The Supreme Court of Canada Further Constraining Public Interest Standing" (1994), 32 Alta L. Rev. 19. The general rule is that standing will be denied to public interest groups if there is another reasonable and effective way to bring the issue before the court.

[52] University of Toronto Press, 1968.

so-called "adjudicative facts" and evidence designed to prove so called "legislative facts" and argues that with respect to the latter, there should be a wider regime of admissibility. This would lead to a greater use of judicial notice, Brandeis briefs,[53] amicus curiae interventions and generally the lessening of some of the stricture in the rules of evidence. This, of course, to some extent already exists in constitutional cases as evidenced by the decision, for example, in the *Anti-Inflation Reference*.[54] But in addition, there are words in the Charter which invite the courts to admit wider kinds of evidence. For example, in s. 1 , there is a specific reference to the term "demonstrably justified". Whether something is demonstrably justified or not must surely be determined on the basis of either judicial notice, or evidence, or both, and that seems to invite consideration of a broader range of evidence than can be received. Elsewhere in the Charter, for example, in the section on minority language education, there is mention of the notion of "where numbers warrant". Obviously, a court has to receive demographic evidence in order to determine whether, in fact, the "numbers warrant" the expenditure of public funds to provide minority language education.[55]

Mr. Justice Strayer, in a more recent work,[56] acknowledges that there has been a significant widening of admissibility in constitutional cases in recent years. His earlier concerns relating to the restricted admissibility of the so-called 'legislative facts' have been significantly reduced during the past decade. In fact, Mr. Justice Strayer does not employ the terms 'adjudicative facts' and 'legislative facts' in his latest book. Rather, he makes the following remarks which are reflective of the new reality under which admissibility is no longer the issue it once was in constitutional cases.

> Having thus identified many of the kinds of facts which are relevant in constitutional adjudication, and the general considerations which ought to guide the courts in determining relevancy, we can examine the rules respecting admissibility of particular forms of evidence. In doing so it is important to keep in mind that not only have the Supreme Court Justices in recent years confirmed the relevancy of extrinsic evidence of effect, but they have also cautioned against any "general principle of admissibility or inadmissibility" of such evidence or against "any inflexible rule governing the admissibility of extrinsic materials in constitutional references. The effect of such a rule might well be to exclude logically relevant and highly probative evidence". This suggests that admissi-

---

[53] See *R. v. Chabot*, [1980] 2 S.C.R. 985, 18 C.R. (3d) 258, 55 C.C.C. (2d) 385, 117 D.L.R. (3d) 527, 34 N.R. 361.

[54] *Reference re Anti-Inflation Act*, [1976] 2 S.C.R. 373, 68 D.L.R. (3d) 452, 9 N.R. 541.

[55] See Yves L.J. Fricot, "The challenge of legislation by means of the Charter: evidentiary issues" (1984), 16 Ottawa L. Rev. 565.

[56] B.L. Strayer, The Canadian Constitution and the Courts: Function and Scope of Judicial Review, 3rd ed. Toronto: Butterworths, 1988. See also Hogg, P.W., *Constitutional Law in Canada*, 3rd ed. Toronto: Carswell, 1992 and *Danson v. Ontario (Attorney General)*, [1990] 2 S.C.R. 1086, 74 O.R. (2d) 763 (note), 112 C.P.C. (2d) 165, 50 C.R.R. 59, (*sub nom. R. v. Danson*) 73 D.L.R. (4th) 686, 112 N.R. 362, 41 O.A.C. 250

bility may be a problem for relevant evidence only where its weight is so insubstantial that it should not be put before the court.

. . .

Traditionally in cases involving only statutory interpretation such evidence has been held to be inadmissible.

. . .

With respect to the characterization of laws, the admissibility of statements of legislators and of governmental pronouncements on the purpose or effect of legislation has evolved markedly.

. . .

Dickson J., writing for the court in *Reference re Residential Tenancies Act*, in the context of warning against inflexible rules which might exclude "logically relevant and highly probative" extrinsic evidence in constitutional cases, observed that where the object or purpose of an Act had to be considered speeches made in the Legislature at the time of its passage "are inadmissible as having little evidential weight". Here, however, the criterion appears to be weight, a more flexible test, and no absolute bar to such evidence is implied.

. . .

It has also become accepted that the meaning of provisions of the Constitution can be clarified by resort to legislative debates and similar materials purporting to indicate the intention of the framers. This is true even with respect to pre-1982 constitutional provisions. For example, in *A.G. Can. v. C.N. Transportation Ltd.*, et al. Laskin C.J. mentioned the examination he had made of the Confederation Debates to seek illumination on the meaning of the criminal law power in head 91 [27] of the *Constitution Act, 1867*. In *Reference re Manitoba Language Rights* resort was had by the court to the Confederation Debates to assist in interpreting s. 133 of the 1867 Act, this being a guide to the proper interpretation of the *Manitoba Act, 1870*.

. . .

There is need for further consideration of the use of the *travaux préparatoires* leading up to the adoption of the Charter and the other amendments in 1982. It is true, of course, that the opinions of individual ministers or officials can not be taken out of context as proof of the intent of those various governments and the Parliament of Canada which collectively expressed the consensus of the Canadian people on the contents of the Charter. But a more extensive examination of the committee proceedings, and of other available materials on positions of various governments and parliamentarians, may indeed be very useful in gaining an understanding of that consensus, which is after all the only source of legitimacy for judicial review under the Charter. Those materials might well include speeches in Parliament, if such speeches for example explained the concerns which led to a compromise or the choice of certain language in the Charter. All of these matters should be admissible, but viewed very carefully as to the weight which should be accorded to them having regard to the particular circumstances.[57]

One of the most important aspects of our new Charter raises the question of what types of precedent are relevant and should be receivable by our courts. A language comparison between the Charter and the Canadian Bill of Rights indicates some language similarity. Therefore, the existing jurisprudence under the Canadian Bill of Rights would be relevant. In other sections, the Charter is comparable to the U.S. Bill of Rights; therefore, American jurisprudence would also be relevant. But also, European precedents will assist a court in interpreting a Charter provision, since, for example, the limitations clause in s. 1 is borrowed heavily from

---

[57] *Ibid.*, pp. 275, 277, 280, 281. 282.

various international instruments. In this connection, one might particularly refer to Mr. Justice D.C. McDonald's book, *Legal Rights in the Canadian Charter of Rights and Freedoms*,[58] with respect to a discussion of the various relevant international instruments.

There is a presumption of constitutionality or constitutional validity in our law. Does this presumption apply equally in respect of the Charter, that is, must the courts presume that an act is constitutionally valid when measured against the Charter with the onus of proof falling on those who allege that a given statute is constitutionally invalid?

The Supreme Court of Canada has, in fact, said that the presumption of constitutionality does not apply to the Charter. As a result, the initial onus in proving that a Charter right has been violated falls on the party alleging the violation. However, if that party is successful in proving that the Charter right has been infringed, the onus shifts onto the government to attempt to justify the violation as a reasonable limit as can be demonstrably justified in a free and democratic society, under the terms of s. 1. In both instances, the burden of proof is that of a civil burden; namely, a balance of probabilities or a preponderance of evidence.[59]

One should also, in this context, refer to Canada's international obligations under the various international instruments. One should then consider whether there exists a presumption that our domestic statutes conform to our international obligations.

Consider the following key issues in connection with the process of Charter adjudication/interpretation.

(a) Role of the Judiciary

Clearly a major change in our legal system relates to the role of the judiciary. Previously our judges were largely responsible for the interpre-

---

[58] 2nd ed. (Calgary: Carswell, 1989).

[59] See, for example, *R. v. Oakes*, [1986] 1 S.C.R. 103, 50 C.R. (3d) 1, 19 C.R.R. 308, 24 C.C.C. (3d) 321, 26 D.L.R. (4th) 200, 14 O.A.C. 335, 65 N.R. 87. For further discussions of s. 1, see also *Ford v. Quebec (A.G.)*, [1988] 2 S.C.R. 712, 36 C.R.R. 1, 54 D.L.R. (4th) 577, 10 C.H.R.R. D/5559, 19 Q.A.C. 69 (*sub nom Chaussure Brown's Inc. v. Québec (P.G.)*), 90 N.R. 84; *Irwin Toy Ltd. v. Québec (A.G.)*, [1989] 1 S.C.R. 927, 25 C.P.R. (3d) 417, 39 C.R.R. 193, 58 D.L.R. (4th) 577, 24 Q.A.C. 2, 94 N.R. 167; and *R. v. Edwards Books and Art Ltd.*, [1986] 2 S.C.R. 713, 55 C.R. (3d) 193 (*sub nom. R. v. Videoflicks*), 28 C.R.R. 1, 30 C.C.C. (3d) 385 (*sub nom. R. v. Nortown Foods Ltd.*), 35 D.L.R. (4th) 1, 87 C.L.L.C. 14,001, 19 O.A.C. 239, 71 N.R. 161. With respect to the issue of the presumption of constitutionality, see *Metropolitan Stores (MTS) Ltd. v. Man. Foods & Commercial Workers, Local 832*, [1987] 1 S.C.R. 110 (*sub nom. Manitoba (A.G.) v. Metropolitan Stores (MTS) Ltd.*) 25 Admin L.R. 20, 18 C.P.C. (2d) 273, [1987] 3 W.W.R. 1, 87 C.L.L.C. 14,015 (*sub nom. Manitoba (A.G.) v. Metropolitan Stores (MTS) Ltd.*), 38 D.L.R. (4th) 321, 73 N.R. 341, [1987] D.L.Q. 235 (headnote).

tation of our laws. Although that responsibility has not changed in and of itself, what has occurred is a usurpation of the doctrine of parliamentary sovereignty by a regime under which the final say on legislative policy rests with the judiciary pursuant to the power given judges under s. 52 of the Constitution Act. This role should be contrasted with the "construe and apply" mandate given the judiciary under the Canadian Bill of Rights,[60] or the mandate given the courts under other human rights legislation. Plainly and simply there has been a shift from a regime of parliamentary sovereignty to a system whereby the ultimate power rests in the Constitution as interpreted by a judge with powers under s. 24 to fashion new remedies in appropriate circumstances.

(b) Interpretation

Obviously, neither the federal Interpretation Act nor a provincial Interpretation Act can be binding on the interpretation of a constitution. They might be persuasive but they cannot be viewed as binding. Although the Constitution Act is technically a U.K. statute, it would be ironic to rely upon the United Kingdom Interpretation Act in interpreting the Canadian Constitution in view of the symbolic significance of the act of patriation. Accordingly, the correct view is that all interpretation acts are relevant and persuasive but that none is binding, which leads to the conclusion that the judiciary must perhaps proceed on its own instincts rather than be bound by one particular instrument in interpreting the Constitution.

(c) Generally

First, in connection with s. 1, there are various issues which ought to be raised. In respect of the question of "demonstrably justified in a free and democratic society", the issue has arisen as to who bears the onus of proving this. This has already been determined and is discussed above. As to what constitutes a free and democratic society, one might reflect upon the views of U.S. Circuit Court of Appeal Judge Aldisert, who says simply that it means Canada and therefore invites a consideration of Canadian traditions and history in order to determine what constitutes a free and democratic society and a reasonable limit therein.[61] Others have expressed the view that, given, for example, the Japanese-Canadian chapter in our history, Canada is perhaps not the best example of a free and democratic society in interpreting s. 1.

---

[60] See B. Hovius, "The Legacy of the Supreme Court of Canada's Approach to the Canadian Bill of Rights: Prospects for the Charter" (1982), 28 McGill L.J. 1. See also the Edmonton Journal, 11th April 1983.

[61] From an address delivered at the University of Alberta, January 1981.

Although the *Oakes* decision[62] (and other cases) have not defined a "free and democratic society" as such, they have provided the means by which a court determines a reasonable limit as can be demonstrably justified in a free and democratic society.

With respect to the question of the application of the Charter, ss. 32 and 33 clearly indicate that the Charter applies to Parliament and the federal government, as well as to the legislatures and the provincial governments, but this raises the issue as to what constitutes "government". To what extent are Crown agencies and Crown corporations covered by the Charter? Does Petro-Canada or the C.B.C. fall within this terminology? Professor Dale Gibson has argued that because the word "only" is not included in the charging words of s. 32, the private sector as well as the public sector may be covered by the Charter.[63]

This matter has been determined by the Supreme Court of Canada in *R.W.D.S.U. v. Dolphin Delivery*, [1986] 2 S.C.R. 573, [1987] 1 W.W.R. 577, 9 B.C.L.R. (2d) 273, 38 C.C.L.T. 184, 33 D.L.R. (4th) 174, 25 C.R.R. 321, 87 C.L.L.C. 14,002, 71 N.R. 83, where it has decided that the Charter applies only to the public sector.[64]

(d) New Terminology

The courts have had to interpret the terminology of the Charter, including some phraseology which is relatively new. The key areas of interpretation are as follows:

---

[62] *Supra*, note 34.

[63] Dale Gibson, *The Law of the Charter: General Principles* (Calgary: Carswell, 1986), p. 112.

[64] For further discussions on the relationship of the Charter to the private sector and, generally, on the scope or reach of the Charter, see *Slaight Communications Inc. v. Davidson*, [1989] 1 S.C.R. 1038, 26 C.C.E.L. 85, 59 D.L.R. (4th) 416, 89 C.L.L.C. 14,031, (*sub nom. Davidson v. Slaight Communications Inc.*), 93 N.R. 183; *McKinney v. Univ. of Guelph*, [1990] 3 S.C.R. 229; *Harrison v. University of British Columbia*, [1990] 3 S.C.R. 451, 52 B.C.L.R. (2d) 105, [1991] 1 W.W.R. 681, (*sub nom. Connell v. University of British Columbia*) 91 C.L.L.C. 17,001, 13 C.H.R.R. D/317, 2 C.R.R. (2d) 193, 77 D.L.R. (4th) 55, 120 N.R. 1; *Stoffman v. Vancouver General Hospital*, [1990] 3 S.C.R. 483, 52 B.C.L.R. (2d) 1, (*sub nom. Vancouver Gerneral Hospotal v. Stoffman*), [1991] 1 W.W.R. 577, (*sub nom. Vancouver General Hospital v. Stoffman*) 91 C.L.L.C. 17,003, 13 C.H.R.R. D/337, 2 C.R.R. (2d) 215, 118 N.R. 241 and *Douglas/Kwantlen Faculty Assn. v. Douglas College*, [1990] 3 S.C.R. 570, 50 Admin. L.R. 69, 52 B.C.L.R. (2d) 68, [1991] 1 W.W.R. 643, (*sub nom. Douglas College v. Douglas/Kwantlen Faculty Assn.*) 91 C.L.L.C. 17,002, 13 C.H.R.R. D/403, 2 C.R.R. (2d) 157, 77 D.L.R. (4th) 94, 118 N.R. 340, and *Blainey v. Ont. Hockey Assn.* (1986), 54 O.R. (2d) 513, 10 C.P.R. (3d) 450, 21 C.P.R. 44, 7 C.R.R. 44, 7 C.H.R.R. 44, 7 C.H.R.R. D/3529, 26 D.L.R. (4th) 728, 14 O.A.C. 194 (C.A.), leave to appeal to S.C.C. refused (1986), 58 O.R. (2d) 274, 10 C.P.R. (3d) 450n, 21 C.R.R. 44n, 7 C.H.R.R. D/3529n, 72 N.R. 76n, 17 O.A.C. 399n (*sub. nom. Ont. Hockey Assn. v. Blainey*) (S.C.C.).

1. "Reasonable limits" in s. 1.

2. "Demonstrably justified in a free and democratic society" in s. 1.

3. "Principles of fundamental justice" in s. 7.

4. "Unreasonable search and seizure" in s. 8.

5. "Arbitrarily detained or imprisoned" in s. 9.

6. "Unreasonable delay" and "reasonable time" in s. 11.

7. "A court of competent jurisdiction" and "such remedy as the court considers appropriate and just in the circumstances" in s. 24.

As indicated earlier, the main constitutional concern in Canada prior to 17th April 1982 was with the jurisdiction to pass laws of the various sovereign legislative bodies. As of 17th April 1982, the constitutional orientation in Canada has changed to concern with content and jurisdiction, which is to say that the constitutionality or validity of laws will be tested on the basis of whether they conform to the jurisdictional constraints imposed by the division of legislative powers and whether they conform to the boundaries of content imposed by the Canadian Charter of Rights and Freedoms. Having examined the latter, our attention will now turn to examining the former, namely, the jurisdictional concerns that have been with us since 1867 and that will, no doubt, continue into the future.

The B.N.A. Act of 1867 (now renamed the Constitution Act of 1867) was primarily concerned with jurisdiction, but it was also concerned with questions relating to the establishment of a body politic for the new nation created at Confederation. In examining the provisions of the B.N.A. Act, it is important to bear in mind that this Act continues in force as the Constitution Act of 1867 by virtue of its (and all amendments thereto) inclusion in the Schedule to the Constitution Act of 1982, which specifically states in s. 52(2) that the Constitution of Canada includes, among other things, all the matters contained in the Schedule to the Constitution Act of 1982.

The B.N.A. Act of 1867 (hereinafter referred to as the Constitution Act of 1867) was extraordinarily vague in defining many of the elements of our constitutional system. In other words, a reading of the Constitution Act of 1867 alone by a stranger to the Canadian political system would in and of itself leave that person with a serious misimpression as to the nature of our political order. For example, the Constitution Act of 1867 mentions a governor, advised by a council, having what appears to be autocratic and dictatorial authority, including the power to convene Parliament, prorogue Parliament, dissolve Parliament, call an election, appoint senators, command the armed forces, and conduct many other responsibilities under provisions contained in the Act. It makes no mention of a Prime Minister, of a cabinet, or political parties. With limited exceptions, it makes no mention of the procedure by which constitutional amendments are effected. It is only through the application of the unwritten component of the constitution, comprised principally of conventions, customs and usages derived from British constitutional history and developed through the political and constitutional experience of Canada since attaining her nationhood, that the ambiguity and misimpression that arises out of a literal interpretation of the Constitution Act of 1867 may be resolved and corrected. In other words, the simplistic and autocratic impression arising out of a literal reading of the Constitution Act of 1867 is greatly modified by the application of the customs and usages which define accurately the nature of our constitutional system.

The principal features of the Constitution Act of 1867 are as follows:

(1) The preamble, which states essentially that our constitution is similar in principle to that of the United Kingdom;

(2) The provisions relating to the union of the four provinces of Nova Scotia, New Brunswick, Ontario and Quebec in 1867;

(3) The establishment of a federal executive;

(4) The establishment of a federal legislative body; this includes the Senate and the House of Commons;

(5) The establishment of provincial executives;

(6) The establishment of provincial legislatures;

(7) The distribution of legislative powers;

(8) Miscellaneous provisions relating to such matters as education, language rights, courts,[65] agricultural marketing, etc.

The essential values which are promoted by the Constitution Act of 1867 relate, primarily, to a desire on the part of the drafters of our constitution to achieve a strong central government. It is interesting to note

---

[65] It is interesting to note that the Constitution Act of 1867 does not establish a supreme court for Canada. Section 101 allows Parliament to create such a court, and Parliament did so in 1875. The Supreme Court of Canada was established, however, under a regular statute of Parliament and, although quasi-constitutional in nature, the law establishing the court could conceivably have been repealed by Parliament at any time. However, the court has essentially been entrenched as part of the Constitution under the Constitution Act of 1982, with any changes to its enabling statute subject to the 1982 amendment procedure. This process of entrenchment is further enhanced by the Meech Lake Constitutional Accord.

that the opposite notion was promoted in the drafting of the United States Constitution, a document which emphasized strong states' rights. Ironically, one might argue that the original American desire for strong states' rights has, throughout the nation's history, been transformed, de facto, into a strong central government, while the original Canadian notion of a strong central government has been transformed into an increase in provincial power. However, it is clear that a strong central government was one of the initial concerns arising from such practical considerations as, for example, the achievement of efficiency in expanding trade and commercial enterprises and the creation of a strong defence against the United States.

In addition, one can imply certain values promoted by the Constitution Act of 1867 from a reading of the preamble to the Act, which contains what has been termed "the implied Bill of Rights". The preamble states, essentially, that the drafters of our constitution desired to establish a constitution similar in principle to that of the United Kingdom, which has been interpreted as importing into the Canadian constitutional system certain values contained in the British system. These values include the principles enunciated in the Magna Carta, the British Bill of Rights, and the Petition of Rights, and refer to such notions as freedom of speech, freedom of association and assembly, freedom of the press, and fair play. However, more importantly, and more specifically, this implied Bill of Rights has imported into our constitutional system the British doctrines of parliamentary sovereignty, the rule of law, and responsible government.

The doctrine of parliamentary sovereignty means that Parliament is supreme and can make or unmake any law. The British view of parliamentary sovereignty is best stated by Professor A.V. Dicey in his classic treatise *Introduction to the Study of the Law of the Constitution*[66], and has subsequently been restated by Professor Wade.[67] In brief, the Diceyan-Wade model of parliamentary sovereignty contains the following two essential elements:

(a) that Parliament can make or unmake any law; and

(b) that no body or person has a right to override or set aside the legislation of Parliament.

The key question is whether the Diceyan-Wade model of parliamentary sovereignty applies to the Canadian federation. If it does, Parliament would, of course, be supreme only in respect of those matters coming

---

[66] London: Macmillan, 1959, p. 39.

[67] E.C.S. Wade, *Constitutional and Administrative Law* (Essex: Longman Group, 1985), p.64.

within the legislative competence of the Parliament of Canada under the provisions of the Constitution Act of 1867 and the provinces would be sovereign only in respect of those matters which fall within provincial jurisdiction under the provisions of the Constitution Act of 1867. This modification notwithstanding, is it reasonable to assume that the Diceyan-Wade model of the doctrine of parliamentary sovereignty applies in all other respects to the Canadian federation? Although the doctrine of parliamentary sovereignty has been regarded as embodying the essential component of the British constitution, the applicability of the doctrine in the Canadian context has been controversial for two reasons. First, the Diceyan-Wade notion of parliamentary sovereignty ignores the whole process of judicial review. Secondly, and this is probably more fundamental, the Diceyan notion does not take into account the possibility that Parliament or a provincial legislature may "entrench" a given statutory provision by requiring that a particular "manner and form" be satisfied before that "entrenched" provision may be altered. "Entrenching" a provision refers to the notion that that provision may not be altered by simple majority. A "manner and form" is the requirement, other than simple majority, which must be satisfied in order to alter an "entrenched" provision. The imposition of a "manner and form" requirement in a given statute binds future Parliaments to conform to the particular "manner and form" requirement in order to amend that statute. One authority for the validity of a "manner and form" requirement is the case of *Bribery Commr. v. Ranasinghe*, [1965] A.C. 172, [1964] 2 All E.R. 785 (P.C.). This notion of "manner and form" as a limitation on the applicability of the Diceyan definition of parliamentary sovereignty in Canada is discussed at length in Chapter 3 of W.S. Tarnopolsky's *The Canadian Bill of Rights*.[68] Professor Tarnopolsky (as he then was), in discussing the possible entrenchment of the Canadian Bill of Rights in the Canadian constitution, makes these comments:

1) There is serious doubt among high authorities even as to the validity of Dicey's contention that the United Kingdom Parliament is sovereign in the terms he used.

2) Even if the United Kingdom Parliament could be described as being sovereign, this does not mean that in enacting legislation it can ignore the "manner and form" required by law for passing that legislation.

3) Regardless of the conclusion that is reached in viewing the United Kingdom Parliament. The Canadian Parliament could never be said to have been sovereign in the Diceyan sense, nor in the modern sense put forth by Professor Wade.

4) Even if one were to conclude that the Canadian Parliament is sovereign in the sense that it cannot be prevented from passing any legislation within its jurisdiction, it cannot ignore a "manner and form" requirement for passing valid Acts of Parliament even if Parliament can change the "manner and form" requirement by simple statute.

---

[68] 2nd ed. (Toronto: McClelland and Stewart, 1975).

5) The *Canadian Bill of Rights* could be entrenched in the B.N.A. Act by requiring that any amendments be in a specified "manner and form", and by further requiring a specified "manner and form" for amending this requirement.[69]

Indeed, the primacy provision contained in the Canadian Bill of Rights is, in itself, a "manner and form" requirement. That provision requires that all federal statutes must conform to the substantive provisions contained in the Canadian Bill of Rights unless Parliament, in enacting a statute, specifically provides that that statute shall operate notwithstanding the Canadian Bill of Rights. In effect, this primacy provision validly binds future Parliaments, in that in order to avoid the operation of the Canadian Bill of Rights, future Parliaments must specifically so provide. This requirement runs contrary to the Diceyan notion of parliamentary sovereignty.[70]

The implied Bill of Rights contained in the preamble to the Constitution Act of 1867 also imports into our constitutional system the doctrine of "rule of law":

(1) the supremacy of regular law as opposed to the influence of arbitrary power, excluding the existence of arbitrariness, prerogative, or even of wide discretionary authority on the part of the government;

(2) equality before the law, excluding the idea of any exemption of officials or others from the duty of obedience to the law which governs other citizens;

(3) the law of the constitution is not the source but the consequence of the rights of individuals as defined and enforced by the courts.[71]

These elements of "rule of law" have been restated in terms of a modern context by professor H. W. Jones:

(1) in a decent society it is unthinkable that government, or any officer of government, possesses arbitrary power over the person or the interests of the individual;

(2) all members of society, private persons and government officials alike, must be equally responsible before the law; and

(3) effective judicial remedies are more important than abstract constitutional declarations in securing the rights of the individual against encroachment by the state.[72]

For a fuller discussion of "rule of law" the reader may consult Chapter 4 of Tarnopolsky's *The Canadian Bill of Rights.* In addition, see the

---

[69] *Ibid.*, p. 104.

[70] Section 33 of the Charter of Rights and Freedoms, the so-called "opting out" or "notwithstanding clause", is akin to or in the nature of a constitutional "manner and form" requirement. See also *R. v. Mercure*, [1988] 1 S.C.R. 234, [1988] 2 W.W.R. 577, 39 C.C.C. (3d) 385, 48 D.L.R. (4th) 1, 83 N.R. 81 (*sub nom. Mercure v. Saskatchewan*), 65 Sask. R. 1 (S.C.C.); and *Re Canada Assistance Plan*, [1991] 2 S.C.R. 525, 1 Admin. L.R. (2d) 1, 58 B.C.L.R. (2d) 1, [1991] 6 W.W.R. 1, (*sub nom. Reference re Canada Assistance Plan (British (Columbia))* 83 D.L.R. (4th) 297, 127 N.R. 161, 1 B.C.A.C. 241, 1 W.A.C. 241.

[71] A.V. Dicey, *supra*, note 41, pp. 202-203, footnote 3.

[72] H.W. Jones, "The Rule of Law and the Welfare State" (1958), 58 Colum. L. Rev. 149.

case of *Roncarelli v. Duplessis*, [1959] S.C.R. 121, 16 D.L.R. (2d) 689. More recently, the concept of rule of law (together with the new so-called 'doctrine of necessity') is discussed in *Re Manitoba Language Rights*, [1985] 1 S.C.R. 721, [1985] 4 W.W.R. 385, 19 D.L.R. (4th) 1, 35 Man. R. (2d) 83, 59 N.R. 321.

The foregoing discussion has pointed to some implied values arising out of the express provisions contained in the Constitution Act of 1867, together with some express values arising out of the whole scheme of the Act. Accordingly, despite its rather benign or sterile appearance at first glance, the Constitution Act of 1867 does in fact have a value orientation. Nonetheless, much has changed with respect to value orientation with the inclusion of an entrenched charter of rights. All kinds of values arise in the Canadian Charter of Rights and Freedoms, including those related to fundamental freedoms (expression, the holding of religious beliefs, and the exercise of association and peaceful assembly), mobility from province to province, protections related to the criminal justice system, egalitarianism, multiculturalism and others. Furthermore, these values have, by virtue of s. 1 of the Charter, been put in the context of what should be tolerated in a free and democratic society. Indeed, the change of constitutional orientation from that of jurisdiction to one of content and jurisdiction represents, at the very least, a codification or perhaps a new recognition that certain values ought to be promulgated through our nation's highest law so that they are advanced in the most effective way. In institutional terms, there is yet another value recognition which flows from the entrenchment of a charter of rights in the Constitution. Put simply, we now recognize that in the protection and preservation of civil liberties, the notion of parliamentary sovereignty or supremacy must be subservient to the Constitution. And to this end, subject to s. 33 of the Charter, we entrust our judiciary with the responsibility of ensuring that having regard to the content of laws, the Constitution reigns supreme over ordinary legislative enactment. So clearly, by virtue of the recognition and advancement of specific values and by virtue of the institutional arrangements by which we protect those values, the highest law of the land is now a much more value-oriented instrument than it was prior to 17th April 1982.

Reference will be made to convention, custom and usage as the principal unwritten components of the Canadian constitution, in the discussion on constitutional amendment later in this chapter.

CONSTITUTIONAL BASIS OF LEGISLATIVE AUTHORITY

The most important provisions in the Constitution Act of 1867 are those provisions distributing legislative jurisdiction between the Parliament of

Canada on one hand, and the provincial legislatures on the other. The two main sections of the Constitution Act of 1867 concerned with the division of powers are ss. 91 and 92, although there are other sections dealing with this as well.

Section 91 reserves exclusively to the Parliament of Canada a general grant of legislative authority, together with exclusive legislative jurisdiction in respect of various matters contained in the twenty-nine enumerations following the general grant. Similarly, s. 92 reserves to the provincial legislatures exclusive legislative authority in respect of those matters falling within the sixteen enumerations contained in s. 92. There is one exception, however, in s. 92 and that relates to s. 92(10) (a), (b) and (c) which, by operation of s. 91 (29), bring certain matters within federal jurisdiction.

The relevant provisions contained in the Constitution Act of 1867 in respect of the division of powers follow:

VI. DISTRIBUTION OF LEGISLATIVE POWERS

Powers of the Parliament

91. It shall be lawful for the Queen, by and with the Advice and Consent of the Senate and House of Commons, to make Laws for the Peace, Order, and good Government of Canada, in relation to all Matters not coming within the Classes of Subjects by this Act assigned exclusively to the Legislatures of the Provinces; and for greater Certainty, but not so as to restrict the Generality of the foregoing Terms of this Section, it is hereby declared that (notwithstanding anything in this Act) the exclusive Legislative Authority of the Parliament of Canada extends to all Matters coming within the Classes of Subjects next herein-after enumerated; that is to say,—

. . .

1A.	The Public Debt and Property.
2.	The Regulation of Trade and Commerce.
2A.	Unemployment insurance.
3.	The raising of Money by any Mode or System of Taxation.
4.	The borrowing of Money on the Public Credit.
5.	Postal Service.
6.	The Census and Statistics.
7.	Militia, Military and Naval Service, and Defence.
8.	The fixing of and providing for the Salaries and Allowances of Civil and other Officers of the Government of Canada.
9.	Beacons, Buoys, Lighthouses, and Sable Island.
10.	Navigation and Shipping.
11.	Quarantine and the Establishment and Maintenance of Marine Hospitals.
12.	Sea Coast and Inland Fisheries.
13.	Ferries between a Province and any British or Foreign Country or between Two Provinces.
14.	Currency and Coinage.
15.	Banking, Incorporation of Banks, and the Issue of Paper Money.
16.	Savings Banks.
17.	Weights and Measures.
18.	Bills of Exchange and Promissory Notes.
19.	Interest.
20.	Legal Tender.
21.	Bankruptcy and Insolvency.
22.	Patents of Invention and Discovery.

23. Copyrights.
24. Indians, and Lands reserved for the Indians.
25. Naturalization and Aliens.
26. Marriage and Divorce.
27. The Criminal Law, except the Constitution of Courts of Criminal Jurisdiction, but including the Procedure in Criminal Matters.
28. The Establishment, Maintenance, and Management of Penitentiaries.
29. Such Classes of Subjects as are expressly excepted in the Enumeration of the Classes of Subjects by this Act assigned exclusively to the Legislatures of the Provinces.

And any Matter coming within any of the Classes of Subjects enumerated in this Section shall not be deemed to come within the Class of Matters of a local or private Nature comprised in the Enumeration of the Classes of Subjects by this Act assigned exclusively to the Legislatures of the Provinces.

Exclusive Powers of Provincial Legislatures

92. In each Province the Legislature may exclusively make Laws in relation to Matters coming within the Classes of Subject next herein-after enumerated; that is to say, —

1. The Amendment from time to time, notwithstanding anything in this Act, of the Constitution of the Province, except as regards the Office of the Lieutenant Governor.
2. Direct Taxation within the Province in order to the raising of a Revenue for Provincial Purposes.
3. The borrowing of Money on the sole Credit of the Province.
4. The Establishment and Tenure of Provincial Offices and the Appointment and Payment of Provincial Officers.
5. The Management and Sale of the Public Lands belonging to the Province and of the Timber and Wood thereon.
6. The Establishment, Maintenance, and Management of Public and Reformatory Prisons in and for the Province.
7. The Establishment, Maintenance, and Management of Hospitals, Asylums, Charities, and Eleemosynary Institutions in and for the Province, other than Marine Hospitals.
8. Municipal Institutions in the Province.
9. Shop, Saloon, Tavern, Auctioneer, and other Licences in order to the raising of a Revenue for Provincial, Local, or Municipal Purposes.
10. Local Works and Undertakings other than such as are of the following Classes: —
    a. Lines of Steam or other Ships, Railways, Canals, Telegraphs, and other Works and Undertakings connecting the Province with any other or others of the Provinces, or extending beyond the Limits of the Province:
    b. Lines of Steam Ships between the Province and any British or Foreign Country:
    c. Such Works as, although wholly situate within the Province, are before or after their Execution declared by the Parliament of Canada to be for the general Advantage of Canada or for the Advantage of Two or more of the Provinces.
11. The Incorporation of Companies with Provincial Objects.
12. The Solemnization of Marriage in the Province.
13. Property and Civil Rights in the Province.
14. The Administration of Justice in the Province, including the Constitution, Maintenance, and Organization of Provincial Courts, both of Civil and of Criminal Jurisdiction, and including Procedure in Civil Matters in those Courts.
15. The Imposition of Punishment by Fine, Penalty, or Imprisonment for enforcing any Law of the Province made in relation to any Matter coming within any of the Classes of Subjects enumerated in this Section.
16. Generally all Matters of a merely local or private Nature in the Province.

Education

93. In and for each Province the Legislature may exclusively make Laws in relation to Education, subject and according to the following Provisions: —

(1) Nothing in any such Law shall prejudicially affect any Right or Privilege with respect to Denominational Schools which any Class of Persons have by Law in the Province at the Union:

(2) All the Powers, Privileges, and Duties at the Union by Law conferred and imposed in Upper Canada on the Separate Schools and School Trustees of the Queen's Roman Catholic Subjects shall be and the same are hereby extended to the Dissentient Schools of the Queen's Protestant and Roman Catholic Subjects in Quebec:

(3) Where in any Province a System of Separate or Dissentient Schools exists by law at the Union or is thereafter established by the Legislature of the Province, an Appeal shall lie to the Governor General in Council from any Act or Decision of any Provincial Authority affecting any Right or Privilege of the Protestant or Roman Catholic Minority of the Queen's Subjects in relation to Education:

(4) In case any such Provincial Law as from Time to Time seems to the Governor General in Council requisite for the due Execution of the Provisions of this Section is not made, or in case any Decision of the Governor General in Council on any Appeal under this Section is not duly executed by the proper Provincial Authority in that Behalf, then and in every such Case, and as far only as the Circumstances of each Case require, the Parliament of Canada may make remedial Laws for the due Execution of the Provisions of this Section and of any Decision of the Governor General in Council under this Section . . .

Old Age Pensions

94A. The Parliament of Canada may make laws in relation to old age pensions and supplementary benefits, including survivors' and disability benefits irrespective of age, but no such law shall affect the operation of any law present or future of a provincial legislature in relation to any such matter.

Agriculture and Immigration

95. In each Province the Legislature may make Laws in relation to Agriculture in the Province, and to Immigration into the Province; and it is hereby declared that the Parliament of Canada may from Time to Time make Laws in relation to Agriculture in all or any of the Provinces, and to Immigration into all or any of the Provinces; and any Law of the Legislature of a Province relative to Agriculture or to Immigration shall have effect in and for the Province as long and as far only as it is not repugnant to any Act of the Parliament of Canada . . .

THE THIRD SCHEDULE

Provincial Public Works and Property to be the Property of Canada

1. Canals, with Lands and Water Power connected therewith.
2. Public Harbours.
3. Lighthouses and Piers, and Sable Island.
4. Steamboats, Dredges, and public Vessels.
5. Rivers and Lake Improvements.
6. Railways and Railway Stocks, Mortgages, and other Debts due by Railway Companies.
7. Military Roads.
8. Custom Houses, Post Offices, and all other Public Buildings, except such as the Government of Canada appropriate for the Use of the Provincial Legislatures and Governments.
9. Property transferred by the Imperial Government, and known as Ordnance Property.

10. Armouries, Drill Sheds, Military Clothing, and Munitions of War, and Lands set apart for general Public Purposes.

. . .

MISCELLANEOUS PROVISIONS

109. All Lands, Mines, Minerals, and Royalties belonging to the several Provinces of Canada, Nova Scotia, and New Brunswick at the Union, and all Sums then due or payable for such Lands, Mines, Minerals, or Royalties, shall belong to the several Provinces of Ontario, Quebec, Nova Scotia, and New Brunswick in which the same are situate or arise, subject to any Trusts existing in respect thereof, and to any Interest other than that of the Province in the same . . .

121. All Articles of the Growth, Produce, or Manufacture of any one of the Provinces shall, from and after the Union, be admitted free into each of the other Provinces . . .

125. No Lands or Property belonging to Canada or any Province shall be liable to Taxation . . .

132. The Parliament and Government of Canada shall have all Powers necessary or proper for performing the Obligations of Canada or of any Province thereof, as Part of the British Empire, towards Foreign Countries, arising under Treaties between the Empire and such Foreign Countries.

133. Either the English or the French Language may be used by any Person in the Debates of the Houses of the Parliament of Canada and of the Houses of the Legislature of Quebec; and both those Languages shall be used in the respective Records and Journals of those Houses; and either of those Languages may be used by any Person or in any Pleading or Process in or issuing from any Court of Canada established under this Act, and in or from all or any of the Courts of Quebec.

The Acts of the Parliament of Canada and of the Legislature of Quebec shall be printed and published in both those Languages.

The matters contained in the pre-patriation s. 91(1) are still part of the Constitution, but they are now included in ss. 3-5 of the Charter, together with a related provision concerned with the right to vote.

It is not appropriate, in a text of this nature, to outline in detail the respective legislative jurisdictions of the Parliament of Canada and of the provincial legislatures in respect of those matters contained in the more important enumerated heads of ss. 91 and 92 of the Constitution Act of 1867. To do so properly would require a detailed analysis, not within the purport of an introductory text. However, so that the reader may appreciate the limitations placed upon the various legislative bodies in Canada, it might be appropriate to outline, in a brief and summary form, the division of legislative jurisdictions in respect of some of the more important enumerated heads.

Under the general power of Parliament, contained in s. 91 of the Constitution Act of 1867, the Parliament of Canada is given exclusive legislative authority to enact laws in respect of the peace, order and good government of Canada. The peace, order and good government clause, however, has met with various interpretations over the years. Under the emergency doctrine, Parliament may legislate, under the peace, order and good government clause, in respect of emergency situations arising out of war or famine, or conditions arising out of war or famine but which survive the termination of the period of war or famine. In addition, in one case, it was held that national intemperance was a type of emergency contemplated under the emergency doctrine. Finally, as a result of the reference case[73] concerning the constitutionality of the Anti-Inflation Act, S.C. 1974-75-76, c. 75,[74] certain types of economic emergencies might give rise to appropriate federal legislation. In effect, upon the application of the emergency doctrine, Parliament may encroach upon those matters falling within provincial legislative authority under the provisions contained in s. 92 of the Constitution Act of 1867.

Under the 'national dimensions' doctrine, Parliament is given authority to legislate, under the peace, order and good government clause, in respect of those matters which affect the Dominion as a whole. It is difficult to rationalize the list of ad hoc matters which have been held to be within federal jurisdiction under this doctrine, but they include such matters as nuclear energy, aeronautics and the national capital region. Under this doctrine Parliament may again encroach upon those matters falling within provincial jurisdiction.

The most recent statement by the Supreme Court of Canada on the scope of the 'national dimensions' or 'national concerns' doctrine was made in *R. v. Crown Zellerbach Can. Ltd.*, [1988] 1 S.C.R. 401, [1988] 3 W.W.R. 385, 25 B.C.L.R. (2d) 145, 40 C.C.C. (3d) 289, 49 D.L.R. (4th) 161, 84 N.R. 1. In that case, the court held:

1. The national concern doctrine is separate and distinct from the national emergency doctrine of the peace, order and good government power, which is chiefly distinguishable by the fact that it provides a constitutional basis for what is necessarily legislation of a temporary nature.

2. The national concern doctrine applies to both new matters which did not exist at Confederation and to matters which, although originally matters of a local or private nature in a province, have since, in the absence of national emergency, become matters of national concern.

3. For a matter to qualify as a matter of national concern in either sense it must have a singleness, distinctiveness and indivisibility that clearly distinguishes it from matters of provincial concern and a scale of impact on provincial jurisdiction that is reconcilable with the fundamental distribution of legislative power under the Constitution.

4. In determining whether a matter has attained the required degree of singleness, distinctiveness and indivisibility that clearly distinguishes it from matters of provincial concern it is relevant to consider what would be the effect on extra-provincial interests of a provincial failure to deal effectively with the control or regulation of the intraprovincial aspects of the matter.[75]

---

[73] *Reference re Anti-Inflation Act*, [1976] 2 S.C.R. 373, 68 D.L.R. (3d) 452, 9 N.R. 541.
[74] Since repealed: see S.C. 1988, c. 2, s. 68 (Sched. IV, item 33).
[75] 49 D.L.R. (4th) 161 at 184.

Finally, the peace, order and good government clause has been regarded as a residuary power in respect of those matters not falling within any of the specific enumerations in either s. 91 or 92. This was illustrated in the *Hauser*[76] case, where the residuary power was invoked to justify federal narcotics legislation, but it was suggested in that case that residual matters are only those which did not exist at Confederation. It was even suggested by some judges that residual matters must also be in the nature of emergencies, although that notion was not in accord with the view of the majority.

Generally speaking, under s. 91(2) of the Constitution Act of 1867, the Parliament of Canada has exclusive legislative jurisdiction over the regulation of international and extraprovincial trade. The provinces, on the other hand, possess exclusive jurisdiction over purely intraprovincial trade. However, this distinction has become somewhat blurred in recent cases as a result of an application by the courts of a "functional" or "flow of trade" analysis. Under a functional analysis, the courts often ask to what extent it is possible to sever an apparently intraprovincial operation, functionally speaking, from the whole of an extraprovincial operation. Recent cases leave some doubt as to what truly remains "intraprovincial trade" in view of the modern, highly interrelated economics of the various trading jurisdictions. (See, for example, the *C.I.G.O.L.*[77] and *Central Canada Potash*[78] cases.) The Supreme Court of Canada has also recently explored in detail the notion of a general trade and commerce power (i.e., the so-called 'second branch' of s. 91(2) (see *Vapor Canada Ltd. v. MacDonald*, [1977] 2 S.C.R. 134, 22 C.P.R. (2d) 1, 7 N.R. 477, 66 D.L.R. (3d) 1); the *Labatt's*[79] case and see, for an analysis as to the circumstances under which Parliament may exercise this jurisdiction, *Canadian National Transportation v. Canada (A.G.)*.[80]

---

[76] *R. v. Hauser*, [1979] 1 S.C.R. 984, [1979] 5 W.W.R. 1, 8 C.R. (3d) 89, 98 D.L.R. (3d) 193, 46 C.C.C. (2d) 481, 26 N.R. 541, 16 A.R. 91.

[77] *Can. Indust. Gas & Oil Ltd. v. Sask.*, [1978] 2 S.C.R. 545, [1977] 6 W.W.R. 607, 80 D.L.R. (3d) 449, 18 N.R. 107.

[78] *Central Can. Potash Co. v. Sask.*, [1979] 1 S.C.R. 42, [1978] 6 W.W.R. 400, 6 C.C.L.T. 265, 88 D.L.R. (3d) 609, 23 N.R. 481.

[79] *Labatt Breweries of Can. Ltd. v. A.G. Can.*, [1980] 1 S.C.R. 914, 9 B.L.R. 181, N.R. 496.

[80] [1983] 2 S.C.R. 206, 28 Alta. L.R. (2d) 97, [1984] 1 W.W.R. 193, 38 C.R. (3d) 97, 7 C.C.C. (3d) 449, 76 C.P.R. (2d) 1, 3 D.L.R. (4th) 16, 49 A.R. 39, 49 N.R. 241. Those circumstances are as follows:

    (1) the impugned legislation must be part of a general regulatory scheme;

    (2) the scheme must be monitored by the continuing oversight of a regulatory agency;

    (3) the legislation must be concerned with trade as a whole rather than with a particular industry,

    (4) the legislation should be of a nature that the provinces jointly or severally would be constitutionally incapable of enacting; and

The Parliament of Canada, under s. 91(27) of the Constitution Act of 1867, is granted exclusive legislative jurisdiction in respect of criminal law and procedure, although not in respect of the constitution of courts of criminal jurisdiction. A key issue, therefore, is the domain of criminal law. Criminal law has been defined in many ways and most often in a very wide sense to include subject matters which, by their very nature, fall within the domain of criminal jurisprudence. These matters, generally, are contained in legislation promoting public peace, order, security, health or morality. In other words, the court examines an impugned statute and asks, in terms of its operational effects, whether that statute was enacted with a view to a public purpose which can support it as being in relation to criminal law. To support the legislation as a valid exercise of criminal law, the ordinary, though not exclusive, object of that law must be directed at public peace, order, security, health or morality.

On the other hand, the provinces can legislate in respect of purely regulatory matters as well as those matters referred to as "quasi-criminal" in nature. A quasi-criminal matter is one which is enacted with a view to suppressing conditions which are calculated to foster the development of crime. A quasi-criminal provincial statute is constitutionally permissible. However, a province cannot, under the guise or colour of quasi-criminal legislation, legislate matters which are truly criminal in nature and thus fall under s. 91(27).

Federal jurisdiction over radio, television, cable and pay television and other similar forms of communication, including satellite communication, as well as federal jurisdiction over interprovincial railway and trucking operations, are derived from the exceptions contained in s. 92(10)(a) of the Constitution Act of 1867.

The Parliament of Canada has jurisdiction in respect of both direct and indirect taxation, while the provincial jurisdiction is limited to direct taxation within the province for provincial purposes. One major difficulty is the categorization of taxes as either direct or indirect.

The foregoing is only a sampling of the various enumerations in ss. 91 and 92, and the discussion under each of these enumerations is very

---

(5) the failure to include one or more provinces or localities in a legislative scheme would jeopardize the successful operation of the scheme in other parts of the country.

These factors were further reviewed in *General Motors of Canada Limited v. City National Leasing*, [1989] 1 S.C.R. 641 where the former Chief Justice stated that:

. . . the five factors provide a preliminary check-list of characteristics, the presence of which in legislation is an indication of validity under the trade and commerce power. These indicia do not, however, represent an exhaustive list of traits that will tend to characterize general trade and commerce legislation. Nor is the presence or absence of any of these five criteria necessarily determinative. . .

limited, given the scope of this text. However, one can appreciate the limitations which legislators must accept on both the federal and provincial levels, given both the express provisions contained in the Constitution Act of 1867 along with the limitations arising out of the interpretation by the courts of those express provisions.

The division of legislative jurisdiction in ss. 91 and 92 of the Constitution Act of 1867 has given rise to what has been referred to as the "watertight compartment theory". By this theory, the doctrine of exclusivity has created two watertight legislative compartments. Accordingly there is a certain constitutional rigidity in Canada which must be surmounted by various means. First, the courts have allowed the notion of permissible or administrative interdelegation. While it is not constitutionally permissible for Parliament, for example, to pass a law delegating its exclusive legislative jurisdiction in respect of a given matter to the legislative assembly of a province, it can, nonetheless, delegate part of its exclusive legislative jurisdiction to a subordinate agency of a provincial legislature.[81] Secondly, flexibility has been achieved through agreements reached at federal-provincial conferences[82] which subsequently form the basis of a mutually agreed-upon legislative scheme. These agreements include conditional grants or grants-in-aid which tie certain conditions to the provision of funds from the federal government to the province. These conditions usually relate to how these funds are to be spent. Thus, even though the money is to be spent with respect to a matter within provincial jurisdiction, the tying of conditions gives the federal government some say as to the exercise of a matter normally within provincial jurisdiction.[83] In recent years, equalization payments have played a major role in federal/provincial fiscal arrangements. Indeed, equalization has become constitutionally entrenched as a separate Part of the Canada Act of 1982.

Another device to provide flexibility in the Constitution is the amending formula. Certain portions of the Constitution Act of 1867 used to be amendable by an Act of the Parliament of Canada according to the provision contained in the old s. 91(1). This power of amendment allowed

---

[81] See *Nova Scotia (Attorney General) v. Canada (Attorney General)*, [1951] S.C.R. 31, [1950] 4 D.L.R. 369; *Prince Edward Island (Potato Marketing Board) v. H.B. Willis Inc.*, [1952] 2 S.C.R. 392, [1952] 4 D.L.R. 146 and *Couglin v. (Ontario Highway Transport Board)*, [1968] S.C.R. 569, 68 D.L.R. (2d) 384.

[82] The Meech Lake and Charlottetown Constitutional Accords regularized or constitutionalized the federal-provincial consultative process by requiring at least one First Ministers' meeting annually.

[83] The Meech Lake and Charlottetown Constitutional Accords altered this in that they allowed a province to opt out of such a federal program provided that the province established its own program having objectives compatible with the national objectives. If it did so, the federal government would have been required to provide reasonable compensation to the province.

Parliament to unilaterally amend only those matters which fell purely within federal jurisdiction. Section 91(1) was a 1949 amendment to the Constitution Act of 1867, enacted as a complement to s. 92(1), which allowed the provincial legislature to unilaterally amend only those matters which fell purely within provincial jurisdiction. However, there were other matters which could only be amended, through the application of certain conventional rules and procedures, by an Act of the Parliament of Great Britain. These matters were set out in s. 91(1) of the Constitution Act of 1867:

> . . . matters coming within the classes of subjects by this Act assigned exclusively to the Legislatures of the provinces, or as regards rights or privileges by this or any other Constitutional Act granted or secured to the Legislature or the Government of a province, or to any class of persons with respect to schools or as regards the use of the English or the French language or as regards the requirements that there shall be a session of the Parliament of Canada at least once each year, and that no House of Commons shall continue for more than five years from the day of the return of the Writs for choosing the House: Provided, however, that a House of Commons may in time of real or apprehended war, invasion or insurrection be continued by the Parliament of Canada if such continuation is not opposed by the votes of more than one-third of the members of such House.

The conventional rules and procedures under which an amendment affecting any of the above matters would be effected were thought to be as follows:

> The first general principle that emerges in the foregoing resume is that although an enactment by the United Kingdom is necessary to amend the British North America Act, such action is taken only upon formal request from Canada No Act of the United Kingdom Parliament affecting Canada is therefore passed unless it is requested and consented to by Canada. Conversely, every amendment requested by Canada in the past has been enacted.

> The second general principle is that the sanction of Parliament is required for a request to the British Parliament for an amendment to the British North America Act.

> This principle was established early in the history of Canada's constitutional amendments, and has not been violated since 1895. The procedure invariably is to seek amendments by a joint Address of the Canadian House of Commons and Senate to the Crown.

> The third general principle is that no amendment to Canada's Constitution will be made by the British Parliament merely upon the request of a Canadian province. A number of attempts to secure such amendments have been made, but none has been successful. The first such attempt was made as early as 1868, by a province which was at that time dissatisfied with the terms of Confederation. This was followed by other attempts in 1869, 1874, and 1887. The British Government refused in all cases to act on provincial government representations on the grounds that it should not intervene in the affairs of Canada except at the request of the federal government representing all of Canada.

> The fourth general principle is that the Canadian Parliament will not request an amendment directly affecting federal-provincial relationships without prior consultation and agreement with the provinces. This principle did not emerge as early as others but since 1907, and particularly since 1930, has gained increasing recognition and acceptance. The nature and the degree of provincial participation in the amending process, however, have not lent themselves to easy definition.

> There have been five instances — in 1907, 1940, 1951, 1960, and 1964 — of federal consultation with all provinces on matters of direct concern to all of them. There has been only one instance up to the present time in which an amendment was sought after

consultation with only those provinces directly affected by it. This was the amendment of 1930, which transferred to the Western provinces natural resources that had been under the control of the federal government since their admission to Confederation. There have been ten instances [in 1871, 1875, 1886, 1895, 1915, 1916, 1943. 1946, 1949 and 1949 (2nd Sess.)] of amendments to the Constitution without prior consultation with the provinces on matters that the federal government considered were of exclusive federal concern. In the last four of these, one or two provinces protested that federal-provincial consultations should have taken place prior to action by Parliament.[84]

As indicated earlier, as part of the events leading up to the enactment of the Canada Act by the U.K. Parliament, the question arose as to whether the Parliament of Canada could unilaterally request, by Resolution of both Houses of Parliament, that Her Majesty place before the U.K. Parliament the new constitutional package. This issue was litigated through the courts, including a final determination of the matter by the Supreme Court of Canada (all of which occurred prior to obtaining the agreement of nine of the provinces and the federal government to make the request to the U.K. Parliament). As a result, the case raised the issue as to whether essentially political questions should be dealt with as legal matters. Indeed, the concern expressed by some of the twenty-two judges who heard the case in Manitoba, Quebec, Newfoundland and in the Supreme Court of Canada was that while this concern may be real, it does not take into account a recognition that in most constitutional cases the matters come before the court as a result of some political disagreement.

In any event, the issue which came before the courts was simply whether the Parliament of Canada had jurisdiction to unilaterally make the request to the Queen in the United Kingdom. That, in turn, raised the issues as to what were the various rules regarding the amending of the Constitution and, secondly, as to what was the status of convention in Canadian constitutional law. Ultimately, the Supreme Court of Canada[85] concluded that in view of the fact that the new constitutional package contained an entrenched Charter of Rights which, in turn, contained provisions that directly affected the power of Parliament and the provincial legislatures to pass laws in respect of matters within their respective jurisdictions, the new package did therefore directly affect federal/provincial relations. Given that conclusion, the question remained as to whether Parliament nonetheless had the authority to unilaterally make the request to the United Kingdom. The Supreme Court held that, strictly speaking, there was no legal bar to the Parliament of Canada doing this. However, it also held that there was a convention to the effect that if an amendment to the Con-

---

[84] *The Amendment of the Constitution of Canada* 4-7 (1965), A White Paper issued by the Honourable Guy Favreau, Minister of Justice.

[85] *Manitoba (A.G.) v. Canada (A.G.)*, [1981] 1 S.C.R. 753, [1981] 6 W.W.R. 1, 125 D.L.R. (3d) 1 (*sub nom. Reference re Amdt. of Constitution of Can.*), 11 Man. R. (2d) 1, 34 Nfld. & P.E.I.R. 1, 95 A.P.R. 1, 39 N.R. 1.

stitution directly affected federal/provincial relations, that is to say the division of legislative jurisdiction, then the consent of not all, but a substantial number, of the provinces must be obtained before Parliament could proceed with the proposed amendment. Accordingly, the Supreme Court of Canada held that the unilateral request of the Parliament of Canada to Her Majesty in the United Kingdom to place the new constitutional package before the U.K. Parliament was proper in a strict legal sense, but improper in a conventional sense. Subsequent to this decision, the consent of a substantial number of the provinces was obtained and the Resolution was enacted by Parliament, satisfying both the legal and conventional requirements under the old B.N.A. Act as interpreted by the Supreme Court of Canada.

The case raises two important points concerning the role of convention in our constitutional law. The first point relates to the establishment of a convention. Clearly, conventions are customs or traditions or usages which, through the passage of time and consistency of application, have hardened or crystallized into conventions. Also, as a result of the above case, it is clear that a convention can never become a law, that is, a custom or usage can become a convention, but a convention cannot become law. The difficult question that remains, therefore, is how to know when custom or usage has, in fact, crystallized into convention. Clearly, this would be determined by the courts in each instance depending upon the individual circumstances. The second point relates to the status of convention in our legal system. It is now clear that a convention is not enforceable by a court. In the case of a government disobeying a convention, the only remedy or sanction is by way of political consequence. For example, with respect to the new constitutional package, the pronouncement by the Supreme Court of Canada that the federal government's plans were legally correct but conventionally incorrect served, no doubt, in part to motivate the federal government and the provincial governments to conduct one final effort at political compromise which, in fact, led to a final agreement.

The new Constitution does contain a comprehensive amending formula. The general rule is that a matter which directly affects federal/provincial relations can be amended by consent of the federal government and two-thirds of the provinces, provided those provinces constituting the two-thirds contain 50 per cent of the population of Canada. There are special amendment procedures relating to special matters, some of which require unanimity for amendment.[86] Interestingly, one of those special matters relates

---

[86] The Meech Lake Constitutional Accord increases the number of matters requiring unanimity for amendment. See the discussion of the Meech Lake Accord at the beginning of this chapter.

to the composition of the Supreme Court of Canada. As a result of those provisions in ss. 41 and 42 of the Constitution Act of 1982, in effect, the Supreme Court of Canada is given constitutional status, notwithstanding the fact that the Supreme Court of Canada is constituted under an ordinary statute of Parliament. In effect, the Constitution Act has elevated the Supreme Court of Canada to constitutional status.[87]

Accordingly, the devices of federal/provincial negotiations (and the resulting agreements), interdelegation, and amendment have provided for some flexibility in our constitution.[88]

As indicated earlier, the main heads of legislative jurisdiction in ss. 91 and 92 have been subject to various interpretations at various stages of our history. Generally, the notion of a strong central government was emasculated by interpretations of the Judicial Committee of the Privy Council in the 1920's and 1930's. However, stronger federal legislative authority has been restored by the Supreme Court of Canada since it became the final court of appeal for all criminal and civil matters in 1949.

CONSTITUTIONAL BASIS OF JUDICIAL AUTHORITY

The constitutional basis of judicial authority in Canada is provided for in ss. 96 to 101 of the Constitution Act of 1867. These sections are set out as follows:

VIII. JUDICATURE

96. The Governor General shall appoint the Judges of the Superior, District, and County Courts in each Province, except those of the Courts of Probate in Nova Scotia and New Brunswick.

97. Until the laws relative to Property and Civil Rights in Ontario, Nova Scotia, and New Brunswick, and the Procedure of the Courts in those Provinces, are made uniform the Judges of the Courts of those Provinces appointed by the Governor General shall be selected from the respective Bars of those Provinces.

98. The Judges of the Courts of Quebec shall be selected from the Bar of that Province.

99. (1) Subject to subsection (2) of this section, the judges of the superior courts shall hold office during good behaviour, but shall be removable by the Governor General on address of the Senate and House of Commons.

(2) A judge of a superior court, whether appointed before or after the coming into force of this section, shall cease to hold office upon attaining the age of seventy-five years, or upon the coming into force of this section if at that time he has already attained that age.

---

[87] This process of constitutionalizing the Supreme Court of Canada has been further solidified by the Meech Lake Constitutional Accord. See the discussion of the Meech Lake Constitutional Accord at the beginning of this chapter.

[88] The opting out provisions of the Meech Lake Constitutional Accord in respect of national social programs may, in fact, provide for greater flexibility. Some, however, have argued that the opting out provision may lead to a "Balkanization" of the provinces.

100. The Salaries, Allowances, and Pensions of the Judges of the Superior, District, and County Courts (except the Courts of Probate in Nova Scotia and New Brunswick), and of the Admiralty Courts in Cases where the Judges thereof are for the Time being paid by Salary, shall be fixed and provided by the Parliament of Canada.

101. The Parliament of Canada may, notwithstanding anything in this Act, from Time to Time provide for the Constitution, Maintenance, and Organization of a General Court of Appeal for Canada, and for the Establishment of any additional Courts for the better Administration of the Laws of Canada.

Section 92(14) of the Constitution Act of 1867 provides an additional basis of judicial authority:

92. In each Province the Legislature may exclusively make Laws in relation to Matters coming within the Classes of Subjects next herein-after enumerated; that is to say. . .

14. The Administration of Justice in the Province, including the Constitution, Maintenance, and Organization of Provincial Courts, both of Civil and of Criminal Jurisdiction, and including Procedure in Civil Matters in those Courts.

The above provisions may be summarized in the following way:

The Parliament of Canada is granted legislative competence to enact laws providing for the establishment of certain courts and tribunals under the provisions of s. 101 of the Constitution Act of 1867. The various provincial legislatures are given authority to enact laws to provide for the establishment of certain provincial courts and tribunals under the provisions of s. 92(14) of the Constitution Act of 1867 (read together with the exclusion of federal jurisdiction to do so in s. 91(27) of the Constitution Act of 1867).

There are essentially three provisions of the Constitution Act of 1867 providing for the appointment of judges. First, s. 101 gives Parliament authority to enact laws establishing certain federal courts and tribunals and, by implication, also gives Parliament authority to pass legislation respecting the appointment of judges to these courts,[89] the salaries of these judges, their tenure of office and their removal. Secondly, ss. 96 to 100 provide for, among other things, the federal appointment of judges to serve on county or district, and superior courts established by the province under the provisions of s. 92(14). And thirdly, s. 92(14) provides for, by implication, the appointment of judges at the provincial level to serve on provincial courts established under s. 92(14). In summary then, the Constitution Act of 1867 provides for:

1. Federal courts and tribunals constituted under federal legislation enacted pursuant to legislative authority granted Parliament under s. 101 of the Constitution Act of 1867, with federally appointed judges pursuant to this same section.

---

[89] The Meech Lake and Charlottetown Constitutional Accords, however, provided a formal role for the provinces in the appointment of judges to the Supreme Court of Canada.

2. Provincial courts constituted under provincial legislation enacted pursuant to legislative authority granted under s. 92(14) of the Constitution Act of 1867, with federally appointed judges pursuant to the provisions contained in ss. 96 to 100 of the Constitution Act of 1867.

3. Provincial courts constituted under provincial legislation enacted pursuant to legislative authority granted under s. 92(14) of the Constitution Act of 1867, with provincially appointed judges pursuant to the provisions contained in this same section.

A more detailed description of the judiciary in Canada is set out in the chart on the following page.

The foregoing is reviewed again in Chapter 9, together with a discussion on the process of appointment of judges.

CONSTITUTIONAL PROCEDURE

At one time, the final court of appeal in all civil and criminal cases was the Judicial Committee of the Privy Council. Then, after certain amendments to the Criminal Code and after a series of cases,[90] the Supreme Court of Canada became the final court of appeal in all criminal cases. However, civil cases could still be appealed to the Judicial Committee of the Privy Council. Finally, in 1949, the Supreme Court of Canada became the final court of appeal for all civil and criminal cases.[91] The jurisdiction of the Supreme Court of Canada is set out in the Supreme Court Act, R.S.C. 1985, c. s-26. The Act was amended significantly in 1975 to abolish the prevailing civil monetary jurisdiction with the result that now the Supreme Court is able to choose the cases it regards as raising matters of national importance or important issues of law, and to decide only those cases. The criminal appeal jurisdiction, however, remains unchanged. This amendment has strengthened the authority of the Supreme Court in adjudicating matters of legal and national importance. Commenting on the specific consequences arising out of this amendment, the Chief Justice of Canada remarked that the new system increased the quality of the court's work and created a marked reduction in the backlog that existed prior to the 1975 amendment, with the result that the court is now permitted to sit in a full bench of nine judges for at least two-thirds of all appeals.[92]

---

[90] *British Coal Corp. v. R.*, [1935] A.C. 500, [1935] 2 W.W.R. 564, 64 C.C.C. 145, [1935] 3 D.L.R. 401 (P.C.); *Nadan v. R.*, [1926] A.C. 482, [1926] 1 W.W.R. 801, 45 C.C.C. 221, [1926] 2 D.L.R. 177 (P.C.).

[91] *Ontario (A.G.) v. Canada (A.G.)*, [1947] A.C. 127, [1947] 1 W.W.R. 305, [1947] 1 D.L.R. 801 (P.C.).

[92] See The Globe & Mail, 3rd February 1977.

LEVEL OF COURT	NAME OF COURT ENABLING STATUTE	ESTABLISHING COURT	APPOINTING AUTHORITY	SALARY	TENURE OF OFFICE	RETIREMENT
Federal	Supreme Court of Canada	Supreme Court Act (enacted pursuant to s.101 of the Constitution Act, 1867)	The Governor in Council (i.e., Minister of Justice)	Set by the Judges Act	During good behaviour (pursuant to the Supreme Court Act and provisions in the Judges Act)	75 (pursuant to the Supreme Court Act)
Federal	Federal Court of Canada	Federal Court Act (enacted pursuant to s.101 of the Constitution Act, 1867)	The Governor in Council (i.e., Minister of Justice)	Set by the Judges Act	During good behaviour (pursuant to the Federal Court Act and provisions in the Judges Act)	75 (pursuant to the Supreme Court Act)
Provincial	Federal Administrative Tribunals	Various enabling statutes (enacted pursuant to s.101 of the Constitution Act, 1867)	See various enabling statutes	See various enabling statutes	See various enabling statutes	See various enabling statutes
Provincial	Court of Appeal, Court of Queen's Bench, or a single Supreme Court (Appellate and Trial Divisions)	Judicature Act (pursuant to s.92(14) of the Constitution Act, 1867)	The Governor General pursuant to s.96 of the Constitution Act, 1867 (i.e., Minister of Justice)	Set in the Judges Act (pursuant to s.100 of the Constitution Act, 1867)	Pursuant to s.99 of the Constitution Act, 1867, during good behaviour (and subject to additional provisions in the Judges Act)	75 (pursuant to s.99(2) of the Constitution Act, 1867)

LEVEL OF COURT	NAME OF COURT ENABLING STATUTE	ESTABLISHING COURT	APPOINTING AUTHORITY	SALARY	TENURE OF OFFICE	RETIREMENT
Provincial	District or County Court	District Court Act (pursuant to s.92(14) of the Constitution Act, 1867)	The Governor General pursuant to s.96 of the Constitution Act, 1867 (i.e., Minister of Justice)	Set in the Judges Act (pursuant to s.100 of the Constitution Act, 1867)	During good behaviour (pursuant to the Judges Act)	70 (pursuant to the Judges Act)
Provincial	Provincial Courts	Varies from province to province but a common formulation might be a single court with various divisions (criminal, family, juvenile and small claims) or might be two or more courts as constituted by various statutes.	See various enabling statutesSet in particular enabling statutes	Set in particular enabling statutes	Set in particular enabling statutes which vary from province to province; in most provinces at age 70	
Provincial	Provincial Administrative Tribunals	Various enabling statutes	Pursuant to various enabling statutes	Pursuant to various enabling statutes	Pursuant to various enabling statutes	Pursuant to various enabling statutes

How does a constitutional case arise? Often it can arise in the course of private litigation. Also there is the possibility of a reference under the provisions of a provincial Constitutional Questions Act or a reference under the provisions of the federal Supreme Court Act. As a result of the application of *Thorson v. A.G. Can.*[93] a taxpayer now has the *locus standi* to challenge the constitutionality of a public statute where the issue sought to be raised is a justiciable one, where all members of the public alike are affected by the legislation and no person or class of persons has any particular or special interest in the matter, and where the legislation is not regulatory in nature but is declaratory and directory and creates no offences and imposes no penalties, but does involve the expenditure of public money by creating an administrative structure which oversees the implementation of the legislation. It is doubtful that in the federal system it is a necessary precondition to a private individual initiating proceedings on his own to test the constitutional validity of federal legislation, that he first request the federal Attorney General to commence such proceedings, since in such a system the Attorney General is the officer of the government who is obliged to enforce the legislation.

These conditions were somewhat relaxed in *McNeil v. N.S. Bd. of Censors,*[94] where the Supreme Court of Canada held that the distinction between a regulatory statute and a declaratory statute was not

> a distinction that could be controlling, especially in the light of the reserve of discretion in the Court, and more especially because a word or the term "regulatory" is not a term of art, not one susceptible of an invariable meaning which would in all cases serve to distinguish those in which standing to a taxpayer or citizen would be granted and those in which it would not.

Moreover, the Chief Justice held that a challenge to a regulatory statute is permissible, in the discretion of the court, if the provisions contained in the regulatory statute strike at the members of the general public as the central aspect of the regulatory statute.

More recently, in the *Borowski* case, a challenge to the abortion provisions contained in the Criminal Code on the basis of their alleged nonconformity to the provisions of the Canadian Bill of Rights, the Supreme Court of Canada relaxed the above rules of standing even further. Speaking for the majority, Mr. Justice Martland stated as follows:

---

[93] [1975] 1 S.C.R. 138, 43 D.L.R. (3d) 1, 1 N.R. 225. Applied in *Finlay v. Canada (Minister of Finance)*, [1986] 2 S.C.R. 607, [1987] 1 W.W.R. 603, 23 Admin. L.R. 197, 17 C.P.C. (2d) 289, 33 D.L.R. (4th) 321, 8 C.H.R.R. D/3789, 71 N.R. 338. See discussion of this decision *infra*.

[94] [1976] 2 S.C.R. 265, 32 C.R.N.S. 376 at 379, 55 D.L.R. (3d) 632, 12 N.S.R. (2d) 85, 5 N.R. 43.

[T]o establish status as a plaintiff in a suit seeking a declaration that legislation is invalid, if there is a serious issue as to its invalidity, a person need only to show that he is affected by it directly or that he has a genuine interest as a citizen in the validity of the legislation and that there is no other reasonable and effective manner in which the issue may be brought before the court.[95]

The tests enunciated in the *Thorson, McNeil* and *Borowski* trilogy were applied in the Supreme Court of Canada in *Finlay v. Canada (Minister of Finance)*.[96] Speaking for the court, Le Dain J. stated:

. . . in my view . . . the judgments of this court in *Thorson, McNeil* and *Borowski* cannot be regarded as providing clear and direct authority for the recognition of public interest standing, as a matter of judicial discretion, to bring a non-constitutional challenge by an action for a declaration to the statutory authority for public expenditure or other administrative action. It is fair to say, however, that they do not clearly exclude such recognition. The issue, then, as I see it, is whether the principle reflected in *Thorson, McNeil* and *Borowski* should be extended by this court to such cases. This question raises again the policy considerations underlying judicial attitudes to public interest standing, and in particular, whether the same value is to be assigned to the public interest in the maintenance of respect for the limits of administrative authority as was assigned by this court in *Thorson, McNeil* and *Borowski* to the public interest in the maintenance of respect for the limits of legislative authority.

In my view an affirmative answer should be given to this question. The recognized standing of the Attorney-General to assert a purely public interest in the limits of statutory authority by an action of his own motion or on the relation of another person is a recognition of the public interest in the maintenance of respect for such limits. For the reasons indicated in *Thorson*, I do not think that his refusal to act in such a case should bar a court from the recognition, as a matter of discretion in accordance with the criteria affirmed in *Borowski*, of public interest standing in a private individual to institute proceedings. The traditional judicial concerns about the expansion of public interest standing may be summarized as follows: the concern about the allocation of scarce judicial resources and the need to screen out the mere busybody; the concern that in the determination of issues the courts should have the benefit of the contending points of view or those most directly affected by them and the concern about the proper role of the courts and their constitutional relationship to the other branches of government. These concerns are addressed by the criteria for the exercise of the judicial discretion to recognize public interest standing to bring an action for a declaration that were laid down in *Thorson, McNeil* and *Borowski*. I shall deal with each of them in relation to the question of the respondent's standing in the present case.

The concern about the proper role of the courts and their constitutional relationship to the other branches of government is addressed by the requirement of justiciability, which Laskin J. held in *Thorson* to be central to the exercise of the judicial discretion whether or not to recognize public interest standing. Of course, justiciability is always a matter of concern for the courts, but the implication of what was said by Laskin J. in *Thorson* is that it is a matter of particular concern in the recognition of public interest standing.

. . .

The judicial concern about the allocation of scarce judicial resources and the need to screen out the mere busybody is addressed by the requirements affirmed in *Borowski* that there be a serious issue raised and that a citizen have a genuine interest in the issue.

---

[95] *Borowski v. Canada (Minister of Justice)*, [1981] 2 S.C.R. 575 at 598, [1982] 1 W.W.R. 97, 24 C.R. (3d) 352, 24 C.P.C. 62, 64 C.C.C. (2d) 97, 130 D.L.R. (3d) 588, 12 Sask. L.R. 420, 39 N.R. 331. Applied in *Finlay v. Canada Minister of Finance)*, *infra*.

[96] [1986] 2 S.C.R. 607, [1987] 1 W.W.R. 603, 23 Admin. L.R. 197, 17 C.P.C. (2d) 289, 33 D.L.R. (4th) 321 (*sub nom. Canada (Minister of Finance) v. Findlay*), 8 C.H.R.R. D/3789, 71 N.R. 338 (*sub nom. Finlay v. Canada*).

. . .

> The judicial concern that in the determination of an issue a court should have the benefit of the contending views of the persons most directly affected by the issue—a consideration that was particularly emphasized by Laskin C.J.C. in *Borowski*—is addressed by the requirement affirmed in *Borowski* that there be no other reasonable and effective manner in which the issue may be brought before a court. In *Thorson*, *McNeil* and *Borowski* that requirement was held to be satisfied by the nature of the legislation challenged and the fact that the Attorney-General had refused to institute proceedings although requested to do so.

. . .

> In so far as a prior request to the Attorney-General to intervene might be considered to be necessary in certain cases to show that there is no other way in which the issue may be brought before a court I do not think it should be regarded as necessary in a case such as this one, where it is clear from the position adopted by the Attorney-General in the case that he would not have consented to the institution of proceedings.[97]

Two recent cases in the Supreme Court of Canada add a slightly new dimension to the issue of standing. With respect to the standing of public interest groups, Mr. Justice Cory wrote in *Canadian Council of Churches v. R.*, [1992] 1 S.C.R. 236, 2 Admin. L.R. (2d) 229, 5 C.P.C. (3d) 20, (*sub nom: Canadian Council of Churches v. Canada (Minister of Employment & Immigration)*) 8 C.R.R. (2d) 145, 88 D.L.R. (4th) 193, (*sub nom. Canadian Council of Churches v. Canada*) 132 N.R. 241, 49 F.T.R. 160 (note), 16 Imm. L.R. (2d) 161 that:

> the recognition of the need to grant standing in some circumstances does not amount to a blanket approval to grant standing to all who wish to litigate an issue.

In this particular case, he denied standing to the applicant on the basis that there was another reasonable and effective way to bring the matter before the courts (namely, those who were directly affected by the impugned legislation and whose cases may already be before the courts). More recently, in a judgement written be Mr. Justice Major, it was held that, notwithstanding that a party may be directly affected by impugned legislation, standing might still be denied if there were another reasonable and effective way to bring an issue before the courts. See *Hy & Zel's Inc. v. Ontario (Attorney General)*, [1993] (1994), 3 S.C.R. 675, 18 C.R.R. (2d) 99, 107 D.L.R. (4th) 634, (*sub nom. Magder (Paul) Furs Ltd. v. Ontario (Attorney General)* 160 N.R. 161, 67 O.A.C. 81.

As a result of the above decisions, particularly in light of the *Borowski* and *Finlay* cases, it is probable that under s. 52(1) of the Constitution Act of 1982, there is considerable latitude for the average citizen to come forth and challenge the constitutionality of public statutes on the basis of their nonconformity to the provisions contained in the Canadian Charter of Rights and Freedoms. The reader will recall that s. 52(1) says that the

---

[97] [1986] 2 S.C.R. 630 *et seq.*

Constitution of Canada (including the Canadian Charter of Rights and Freedoms) is the supreme law of Canada and any law that is inconsistent with the Constitution is of no force and effect to the extent of the inconsistency. As such, with the above line of cases relating to standing requirements, it is suggested by many that s. 52(1) will become the vehicle by which the average citizen has access to the courts to challenge the constitutionality of legislation which contains provisions contrary to the Canadian Charter of Rights and Freedoms.

Under the provisions of various statutes, there are requirements that notice be given to the appropriate Attorney- General and to the federal Minister of Justice before a challenged statute may be declared unconstitutional. Under these provisions, the person receiving notice has a right to intervene and a right to be heard. In addition, often third parties, usually governments, but on occasion labour unions, trade associations and private interest groups, apply to the court to intervene and make representations in a case in which they are not directly interested. These interventions are often allowed, solely in the discretion of the court, and, in the case of provincial governments, are rarely refused.[98]

According to Professor Barry Strayer (now Mr. Justice Strayer) in his earlier treatise *Judicial Review of Legislation in Canada*,[99] and in his later treatise *The Canadian Constitution and the Courts: Function and Scope of Judicial Review*,[100] the whole process of constitutional decision-making is somewhat different from the process of simple statutory interpretation. The process engaged in by the courts in constitutional cases is, rather, one of "constitutional adjudication". Special doctrines of interpretation such as the aspect, ancillary or necessarily incidental, and trenching doctrines are employed. But in determining the constitutionality of an impugned statute the court must still address itself to the central question as to the intent of the legislature in enacting that statute. In this connection, Professor Strayer argues for broadened rules of evidence so as to permit more evidence to be adduced in connection with the legislative history of an impugned statute in order to determine the intent of the legislature in enacting that statute. Mr. Justice Strayer, in his later work, suggests that this has now largely been achieved and therefore there is not a compelling need for a further relaxation in the application of the rules of evidence.

Traditionally, the rule of evidence in respect of legislative history is

---

[98] For a more in-depth treatment of the law of intervention, see Paul R. Muldoon, *Law of Intervention: Status and Practice* (Aurora: Canada Law Book, 1989).

[99] University of Toronto Press, 1968.

[100] 3rd ed. (Toronto: Butterworths, 1988).

a narrow and restrictive one (see Chapter 11). However, Professor Strayer argues for the admissibility of evidence in order to determine what he refers to as "legislative facts". That is, in deciding constitutional cases, the court ought to be aware of general facts concerning the economic, social and political context of legislation. In order to ascertain these facts, Professor Strayer then argues for the admissibility of statements made by members of legislative bodies, reports of legislative committees and Royal Commissions, direct evidence, and other types of evidence now excluded under the existing rule concerning the admissibility of legislative history.

The thrust of Dr. Strayer's thesis emphasizes, as Professor Cheffins maintains, that constitutional law cannot be isolated, as can the law of trust, for example, from political, economic and social reality. Students of constitutional law must regard this discipline as all-encompassing; it cannot be compartmentalized and insulated from the realities of the other components which define modern Canadian society.

This view has been recognized judicially. For example, in the *Anti-Inflation*[101] case, referred to earlier, the courts took into account all sorts of extrinsic evidence, including the effect of severe inflation and recession on the value of the Canadian dollar on international money markets. Another example is the recent decision in *R. v. Crown Zellerbach Can. Ltd.*[102] In this case, the Supreme Court of Canada considered extrinsic evidence in determining whether legislation regulating ocean dumping was a matter falling under the national concern doctrine of the federal peace, order and good government clause.[103]

There are several other examples in cases decided over the past few years which, consistent with Dr. Strayer's thesis, have permitted the use of extrinsic evidence in the constitutional law area. This will become increasingly important in the making of judicial determinations under the Canadian Charter of Rights and Freedoms. For example, s. 1 of the Charter, the so-called "limitations" clause, provides that every right in the Charter is guaranteed subject only to such reasonable limits prescribed by law as

---

[101] *Reference re Anti-Inflation Act*, [1976] 2 S.C.R. 373, 68 D.L.R. (3d) 452, 9 N.R. 541.

[102] [1988] 1 S.C.R. 401, [1988] 3 W.W.R. 385, 25 B.C.L.R. (2d) 145, 40 C.C.C. (3d) 289, 49 D.L.R. (4th) 161, 84 N.R. 1. A more detailed discussion of this case is provided earlier in this chapter.

[103] Specifically, the evidence considered was as follows:
1. *The Review of the Health of the Oceans* by UNESCO in 1982.
2. *1980 Annual Report: A perspective on the Problem of Hazardous Substances in the Great Lakes Basin Ecosystem* by the Great Lakes Science Advisory Board to the International Joint Commission, Toronto 1980.
3. The Appendix to the above report entitled "Assessment of Airborne Contaminants in the Great Lakes Basin Ecosystem".

can be demonstrably justified in a free and democratic society. The use of the term "demonstrably" invites, one might argue, the increased use of either judicial notice and/or extrinsic evidence. There are other examples as well and these were referred to at an earlier point in this chapter.[104] Clearly, in view of the expanded role of the judiciary under a regime of entrenched rights, together with a broader standing requirement than previously existed, courts are no longer constrained, at least in constitutional cases, by strict, narrow evidentiary rules that might have worked a hardship on the judicial decision-making process in the past.

There has always been debate as to whether the law of civil liberties falls within the domain of constitutional law. Several years ago the only issue concerning civil liberties was not whether legislation was bad or evil, but rather whether the legislative body enacting the given piece of legislation had the constitutional authority to do so. But then there were many instances in which the courts invoked the constitutional division of powers in order to declare *ultra vires* a statute containing provisions tending to derogate from notions of egalitarianism and individual liberty. Now, with the entrenchment of the Canadian Charter of Rights and Freedoms in the Constitution, civil liberties are clearly constitutional concerns. Notwithstanding this, the reader should be aware of the many developments in the area of the law of civil liberties in the past quarter century.

In 1960, the Canadian Bill of Rights was enacted. Essentially, the Canadian Bill of Rights is a statutory code of conduct to which all other federal statutes must conform. These statutory guidelines ensure that no federal statutes violate certain protected human rights set out in the Canadian Bill of Rights, unless a federal statute specifically states that it shall operate notwithstanding the Canadian Bill of Rights (see earlier discussion).

The provisions of the Canadian Bill of Rights are still relevant in view of the provision contained in s. 26 of the Charter which states that the "guarantee in this Charter of certain rights and freedoms shall not be construed as denying the existence of any other rights or freedoms that exist in Canada". As such, the Canadian Bill of Rights continues in force.

Some of the provisions of the Canadian Bill of Rights are set out as follows:

> The Parliament of Canada, affirming that the Canadian Nation is founded upon principles that acknowledge the supremacy of God, the dignity and worth of the human person and the position of the family in a society of free men and free institutions;
> Affirming also that men and institutions remain free only when freedom is founded upon respect for moral and spiritual values and the rule of law;
> And being desirous of enshrining these principles and the human rights and fundamental freedoms derived from them, in a Bill of Rights which shall reflect the respect of

---

[104] See the section dealing with the Significance of Entrenchment, *supra*.

Parliament for its constitutional authority and which shall ensure the protection of these rights and freedoms in Canada:

Therefore Her Majesty, by and with the advice and consent of the Senate and House of Commons of Canada enacts as follows:

1. It is hereby recognized and declared that in Canada there have existed and shall continue to exist without discrimination by reason of race, national origin, colour, religion or sex, the following human rights and fundamental freedoms, namely,

    (a) the right of the individual to life, liberty, security of the person and enjoyment of property, and the right not to be deprived thereof except by due process of law;

    (b) the right of the individual to equality before the law and the protection of the law;

    (c) freedom of religion;

    (d) freedom of speech;

    (e) freedom of assembly and association; and

    (f) freedom of the press.

2. Every law of Canada shall, unless it is expressly declared by an Act of the Parliament of Canada that it shall operate notwithstanding the *Canadian Bill of Rights*, be so construed and applied as not to abrogate, abridge or infringe or to authorize the abrogation, abridgment or infringement of any of the rights or freedoms herein recognized and declared, and in particular, no law of Canada shall be construed or applied so as to

    (a) authorize or effect the arbitrary detention, imprisonment or exile of any person;

    (b) impose or authorize the imposition of cruel and unusual treatment or punishment;

    (c) deprive a person who has been arrested or detained
        (i) of the right to be informed promptly of the reason for his arrest or detention,
        (ii) of the right to retain and instruct counsel without delay, or
        (iii) of the remedy by way of habeas corpus for the determination of the validity of his detention and for his release if the detention is not lawful;

    (d) authorize a court, tribunal, commission, board or other authority to compel a person to give evidence if he is denied counsel, protection against self crimination or other constitutional safeguards;

    (e) deprive a person of the right to a fair hearing in accordance with the principles of fundamental justice for the determination of his rights and obligations;

    (f) deprive a person charged with a criminal offence of the right to be presumed innocent until proved guilty according to law in a fair and public hearing by an independent and impartial tribunal, or of the right to reasonable bail without just cause; or

    (g) deprive a person of the right to the assistance of an interpreter in any proceedings in which he is involved or in which he is a party or a witness, before a court, commission, board or other tribunal, if he does not understand or speak the language in which such proceedings are conducted.

It is interesting to note that some rights contained in the Canadian Bill of Rights are not contained in the Canadian Charter of Rights and Freedoms while others are contained in the Charter and not in the Bill. It appeared to the legal profession in 1960 that the enactment of the Canadian Bill of Rights heralded a new era in the development of the law of civil liberties in Canada. To the legal profession in 1982, however, the 1960 enactment did not have the importance that many thought it would. And, to the legal profession in 1990, the Canadian Bill of Rights has experienced a renewed significance.[105]

The status of the Canadian Bill of Rights in 1982 was not entirely clear. Most lawyers could not reconcile the decisions of the Supreme Court of Canada in *R. v. Drybones*,[106] *Canada (A.G.) v. Lavell*, [107]and *Canada (A.G.) v. Canard*.[108] One thing was clear, however, and that is that the spirit, if not the substance of *Drybones* had been significantly whittled down since it was rendered. Some experts did not regard this as the death of the Canadian Bill of Rights as a viable instrument in ensuring the preservation of the political, egalitarian and legal civil liberties of Canadians, but rather they regarded those recent cases as merely growing pains in the development of the law of civil liberties in Canada. Many experts continually pointed to the American experience, arguing that it took the American judiciary almost two hundred years to develop the law of civil liberties whereas the Canadian experience was limited to merely twenty-three years and we were perhaps expecting too much to happen too quickly.

In view of the entrenchment of the Canadian Charter of Rights and Freedoms in the Canadian constitution the issue was regarded as somewhat moot, but, as it turns out, the Canadian Bill of Rights has assumed a renewed importance during the Charter era. It has, in fact, played a significant role in several Charter cases.[109] This renewed importance may not however be as significant as one might think.[110]

In addition to the Bill of Rights, there have been other developments in the law of civil liberties during the past quarter century. All the provinces

---

[105] See footnote 109.

[106] [1970] S.C.R. 282, 71 W.W.R. 161, 10 C.R.N.S. 334, [1970] 3 C.C.C. 355, 9 D.L.R. (3d) 473, Applied in *MacBain v. Can. Human Rights Comm.*, [1985] 1 F.C. 856, 16 Admin. L.R. 109, 85 C.L.L.C. 17,023, 18 C.R.R. 165, 22 D.L.R. (4th) 119, 6 C.H.R.R. D/3064, 62 N.R. 117 (C.A.); and *Waskaganish Band v. Blackned*, [1986] 3 C.N.L.R. 168 (Que. Prov. Ct.). Distinguished in *Int. Assn. of Longshoremen, Loc. 1657 v. R.* (1979), 114 D.L.R. (3d) 335 (Que. C.A.); and *R. v. Rocher*, [1982] 3 C.N.L.R. 122, reversed [1983] N.W.T.R. 123, [1983] 3 C.N.L.R. 137, which was reversed [1984] N.W.T.R. 288, [1985] 2 C.N.L.R. 151, 16 C.C.C. (3d) 89, 14 D.L.R. (4th) 210, 55 A.R. 387 (C.A.).

[107] [1974] S.C.R. 1349, 23 C.R.N.S. 197, 11 R.F.L. 333, 38 D.L.R. (3d) 481.

[108] [1976] 1 S.C.R. 170, [1975] 3 W.W.R. 1, 52 D.L.R. (3d) 548, 4 N.R. 91. Applied in *R. v. Lefthand*, [1985] 4 W.W.R. 577, 37 Alta. L.R. (2d) 223, [1985] 3 C.N.L.R. 157, 19 C.C.C. (3d) 534, 19 D.L.R. (4th) 720, 66 A.R. 331 (C.A.).

[109] See especially *Singh v. Canada (Minister of Employment & Immigration)*, [1985] 1 S.C.R. 177, 12 Admin. L.R. 137, 14 C.R.R. 13, 17 D.L.R. (4th) 422, 58 N.R. 1; and *Andrews v. Law Society (B.C.)*, [1989] 1 S.C.R. 143, [1989] 2 W.W.R. 289, 34 B.C.L.R. (2d) 273, 25 C.C.E.L. 255, 36 C.R.R. 193, 56 D.L.R. (4th) 1, 10 C.H.R.R. D/5719, 91 N.R. 255.

[110] Since 1990 and about mid-1995, there have been some 21 cases in which the Canadian Bill of Rights has been invoked. Of these 21 cases, none were argued solely on the basis of the Canadian Bill of Rights and the only successful cases were those in which the Canadian Bill of Rights was argued in conjunction with the Canadian Charter of Rights and Freedoms.

and the federal government have enacted anti-discrimination legislation. While a bill of rights is a statutory code of conduct to which all other statutes must conform, anti-discrimination legislation is concerned with protection against private discriminatory conduct. This, too, is an area covered by ss. 15 and 28 of the Canadian Charter of Rights and Freedoms, and, like the Canadian Bill of Rights, by virtue of s. 26 of the Charter, those provincial and federal anti-discrimination laws continue in force.

In addition to the above, there is other legislation directed at providing protection and ensuring preservation of our civil liberties. For example, the institution of ombudsman has now been established in most provinces. Indeed, the International Conference of Ombudsmen, held every four years, was first held in Edmonton in 1976. Somewhat akin to the function served by the office of the ombudsman is the current legislative development ensuring the protection of privacy and providing for freedom of information, including the federal Access to Information Act enacted in June of 1982.[111] Moreover, access to information legislation has been enacted in every province and in some municipalities.

Accordingly, the reader can appreciate that the law of civil liberties in Canada is a dynamic and developing area in which legislation, at all levels of government, is presently under consideration. It will provide protection for the individual in the face of private discrimination, large, impersonal modern bureaucracy and, generally, against legislation violating fundamental human liberties. This will be particularly so in view of the entrenchment of the Charter of Rights and Freedoms in the new Constitution.

The law of civil liberties cannot properly be the subject of a detailed discussion in a treatise of this nature; however, the reader should appreciate the extent to which the law is presently responding to issues of this nature. For further discussion of these issues, the reader might consult the various works cited in the bibliography at the end of this chapter.

The whole field of Canadian constitutional law forms the major substructure of the Canadian legal and political system and it cannot be given proper treatment in merely a single chapter. However, it is hoped that the reader will appreciate the constitutional basis underlying the distribution of legislative authority as well as the constitutional basis underlying the creation of courts and the appointment of judges in Canada.

---

[111] This Act came into force on 1st July 1983. See now the Access to Information Act, R.S.C. 1985, c. A-1. The similarity in function between the office of Ombudsman and the role of an information/privacy commissioner is underscored by the fact that in the province of Manitoba, for example, the Ombudsman is responsible for both Ombudsman and privacy/access to information legislation.

At the time of this writing, there is still much concern in Canada in connection with changes in the distribution of legislative power. More pressing, however, Canadians are currently concerned with the ultimate constitutional issue, namely, the possible separation of the province of Quebec. In addition, there are concerns relating to other ongoing constitutional developments. As a result, to some extent, the situation presently is in a state of flux. That fact, taken together with the continuing evolution of a new era characterized by an entrenched charter of rights, makes the study of Canadian constitutional law a dynamic and exciting exercise.

SELECTED BIBLIOGRAPHY OF ARTICLES AND TREATISES ON THE CONSTITUTIONAL BASIS OF JUDICIAL AND LEGISLATIVE AUTHORITY IN CANADA

CHARTER BOOKS AND ARTICLES

ARTICLES

Black, W. "A Walk Through the Charter". (1986), Balance 47.

Christian, T.J. "Sweeping Constitutional Changes in Canada". (1987), 36 Int. and Comp. L. Q. 139.

Dekany, A.C. "An Overview of the Charter of Rights and Freedoms". (1987), 6 Advocates' Soc. J. 14.

Del Buono, V.M. "The Implications of the Supreme Court's Purpose Interpretation of the Charter". (1986), 48 C.R. (3d) 121.

Kaufman, F. "The Canadian Charter: A Time for Bold Spirits, Not Timorous Souls". (1986), 31 McGill L.J. 456.

McConnell, W.H. "Constitutional Law; Recent Developments in Canadian Law". (1986), 18 Ottawa L. Rev. 721.

Petter, A. "The Politics of the Charter". (1986), 8 Sup. Ct. L. Rev. 4-73.

"Ripples Off Meech Lake: Disadvantaged Groups Should Take a Good Hard Look At What Their Provincial Governments Are Doing to Equality Rights 'Guaranteed' in the Charter". (1987), 3 Can. Human Rights Advocate 9:11.

TREATISES

Anderson, J.C. *The Effects and Implications of our Charter on the Education System.* Toronto: Canadian Education Association, 1986.

Anisman, P., and A.M. Linden (eds.). *The Media, the Courts and the Charter.* Toronto: Carswell, 1986.

Bayefsky, A.F., and M.A. Eberts. *Equality Rights and the Canadian Charter of Rights and Freedoms.* Toronto: Carswell, 1985.

Beaudoin, G.-A. (ed.). *Charter Cases 1986-87.* Cowansville: Les Editions Yvon Blais, 1987.

Beaudoin, G.-A. (ed.). *Your Clients and the Charter — Liberty and Equality: Proceedings of the October 1987 Colloquium of the Canadian Bar Association in Montreal.* Montreal: Les Editions Yvon Blais, 1988.

Beaulieu, C. *Droits et libertés au pouvoir judicaire.* Montréal: Les Éditions Thémis, 1994.

Boyle, C.L.M. *et al.* (eds.). *Charterwatch: Reflections on Equality.* Toronto: Carswell, 1986.

Brooke, J. *The Charter of Rights and Freedoms and Its Effect on Canadians.* Ottawa: Library of Parliament, 1982.

Canadian Bar Association and Department of Justice, *The Charter: 10 Years Later: Proceedings of the April 1992 Colloquium of the Canadian Bar Association and Department of Justice.* Cowansville: Editions Y. Blais, 1992.

Canadian Human Rights Foundation. *Multiculturalism and the Charter: A Legal Perspective.* Toronto: Carswell, 1987.

Carson, B. *The Charter of Rights and Freedoms: Legal Rights.* Ottawa: Library of Parliament, 1987.

Carter, D. *The Canadian Charter of Rights and Freedoms: implications for industrial relations and human resource practitioners.* Kingston: Industrial Relations Centre, Queens U. P., 1991.

Fogarty, K.H. *Equality Rights and their Limitations in the Charter.* Toronto: Carswell, 1987.

Gibson, D. *The Law of the Charter: General Principles.* Calgary: Carswell, 1986.

A Guide to the Canadian Charter of Rights and Freedoms. Community Law Program of Windsor, Faculty of Law, University of Windsor, 1982.

Herriges, G.M. *A Manual on the Charter of Rights and Freedoms.* Saskatoon: Sask. Human Rights Commission and Sask. Association on Human Rights, 1983.

McDonald, D.C. *Legal Rights in the Canadian Charter of Rights and Freedoms.* 2nd ed. Calgary: Carswell, 1989.

Magnet, J.E. *Constitutional Law of Canada. Volume 2: Canadian Charter of Rights and Freedoms.* 3rd ed. Toronto: Carswell, 1987.

Mandel, M. *The Charter of Rights and the Legalization of Politics in Canada.* Toronto: Wall and Thompson, 1989.

Monahan, P. *Politics and the Constitution: The Charter, Federalism and the Supreme Court of Canada*. Toronto: Carswell, 1987.

Salhany, R.E. *The Origin of Rights*. Toronto: Carswell, 1986.

Tarnopolsky, W.S., and G.-A. Beaudoin (eds.). *Canadian Charter of Rights and Freedoms: Commentary*. Toronto: Carswell, 1982.

Trakman, L. *Reasoning with The Charter*. Markham: Butterworths, 1991.

Weiler, J., and R.M. Elliot (eds.). *Litigating the Values of a Nation: The Canadian Charter of Rights and Freedoms*. Calgary: Carswell, 1986.

THE CONSTITUTION GENERALLY

ARTICLES

Abel, A.S. "Constitutional Charter for Canada". (1978), 28 U.T.L.J. 265.

Abel, A.S. "Re Official Languages Act: A Comment". (1974), 20 McGill L.J. 595.

Abel, A.S. "The Neglected Logic of 91 and 92". (1969), 19 U.T.L.J. 487.

Abel, A.S. "The Role of the Supreme Court in Private Law Cases". (1965), 4 Alta. L. Rev. 39.

Abel, A.S. "What Peace, Order and Good Government?" (1968), 7 Western Ont. L. Rev. 1.

Alexander, E.R. "A Constitutional Strait Jacket for Canada". (1965), 43 Can. Bar Rev. 262.

Atkey, R.G. "The Role of the Provinces in International Affairs". (1971), 26 Int. J. 249.

Beaudoin, G.-A. "Le bilinguisme et la Constitution". (1973), 4 R. Gen. 321.

Beaudoin, G.-A. "La Cour suprême et la protection des droits fondamentaux". (1975), 53 Can. Bar Rev. 675.

Beaudoin, G.-A. "Linguistic Rights in Canada". In R. St. J.

McDonald and J.P. Humphrey (eds.). *The Practice of Freedom*. Toronto: Butterworths, 1979.

Beckton, C.F. "A.G. for Canada v. Claire Dupond: The Right to Assemble in Canada?" (1979), 5 Dalhousie L.J. 169.

Beetz, J. "Le contrôle juridicionnel du pouvoir législatif et les droits de l'homme dans la Constitution du Canada". (1958), 18 R. du B. 361.

Brent, A.S. "The Right to Religious Education and the Constitutional Status of Denominational Schools". (1976), 40 Sask. L. Rev. 239.

Brun, H. "La Charte des droits et libertés de la personne: domaine d'application". (1977), 37 R. du B. 179.

Brun, H., and G. Tremblay. "Les langues officielles au Canada". (1979), 20 C. de D. 69.

Caron, M. "Le Code civil québécois: instrument de protection des droits et libertés de la personne?" (1978), 56 Can. Bar Rev. 197.

Carr, R.M. "Division of Legislative Powers under the British North America Act — The Case for Fully Concurrent Powers". (1971), 4 Man. L.J. 297.

Cline, E., and M.J. Finley. "Whither the Implied Bill of Rights?" (1980-81), 45 Sask. L. Rev. 137.

Conklin, W.E. "Constitutional Ideology, Language Rights and Political Disunity in Canada". (1979), 28 U.N.B.L.J. 39.

Crommelin, M. "Jurisdiction over Onshore Oil and Gas in Canada". (1975), 10 U.B.C.L. Rev. 86.

Diefenbaker, J.G. "A Half-Century Encounter with Civil Liberties". (1972-73), 5 Man. L.J. 255.

Driedger, E.A. "Statute of Westminster and Constitutional Amendments". (1968), 11 Can. Bar J. 348.

Fairley, H.S. "Developments in Constitutional Law: the 1983-84 Term". (1985), 7 Sup. Ct. L. Rev. 63.

Finkelstein, N. "Constitutional Law — Section 91(2) of the Constitution Act 1867 — Competition Legislation". (1984), 62 Can. Bar Rev. 182.

Fraser, I.H. "Some Comments on Subsection 92(10) of the Constitution Act, 1867". (1984), 29 McGill L.J. 557.

Gibson, D. "Constitutional Jurisdiction Over Environmental Management in Canada". (1973), 23 U.T.L.J. 54.

Gibson, D. "Constitutional Law". (1967), 2 Man. L.J. 283.

Gibson, D. "Constitutional Law — Federalizing the Judiciary". (1966), 44 Can. Bar Rev. 674.

Gibson, D. "Interjurisdictional Immunity in Canadian Federalism". (1969), 47 Can. Bar Rev. 40.

Gibson, D. "The Constitutional Context of Canadian Water Planning". (1969), 7 Alta. L. Rev. 71.

Hanssen, K. "The Federal Declaratory Power Under the British North America Act: With an Appendix". (1968), 3 Man. L.J. 87.

Head, I.L. "The Canadian Offshore Minerals Reference: The Application of International Law to a Federal Constitution". (1968), 18 U.T.L.J. 131.

Head, I.L. "The Legal Clamour over Canadian Off-shore Minerals". (1967), 5 Alta. L. Rev. 312.

Hogg, P.W. "Judicial Review on Federal Grounds: Canada compared to the United States". [1986] Sup. Ct. Conf. 25.

Hogg, P.W. "Constitutional Power Over Language". [1978] L.S.U.C. Special Lectures 229.

Hogg, P.W., and W. Grover. "The Constitutionality of the Competition Bill". (1976), 1 Can. Bus. L.J. 197.

Kaiser, G.E. "Constitutional Aspects of the Regulation of Canadian Computer Technology". [1971] Queen's L.J. 97.

Katz, L. "Constitutional Problems of a Unified Family Court System". (1974), 6 Man. L.J. 211.

Kovach, A.J. "An Assessment of the Merits of Newfoundland's Claim to Offshore Mineral Resources". (1975), 23 Chitty's L.J. 18.

Krauss, M. "Interpretation de lois — historie législative". (1980), 58 Can. Bar Rev. 756.

La Forest, G. "The Labour Conventions Case Revisited". (1974), 12 Can. Year Book Int. L. 137.

Laskin, B. "Occupying the Field: Paramountcy in Penal Legislation". (1963), 41 Can. Bar Rev. 234.

Laskin, B. "The Canadian Constitution After the First Century, Part I". (1967), 45 Can. Bar Rev. 395.

Lederman, W.R. "The Concurrent Operation of Federal and Provincial Laws in Canada". (1962-63), 9 McGill L.J. 185.

Lederman, W.R. "Unity and Diversity in Canadian Federalism: Ideals and Methods of Moderation". (1976), 14 Alta. L. Rev. 34.

Leon, J.S. "Cruel and Unusual Punishment: Sociological Jurisprudence and the Canadian Bill of Rights". (1978), 36 U.T. Fac. L. Rev. 222.

Lyon, J.N. "The Central Fallacy of Canadian Constitutional Law". (1976), 22 McGill L.J. 40.

Lysyk, K.M. "The Unique Constitutional Position of the Canadian Indian". (1967), 45 Can. Bar Rev. 513.

McEvoy, J.P. "Atlantic Canada: the Constitutional Offshore Regime". (1984), 8 Dalhousie L.J. 284.

MacKenzie, J.A. "Planning of the B.N.A. Act". (1974), 6 Ottawa L. Rev. 332.

McNairn, C.H. "Aeronautics and the Constitution". (1971), 49 Can. Bar Rev.411.

McNairn, C.H. "Transportation, Communication and the Constitution: The Scope of Federal Jurisdiction". (1969), 47 Can. Bar Rev. 355.

MacPherson, J.C. "Developments in Constitutional Law: The 1978-79 Term". (1980), 1 Sup. Ct. L. Rev. 77.

MacPherson, J.C. "Developments in Constitutional Law: The 1979-80 Term". (1981), 2 Sup. Ct. L. Rev. 49.

McWhinney, E. "The Supreme Court of Canada and the Constitutional Division of Powers". [1986] Sup. Ct. Conf. 55.

McWhinney, E. "Techniques of Constitutional Interpretation". (1967), 5 Col. I. Dr. Comp. 67.

Mallory, J.R. "The B.N.A. Act: Constitutional Adaptation and Social Change". (1967), 2 Thémis 127.

Martin, C. "Newfoundland's Case on Offshore Minerals, A Brief". (1975), 7 Ottawa L. Rev. 34.

Marx, H. "Language Rights in the Canadian Constitution". (1967), 2 Thémis 239.

Monahan, P.J. "At Doctrine's Twilight: the Structure of Canadian Federalism". (1984), 34 U.T.L.J. 47.

Morin, J. "A Constitutional Court for Canada". (1965), 43 Can. Bar Rev. 545.

Morris, G.L. "Canadian Federalism and International Law". (1974), Can. Persp. 55.

Morris, G.L. "The Treaty-Making Power: A Canadian Dilemma". (1967), 45 Can. Bar Rev. 478.

Moull, W.D. "Natural Resources: Provincial Proprietary Rights, the Supreme Court of Canada, and the Resource Amendment to the Constitution". (1983), 21 Alta. L. Rev. 472.

Moull, W.D. "Pricing Alberta's Gas—Cooperative Federalism and the Resource Amendment". (1984), 22 Alta. L. Rev. 348.

Moull, W.D. "Section 97A of the Constitution Act, 1867". (1983), 61 Can. BarRev. 715.

Mullan, D. "Standing After McNeil". (1976), 8 Ottawa L. Rev. 32. Nadin-Davis, R.P. "Comment: Civil Liberties—Right to Counsel". (1980), 58 Can. Bar Rev. 686.

Proulx, D. "Egalité et discrimination dans la Charte des droits et libertés de la personne: étude comparative". (1980), 10 R.D.U.S. 381.

Proulx, D. "La suprématie des droits et libertés de la personne et la question constitutionnelle au Canada". (1981), 12 R. Gen. 413.

Richardson, D., and Z. Quigley. "The Resources Industry, Foreign Ownership and Constitutional Methods of Control". (1975), 39 Sask. L. Rev. 92.

Russell, P.H. "Constitutional Reform of the Canadian Judiciary". (1969), 7 Alta. L. Rev. 103.

Sanders, D. "Aboriginal Peoples and the Constitution". (1981), 19 Alta. L. Rev. 410.

Schmeiser, D.A. "The Case Against Entrenchment of a Canadian Bill of Rights". (1973), 1 Dalhousie L.J. 15.

Scmneiser, D.A. "The Entrenchment of a Bill of Rights". (1981), 19 Alta. L. Rev. 375.

Scott, F.R. "Canadian Federalism: The Legal Perspective". (1967), 5 Alta. L. Rev. 262.

Scott, F.R., and W.R. Lederman. "A Memorandum Concerning Housing, Urban Development and the Constitution of Canada". (1972), 12 Plan. Can. 33.

Smiley, D.V. "Canadian Federalism and the Spending Power: Is Constitutional Restriction Necessary?" (1969), 17 Can. Tax J. 467.

Strayer, B.L. "Amendment of the Canadian Constitution: Why the Fulton-Favreau Formula?" (1966), 1 Can. Legal Studies 119.

Strayer, B.L. "The Flexibility of the B.N.A. Act". In T.0. Lloyd (ed.). *Agenda 1970.* Toronto: University of Toronto Press, 1968.

Sullivan, R.E. "Interpreting the Territorial Limitations on the Provinces". (1985), 7 Sup. Ct. L. Rev. 511.

Swan, J. "The Canadian Constitution, Federalism and the Conflict of Laws". (1985), 63 Can. Bar Rev. 271.

Swinton, K. "Bora Laskin and Federalism". (1985), 33 U.T.L.J. 353.

Tarnopolsky, W.S. "Just Desserts or Cruel and Unusual Treatment or Punishment? Where Do We Look for Guidance?" (1978), 10 Ottawa L. Rev. 1.

Tarnopolsky, W.S. "The Canadian Bill of Rights from Diefenbaker to Drybones". (1971), 17 McGill L.J. 437.

Tarnopolsky, W.S. "The Effectiveness of Constitutional Guarantees and other Governmental Declarations on Human Rights and Fundamental Freedoms". (1967), 5 Col. I, Dr. Comp. 117.

Tarnopolsky, W.S. "The Historical and Constitutional Context of the Proposed Canadian Charter of Rights and Freedoms". (1981), 44 Law and Contemporary Problems 169.

Tarnopolsky, W.S. "The Supreme Court and Civil Liberties". (1976), 14 Alta. L. Rev. 58.

Taylor, M.R. "The Status of Individual Rights and Freedoms under the Constitution Act, 1981". (1982), 40 Advocate 119.

Thompson, A.R. "Implications of Constitutional Change for the Oil and Gas Industry". (1969), 17 Alta. L. Rev. 369.

Trudeau, P.E. "Constitutional Reform and Individual Freedoms". (1969), 8 Western Ont. L. Rev. 1.

Trudeau, P.E. "Les Droits de l'homme et la suprematie parlementaire". In A. Gotlieb (ed.). *Les Droits de l'homme, le féderalisme et les minoritiés.* Toronto: Institut canadien des affaires internationales, 1970.

Weiler, P.C. "The Supreme Court of Canada and Canadian Federalism". (1973), 11 Osgoode Hall L.J. 225.

ARTICLES

Bowal, P. "The New Ontario Judicial Alternative Dispute Resolution Model". (1995), 34 Alta. L. Rev. 206.

Davis, O. "Alternative Resolutions Inc." (1995), 34 Alta. L. Rev. 281.

Di Marzo, L. "Dispute Resolution Provisions of the *Agreement on Internal Trade*". (1995), 34 Alta. L. Rev. 240.

Elliott, D. C. "Med/Arb: Fraught with Danger or Ripe with Opportunity?" (1995), 34 Alta. L. Rev. 163.

Goss, J. "An Introduction to Alternative Dispute Resolution". (1995), 34 Alta. L. Rev. 1.

Gould, D.G., Q.C. "Canadian Dispute Resolution Corporation." (1995), 34 Alta. L. Rev. 284.

Gross, E.L. "The Expert Witness and Mediation". (1995), 34 Alta. L. Rev. 69.

Haigh, D.R., Q.C., A.K. Kunetzki and C.M. Antony. "International Commercial Arbitration and the Canadian Experience." (1995), 34 Alta. L. Rev. 137.

Hartnett, W.J. "The Canadian Foundation for Dispute Resolution". (1995), 34 Alta. L. Rev. 287.

Hurlburt, W.H., Q.C. "A New Bottle for Renewed Wine: The *Arbitration Act, 1991*". (1995), 34 Alta. L. Rev. 86.

MacLean, L. and J. McNiven. "The Complaint Resolution Project". (1995), 34 Alta. L. Rev. 54.

Marshall, M.A. and L.C. Reif. "The Ombudsman: Maladministration and Alternative Dispute Resolution". (1995), 34 Alta. L. Rev. 215.

Moore, The Hon. W.K. "Mini-Trials in Alberta". (1995), 34 Alta. L. Rev. 194.

Pentelechuk, D. "Rule 219: Stairway to Heaven". (1995), 34 Alta. L. Rev. 180.

Portlock, P. "Alberta Arbitration and Mediation Society". 34 Alta. L. Rev. 279.

Swanson, E.J. "Alternative Dispute Resolution and Environmental Conflict: The Case for Law Reform". (1995), 34 Alta. L. Rev. 267.

Trace, K. "The Art of Skilful Negotiating." (1995), 34 Alta. L. Rev. 34.

Wright, E. "Dispute Settlement Centre — BBB". (1995), 34 Alta. L. Rev. 290.

TREATISES

Abel, A.S. *Toward a Constitutional Charter for Canada.* Toronto: University of Toronto Press, 1980.

Bakan, J., and D. Schneiderman (eds.). *Social Justice and the Constitution: Perspectives on a Social Union for Canada.* Ottawa: Carleton University Press, 1992.

Banting, K.G. *The Welfare State and Canadian Federalism.* 2nd ed. Kingston and Montreal: McGill-Queen's University Press, 1987. Beaudoin, G.-A. *Essais sur la Constitution.* Ottawa: Editions de l'Université d'Ottawa, 1979.

Beaudoin, G.-A., and E. Ratushny. *The Canadian Charter of Rights and Freedoms.* 2nd ed. Toronto: Carswell, 1989.

Beatty, D. *Constitutional Law in Theory and Practice.* Toronto: University of Toronto Press.

Beck, J.M. The Shaping of Canadian Federalism: Central Authority or Provincial Right? Toronto: Copp Clark Publishing Co., 1971.

Berger, T. *Fragile Freedoms.* Toronto: Clarke Irwin, 1982.

Browne, G.P. *Documents on the Confederation of British North America.* Toronto: McClelland and Stewart, 1969.

Brun, H. *Droit Constitutionnel.* Cowansville: Les Editions Yvon Blais, 1982.

Cheffins, R.I., and P.A. Johnson. *The Revised Canadian Constitution: Politics as Law.* Toronto: McGraw-Hill Ryerson, 1986.

Cheffins, R.I., and R.N. Tucker. *The Constitutional Process in Canada.* 2nd ed. Toronto: McGraw-Hill Ryerson, 1976.

Chevrette, F., and H. Marx. *Droit Constitutionnel: notes et jurisprudence.* Montreal: Les Presses de l'Université de Montréal, 1982.

Cohen, L., and P. Smith. *The Vision and the Game: Making the Canadian Constitution.* Calgary: Detselig Enterprises, 1987.

Cook, R. *Canada and the French-Canadian Question*. Toronto: Macmillan of Canada, 1966.

Creighton, D.G., C.P. Stacey, P.B. Waite, W. Ullmann, A.G. Bailey, and G.F.G. Stanley. *Confederation*. Toronto: University of Toronto Press, 1967.

Crepeau, P.A., and C.B. Macpherson (eds.). *The Future of Canadian Federalism*. Toronto: University of Toronto Press, 1965.

Dawson, R.M. *The Government of Canada*. 5th ed. rev. by N.M. Ward. Toronto: University of Toronto Press, 1970.

Dawson, R.M., and W.F. Dawson. *Democratic Government in Canada*. 4th ed. rev. by N.M. Ward. Toronto: University of Toronto Press, 1971.

de Smith, S.A. *Constitutional and Administrative Law*. 5th ed. Harmondsworth: Penguin, 1985.

de Smith, S.A. *Judicial Review of Administrative Action*. 3rd ed. London: Stevens, 1973.

Dicey, A.V. *Introduction to the Study of the Law of the Constitution*. 10th ed. rev. by E.C.S. Wade. London: Macmillan, 1959.

Doerr, A., and M. Carrier. *Women and the Constitution in Canada*. Ottawa: Can. Advisory Council on the Status of Women, 1981.

Funston, B.W., & E. Meehan. *Canadian Constitutional Law in a Nutshell*. Toronto: Carswell, 1994.

Funston, B.W., & E. Meehan. *Canadian Constitutional Documents Consolidated*. Toronto: Carswell, 1994.

Gall, G. (ed.). *Civil Liberties in Canada*. Toronto: Butterworths, 1982.

Heuston, R.F.V. *Essays on Constitutional Law*. 2nd ed. London: Stevens, 1 964.

Hockin, T.A. *Government in Canada*. Toronto: McGraw-Hill Ryerson, 1976.

Hogg, P.W. *Canada Act 1982 Annotated*. Toronto: Carswell, 1982.

Hogg, P.W. *Constitutional Law of Canada*. 2nd ed. Toronto: Carswell, 1985.

Holdsworth, Sir Wm. *A History of English Law*. 7th ed. by A.L. Goodhart and H.G. Hanbury, Vols. I and II. London: Methuen, 1956.

Jennings, Sir W. Ivor. *The Law and the Constitution*. 5th ed. London: University of London Press, 1959.

Jones, D.P. *A Constitutionally Guaranteed Role for the Courts*.Toronto: Carswell, 1979.

Kallen, E. *Ethnicity and Human Rights in Canada*. Toronto: Gage Publishing, 1982.

Kelsen, H. *General Theory of Law and the State*. New York: Russell and Russell, 1961.

Kennedy, W.P.M. *Essays in Constitutional Law*. Oxford, London, 1934.

La Forest, G.V. *The Allocation of Taxing Power under the Canadian Constitution*. 2nd ed. Toronto: Canadian Tax Foundation, 1981.

La Forest, G.V. *Disallowance and Reservation of Provincial Legislation*. Ottawa: Department of Justice, 1955.

La Forest, G.V. *Natural Resources: Public Property, Under the Canadian Constitution*. Toronto: University of Toronto Press, 1969.

Laskin, B. *Laskin's Canadian Constitutional Law*. 5th ed. rev. by N. Finkelstein. Toronto: Carswell, 1986.

Lederman, W.R. *The Courts and the Canadian Constitution*. Toronto: McClelland and Stewart, 1964.

Lefroy, A.H.F. *Canada's Federal System*. Toronto: Carswell, 1913.

Lyon, J.N., and R.G. Atkey. *Canadian Constitutional Law in a Modern Perspective*. Toronto: University of Toronto Press, 1970.

MacKinnon, F. *The Crown in Canada*. Calgary: McClelland and Stewart West, 1976.

Mackintosh, W.A. *The Economic Background of Dominion-Provincial Relations*. Toronto: McClelland and Stewart, 1964.

Magnet, J.E. *Constitutional Law of Canada*. 3rd ed. Toronto: Carswell, 1987.

Mallory, J.R. *The Structure of Canadian Government*. Rev. ed. Toronto: Gage, 1984.

Manning, M. *Rights, Freedoms and the Courts: A Practical Analysis of the Constitution Act, 1982*. Toronto: Emond-Montgomery, 1982.

Marshall, G. *Constitutional Theory*. Oxford: Clarendon, 1971.

Marshal], G. *Parliamentary Sovereignty and the Commonwealth*. Oxford: Clarendon, 1957.

Marshall, G., and C.G. Moodie. *Some Problems of the Constitution*. Rev. 4th ed. London: Hutchinson, 1967.

McRuer Report. *Royal Commission of Inquiry into Civil Rights*. Queen's Printer, Toronto: Report No. 1, Vols. I-III, 1968; Report No. 2, Vol. IV, 1969; Report No. 3, Vol. V, 1971.

McWhinney, E. *Judicial Review*. 4th ed. Toronto: University of Toronto Press, 1969.

Meekison, J.P. *Canadian Federalism: Myth or Reality*. 3rd ed. Toronto: Methuen, 1977.

Mitchell, J.D.B. *Constitutional Law*. 2nd ed. Edinburgh: W. Green, 1968.

Molgat, Senator G.L., and M. MacGuigan. *Constitution of Canada - Final Report of Special Joint Committee of the Senate and of the House of Commons*. Ottawa: Information Canada, 1972.

Monahan, P. *Politics and the Constitution: The Charter, Federalism and the Supreme Court of Canada*. Toronto: Carswell, 1987.

Morton, F.L. (ed.). *Law, Politics and the Judicial System in Canada*. Calgary: University of Calgary Press, 1984.

Ontario Advisory Committee on Confederation: Background Papers and Reports, Vol. I. Queen's Printer of Ontario, 1967.

Ontario Advisory Committee on Confederation: Background Papers and Reports, Vol. II. Queen's Printer of Ontario, 1970.

Ontario Advisory Committee on Confederation: 2nd Report on Confederation: The Federal-Provincial Distribution of Powers. Toronto, 1979.

Ouellet, F., L.A.H. Smith, D.G. Creighton, and W.H. Parker. *Constitutionalism and Nationalism in Lower Canada*. Toronto: University of Toronto Press, 1969.

Rand, J.C. *Some Aspects of Canadian Constitutionalism*. Toronto: York University Law Library, 1980.

Reesor, B. *The Canadian Constitution in Historical Perspective*. Whitby, Prentice Hall, 1992.

Report of the Royal Commission on *Bilingualism and Biculturalism*, Vols. I-IV. Ottawa: Queen's Printer, 1967-1970.

Report of the Royal Commission of Inquiry on *Constitutional Problems* (Tremblay Report). Quebec, 1956.

Report of the Royal Commission on *Dominion-Provincial Relations* (Rowell-Sirois Report). Canada, 1940.

Report of the Select Committee on Constitutional Reform, Ontario Legislative Assembly—Select Committee. Ottawa, 1980.

Report of the Special Joint Committee of the Senate and House of Commons on *The Constitution of Canada*. Ottawa: Queen's Printer, 1972.

Riddell, W.R. *The Constitution of Canada*. New Haven, Conn.: Yale University Press, 1917.

Robertson, S. *Courts and the Media*. Toronto: Butterworths, 1981.

Russell, P.H. *Leading Constitutional Decisions*. 2nd ed. Toronto: McClelland and Stewart, 1973.

Saint-Laurent, D. *Principles de Droit Constitutionnel et Penal*. Mont Royal: Modulo, 1986.

Salhaney, R.E. *The Origin of Rights*. Toronto: Carswell, 1985.

Sawer, G. *Modern Federalism*. Smithers and Benellie, 1969.

Schmeiser, D.A. *Civil Liberties in Canada*. Oxford, London, 1964.

Scott, F.R. *The Canadian Constitution and Human Rights*. Toronto: Canadian Broadcasting Corporation, 1959.

Scott, F.R. *Civil Liberties in Canada*. Toronto: University of Toronto Press, 1959.

Secretary's Report on *The Constitutional Review 1968-1971* by the Canadian Intergovernmental Conference Secretariat. Ottawa: Information Canada, 1974.

Sharp, M. *Federalism and International Conferences on Education*. A Supplement to Federalism and International Relations. Ottawa: Queen's Printer, 1968.

Smiley, D.V. *Canada in Question: Federalism in the Seventies*. 2nd ed. Toronto: McGraw-Hill Ryerson, 1976.

Smiley, D.V. *Constitutional Adaptation and Canadian Federalism Since 1945*. Ottawa: Information Canada, 1970.

Smith, A. *The Commerce Power in Canada and the United States*. Toronto: Butterworths, 1963.

Stanley, M. *Short History of the Canadian Constitution*. Toronto: Ryerson Press, 1969.

Strayer, B.L. *Judicial Review of Legislation in Canada*. Toronto: University of Toronto Press, 1968.

Strayer, B.L. *The Canadian Constitution and the Courts: The Function and Scope of Judicial Review*. 2nd ed. Toronto: Butterworths, 1983.

Strayer, B.L. *The Patriation and Legitimacy of the Canadian Constitution*. Saskatoon: University of Saskatchewan Press, 1982.

Tarnopolsky, W.S. *Discrimination and the Law: Including Equality Rights Under the Charter*. Don Mills: De Boo, 1985.

Tarnopolsky, W.S. (ed.). *Some Civil Liberties Issues of the Seventies*. Toronto: Carswell, 1975.

Tarnopolsky, W.S. *The Canadian Bill of Rights*. 2nd ed. Toronto: McClelland and Stewart, 1975.

Tarnopolsky, W.S., and G.-A. Beaudoin (eds.). *The Canadian Charter of Rights and Freedoms: Commentary*. Toronto: Carswell, 1982.

Tarnopolsky, Wright, Beaudoin and Cody-Rice. *Newspapers and the Law; Les quotidiens et la loi*. Annexed to the Kent Report. Ottawa: Supply and Services, 1981.

Trudeau, P.E. *A Canadian Charter of Human Rights*. Ottawa: Queen's Printer, 1968.

Trudeau, P.E. *Charte canadienne des Droits de l'homme*. Ottawa: Queen's Printer, 1968.

Trudeau, P.E., and T. Axworthy (eds.). *Towards a Just Society*. Markham: Viking, 1990.

Varcoe, F.P. *The Constitution of Canada*. Toronto: Carswell, 1965.

Waite, P.B. *The Confederation Debates in the Province of Canada/1865*. Toronto: McClelland and Stewart, 1963.

Waite, P.B. *The Life and Times of Confederation, 1865-1867*, Politics, Newspapers and the Union of British North America". Toronto: University of Toronto Press, 1962.

Weiler, P. *In the Last Resort. A Critical Study of the Supreme Court of Canada*. Toronto: Carswell/Methuen, 1974.

Wheare, K.C. *The Constitutional Structure of the Commonwealth*. Oxford, 1960.

Wheare, K.C. *Federal Government*. 4th ed. Oxford, 1963.

Wheare, K.C. *The Statute of Westminster and Dominion Status*. 5th ed. Oxford, 1953.

Whyte, J.D., and W.R. Lederman. *Canadian Constitutional Law - Cases, Notes and Materials on the Distribution and Limitations of Legislative Powers Under the Constitution of Canada*. Toronto: Butterworths, 1975.

Whyte, J.D. *The Constitution and Natural Resource Revenue*. Kingston: Institute of Intergovernmental Relations, Queen's University, 1982.

Zlotkin, N.K. *Unfinished Business: Aboriginal Peoples and the 1983 Constitutional Conference*. Kingston: Institute of Intergovernmental Relations, Queen's University, 1983.

THE FUTURE OF CANADA

TREATISES

Citizens Forum on Canada's Future, *Citizens Forum on Canada's Future: Report to the People and Government of Canada*. Ottawa: Supply and Services Canada, 1991.

Clark, Rt. Hon. J., *A Nation Too Good to Lose: Renewing the Purpose of Canada*. Toronto: Ken Porter Books Ltd., 1994.

Cook, R., *Canada, Quebec and the Uses of Nationalism*, 2nd ed. Toronto: McLelland & Stewart, Inc., 1995.

Côté, M., & Johnson, D., *If Quebec Goes ...: The Real Cost of Separation* Toronto: Stoddart Books, 1995.

Freeman, A. and Grady, P., *Dividing the House: Planning for a Canada Without Quebec.* Toronto: Harper Collins Publishers Ltd., 1995.

If You Love this Country: 15 Voices in a United Canada. Toronto: Penguin Books, 1995.

Jeffrey, B., *Strange Bedfellows, Trying Times: October 1992 and the Defeat of the Powerbrokers.* Toronto: Key Porter Books, 1993.

Johnson, W., *A Canadian Myth: Quebec, Between Canada and the Illusion of Utopia.* Montreal, Toronto: Robert Davies Publishing, 1994.

Lamont, L., *Breakup: The Coming End of Canada and the Stakes in America.* Toronto: Ken Porter Books Ltd., 1995.

Russell, P., *Constitutional Odyssey.* Toronto: University of Toronto Press, 1993.

Chapter 6

THE INSTITUTIONS: THE ROLE OF COURTS IN CANADA

INTRODUCTION

An inquiry into the role of courts in Canada necessarily involves an inquiry into the role and function of judges. That inquiry, however, is the subject of a major discussion in Chapter 9. Judges sit in various different courts; the hierarchy of courts within the Canadian judiciary is also made the subject of two discussions in this treatise. In the preceding chapter, we directed our attention to the constitutional basis of judicial authority in Canada; in the following chapter, we will be examining that same hierarchy in terms of the various functions of the different courts at the various levels. Accordingly, the purpose of this chapter is to bridge the gap between our knowledge of the constitutional basis for the establishment of courts in Canada and the later discussions (in Chapters 7 and 9) of the functions of the various courts and the role of the judge in exercising those functions. This chapter will discuss, by way of a general introduction, the role and function of courts in Canada.

THE ATMOSPHERE OF THE COURTS

There are, essentially, two features which describe the atmosphere in Canadian courts.[1] The first feature is a custom or convention that the proceedings are to be held openly and in public. The second feature is that proceedings are to be conducted in an atmosphere of decorum and dignity commensurate with the seriousness or importance of the work engaged in by our courts.

---

[1] See, generally, D.J. Galligan, *Discretionary Powers: A Legal Study of Official Discretion* (New York: Oxford University Press, 1986); Henry Julian Abraham, *The Judicial Process: An Introductory Analysis of the Courts of the U.S., England and France*, 6th ed. (New York: Oxford University Press, 1993); and Chester James Antieau, *Adjudicating Constitutional Issues* (New York: Ocean Publications, 1985).

1. THE OPEN COURT

A legal philosopher, Jeremy Bentham, once said:

> In the darkness of secrecy, sinister interest and evil in every shape have full swing. Only in proportion as publicity has place can any of the checks applicable to judicial injustice operate. Where there is no publicity there is no justice. Publicity is the very soul of justice. It is the keenest spur to exertion and the sheerest of all guards against improbity. It keeps the judge himself while trying under trial. The security of securities is publicity.[2]

The view espoused above reflects a tradition of our Anglo-Canadian legal system. That tradition, of course, arose out of a sad and perverse chapter in our legal history, associated with the proceedings of the Star Chamber and similar expressions of manifest injustice and unfairness throughout our legal history. In short, the scrutiny and vigilance which arise out of the publicity of proceedings held in our courts are regarded as essential in ensuring the preservation of justice and in ensuring public acceptance, confidence and credibility in our courts as vital institutions in society.

Notwithstanding the foregoing, however, there are instances where the desire for publicity conflicts with the responsibility of our courts to provide for the protection of the rights of certain classes of persons appearing before the courts. For example, under the Young Offenders Act, R.S.C. 1985, c. Y-1 , the proceedings of a youth court may be held in camera.[3] This is done at the discretion of the presiding judge. The test is whether the evidence that is to be admitted would be injurious or prejudicial to a young accused, a young witness, or a young victim, or whether the in camera proceedings would be in the interest of public morals or the maintenance of public order or the proper administration of justice. The rationale here for in camera hearings is to protect both the young offender and the public.

There are other instances in the law in which our parliamentarians have felt it advisable that the proceedings of courts be held in camera. For example, under the Criminal Code, R.S.C. 1985, c. C-46, s. 539, upon an application by counsel for an accused person at a preliminary inquiry, the judge must order that the proceedings of that preliminary inquiry, excepting only the disposition at the end of the inquiry, not be publicized until there is,

---

[2] Quoted from the Ontario Law Reform Commission, "Report on Administration of Ontario Courts", Part I, 1973, p. 205.
[3] See *Southam Inc. v. R.* (1984), 48 O.R. (2d) 678, 42 C.R. (3d) 336, 16 C.C.C. (3d) 262, 12 C.R.R. 212, 14 D.L.R. (4th) 683 (H.C.), affirmed (1986), 53 O.R. (2d) 663, 50 C.R. (3d) 241, 25 C.C.C. (3d) 119, 20 C.R.R. 7, 26 D.L.R. (4th) 479, 12 O.A.C. 394 (C.A.), leave to appeal to S.C.C. refused (1986), 50 C.R. (3d) xxv (note), 25 C.C.C. (3d) 119n, 20 C.R.R. 7n, 26 D.L.R. (4th) 479n, 68 N.R. 398 (note), 160 O.A.C. 80 (note) (S.C.C.)

subsequently, a conviction at trial. Publication of the name of the complainant or victim of a sexual assault is also banned.[4]

One should, however, draw a distinction between the departures from the principle of the open court contained in the instances described above. In youth court proceedings, the entire matter may be held in private, while in respect of the two examples under the Criminal Code set out above, the proceedings are still held in public and anyone may enter the court, but there is a ban on publication.[5] This distinction aside, the common denominator linking all of these examples is a desire on the part of our legislators (and, by implication, on the part of our courts) that the rights of certain classes of persons appearing before the courts be protected. It is a question of balancing the protections arising out of the concept of the open court, including the desire for publicity and the public's right to know, with the protection of the rights of certain classes of private individuals appearing before the courts, including the harm that would come to those persons in the event of publicity. Nonetheless, the occasions which require a derogation from the concept of the open court are conventionally rare because both traditionally and in the present, that balance is strongly tilted towards the desire to conduct proceedings openly and in public.[6] But recent media disclosures suggest to many that the number of publication bans (of various kinds) has dramatically increased. No one really knows if this is the case as there appears to be no empirical studies of the question. It could be that our society values openness more so than in the past and the public, through the media, is becoming more sensitive and aware of the imposition of publication bans. It could be that some judges, in seeing their colleagues impose publication bans, feel a greater ease or comfort in doing so themselves. Or, it could be that, in a time when media and other interests in Canada are lobbying for cameras in the courtroom and are comparing Canada to (primarily) the U.S.

---

[4] See s. 486 (3), (4) of the Criminal Code. See, for example, *R. v. K.(V.)* (1991), 4 C.R. (4th) 338, 68 C.C.C. (3d) 18 (B.C. C.A.); *Southam Inc. v. R.* (1989), 69 C.R. (3d) 229, *(sub nom. R. v. Southam Inc.)* 47 C.C.C. (3d) 21, 44 C.R.R. 175, 32 O.A.C. 274, reversing (1987), 40 C.C.C. (3d) 218 (Ont. H.C.), additional reasons at (November 18, 1987), Doc. 279/87 (Ont H.C.); *Canadian Newspapers Co. v. Canada (A.G.),* [1988] 2 S.C.R. 122, 65 O.R. (2d) 637 (note), 65 C.R. (3d) 50, 43 C.C.C. (3d) 24, *(sub nom. Cdn. Newspapers Co. v. Canada (A.G.))* 38 C.R.R. 72, 52 D.L.R. (4th) 690, *(sub nom. Cdn. Newspapers Co. v. Canada)* 87 N.R. 163, 32 O.A.C. 259.

[5] In addition to the preceding examples, s. 648(1) of the Criminal Code provides:

> 648(1) Where permission to separate is given to numbers of a jury under subsection 647(1), no information regarding any portion of the trial at which the jury is not present shall be published, after the permission is granted, in any newspaper or broadcast before the jury retires to consider its verdict.
>
> (2) Every one who fails to comply with subsection (1) is guilty of an offence punishable on summary conviction.

[6] For a discussion of the American position on similar issues, see U.S. News & World Report, 14th August 1978.

experience in this regard, that the public is becoming more sensitized to the issue of ready accessibility to court proceedings. Maybe, some, in the light of the O.J. Simpson trial, feel we are being deprived of the 'educative' value (or, as some would say, the 'entertainment' value) of greater public exposure. In any event, irrespective of whether the instances of publication bans have increased in recent years, clearly, they are being more noticed and scrutinized by the media and other commentators.[7]

Furthermore, it appears that often publication bans simply do not work in our technological 'global village'. For example, with the wide spread use of the computer Internet, cross-border television transmissions and

---

[7] To illustrate this heightened awareness, there have been a number of newspaper articles on publication bans, including bans related to the Bernardo/Homolka trial, the Martensville trial, and the McCain brothers, The Boys of St. Vincent and the Valour and the Horror and other legal actions. See, for example, "Media lawyers argue publication ban not justified", Edmonton Journal, May 2, 1991; "Publication ban lifted on physicians sexual assault trial", Edmonton Journal, May 4, 1991; "It's no secret: what we don't know can hurt us", Vancouver Sun, July 15, 1993; "Collision of rights: A growing trend in Canadian court to ban publication of news about certain cases is leading to a clash between two fundamental Charter rights", Canada and the World 59 (8) (April 1994); "Judges' ban in sex-slaying trial costs Canada in freedom rating", Vancouver Sun, May 4, 1994; "Can justice unseen be justice done? Judges deny public access in two of Canada's most sensational trials", Western Report 8 (26) July 26, 1993; "Cone of Silence lifted in trial of transit worker", Edmonton Journal, January 6, 1995; "Keep tapes off TV — Family: Bernardo judge hears emotional plea", Edmonton Journal, April 6, 1995; "Molester's identity to be known", Edmonton Journal, October 7, 1994; "Paper ignores ban" Edmonton Journal, March 31, 1994; "Journal fined $1,500 for breaching ban", Edmonton Journal, July 8, 1993; "Sun fined $5,000 on contempt charge", Edmonton Journal, July 7, 1993; "A bad gag order in Canada", The New York Times, December 4, 1993; "Unspeakable Crimes: This story can't be told in Canada and so all Canada is talking about it...", The Washington Post, November 23, 1993; "Court reserves decision on publication ban", Edmonton Journal, March 11, 1993. See also, editorials in the Toronto Globe & Mail, September 15 and 21, 1993; "Behind closed courtroom doors" and "Feuds, trials and TV shows all hit by bans", Edmonton Journal, September 26, 1993; "Radio, TV join opponents of proposed trial media ban", Toronto Star, December 11, 1994; "Cable companies caught in middle of Homolka ban" and "Precedent for charging U.S. media set in '54", The Globe & Mail, December 4, 1993; "Closing of courtrooms to media no longer rare", The Globe & Mail, September 15, 1993; "A victory for free speech", Maclean's, December 19, 1994; "Public could face Bernardo hearing ban", Toronto Star, September 16, 1993; and "Case closed: Open courts are fundamental to our democracy. Can't the public be trusted?", Montreal Gazette, September 21, 1993. In addition, see Debby Waldman and Mary McIntosh, "Understanding Canadian Bans on Trial Coverage", Editor & Publisher, May 7, 1994; Debby Waldman and Mary McIntosh, "The Ban", Columbia Journalism Review, July/August 1994; Marcia Kaye, "No right to know?" Canadian Living, July 1994; and James Bacque, "Karla's Threat to the Internet", Saturday Night, October 1994. More recently in respect of the Bernardo trial, see "Does public have right to see video evidence?", Toronto Star, Febuary 3, 1995; and "Bernardo isn't a Canadian Simpson", Edmonton Journal, May 7, 1995; "Common sense and the jury", The Globe & Mail, May 9, 1995. With respect to the Marilyn Tan trial, a prominent witness asked to testify "from behind a screen and retain anonymity" (see The Globe & Mail, May 9, 1995) but this was denied by a judge who stated: "The administration of justice would fall into disrepute if the wealthy and powerful could use the fact of that wealth and power to get exceptions to the rule because they have more to lose than less advantaged citizens who find themselves in similar circumstances," Edmonton Journal, May 9, 1995) and The Globe & Mail, August 18, 1995.

the like, the effectiveness and/or enforceability of publication bans becomes tenuous.[8]

Notwithstanding this, one might consider the remarks of the late Dr. Max Wyman, a former president of the University of Alberta and a commissioner on the Kirby Commission studying the lower courts in the province of Alberta:

> I began to wonder what had happened to Jeremy Bentham's *security of securities*, and why our open courts do not seem to apply any checks to the appearance of judicial injustice. The names of people, not charged with any offence, are often bandied about in those open courts, and the news media have the power to disseminate to the world, in a matter of hours, serious innuendos concerning people who have no defence. I've begun to wonder whether those open courts, as they have now come to be, may be destroying more lives than they save . . . I began to wonder what safeguards were being taken to guard innocent people, wrongly accused of crime, from suffering such stigma. It seems to me that the open court, with the attendant publicity, is an open invitation to all and sundry to jump to the wrong conclusion.
>
> If the presumption of innocence is to mean anything in our system of law, the privacy of people should be guarded up to, and until, an actual conviction takes place. Does the public really have a right to know that people have been accused of crimes even when adjudication later deems them to be innocent of those crimes? I think not.
>
> The confusion that now reigns in those open courts has now become so great that some people answer to the wrong name, and plead guilty to the wrong charges, and it takes months to discover and rectify situations like this. Indeed, I now see none of the benefits that Bentham so clearly saw for those open courts. Although I hardly advocate a return to the Star Chamber, I do advocate a serious re-examination of the proper role an open court should play in our scheme of things. If the purpose of an open court is to protect the accused, then the accused should have an unprejudiced choice as to whether he or she wants to have his or her case heard in an open court.[9]

---

[8] See, for example, "The 'Current Affair' Affair", The Globe & Mail, December 4, 1993; "Canadian slayings shrouded in secrecy" and "Canadians fear arrest if they defy ban on selling Detroit papers", The Detroit News, November 28, 1993; and "The Ban has backfired: Let Teale facts flow", The Kingston Whig-Standard, December 3, 1993.

[9] Comments on the Criminal Law and the Legal Process. May 1975. Those readers who are interested in a more detailed examination of the relationship between the press as an institution in society, on one hand, and the law and the Canadian legal system, on the other hand, including the application of the fundamental notion of freedom of the press, may consult the following treatises:Robert Martin and G. Stuart Adam, *A Sourcebook of Canadian Media Law,* 2nd ed. (Ottawa: Carleton University Press, 1994); Richard V. Erickson, Patricia M. Baranek, and Janet B.L. Chan, *Representing Order: Crime, Law, and Justice in the News Media* (Toronto: University of Toronto Press, 1991); David Schneiderman (ed.), *Freedom of Expression and the Charter* (Toronto: Carswell, 1991); John D. Richard, *The Charter and the Media* (Ottawa: Canadian Bar Foundation, 1985); Gordon F. Proudfoot, *Privacy Law and the Media in Canada* (Ottawa: Canadian Bar Foundation, 1984); David M. Lepofsky, *Open Justice: The Constitutional Right to Attend and Speak about Criminal Proceedings* (Toronto: Butterworths, 1985); Wilfred H. Kesterton, *The Law and the Press in Canada* (Toronto: McClelland and Stewart, Carleton Library Series, 1976); G. Stuart Adam (ed.), *Journalism, Communication and the Law* (Scarborough: Prentice-Hall of Canada Ltd., 1976); Clare F. Beckton, *Law and the Media in Canada* (Toronto: Carswell, 1982); Stuart M. Robertson, *Courts and the Media* (Toronto: Butterworths, 1981); and Michael G. Crawford, *The Journalist's Legal Guide,* 2nd ed. (Toronto: Carswell, 1990). Some recent articles include Daniel J. Henry and Brian MacLeod Rogers, "Open justice

There is an inherent power vested in all judges generally to supervise and control the proceedings in their courts which allows a judge to close his courtroom to the press and/or public if there is a legitimate reason for doing so. Occasionally this is done where the evidence assumes a particularly salacious character. This whole question concerning the relationship between the open court and freedom of the press, and the desire in certain circumstances either to hold proceedings in camera or to order, upon pain of a citation of contempt of court, a ban on publication was, in fact, the subject of controversy a few years ago. In an Ontario case, a trial judge ordered a ban on the publication of the evidence adduced at trial of a criminal matter, without more than the vaguest of reasons for doing so. This subsequently gave rise to editorial condemna-

---

and the presumption of innocence: a response to a proposed ban on identifying those accused of sexual crimes" (August 1990) 1 Media & Communications L.R. 128-137; A. Wayne MacKay, "Freedom of expression: is it all just talk?" (December 1989) 68 Can. Bar Rev. 713-764; Mark Crawford, "Regimes of tolerance: a communitarian approach to freedom of expression and its limits" (Winter 1990) 48 U.T. Fac. L.R. 1-21; Christine Boyle, "Publication of identifying information about sexual assault survivors" (case comm.); *R. v. Canadian Newspapers Co.* (1988), 43 C.C.C. (3d) 24 (S.C.C.); (1989-90) 3 Can. J. Women & L. 602-614; Marlys Edwardh and Daniel Brodsky, "Media access to refugee proceedings in Canada" (1991), 29 Alta. L. Rev. 701-711; Richard G. Dearden and Jim Cruickshank, "Problems of proof for the media in freedom of the press Charter cases" (1991) Spec. Lect. L.S.U.C. 97-140; V. Gogolek, "Secret Trials: A look behind the closed doors," National, April 1995; Pierre N. Leval, "The continuing battle between the courts and the press" Cambridge Lectures 1989, ed. Frank E. McArdle (Montreal: Editions Y. Blais, 1990), 51-58; M. David Lepofsky, "The Role of "The Press" in freedom of the press" (September 1992) 3 Media & Communications L.R. 89-119; M. David Lepofsky, "Open Justice 1990: The Constitutional Right to Attend and Report on Court Proceedings in Canada" in D. Schneiderman, ed., *Freedom of the Press and the Charter* (Calgary: Thompson, 1991) 3; M. David Lepofsky, "Section 2(b) of the *Charter* and the Media coverage of Criminal Court Proceedings" (1983), 34 C.R. 63; Harold J. Levy, "Press-umed Innocent" in D. Schneiderman, ed., *Freedom of Expression and the Charter* (Calgary: Thomson Professional Publishing Corp., 1991) 85; Allen M. Linden, "Limitations of Media Coverage of Legal Proceedings," in P. Anisman and A.M. Linden, eds., *The Media, the Courts, and the Charter* (Toronto: Carswell, 1986) 301; A.W. Mewett, "Public Criminal Trials" (1978), 21 Crim. L.Q. 199; M. Radin, "The Right to a Public Trial" (1932), 6 Temple L.Q. 381; S.A. Radke, "Pretrial Publicity and the Criminal Justice System", (Ll.M. Thesis, University of Alberta, 1991); D.H. Jack, "Striking a balance between freedom of expression and the discretion of the court to seal court files" (case comm.) *National Bank of Canada v. Melnitzer* (1991), 84 D.L.R. (4th) 315 (Ont. Gen. Div.) (September 1992) 14 Advocates' Q. 210-221; Lynda Shorten, "Fractured silence: the use and abuse of publication bans" (December 1993) 17 Can. Lawyer No. 9, 10-12; D.F. Bur and J.K. Kehoe, "Developments in Constitutional Law: the 1991-92 term [of the Supreme Court of Canada]" (1993), 4 Sup. Crt. L. Rev. 49-176; John Pearson Allen and Thomas Allen, "Publication restrictions and criminal proceedings" (Febuary 1994) 36 Crim. L.Q. 168-1841; J.E. Jefferson, "Loosening the Gag: Free Press and Fair Trial" (1985), 43 U.T. Fac. L. Rev. 100; Clare F. Beckton, "Freedom of Expression (s. 2 (b))", in W. S. Tarnopolsky and G.A. Beaudoin, eds., *The Canadian Charter of Rights and Freedoms, Commentary* (Toronto: Carswell, 1982) 75; Law Reform Commission of Canada, "Public and Media Access to the Criminal Process" (Working Paper 56) (Ottawa: Law Reform Commission of Canada, 1987); Clare F. Beckton, "Freedom of Expression in Canada — How Free?" (1983), 13 Man. L.J. 583, and Robert Martin, "An Open Legal System" (1985), 23 U.W.O. L. Rev. 169.

tion.[10] In addition, one often reads of the fate which awaits, upon imprisonment, persons convicted of sexually related crimes, especially those committed on children. In order to protect the lives of those individuals, some persons have suggested that there be a restriction on the publication of their names at trial.

The issue of the open court has recently been the subject of considerable litigation. For example, in *R. v. N.*, [1980] 1 W.W.R. 68, 15 B.C.L.R. 218, 10 C.R. (3d) 68, 48 C.C.C. (2d) 97, 11 R.F.L. (2d) 45, 102 D.L.R. (3d) 417, the British Columbia Court of Appeal held that a Juvenile Court Judge had the discretion under s. 12(1) of the Juvenile Delinquents Act to permit the members of the public to attend at the trial of a child charged with a delinquency. Essentially, the Court of Appeal held that the words "without publicity" in the above section do not mean "in camera". Accordingly, the Juvenile Court Judge had the discretion to allow members of the public to attend juvenile proceedings.

The Juvenile Delinquents Act has since been replaced by the Young Offenders Act. The Act gives a presiding judge discretion to hold proceedings involving young persons in camera. Unlike s. 12(1) of the old Juvenile Delinquents Act, which stated that the judge must hold the proceedings in camera, s. 39 of the Young Offenders Act gives a judge the discretion to exclude certain persons from all or part of the proceedings. One can assume that the drafters of the Young Offenders Act recognized the importance of openness as a principle that must be balanced in appropriate circumstances with the requirements of secrecy in the conduct of certain proceedings. Section 39 is as follows:

39. (1) Subject to subsection (2), where a court or justice before whom proceedings are carried out under this Act is of the opinion

    (*a*) that any evidence or information presented to the court or justice would be seriously injurious or seriously prejudicial to

---

[10] For some other instances over the past few years where this issue has arisen, see the following newspaper reports:

    (i) Unprecedented ban on reporting of evidence *and* decision at bail hearing of child charged with murder — see the Edmonton Journal, 5th August 1981.

    (ii) Rejection of a defence request to exclude press from guilty plea concerning a sexual offence committed by an adult on a juvenile — see the Edmonton Journal, 13th April 1981.

    (iii) Similar issues were recently considered by the Supreme Court of the United States — see Newsweek Magazine, 27th August 1979 and U.S. News & World Report, 20th August 1979.

    (iv) A Provincial Judge ordered a ban on the reporting of a bawdy house trial, including the identification of those witnesses who had "paid for sex" — see the Edmonton Journal, 29th August 1979. The order was subsequently upheld by a Supreme Court Judge — see the Edmonton Journal, 29th September 1979. But it was later overruled by a Court of Appeal decision — see the Edmonton Journal, 29th October 1979.

(i) the young person who is being dealt with in the proceedings,

(ii) a child or young person who is a witness in the proceedings,

(iii) a child or young person who is aggrieved by or the victim of the offence charged in the proceedings, or

(b) that it would be in the interest of public morals, the maintenance of order or the proper administration of justice to exclude any or all members of the public from the court room,

the court or justice may exclude any person from all or part of the proceedings if the court or justice deems that person's presence to be unnecessary to the conduct of the proceedings.

(2) Subject to section 650 of the Criminal Code and except where it is necessary for the purposes of subsection 13(6) of this Act, a court or justice may not, pursuant to subsection (1), exclude from proceedings under this Act

(a) the prosecutor,

(b) the young person who is being dealt with in the proceedings, his parent, his counsel or any adult assisting him pursuant to subsection 11(7);

(c) the provincial director or his agent; or

(d) the youth worker to whom the young person's case has been assigned.

(3) The youth court, after it has found a young person guilty of an offence, or the youth court or the review board, during a review of a disposition under sections 28 to 32, may, in its discretion, exclude from the court or from a hearing of the review board, as the case may be, any person other than

(a) the young person or his counsel,

(b) the provincial director or his agent,

(c) the youth worker to whom the young person's case has been assigned, and

(d) the Attorney General or his agent,

when any information is being presented to the court or the review board the knowledge of which might, in the opinion of the court or review board, be seriously injurious or seriously prejudicial to the young person.

(4) The exception set out in paragraph (3)(a) is subject to subsection 13(6) of this Act and section 650 of the Criminal Code.

Section 486 of the Criminal Code also provides for circumstances under which members of the public (i.e., the general public and the media) may be excluded from court. A judge may make such an order in the interest of public morals, the maintenance of order and the proper administration of justice.

The Young Offenders Act also contains a provision in relation to a publication ban. It states as follows:

38(1) Subject to this section, no person shall publish by any means any report

(a) of an offence committed or alleged to have been committed by a young person, unless an order has been made under Section 16 with respect thereto, or

(b) of a hearing, adjudication, disposition or appeal concerning a young person who committed or is alleged to have committed an offence

in which the name of the young person, a child or a young person who is a victim of the offence or a child or a young person who appeared as a witness in connection with the offence, or in which any information serving to identify such person or child, is disclosed.

The Act also allows persons aged 14 and over to be transferred to an adult court at a hearing to make this determination. The Act specifies:

17. (1) Where a youth court hears an application for a transfer to ordinary court under section 16, it shall
    (a) where the young person is not represented by counsel, or
    (b) on application made by or on behalf of the young person or the prosecutor, where the young person is represented by counsel,
    make an order directing that any information respecting the offence presented at the hearing shall not be published in any newspaper or broadcast before such time as
    (c) an order for a transfer is refused or set aside on review and the time for all reviews against the decision has expired or all proceedings in respect of any such review have been completed; or
    (d) the trial is ended, if the case is transferred to ordinary court.
    (2) Every one who fails to comply with an order made pursuant to subsection (1) is guilty of an offence punishable on summary conviction.

The Criminal Code also contains various sections which provide for publication bans. Section 276 prohibits the publication of evidence of a complainant's past sexual history in cases related to sexual offences. Sections 486 (3) and 486 (4) provide for circumstances in which a judge may prohibit the identification of a witness, including the suppression of any evidence that might identify a witness.[11] Section 517 permits a judge to order a publication ban respecting matters raised at a judicial interim release hearing. Section 539 requires a judge, upon application of an accused, to ban the publication of evidence at a preliminary inquiry until the accused is discharged at the preliminary inquiry or, if not discharged, until the disposition of the matter at trial. Finally, section 648 of the Criminal Code, in the case of a trial by jury, prohibits the publication of evidence adduced when the jury is not present. Typically, this occurs during a *voir dire* (for example, a trial within a trial to determine whether a confession was voluntarily given). However, it can also apply in other circumstances. For example, in the Bernardo trial, any pre-trial motions, between the time an unsequestered jury is chosen and the time that *viva voce* (oral) and documentary evidence are given, are prohibited from publication.[12]

There have been a number of similar cases arising out of the provisions contained in the Canadian Charter of Rights and Freedoms. Some newspapers have raised the issue in connection with s. 2 of the Charter, which provides that:

[e]veryone has the following fundamental freedoms: . . .
(*b*) freedom of . . . expression, including freedom of the press and other media of communication . . .

---

[11]See for example, in connection with the Marilyn Tan trial, The Globe & Mail, May 9, 1995 and the Edmonton Journal, May 9, 1995.
[12]See the Edmonton Journal, May 10, 1995.

In addition, s. 11 provides that:

[a]ny person charged with an offence has the right . . .
(*d*)   to be presumed innocent until proven guilty according to law in a fair and public hearing . . .

It should be noted that, unlike s. 2, the benefit of this section is restricted to persons charged with criminal offences.

The courts have considered the scope of the above sections (especially s. 2(*b*)) on several occasions. For a sense of how the courts are reacting to these sections (again, especially s. 2(*b*)), see the following recent cases:

Access to Judicial Proceedings

Southam Inc. v. Coulter (1990), (*sub nom. Southam Inc. v. Coulter*) 75 O.R. (3d) 1, 60 C.C.C. (3d) 267, 40 O.A.C. 341 (C.A.); *R.v. Needham* (1992), 72 B.C.L.R. (2d) 331, (*sub nom. Needham v. British Columbia*) 76 C.C.C. (3d) 146, 95 D.L.R. (4th) 754 (C.A.); *R. v. Squires* (1992), 11 O.R. (3d) 385, 18 C.R. (4th) 22, 78 C.C.C. (3d) 97, 12 C.R.R. (2d) 193, 59 O.A.C. 281 (C.A.), leave to appeal to S.C.C. refused (1993), 15 O.R. (3d) xvi (note), 25 C.R. (4th) 103n, 83 C.C.C. (3d) vii (note), 16 C.R.R. (2d) 384n, 164 N.R. 80 (note), 67 O.A.C. 158n (S.C.C.); *Ruby v. Canada (Solicitor General)* (1994), 22 C.R.R. (2d) 324, 80 F.T.R. 81 (F.C.T.D.); and *Canadian Broadcasting Corp. v. New Brunswick (Attorney General)* (1994), 32 C.R. (4th) 334, 378 A.P.R. 161, 91 C.C.C. (3d) 560, 116 D.L.R. (4th) 506, 148 N.B.R. (2d) 161 (C.A.), leave to appeal to S.C.C. granted (1995), 95 C.C.C. (3d) vi (note), 120 D.L.R. (4th) vii (note) (S.C.C.).

Publication Bans

R. v. Zayet (1992), 16 W.C.B. (2d) 166 (Ont. Gen. Div.); *National Bank of Canada v. Melnitzer* (1991), 5 O.R. (3d) 234, 2 C.P.C. (3d) 106, 84 D.L.R. (4th) 315 (Gen. Div.); *Northwest Territories (Workers' Compensation Board) v. Schott,* [1993] N.W.T.R. 294 (S.C.); *Canadian Broadcasting Corp. v. R.* (1992), 81 C.C.C. (3d) 431 (*sub nom. Canadian Broadcasting Corp. v. Canada*), 116 N.S.R. (2d) 126, 320 A.P.R. 126 (S.C.); and *R. v. Wilson* (1993), 20 W.C.B. (2d) 290 (Ont. Gen. Div.).

Freedom of the Press

R. v. Robinson-Blackmore Printing and Publishing Co. (1989), 229 A.P.R. 46, 47 C.C.C. (3d) 366, 48 C.R.R. 327, (*sub nom. R. v. Harris*) 73 Nfld. & P.E.I.R. 46 (Nfld. T.D.); *Alberta (Attorney-General) v. Interwest Publications Ltd.* (1990), 74 Alta. L.R. (2d) 372, [1990], 5 W.W.R. 498, 108 A.R. 173, 58 C.C.C. (3d) 114, 73 D.L.R. (4th) 83 (Q.B.); *MacLeod v.*

Canada (Chief of Defence Staff, Canadian Armed Forces) (1990), 2 C.R. (3d) 213, [1991] 1 F.C. 114, (*sub nom. MacLeod v. Canada (Canadian Armed Forces (Chief, Defence Staff))*) 38 F.T.R. 129 (Fed T.D.); *New Brunswick Broadcasting Co. v. Nova Scotia (Speaker, House of Assembly)*, [1993] 1 S.C.R. 319, 118 N.S.R. (2d) 181, 327 A.P.R. 181, 13 C.R.R. (2d) 1, 100 D.L.R. (4th) 212, 118 N.S.R. (2d) 181; *Société Radio-Canada c. Nouveau-Brunswick (Procureur général)*, [1991] 3 S.C.R. 459, 119 N.B.R. (2d) 271, 9 C.R. (4th) 192, 300 A.P.R. 271, 67 C.C.C. (3d) 544, (*sub nom. Société Radio-Canada/Canadian Broadcasting Corp. v. New Brunswick (Attorney General)* 7 C.R.R. (2d) 270, (*sub nom. Canadian Broadcasting Corp. v. New Brunswick (Attorney General)*) 85 D.L.R. (4th) 57, 130 N.R. 362; *Société Radio-Canada c. Lessard*, [1991] 3 S.C.R. 421, 9 C.R. (4th) 133, (*sub nom. Canadian Broadcasting Corp. v. Lessard*) 67 C.C.C. (3d) 517, (*sub nom. Société Radio-Canada/Canadian Broadcasting Corp. v. Lessard*) 7 C.R.R. (2d) 244, 130 N.R. 321.

Some earlier cases are set out as follows:
Southam Inc. v. Min. of Employment & Immigration, [1987] 3 F.C. 329, 3 Imm. L.R. (2d) 226 (*sub nom. Southam Inc. v. Can. (Min. of Employment & Immigration)*), 13 F.T.R. 138, 33 C.R.R. 376 (T.D.); *R. v. Begley* (1982), 38 O.R. (2d) 549, 70 C.C.C. (2d) 264, 141 D.L.R. (3d) 349 (*sub nom. Re Southam Inc. and R.*) (H.C.); *R. v. Banville* (1983), 34 C.R. (3d) 20, 3 C.C.C. (3d) 312, 145 D.L.R. (3d) 595, 45 N.B.R. (2d) 134, 118 A.P.R. 134 (Q.B.); *Global Communications Ltd. v. Canada (A.G.)* (1983), 42 O.R. (2d) 13, 34 C.R. (3d) 52 (*sub nom. Re Smith*), 5 C.R.R. 38, 148 D.L.R. (3d) 331, 5 C.C.C. (3d) 346 (H.C.), affirmed (1984), 44 O.R. (2d) 609, 38 C.R. (3d) 209, 5 D.L.R. (4th) 634, 10 C.C.C. (3d) 97, 7 C.R.R. 22, 2 O.A.C. 21 (*sub nom. Global Communications Ltd. v. California*) (C.A.); *R. v. Robinson* (1983), 41 O.R. (2d) 764, 34 C.R. (3d) 92, 5 C.C.C. (3d) 230, 148 D.L.R. (3d) 185 (H.C.); *R. v. R. (T.)* (1984), 10 C.C.C. (3d) 481, 7 D.L.R. (4th) 205, 52 A.R. 149 (Q.B.); *R. v. Canadian Newspapers Co.* (1984), 16 C.C.C. (3d) 495, 13 C.R.R. 43, 31 Man. R. (2d) 187 (*sub nom. Canadian Newspapers Co. v. Swail*) (C.A.); *Cdn. Newspapers Co. v. Canada (A.G.)*, (1985), 49 O.R. (2d) 557, 44 C.R. (3d) 97 (*sub nom. Cdn. Newspapers Co. v. A.G. Can.*; *R. v. D.D.*), 17 C.C.C. (3d) 385, 7 O.A.C. 161, 16 D.L.R. (4th) 642, 14 C.R.R. 276, reversed [1988] 2 S.C.R. 122, 65 O.R. (2d) 637n, 65 C.R. (3d) 50, 43 C.C.C. (3d) 24, 52 D.L.R. (4th) 690, 38 C.R.R. 72, (*sub nom. Cdn. Newspapers Co. v. Canada*) 87 N.R. 163, 32 O.A.C. 259, 38 C.R.R. 72; *Hirt v. College of Physicians & Surgeons (B.C.)*, [1985] 3 W.W.R. 350, 60 B.C.L.R. 273, 17 D.L.R. (4th) 472 (C.A.); *Toronto Sun Publishing Corp. v. Alberta (A.G.)*, [1985] 6 W.W.R. 36, 39 Alta. L.R. (2d) 97, 62 A.R. 315 (C.A.); *R. v. Unnamed Person* (1985), 22 C.C.C. (3d) 284, 10 O.A.C. 305, 20 C.R.R. 188 (C.A.); *Lortie v. R.*, [1985] C.A. 451, 46 C.R. (3d) 322, 21

C.C.C. (3d) 436 (C.A. Qué.); *R. v. McArthur* (1984), 13 C.C.C. (3d) 152, 10 C.R.R. 220 (Ont. H.C.); *Edmonton Journal v. Alberta (Attorney General)*, 53 Alta. L.R. (2d) 193, [1987] 5 W.W.R. 385, 78 A.R. 375, 34 C.R.R. 111, 41 D.L.R. (4th) 502 (C.A.), reversed [1989] 2 S.C.R. 1326, 71 Alta. L.R. (2d) 273, 41 C.P.C. (2d) 109, [1990] 1 W.W.R. 577, 103 A.R. 321, 45 C.R.R. 1, 64 D.L.R. (4th) 577, 102 N.R. 321; *R. v. Dacey* (1988), 84 N.S.R. (2d) 97, 213 A.P.R. 97 (Prov. Ct.); *Southam Inc. v. R.* (1987), 37 C.C.C. (3d) 139 (Ont. H.C.); *Cdn. Newspapers Co. v. Canada (A.G.)*, [1987] 1 W.W.R. 262, 28 C.C.C. (3d) 379, 31 D.L.R. (4th) 601 (Man. Q.B.); *Coates v. Citizen (The)* (1986), 11 C.P.C. (2d) 96, 29 D.L.R. (4th) 523 (*sub nom. Citizen (The) v. Coates*), 74 N.S.R. (2d) 143, 180 A.P.R. 143 (C.A.); *Cdn. Newspaper Co. v. Directeur des services de la voie publique & de la circulation routière de Québec) (Ville)*, 33 M.P.L.R. 28, [1987] R.J.Q. 1078, 36 D.L.R. (4th) 641 (*sub nom. Cdn. Newspaper Co. v. Public Road & Traffic Services of Quebec (City)*), 30 C.R.R. 299 (C.S. Qué.); *Can. Newspaper Co. v. Victoria (City)* (1989), 40 B.C.L.R. (2d) 297, [1990] 2 W.W.R. 1, 46 C.R.R. 271, 63 D.L.R. (4th) 1 (C.A.); *Manitoba (A.G.) v. Groupe Québecor Inc.*, [1987] 5 W.W.R. 270, 59 C.R. (3d) 1, 37 C.C.C. (3d) 421, 45 D.L.R. (4th) 80, 31 C.R.R. 313 (*sub nom. A.G. for Man. v. Groupe Quebecor Inc.*), 47 Man. R. (2d) 187 (C.A.); *Snyder v. Montreal Gazette Ltd.*, [1988] 1 S.C.R. 494, 43 C.C.L.T. 216, 49 D.L.R. (4th) 17, [1988] R.R.A. 220, 12 Q.A.C. 83, 82 N.R. 371; and *Coates v. Citizen (The)* (1988), 44 C.C.L.T. 286; 85 N.S.R. (2d) 146, 216 A.P.R. 146 (T.D.).

Section 2(*b*) was recently applied and considered in the Supreme Court of Canada. See *Moysa v. Alberta (Labour Relations Bd.)* (1986), 45 Alta. L.R. (2d) 37, 28 D.L.R. (4th) 140, 25 C.R.R. 346, 71 A.R. 70, (Q.B.), affirmed (1987), 52 Alta. L.R. (2d) 193, 17 C.P.C. (2d) 91, 43 D.L.R. (4th) 159, 79 A.R. 118 (C.A.), affirmed [1989] 1 S.C.R. 1572, [1989] 4 W.W.R. 596, 67 Alta. L.R. (2d) 193, 34 C.P.C. (2d) 97, 89 C.L.L.C. 14,028, 60 D.L.R. (4th) 1, 96 N.R. 70, 97 A.R. 368.

In order to protect against any improprieties on the part of the press, including any abuses in relation to press coverage of judicial proceedings, several so-called "press councils" have been established throughout Canada. These press councils are essentially bodies which conduct a form of self-regulation arising out of complaints against participating newspapers.[13]

---

[13] See, for example, "A Report on the Alberta Press Council", Edmonton Journal, 20th December 1976. Virtually every daily (and some weekly) newspapers now belong to a provincial press council. In addition, many newspapers have a form of self-regulation in the form of an "ombudsman" to whom people can complain. While this may be helpful, the individual serving in this capacity is not in reality an ombudsman for he lacks independence from his employer/newspaper.

Finally, Dr. Wyman is not alone, in his views set out above, in expressing a desire that a re-examination of the concept of the open court be conducted.[14] For example, the executive director of the Alberta Council on Aging recently made these remarks:

> . . . the council maintains the media, especially the printed media, "doesn't realize the implications of what they are printing."
>
> Printing the names, ages and addresses "is a form of persecution and a violation of human rights as these people have no say in having this information published" . . . The council is calling on all editors and publishers to review stories of violent crimes and think about the consequences before releasing names, ages, and addresses . . . The council is not questioning the freedom of the press but their prerogative to infringe on human rights.[15]

Accordingly, at least in respect of the criminal law, the notion of the freedom of the press and the concept of the open court are not without some current challenge. However, these criticisms notwithstanding, the concept of the open court, including the associated publicity which arises therefrom, represents essentially a fundamental protection afforded to those persons appearing in proceedings before our courts which defines an essential feature of the atmosphere surrounding the conduct of proceedings in Canadian courts.

Some recent articles on press councils include "Growing pains threaten existence of press watchdog", [Quebec Press Council] Montreal Gazette, May 13, 1990; "Press council tries to bridge readers-papers' gap: opinion split over 7 year-old body's effectiveness", Halifax Chronicle Herald, June 9, 1990; "Here's a code of ethics that press councils might adopt", Montreal Gazette, July 23, 1990; "Complaints against Journal dismissed", Edmonton Journal, October 5, 1994; "Press council dismisses complaint", Edmonton Journal, March 11, 1993; and, "Press council rejects complaints", Edmonton Journal, March 5, 1993.

See also Macdonald and Russell, *Journalists' Attitudes Towards the Police and the Judiciary* (Toronto: Canadian Daily Newspaper Publishers Association, 1978); Parker, *Collision Course? Free Press and the Courts*, from a symposium of lawyers and journalists at Osgoode Hall Law School (Toronto: Ryerson Polytechnical Institute, 1966); LaMarsh, "Abuse of Power by the Media", [1979] Lectures L.S.U.C. 651; Atkey, "Freedom of Information: The Problem of Confidentiality in the Administrative Process" (1980), 18 U.W.O.L. Rev. 153.

The move towards promoting continued self-regulation on the part of the newspapers has been particularly heightened since the report of the Kent Royal Commission on Newspapers was released in 1982. The Commission recommended, among other things, the enactment of a Newspaper Act to control the monopolistic and oligopolistic practices of the large newspaper chains. At the time of this writing the federal government has agreed to proceed on this recommendation, notwithstanding the newspaper industry's claims that a Newspaper Act would constitute an infringement of the freedom of the press.

[14] See David M. Lepofsky, *Open Justice: The Constitutional Right to Attend and Speak about Criminal Proceedings* (Toronto: Butterworths, 1985). See also the following articles: F.R. Smith, "Free Press — Fair Trial, a Question of Balance" (1985), 19 U.B.C. L. Rev. 73; J.E. Jefferson, "Loosening the Gag: Free Press and Fair Trial" (1985), 43 U.T. Faculty L. Rev. 100; and Law Reform Commission of Canada, "Public and Media Access to the Criminal Process" (Working Paper 56) (Ottawa: Supply and Services Canada, 1987).

[15] The Edmonton Journal, 18th December 1976. In the United States, the use of so-called "gag orders" by the courts arouses far more concern, reaction, and editorial criticism than that arising out of the employment of similar restrictions on publicity in Canada.

2. DIGNITY AND DECORUM

The television and motion picture portrayal of American courts that is familiar to many lay persons is certainly not applicable to Canadian courts. Although Canadian courts perhaps do not conduct their proceedings with the same strictness and formality exercised by their British counterparts, nonetheless there exists an air of formality in Canadian courts. Judges are addressed in certain formal ways and the manner in which counsel addresses the court depends, in turn, upon the particular level of the judiciary occupied by that court. Judges are often gowned and, depending upon the level of the judiciary and the nature of the proceedings, counsel are also gowned.

While some may argue that these formalities constitute a certain stuffiness, if not elitism, on the part of judges and lawyers, the counter argument is more persuasive. This argument holds that by conforming to certain formalities, the court achieves the prestige it deserves, given the important function it exercises in society. Arising out of this prestige, the proceedings before our courts will then be conducted in an atmosphere of dignity and decorum. This is not to say that Canadian courts are humourless institutions. On the contrary, members of the legal profession in Canada are able to relate many anecdotes arising out of experiences in Canadian courts. The notions of dignity and decorum, however, are designed to serve essentially two fundamental objectives. The first is that, in order to ensure that the objectives of fairness and justice are achieved, proceedings should never stoop to a level of frivolity. Secondly, in regarding judicial proceedings as a search for truth and justice, Canadian judges and lawyers strongly adhere to the notion that this search ought not to be conducted in an atmosphere of showmanship, dramatics, flamboyance or sensationalism. In short, an atmosphere of dignity and decorum is regarded as best suited to the search for truth and, ultimately, the attainment of justice.[16] That is why, at least in respect of proceedings in Canadian courts, the American television and motion picture image of court proceedings is generally inaccurate. That is also why, in defining the nature of the atmosphere surrounding Canadian courts, one must add to the concept of the open court the additional notions of dignity and decorum.

---

[16] Recently, in a well-publicized case, an Ontario lawyer was convicted at trial but acquitted on appeal for contempt of court. It was alleged that he had "scandalized the court", a common law criminal offence that has been preserved in the Criminal Code (s. 9). See *R. v. Kopyto* (1987), 62 O.R. (2d) 449, 61 C.R. (3d) 209, 39 C.C.C. (3d) 1, 47 D.L.R. (4th) 213, 24 O.A.C. 81 (C.A.).

Also, two Ontario judges warned lawyers and members of the public that they would not proceed in divorce cases unless those who appeared before them were properly dressed. For an analysis of those pronouncements, see the article appearing in the Edmonton Sun, 1st February 1982.

3. TELEVISION IN THE COURTROOM

Probably the most dramatic development over the past few years in connection with the issues of openness and dignity and decorum in our courts relates to the use of television in the courts. Television has now been allowed in some U.S. courts for a number of years.[17]

In Canada, the Supreme Court of Canada allowed television cameras to be present during the historic pronouncement of its decision on the unilateral patriation of the Canadian constitution, and in Ontario there has been some significant work done on an experimental basis in connection with television in the courtrooms.[18] In addition, under Ontario law,

---

[17] For a brief discussion of the American position, see U.S. News & World Report, 9th February 1981. The U.S. cable television channel, Court T.V. broadcasts proceedings in the courts on a regular basis. Of course, the experience of the O.J. Simpson trial dramatically underscored the debate as to the advisability of television coverage of judicial proceedings. See for example, The Calgary Herald, October 7, 1995.

[18] In particular, one might refer to the Ontario experiment and the related study thereof conducted by the Radio Television News Directors Association of Canada (R.T.N.D.A.). This study, entitled *Electronic Public Access to Court: A Proposal for its Implementation Today*, was submitted on 18th November 1982. It was prepared by the R.T.N.D.A. Special Committee on Electronic Public Access (Mr. Con Stevenson (CKOC) Chairman; Mr. Craig Armstrong (CBC — Toronto); Mr. Gordon Haines (CITY-TV); and Mr. Daniel Henry (CBC, Legal Counsel)). This report presents an excellent argument in favour of television cameras in the courtroom. In Ontario the Courts of Justice Act permits cameras in the courtroom if the judge and all parties agree to it. The media have generally taken the position that the Act does not go far enough. As a result a constitutional challenge was launched and is presently before the courts. Readers who are interested in pursuing this topic further may consult the following articles: "Time has come for cameras in court", Halifax Chronicle Herald, August 3, 1990; "Cable TV will take [US] viewers to court, 24 hours a day", Montreal Gazette, December 15, 1990; "Is Canada ready to let TV into the courtroom?", Toronto Star, July 29, 1991; "TV trials: should cameras cover the courts? [Views for and against the idea]", Toronto Star, December 16, 1991; "Trial-TV is exploding, not educating", Halifax Chronicle Herald, December 12, 1991; "Cameras in the courtroom can taint "common" sense Rick Salutin says", The Globe & Mail, December 27, 1991; "Dahmer will face jury and television cameras: widespread coverage shows how once-controversial issue of courtroom TV is now routine", The Globe & Mail, January 10, 1992; Supreme Court may soon admit TV cameras: top Justices have agreed to experiment, Lamer tells press gallery", Montreal Gazette, March 26, 1992; "Judge bars Vander Zalm trial cameras", Vancouver Sun, May 15, 1992; "Bryan Schwartz focuses on question of whether some trials should be televised", The Globe & Mail, September 1, 1992; "Former Justice now backs TV cameras in courtrooms: [Gregory Evans]" Toronto Star, May 4, 1992; "Camera access to courtrooms: Canadian, US, and Australian experiences", Bibl. Canadian Journal of Communication, 18 (1) (Winter 93); "The verdict: supremely boring television", The Globe & Mail, March 3, 1993; "Right-to-die case to get TV coverage", Winnipeg Free Press, April 21, 1993; "Cameras go back to Supreme Court", The Globe & Mail, May 21, 1993; "Networks may have to share OJ trial", The Globe & Mail, July 25, 1994; John Maclean, "Fuzzy Picture Emerges on TV in Supreme Court" (1985), 9 Can. Lawyer 36(2), D.J. Henry, "Televised Court Proceedings: The Case for Implementation Today" (1984), 3 Advocates' Soc. J. 19, A.W. Mewett, "Television in the Courtroom" (editorial) (1984), 26 Crim. L.Q. 385. See also The Globe & Mail, 4th July 1988, 2nd December 1987, 18th November 1987, 25th September 1987, 28th August 1987, 24th August 1987, 27th July 1987, 5th June 1987, 19th February 1986, 3rd February 1986, 27th September 1985, 11th February 1985, 21st January 1985,

s. 67 of the Judicature Act[19] and, subsequently, s. 146 of the Courts of Justice Act, [20] provide for a general prohibition of cameras in the court. But these provisions permit an exception for educational and instructional purposes with the consent of all parties as well as the judge. This provision (i.e., s. 67 of the Judicature Act) was constitutionally tested in *R. v. Squires*.[21] In that case, the impugned provision was held to be in violation of s. 2 of the Charter but was nonetheless upheld as a "reasonable limit" under s. 1. Leave to appeal to the Supreme Court of Canada was denied. None of the other provinces have similar provisions to those described above and therefore, in all provinces, (including Ontario, subject to the above provisions) the issue of cameras in the court remains a discretionary matter.[22] However, while on the one hand, it might be argued that television provides an openness in court proceedings readily available to all, on the other hand, it is arguable that television in the courtroom could have the effect of detracting from the dignity and decorum to which we have become accustomed.

Clearly, the progress of this development should depend on a careful assessment of the current experiments involving the use of television in our courts with a view to achieving a balance between the desire to attain openness and the desire to protect the important notions of dignity and decorum from the dangers of sensationalism.

THE FUNCTION OF COURTS IN CANADA

Generally speaking, the role of our courts is to provide a fair and just resolution of the various problems and conflicts that are brought before

---

12th November 1984, 28th September 1984, 27th September 1984, 9th March 1984, 27th January 1984 and 13th May 1983.

[19] R.S.O. 1980, c. 223.

[20] R.S.O. 1990, c. C.43.

[21] *R. v. Squires* (1986), 50 C.R. (3d) 320, (*sub nom. R. v. Squires (No. 2)*) 25 C.C.C. (3d) 44, 23 C.R.R. 31 (Ont. Prov. Ct.), affirmed (1989), 69 C.R. (3d) 337 (Ont. Dist. Ct.), affirmed (1992), 11 O.R. (3d) 385, 18 C.R. (4th) 22, 78 C.C.C. (3d) 97, 59 O.A.C. 281, 12 C.R.R. (2d) 193 (C.A.), leave to appeal to S.C.C. refused (1993), 15 O.R. (3d) xvi (note), 25 C.R. (4th) 103n, 83 C.C.C. (3d) vii (note), 16 C.R.R. (2d) 384n, 67 O.A.C. 158n, 164 N.R. 80n (S.C.C.).

[22] This issue also achieved some prominence in Ontario several years ago in respect of the public inquiry into the deaths of infants at Toronto's Hospital for Sick Children (the so-called Grange inquiry). See D. Eisler, "Grange says T.V. coverage could improve court's image", National, February 1986, p. 29. More recently, the Canadian Broadcasting Corporation launched an application to permit the broadcasting of the *Bernardo* trial. This application, however, was refused. Also, the Canadian Bar Association several years ago recommended that a two year trial period be implemented, with strict criteria applied. See *Report of the Canadian Bar Association's Special Committee on Cameras in the Courts*. July, 1987. For some other commentary on this issue, see A.W. Mewett, "Television in the courtroom" (1984), 26 C.L.Q. 385 and L.H. Abugov, "Televising Court Trials in Canada: We Stand on Guard for a Legal Apocalypse" (1979), 5 Dal. L.J., 694.

them. The attainment of justice, through the instrumentality of fair and impartial proceedings, defines the essential nature of the function of our system of courts in Canada. Indeed, if all the lawyers in Canada were canvassed as to what views, if any, they all had in common, probably only one view would emerge: that procedural fairness is essential in the quest for justice.

In terms of resolving particular disputes before the courts, one must view the role of the courts (and, by implication, the role of judges) in terms of providing objective arbitration of particular disputes. However, that definition by itself would probably be insufficient. One would, in addition, have to examine the nature of the process of objective arbitration. Essentially, that process is an exercise in the search for truth. Upon the discovery of the truth, through an application of our rules of procedure and rules of evidence, the courts then exercise a decision-making jurisdiction, after which the appropriate disposition is made.

Broadly speaking, however, there is one final component necessary in order to define the role of courts in the Canadian legal system. That final component is, essentially, the method by which the courts conduct the foregoing search for truth. And that method is in the nature of an application of the rules of procedure and evidence in the context of an adversarial system. In short, our system of judicial decision-making is based on the assumption that the search for truth is best conducted in the context of an adversarial system. Moreover, in resolving particular disputes, it is through the instrumentality of that system that our courts ensure fairness and the attainment of just results.

Mr. Justice Antonio Lamer, a former Chairman of the Law Reform Commission of Canada and now Chief Justice of the Supreme Court of Canada, described the role and function of our courts as providing a "conflict resolution service". In addition, our courts exercise a secondary function: namely the provision of a forum for the dramatic reaffirmation of transgressed societal values. Chief Justice Lamer referred to this as the "dramatization function". Moreover, he indicated that both the conflict resolution and dramatization functions share the following essential characteristics:

1. Adjudicative
2. Authoritative
3. Adversarial
4. Visible, mandatory, official and presided over by a judicial officer
5. Applying predetermined, objective norms

Finally, Chief Justice Lamer described the role exercised by administrative tribunals as arbitrative in nature, possessing the same essential characteristics as listed above.[23]

ARBITRATION AND ADJUDICATION IN THE CONTEXT OF AN ADVERSARIAL SYSTEM

In order to understand the process of judicial decision-making utilized by our courts in resolving disputes, it is necessary first to characterize the process of "adjudication" and, secondly, to examine the nature of the "adversarial system".

Professor Paul Weiler made these remarks concerning the above in a significant article on the process of judicial decision-making:

> The first characteristic of "adjudication" is that it has the function of settling disputes (between private individuals or groups, or the government and the individual). These disputes are not future-oriented debates over general policy questions, although, as we shall see, the latter can enter into the final resolution of the problem. Rather, the disputes which are necessary to set the process of adjudication in motion involve "controversies" arising out of a particular line of conduct which causes a collision of specific interests. There is no *logical* or *factual* necessity about this proposition. There can be exceptions and the question of defining the limits of the adjudicative function can be difficult and debatable in the marginal areas.
>
> The legal problems presented to adjudication can be at least several degrees removed from a purely private and concrete dispute. At the other extreme is the decision of a court, completely on its own motion, to issue a statement establishing or changing an existing rule of law, with no argument of counsel at all. This is rare, but not unheard of, as is shown by the recent example of the House of Lords overruling the *London Street Tramways* rule of the inviolability of its own precedents. Much more common is the use by the court of an opinion disposing of a particular dispute to issue general statements about the law that are not absolutely "necessary" for the decision. Intermediate between these two is the case of the advisory opinion, where the court is asked for its opinion on the constitutional legality of proposed legislation.[24]

In addition, Professor Weiler points out that, on occasion, the function of courts is to exercise a role which is different from adjudication. In this connection, he refers to the process of "mediation".

> Not all modes of settling specific, concrete, "private" disputes can be characterized as adjudication, though. Another possible technique is that of "mediation". Essentially, this process is designed to induce an agreement of the parties as to the specific type of settlement which is preferable in the interests of each at the time of settlement. By contrast, adjudication results in an authoritative settlement which is imposed on one (or both) of the parties whatever be his attitude toward it. Not all authoritative settlements can be properly attributed to adjudication, especially those which purport to be nothing more than the fiat of one who wields "legitimated power" because of his position in a hierarchical system (nor, by the way, those that proceed from chance, as the throw of the dice). Although this conclusion might be obvious, it has an interesting corollary for the exercise by the decision-maker of a type of managerial or discretionary function.

---

[23] "Are We Over-judicialized", address delivered to the Canadian Institute for the Administration of Justice, 18th February 1977.

[24] Two Models of Judicial Decision-Making (1968), 46 Can. Bar Rev. 406 at 410.

Why this type of forward-looking disposition of the problem (which shifts values between the parties in the light of society's best future interests) is inconsistent with adjudication can only be seen by considering the "adversary" nature of the latter.[25]

Finally, Professor Weiler characterizes the adversarial process in the following way:

An adversary process is one which satisfies, more or less, this factual description: as a prelude to the dispute being solved, the interested parties have the opportunity of adducing evidence (or proof) and making arguments to a disinterested and impartial arbiter who decides the case on the basis of this evidence and these arguments. This is by contrast with the public processes of decision by "legitimated power" and "mediation agreement", where the guaranteed private modes of participation are voting and negotiation respectively. Adjudication is distinctive because it guarantees to each of the parties who are affected the right to prepare for themselves the representations on the basis of which their dispute is to be resolved.

This is the minimum descriptive content of adjudication as an adversary institution.[26]

EFFECTIVENESS OF OUR SYSTEM OF COURTS — THE IMPORTANCE OF SCRUTINY AND RESPONSIVENESS

However one defines the adversarial system, and the process by which the courts conduct their arbitrative and adjudicative functions, the key issue is whether the Canadian model, in fact, "works". Indeed, the search for a definition or a universal description of the Canadian model of judicial decision-making is more or less in the nature of an academic exercise, because, first, among judges themselves, there is no uniformity of opinion as to their role and function, and secondly, because a definition is unimportant; what is important is whether our system "works".

For a judicial system to "work", it must be able to successfully achieve the objectives of that system. In Canada, it is doubtful that members of the legal profession, including both judges and lawyers, as well as members of the public at large, share a uniformity of opinion as to what these objectives are. However, at the very least, most Canadians would presumably agree that as a fundamental objective of the Canadian legal system, our courts must entertain a search for truth, and that that search for truth must be conducted in a manner and with the result that might, broadly speaking, be characterized as the dispensation of justice. In turn, the dispensation of justice must not only be directed at those persons appearing before our courts, but also at the same time it must be directed to the best interests of society at large. This rather broad and generic description of the fundamental objectives underlying the process of judicial decision-making in Canada is set out to assist in the answering of that basic, but vitally important, question raised above. Does the Canadian

---

[25] *Ibid.*, pp. 411-412.
[26] *Ibid.*, p. 412.

legal system "work"? In other words, is our system successful in achieving the fundamental objectives set out above?

Clearly, no system can be perfect. It is important, however, to ensure that those persons who are involved with the Canadian legal system, namely, judges, lawyers, law reformers, law teachers, legislators, the press and members of the public at large, always strive for the achievement of perfection. Moreover, those persons ought to subject the Canadian legal system to continual scrutiny, periodic review and, where advisable, necessary reform. Continual scrutiny of the Canadian legal system by all those connected with it probably provides the best safeguard in ensuring that the legal system successfully achieves its fundamental objectives.

Generally speaking, most observers would agree that our legal system is successful in achieving its basic objectives. However, in order to ensure that our legal system maintains its effectiveness in accomplishing these objectives, and in order to maintain its integrity as a vital institution in Canadian society, the legal system must not fall prey to two dangers. Judges, lawyers and judicial administrators should not react negatively to the scrutiny suggested above. Indeed, they must themselves take an active part in the conduct of that scrutiny. For example, the chief judges and chief justices of the various benches in several provinces have recently taken an active role in reducing the problem of a large backlog of cases. On the theory that justice delayed is justice denied, these chief judges and chief justices have, often upon their own initiative, taken the necessary measures in order to solve or, at the very least, reduce this particular problem. And indeed, many of these chief judges and chief justices have been quite successful in reducing the backlog.[27]

Over the past few years, this backlog has led to a number of cases under the Canadian Charter of Rights and Freedoms. In particular, it has led to a number of challenges under s.11(b) of the Charter. Section 11(b) provides that:

---

[27] One issue of some controversy relates to whether the function of judicial administration should remain in the hands of the chief judge or chief justice of every bench in Canada, or alternatively, whether that function should reside in the hands of professionally trained court administrators. Generally speaking, the response of the courts to this suggestion of reform has been somewhat negative. The reason, however, does not relate to any notion of responsiveness or lack thereof, but rather, is related to a serious and fundamental concern on the part of our courts. Specifically, that concern is that a withdrawal of the judicial administrative function into the hands of a civil servant might effectively do harm to the notion of judicial independence. Given the importance of judicial independence from government, the argument against a withdrawal of the judicial administrative function to specialized personnel is a compelling one. However, the controversy still continues. See G.D. Watson, "The Judge and Court Administration" in A.M. Linden (ed.), *The Canadian Judiciary* (Toronto: Osgoode Hall, 1976), p. 163; Perry S. Millar and C. Baar, *Judicial Administration in Canada* (Kingston: McGill-Queen's University Press, 1981); and J. Deschênes C.J., *Masters in Their Own House* (Ottawa: Canadian Judicial Council, 1981).

any person charged with an offence has the right...
(b) to be tried within a reasonable time.

The two leading cases in this regard are *R. v. Askov*, [1990] 2 S.C.R. 1199, 75 O.R. (2d) 673, 79 C.R. (3d) 273, 59 C.C.C. (3d) 449, 49 C.R.R. 1, 74 D.L.R. (4th) 355, 113 N.R. 241, 42 O.A.C. 81, reversing (1987), 60 C.R. (3d) 277, 37 C.C.C. (3d) 289, 33 C.R.R. 319, 22 O.A.C. 299 (C.A.), and *R. v. Morin*, [1992] 1 S.C.R. 771, 12 C.R. (4th) 1, 71 C.C.C. (3d) 1, 134 N.R. 321, 8 C.R.R. (2d) 193, 53 O.A.C. 241.

However, scrutiny of the legal system is not, in itself, sufficient. It is also important for our courts to be responsive to suggestions of possible reform, where those suggestions are well founded and necessary. In order to be responsive, it is necessary that our courts regard themselves as ultimately responsible to society at large. Because our judges occupy a special and unique position in society, there is always the danger that our courts might become somewhat isolated; with isolation, these institutions might also lose touch with the community at large.[28] However, this isolation will not occur if the members of the Canadian judiciary regard our system of courts as not merely components of our legal system, but rather as vital institutions mandated by society to ultimately serve society. With this notion in mind, our courts will possess a character of responsiveness.

Through the instrumentality of scrutiny and responsiveness, the Canadian legal system can continue to be successful in achieving its fundamental objectives and to enjoy the collective trust vested in it by the society at large. Our courts will remain the beneficiaries of the reputation of integrity they have earned, and will continue to command the confidence of all persons in society.[29]

---

[28] Some degree of isolation is, however, necessary. For a further consideration of the constraints of judicial life, see the discussion on the role of the judge set out in Chapter 9.

[29] For some recent journalistic reflections on our courts, see the following sources: (1) On the Supreme Court of Canada, "How top judges came to grips with Charter" [Series: Inside the Supreme Court], Toronto Star, May 20, 1990, May 21, 1990 and May 22, 1990; "The judges: the inner workings of Canada's top court", [Series], Vancouver Sun, April, 11, 1992, April 12, 1992, April 14, 1992; Maclean's Magazine, 11th January 1988 and 12th December 1988; and (2) On the selection of judges, "Supreme Court redone in conservative hues: the way judges are chosen leaves a lot to be desired", The Globe & Mail, April 19, 1990; "Better the devil we don't know: the US method of appointing supreme court justices may not be perfect, but it's a lot better than ours", The Globe & Mail, September 24, 1990; "Canada's senior judges rise to power almost anonymously: as Supreme Court gets more powerful, many argue that Canadians must know more about key players", The Globe & Mail, Oct. 12, 1991; Financial Post, 20th February 1989 and 27th March 1989. For some earlier journalistic thoughts on our courts see: (1) On the Supreme Court of Canada see Maclean's Magazine, 12th February 1979, and (2) On the Canadian legal system, generally, see "Justice in the 1980's", a four-part series appearing in the Toronto Star, 8th-11th February 1982.

CANADIAN COURTS AS INSTITUTIONS IN SOCIETY

In the above section of this chapter, reference was made to two important notions. First, it was suggested that our courts are not only components of the legal system, but also they are, at the same time, vital and independent institutions in society at large. Secondly, it was also suggested that in order for our courts to effectively achieve their fundamental objectives, they must possess the confidence and trust of the members of society. In order to enjoy this confidence and trust, our courts must possess a reputation of the highest integrity.

The importance of the first notion relates to the role and responsibility of courts in society. Society must regard our system of courts and the courts must regard themselves as mandated by society, concerned with the interests of society, and as ultimately responsible and accountable to society. The importance of the second notion relates to fundamental considerations of power and authority. Persons in authority are only able to exercise power over those that they govern, without force, if they enjoy the trust and confidence of those that they govern. This is true of the relationship between parent and child, teacher and student, employer and employee, politician and constituent, and others. It is also true of our courts in relation to all members of society, whose lives and affairs our courts govern. In order to gain that trust our courts must be regarded by all as singularly vital and independent institutions possessing the utmost of integrity. Traditionally, our courts have always enjoyed the prestige they deserve, largely owing to the nature of the important functions that they exercise. In addition, our courts have earned an added measure of integrity through their just exercise of the judicial decision-making process. Built into that decision-making process are certain devices which ensure the preservation of the integrity of our courts. The most important device is the power of the court to find a person in contempt of court in certain circumstances. This power is, essentially, the method by which our courts ensure the respect of those persons appearing before them.[30] The engendering of respect in this way contributes to the maintenance of the integrity of our courts as vital institutions in society.

---

[30] There is, in law, more than one type of contempt; and, in addition, there is more than one type of circumstance in which a person could be found in contempt. With respect to the latter, a person need not appear in court to be in contempt of court. For example, the reader might recall the so-called "judges affair", where a cabinet minister was found guilty of contempt of court arising out of intemperate criticism by the cabinet minister of a decision in a case, adjudicated following an investigation conducted by his department. Also, a violation of the terms of certain types of orders issued by a court constitutes a contempt of court. For example, the violation of a prohibition order under the Competition Act, R.S.C. 1985, c. C-34, is, essentially, in the nature of a contempt of court.

ALTERNATIVE DISPUTE RESOLUTION MECHANISMS (A.D.R.)

Recently, there has developed a trend toward the resolution of certain kinds of disputes outside the normal and formal courtroom setting. From the popular television program, "People's Court" to the establishment of a "Private Court" in Metropolitan Toronto, this new development has taken several forms. Essentially, whatever the form, they are all variations of a basic model of arbitration where parties submit their competing claims to an independent, non-governmental tribunal and agree by contract to be bound by the tribunal's decision. There are, of course, differences from model to model but essentially they share many common elements. Although relatively new in Canada, the alternative dispute resolution movement is well advanced in the United States. In fact, there are associations and publications that have arisen around alternative dispute resolution and, moreover, many former judges, some retired and some having left the judiciary, fill positions in these various bodies.[31]

Essentially, there are six kinds of alternative dispute resolution forms and functions. They are as follows:

    (1) negotiation
    (2) conciliation
    (3) mediation
    (4) arbitration
    (5) hybrid alternative mechanisms
        (i) "rent-a-judge"
        (ii) mediation–arbitration
        (iii) "mini-trial"
        (iv) neighbourhood/community justice movement
    (6) diversion of cases out of the court system.

CONCLUSIONS

If one were to list the three most important institutions in society, that list would contain, broadly speaking, our legislative bodies, our bureaucracies and our courts. But if one were to ask upon which of these institutions we must rely in the event of disputes between legislative bodies, between a citizen and the bureaucracy, and between citizen and citizen,

---

[31] The University of Alberta has recently established the John V. Decore Alternative Dispute Resolution Centre in the Faculty of Law as a formal component in its legal education and public service delivery program. The A.D.R. concept has other applications as well. For example, in Edmonton, in lieu of the formal criminal justice process in minor offences, the Crown and accused, in certain circumstances, are able to participate in the Victim Offender Mediation Project.

the answer would, of course, be our courts. Our system of courts is not only a fundamental component of the Canadian legal system; it is also an important and independent institution within society. Indeed, given the special importance in the event of disputes arising between the other major institutions in society, our system of courts must be regarded as no less than an essential structural component of society itself.

In this chapter, we have examined the Canadian system of courts on a somewhat general level. In the next chapter, we will examine the hierarchy of the various courts in Canada and discuss the specific functions exercised by each of those courts.

SELECTED BIBLIOGRAPHY ON ALTERNATIVE
DISPUTE RESOLUTION MECHANISMS[32]

*The 1986 Isaac Pitblado Lectures on Alternative Dispute Resolution —
Emerging Mechanisms and Professional Responsibilities in Dispute
Resolution.* (Winnipeg: University of Manitoba, November 1986).

Abella, Rosalie S. "Towards Judicialization or Dejudicialization". (1988), 22 Law Soc. Gazette 220.

Ackerman, Robert M. "Defamation and Alternative Dispute Resolution: Healing the Sting". [1986] Missouri J. of Dispute Resolution 1.

*ADR: A Practical Guide to Resolve Construction Disputes: Alternative
Dispute Resolution in the Construction Field.* (Dubuque, Iowa: Kendall/Hunt Pub., 1994).

"Alternative Dispute Resolution: A Special Issue". (January 1988), 51 Texas Bar J. 14.

*Alternative Dispute Resolution 1990 = Le reglement des conflits parallele
1990.* Toronto: The Standing Committee on the Administration of Justice, 1990.

"Alternative Dispute Resolution: A Symposium". (1984), 29 Villanova L. Rev. 1219.

Alternative Dispute Resolution: An ADR Primer. 3rd ed. (Chicago: ABA Standing Committee on Dispute Resolution, 1989).

"Alternative Dispute Resolution and the Courts". (Febuary/March 1986), 69 Judicature 252.

"Alternative Dispute Resolution and Siting of Hazardous Waste Facilities: The Pennsylvania Proposal in Light of the Wisconsin and Massachusetts Statutes". (Summer 1986), 5 Temple Environmental Law & Technology Journal 58.

---

[32] The author wishes to gratefully acknowledge the work of the Alberta Law Reform Institute in the preparation of a significant part of this selected bibliography.

Alternative Dispute Resolution: Bane or Boon to Attorneys? Panel discussion series. Topic 1-1982. (Chicago: ABA Special Committee on Alternative Means of Dispute Resolution, 1982).

Alternative Dispute Resolution: A Handbook for Judges. 2nd ed. (Washington, D.C.: American Bar Association Standing Committee on Dispute Resolution, Public Service Division, Governmental Affairs Group, 1991).

Alternative Dispute Resolution in Action in Canada = La practique au Canada des solutions de rechange au reglement des conflits (Ottawa: n.p., 1991).

"Alternative Dispute Resolution in Farmer Lender Disputes: Mandatory Mediation in Minnesota". (January 1988), 5 Law & Inequality 487.

"Alternative Dispute Resolution in the Law Curriculum". (June 1984), 34 J. Leg. Educ. 229.

"Alternative Dispute Resolution in the University Community: The Power and Presence of the American Association of University Professors (AAUP)". (1988), 3 Ohio State J. of Dispute Resolution 437.

Alternative Dispute Resolution: Practice and Perspectives. B.N.A. Special Report. (Washington, D.C.: Bureau of National Affairs, 1990).

"The Alternative Dispute Resolution Promotion Act of 1986: A Critical Analysis". (1987), 31 Saint Louis U.L.J. 981.

"Alternative Dispute Resolution Symposium". (Winter 1985), 37 U. Fla. L. Rev. 1.

"Alternative Dispute Resolution Techniques". (1984), 53 Antitrust L.J. 271.

Alternative Dispute Resolution: Training and Accreditation of Mediators. (Sydney: New South Wales Law Reform Commission, 1991).

Alternative Dispute Resolution: What's all the Fuss and Where is it Going? (Toronto: Canadian Bar Association — Ontario Continuing Legal Education, 1988).

"Alternative Methods of Dispute Resolution". (1986), 65 Michigan Bar J. 875.

Alternatives: The Report of the Dispute Resolution Subcommittee (Toronto: Law Society of Upper Canada, 1993).

Alvarez, Henri C. "The Role of Arbitration in Canada — New Perspectives". (1987), 21 U.B.C.L. Rev. 247.

Arbitration Canada. "ADR Vital, Says Judge". (April 1989), 2:2 Arbitration Canada.

Arbitration Canada. "Dispute Resolution Saves Business Millions". (Summer 1988), 1:4 Arbitration Canada.

Bacigal, Ronald J. "An Empirical Case Study of Informal Alternative Dispute Resolution". (1988), 4 Ohio State J. on Dispute Resolution 1.

Banks, Robert S. "Alternative Dispute Resolution: A Return to Basics". (1987), 61 Aust. L.J. 569.

Barnette, Curtis H. "The Importance of Alternative Dispute Resolution: Reducing Litigation Costs as a Corporate Objective". (1984), 53 Antitrust L.J. 277.

Bevan, Alexander H. *Alternative Dispute Resolution: A Lawyer's Guide to Mediation and Other Forms of Dispute Resolution.* (London: Sweet & Maxwell, 1992).

Blair, Robert A. "Ontario Courts Test Court-based ADR" (edited remarks delivered at a colloquium held at the University of Toronto Law School on Dec. 8, 1993) (January 1994) 3 Can. Corp. Counsel 51-54.

Bradley, James (Honourable). "Environmental Mediation in Windsor and Essex". (1986), 2 Can. Environmental Mediation Newsletter 1.

Branson, C.O.C. "A View from the Centre [British Columbia International Commercial Arbitration Centre]" (November 1993) 51 Advocate (Van.) 383-385; (September 1993) 701-703; (May 1994) 52 Advocate (Van.) 383-385.

Brazil, Wayne D., Michael A. Kahn, Jefferey P. Newman, and Judith Z. Gold. "Early Neutral Evaluation: an Experimental Effort to Expedite Dispute Resolution". (1986), 69 Judicature 279.

"The California Rent-a-Judge Experiment: Constitutional and Policy Considerations of Pay-as-You-Go-Courts". (1981), 94 Harvard L. Rev. 1592.

Carbonneau, Thomas E. *Alternative Dispute Resolution: Melting the Lances and Dismounting the Steeds.* (Urbana: University of Illinois Press, 1989).

Carrington, Paul D. "Civil Procedure and Alternative Dispute Resolution". (June 1984), 34 J. Leg. Educ. 298.

Collins, Sean. " 'Private Court' Can Speed Resolution of Family Law Disputes, Organizers Say". (June 1988), National.

Consumer Dispute Resolution: Exploring the Alternatives (Chicago: American Bar Association, Special Committee on Alternative Dispute Resolution, Public Services Group, U.S. Dept. of Consumer Affairs, National Association of Consumer Agency Administrators, 1983).

Cooley, J. "Arbitration v. Mediation — Explaining the Differences". (1986), 69 Judicature 264.

Coughlan, Stephen G., "The 'Adversary System': Rhetoric or Reality?" (Fall 1993) 8 Can. J. L. & Soc. 139-170.

Craver, Charles B. *Effective Legal Negotiation and Settlement.* 2nd ed. (Charlottesville, Virginia: Michie Co., 1993).

Davidson, Paul. "Dispute Settlement in Commercial Law Matters". (1982-83), 7 Can. Bus. L.J. 197.

Delgado, Richard, and Chris Dunn. "Fairness and Formality: Minimizing the Risk of Prejudice in Alternative Dispute Resolution". (1985), Wis. L. Rev. 1359.

Dispute Resolution: A Directory of Methods, Projects and Resources, Research paper no. 19 (Edmonton: Alberta Law Reform Institute, 1990).

Dispute Resolution Program Directory. (Washington, D.C.: ABA Special Committee on Alternative Means of Dispute Resolution, 1980).

"Dispute Resolution: A Symposium". (1988), 37 U.N.B.L.J. 75.

Dittenhoffer, Tony, and Richard V. Ericson. "The Victim/Offender Reconciliation Program: A Message to Correctional Reformers". (1983), 33 U.T.L.J. 315.

Dore, Karl J. "The Rentalsman as an Alternative to the Courts in Landlord and Tenant Dispute Resolution". (1988), 37 U.N.B.L.J. 146.

Doyle, Stephen Patrick and Roger Silve Haydock. *Without the Punches: Resolving Disputes without Litigation.* Minneapolis: Equilaw, 1991).

A Drafter's Guide to Alternative Dispute Resolution. (Chicago: American Bar Association, 1991).

Dunn, Richard D. "Mediation — A Viable Method of Alternative Dispute Resolution". (1986), 65 Michigan Bar J. 894.

Effective Dispute Resolution, New Horizons. (Edmonton: Legal Education Society of Alberta, 1991).

Foskett, David Q.C. *The Law and Practice of Compromise.* 3rd ed. (London: Sweet & Maxwell, 1991).

Fulton, Maxwell J. *Commercial Alternative Dispute Resolution* (Sydney: Law Book Co., 1989).

Galanter, Marc. "The Emergence of the Judge as a Mediator in Civil Cases". (1986), 69 Judicature 256.

Gilkey, Roderick. "Alternative Dispute Resolution: Hazardous or Helpful?" (Spring 1987), 36 Emory L.J. 575.

Grygier, Tadeusz. "Crime Prevention by Conflict Resolution", (1994) 10 *Jus. Report* No. 1, 7-9.

Guidance on the Use of Alternative Dispute Resolution in EPA Enforcement Cases. (Washington, D.C.: U.S. Environmental Protectionedit Agency, 1987).

Handbook on Alternatives for Dispute Resolution. (American College of Trial Lawyers, 1991).

Kahneman, Daniel. *Conflict Resolution: A Cognitive Perspective.* Legal Theory Workshop W.S. 1992-93 (11) (Toronto: University of Toronto, Faculty of Law, 1993).

Kanowitz, Leo. "Alternative Dispute Resolution and the Public Interest". (1986/87), 38 Hastings L.J. 239.

Keegan, Judith M. "The Peacemakers: Biblical Conflict Resolution and Reconciliation as a Model Alternative to Litigation". (1987), Missouri J. of Dispute Resolution 11.

Lambros, T. "Summary Jury Trial — An Alternative Method of Dispute Resolution". (1986), 69 Judicature 286.

Languedoc, Colin. "Mediation is the Message: Why C.A.'s Can Resolve Disputes more Creatively than the Courts". (February 1993) 126 C.A. Mag. No. 2, 32-35.

Linden, Allen M. (Mr. Justice). "In Praise of Settlement: Towards Cooperation, Away from Confrontation". (1984), 7 Can. Community L.J. 9.

Lover, John G. *Alternative Dispute Resolution for the Community: An Annotated Bibliography.* (Victoria, B.C.: UVic Institute for Dispute Resolution, 1990).

Lowry, M.J. "Law School Socialization and the Perversion of Mediation in the United States". (1983), 3 Windsor Yearbook of Access to Justice 245.

Lynch, Hon. Eugene F., *et al. Negotiation and Settlement.* (New York: Lawyers Cooperative Publishing, 1992).

Makin, Kirk. "Toronto Rent-A-Judge Firm Founded by Group of Leading Civil Lawyers". (Thursday, May 19, 1988), 43 The Globe & Mail 198.

Marks, Jonathan B. "An Overview of Alternative Dispute Resolution Techniques, Successes and Obstacles". (1984), 53 Antitrust L.J. 283.

Mazurak, Stephen A. "Alternative Dispute Resolution of Employment Claims: Exclusivity, Exhaustion and Preclusion". (Summer 1987), 64 U. of Detroit L. Rev. 623.

Mirsky, Ellis R., chairman. *Dispute Resolution Alternatives Supercourse.* (New York: Practising Law Institute, 1993).

Nagel, Stuart S. *Multi-Criteria Methods for Alternative Dispute Resolution, with Microcomputer Software Application.* (New York: Quorum Books, 1990).

New Zealand's Waitangi Tribunal: An Alternative Dispute Resolute Mechanism. (Ottawa: Canadian Bar Association, 1986).

Osborne, B. "The Pre-Trial and Dispute Resolution". *Continuing Legal Education, Practical Approaches to Dispute Resolution* (Can. Bar Assn., 1986).

Pearson, B. "An Evaluation of Alternatives to Court Adjudication". (1982), 7 Justice System J. 420.

Pirie, Andrew J. "The Lawyer as Mediator: Professional Responsibility Problems or Profession Problem?" (1985), 63 Can. Bar Rev. 378.

Portlock, Peter. "Dispute Resolved through Mediation". (May 1994) 18 L. Now, No. 8, 9-12.

Posner, Richard A. "The Summary Jury Trial and Other Methods of Alternative Dispute Resolution: Some Cautionary Observations". (Spring 1986), 53 U. of Chicago L. Rev. 366.

Pounsett, Donald F. "Litigation and Alternative Methods of Dispute Resolution in Canada", (Part 1) (June 1991) 4 Can.-U.S. Trade 33-37 and (Part 2) (July 1991) 4 Can.-U.S. Trade 41-44.

Quan, Judy. *Legal Assistant's Guide to Alternative Dispute Resolution*. (n.l.: Clark Boardman Callaghan, 1994).

"Private Judging: An Effective and Efficient Alternative to the Traditional Court System". (Spring 1987), 21 Valparaiso U.L. Rev. 681.

Raven, Robert D. "Alternative Dispute Resolution: Expanding Opportunities". (June 1988), 43:2 Arbitration Journal 44.

Report of the Canadian Bar Association Task Force on Alternative Dispute Resolution: A Canadian Perspective. (Ottawa: C.B.A., 1989).

Rosenberg, M. "QUERY: Can Court-Related Alternatives Improve Our Dispute Resolution System". (1986), 69 Judicature 254.

Roth, Bette J., Randall W. Wuluff, and Charles A. Cooper (eds.). *The Alternative Dispute Resolution Practice Guide*. (New York: Lawyers Co-op, 1993).

Rudin, Jonathon. *Native Alternative Dispute Resolution Systems: The Canadian Future in Light of the American Past*. (Toronto: Ontario Native Council on Justice, 1993).

Scaglion, R. "The Effects of Mediation Styles on Successful Dispute Resolution: the Abelam Case". (1983), 3 Windsor Yearbook of Access to Justice 256.

Sharma, Robin S. "Alternate Dispute Resolution Moves into the '90's". (Febuary 1990) 16 N.S.L. News 61(4).

Shavell, Steven. *Alternative Dispute Resolution, an Economic Analysis*. Law and Economics Workshop W.S. 1992-93 (5) (Toronto: University of Toronto, Faculty of Law, 1992).

Simpson, Stuart. "I Won't See You in Court: Alternate Dispute Resolution Choices" (May 1994) 18 L. Now, No. 8, 6-8.

Solutions de rechange au reglement des conflits. (Saint Foy, Quebec: Presses de l'Universite Laval, 1993).

Sopinka, John. "What can we do to make the current system of Dispute Resolution work better?" [paper presented at a conference held in Cleveland, Ohio, April 12-14, [1991] (1991) 17 *Can.-U.S. L. J.* 519-532.

Stevenson, M., G. Watson, and E. Weissman. "The Impact of Pre-Trial Conferences: An Interim Report on the Ontario Pre-Trial Conference Experiment". (1977), 15 Osgoode Hall L.J. 591.

"Symposium: Alternative Dispute Resolution in Canada — United States Trade Relations". (1988), 40:2 Maine L. Rev. 223.

Tannis, Ernest G. *Alternative Dispute Resolution that Works.* (North York, Ont.: Captus Press, 1989).

Thompson, Claud R., "Disposition Without Trial". (Dec. 1992) 11 Advocates' Soc. J. No. 4 21-25.

Vidmar, Neil. "The Small Claims Court: A Reconceptualization of Disputes and an Empirical Investigation". (1984), 18 Law and Soc. Rev. 515.

Watson, Garry, *et al.* (eds.). *Dispute Resolution and the Civil Litigation Process.* Canadian perspectives on law and the legal process series. (Toronto: Emond Montgomery Publication, 1991).

Whittington, Barbara. *Mediation, Power & Gender: A Critical Review of Selected Readings.* (Victoria, B.C.: U. Vic. Institute for Dispute Resolution, 1992).

Wolman, Frank W. "Arbitration: An Alternative to Litigation." (August 1993) 103 Mun.World No. 8, 18.

Woodman, Gordon R. "The Alternative Law of Alternative Dispute Resolution". (March 1991) 32 Les cahiers de droit 3-31.

Chapter 7

HIERARCHY OF FEDERAL AND PROVINCIAL COURTS AND DIVISION OF RESPONSIBILITY

Thus far, we have examined Canadian courts as vital components of the Canadian legal system and of Canadian society. We have entertained a discussion as to the constitutional basis of judicial authority in Canada, and examined the judiciary in terms of its functions, broadly defined. The present chapter will concern itself with the particular functions exercised by courts at various levels of the judiciary. It is important to realize at the outset that the specific courts each exercise specific functions. While it is true that Canadian courts, generally speaking, exercise a common function (a function characterized in the last chapter as being in the nature of arbitration and/or adjudication), this common function must be defined in terms of specific jurisdictions, depending upon the particular stratum occupied by a given court in the judicial hierarchy. The jurisdictional variations among the various courts relate to distinctions based upon differing monetary jurisdictions, or to jurisdictional limitations based upon various specific areas of the law or to other considerations.

One important consideration, however, is a constitutional limitation imposed upon certain provincial courts. More specifically, those courts constituted by provincial statute with judges provincially appointed cannot, constitutionally, exercise the same or similar functions as those exercised by courts which are constituted by provincial statutes with judges federally appointed. The latter courts are often referred to as "s. 96 courts". These courts are governed by the provisions set out in ss. 96 to 100 of the Constitution Act of 1867. Those provisions were set out earlier in Chapter 5; among other things, they provide for the federal appointment of judges in these particular types of provincially constituted courts.

Specifically, the s. 96 courts are the courts of superior jurisdiction in a province (namely, the supreme court of a province, including both the appellate and trial divisions, and both of those courts in those provinces where the two divisions are constituted as separate courts) and the county or district courts of a province.[1]

On occasion, a provincially constituted court with judges provincially appointed, or a provincially constituted administrative tribunal with a hearing officer provincially appointed, will hear and adjudicate a given matter which arguably falls within the domain of a county or district, or superior court of a province. In this event, the decision of the judge or the hearing officer may be challenged on the basis that the court or tribunal had no jurisdiction to hear the matter, in that such a court or tribunal was exercising a function normally reserved to s. 96 courts. As a result of various constitutional challenges on this basis, the jurisprudence has provided several tests to assist in the determination as to whether a particular function exercised by a court is a s. 96 function.[2]

---

[1] The county or district courts in all provinces where they existed have been merged or amalgamated in recent years with the superior courts of trial jurisdiction. Some time ago, the province of Nova Scotia established a Task Force to examine the province's court system. See The Globe & Mail, 4th January 1990. Regarding the merging of British Columbia's two-tier court system, see the Globe and Mail, 10th May 1989. With respect to possible reform of the criminal courts, see Law Reform Commission of Canada Working Paper No. 59, "Toward a Unified Criminal Court", 1989. See also the further discussion of the merger/amalgamation of the county or district courts at a later point in this chapter.

[2] For a discussion of the various tests enunciated by the courts in determining whether a given matter is reserved to a s. 96 court, see the following leading cases: *Reference re An Act to Amend Chapter 401 of the Revised Statutes, 1989, the Residential Tenancies Act, S.N.S. 1992, c. 31* (1994), 24 Admin. L.R. (2d) 196, (*sub nom. Reference Re Residential Tenancies Act (Nova Scotia)*) 130 N.S.R. (2d) 346, 367 A.P.R. 346, (*sub nom. Reference re: Act to Amend Chapter 401 of the Revised Statutes, 1989, the Residential Tenancies Act (N.S.), s.s. 7, 8 (2)*) 115 D.L.R. (4th) 129 (C.A.); *Chambre des Notaires du Québec c. Haltrecht* (1992), R.J.Q. 947 (C.A.); leave to appeal to S.C.C. refused (*sub nom. Haltrecht v. Chambre des Notaires du Québec*) (1992), 145 N.R. 399 (note), (*sub nom. Haltrecht c. Chambre des Notaires du Québec*) 56 Q.A.C. 104 (note) (C.S.C.) *R. v. L. (B. L.)*, [1991] 1 S.C.R. 285, 119 N.S.R. (2d) 181, 330 A.P.R. 181, (*sub nom. R. v. F. (J.T.)* 62 C.C.C. (3d) 190, 121 N.R. 114, affirming (1989), 90 N.S.R. (2d) 355, 230 A.P.R. 355 (C.A.); *Reference re Adoption Act (Ontario)*, [1938] S.C.R. 398, 71 C.C.C. 110, [1938] 3 D.L.R. 497; *Saskatchewan (Labour Relations Bd.) v. John East Iron Works Ltd.*, [1948] 2 W.W.R. 1055, [1949] A.C. 134, [1948] 4 D.L.R. 673 (P.C.); *Dupont v. Inglis*, [1958] S.C.R. 535, 14 D.L.R. (2d) 417; *Concerned Citizens of British Columbia v. Capital Regional District,* [1980] 6 W.W.R. 193 (S.C.), affirmed [1981] 1 W.W.R. 359, 25 B.C.L.R. 273, 118 D.L.R. (3d) 257, 14 M.P.L.R. 118. (C.A.), reversed [1982] 2 S.C.R. 842, [1983] 2 W.W.R. 481, 141 D.L.R. (3d) 385, 45 N.R. 95; *Reference re Residential Tenancies Act (Ontario)*, [1981] 1 S.C.R. 714, 123 D.L.R. (3d) 554, 37 N.R. 158; *Re First Investors Corp.*, [1988] 4 W.W.R. 22 (*sub nom. Re Associated Investors of Can. Ltd.*), 58 Alta. L.R. (2d) 38, 86 A.R. 126 (Q.B.), affirmed [1988] 5 W.W.R. 65, 59 Alta. L.R. (2d) 334, 52 D.L.R. (4th) 168, 87 A.R. 273 (C.A.); *Citation Industries Ltd. v. C.J.A., Local 1928* (1988), 30 B.C.L.R. (2d) 230 (S.C.), reversed (1988), 33 Admin. L.R. 59, 53 D.L.R. (4th) 360 (C.A.); *Kapoor v. Saskatchewan (Rent Appeal Comm.)*, [1988]

In addition to the above constitutional limitation, the specific functions to be exercised by courts at various levels must be determined by reference to two sources. Often the statute establishing a given court will set out the specific functions reserved for that court. In addition, various other statutes within a jurisdiction might also dictate the functions reserved for a given court. For example, the Federal Court has particular matters reserved to its trial and appellate divisions by virtue of the provisions contained in the Federal Court Act, R.S.C. 1985, c. F-7, and various other federal statutes. A more striking example may be found in connection with the superior court of a province. For instance, a superior court of a province might be given authority to adjudicate particular matters under the provisions of the enabling statute which establishes that court. In addition many particular statutes, both federal and provincial, assign specific functions to the supreme court of every province. Moreover, the Judicature Act and the rules of court or the rules of practice, which are essen-

---

5 W.W.R. 273, 52 D.L.R. (4th) 98, 68 Sask. R. 43 (C.A.), leave to appeal to S.C.C. refused [1988] 4 W.W.R. lxx (note), 57 D.L.R. (4th) viii (note), 102 N.R. 153n (S.C.C.); *R. v. Morgentaler* (1988), 52 O.R. (2d) 353, 48 C.R. (3d) 1, 22 C.C.C. (3d) 353, 17 C.R.R. 223. 22 D.L.R. (4th) 641, 11 O.A.C. 81 (C.A.), reversed [1988] 1 S.C.R. 30, 63 O.R. (2d) 281n, 62 C.R. (3d) 1, 37 C.C.C. (3d) 449 *(sub nom. Morgentaler v. R.)*, 31 C.R.R. 1, 44 D.L.R. (4th) 385, 26 O.A.C. 1, 82 N.R. 1; *R. v. W. (D.A.)*, [1991] 1 S.C.R. 291, 101 N.S.R. (2d) 356, 275 A.P.R. 356, 61 C.C.C. (3d) 574, 121 N.R. 118, affirming (1989), 92 N.S.R. (2d) 92, 237 A.P.R. 92, 49 C.C.C. (3d) 284 (C.A.), reversing (1988), *(sub nom. R. v. W. (D.A.)*; *R. v. C. (C.F.))* 86 N.S.R. (2d) 392, 218 A.P.R. 392, 44 C.C.C. (3d) 138 (T.D.); *Reference re Young Offenders Act (Canada) (sub nom. Reference re Young Offenders Act (P.E.I.))* [1991] 1 S.C.R. 252, 278 A.P.R. 91, 62 C.C.C. (3d) 385, *(sub nom. Reference re Young Offenders Act, s. 2 (P.E.I.))* 77 D.L.R (4th) 492, 89 Nfld. & P.E.I.R. 91, *(sub nom. Reference re Young Offenders Act & Youth Court Judges)* 121 N.R. 81; *Québec (A.G.) v. Grondin; L'atelier 7 Inc. v. Babin*, [1983] 2 S.C.R. 364, 3 Admin. L.R. 267, 4 D.L.R. (4th) 605, 50 N.R. 50; *Smale v. Wintemute*, [1986] 1 W.W.R. 268, 40 Alta. L.R. (2d) 237, 22 D.L.R. (4th) 198, 62 A.R. 369 (C.A.); *Massey-Ferguson Industries Ltd. v. Saskatchewan* [1981] 2 S.C.R. 413, [1981] 6 W.W.R. 596, 127 D.L.R. (3d) 513, 39 N.R. 308; *Nova Scotia (A.G.) v. Gillis* (1980), 39 N.S.R. (2d) 97, 71 A.P.R. 97, 111 D.L.R. (3d) 349 (C.A.); *Jones v. Edmonton Catholic School District No. 7*, [1977] 2 S.C.R. 872, [1976] 6 W.W.R. 336, 1 M.P.L.R. 112, 70 D.L.R. (3d) 1, 11 N.R. 280, 1 A.R. 100; *Crevier v. Québec (A.G.)*, [1981] 2 S.C.R. 220, 127 D.L.R. (3d) 1; 38 N.R. 541; *Séminaire de Chicoutimi v. Québec (A.G.)*, [1973] S.C.R. 681; *Canadian Broadcasting Corp. v. Cordeau*, [1979] 2 S.C.R. 618, 14 C.P.C. 60, 48 C.C.C. (2d) 289, 101 D.L.R. (3d) 24, 28 N.R. 541 *(sub nom. C.B.C. v. Que. Police Comm.)*; *Reference re s. 6 of Family Relations Act (British Columbia)*, [1980] 6 W.W.R. 737, 18 R.F.L. (2d) 17, 23 B.C.L.R. 152, 116 D.L.R. (3d) 221 (C.A), varied [1982] 1 S.C.R. 62, [1982] 3 W.W.R. 1, 26 R.F.L. (2d) 113, 36 B.C.L.R. 1, 40 N.R. 206; *Tomko v. Nova Scotia (Labour Relations Board)*, [1977] 1 S.C.R. 112, 76 C.L.L.C. 14,005, 69 D.L.R. (3d) 250, 14 N.S.R. (2d) 191, 7 N.R. 317 [Fr.], 10 N.R. 35 [Eng.]; *Pepita v. Doukas*, [1980] 1 W.W.R. 240, 16 B.C.L.R. 120, 101 D.L.R. (3d) 577 (C.A.); *C.U.P.E. v. Guelph General Hospital* (1978), 22 O.R. (2d) 348, 13 C.P.C. 206, 93 D.L.R. (3d) 359 (H.C.); *Mississauga (City) v. Peel (Regional Municipality)*, [1979] 2 S.C.R. 244, 9 M.P.L.R. 81, 97 D.L.R. (3d) 439, 26 N.R. 200, 9 O.M.B.R. 129; *Reference re Proposed Legislation Concerning Leased Premises and Tenancy Agreements (sub nom. Re Constitutional Questions Act (Alberta))*, [1978] 6 W.W.R. 152, 7 R.P.R. 104, 11 A.R. 451, 89 D.L.R. (3d) 460 (C.A.); *Re Miramichi Lumber Co.* (1977), 83 D.L.R. (3d) 545, 20 N.B.R. (2d) 35, 34 A.P.R. 35 (C.A.); *Québec (A.G.) v. Farrah*, [1978] 2 S.C.R. 638, 86 D.L.R. (3d) 161, 21 N.R. 595.

CHART 1

THE SYSTEM OF COURTS IN CANADA GENERALLY

A. *Federal Courts — Courts constituted under federal statutes with judges federally appointed.*

Supreme Court of Canada

- The Chief Justice of the Supreme Court is also the Chief Justice of Canada
- Eight Puisne Justices

Federal Court of Canada

- Appellate Division
- Trial Division

Tax Court of Canada

- Replaces Tax Review Board[3]

B. *Provincial Courts — Courts constituted under provincial statutes with judges federally appointed.*

Courts of Superior Jurisdiction of a Province
or the
Supreme Court of a Province

Appellate Division

- This court is often referred to as the Court of Appeal of the province
- The Chief Justice of the Appellate Division is also the Chief Justice of the province

Trial Division

- In some provinces, such as Manitoba, for example, the two divisions here are separate courts constituted by separate statutes, with the trial court known as the Court of Queen's Bench. In turn, the Court of Queen's Bench of Manitoba is itself subdivided into three divisions — the general division, the family division and the surrogate division.
- Often this court is simply referred to as the Supreme Court of the province
- The Chief Justice of this court is properly referred to as the Chief Justice of the Trial Division

NOTE: In the province of Ontario, there is a further subdivision with the creation of the Divisional Court. The Divisional Court has an administrative law jurisdiction in respect of the granting of prerogative remedies. In addition, in December of 1976, the Supreme Court of Ontario was further subdivided to create a family law division. All of this changed in 1990 as the province of Ontario embarked on major court reform. This dramatic initiative will be discussed later in this chapter.

County or District Courts

- In certain circumstances, the District or County Court judges exercise the jurisdiction of local judges of the Supreme Court of a province

Surrogate Courts

- Usually, judges of the County or District Court serve in the capacity of Surrogate Court Judges

NOTE: As indicated elsewhere, most of the provinces have or are about to merge their county or district courts with their superior courts. The result of such an amalgamation is the elimination of an intermediate court of trial jurisdiction with judges who are federally appointed.[4]

---

[3] In 1983, the Tax Review Board was replaced by the Tax Court of Canada. See S.C. 1980-81-82-83, c. 158.

[4] When this occurs, judges of the newly amalgamated court of superior jurisdiction assume the surrogate court responsibilities.

C. *Provincial Courts — Courts constituted under provincial statutes with judges provincially appointed*

Provincial Courts

Youth Court	Family Court	Provincial Court (Criminal Jurisdiction)	Small Claims Court or Civil Division of Provincial Court

NOTE: In some provinces, by the operation of various enabling statutes, two or more of the above courts are combined into a single court, with various divisions. For example, in Ontario the Provincial Court is divided into Family, Criminal and Civil Divisions. Alternatively, some provinces provide concurrent jurisdiction for judges serving on one or more of the above courts to deal with matters arising in another of the above courts. For example, in Alberta, under the Provincial Court Act, R.S.A. 1980, c. P-20, a judge of the Provincial Court has jurisdiction to sit in either, some or all of the criminal, civil, family or youth divisions.[5]

tially regulations under the Judicature Act, also assign specific functions to the superior court. Therefore one must look not only to the enabling statute, but also to all of the regular statutes of both Parliament and the provincial legislature, including, in particular, the Judicature Act of the province and the rules of practice or rules of court, in order to define the jurisdiction of the supreme court of a province.

Prior to studying the various functions assigned to the specific courts, it is useful to know the names of the various courts and where they fall within the judicial hierarchy. Accordingly, set out on the chart "The System of Courts in Canada Generally", *supra* is a diagrammatic representation of all the major courts within the Canadian judicial hierarchy. It is not exhaustive; some minor courts at the municipal level, for example, are not included, and there is no mention of administrative tribunals at either the federal or provincial level. The chart is intended to apply to all of the provinces of Canada, but there are, in reality, significant differences from province to province, some of which are contained in notations in the chart. The reader should appreciate that the court system within a particular province may differ from the general model described.

Because, as indicated earlier, one must look to so many different sources in defining the jurisdiction of particular courts, it is difficult to describe,

---

[5] For the transition from the former juvenile division to the Youth Court, see the Young Offenders Act, S.A. 1984, c. Y-1, s. 38. For the transition from the former small claims division to the new civil division, see the Provincial Court Act, S.A. 1989, c. 18, s. 2, effective January 15, 1990. The monetary jurisdiction of this division was increased from $1,000 to $4,000 in s. 4 (also, effective January 15, 1990) of the same statute.

at least in respect of provincially constituted courts across Canada, the specific functions of those courts. However, the various provincially constituted courts do share certain functions which are common from province to province. Of course, federally constituted courts exercise the same functions uniformly throughout all provinces.

Set out below are several diagrammatic representations defining the functions assigned to each of these courts. On occasion, reference is made in the following diagrams, by way of example, to specific functions assigned to particular courts in the provinces of Ontario, Quebec and Alberta. With the possible exception of the province of Quebec, the various functions described are exercised by similar courts in all provinces. One major difference is, however, the manner in which a particular province constitutes particular courts. For example, one province may constitute its courts of superior jurisdiction with trial and appellate divisions, while another province may establish two separate courts with two enabling statutes. Or, as in the case of Ontario, a province may create a third division of its superior court (namely, in this example, the Divisional Court).[6] One province may constitute its provincial court with criminal, small claims, family and juvenile divisions, while another constitutes those courts as separate entities established under separate enabling statutes. Also, the monetary jurisdictions of the various courts of civil jurisdiction may differ from province to province. Accordingly, the following charts are not intended to be exhaustive, as that would require a detailed examination of all the various statutes which assign particular functions to various courts in all provinces. Rather, they are intended to provide the reader with an appreciation of the types of matters dealt with by the various courts, at all levels of the judiciary, including especially the particular types of matters reserved for s. 96 courts under the Canadian constitution.

From an examination of the following diagrams, one should appreciate the diversity of matters which come before our courts. Judges must decide cases arising out of a multitude of areas of human concern reflected in the many specialized areas of the law. Accordingly, a judge must be thoroughly cognizant of the many areas of the law over which he is given jurisdiction.

---

[6] Reference has already been made to major court reform in Ontario. This will be discussed below.

CHART 2
SUPREME COURT OF CANADA

- The Supreme Court of Canada is the highest court in Canada
- Nine justices: one Chief Justice, who also serves as the Chief Justice of Canada, and eight Puisne Justices, all federally appointed

(a) *Criminal Cases*
- Adjudicates appeals from decisions of the provincial courts of appeal affecting verdict in respect of:
    - (i) indictable offences, with leave, where there has been no dissenting opinion in the court of appeal on questions of law (Criminal Code, Pt. XXI (CC))
    - (ii) indictable offences, without leave, where there has been a dissenting opinion in the court of appeal on questions of law (Criminal Code, Pt. XXI (CC))
    - (iii) summary conviction offences, with leave, on questions of law (Supreme Court Act, s. 40(3)).

(b) *Civil Cases*
- Appeals heard under a 1975 amendment to the Supreme Court Act only if leave is given on any matter of public importance or on an important issue of law or of mixed law and fact
- Cases do not have to involve a sum of money exceeding a set amount

(c) *Reference Jurisdiction*
- Can also give opinions on constitutional and other matters which involve:
    - (a) the interpretation of the Constitution Act
    - (b) the interpretation of federal or provincial legislatures
    - (c) the powers (jurisdiction) of Parliament or the provincial legislatures
    - (d) any matter which is referred to the Supreme Court under the provisions contained in the Supreme Court Act, R.S.C. 1985, c. S-26.

CHART 3
FEDERAL COURT OF CANADA[7]

- Approximately thirty-five federally appointed judges
- One Chief Justice and One Associate Chief Justice

Appeal Division
or Federal Court of Appeal
- Hears appeals from the Trial Division of the Federal Court
- Adjudicates applications to renew and set aside decisions of federal boards, commissions or other tribunals, only on specific grounds
- Determines questions of law, jurisdiction or practice referred by federal boards, commissions or other tribunals
- Adjudicates appeals under various federal Acts others than the Income Tax Act, the Estate Tax Act and the Canadian Citizenship Act

Trial Division
- Exclusive jurisdiction:
    - (a) to hear applications for writs in relation to anyone in the Canadian Armed Forces stationed outside Canada
    - (b) to grant equitable relief against any federal board, commission or other tribunal

---

[7] By Order-in-Council of May 30, 1995 (P.C. 1995-852), on the recommendation of the Minister of Justice, the Governor General in Council requested the Auditor General of Canada
(a) to inquire into
    (i) the possible merger and regionalization of the Trial Division of the Federal Court of Canada and of the Tax Court of Canada, and
    (ii) the possible consolidation of the administrative support services of the Courts; and
(b) to report to the Minister of Justice on the matters referred to in paragraph (a).

(c) to hear matters of copyright, trademark, industrial design and patents of invention
- Original jurisdiction and, unless otherwise provided, exclusive jurisdiction in claims against the Crown
- Residuary jurisdiction:
  (a) where no other Canadian court has jurisdiction
  (b) in matters of Federal Court jurisdiction not specifically assigned to the Federal Court, Appeal Division
- Shares concurrent jurisdiction with other courts over:
  (a) bills of exchange and promissory notes
  (b) aeronautics
  (c) interprovincial works and undertakings
  (d) claims by the Crown or Attorneys General
  (e) actions against an officer or servant of the Crown for acts or omissions committed in carrying out his duty
  (f) admiralty
- Also adjudicates:
  (a) federal-provincial or interprovincial disputes where legislatures agree
  (b) citizenship appeals

CHART 4
TAX COURT OF CANADA[8]

- Approximately twenty-three federally appointed judges
- One Chief Justice and One Associate Chief Justice

- In 1983, the Tax Review Board was replaced by the Tax Court of Canada.
- Hears appeals in respect of assessments made under the Income Tax Act and the Canada Pension Plan Act

CHART 5
OTHER FEDERALLY CONSTITUTED COURTS

- Court Martial Appeal Court of Canada[9]
- Court of Canadian Citizenship [10]

CHART 6
THE PROVINCIAL SUPERIOR OR SUPREME COURTS

- Federally appointed judges

Appellate Division or Court of Appeal
- Appeals from Surrogate Court over a given monetary amount
- Adoption appeals from a District or County Court
- Family matter appeals from the Supreme Court, Trial Division
- Civil matter appeals from District or County Court and Supreme Court, Trial Division
- Appeals of criminal cases
- Appeals of indictable young offenders cases
- Applications for new trials
- All questions or issues of law

[8] *Ibid.*

[9] Judges in this Court are appointed from among existing federally-appointed judges (i.e., from Federal Court judges) and/or from provincial superior court judges.

[10] This Court is really a federal administrative tribunal despite its designation as a 'court'. In any event, the Canadian Citizenship Court is about to be abolished.

CHART 6 — *Continued*

Trial Division or Court of Queen's Bench
- This court has almost unlimited scope
- Indictable offences under s. 469 of the Criminal Code, R.S.C. 1985, c. C-46
- Indictable offences by election (with or without a jury)
- Appeals of summary conviction offences (see s. 812 of the Criminal Code)
- Appeals of summary conviction young offenders cases
- All civil matters over a given monetary amount
- Divorces, judicial separations and guardianships
- Appeals from Family Court
- Administrative law jurisdiction in respect of applications to review and set aside decisions of provincial boards, commissions, etc.

CHART 7
COUNTY OR DISTRICT COURTS[11]

- Federally appointed judges

- Indictable offences by election (with a judge alone or a judge and jury)
- Appeals of summary conviction offences (see ss. 812 and 822 of the Criminal Code)
- All civil matters within a given monetary jurisdiction
- All appeals from Provincial Court (Civil Division)

SURROGATE COURTS[12]

- Federally appointed judges

- Testamentary matters and causes
- Issues and revokes grants of probate and administration[13]
- Appoints, controls or removes guardians
- Determining entitlements to succession

---

[11] This chart is relevant only historically, as every province that had a county or district court has abolished or merged it with the provincial trial division of superior jurisdiction or separate trial court of superior jurisdiction. The main reason for these mergers was related to a desire to streamline the court system since both of the merged courts were largely serving in overlapping capacities. The three most recent mergers occurred in British Columbia (see Supreme Court Act, S.B.C. 1989, c. 40), Nova Scotia (see Provincial Court Act, S.N.S. 1992, c. 16) and Saskatchewan (see S.S. 1992, c. 62).

[12] In the past, surrogate court responsibilities were exercised by the county or district courts. The same judges would, in respect of a surrogate matter, be designated as surrogate court judges and, in respect of other matters, would be designated as county or district court judges. Procedurally, in respect of surrogate matters, separate forms would have to be filed by lawyers appearing before them. Upon the elimination/merger/amalgamation of the county or district courts, either the new merged court assumed the former surrogate responsibilities, either as provincial superior court judges serving in surrogate capacities or as provincial superior court judges exercising a new, expanded jurisdiction. For example, the province of Ontario has abolished the Surrogate Court and has assigned the former surrogate responsibilities to its new Ontario Court of Justice (General Division) as part of the responsibilities of the newer court and not as a separate and distinct jurisdiction. In other words, the General Division has simply absorbed the responsibilities of the former Surrogate Court.

[13] In a move toward the usage of plain language in the law, Ontario, for example, as of January 1, 1995 has replaced the terms 'probate' and 'administration' with the issuance of a 'Certificate of Appointment of Estate Trustee' ('with a will' or 'without a will').

CHART 8

PROVINCIAL COURTS

• Provincially appointed judges

Youth Court or Provincial Court (Youth Division)
• The judges for this court are appointed from any judges in the province • Jurisdiction covers cases involving the Child Welfare Act, neglected children and young offenders under the Young Offenders Act, R.S.C. 1985, c.Y-1[14]

Family Court[15] or Provincial Court (Family Division)
• Maintenance and custody under provincial statutes • Some offences under the Criminal Code (for example, assault of a spouse or a child) • Matters relating to children such as adoption and guardianship

Provincial Court (Criminal Division)
• All summary conviction offences • Indictable offences under s. 553 of the Criminal Code • Indictable offences by election • All preliminary hearings • offences under provincial statutes

Small Claims Court or Provincial Court (Civil Division)

• Statutory and monetary jurisdiction differs for each province
• For example, in Alberta the Provincial Court (Civil Division)
    (a) Is part of the Provincial Court
    (b) Handles claims for debt not exceeding $4,000 and for damages not exceeding $4,000 and for counterclaims for the same amounts
    (c) Does not have jurisdiction in cases involving title to land, devise, bequest or limitation, malicious prosecution, false imprisonment, defamation, criminal conversation, seduction or breach of promise of marriage, replevin, action against a magistrate, or the recovery of taxes
• By contrast, in Ontario the court has small claims jurisdiction up to $6,000[16]
• In both Ontario and Alberta, although the parties may be represented by lawyers, they need not be
• In British Columbia, the monetary limit for a civil claim has recently been increased to $10,000
• In Quebec, claims may not exceed $1,000

---

[14] See footnote 5, *supra*. The most recent example of the provincial response to the federal Young Offenders Act, R.S.C. 1985 c. Y-1, was in New Brunswick where the provincial court was designated as a youth court for the purpose of the complementary federal legislation. See Provincial Court Act, S.N.B. 1991, c. 18.

[15] Several provinces have adopted a unified family court system in which all matters relating to the family, including divorce, are heard by superior court judges.

[16] O. Reg. 92/93.

CHART 9
QUEBEC COURT SYSTEM

- Provincial court constituted under provincial statutes
- Judges federally appointed
- This court has jurisdiction to hear both civil and criminal cases on appeal

---

Superior Court

- Provincial court constituted under provincial statutes
- Judges federally appointed
- This court has some civil jurisdiction
- Adjudicates appeals under Pt. XXVII of the Criminal Code

PROVINCIAL COURTS

Court of Quebec

- Comprising what was formerly known as Provincial Court, Court of the Sessions of the Peace, Small Claims Court and Youth Court
- Judges provincially appointed
- Divided into Montreal regional section for the western part of the province and Quebec regional section for the eastern part of the province
- Each regional section consists of three divisions: Civil Division; Criminal and Penal Division; and Youth Division
- There is also an Expropriation Division set up under the Expropriation Act
- Civil Division hears cases where amount in dispute is less than $15,000, but not applications for support or those reserved for the Federal Court of Canada
- Small Claims Division of Civil Division deals with claims for $1,000 or less. Parties are to appear without representation of a lawyer unless case is complex and representation is authorized
- Criminal and Penal Division deals with criminal offences reserved for jurisdiction of Court of Quebec and offences which are not within exclusive jurisdiction of the Superior Court where the accused has elected the matter to be heard in the Criminal and Penal Division. Also has jurisdiction in penal matters for offences against provincial and federal statutes
- Youth Division adjudicates in adoption cases and under the Youth Protection Act and hears cases in first instance in criminal and penal matters where accused is under 18 years of age

---

Municipal Courts

- Provincial courts constituted under provincial statutes
- Judges provincially appointed

MAJOR COURT REFORM IN THE PROVINCE OF ONTARIO

Many provinces have undergone changes to their judicial systems over the past decade. Reference, for example, was made earlier in this chapter to the merger or amalgamation of county or district and superior courts in every province. The province of Ontario, however, had conceived of the most far-reaching and dramatic reform that has occurred in any province since Confederation.

In 1986, Mr. Justice Thomas Zuber of the Ontario Court of Appeal was appointed to conduct a major study of the Ontario Court system. The study, like others before it, was prompted by the necessity of improving the administration of justice and particularly by the need to address the continuing problems of escalating costs and long delays in our court system, which are generally recognized as the two main impediments to access to justice in our legal system. In any event, Mr. Justice Zuber looked at Ontario's present court structure, with the objective of making recommendations to improve the availability and quality of justice to all residents of Ontario. In 1987, Mr. Justice Zuber released his report. On 1st May 1989, the Honourable Ian Scott, the Attorney General of Ontario, introduced into the Ontario legislature Bill 2, An Act to amend the Courts of Justice Act, 1984. Its purpose was to reform and improve Ontario's trial court system. The Bill, although taking into account some of Mr. Justice Zuber's recommendations, went much further than the Zuber report. Its main feature was the establishment of a unified trial court structure. The proposal was based on three underlying principles. It envisaged a regional, as opposed to a centralized, structure. It contemplated a single trial court eventually, with the judges of that single court dealing with matters now within the jurisdiction of the district[17] and superior courts on one hand, as well as the provincial courts on the other. The third principle was to ensure an efficient and co-operative management of the new system.

The change was brought about in two phases. Phase I, the details of which were contained in Bill 2, an amendment to the Courts of Justice Act[18], was implemented in 1990. It established the new Ontario Court of Justice, a court containing two divisions. One division is the General Division (including the Small Claims Court). The other division is the Provincial Division (which, in turn is subdivided into Family and Criminal subdivisions). The Unified Family Court still remains as a separate court after Phase I was completed. In essence, the major part of the change

---

[17] In the mid-1980's, Ontario changed its existing system of having both County and District courts to a system where all judges of those courts became judges of a single District Court for all of Ontario.

[18] An Act to Amend the Courts of Justice Act, 1984, S.O. 1989, c. 55.

PROPOSED RE-STRUCTURING OF ONTARIO TRIAL COURTS

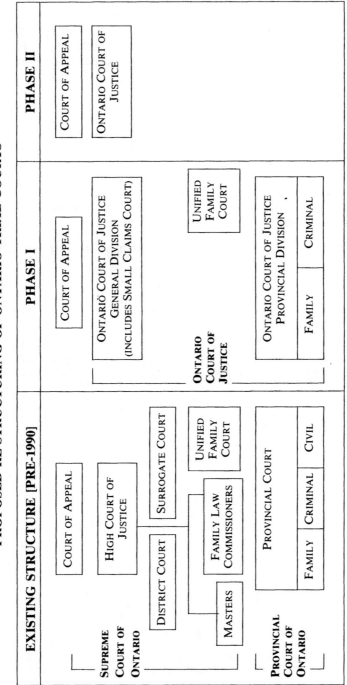

was really no more than the merger or amalgamation of s. 96 trial judges into a single court, a change that has occurred in most provinces. However, what is truly dramatic is Phase II, which merges all Ontario trial courts into a single court. Essentially, it amalgamates the General and Provincial Divisions of the Ontario Court of Justice established in Phase I into a single, one-level trial court that will be functionally divided for criminal, family and civil cases.

Phase II, however, cannot occur without constitutional amendment or, at the very least, without a large measure of federal-provincial co-operation. It will likely require years of discussion and negotiation before it reaches fruition.

Set out above is a chart prepared by the Government of Ontario, in advance of the implementation of Phase I, illustrating, in summary form, the proposed changes to the Ontario court system.[19]

Some recent articles related to court reform are set out as follows:

Baar, C., "The Zuber Report: The Decline and Fall of Court Reform in Ontario", [1988] 8 Windsor Yearbook Access Justice 105.

"Better Access to Justice by Unification of the Courts; A Necessary Solution" (1993), 17 Provincial Judges Journal 3:9.

McDonald, D.C., "Comments on Proposals for a Single Trial Court in the Canadian Provinces", (1991), 15 Provincial Judges Journal 1:21.

Mewett, A.W., "A Unified Criminal Court" (editorial) (1990), 32 Criminal L.Q. 401.

Meyers, R., "Family Violence Court of Manitoba", (1991), 15 Provincial Judges Journal 2:6.

Scott, I., "Court Reform in Ontario", (1989), 13 Provincial Judges Journal 2:10.

THE MILITARY JUSTICE SYSTEM

Recent events in respect of Canadian peacekeeping troops in Somalia have focused public attention on Canada's military justice system. It is appropriate, therefore, to outline, in summary form, some of the key elements of that system.

The relevant legislation falls within federal jurisdiction under the

---

[19] As of mid-1995, it appears that the pursuit of Phase II has not been the subject of any activity. At the least, it has been delayed and may, in fact, have been cancelled. Ontario has not been the only province seeking a merger of its federally and provincially appointed courts. The Attorney-General of New Brunswick expressed a similar interest in the fall of 1994. In this regard, see the earlier *McEvoy* case.

authority of s. 91(7) of the Constitution Act of 1867; namely, Parliament's authority to enact laws related to the "Militia, Military and Naval Service, and Defence". Pursuant to this authority, Parliament has enacted the National Defence Act, R.S.C. 1985, c. N-5. And, pursuant to that statute, the federal government has promulgated the Queen's Regulations and Orders (QR & O) and the Canadian Forces Administrative Orders (CFAO). The foregoing legislative enactments serve as the underpinnings of Canada's military justice system.

Essentially, similar to the civilian justice system's categorization of offenses as either summary or indictable,[20] the military justice system provides for trials of a summary nature and by court martial. The method of procedure depends upon factors relating to the rank of the accused, the nature of the offence and the severity of the punishment. The chart below sets out the essential features of the military justice system.

MILITARY JUSTICE SYSTEM
(A) SUMMARY TRIALS

NATURE OF PROCEEDING	ADJUDICATOR	ACCUSED	POSSIBLE PENALTIES
(1) summary trials by commanding officers[21]	commanding officer (commanding officer has the responsibility to determine if the accused may elect trial by court martial, depending on the offence, and, if so, he/she must offer the accused the election)	officer cadets and non-commissioned members below the rank of warrant officer	30 days detention, or 90 days detention with the approval of higher authority
(2) summary trials by delegated officers[22]	any officer delegated by commanding officer	officer cadets and non-commissioned members below the rank of warrant officer	detention not exceeding fourteen days, severe reprimand, reprimand, a fine not exceeding basic pay for fifteen days, and minor punishments[23]

---

[20] The civilian justice system also contains the so-called hybrid offenses where the Crown can elect to proceed either by summary or indictable procedure. The military justice system also contains a certain degree of flexibility.

[21] National Defence Act, s. 163.

[22] National Defence Act, s. 163(4).

[23] By regulation, the authority of the delegated officer is effectively limited to a severe reprimand. He/she may not order detention nor impose a fine. The delegated officer may,

MILITARY JUSTICE SYSTEM (*Continued***)**

NATURE OF PROCEEDING	ADJUDICATOR	ACCUSED	POSSIBLE PENALTIES
(3) summary trials by superior commanders	superior commander	persons including and between the ranks of warrant officer and major	forfeiture of seniority, severe reprimand, reprimand, fine

(B) COURTS MARTIAL

NATURE OF PROCEEDING	ADJUDICATOR	ACCUSED	POSSIBLE PENALTIES
(1) general court martial (this tribunal deals with the most serious kinds of offences)[24]	five officers with a colonel serving as the minimum rank for the president	a service person of any rank	any punishment (including death) excluding minor punishments
(2) disciplinary court martial[25]	three officers with a major serving as the minimum rank for the president	any service person below the rank of major	dismissal with disgrace, sentence of imprisonment of less than two years, etc., excluding minor punishments
(3) standing court martial[26]	one officer of a rank not lower than the accused who is a barrister or advocate of at least three years standing	any service person below the rank of colonel in respect of certain specified offences	imprisonment for less than two years, etc., excluding minor punishments
(4) special general court martial[27]	a superior court judge or barrister or advocate of at least ten years standing	non-service personnel subject to the Code of Service Discipline	subject to regulation, the same punishment as is applicable to general courts martial

With respect to the various courts martial, an appeal lies to the Court Martial Appeals Court[28] and, with leave, to the Supreme Court of Canada.

---

however, as part of the minor punishment jurisdiction, confine an accused private to his/her ship or barracks for up to fourteen days or impose a 30 days stoppage of leave for anyone below the rank of warrant officer.

[24] National Defence Act, s. 166.

[25] National Defence Act, s. 171.

[26] National Defence Act, s. 177.

[27] National Defence Act, s. 178.

[28] This Court consists of judges who are already serving as justices of provincial superior courts or of the Federal Court of Canada.

For some recent cases on military justice see the following authorities. These cases deal with challenges under the Canadian Bill of Rights and the Canadian Charter of Rights and Freedoms, and deal mostly with the issue of the independence of the adjudicating body. The most important case is *R. v. Genereux*, [1992] 1 S.C.R. 259, 70 C.C.C. (3d) 1, 8 C.R.R. (2d) 89, 88 D.L.R. (4th) 110, 133 N.R. 241. The other leading cases are as follows: *Forster v. MacDonald* (1993), 14 Alta. L.R. (3d) 225, [1994] 3 W.W.R. 364, 146 A.R. 270, 108 D.L.R. (4th) 690 (Q.B.); *R. v. Mackay,* [1980] 2 S.C.R. 370, [1980] 5 W.W.R. 385, 54 C.C.C. (2d) 129, 114 D.L.R. (3d) 393, 33 N.R. 1; *R. v. Deneault* (1994), 167 N.R. 138 (Ct. Martial App. Ct.); *R. v. Forster,* [1992] 1 S.C.R. 339, 70 C.C.C. (3d) 59, 88 D.L.R. (4th) 169, 133 N.R. 333; *R. v. Ingebrigtson* (1990), 61 C.C.C. (3d) 541, 76 D.L.R. (4th) 481, 114 N.R. 381 (C.M.A.C.); *Nye v. R.* (1980), C.M.A.R. 85; and *Sutton v. Johnston,* 1 T.R. 493 (S.C.).

The following is a bibliography of Canadian sources relating to the military justice system.

Articles

Corry, D.J. "Military Law Under the Charter". (1986), 24 Osgoode Hall L.J. 67.

Fay, J.B. "Canadian Military Criminal Law: An Examination of Military Justice" (1975), 23 Chitty's L.J., 120, 156, 195 and 228.

Heard, A.D. "Military Law and the Charter of Rights". (1988), 11 Dalhousie L.J. 514.

Hollies, J.H. "Canadian Military Law". (1961), 13 Military L. Rev. 69.

MacKay, A.W. "Fairness After the Charter; A Rose by any Other Name". (1985), 10 Queen's L.J. 263.

McDonald, "The Trail of Discipline: The Historical Roots of Canadian Military Law" (1985), 1 Judge Advocate General J. 1.

Ray, R. "Law in the Trenches". National, March 1995, p. 12.

Treatises

Rowe, P.J. *Defence: The Legal Implications.* London: Brassey's Defence Publishers, 1987.

Watkin, K.W. *Canadian Military Justice: Summary Proceedings and the Charter.* Ll.M. thesis, Faculty of Law, Queen's University, 1990 (unpublished).

ABORIGINAL JUSTICE

In recent years, there has been a move toward the establishment of an independent or quasi-independent Aboriginal justice system. Underlying this move is a recognition that there are certain values and customs *[in agreement]* historically attached to Aboriginal communities. In addition, the concept of an independent justice system is viewed as being <u>consonant</u> with the notion of the inherent right of Aboriginal self-government. Constitutionally, recognition was given to the inherent right of Aboriginal self-government in the failed Charlottetown Constitutional Accord. Nonetheless, discussions continue in attempting to seek this objective, including the realization of an independent or quasi-independent Aboriginal justice system. One experience that is often raised as a model for such a system is that which occurs in the state of New Mexico in the United States.

Related to the above, there have been several Royal Commissions and public inquiries dealing with the issue of Aboriginal justice. The most prominent of these studies include two such inquiries in Alberta, one in Saskatchewan, one in Manitoba and three at the federal level, including the major Royal Commission on Aboriginal Peoples. Some of these Royal Commissions and public inquiries recommended a form of independent justice in Aboriginal communities. An independent justice system would recognize an important role for elders in the community and would reinforce those values and traditions that are historically intrinsic to those indigenous communities. One suggestion relates to the use of 'sentencing circles' as a more appropriate mechanism of dealing with certain accused in lieu of the regular courts. Other suggestions include a greater use of diversion programs and the implementation of various initiatives in corrections.

Recognizing the benefits (and the entitlements) that would flow from a quasi-independent justice system, the regular courts have begun, in a limited way, to take into account Aboriginal customs and traditions in the sentencing process.[29] But there remains much to accomplish, constitutionally and otherwise, in order to achieve a meaningful, widespread Aboriginal justice system. In short, the development of such a system is an evolutionary process that, at present, is in its early stages.[30]

---

[29] See, for example, The Globe & Mail, June 13, 1995. In this case, a judge banished an aboriginal offender to an isolated island for a year on the recommendation of a community sentencing circle. For a similar case in the United States, see the Edmonton Sun, October 4, 1995.

[30] In a major conference on the public perception of justice, the Grand Chief of the Assembly of First Nations, Ovide Mercredi, commented to the effect that "[a]boriginals are unlikely to play by the rules of the Canadian justice system until their perspective is recognized and included". More particularly, he stated, "[w]e're reluctant to go to court on our treaties because we don't know what the judge will decide. . . . All the different rules work against us". See the Edmonton Journal, October 14, 1995.

The following is a bibliography of some of the leading materials related to the development of various initiatives with respect to Aboriginal justice.

Cadman Sr., W. "Traditional Navajo Justice Revisited". A paper prepared for the Alternative Dispute Resolution Conference, Vancouver, February, 1995.

Chartrand, L. "The Appropriateness of the Lawyer as Advocate in Contemporary Aboriginal Justice Initiatives", (1995), 33 Alta. L. Rev. 874.

Diabo, W., and J.K. Mitchell. "Court of Kahnawake", in *Aboriginal Peoples and the Justice System: Report of the National Round Table on Aboriginal Justice Issues*. Royal Commission on Aboriginal Peoples. Ottawa: Minister of Supply and Services Canada, 1993 at p. 402.

Dumont, J. "Justice and Aboriginal People", in *Aboriginal Peoples and the Justice System: Report of the National Round Table on Aboriginal Justice Issues*. Royal Commission on Aboriginal Peoples. Ottawa: Minister of Supply and Services Canada, 1993 at p. 42.

Giokas, J. "Accommodating the Concerns of Aboriginal Peoples Within the Existing Justice System", in *Aboriginal Peoples and the Justice System: Report of the National Round Table on Aboriginal Justice Issues*. Royal Commission on Aboriginal Peoples. Ottawa: Minister of Supply and Services Canada, 1993 at p. 184.

Greschner, D. "Aboriginal Women, the Constitution and Criminal Justice". (1992), Special Edition U.B.C. Law Rev. 338.

Huculak, Judge B., "From the Power to Punish to the Power to Heal", Justice as Healing: A Newsletter on Aboriginal Concepts of Justice, Native Law Centre, Fall 1995, p. 1.

Indigenous Bar Association. *Symposium on Indian Justice Systems: A Review of Aboriginal Justice Initiatives and Their Implementation in Aboriginal Communities*. Edmonton, June 1991.

Jackson, M. "In Search of the Pathways to Justice: Alternative Dispute Resolution in Aboriginal Communities". (1992), Special Edition U.B.C. L. Rev. 147.

Jackson, M. "Locking up Natives in Canada — A Report of the Committee of the Canadian Bar Association on Imprisonment and Release", June, 1988.

Justice on Trial, Report of the Task Force on the Criminal Justice System and its Impact on the Indian and Metis People of Alberta, (Mr. Justice R.A. Cawsey, Chairman), March, 1991.

Kaiser, H.A. "The *Criminal Code* of Canada: A Review Based on the Minister's Reference". (1992), Special Edition U.B.C. L. Rev. 41

Keenan, D. "Teslin Tlingit Justice Council", in *Aboriginal Peoples and the Justice System: Report of the National Round Table on Aboriginal Justice Issues*. Royal Commission on Aboriginal Peoples. Ottawa: Minister of Supply and Services Canada, 1993 at p. 397.

Louttit, R. "Attawapiskat First Nation Justice Project", in *Aboriginal Peoples and the Justice System: Report of the National Round Table on Aboriginal Justice Issues*. Royal Commission on Aboriginal Peoples. Ottawa: Minister of Supply and Services Canada, 1993 at p. 399.

Law Reform Commission of Canada. *Report on Aboriginal Peoples and Criminal Justice: Equality, Respect and the Search for Justice*, December, 1991.

Lyon, N. "A Perspective on the Application of the *Criminal Code* to Aboriginal Peoples in Light of the Judgment of the Supreme Court of Canada in *R. v. Sparrow*". (1992), Special Edition U.B.C. Law Rev. 306.

Macdonald, R.A. "Recognizing and Legitimating Aboriginal Justice: Implications for a Reconstruction of Non-Aboriginal Legal Systems in Canada", in *Aboriginal Peoples and the Justice System: Report of the National Round Table on Aboriginal Justice Issues*. Royal Commission on Aboriginal Peoples. Ottawa: Minister of Supply and Services Canada, 1993 at p. 232.

Mackay, A.W. "Federal-Provincial Responsibility in the Area of Criminal Justice and Aboriginal Peoples". (1992), Special Edition U.B.C. Law Rev. 314.

Macklem, P. "Aboriginal Justice, the Distribution of Legislative Authority, and the Judicature Provisions of the *Constitution Act, 1867*", in *Aboriginal Peoples and the Justice System: Report of the National Round Table on Aboriginal Justice Issues*. Royal Commission on Aboriginal Peoples. Ottawa: Minister of Supply and Services Canada, 1993 at p. 326.

Macklem, P. "Aboriginal Peoples, Criminal Justice Initiatives and the Constitution". (1992), Special Edition U.B.C. Law Rev. 280.

Mandamin, L. "Aboriginal Justice Systems: Relationships", in *Aboriginal Peoples and the Justice System: Report of the National Round Table on Aboriginal Justice Issues*. Royal Commission on Aboriginal Peoples. Ottawa: Minister of Supply and Services Canada, 1993 at p. 275.

Mandamin, L., D. Callihoo, A. Angus and M. Buller. "The *Criminal Code* and Aboriginal People". (1992), Special Edition U.B.C. Law Rev. 5.

Manson, M. "Justice that Heals: Native Alternatives", Canadian Lawyer, October, 1994.

Monture-OKanee, P.A. and M.E. Turpel. "Aboriginal Peoples and Canadian Criminal Law: Rethinking Justice". (1992), Special Edition U.B.C. Law Rev. 239.

Monture-OKanee, P.A. "Reclaiming Justice: Aboriginal Women and Justice Initiatives in the 1990's", in *Aboriginal Peoples and the Justice System: Report of the National Round Table on Aboriginal Justice Issues*. Royal Commission on Aboriginal Peoples. Ottawa: Minister of Supply and Services Canada, 1993 at p. 105.

Morse, B. and L. Lock. *Native Offenders' Perceptions of the Criminal Justice System*. Ottawa: Department of Justice of Canada (Research Reports of the Canadian Sentencing Commission), 1988.

Nahanee, T. "Dancing with a Gorilla: Aboriginal Women, Justice and the Charter", in *Aboriginal Peoples and the Justice System: Report of the National Round Table on Aboriginal Justice Issues*. Royal Commission on Aboriginal Peoples. Ottawa: Minister of Supply and Services Canada, 1993 at p. 359.

Nungak, Z. "Fundamental Values, Norms, and Concepts of Justice", in *Aboriginal Peoples and the Justice System: Report of the National Round Table on Aboriginal Justice Issues*. Royal Commission on Aboriginal Peoples. Ottawa: Minister of Supply and Services Canada, 1993 at p. 86.

Policing in Relation to the Blood Tribe, Report of a Public Inquiry, (Assistant Chief Judge C.H. Rolf, Commissioner), February, 1991.

R. v. P.(J.A.), [1991] N.W.T.R. 301, 6 C.R. (4th) 126 (Y.T. Terr. Ct.).

Report of the Aboriginal Justice Inquiry of Manitoba: The Justice System and Aboriginal People, (Associate Chief Justice A.C. Hamilton and Associate Chief Judge C.M. Sinclair, Commissioners), August, 1991.

Report of the Saskatchewan Metis Justice Review Committee, (Judge Patricia Linn, Chairperson), January, 1992.

Ross, R. "Duelling Paradigms? Western Criminal Justice versus Aboriginal Community Healing", a Discussion Paper following a conference of the Northern Justice Society. July, 1993.

Ross, R. "Leaving Our White Eyes Behind: The Sentencing of Native Accused". [1989] 3 C.N.L.R. 1.

Rudin, J. "Aboriginal Legal Services Community Council of Toronto", in *Aboriginal Peoples and the Justice System: Report of the National Round Table on Aboriginal Justice Issues*. Royal Commission on Aboriginal Peoples. Ottawa: Minister of Supply and Services Canada, 1993 at p. 394.

Sampson, T. "South Vancouver Island Justice Education Project", in *Aboriginal Peoples and the Justice System: Report of the National Round Table on Aboriginal Justice Issues*. Royal Commission on

Aboriginal Peoples. Ottawa: Minister of Supply and Services Canada, 1993 at p. 390.

Sinclair, Associate Chief Judge M. "Aboriginal Peoples, Justice and the Law", from R., Gosse, et al., *Continuing Poundmaker and Riel's Quest*. Saskatoon: Purich Publishing, 1994.

Stevens, S. "Northwest Territories Community Justice of the Peace Program", in *Aboriginal Peoples and the Justice System: Report of the National Round Table on Aboriginal Justice Issues*. Royal Commission on Aboriginal Peoples. Ottawa: Minister of Supply and Services Canada, 1993 at p. 385.

"The *Morin* decision: an excerpt", Justice as Healing: A Newsletter on Aboriginal Concepts of Justice, Native Law Centre, Fall 1995, p. 5.

"Trial By Healing Circle", Canadian Lawyer, March 1994, p. 7.

Turpel, M.E. "On the Question of Adapting the Canadian Criminal Justice System for Aboriginal Peoples: Don't Fence Me In", in *Aboriginal Peoples and the Justice System: Report of the National Round Table on Aboriginal Justice Issues*. Royal Commission on Aboriginal Peoples. Ottawa: Minister of Supply and Services Canada, 1993 at p. 161.

Webber, J. "Individuality, Equality and Difference: Justifications for a Parallel System of Aboriginal Justice", in *Aboriginal Peoples and the Justice System: Report of the National Round Table on Aboriginal Justice Issues*. Royal Commission on Aboriginal Peoples. Ottawa: Minister of Supply and Services Canada, 1993 at p. 133.

Wildsmith, B.H. "Treaty Responsibilities: A Co-Relational Model". (1992), Special Edition U.B.C. Law Rev. 324.

Yazzie, R. "Navajo Justice Experience — Yesterday and Today", in *Aboriginal Peoples and the Justice System: Report of the National Round Table on Aboriginal Justice Issues*. Royal Commission on Aboriginal Peoples. Ottawa: Minister of Supply and Services Canada, 1993 at p. 407.

Zimmerman, S. " 'The Revolving Door of Despair': Aboriginal Involvement in the Criminal Justice System". (1992), Special Edition U.B.C. Law Rev. 367.

Zion, J.W. "Living Indian Justice: Navajo Peacemaking Today", a paper prepared for the Alternative Dispute Resolution Conference, Vancouver, February, 1995.

Zion, J.W. "Taking Justice Back: American Indian Perspectives", in *Aboriginal Peoples and the Justice System: Report of the National Round Table on Aboriginal Justice Issues*. Royal Commission on

Aboriginal Peoples. Ottawa: Minister of Supply and Services Canada, 1993 at p. 309.[31]

From the foregoing, one can appreciate not only the expertise required of judges in hearing a wide variety of matters, covering virtually all areas of the law, but also the complexity of the model of judicial decision-making discussed earlier. It is not enough to describe the role of courts in Canada as, essentially, adjudicative and/or arbitrative. This general characterization must be broadened if our model of the judicial decision-making process is to accurately describe the role of our courts in exercising the specific functions assigned to them. More important, however, than a search for a broader definition is the question whether our courts are successfully applying this basic model to real-life circumstances. In fact, judges do effectively adapt the basic adjudicative/arbitration model of judicial decision-making in order to resolve the particular matters before our courts.

In summary, the processes of objective adjudication and arbitration cannot be divorced from the context in which they are conducted. In this correction, one should appreciate that these processes are conducted in the context of a flexible and adaptable adversarial system. That is why the Canadian legal system is able to exercise effectively the various specific functions assigned to it and, by doing so, successfully achieve its institutional objectives.

This is an important point in our examination of the Canadian legal system: we have progressed from a consideration of the Canadian legal system as an abstract entity containing various institutions with somewhat generically described functions, to an appreciation of the legal system as a highly structured complex. This complex contains a matrix of institutions, exercising specifically assigned functions, and charged with the resolution of real and highly specific problems, covering virtually all aspects of human life and human affairs. With that juncture in mind, let us now consider the role of judges and lawyers in the Canadian legal system.

APPENDIX A

THE SUPREME COURT OF CANADA

For a detailed study of the Supreme Court of Canada, see Paul Weiler's *In the Last Resort* (Carswell/Methuen, 1974). Set out below are some of

---

[31] The author wishes to gratefully acknowledge the assistance of Alberta lawyer, Leonard (Tony) Mandamin in providing materials included in this bibliography. In addition, it should be noted that Mr. Mandamin is the author of two of the articles set out above.

the key sections of the Supreme Court Act, R.S.C. 1985, c. S-26.[32] The legislative jurisdiction of Parliament to establish a supreme court is set out in s. 101 of the Constitution Act of 1867. Pursuant to that jurisdiction, Parliament established the Supreme Court of Canada in 1875.[33] Also, particular attention should be directed to the amendment in 1974-75-76, c. 18, s. 5, to the Supreme Court Act, contained in s. 41(1) of the Act, set out below.

For those who wish to engage in a study of the development of the Supreme Court of Canada as the final court of appeal in respect of all criminal and civil matters, see the following three cases: *Nadan v. R.*, [1926] A.C. 482, [1926] 1 W.W.R. 801, 45 C.C.C. 221, [1926] 2 D.L.R. 177 (P.C.); *Br. Coal Corp. v. R.*, [1935] A.C. 500, [1935] 2 W.W.R. 564, 64 C.C.C. 145, [1935] 3 D.L.R. 401 (P.C.); *A.G. Ont. v. A.G. Can.*, [1947] 1 W.W.R. 305, [1947] A.C. 127, [1947] 1 D.L.R. 801 (P.C.).

The Supreme Court Act, R.S.C. 1985, c. S-26[34]

. . .

4. (1) The Court shall consist of a chief justice to be called the Chief Justice of Canada, and eight puisne judges.

---

[32] Both the Meech Lake and the Charlottetown Constitutional Accords attempted to amend the Judicature part of the Constitution Act of 1867. They did so by the addition of several new sections. These sections essentially constitutionalized various requirements related to the composition of the Supreme Court of Canada. For example, in the Meech Lake Accord, the judges on the Supreme Court would have been appointed from lists of candidates submitted by the provinces. If a vacancy arose, it would have been filled by a person nominated on such a list provided that the person was acceptable to the Queen's Privy Council for Canada. (In practical terms, this means the Prime Minister since, traditionally, Supreme Court appointments are Prime Ministerial prerogatives.) With respect to the three Quebec positions on the Court, obviously, they would have been appointed from a list of persons submitted by the government of Quebec.

[33] For some recent treatises in connection with the Supreme Court of Canada see, Beaudoin, G.-A. (ed.), *The Supreme Court of Canada: Proceedings of the October 1985 Conference.* Montreal: Les Editions Yvon-Blais Inc., 1986; Bushnell, I., *The Captive Court: a Study of the Supreme Court of Canada.* Montreal: McGill-Queen's University Press, 1992; Monahan, P., *Politics and the constitution: the Charter, federalism, and the Supreme Court of Canada.* Toronto: Carswell/Methuen, 1987; and Snell, J.G., *The Supreme Court of Canada: history of the institution.* Toronto: University of Toronto Press, 1985. See also *Report of the Canadian Bar Association Committee on the Supreme Court of Canada.* Ottawa: C.B.A., 1987. In addition, on the occasion of the 100th anniversary of that event the Canadian Bar Review published a special two-part series to commemorate the anniversary: see (1975), 53 Can. Bar Rev. 459 and 649. In addition, the Canadian Association of Law Teachers made that anniversary the subject of its deliberations at its annual meeting, held in Edmonton in June of 1975. The papers delivered at that meeting are set out in a special edition of the Alberta Law Review: see (1976), 14 Alta. L. Rev. 1.

[34] The Constitution Act of 1982, in a sense, entrenches the Supreme Court of Canada as part of our constitutional fabric. The Supreme Court Act was enacted as an ordinary statute of the Parliament of Canada and could have been repealed at will by Parliament, although many regarded the Supreme Court Act as quasi-constitutional legislation and therefore politically inexpedient to repeal. Now, however, by virtue of ss. 41 and 42 of the Constitution Act of 1982, the unanimous consent of the Parliament of Canada and the legislatures of

(2) The judges shall be appointed by the Governor in Council by letters patent under the Great Seal.

5. Any person may be appointed a judge who is or has been a judge of a superior court of a province or a barrister or advocate of at least ten years standing at the bar of a province.

6. At least three of the judges shall be appointed from among the judges of the Court of Appeal or the Superior Court of the Province of Quebec or from among the advocates of that Province . . .

9. (1) Subject to subsection (2), the judges hold office during good behaviour, but are removable by the Governor General on address of the Senate and House of Commons.

(2) A judge ceases to hold office on attaining the age of seventy-five years . . .

22. All persons who are barristers or advocates in a province may practise as barristers, advocates and counsel in the Court.

23. All persons who are attorneys or solicitors of the superior courts in a province of Canada may practise as attorneys, solicitors and proctors in the Court . . .

25. Any five of the judges of the Court shall constitute a quorum and may lawfully hold the Court. . .

28. (1) No judge against whose judgment an appeal is brought, or who took part in the trial of the cause or matter, or in the hearing in a court below, shall sit or take part in the hearing of or adjudication on the proceedings in the Supreme Court.

(2) In any cause or matter in which a judge is unable to sit or take part in consequence of this section, any four of the other judges of the Supreme Court constitute a quorum and may lawfully hold the Court.

29. Any four judges constitute a quorum and may lawfully hold the Court in cases where the parties consent to be heard before a court so composed . . .

35. The Court shall have and exercise an appellate, civil and criminal jurisdiction within and throughout Canada.

35.1 An appeal lies to the Court from a decision of the Federal Court of Appeal in the case of a controversy between Canada and a province or between two or more provinces.[35]

36. An appeal lies to the Court from an opinion pronounced by the highest court of final resort in a province on any matter referred to it for hearing and consideration by the lieutenant governor in council of that province whenever it has been by the statutes of that province declared that such opinion is to be deemed a judgment of the highest court of final resort and that an appeal lies therefrom as from a judgment in an action.

37. Subject to sections 39 and 42, an appeal to the Supreme Court lies with leave of the highest court of final resort in a province from a final judgment of that court where, in the opinion of the court, the question involved in the appeal is one that ought to be submitted to the Supreme Court for decision. . . .

37.1 Subject to sections 39 and 42, an appeal to the Court lies with leave of the Federal Court of Appeal from a final judgment of the Federal Court of Appeal where, in its opinion, the question involved in the appeal is one that ought to be submitted to the Court for decision.[36]

40 (1) Subject to subsection (3), an appeal lies to the Supreme Court from any final or other judgment of the Federal Court of Appeal or of the highest court of final resort in a province, or a judge thereof, in which judgment can be had in the particular case

---

all of the provinces is required in order to amend the Supreme Court Act to effect a change in the composition of the Supreme Court of Canada. This requirement, in effect, "constitutionalizes" the Supreme Court of Canada.

[35] An Act to Amend the Federal Court Act, the Crown Liability Act, the Supreme Court Act and other Acts in Consequence Thereof, S.C. 1990, c. 8, s. 33.

[36] An Act to Amend the Federal Court Act, the Crown Liability Act, the Supreme Court Act and other Acts in Consequence Thereof, S.C. 1990, c. 8, s. 34.

sought to be appealed to the Supreme Court, whether or not leave to appeal to the Supreme Court has been refused by any other court, where, with respect to the particular case sought to be appealed, the Supreme Court is of the opinion that any question involved therein is, by reason of its public importance or the importance of any issue of law or any issue of mixed law and fact involved in that question, one that ought to be decided by the Supreme Court or is, for any other reason, of such a nature or significance as to warrant decision by it, and leave to appeal from that judgment is accordingly granted by the Supreme Court.[37]

References by Governor in Council

53. (1) The Governor in Council may refer to the Court for hearing and consideration important questions of law or fact concerning
   (a) the interpretation of the *Constitution Acts*;
   (b) the constitutionality or interpretation of any federal or provincial legislation;
   (c) the appellate jurisdiction respecting educational matters, by the *Constitution Act, 1867*, or by any other Act or law vested in the Governor in Council; or
   (d) the powers of the Parliament of Canada, or of the legislatures of the provinces, or of the respective governments thereof, whether or not the particular power in question has been or is proposed to be exercised.

(2) The Governor in Council may refer to the Court for hearing and consideration important questions of law or fact concerning any matter, whether or not in the opinion of the Court *ejusdem generis* with the enumerations combined in subsection (1), with reference to which the Governor in Council sees fit to submit any such question.

(3) Any question concerning any of the matters mentioned in subsections (1) and (2), and referred to the Court by the Governor in Council, shall be conclusively deemed to be an important question.

(4) Where a reference is made to the Court under subsection (1) or (2), it is the duty of the Court to hear and consider it and to answer each question so referred, and the Court shall certify to the Governor in Council, for his information, its opinion on each question, with the reasons for each answer, and the opinion shall be pronounced in like manner as in the case of a judgment on an appeal to the Court, and any judges who differ from the opinion of the majority shall in like manner certify their opinions and their reasons.

(5) Where the question relates to the constitutional validity of any Act passed by the legislature of any province, or of any provision in any such Act, or in case, for any reason, the government of any province has any special interest in any such question, the attorney general of the province shall be notified of the hearing in order that the attorney general may be heard if he thinks fit.

(6) The Court has power to direct that any person interested or, where there is a class of persons interested, any one or more persons as representatives of that class shall be notified of the hearing on any reference under this section, and those persons are entitled to be heard thereon.

(7) The Court may, in its discretion, request any counsel to argue the case with respect to any interest that is affected and with respect to which counsel does not appear, and the reasonable expenses thereby occasioned may be paid by the Minister of Finance out of any moneys appropriated by Parliament for expenses of litigation.

References by Senate or House of Commons

54. The Court, or any two of the judges, shall examine and report on any private bill or petition for a private bill presented to the Senate or House of Commons and referred to the Court under any rules or orders made by the Senate or House of Commons.

---

[37] An Act to Amend the Federal Court Act, the Crown Liability Act, the Supreme Court Act and other Acts in Consequence Thereof, S.C. 1990, c. 8, s. 37.

APPENDIX B

THE COURT SYSTEM OF THE UNITED STATES

By way of comparison, it is interesting to examine the United States court system. In the United States there are basically two court systems, one at the state level and the other at the federal level. The state courts concern themselves with matters falling within state jurisdiction under the American Constitution, while the federal courts concern themselves with matters falling within federal jurisdiction under the American Constitution. With respect to the former, the highest court of appeal is the state Court of Appeal. With respect to the latter, the highest court of appeal is the Supreme Court of the United States. With one exception, one cannot appeal from the decision of a state Court of Appeal to a federal court. The exception relates to the raising of a constitutional matter in the course of proceedings in the state courts. If a constitutional matter is raised, an appeal lies from the state Court of Appeal to courts within the federal court system. Ultimately, this might lead to an appeal to the Supreme Court of the United States.

A summary of the hierarchy of the courts in the dual court system of the United States is set out below:

ORGANIZATION OF UNITED STATES COURT SYSTEM

A. *Federal Courts*[38]

1. Supreme Court of the United States
2. Circuit Courts of Appeal
3. United States District Courts

B. *State Courts*

1. Appellate courts
   (a) Intermediate courts
   (b) Courts of last resort
2. Trial courts of general jurisdiction
3. Courts of special and limited jurisdiction

---

[38] Jurisdiction of federal courts:
  1. Matters relating to citizenship
  2. Federal matters:
     (a) violation of federal statutes
     (b) constitutional issues
  3. Matters falling within the original jurisdiction of the Supreme Court.

The reader should appreciate two fundamental distinctions between the American and Canadian court systems. First, the Canadian courts are derived, essentially, from the British system. (See the discussion on this subject in the Hamlyn Lectures, delivered by the late Chief Justice Bora Laskin, referred to in Chapter 4.) Secondly, as indicated above, the Canadian court system is unified, while the American court system consists of two separate systems of courts.[39]

---

[39] For some recent observations on the Supreme Court of the United States, see Schwartz, B., *A History of the Supreme Court*. New York: Oxford University Press, 1993; Stein, J.W., "Expounding on the Supreme Court", vol. 77 *Judicature* May-June 1994, 331; *The Supreme Court of the United States: Its Beginnings and Its Justices 1790-1991*. Washington, D.C.: Commission on the Bicentennial of the U.S. Constitution, 1992; Wagman, R.J., *The Supreme Court: A Citizen's Guide*. New Jersey: Pharos Books, 1993; Walker, T.G., *The Supreme Court of the United States: An Introduction*. New York: St. Martin's Press, 1993; and Witt, E. (ed.), *The Supreme Court A to Z; A Ready Reference Encyclopedia*, Congressional Quarterly, 1993. For some earlier discussion on the work of the Supreme Court of the United States, see J.M. Arbour and E. Hudon, "Growing Pains and other Things: The Supreme Court of Canada and the Supreme Court of the United States" (1986), 17 R. Gen. 753, and A. Cox, "The Role of the Supreme Court of the United States", [1986] Sup. Ct. Conf. 323.

Chapter 8

THE LEGAL SYSTEM IN QUEBEC

INTRODUCTION

The history of the legal system in Quebec is a characteristically Canadian story about the accommodation of regional interests in a federal structure and the struggle of a minority for identity and self-determination.[1] While it is true that Quebec is Canada's only Civil law[2] jurisdiction, it is also true that in many respects the practice of law in Quebec today might be more familiar to a Bay Street litigator than to a French *avocat*. This is largely a result of the fact that although Quebec's private law system is a based on the Civil law, its public law and court structures are based on the common law.

Several key historical events, discussed below, contributed to this hybrid system, many of which were influenced in varying degrees by the powerful centrifugal forces of federalism. Quebec's legal system may be unique in Canada, but in many respects it is also uniquely Canadian.

Quebec's private law is a member of the Romano-Germanic legal systems.[3] The historical components of that system included customary law and Roman law, drawn from or expressed by such diverse sources as Germanic traditions, Romanist scholarship, royal ordonnances, commercial usage and canon law. There were sharp regional differences in Western Europe in the permutations and combinations of these diverse elements,

---

[1] For a thoughtful analysis of Canada's constitutional tangles, see J. Webber, *Reimagining Canada: Language, Culture, Community, and the Canadian Constitution* (McGill-Queen's University Press, 1994). For a rather more prosaic view, see Conrad Black, "Canada's Continuing Identity Crises" (1995), 74 Foreign Affairs 99.

[2] The term "Civil law" here means the system of law that governs relations between individuals, including the concomitant civil procedure, as distinct from the common law connotation of private law dictating civic relations between individuals in opposition to criminal, military or ecclesiastical law. See Brierley and Macdonald, eds., *Quebec Civil Law: An Introduction to Quebec Private Law* (Toronto: Emond Montgomery, 1994) at par. 3.

[3] See generally, René David, *Les grands systèmes de droit contemporain*, Précis Dalloz, 7ième éd. (France, 1978) No. 83, p. 11.

even within particular countries, with the Romanist influence holding sway in the south and certain Germanic and customary usages prevalent in the north. These elements eventually coalesced in different regional combinations to form the base of unmodified Civil law systems.

As is the case in many Civil law jurisdictions, the private law in Quebec is codified. The first Civil code in Quebec was inspired by the Napoleonic Code of 1804. Like other codes of the nineteenth century, its key feature was that the directing principles of its legal system were derived in a single, authoritative text. The unitary nature of a code in Civil law jurisdictions is central to the Civilian legal structure. Common law lawyers are conditioned by their own legal system to analyze legal issues in terms of the highly developed bodies of law that emerged though the courts of Law and Equity. No such historical division exists in the Quebec system, so that the administration of justice in private law matters is better considered as an integrated set of unified rules.

For example, the use of the term "equity" in the Civil Code of Quebec is literal rather than remedial. Art. 1434 of the Civil Code of Quebec provides that contracts bind the parties not only in respect of what is expressed, but also what is incident to the contract in virtue of "equity", usage or law. "Equity" in this context refers to the ordinary, plain meaning of the word as a method of interpreting contracts rather than a separate set of rules for resolving disputes.

It also is important for readers trained in the Common law to understand that the reduction of law to statute is conceptually distinct from the exercise of codification in the Civil law. The differences between the two systems are frequently described in terms of the contrasts between the rule of experience and inductive thinking on the one hand, and the rule of reason and deductive thinking on the other.[4] Civil law systems have a fundamentally different understanding of the role of codification as an exercise in social construction — or reconstruction[5] — and in the articulation of normative rules as an expression of a society's principles and values. An elegant expression of these differences is described by two of Quebec's leading scholars in this area, Brierley and Macdonald:

> The legislative style of a Code differs from that of a statute both in the degree of abstraction at which it is cast and in its normative referent. A statue or regulation is usually directed to a particular problem, defined not in terms of a legal category, but in terms of the application of a legal category to an identifiable set of facts. The form of a statute therefore tends to be casuistic and remedial. In contrast, an artfully drawn Civil Code

---

[4] See W. Friedman, "*Stare Decisis* at Common Law and under the Civil Code of Quebec" (1953), 31 Can. Bar Rev. 723.

[5] The revision of the Civil Code of Lower Canada which culminated in the 1991 Civil Code of Quebec is referred to as the *projet de société* or social contract.

will contain [. . .] expressions of legal norms articulated at a level of abstraction that allow them to serve over a wide variety of particular instances. . . a Code aspires to promise meaningful generalities that can accommodate a range of future facts in all their diversity.[6]

Quebec's private law is thus unique in Canada and developed within the context of its own traditions. It coexists, however, with a public law system that is shared with the rest of Canada which is based on a Common law system.[7] Matters such as criminal, constitutional and administrative law fall under this public law rubric. In addition, although civilian in its origins, Quebec's civil procedure is increasingly influenced by common law and U.S. models.[8]

Because the Quebec legal system acquired a criminal law system and key institutions based on English law, the organization of the courts and the exercise of judicial powers have been largely the product of English traditions governing the administration of justice which were, by and large, imported from England.[9] The implications for modern law practice in Quebec were significant, and are not merely historical relics. Because of the continuing influence of a significant English speaking minority, largely based in the city of Montreal, English remains a current language in the courts.[10] The Quebec legal system is thus bijural and bilingual in both theory and in practice.[11]

---

[6] Brierley and Macdonald, *supra,* note 2 at par. 91.

[7] For discussions of the centrality of the public/private debate in Quebec's legal system, see Macdonald, "Understanding Civil Law Scholarship in Quebec" (1985), 23 Osgoode Hall L.J. 573; Yalden, *Unité et Différence*: The Structure of Legal Thought in Late Nineteenth Century Quebec" (1988), 46 U. of T. L.J. 365.

[8] The Code of Civil Procedure contains the rules for practice and procedure generally before the Quebec courts, excluding criminal procedure and divorce, and also excluding matters dealt with by statute such as the *Special Procedure Act,* R.S.Q. 1977, c. P-27.

[9] Judges of the Superior Court of Quebec, the superior court of record, are endowed with the judicial powers usually identified with the Common law, namely the power to make such orders as are required to give effect to judgments, such as those powers traditionally associated with prerogative writs, excepting those powers which are implicit in the exercise of royal prerogative such as *parens patriae* because of the original jurisdiction of that court. Brierley and Macdonald, *supra,* note 2 at par. 48.

[10] In practice, both languages are pleaded before the courts. In Montreal, which has the heaviest case load in the province, one frequently sees lawyers, witnesses and the judiciary moving seamlessly and unannounced between the two languages.

[11] For example, art. 2615 of the 1866 Civil Code of Lower Canada provided that the English and French versions of the *Civil Code of Lower Canada* were equally authoritative. Although the *Charter of the French Language* ("Bill 101") established French as the official language of Quebec after the Parti Québécois' victory in 1976, the Supreme Court of Canada decided in *Blaikie c. Québec (Procureur général)*, [1979] 2 S.C.R. 1016, 49 C.C.C. (2d) 359, 30 N.R. 225, that provisions making French the predominant language of the legislature and the courts were unconstitutional.

HISTORICAL BACKGROUND

There is always a danger of inaccuracy when attempting to briefly enumerate any litany of events in a complex history. Nevertheless, authors generally tend to agree on the following key events shaping Quebec's legal history: (1) the Royal measures of Louis XIV in 1663 and 1664, which ordered that New France would receive the same form of justice as that of the then current French system, and particularly the reception of the *Coutume de Paris*;[12] (2) the Quebec Act of 1774;[13] (3) the 1857 decision to codify the Civil law and the enactment of the *Civil Code of Lower Canada* on August 1, 1866; (4) Confederation in 1867; (5) the Quiet Revolution in the 1960's and the reform or "social project" initiated in 1965 and culminating in the new *Civil Code of Québec* in 1991.[14] Each of these events will be examined briefly.

New France was a possession and a colony of the French Crown, discovered and claimed in the sixteenth century and colonized in the seventeenth century. It covered the vast expanse of territory including what we now call Hudson's Bay, Labrador, Quebec, Ontario, New Brunswick, and swathes of what is today the southeastern United States.

From 1627 to 1663, New France was governed by the *Compagnie des Cent Associés* under a system of seigniorial grants of land. Rapid colonization and a push for a broader administrative organization led to a Royal edict establishing the *Compagnie des Indes Occidentales* in 1664.[15]

In the fifteenth century, King Charles VII of France had initiated a process of reducing the various forms of *droit commun coutumier* (customary "common" law) to writing, which culminated in the sixteenth century with the drafting of approximately 360 local or general customs.[16] In 1580, one of the most influential *coutumes*, that of Paris, was reduced to a written form known as the *Coutume de Paris*.[17] This *coutume* was to be of enormous importance for New France.

---

[12] Specifically, that law which was found in the *parlement* of Paris at that time.

[13] *An Act for making more effectual Provision for the Government of the Province of Quebec in North America*, (U.K.) 14 Geo. III, c. 83 (1774).

[14] This occurred against the backdrop of the "repatriation" of the Canadian constitution and the "entrenchment" of a Federal Bill of Rights in the *Charter of Rights and Freedoms*. Quebec did not formally accede to the 1982 Constitution. The ensuing bitterness over this perceived betrayal contributed in large measure to resurgence of the independence movement, notably following the failures of the Conservative government's attempts to heal the ruptures of the early Eighties.

[15] *Edit d'établissement de la Compagnie des Indes Occidentales*, mai 1664.

[16] *Ordonnance de Montils-les-Tours* (1454), art. 125. Cited in Morel, *Histoire du droit: Sources et Formation du droit* (édition révisée, 10ième éd.) (Université de Montréal, 1991) at par. 8.

[17] A shorter prior version of the *Coutume de Paris* was prepared in 1510, but the revised version of 1580 is the most influential version. Brierley and Macdonald point to F. Olivier

1. THE ROYAL MEASURES OF 1663-64[18]

The Royal measures of Louis XIV vested the *Conseil souverain* with full powers of executive, legislative and judicial authority and gave to New France its first true government, based on that of France. Article XXXIII of the May Edict declared that the laws and ordinances of the Kingdom would be established in New France, and in particular, the *Coutume* of Paris was to be established in order to minimize the "diversity" that was prevalent in French law at that time. The concern about "diversity" was well founded. French law at the time of the reception of 1663-64 was a rich brew of customary law, royal edict, Romanist influence, commercial usage and canon law. Lack of national uniformity had spawned diverse local practices that varied significantly across France. In addition to the *coutumes* as a source of law, Roman law and Romanist scholarship played an important suppletive role in sixteenth and seventeenth century France, particularly in the south of France.

The *Coutume de Paris*, for example, dealt primarily with moveable and immoveable property law, dowry, community of property, successions etc., but fell short of setting out a complete "code" of private relations between citizens. Romanist sources provided the substantive law of obligations (the body of law providing the rules of responsibility between persons, including what a Common law lawyer would call tort and contract law) and, along with canon law, supplied the laws respecting filiation, marriage and certain aspects of commercial law.

The *Conseil souverain* governed by royal edicts and from time to time, local authorities issued their own edicts and regulations. In 1703, the administration of justice in New France was given to a legislative and judicial council which had the responsibility of implementing the Royal measures. This council was styled the *Conseil supérieur* and acted as a central authority. It issued judgments and general commands in matters of property, safety regulations, agricultural matters and the like.

In the larger political framework, eighteenth century France's ambitions for her North American colonies were weakening. Rising tensions between England and France in Europe had their echoes in North America. As the French hold on her territories diminished, the English skirmishes and invasions grew more aggressive until a series of battles in 1759-1760, which ended in the defeat of the French in the famous battle of the

---

Martin's commentary, *Histoire de la Coutume de Paris* (Paris: Erns Laloux, 1922-1930), 3 vols. as the definitive modern work on the subject. Brierley and Macdonald, *supra*, note 2 at par. 9, fn. 5.

[18] *Edit d'avril 1663* in *Edits & ordonnances* [etc.] I, 37; *Edit de mai 1664, ibid.*, I, 40 cited in Brierley and Mcdonald, *supra*, note 2 at par. 8, fn. 2.

Plains of Abraham. The capitulation of the French was signed on September 8, 1760 and the colony of New France became an English possession, governed under military rule until 1763. During the military rule French Civil law survived, subject to the Crown's pleasure. The formal change of sovereignty took place in 1763 pursuant to the Treaty of Paris.[19]

George III issued a Royal Proclamation on October 7, 1763 which gave extensive powers to the Governor to create courts of justice in both criminal and civil matters, "according to Law and Equity, and as near as may be agreeable to the Laws of England." The new authorities tried to impose English law, in part through local measures issued under the authority of the Royal Proclamation. These unpopular measures resulted in a virtual boycott of the new judicial system by the French inhabitants, who resorted to private arbitration and forced the creation of an inferior tribunal, the Court of Common Pleas where French lawyers could plead. The problems with the new local measures were both theoretical and practical, since English writers were of the view that in order to impose new law, the Sovereign must actually change the laws, and not merely authorize a vague compliance with English law. According to Blackstone:

> [I]n conquered or ceded countries, that have already laws of their own, the King may indeed alter and change those laws, but till he does actually change them, the ancient laws of the country remain, unless such as are against the law of God, as in the case of an infidel country.[20]

The ensuing uncertainty and chaos cried out for a solution, which the Parliament of Westminster provided in 1774.

2. THE QUEBEC ACT OF 1774

Despite the fitful early attempts to impose English law in all respects, the general view was that they were void of effect and as mentioned above, had been utterly rejected by the French inhabitants, a dilemma that the English themselves clearly recognized:[21]

> . . .whereas the Provisions, made by the said Proclamation, in respect of the Civil Government. . . have been found upon experience, to be inapplicable to the State and Circumstances of said Province. . .[22]

---

[19] For a classic historical study of the history of French Canada, see François Xavier Garneau, *Histoire du Canada français* (Paris: François Beauval), in ten volumes.

[20] Blackstone, *Commentaries on the Laws of England*, Introduction, Section IV.

[21] For example, two petitions were sent to the King in 1770 and 1773, complaining of the loss of the French laws and procedures, and of the cost of legal services. See also *Campbell v. Hall* (1774), [1558-1774] All E.R. Rep 252 (K.B.), *per* Lord Mansfield.

[22] *An Act for making more effectual Provision for the Government of the Province of Quebec in North America*, (U.K.) 14 Geo. III, c. 83 (1774), par. 4.

The *Quebec Act* of 1774 replaced all prior laws, including the Royal Proclamation, and received Royal Assent on June 22, 1774. In essence, and over the objections of the English inhabitants, the *Quebec Act* left in place the local Civil law used by the French, except to the extent that it was deemed incompatible with the legal system imposed by the English sovereign.[23] The preservation of the Quebec's private law as it existed prior to the conquest was thereby assured by the *Quebec Act* of 1774.

The essential features of the *Quebec Act* of 1774 were that in all matters respecting property and civil rights, "Resort shall be had to the laws of Canada", that the system of land holding was altered to free and common soccage. Subject to the English sovereign, the free exercise of the Roman Catholic religion was to continue. These provisions, along with the imposition of the English criminal law and the principle of freedom of willing at once secured the place of the Civil law within the constitutional structure of Canada and established patterns of divisions of legislative authority that would be reflected at the time of Confederation one hundred years later.

Two further important events, the division of the province of Quebec into Upper and Lower Canada in 1791 and the Act of Union in 1840, set the constitutional place for Quebec in a Canadian state.

3. THE CODIFICATION OF 1866[24]

Nineteenth century Quebec was an agricultural, rural society whose mores were bound up closely with the strong institutional presence of the Roman Catholic church. Commercial centres such as Montreal and Three Rivers flourished during this period, but the overwhelming features of Quebec society were essentially those of an agrarian, family-oriented French-speaking people.

Nevertheless, the emerging capitalist and mercantile classes of the developing commercial centres had their influence as well, an influence whose force was felt in a push toward freedom of contract, the recognition of freedom of religion and a focus on the person *qua* individual.

The legal isolation of the Civil law in Quebec in a sea of Common law and the ongoing influence of Common law sources prompted commentators of the period to notice a deterioration in the Civil law and increasing uncertainty about what the law actually was. Lord Durham sent a report in 1839 that severely criticized the legal situation in a famous passage:

---

[23] Brierley and Macdonald, *supra,* note 2 at par. 14.

[24] The *Civil Code of Lower Canada* was proclaimed on May 26, 1866 (Canada Gazette, 1824, at 1877) and came into force on August 1, 1866.

The law of the Province and the administration of justice are, in fact, a patch-work of the results of the interference, at different times, of different legislative powers, each proceeding on utterly different and generally incomplete views, and each utterly regardless of the other. The law itself is a mass of incoherent and conflicting laws, part French, part English, and with the line between each very confusedly drawn.

In 1851, the first school of law was established in Montreal with six students and the first Faculty of Law was established at McGill University in 1853. A law faculty at Laval was established one year later. But they had little to work with, as one article of the times plaintively complained:

Is there a country in the civilized world, wherein so few scientific books or pamphlets have appeared, as Lower Canada? Have we a solitary work on any branch of legal science written by a Lower Canadian, worthy of the name of treatise of Law, and to which reference can be made in Court as of authority. . . .With two different systems of law partially in force, no one has been found sufficiently patriotic or painstaking to write Commentaries on the Law of Lower Canada [.].[25]

It was clear that some form of review or reform would be required. In 1857 it was decided that a commission would be appointed to codify the Civil law of Lower Canada.[26] On June 10, 1957, Georges-Etienne Cartier tabled the legislation, which provided for the appointment of three commissioners and two bilingual secretaries, whose task was to "reduce into one code. . .those provisions of the laws of Lower Canada which relate to civil matters and are of a general and permanent character".[27]

The codification was carried out with startling efficiency over a period of less than ten years. With relatively few resources, the commissioners[28] organized and reduced to written form the corpus of Civil and commercial law of Lower Canada in both English and in French. Rather than adopting the revolutionary tone of the French Code, the 1866 Code is viewed by scholars as a consolidating, technical exercise rather than a social statement.[29]

The 1866 Code had a number of other important features that are worth mentioning here. First, because of its bilingual nature, each of the English and French versions was drafted and enacted together and considered to be authoritative. The codifiers specified that the version most consistent with existing law was to prevail. A linguistic balance was maintained on the 1857 Commission, so that both texts were drafted as the codification progressed, with the result that both the English and French

---

[25] *The Examiner — L'Observateur* (janvier, 1861) at 4-5.

[26] *An Act respecting the Codification of the Laws of Lower Canada relative to Civil matters and Procedure*, Stats. Prov. Can. 1857, c. 43.

[27] *Ibid.* art. 4.

[28] The commissioners were prominent jurists of the day: René-Edouard Caron, Charles Dewey Day, Augustin-Norbert Morin, and subsequently Joseph-Ubalde Beaudry.

[29] See Brierley and Macdonald, *supra*, note 2 at par. 21-22.

versions were not only original, but were also successful texts from the standpoint of drafting and coherence.[30] Second, unlike the French Code, the 1866 Code did not expressly repeal all law prior to the date of its coming into force. Indeed, art. 2613 of the 1866 Code specifically stated the law prior to August 1, 1866 remained in force except to the extent that it was altered by the 1866 Code.

The 1866 Code is therefore at once derivative and original in its conception and content. It is derivative in the sense that it can properly be considered a "descendant" of the French Code in its organization and drafting style. It is original in that its drafters took care to reflect the law of Quebec as it existed at that time and avoided the wholesale introduction of a foreign text into local law. The 1866 Code contains not only those elements that were transplanted from the French Code, but also surviving customary law and law that was derived from English sources, particularly respecting certain aspects of commercial law, the law of evidence and the principle of freedom of willing.

The 1866 Code closely follows the organizational structure of the Napoleonic Code of 1804. Three books dealt with persons (i.e. status, capacity, etc.), property, the methods of acquisition of property and a fourth book dealt with commercial law.

One year after the coming into force of the 1866 Code, Canadian confederation took place, and the Canadian political and legislative structure was established.

4. CONFEDERATION

Canada became a federal state in 1867 pursuant to the *British North America Act*, which was renamed the *Constitution Act, 1867*[31] following the "patriation" of the constitution by Pierre Trudeau's Liberals in 1982. The 1867 constitution re-affirmed the divisions of powers that had been established by the *Quebec Act* of 1774 with respect to property and civil rights. Provincial jurisdiction was also retained in respect of heads of power such as education and matters of a local and private nature generally.

---

[30] Skipping ahead a century, it is noteworthy that the economy of the 1866 Code compares favourably to Quebec's second codification initiated in 1965. That "revision" lumbered through commissions, Ministers of Justice, consultations and commentaries, with the assistance of dozens of authors, computerized technical assistance and myriad legislative drafters for over a quarter century before delivering up a new Civil code. It has been argued that the success of the drafting technique in the new Quebec Civil Code is less felicitous than that of its predecessor, and it is certainly true that the English version is less impressive than its French counterpart.

[31] (U.K.) 30 & 31 Vict., c. 3.

Initially, the impact of Confederation on the Civil law was minimal. Over the years, national public standards in matters such as banking law, divorce, matters affecting peace, order and good government, inter-provincial travel, federal employment and corporate law, etc., resulted in the sometimes muscular exercise of federal jurisdiction. A vast body of public law has appeared which was applied throughout the country with results that were sometimes incompatible with Civil law.[32]

5. THE SIXTIES AND THE "SOCIAL PROJECT" OF REVISION

The 1866 Code proved to be an enormously stable piece of legislation, and largely because of its symbolic stature, there was some reluctance to modify it in any significant way.[33] For example, authors point to numerous extra-Codal statutes dealing with a variety of private and quasi-private matters in a wide range of areas, including guardianship, change of name and partnership declarations, all of which could easily have been incorporated in an amended Code but were instead relegated to separate statutes.[34]

However, partly as a result of federalist forces mentioned in the preceding section, concerns were expressed in the 1960's as to the relevance of the 1866 Code.[35] Coupled with the growing national and nationalistic pride of the so-called "Quiet Revolution" in Quebec, there was a push for reform and a renewal of the 1866 Code as part of a social project or constitution reflecting the aspirations of a distinct people. In short, there was a perceived need to modernize the Code. Early efforts appeared in 1955 in the form of enabling legislation[36] and the creation of the Civil Code Revision office under the auspices of a leading Civilian scholar, Paul-André Crépeau.

In 1977, the Report on the Civil Code was presented to the then Minister of Justice under the separatist government, the Parti Québécois, and a Draft Civil Code was published in 1978.[37] Subsequently, the responsibility for the revision of the Civil Code was transferred directly to the Minister of Justice of the Province of Quebec. Public consultations were held in order to establish a range of priorities.

---

[32] Brierley and Macdonald point in particular to the federal enactments respecting divorce and the forms of security available to banks. See Brierley and Macdonald, *supra*, note 2 at pars. 44-45; Macdonald, "Security under Section 178 of the *Bank Act*: A Civil Law Analysis" (1983), 43 R. du Barreau 1007.

[33] This observation is made by Brierley and Macdonald, *supra*, note 2 at 68-70.

[34] *Ibid.* at par. 69.

[35] See, notably, Beaudoin, "Le Code civil québécois: crise de croissance ou crise de vieillesse" (1966), 44 Can. Bar Rev. 391.

[36] An *Act respecting the Revision of the Civil Code*, S.Q. 1954-55, c. 47.

[37] Civil Code Revision Office, Report on the Québec Civil Code, 2 vols. (Québec: éditeur officiel du Québec, 1978).

In 1980 a new Civil Code was partially enacted in order to deal with the perceived urgency of reform and modernization, namely in respect of the provisions dealing with the family.[38] These provisions introduced new law in marriage and matrimonial regimes, divorce, filiation and parental authority and obligations of support, although certain of the provisions dealing with divorce and nullity of marriage have not been proclaimed as a result of continuing federal jurisdiction in these matters.

Consultations were held in 1982 and 1983 regarding the law of persons, successions and property. Between 1986 and 1988 draft bills were prepared on security interests, registration of rights, obligations, evidence, prescription and private international law. In addition, matters with a more public character such as international adoptions and guardianship were also being reformed significantly. Draft legislation was presented in 1990 by the then Minister of Justice, Gilles Remillard, and further study and consultations took place which culminated in a final draft which was enacted in December 1991.[39] On January 1, 1994, the Civil Code of Quebec (C.C.Q.) came into force. Its mission as a social project or legal "blueprint" is clearly announced by the Preliminary Provision:

> The Civil Code of Quebec, in harmony with the *Charter of Human Rights and Freedoms* and the general principles of law, governs persons, relations between persons, and property.
>
> The Civil Code comprises a body of rules which, in all matters within the letter, spirit or object of its provisions, lays down the *jus commune*, expressly or by implication. In these matters, the Code is the foundation of all other laws, although other laws may complement the Code or make exception to it.

SOURCES OF LAW[40]

1. LAW, GENERAL PRINCIPLES AND CUSTOM

The sources of law are used to identify and locate the formal rules which govern the Civil law. There is no universally accepted and complete inventory of exactly what the sources of law are in Civil law jurisdictions, but there is broad consensus that a written code is necessarily the base on which all other law rests, and a recognition that custom plays a primary role as well, albeit as a "subsidiary" primary source of law.[41] In addition to

---

[38] *Act to establish a new Civil Code of Québec and to reform family law*, S.Q. 1980, c. 39; *Act to provide for the carrying out of the family law reform and to amend the Code of Civil Procedure*, S.Q. 1982, c. 17.

[39] See *Commentaires du ministre de la Justice* (Les Publications du Quebec, 1993) Tome 1.

[40] This section deals exclusively with the sources of law in private law and hence the public law as it applies in Quebec is necessarily excluded.

[41] Brierley and Macdonald, *supra*, note 2 at par. 94.

the law and custom, caselaw and doctrine (scholarly commentary) are important but play a secondary or interpretive role.

As the Preliminary Provision of the C.C.Q. announces, the Civilian tradition of the primacy of the code as an imperative source of law is both retained and renewed. In this sense, the C.C.Q. occupies a similar place in Civil law as the unlegislated common law in Common law jurisdictions.[42]

The C.C.Q. is comprehensive and normative in nature, and significantly, is apparently perceived by the Legislator to be on equal or near equal footing with quasi-constitutional legislation such as the provincial human rights legislation, the Quebec *Charter of Rights and Freedoms*. In effect, the Preliminary Provision confirms that it is the primary source of law, interpreted "in harmony" with the Quebec *Charter of Rights and Freedoms*.

The first paragraph of the Preliminary Provision refers as well to the "general principles of law" which the Minister of Justice describes as those principles which, although not explicitly present in the C.C.Q., are nevertheless "supereminent" and inspire the C.C.Q.. The notion of general principles as a new, primary source of law reflects the thinking of French scholars to the effect that supereminent principles are separate from the law but nevertheless primary in their imperative nature.[43] This thinking appears to have found its way directly into the C.C.Q.

The second paragraph of the Preliminary Provision also specifies that the C.C.Q. "lays down" the *jus commune* or, in the French version, *droit commun*. This term refers to the "general law", and reflects a standard reference found in other Civil law jurisdictions.[44] However, the terms are not identical in meaning, and their presence in the two versions of the Preliminary Provision is explained by Hans W. Baade as follows:

> "[D]roit commune embodies the Civil Code instead of legislation outside of the Code and not suppletory to it. *Jus commune*, on the other hand, is a term traditionally employed (and presently used to describe Roman law as received and applied in European countries and their colonies before the nineteenth and twentieth-century codification. When used together, these two terms have one central meaning for Civil lawyers: the civil law, received and/or codified, is the real common law, reflecting the senior legal tradition.[45]

2. CASE LAW

Most Common law lawyers know that decided cases do not occupy the same central place in the Civilian tradition as in the Common law. The

---

[42] Brierley and Macdonald, *supra*, note 2 at par. 97.

[43] See, *e.g.* R. David, *French Law: Its Structure, Sources and Methodology*, trans. M. Kindred (Baton Rouge: Louisiana State University Press, 1972) at 194 ff.

[44] Notably Spain and Mexico. See Baade's book review of Brierley and Macdonald, *supra*, note 2 (1995), 40 McGill Law J. 571 at 571.

[45] Baade, *ibid.* at 571-572.

reasons for this are historical and are grounded in the hostility of the French Revolution to the courts of the *ancien régime* which purported to engage in law making in a manner that was perceived to be profoundly undemocratic.[46] The *Cour de cassation* of the Republic, therefore, had no authority to pronounce a decision on a case, but rather could only quash lower court decisions. This in turn led to the notion that there is no such thing as *stare decisis* or binding precedent in the French system. The classical expression of the role of the courts in France was that *jurisprudence* is not a primary legal source but rather an authority in fact.[47]

In France, however, decided cases are assuming more importance, and the rule that a *jurisprudence constante*, or consistent line of decided cases, is required in order to establish an authoritative principle has given way to an acknowledgement that even a single case from the highest court may suffice.[48]

In Quebec, the role of decided cases has been enormously controversial. The inherent tension between the forces that demanded "purity" in the private Civil law system clashed not only with the growing importance of case law in other Civil law jurisdictions, but with the natural tendency of the court structure in Quebec to develop a judicial style that reflected its Common law structures.

Quebec judges tend now to write lengthy judgments setting out facts, reasons and conclusions in much the same style as one sees in Common law jurisdictions. Contrary to the traditional short, non-discursive form of judgments in Civil law systems which give no insight into judicial reasoning, the current trend lends itself to the development of legal principles and their applications to fact patterns that are not necessarily on all fours with those in a given precedent. Inevitably, these tensions created serious questions as to the proper place and role of decided cases.[49]

In practice, however, the issue is largely moot. Cases are cited before the Quebec courts in much the same manner and with the same deference for appellate decisions as one might find in a Canadian court in a Common law jurisdiction. Even if the theory may vary, lower courts have adopted a *de facto* principle of stare decisis.[50]

---

[46] See B. Nicholas, *French Law of Contract* (Butterworths: London 1982) at 12.

[47] *Ibid.* at 13. See also Esmein, "La jurisprudence et la loi" (1952), 50 Rev.trm.dr.civ. 17.

[48] See Brierley and Macdonald, *supra,* note 2 at par. 101.

[49] See, *e.g.*, J. Deschênes, "Le Rôle législatif du pouvoir judiciaire" (1974), 5 R.D.U.S. 1.

[50] See generally, A. Harvison Young, "*Stare Decisis* — Quebec Court of Appeal — Authority v. Persuasiveness" (1993), 72 Can. Bar Rev. 91.

3. DOCTRINE

Doctrine is a body of writings by learned experts or scholars and is fundamentally academic in its approach. It has a unique and important place in Civil law systems, as a vehicle for interpretation, criticism and systematic exposition of the law. Although doctrine is not necessarily recognized as a formal source of law,[51] it is nevertheless heavily relied on by the courts. The role of doctrine in Civil law, as distinct from that of decided cases in English law is that:

> The English judgment fulfils in fact two functions. In its *ratio decidendi* it constitutes a source of law; in its discursive element it provides a part of what is supplied in French law by doctrine. The part which [the English judgment] cannot provide is large-scale systematic exposition, and it is only in the course of the last 100 years that this gap has gradually been filled, as it always has been in France, by academic writing.[52]

In Quebec, the important place of doctrine is retained and indeed enhanced by a significant body of scholarly works in the Civil law in both its domestic and comparative aspects. As in France, doctrine in Quebec emanated primarily from the universities, and authors now include practitioners, government officials and committees as well as scholars.[53]

ORGANIZATION OF THE JUDICIARY

There is no separate court structure established in Quebec in respect of pure Civil law matters. Consequently, Civil law, criminal, administrative, municipal and constitutional matters are all heard by a court system that is similar to that found in the rest of Canada. Judges are usually appointed from the Bar, and are not trained as career judges as is the case in some European countries such as France.

Under s. 101, *Constitution Act, 1867,* matters assigned to federal jurisdiction are allocated to the Federal Court of Canada in virtue of the *Federal Court Act.* The Federal Court jurisdiction includes tax, maritime, immigration, intellectual property matters and Crown liability. The Federal Court has had no appreciable impact on the Civil law in Quebec.

Before 1949, the final court of appeal in Civil law matters was the Judicial Committee of the Privy Council in London, England, Following the abolition of appeals to the Privy Council, the Supreme Court of Canada was established for the entire country, including final appeal in respect

---

[51] In Quebec, see Popovici, "Dans quelle mesure la jurisprudence et la doctrine sont-elles source de droit au Quebec?" (1973), 8 R.J.T. 189.

[52] Nicholas, *supra,* note 46, at 18.

[53] For a review of the doctrine in Quebec law, see Normand, "Une analyse quantitative de la doctrine en droit civil québécois" (1982), 23 C. de D. 1009.

of Civil law matters. The Supreme Court of Canada is comprised of nine justices, three of whom must be from the Province of Quebec.

1. THE SUPERIOR COURT OF QUEBEC

The *Constitution Act, 1867* provides that Quebec has the same judicial organization and methods of appointments to the judiciary as the other Canadian provinces. The court of original and general jurisdiction is the Superior Court of Quebec. Initially established in 1849, it hears all Civil cases not expressly assigned to other courts in first instance.[54]

The Court also has exclusive jurisdiction in matters of divorce, bankruptcy, alimentary pensions and Crown rights. Since the Superior Court possesses all the judicial powers to make such orders as appropriate, as is the case in the English courts, powers such as the issuance of injunctions and writs of seizure before judgment lie exclusively with the Superior Court.

2. THE COURT OF QUEBEC

With the exception of alimentary pensions, the Court of Quebec has jurisdiction on all matters where the sums claimed or the value of the thing demanded is less than $15,000.[55] It also has exclusive jurisdiction in respect of youth protection, adoption and certain municipal tax and school board matters.

3. THE COURT OF APPEAL

The Court of Appeal of Quebec is the general court of appeal in the Province of Quebec in Civil law matters. It was created in 1849 and until 1971 was known as the Court of King's Bench, or Queen's Bench. The Court of Appeal sits in both Montreal and in Quebec City, and sits in panels of three to five judges on the merits of an appeal. Procedural matters are decided by a single justice of the Court of Appeal.

LEGAL EDUCATION IN QUEBEC

Only lawyers and notaries are entitled to practice law in the Province of Quebec through the Bar of Quebec and the Board of Notaries, respectively.

Lawyers are both barristers and solicitors in the Province of Quebec.

---

[54] Art. 31, *Civil Code of Procedure.*
[55] Art. 34, C.C.P.

All lawyers who have completed the requisite university training,[56] bar admission course and articles may practice law and plead before the courts. Lawyers in good standing of Bars of other Canadian provinces may transfer to Quebec without the need to do the Bar admission course. However, the successful completion of three examinations is required.[57]

The notary is similar to the French *notaire* and is both a practitioner for clients and a public official responsible for the redaction of official documents recorded in a prescribed manner. Notaries have limited rights of appearance before the courts in certain non-contested matters such as the probating of wills.

Six universities offer a degree in Civil law (McGill University, Université de Montreal, Université du Québec à Montréal, Université de Laval and Université de Sherbrooke in Québec, and the Civil law faculty of the University of Ottawa in Ontario. At both McGill and Ottawa it is possible for a student to obtain both Common law and Civil law degrees.

PRINCIPAL FEATURES OF THE CIVIL CODE OF QUEBEC[58]

On January 1, 1994, the Civil Code of Quebec ("C.C.Q.") replaced the Civil Code of Lower Canada and certain related amendments in family law and the law of successions. The C.C.Q. comprises ten books:

Book One: Persons;
Book Two: The Family;
Book Three: Successions;
Book Four: Property;
Book Five: Obligations;
Book Six: Prior Claims and Hypothecs;
Book Seven: Evidence;
Book Eight: Prescription;
Book Nine: Publication of Rights; and
Book Ten: Private International Law.

The following sections provide a general overview of the topics dealt with in the new C.C.Q. and highlight some major changes from prior law that may be of interest.

---

[56] University training became obligatory in 1945.

[57] Two examinations are required in Civil law and one in public law.

[58] The C.C.Q. was introduced on December 18, 1990, passed in principle on June 4, 1991, enacted December 18, 1991 and assented to on December 18, 1991.

BOOK ONE: PERSONS

Book One is concerned with the law of persons, starting with the principle of the full enjoyment and exercise of civil rights by each person, with a special mention of children's rights. Certain "personality rights" are protected, with an emphasis on personal privacy (*e.g.* respect of reputation and privacy) and the integrity of the person (*e.g.* rules respecting the adminstration of medical and other related care, confinement, and respect of the body after death).

Book One also deals with the rules on names and civil status, including lawful change of name, change of designation of sex, and domicile and residence. The rules on absence, declaratory judgment of death, and proof of death are found here as well.

The rules on the capacity of persons establish the law respecting majority and minority, tutorship to minors and the protective supervision of persons of full age.

Finally, Book One deals with legal persons, their creation, the effects of their juridical personality, the obligations and disqualification of directors, and the judicial attribution of personality. The operations, dissolution and winding-up of legal persons are also addressed.

BOOK TWO: THE FAMILY

Book Two introduces some new rules concerning filiation and also addresses the emerging technologies respecting medically assisted reproduction and their effects in law.

Title One deals with marriage and solemnization of marriage, the effects of marriage and provisions relating to the rights and duties of the spouses. The rules respecting family patrimony, including the family residence, and general rules governing the choice of a matrimonial regime are dealt with as well. Chapter II sets out the rules respecting adoption.

Titles Three and Four cover, respectively, the obligation of support between family members and the principle of parental authority.

BOOK THREE: SUCCESSIONS

This Book reaffirms the tradition in Quebec of freedom of testation, although in 1989 some qualifications to this principle were established by claims for alimentary pension by surviving dependents of a deceased spouse. This derogation from the principle of freedom of testation appears as well in the C.C.Q.

Title One deals with the opening of successions and establishes the qualities required for succession. Title Two deals with the transmission of successions and Title Three establishes the rules on the legal devolution of successions, defining degrees, generations and direct and collateral lines of ascent and descent.

Title Four addresses wills, the capacity required of the testator and the forms of wills, their probating and proof.

Title Five sets out the rules on the liquidation of successions and Title Six contains the rules on partition, whereby persons who are in undivided ownership can force division of the jointly owned property. It also deals with the right to maintain undivided ownership.

BOOK FOUR: PROPERTY

Title One of Book Four describes the kinds of property that exist at Civil law in Quebec. Briefly, the types of property include movable and immovable property; property in relation to its proceeds; property in relation to persons having rights thereto or possession, and other relationships creating a property right. This latter category includes the acquisition of vacant property, things without an owner, or lost or forgotten movables.

Title Two defines the right of ownership. Specific rules are set out in respect of the ownership of immoveables, such as limits and boundaries of land, waters, trees, access to and protection of another's land, views, rights of way, and common fences and works, and rules respecting nuisance. Title Three deals with the modes of ownership, which include undivided co-ownership, divided co-ownership and superficies. Title Four describes the components of the right of ownership, namely usufruct, use, servitude and emphyteusis and Title Five sets out some restrictions on the free disposition of property.

Title Six addresses an issue that has long been troublesome in Quebec law, namely the law of Trusts. Since the Quebec law of property does not recognize equitable ownership, the practical requirement of some kind of a comparable vehicle has created a new patrimony.[59] The practical solution adopted in the C.C.Q. is that the Trust patrimony is autonomous and distinct from that of the Trustee, the settlor or the beneficiary. In short, no one can be said to "own" the Quebec Trust.[60]

---

[59] Trusts have existed in Quebec, albeit in a very different form than that known in the Common law, since 1888.

[60] Article 1261, C.C.Q.

The rules governing administration of the property of others are also contained in this Book, and include the permitted activities of administrators, the rules of administration, and the obligations of the administrator towards beneficiaries and third persons.

BOOK FIVE: OBLIGATIONS

Book Five deals first with obligations in general, and second, with nominate contracts.

The general theory of obligations includes fundamental principles that underpin the Civil law, namely that an obligation can arise from a contract or from any act or fact to which law attaches the effects of obligation. In essence, this means that the theories of both contractual liability and delict (tort) arise from the same principle, and in the past, parties have been able to sue in either contract or in delict, at their choice, for injury arising from the same circumstances.[61] However, the new C.C.Q. attempts to restrict access to the range of choice in the new art. 1458 which provides that:

> Art. 1453. Every person has a duty to honour his contractual undertakings.
>
> Where he fails in this duty, he is liable for any . . .injury he causes . . .; neither he nor the other party may in such a case avoid the rules governing contractual liability by opting for the rules that would be more favourable to them.

Despite this clear legislative direction, the Quebec Court of Appeal recently decided that there is nevertheless no impediment to seeking both recourses on a subsidiary basis (as opposed to alternatively).[62]

Chapter III of this Book sets out the rules respecting Civil liability. Under the 1866 Code, the central principle of Civil liability was elegantly described as follows:

> Art. 1053 C.C.L.C. Every person capable of discerning right from wrong is responsible for the damage caused by his fault to another, whether by positive act, imprudence, neglect or want of skill.

The same principle is established by the C.C.Q., albeit rather more ponderously:

> Art. 1457. Every person has a duty to abide by the rules of conduct which lie upon him. according to the circumstances, usage or law, so as not to cause injury to another.

---

[61] The principle of *cumul* was affirmed by the Supreme Court of Canada in a controversial case, *Wabasso Ltd. v. National Drying Machine Co.*, [1981] 1 S.C.R. 578, 19 C.C.L.T. 177, 38 N.R. 224.

[62] *Syndicat du garage du cours Le Royer v. Gagnon*, [1995] R.J.Q. 1313 (C.A.).

Where he is endowed with reason and fails in this duty, he is responsible for the injury he causes to another person and is liable to reparation for the injury, whether it be bodily, moral or material in nature.

He is also liable, in certain cases, to reparation for injury caused to another by the act or fault of another person or by the act of things in his custody.

Title Two of Book Five provides the special rules relating to the *sui generis* contracts called "nominate" contracts, which have their own particular rules. These include sale, gifts, lease, affreightment, carriage, employment, contracts of enterprise and contracts for services, mandate (agency), partnership and association, deposit, loan, suretyship, annuities, insurance, gaming and wagering contracts, transactions and arbitration agreements.

Finally, the C.C.Q. has introduced products liability legislation at art. 1468(1) which imposes liability on manufacturers for safety defects.

BOOK SIX: PRIOR CLAIMS AND HYPOTHECS

Book Six deals with security interests through the body of legal rules governing prior claims and hypothecs.

The Title dealing with hypothecs includes the categories of immovable hypothecs (on real property), movable hypothecs (on chattels), floating hypothecs, and legal hypothecs, as well as the procedures for the enforcement and extinction of these secured claims.

The important innovation in this area is the hypothec on the moveable, the equivalent of a chattels mortgage, which did not exist in Quebec prior to the C.C.Q., except in limited circumstances where the creditor was in possession of the moveable. Non-possessory security interests in moveable property are now recognized in the Quebec system, subject to requirements of registration ("publication").

BOOK SEVEN: EVIDENCE

The law of evidence in Quebec is largely inspired by Common law rules of evidence. The rules respecting burden of proof, admissibility, judicial notice, testimony, probative value, presumptions and admissions will all be familiar to Common law lawyers. The C.C.Q. also introduces proof by means of production of material things.

BOOK EIGHT: PRESCRIPTION

Prescription is divided into two categories, namely acquisitive prescription and extinctive prescription.

The Title devoted to acquisitive prescription sets out the conditions under which it operates and the periods required to acquire rights by the passage of time.

Title Three sets out the special rules relating to extinctive prescription. The most important rule is that an action to enforce a personal right or movable real right is prescribed by three years, if the prescriptive period is not otherwise established. In cases where the Code is silent, the period is ten years.

BOOK NINE: PUBLICATION OF RIGHTS

Book Nine deals with the registration or publication of rights through the applicable register. The effects of publication are essentially that rights can be set up against third persons, and this Book establishes the relative rank of rights and the protection for third persons acting in good faith.

BOOK TEN: PRIVATE INTERNATIONAL LAW

Book Ten sets out the rules governing conflict of laws and the choice of which legal system has jurisdiction over a given legal issue. The subjects are divided into four categories of Civil law, namely persons, property, obligations and procedure.

Title Three deals with the international jurisdiction of Quebec authorities. It is divided into two chapters, one containing general provisions, and the other containing the special provisions relating to matters of an extrapatrimonial and family nature or of a personal and patrimonial nature, and to real and mixed actions.

A major change in this area is in the recognition of foreign judgments because contrary to the situation existing prior to January 1, 1994, Quebec law no longer permits the re-examination of foreign judgments by courts viewed as competent by Quebec. The view of leading scholars such as Professor H.P. Glenn was that the prior law in the 1866 Code was unwarranted.[63] Review of foreign judgments is now prohibited by the C.C.Q. except in respect of foreign proceedings instituted before January 1, 1994.

---

[63] See Brierley and Macdonald, *supra,* note 2 at par. 854.

Chapter 9

THE ROLE OF LAWYERS
AND JUDGES

INTRODUCTION

No matter how well-designed the system of law and no matter how appropriate the institutions created to function within that system, its effective application depends upon the efforts of those who man the institutions. Basically, those persons who man the legal system and the institutions contained in that system fall within one of the following categories:

1. Lawyers (serving in the separate and unique functions of barristers and solicitors, law reformers, teachers and many related vocations);

2. Judges (at various levels within the judicial system with various responsibilities in accordance with the governing statute setting out the jurisdiction of the court over which they preside);

3. Specialized administrative personnel, some of whom assist lawyers and some of whom assist judges; and

4. Staff of the various departments, agencies, boards and commissions of government at all levels, which bodies are responsible for the various aspects of the administration of justice.

Obviously, the key persons in our legal system are the judge and the lawyer, but, as indicated above, there are others. The lawyer is often assisted by paralegal personnel such as professional title searchers, law clerks (many of whom are now trained in special courses at the community college or technical school level), legal secretaries and others.[1] Also,

---

[1] For a discussion of paralegal training in Canada, see D.C. Thompson, *How to Become a Lawyer in Canada* (Edmonton: Acorn Books, 1979) and Taman, "The Emerging Legal Paraprofessionals", in Slayton and Trebilcock (eds.), *The Professions and Public Policy* (Toronto: University of Toronto Press, 1978). More recently, see *Submission to the Standing Committee on the Administration of Justice, Legislative Assembly of Ontario re:*

judges (that is, courts) are assisted by court clerks, court reporters, registrars and others. Finally, both lawyers and judges are assisted by external government agencies, including such personnel as official guardians, public trustees and the like.[2]

All of these people share the responsibility of ensuring the efficient functioning of the institutions within the legal system. Therefore, they must work co-operatively one with the other to ensure the fair, just and efficient administration of justice. In addition, they must work co-operatively with those manning other institutions in society. For example, accountants and medical professionals are often called upon in the course of the lawyer's or judge's conduct of his everyday responsibilities.

We must focus our attention on judges and lawyers, for it is they who are specifically trained and best understand the nature and purpose of our legal system and it is they who play the most dramatic and significant role in ensuring the effective functioning of that system. Historically, the training of lawyers was conducted entirely on an apprenticeship basis; now, in Canada, legal training is a very formalized and institutionalized process. In the past many judges were not trained as lawyers; although presently in Canada there are still some judges who are not lawyers, their number is small and dwindling. They sit exclusively on lower court benches and all new appointments reflect the conventional wisdom that members of the judiciary should properly be members of the legal profession. Most judges are appointed from the ranks of senior practising lawyers, although some are now being appointed from the ranks of legal academicians. The latter kind of appointment, although fairly common in the United States, was, until recently, relatively infrequent in Canada. The training of lawyers and the appointment of judges will be discussed, among other things, in the topics set out below.

Bill 42, An Act to Regulate the Activities of Paralegal Agents (Toronto: Can. Bar Assn., Ont. 1987); M.M. Jennings, "Paralegals — trends for development" (1987), 26 Law Office Economics and Management 279; D.W. Phillips, "The Paralegal" (1986-87), 1 Can. Fam. L.Q. 173; M.O. Mungoran, "The law clerk and the corporation" (1987), 4 Business and Law 54; D. Crump, "What a Legal Assistant can do for you" (1981), 44 Texas Bar J. 739; "Lawyers and Legal Assistants: the excellence equation", Edmonton: Legal Education Society of Alberta, 1987; J. Harwell, "The paralegal: An effective part of the legal service team" (1987), 23 Tennessee Bar J. 37; M.E. Moon, A.K. Lashinger and G.M. Redic, "The Paralegal Malpractice: new profession, new responsibility" (1982), 18 Trial 40; R.W. Lockwood, "The role of the paralegal in the civil commitment process" (1981), 10 Capital Univ. L. Rev. 721; C. Perko and K. Braeman, "A decade of paralegals in the law office: a progress report" (1982), 29 Federal Bar News & J. 77; G.A. Munneke and F. Utley, "If the grass looks greener outside the bar, how do you decide on a nonlegal career?" (1986), 13 Nat. (C.B.A.) 4:34; S. Braungart, "Jobless young lawyers learn of alternative career possibilities (Alta.)" (1986), 13 Nat. (C.B.A.) 7:11.

[2] Recently, so-called 'legal agents' have begun to play a role in the legal system. Essentially, they are non-legally trained persons who are performing some functions traditionally reserved for lawyers. For a discussion of 'legal agents', see Chapter 13.

LAWYERS

1. TRAINING OF LAWYERS

Dr. Max Wyman, a former Chairman of the Alberta Human Rights Commission, a member of the Kirby Commission of Inquiry, and a former President of the University of Alberta, made these remarks on the objectives of legal education in an address to a class of first-year law students:

> Although I have no knowledge of the curriculum of the Faculty of Law, I would hope that it would make new students of law not mechanics of the law. To spend an inordinate amount of time teaching how to draft wills or transfer titles is not, in my opinion, a justified use of university time. You can learn such matters faster and better in actual practice in a law office. To teach you, by the case law approach, how to search legal literature for the perfect defence of a client may be justified, but that will not make you students of the law.
>
> To be students of the law you must be prepared to study some of the big ideas of the law, and big ideas do exist in abundance in the literature of the law. You must be prepared to examine critically the present purpose and scope of the law, and to decide whether that purpose and scope is still consistent with social mores of our time. Indeed as students of the law, you must be prepared to challenge the statements of your teachers, always demanding an understanding of what they say, always demanding a proof of what they say. If you are content to regurgitate that which you are taught, then you must become a legal mechanic, not legal scholars.[3]

Generally speaking, a prospective lawyer must (with some exceptions) undertake successful studies at the undergraduate level at a Canadian university. Most law schools admit students who have performed well in a general Bachelor's Degree program. Some universities, however, admit law students with two years or less of undergraduate training. Some students enter law possessing graduate degrees in all sorts of fields, in the humanities, social sciences, and the natural sciences, while others are already trained in other professions such as engineering and medicine. Some students return to law school after many years in business and industry. Because of the large number of applicants and the limited number of first-year places, obviously no student automatically obtains admission; he or she has to perform well in competition with all other applicants. Once admitted, a student is required to take three years of full-time academic study in a faculty of law. In Canada, as of the date of this writing, there are no night programs and there are about five part-time programs leading to a law degree,[4] although there has been discussion of such

---

[3] An address to the Faculty of Law, University of Alberta, 3rd to 7th November 1975.

[4] The first program was that offered at the College of Law at the University of Saskatchewan in Saskatoon. Subsequently, programs were established at the University of Victoria and the University of Manitoba. In addition, a short-term pilot project was commenced at Queen's University during the 1989-90 academic year. At about the same time a part-time LL.B. program was approved in principle at the University of Toronto.

training. In contrast, in the United States, many such programs are accredited.[5]

Upon graduation, a student is generally required to serve a one-year period of articles of clerkship under a practising member of the bar of that province.[6] This period provides the graduating law student with an opportunity to learn from an experienced practitioner many of the techniques and procedures not included in the academic courses given at law schools.[7] Upon completing his term of articles in, and the bar admission course of a particular province, the student becomes a member of the Law Society of that particular province.[8] Generally, a student who graduates from a law school in Canada with a common law degree may, after serving his period of articles in and successfully completing the bar admission course of any common law province, be called to the bar of (that is, become a member of) the Law Society of that province. This transferability does not as readily exist in respect of the province of Quebec for the reason that the province of Quebec has a civil law system requiring different formal legal training in university.[9]

There are other ways of becoming eligible for membership in the law society of another province and these derive from the statute governing the legal profession in that province. A fairly common method for the lawyer who has been a practising member of one province for a number of years is to successfully complete transfer examinations set by the

---

[5] There are currently several developments occurring in relation to the training of lawyers. These current developments are discussed in Chapter 13. For a further discussion of legal education in Canada, see D.C. Thompson, *How to Become a Lawyer in Canada* (Edmonton: Acorn Books Ltd., 1979); the Hon. Mr. Justice R.J. Matas, Admission and Education Committee of the Law Society of Manitoba; The Council of the Faculty of Law of the University of Manitoba, "Report of the Special Committee on Legal Education" (1979), and the subsequent article, the Hon. Mr. Justice R.J. Matas, "Legal Education in the Wake of the 60's" (1979), 44 Sask. L. Rev. 63; and A.G. Amsterdam, "The lawyering revolution and legal education", [1985] Cambridge Lect. 11. See also the Bibliography on "Legal Education in Canada", appended to this chapter.

[6] The period of articles actually varies from province to province. For example, in Nova Scotia the period is ten months while in New Brunswick it is forty-four weeks. In Quebec it is six months, while in Manitoba it is 50 weeks. In British Columbia it is nine months. Most provinces now conduct the Bar Admission Course at various times during the period of articles. See A.C. Hutchinson, "Articling", National, August/September, 1994.

[7] Apparently, many new lawyers are unhappy with various aspects of their training. See the Financial Post, 31st January 1981.

[8] The Law Society of Upper Canada recently instituted a Practice Advisory Service which is designed, among other things, to advise and assist new or inexperienced lawyers on the opening or administration of a law practice. Also in Ontario, several lawyers recently established a "Mentor Program", the first of its kind in North America, where junior members of the criminal bar are teamed up with senior members, in order to provide a system or network for informal advice. See Maclean's Magazine, 20th July 1981.

[9] Recently, following a major revision of the Quebec Civil Code, all Quebec lawyers, irrespective of their experience, were required to take a mandatory course offered by the Barreau du Québec on the new Code. See Canadian Lawyer, February 1994.

law society of the province to which he or she wishes to transfer. The eligibility to write these exams is often based on a minimum number of years of practice in the former province. The successful transferee is not then precluded from retaining his membership in the province from which he or she is transferring; many lawyers are members of more than one law society. Also, lawyers from one province will appear before the court of another province on an occasional or ad hoc basis for a particular case without being formally enroled as a member of the bar of that province. However, the general and most common method of entering the legal profession is, after earning a Bachelor of Laws degree, to serve a period of articles in a particular province and then pass the bar admission course of that province.

Once a student is called to the bar of a particular province, he becomes in Canada a barrister, solicitor and notary public. Unlike the United Kingdom, where a person practises as either a barrister or solicitor but not both, there is no legally sanctioned distinction in Canada and therefore a practising lawyer may perform as a barrister and/or a solicitor. Generally speaking, the functional distinction is that a barrister articulates a client's case in a court of law in the course of litigation, whereas a solicitor performs more or less technical procedures such as drafting of agreements and wills and other types of work generally referred to as "office" or "desk" work.[10]

2. CAREERS OPEN TO LAWYERS

Upon graduation, the new barrister and solicitor need not enter into the practise of law. In the United States, it is estimated that just over 50 per cent of the lawyers practise law. In Canada, historically, and this is essentially true today, most law school graduates want to become members of the bar and practise their chosen profession. However, following the trend in the United States, and in response to a more crowded marketplace, many lawyers are entertaining the idea of using their law degrees for other related vocations. Thus it is somewhat misleading to refer to a single "career in law" as such. Legal training affords an individual the opportunity to engage in many careers, and often a lawyer changes from one "career" to another during the course of his or her working life. Set

---

[10] The usual designation on a lawyer's letterhead and business card is that of "barrister and solicitor". A Calgary law firm whose members restricted their practice to court work designated themselves as "barristers at law". This was disallowed by the Law Society of Alberta for the reason that the designation implied specialization which was not formally recognized by the Law Society. See St. John's Report, 30th March 1979.

out below is a summary of the various opportunities available to the new graduating lawyer.[11]

A career in law can mean, as it does to most persons, the day-to-day practice of law. In this capacity the lawyer interacts directly with clients to accomplish one or both of two objectives. One is to order and regulate the affairs of his clients, be they individual or corporate clients. This is the practice of preventive law in order to ensure that the client's affairs are conducted in accordance with the rules set done by statutes and various other sources. The other is to articulate a client's case in a court of law if the client is accused of committing a criminal offence or sued in a civil action.

One recent development in respect of private practice is the movement toward accredited specialization in a given area of the law. Some jurisdictions now permit a lawyer to be formally designated as a specialist in certain areas. For example, in Ontario, the Law Society of Upper Canada has created a Specialist Certification Program. This program, in existence since 1986, permits lawyers to apply to a Specialist Certification Board for certification as a specialist in one or more areas such as Civil Litigation, Criminal Law, Family Law, Immigration Law, Intellectual Property law, Labour law, etc.[12] There is a further discussion of specialization in Chapter 13. In addition, the Law Society of Alberta, for example, is currently about to initiate a program of specialization. Some provincial law societies permitted lawyers to publicly advertise that they restrict their practices to certain specialized areas, although this is far removed from a true system of accredited specialization.[13] The Canadian Bar Association also undertook a major study of specialization.[14] As a result of those early developments, much has occurred to promote and advance the notion of specialization, which has led to the expanding institutionalization of specialization as a regularized characteristic of the legal profession in Canada.[15] This major change is discussed in some detail in Chapter 13.

---

[11] J.P. Ryan, "The Lawyer as Mediator: a new role for lawyers in the practice of nonadversarial divorce" (1986), 1 C.F.L.Q. 105; E. Ratushny, "The Role of the Legal Academic — Beyond Orwell" in R. Abella and M. Rothman (eds.), *Justice Beyond Orwell,* Canadian Institute for the Administration of Justice (Montreal: Les Editions Yvon Blais, 1985); L. Weber, "Locked in a gilded cage" (1986), 10 Can. Lawyer 5:37; and D. Fromm and M. Webb, "The Work Experience of U. of A. Law Graduates" (1986), 23 Alta. L. Rev. 366.

[12] See Ontario Reports, September 24, 1993 p. xii. See also Law Society of Upper Canada, Benchers Bulletin, May 1993.

[13] See; *Canada (A.G.) v. Law Society (B.C.); Jabour v. Law Society of B.C.*, [1982] 2 S.C.R. 307, [1982] 5 W.W.R. 289, 37 B.C.L.R. 145, 19 B.L.R. 234, 137 D.L.R. (3d) 1, 66 C.P.R. (2d) 1, 43 N.R. 451.

[14] See the *National*, March 1983, p. 4.

[15] See V. Paisley, "Specialization: A Challenge to the legal profession" (1984), 3 Advocates' Soc. J. 33; "The Unknown Experts: Legal Specialists in Canada Today", Report of the Canadian Bar Association Special Committee on Specialization in the Legal Profession (1983);

Many lawyers are employed in government service at both the provincial and federal levels acting as government advisors, conducting legal research, drafting legislation and serving as counsel in litigation matters involving the government.

All of the provinces and the federal government have law reform commissions which conduct detailed studies into areas of the law that may require reform and submit reports containing their recommendations to their respective legislatures. Lawyers who enjoy in-depth legal research may find employment with a law reform commission challenging.

Many lawyers work in the business world, whether as lawyers in corporate legal departments or as businessmen using their legal training indirectly.

Opportunities are available to lawyers in the teaching profession. Teaching law to law students in the various faculties of law in Canada, or to paralegals or legal secretaries in the various community colleges provides a rewarding career to those who wish to interact with students and at the same time conduct scholarly legal research.

It is becoming less unusual to find lawyers who are also members of other professional associations. For example, there are many persons in Canada who hold both law and medical degrees, and these persons often act as coroners or engage in advisory work for the government or for private industry in connection with medico-legal matters.

In short, law is truly a multi-faceted profession and legal training affords a person an opportunity to engage in all sorts of professional opportunities.[16]

"Legal Specialization", Special Committee on Specialization, American Bar Association (1974-75); Report of the Special Committee on Specialization, Law Society of Upper Canada, Communqué No. 10 (1972); *The Legal Profession and Quality of Service: Further Reports and Proposals,* Report and Materials of a National Workshop on Quality of Legal Services (October 1980), as a sequel to the National Conference on Quality of Legal Services (October 1978) (see particularly the research paper on "Recent Developments in Specialization Regulation of the Legal Profession"); and Report of the Joint Committee on Specialization of the Law Society of B.C. and the B.C. Branch of the Canadian Bar Association on a pilot programme for the certification of legal specialists in B.C. (1977).

See also the following articles in the Lawyers Weekly: "The Time has Come to Certify Specialists", 26th August 1983; "Specialization report adopted", 9th September 1983; " 'Preferred area of Practice' replaced by term of art 'Practice restricted to' ", 13th July 1984; "Two Year trial Program will recognize specialists in Criminal and Civil litigation", 14th June 1985; "Trade Names permissible for Law Firms", 7th February 1986; "Deaf Lawyer hears call of justice as advocate for disabled", 7th November 1986.

[16] See Hoffmann, P., *Career Handbook for Law Students 1993*. Toronto: Carswell, 1992. In Ontario, the Law Society has held several alternative career seminars. In Alberta, both the Women's Law Forum and the Law Society of Alberta have held similar programs.

The reader can appreciate that generally the role of the lawyer is difficult to define, and depends essentially upon how legal training has been utilized upon graduation.

One current concern relates to the number of lawyers who are entering the profession. The existing bar is concerned, as can be expected, with marketplace economics. Indeed, the proliferation of lawyers is so great that, for example, in Alberta, the average number of years of practice experience since graduation is approximately 4 or 5 years. In Ontario, the Law Society of Upper Canada established a Special Committee on Numbers of Lawyers to consider this issue, and it reported to convocation (i.e., the "Benchers" or legislative body of the society in general meeting) that

(1) given existing economic circumstances, more lawyers are engaged in private practice than are needed;

(2) the Law Society should not place arbitrary limits on the number of persons entering the profession;

(3) the law schools should review the number of persons entering the first year of their law programmes; and

(4) members of the public considering a legal career should be educated as to the economic difficulties facing practitioners.[17]

Increasingly, law societies and law schools are establishing placement offices to assist new lawyers in finding employment opportunities. For example, in Ontario, the Law Society of Upper Canada has created such an office while, in Alberta, the Faculty of Law of the University of Alberta has also created such an office.

3. THE LAWYER-CLIENT RELATIONSHIP

Let us now direct our attention to the practising lawyer. In this capacity, he has two responsibilities. First, he must articulate and advance the

[17] See Law Society of Upper Canada, Communique No. 130, 27th January 1983. For reaction to the above conclusions, see the Financial Post, 12th March 1983 and the editorial appearing in the Edmonton Journal, 7th February 1983. For some further discussion on the "oversupply" of lawyers, see the Toronto Star, 13th March 1983, p. A16, and, generally, with respect to the "oversupply" of professionals, including lawyers, the column written by J. McArthur appearing in the Toronto Star, 10th March 1983.

The "oversupply" of lawyers has led to competition among lawyers in the marketplace both in Canada and the United States. See the Toronto Star, 10th June 1979 and the Edmonton Journal, 12th June 1979 (in connection with a so-called "price-cutting war" in Ontario); Newsweek Magazine, 26th February 1979 (in connection with cut-rate divorce); Time Magazine, 9th October 1978 (in connection with supermarketing legal services); Consumer Reports, September 1979 (for advice on paying less for a lawyer); the New York Times, 26th August 1979 (on marketing legal services in large, multibranch firms); the Edmonton Sun, 18th December 1981 (on "bargain-basement" divorce fees).

best interests of his client; it is often said that he must be the champion of his client's interests.[18] This is particularly important in the field of criminal law where an accused client faces a prosecutor possessing access to all the powerful investigatory machinery of the state. The lawyer must consider his client's interests as paramount and his client must be able to rely on the assumption that his lawyer will do so. This basic mutual understanding will undoubtedly foster the confidence and trust that must underlie the lawyer-client relationship. In order to preserve and protect this confidence, the law has recognized a special and unique privilege with respect to communications between a lawyer and his client. The common law provides that communication, written or oral, flowing from a client to his lawyer is privileged, that is, it may not be disclosed by the lawyer in a court of law or to a tribunal or otherwise unless and until such time as the client waives this privilege. The privilege will not exist in the event that any communication between a client and his lawyer involves criminal conduct by the lawyer himself. The important point is that this privilege is vital to the confidential and trusting relationship between a client and solicitor and is recognized nowhere else in the common law. For example, contrary to popular belief, there is no privilege at common law between a doctor and his patient even when the doctor is a psychiatrist, nor is there privilege between a priest and his parishioners or between a journalist and his confidential sources.[19] However, in various states in the United States and in some provinces in Canada these other "privileges" have been created by statutes. For example, in the province of Newfoundland a privilege between priest and penitent has been created by statute. Sometimes, lawyers find themselves in situations where they have a conflict of interest. These situations often involve difficult ethical dilemmas. In most cases, these situations arise as a result of lawyers acting for greater than a single interest in a given transaction, a practice that should be strongly discouraged.[20]

The law's recognition of the need for a vital and trusting relationship between a lawyer and his client through the rule relating to privilege is consistent with the notion that the lawyer's essential responsibility is to protect and to articulate the interests of his client.

---

[18] See Manes, D. and Silver, M., *Solicitor-Client Privilege in Canadian Law* (Markham: Butterworths, 1993).

[19] See *Moysa v. Alta. (Labour Relations Bd.)*, [1989] 1 S.C.R. 1572, [1989] 4 W.W.R. 596, 67 Alta. L.R. (2d) 193, 34 C.P.C. (2d) 97, 89 C.L.L.C. 14,028, 60 D.L.R. (4th) 1, 96 N.R. 70, 97 A.R. 368, 40 C.R.R. 197.

[20] See Law Society of Upper Canada, Errors and Omissions, November 1992.

4. THE LAWYER'S ROLE AS AN OFFICER OF THE COURT

The lawyer's second responsibility is to act at all times as an officer of the court. In taking his oath as a member of the bar of a particular province, the lawyer promises to serve the judicial system at all times as an officer of the court.[21] In serving as an officer of the court, the lawyer must always consider the public good and must work to preserve the integrity of a free and democratic society. He must protect, preserve and respect the institutions within the legal system, and he has a special obligation to ensure that unfairness and injustice do not occur in a court of law. This means, for example, that he must advance the case law, both in support of and against his client's position, so that a judge can adjudicate a particular dispute with a full knowledge of the relevant law. Likewise, the Crown prosecutor in a criminal trial, as an officer of the court, must strive to ascertain the truth as he seeks to prove the case against the accused. Once the truth is ascertained, it is up to the judge to register a conviction against or an acquittal in favour of the accused.

There is no question that the dictates of our system require that a lawyer exercise a special role in society as an officer of the court placing the interests of justice and fairness ahead of the narrower interests of his particular client. However, at the same time, the lawyer must regard his client's interests as vital. This often leads to a dilemma. Accordingly, codes of ethics have been established to permit lawyers to resolve these difficult situations. We will now examine the relevant codes of ethics governing the behaviour of lawyers in Canada. Lord MacMillan once said:

> The code of honour of the Bar is at once its most cherished possession and the most valued safe-guard of the public. In the discharge of his office the advocate has a duty to his client, a duty to his opponent, a duty to the Court, a duty to the State, and a duty to himself. To maintain a perfect poise amidst the various and somewhat conflicting claims is no easy feat.

The pull of these "conflicting claims" referred to by Lord MacMillan is perhaps more severe on the Canadian lawyer in view of the fact that several codes of ethics govern his or her professional conduct.[22]

5. STANDARDS OF CONDUCT REQUIRED OF LAWYERS

To begin with, the legal profession in every province is governed by provincial statute. This statute generally defines the standard of conduct

---

[21] T. Mathew, "Counsel's duties to the Court and to the client — is there a conflict?" (1984), 3 Advocates' Soc. J. 3.

[22] Recently, in debate before Parliament, the Canadian Bar Association sought an exemption from the provisions of the then proposed Lobbyists Registration Act on the ground that lawyers were already subject to stringent ethical standards as a result of the various codes of professional conduct. The Parliamentary committee studying the legislation, however, rejected this argument. See the Edmonton Journal, October 7, 1994.

required of a barrister and solicitor in the province and, in the event that this standard is not met, it outlines the methods of disciplining the lawyer whose conduct has fallen short of the standard.[23] But it would be misleading to conclude that a lawyer must conform only to the particular standard set out in the statute in a given jurisdiction without reference to any other codes of ethics. If a lawyer's conduct meets the statutory standard of conduct governing the profession in a given province, he will likely not be disciplined, but at the same time, he may very well fall short of other standards set out in more extensive codes of ethics. For example, in the province of Alberta, in addition to the statutory standard which must be met to avoid being disciplined, a lawyer must also conform to the canons of ethics established by the Benchers of the Law Society.[24] These canons set out the various duties that the lawyer has to the state, to the court, to his fellow lawyer, and to himself. In Alberta, for example, under the Legal Profession Act, R.S.A. 1980, c. L-9, a lawyer may be disciplined if his behaviour is "conduct unbecoming" a barrister or solicitor. It may or may not be that the violation of a particular canon of ethics constitutes "conduct unbecoming" a barrister or solicitor. Under a 1981 amendment to the Act, a member or student member of the Law Society may be disciplined for any act or conduct which "is incompatible with the best interests of the public or the members of the Society, or . . . tends to harm the standing of the legal profession generally . . . whether or not that act or conduct is disgraceful or dishonourable and whether or not that act or conduct relates to the practice of law". See the Legal Profession Amendment Act, S.A. 1981, c. 53, s. 47. In any event, a lawyer must not only ensure that his conduct is such that it is "becoming" a barrister or solicitor, but he must also ensure that all the detailed canons of ethics are followed. In Alberta, effective January 1, 1995, a new comprehensive code of conduct was established. The Alberta Code of Professional Conduct deals with such matters as:

1. Relationship of the Lawyer to Society and the Justice System
2. Competence
3. Relationship of the Lawyer to the Profession
4. Relationship of the Lawyer to Other Lawyers

---

[23] S. Braungart, "Investigator hired to assist Bencher in dealing with complaint of misconduct (Alta.)" (1986), 13 Nat. (C.B.A.) 3:15; A. Johnson, "Coming up fast on the inside" (1986), 10 Can. Lawyer 4:23; L.L. Legge, "Freedom of expression of lawyers: the rules of professional contact" (1985), 23 U.W.O.L. Rev. 165; S. Traviss, "Discipline precedents" (1986), 4 Advocates' Soc. J. 13; and J. Butler, "Erosion in Professionalism slowing courts, says Wells" (1985), 12 Nat. (C.B.A.) 10:29.

[24] For a recent discussion of the so-called "grey areas of legal ethics" see G.M. Saylor, " 'Ethical Dilemmas' " Thoughts from Behind Closed Doors", Canadian Lawyer, January 1995, p. 22. For a discussion of the role of the law society, see the Report of the Subcommittee on the Role of the Law Society, a subcommittee of the Research and Planning Committee of the Law Society of Upper Canada. This report is set out in O.R., March 11, 1994, p. ix.

5. Accessibility and Advertisement of Legal Services
6. Conflicts of Interest
7. Confidentiality
8. The Lawyer and The Business Aspects of Practice
9. The Lawyer as Advisor
10. The Lawyer as Advocate
11. The Lawyer as Negotiator
12. The Lawyer in Corporate and Government Service
13. Fees
14. Withdrawal and Dismissal
15. The Lawyer in Activities Other than the Practice of Law[25]

In addition to the statute governing the legal profession in each province as well as the detailed canons of ethics, the various provincial law societies have issued specific rulings in order to provide guidance to the members of the profession in particular areas of ethical uncertainty. In addition to all of the foregoing, some time ago the Canadian Bar Association established its Code of Professional Conduct. In 1987, the Council of the Canadian Bar Association approved the adoption of a new and slightly revised Code of Professional Conduct. Many law societies in Canada are considering adopting the Canadian Bar Association Code in their respective canons of legal ethics. For example, the law societies of British Columbia, Nova Scotia and Prince Edward Island have revised their local rules with a view to incorporating part or all of the C.B.A. Code and adopting it to local circumstances. The law societies of Saskatchewan, Manitoba, Ontario (The Law Society of Upper Canada), Newfoundland and the Northwest Territories are currently studying the C.B.A. Code. In the case of Ontario, the Law Society of Upper Canada (L.S.U.C.) did not specifically adopt the C.B.A. Code in that the C.B.A. Code was largely modelled after the L.S.U.C. rules, with the result that there were not sufficient differences between the Code and the L.S.U.C. rules to warrant an adoption. Moreover, in 1993, the Law Society of Upper Canada commenced a major review of its 'Rules of Professional Conduct'. The review is expected to be complete in 1996.[26] Apart from this major review, the Professional Conduct Committee of the Law Society of Upper Canada does recommend on an ad hoc basis, the amendment of particular rules from time to time. For example, in 1992 it studied the amendment of Rule 5 in connection with conflict of interest and Rule 23 in connection with lawyers and meeting transactions.[27] The Yukon Territory has adopted the C.B.A.

---

[25] Law Society of Alberta, Alberta Code of Professional Conduct, 1995.

[26] See Law Society of Upper Canada, Benchers Bulletin, May 1993.

[27] For a history of the development of Ontario's *Professional Conduct Handbook*, see D. Robinson, "Ethical Evolution: The Development of the Professional Conduct Handbook of the Law Society of Upper Canada" (1995), 29 L. Soc. Gaz. 162.

Code together with some supplementary rules. The Law Society of Alberta, as indicated above, has established its own code of conduct rather than adopting the Canadian Bar Association Code. Until the Canadian Bar Association Code of Professional Conduct is adopted by a given jurisdiction, it is not strictly binding on lawyers; however, it provides some basic guidelines to which lawyers should properly conform.

The 1987 Code of Professional Conduct is as follows:

Rules of the Canadian Bar Association Code of Professional Conduct (adopted by Council, August 1987) (19 rules)

1. The lawyer must discharge with integrity all duties owed to clients, the court, other members of the profession and the public.

2. (a) The lawyer owes the client a duty to be competent to perform any legal services undertaken on the client's behalf.
   (b) The lawyer should serve the client in a conscientious, diligent and efficient manner so as to provide a quality of service at least equal to that which lawyers generally would expect of a competent lawyer in a like situation.

3. The lawyer must be both honest and candid when advising clients.

4. The lawyer has a duty to hold in strict confidence all information concerning the business and affairs of the client acquired in the course of the professional relationship, and should not divulge such information unless disclosure is expressly or impliedly authorized by the client, required by law or otherwise permitted or required by this Code.

5. The lawyer shall not advise or represent both sides of a dispute and, save after adequate disclosure to and with the consent of the clients or prospective clients concerned, shall not act or continue to act in a matter when there is or is likely to be a conflicting interest.

6. (a) The lawyer should not enter into a business transaction with the client or knowingly give or acquire from the client an ownership, security or other pecuniary interest unless:
   (i) the transaction is a fair and reasonable one and its terms are fully disclosed to the client in writing in a manner that is reasonably understood by the client;
   (ii) the client is given a reasonable opportunity to seek independent legal advice about the transaction, the onus being on the lawyer to prove that the client's interests were protected by such independent advice; and
   (iii) the client consents in writing to the transaction.
   (b) The lawyer shall not enter into or continue a business transaction with the client if:
   (i) the client expects or might reasonably be assumed to expect that the lawyer is protecting the client's interests;
   (ii) there is a significant risk that the interests of the lawyer and the client may differ.
   (c) The lawyer shall not act for the client where the lawyer's duty to the client and the personal interests of the lawyer or an associate are in conflict.
   (d) The lawyer shall not prepare an instrument giving the lawyer or an associate a substantial gift from the client, including a testamentary gift.

7. The lawyer who engages in another profession, business or occupation concurrently with the practice of law must not allow such outside interest to jeopardize the lawyer's professional integrity, independence or competence.

8. The lawyer owes a duty to the client to observe all relevant laws and rules respecting the preservation and safekeeping of the client's property entrusted to the lawyer. Where there are no such laws or rules, or the lawyer is in any doubt, the lawyer should take the same care of such property as a careful and prudent owner would when dealing with property of like description.

9. When acting as an advocate, the lawyer must treat the tribunal with courtesy and respect and must represent the client resolutely, honourably and within the limits of the law.

10. The lawyer who holds public office should, in the discharge of official duties, adhere to standards of conduct as high as those that these rules require of a lawyer engaged in the practice of law.

11. The lawyer shall not
   (a) stipulate for, charge or accept any fee that is not fully disclosed, fair and reasonable;
   (b) appropriate any funds of the client held in trust or otherwise under the lawyer's control for or on account of fees without the express authority of the client, save as permitted by the rules of the governing body.

12. The lawyer owes a duty to the client not to withdraw services except for good cause and upon notice appropriate in the circumstances.

13. The lawyer should encourage public respect for and try to improve the administration of justice.

14. Lawyers should make legal services available to the public in an efficient and convenient manner that will command respect and confidence, and by means that are compatible with the integrity, independence and effectiveness of the profession.

15. The lawyer should assist in maintaining the integrity of the profession and should participate in its activities.

16. The lawyer's conduct toward other lawyers should be characterized by courtesy and good faith.

17. The lawyer should assist in preventing the unauthorized practice of law.

18. The lawyer who engages in public appearances and public statements should do so in conformity with the principles of the Code.

19. The lawyer should observe the rules of professional conduct set out in the Code in the spirit as well as in the letter.

The law society established by the provincial statute governing the legal profession in that province is responsible for such matters as:

1. Administering the affairs of the legal profession in that province;

2. Establishing standards for admission to the bar;

3. Setting and collecting annual fees;

4. Arranging errors and omissions insurance;

5. Legal aid;

6. Disciplining of lawyers.

Generally these disciplinary obligations are discharged by the governing body within each law society, usually called the benchers of the law society. Depending upon the particular provisions in the governing statute, the benchers usually establish a discipline committee to investigate an allegation of misconduct on the part of a particular lawyer, hold a hearing if necessary, and depending on the findings, discipline the lawyer accordingly. This formula is basically followed in each province, although there are some differences.

Discipline can take many forms, including everything from frequent auditing of a lawyer's accounts to fining or suspending him.[28] The ultimate sanction is disbarment, where a lawyer is struck from the rolls of the particular law society and is prohibited from engaging in the practice of law. While the governing act generally provides the possibility of reinstatement after a number of years, upon disbarment a person is no longer a member of the legal profession. The most difficult determination throughout this process is whether the lawyer's conduct has amounted to a disciplinary offence.[29] While the governing statute generally defines the standard of conduct that is expected of a lawyer, this is usually couched in general words that provide little guidance as to what in a specific instance constitutes a disciplinary impropriety. To determine this, the body of precedent established in Canada must be examined.

Whether a lawyer's incompetence constitutes a disciplinary offence is a currently controversial issue.[30]enerally speaking, incompetence has not been held to be conduct unbecoming a barrister and solicitor or professional misconduct.[31] The conventional wisdom has been that a client's

---

[28] The discipline of professionals has recently been the subject of continuing education programs. For example, an organization known as INFONEX sponsored a program in Vancouver in October of 1995 styled "Regulation of Professionals and Disciplinary Hearings: A Practical Course". Earlier, the University of Toronto, the Université Laval and the Yves Pratte Foundation sponsored a conference on "The Legal Profession: Maintaining Standards and Avoiding Conflicts" in October, 1992. See the following recent articles in connection with the discipline of lawyers: B. Livesey, "The Tarnished Image", Canadian Lawyer, February 1995, p. 16; "Disbarred for 'Contemptible' Conduct", Canadian Lawyer, January 1995, p. 6; and "Legal Imperatives", Canadian Lawyer, November 1993, p. 15. See also a selection of Law Society of Upper Canada Discipline Digest: October 1992, November 1992, March 1993, June 1993, October 1993, November 1993, March 1994, June 1994, October 1994, January 1995.

[29] For some recent articles dealing with the disciplining of lawyers, see H.J. Kirsh, "Liability of lawyers under s. 35 of the Construction Lien Act: one case in point" (1987), 21 C.L.R. 290; D.P. Iggers and J.P. Twohig, "The Disciplinary process of the Law Society of Upper Canada" (1987), 8 Advocates' Q. 1; L. Weinstein, "Product liability and ethics" (1983), N.Y.L.J. 2; and G.J. Smith, "Legal Professional Malpractice" (1986), 4 Can. J. Ins. L. 7. With respect to some ethical issues arising out of the recent *R. v. Bernardo* (July 27, 1995), Doc. 274/94 (Ont. Gen. Div.) case, see The Globe & Mail, August 18, 1995.

[30] The Law Society of Upper Canada, for example, disseminates a monthly publication entitled "Discipline Digest". This publication reviews the various disciplinary matters before Convocation (i.e., the Benchers of the Law Society sitting as a committee of the whole). In September, 1995, for example, there were 19 cases reported on such alleged matters as misappropriation, conduct unbecoming, acting without client consent, practising while suspended, failure to honour financial obligation, failure to reply, misapplication of trust funds, failure to serve clients and failure to file forms (see Law Society of Upper Canada, Discipline Digest, September 1995).

[31] One should consider the case of *Lockhart v. MacDonald* (1979), 38 N.S.R. (2d) 671, 69 A.P.R. 671 (T.D.), varied (1980), 42 N.S.R. (2d) 29, 77 A.P.R. 29, 118 D.L.R. (3d) 397 (C.A.), which was varied (1980), 44 N.S.R. (2d) 261, 83 A.P.R. 261, 118 D.L.R. (3d) 397 at 420 (C.A.), leave to appeal to S.C.C. refused (1980), 118 D.L.R. (3d) 397n, 35 N.R. 265n (S.C.C.), where, at trial, it was held that a solicitor without specialized training was not competent to provide financial advice. The court held that the acceptance of a retainer constituted an undertaking by the solicitor that he was competent to perform the services for

remedy against an incompetent lawyer is a negligence suit for damages.[32] However, there are several indications that it will soon become a ground for discipline. First, there are a few cases where gross incompetence has been held to be conduct unbecoming or professional misconduct. For example, a case to which the reader might refer is the case of *Baron v. F.*[33] where it was held to be "good cause" to justify suspension of a member if that member was guilty of a series of acts of gross negligence which taken together would bring the legal profession into disrepute. Secondly, the Canadian Bar Association Code of Profession conduct contains a provision that a lawyer owes a duty to his client to be competent. Thirdly, reference may be made to recent amendments to the Legal Profession Act of Alberta.[34] Fourthly, reference may be made to the Legal Profession Act of the province of Saskatchewan, R.S.S. 1978, c. L-10, where gross negligence is specifically recognized as a ground for discipline.

In view of these indicators it is probably reasonable to conclude that incompetence will be recognized as a legitimate ground for discipline, which is a significant departure from the present situation.[35]

Mark M. Orkin in his treatise on *Legal Ethics*[36] indicates that the charging of exorbitant fees might constitute "conduct unbecoming"; however, the Canadian Bar Association Code suggests that there must be some element of fraud or dishonesty involved before such overcharging will con-

---

which he was retained. On appeal, it was held that the solicitor need only demonstrate skill, care and competency in providing a service for his client — he is not obliged to guarantee results. But in Alberta see s. 47(3) of the Legal Profession Amendment Act, S.A. 1981, c. 53, where, for the first time, it is provided that "conduct deserving of sanction includes incompetently carrying on the practice of law and incompetently carrying out duties or obligations undertaken by a member or a student-at-law in his capacity as a member or student-at-law".

[32] See *Banks v. Reid* (1977), 18 O.R. (2d) 148, 4 C.C.L.T. 1, 81 D.L.R. (3d) 730, reversing (1975), 6 O.R. (2d) 404, 53 D.L.R. (3d) 27 (C.A.); *Demarco v. Ungaro* (1979), 21 O.R. (2d) 673, 8 C.C.L.T. 207, 95 D.L.R. (3d) 385, 27 Chitty's L.J. 23 (H.C.); and *Law Society of Man. v. Eadie* (1988), 51 Man. R. (2d) 279, reversed C.A., No. 100/88, 27th May 1988 (unreported). See also K.R. Hamilton, "A lawyer's liability for negligence — care is not enough" (1986), 44 Advocate (Van.) 53; and R.M. Mahoney, "Lawyers — Negligence — Standard of Care" (1985), 63 Can. Bar Rev. 221.

[33] [1945] 4 D.L.R. 525 (Law Soc. of B.C.). This case was considered in *Midgley v. Law Society (Alberta)* (1980), 12 Alta. L.R. (2d) 35, 31 A.R. 118 (Q.B.) (re *in camera* hearing). The *Midgley* case was discussed in the Alberta Report, 21st December 1979 and The Globe & Mail, 13th February 1980. See also remarks by Mr. Midgley in his column in the Edmonton Sun, 11th January 1981.

[34] See *supra*, note 31.

[35] See W.H. Hurlburt, "Incompetent Service, and Professional Responsibility" (1980), 18 Alta. L. Rev. 146. See also Federation of Law Societies of Canada, Canadian Bar Association and the Canadian Institute for the Administration of Justice, *The Legal Profession and Quality of Service* (Report and Materials on the Conference on Quality of Legal Services) (1979), and the *Further Report and Proposals* regarding the same conference (1981).

[36] *Legal Ethics: A Study of Professional Conduct* (Toronto: Canada Law Book, 1957).

stitute a disciplinary offence. Reference may be made to the case of *German v. Law Society (Alberta),* [1974] 5 W.W.R. 217, 45 D.L.R. (3d) 535 (Alta. C.A.), in which a similar issue is raised.[37] In some jurisdictions (such a s
Ontario) the charging of fees on a contingency basis constitutes a breach of ethics,[38] while in other jurisdictions (such as Alberta) such charging is permissible.

The Canadian Bar Association Code provides that a lawyer cannot represent both sides in a dispute and should not act where there is or is likely to be a conflict of interest. That general statement is clarified, of course, by particular rulings of the various provincial law societies. For example, it is a common ruling in several jurisdictions that a lawyer can only act for both the vendor and purchaser in a real estate transaction provided that he inform both parties in advance that he is doing so, receives the consent of both parties, and ceases to act in the event that a conflict of interest arises which cannot be resolved. Orkin points out that a lawyer's failure to disclose a personal interest in a client's action constitutes a serious disciplinary offence. Also, a lawyer who acts against a former client in the same or similar matter in which he previously represented that client has a conflict of interest for which he may be disciplined. Finally, although there are constraints upon a lawyer entering into a contract with a client in which the lawyer may receive a benefit, there is no absolute rule which prohibits a lawyer from contracting with his clients: *Shumiatcher v. Law Society (Saskatchewan)* (1966), 58 W.W.R. 465, 60 D.L.R. (2d) 318 (C.A.), leave to appeal to S.C.C. refused (1967), 61 D.L.R. (2d) 520 (S.C.C.). See also *Heagy v. Institute of Chartered Accountants (Saskatchewan)* (1985), 40 Sask. R. 211 (Q.B.), and *Cymbalisty v. Chiropractors' Assn. (Saskatchewan)* (1985), 39 Sask. R. 103 (Q.B.).

One of the major complaints of members of the public against the legal profession is that lawyers do not sufficiently inform their clients as to the progress of their work or inform clients as to the cost incurred in providing the service.[39] A lawyer does, however, owe a duty to his client to keep him informed, and this includes responding to reasonable requests for information. It is irresponsible and unethical for a lawyer to fail to respond to a telephone call from his client, to fail to keep an appointment, or to fail to meet work deadlines anticipated by his client, to refuse to answer

---

[37] This case was applied in another case involving the medical profession. See *Ringrose v. College of Physicians & Surgeons (Alberta) (No. 2)*, [1978] 2 W.W.R. 534, 83 D.L.R. (3d) 680, 8 A.R. 113 (C.A.).

[38] The Law Society of Upper Canada has been considering the adoption of a contingency fee system since 1988; however, the proposal has had a somewhat checkered history. See C.B.A. National, April 1992.

[39] B. Livesey, *supra.*

written communications, or generally, to not report on the progress and completion of his work. The intentional concealment of material facts from a client or the false representation to a client about the progress of an action constitute grounds for disbarment. In addition, provincial law society rulings and the Canadian Bar Association Code of Professional Conduct indicate that it is "conduct unbecoming" to disclose confidential information or to use it for one's own purposes.

The rules concerning the withdrawal of services are not easy ones to define, although at least some of them are fairly clear. For example, a lawyer owes a duty to an accused person whom he represents to continue to represent him through to the end of his trial. However, as indicated in the Canadian Bar Association Code, counsel can withdraw for good cause provided he has given his client appropriate notice, and indeed, in certain circumstances he must withdraw.

A lawyer has certain duties which he must perform as an officer of the court and failure to carry out these duties will usually render the lawyer liable to being disciplined, usually by disbarment. The following is a list set out in Orkin's *Legal Ethics* of such transgressions constituting disciplinary offences.

1. Deliberately deceiving or misleading the Court
2. Refusing to answer interrogatories
3. Abuse of the judicial process
4. Writing abusive and improper letters to the Court
5. Perjury
6. Forging jurat to an affidavit
7. Falsely representing his instructions
8. Wilfully acting without authority
9. Permitting client to swear a false affidavit
10. Using an affidavit which is false to his own knowledge
11. Making false statements in an affidavit of costs
12. Falsely representing that an injunction has been granted
13. Tampering with a witness
14. Impersonation to obtain payment of moneys out of Court
15. Securing witness of the adverse side to keep out of the way at trial
16. Assisting a criminal to escape the country
17. Procuring release of a prisoner by bribe
18. Falsifying or forging a writ or a deed
19. Suppressing an affidavit
20. Subornation of perjury
21. Arranging sham bail
22. Indemnifying a person putting up bail
23. Tampering with the jury
24. Avoiding service of an Order of the Master requiring a lawyer to pay over money
25. Advising a client to sue a person when the suit is clearly vexatious
26. Being intoxicated in Court
27. Failing to comply with an Order of the Court although only if made against the lawyer in his professional capacity

28. Refusing to assist the Court
29. Aiding client to obtain fraudulent discharge of bankruptcy
30. Wrongfully running up costs
31. Taking unnecessary steps

In addition to the above, the Canadian Bar Association Code indicates that a lawyer should not appear before a judge with whom he or his associates have a business or personal relationship, nor should a lawyer, of course, attempt to influence a court's decision by bribery. The latter conduct would inevitably lead to disbarment.

The Canadian Bar Association Report makes certain comments in connection with a lawyer's conduct of advocacy in a court. For example, a lawyer should not waive his client's rights without the informed consent of his client; in civil matters, a lawyer may not resort to technical arguments for the purpose of delaying or harassing the opposite side; in criminal matters, however, a lawyer may place a greater reliance on technical arguments; if a fair and reasonable settlement can be effected, a lawyer has a responsibility to advise his client to settle; in a criminal trial, under the appropriate circumstances, it is permissible for a lawyer to advise his client to plead guilty to a lesser and included offence; if a lawyer is rude, disruptive, provocative or in any other way conducts himself in court so as to be in contempt of court, this naturally would be grounds for discipline. The lawyer must assist the court by revealing the law he has researched on a particular point, whether it is in favour of or opposed to his client's position. (However, failure to do so, which constitutes a disciplinary offence, would probably not lead to the ultimate sanction of disbarment.)

Orkin points out that a lawyer owes the same obligation towards the discipline committee of his provincial law society as he does to the court. This is given statutory recognition in, for example, the Legal Profession Act of the province of Alberta, where it is "conduct unbecoming" for a lawyer to refuse to co-operate with the discipline committee. Similarly, there have been some disbarments recently as a result of a lawyer's failure to reply to letters from his provincial law society. There is no doubt that such a failure constitutes "conduct unbecoming" and, in fact, represents a serious breach of professional responsibility.

Generally speaking, lawyers have certain professional responsibilities to their colleagues in the legal fraternity. Rulings of the various provincial law societies indicate that a lawyer is expected to reply promptly to communications from his fellow lawyer; however, to use an Alberta example, the wording of this ruling, to the effect that it would be "at the very least discourteous" to fail to reply promptly, would seem to indicate that although this might be "conduct unbecoming" it would most likely not warrant disbarment. The Canadian Bar Association Code indicates that a lawyer is generally expected to deal courteously and fairly with a fellow lawyer and not to indulge in sharp practice. Both the Canadian Bar Association Report and various rulings of the provincial law societies indicate that the tape recording of a communication with another lawyer without his consent is forbidden (and, indeed, it might be the subject of criminal liability under recent amendments to the Criminal Code). The above sources also indicate that it is unethical to communicate on a matter directly with a person represented by counsel without that counsel's consent. Also, of great importance, the Canadian Bar Association Report and the various rulings of the respective provincial law societies indicate that it is a lawyer's duty to report any misconduct on the part of his fellow lawyer. For example, an Alberta ruling indicates that "it is proper and desirable for any member to report such incidents". However, the mild language in which the ruling is phrased suggests that the failure to report such a lawyer might not in every case result in discipline; however, no doubt a failure to report a matter regarding a shortage of trust funds or a serious breach of an undertaking made by a fellow lawyer would constitute "conduct unbecoming".

On occasion, a disciplinary matter attracts considerable publicity. One such recent instance relates to the large and prestigious Toronto law firm of Lang Michener Lawrence and Shaw (formerly known as Lang Michener Lash Johnston). The controversy began when one lawyer with the firm engaged in allegedly illegal activities in relation to his immigration law practice. That led to his expulsion from the firm, the laying of several criminal charges against him and his subsequent disbarment from practice. In addition, two other lawyers, brought into the firm by the above-mentioned lawyer, were engaged in similar activities. As a result, those lawyers were also required to leave the firm and were reprimanded by the Law Society after a disciplinary hearing. Several charges were also laid against one of those lawyers.

The matter became more complicated when five senior partners of the law firm were brought before the Discipline Committee of the Law Society of Upper Canada on allegations of professional misconduct. More specifically, it was alleged that these partners, constituting the executive committee of the firm, had violated two rules of the Law Society. Eventually, these lawyers were found guilty in respect of one of those two rules, in that they had "failed in their duty 'to make a timely disclosure' to the law society of allegations of impropriety and possible illegal activity by a former partner".[40]

---

[40] The Globe & Mail, 19th January 1990. See also The Globe & Mail, 18th January 1990 and 10th January 1990, and the Lawyers' Weekly, 19th January 1990 and 2nd February 1990.

A further complication arose as a result of the allegation by the Senior Counsel Discipline (essentially, the chief investigator) of the Law Society, that four other senior lawyers ought to have also been charged with professional misconduct.[41]

Another aspect of the above matter relates to media access to the various deliberations that occurred.[42] For example, on one hand, the report by the Chair of the Discipline Committee to Convocation in respect of the five senior partners found guilty of professional misconduct was conducted in public while, on the other hand, the reprimand (i.e., the penalty administered to the five senior partners) was carried out in private before the Discipline Committee. This, in and of itself, led to a front page newspaper story styled "Private scolding by panel . . .".[43] This underscores the continuing debate on public accountability of and public input into the affairs of self-governing professions. It also reflects, to some extent, a degree of cynicism on the part of the media and the public in respect of the legal profession.[44]

It is generally considered that the legal profession, because of its position in society and its special knowledge, is under a responsibility to carry out legal reform. Indeed, lawyers and judges have accepted this responsibility and play key roles in changing the law. At the same time, the Canadian Bar Association Report also indicates that it is the lawyer's duty to maintain respect for the legal system as it presently exists. In short, criticism must be reasonable and bona fide.[45] The lawyer must disclose whether, in making criticism, he is acting for a particular client or speaking on his own behalf or speaking in the public interest. A lawyer need not believe in the cause he espouses if he is acting for a client, but if he is acting in the public interest he must truly believe in the validity of the cause.

Similarly, writing in a 1967 edition of the Law Society Gazette, the editor offered the view that a lawyer can only use legal means to change the

---

[41] See The Globe & Mail, 11th January 1990 and general correspondence by the Treasurer to members of the profession dated 13th February 1990. See also Proceedings of Convocation of the Law Society of Upper Canada, 26th January 1990, in 71 O.R. (2d) Part 3, 9th March 1990.

[42] Many law societies have recently opened their disciplinary hearings to public scrutiny. For example, notwithstanding its 114 year old history of secrecy in respect of disciplinary proceedings, the Law Society of Manitoba opened its doors to the prublic incertain cases. See C.B.A. National, May 1991.

[43] See The Globe & Mail, 19th January 1990.

[44] See, for example, the article by Allan Fotheringham entitled "A law unto themselves" appearing in the Edmonton Sun, 11th January 1990.

[45] Recently, a lawyer attracted considerable attention in respect of his criticism of the legal system. See The Globe & Mail, 16th September, 1995.

system. Accordingly, and this is buttressed by the Canadian Bar Association Report, civil disobedience by a lawyer is not permissible.[46] The lawyer cannot counsel, assist or engage in activities against the law. However, as Mr. Justice Mark MacGuigan (then a professor of law and subsequently a Minister of Justice of Canada) indicates in another edition of the Law Society Gazette, a breach of a statute, especially a minor regulatory statute, would not, however, lead to disbarment. On the other hand, in yet another article appearing in the Law Society Gazette, it was suggested that there may be a positive duty to act against an unjust law. This latter view is definitely not held by most lawyers and is most certainly in error. Along similar lines, reference may be made to the case of *Martin v. Law Soc. of B.C.,* [1950] 3 D.L.R. 173 (B.C. C.A.), in which a person was held to be ineligible for admission to the bar of British Columbia because he was a member of the Communist Party and such membership indicated an implicit advocacy for the overthrow of government. While Orkin goes further and suggests that such membership would be grounds for disbarment, there are some lawyers in Canada who do possess similar political views and are not, in fact, nor likely will be, the subject of disciplinary action. Moreover, the climate has changed somewhat since the promulgation of the Canadian Charter of Rights and Freedoms.[47]

Regarding a lawyer's personal life,[48] it is not professional misconduct to be a co-respondent in a divorce action. It is, however, according to certain rulings issued by some provincial law societies, "conduct unbecoming" for a lawyer not to meet his financial obligations.

The Canadian Bar Association Report indicates that a lawyer should help prevent the practice of law by unauthorized persons,[49] and to this

---

[46] See *Midgley v. Law Society (Alberta)* (1980), 12 Alta. L.R. (2d) 35, 31 A.R. 118 (Q.B.), and *Law Society (Manitoba) v. Savino,* [1983] 6 W.W.R. 538, 1 D.L.R. (4th) 285, 23 Man. R. (2d) 293, 6 C.R.R. 336 (C.A.).

[47] The Charter is already changing the face of the legal profession in Canada. See, for example, *Andrews v. Law Society (British Columbia),* [1989] 1 S.C.R. 143, [1989] 2 W.W.R. 289, 34 B.C.L.R. (2d) 273, 25 C.C.E.L. 255, 36 C.R.R. 193, 56 D.L.R. (4th) 1, 10 C.H.R.R. D/5719, 91 N.R. 255, where the requirement that a lawyer be a Canadian citizen was struck down. See also *Black v. Law Society (Alberta),* [1989] 1 S.C.R. 591, [1989] 4 W.W.R. 1, 66 Alta. L.R. (2d) 97, 37 Admin. L.R. 161, 38 C.R.R. 193, 58 D.L.R. (4th) 317, 96 A.R. 352, 93 N.R. 266, where a regulation prohibiting the establishment of interprovincial law firms was also struck down.

[48] It appears that some lawyers have little personal life. See Gibb-Clark, M. and S. Fine, "Will 'slaves to the law' ever be free?", The Globe & Mail, 27th November 1993.

[49] See *R. v. Nicholson* (1979), 8 Alta L.R. (2d) 299, 14 A.R. 450, 46 C.C.C. (2d) 230, 96 D.L.R. (3d) 693 (C.A.), reversing (1978), 5 Alta. L.R. (2d) 98, 12 A.R. 595 (Dist Ct.), where an accused incorporated several companies for the public for a fee. The accused did not present himself as a lawyer, nor did he provide legal advice; he merely filled out the required forms. He was convicted at trial but on appeal the conviction was quashed. The court held that the accused only performed clerical work and that such work cannot be said to be reserved to the legal profession.

end there are rulings of various provincial law societies to the effect that it is "conduct unbecoming" to split fees with unqualified persons.

In respect of legal aid, the Canadian Bar Association Report indicates that a lawyer can decline employment except where he has been assigned by the court to act as counsel. But he should, at the same time, try to prevent a situation in which a person would have no representation, and he should not refuse a brief because a client's cause is unpopular or because he believes the person to be guilty.[50]

One area of difficulty relates to the lawyer's outside interests. And, by outside interests, one is referring to other employment (in business, for example), public office and public appearances. The Canadian Bar Association Report indicates that a lawyer's outside interests should not affect his professional judgment in dealing with his clients. If his outside interests are not related to his practice of law, there is usually no problem unless the outside interests tend to bring the profession into disrepute. Moreover, as Orkin indicates, there are some types of outside activities which can lead to disbarment, and these would include the renting of premises as a brothel (see *Re Weare*, [1893] 2 Q.B.D. 439), acting as a bookmaker, and other dubious outside enterprises.

Some rulings of the provincial law societies indicate that it is a disciplinary offence to carry on any business which makes it difficult for a client to know whether the lawyer is acting as a lawyer or is acting in another capacity. However, to use an Alberta ruling as an example, the wording is again expressed in mild language to the effect that it is "most undesirable" to do so and, therefore, although it is a disciplinary offence to do so, a violation of this ruling is probably not a ground for disbarment. With respect to this rule, the Canadian Bar Association Report indicates that a lawyer must indicate the capacity in which he is acting, especially if he also serves as an accountant, engineer, merchant, land developer, building contractor, real estate, insurance or financial agent, broker, financier, property manager or public relations advisor.

Both the Canadian Bar Association Report and various rulings of the provincial law societies indicate that in the event a lawyer holds public office his official duties are paramount, and if there is a conflict a client should not be accepted or, in the case of an existing client, the lawyer should end the relationship with that client. Moreover, the Canadian Bar Association Report adds that the lawyer holding public office in a given body should not appear before that official body in a professional capacity.

---

[50] See "Members have Role in Monitoring Unauthorized Practice", the Law Society of Upper Canada, The Advisor, October 1993.

Both the Canadian Bar Association Report and various provincial law society rulings indicate that a lawyer cannot solicit appearances on television, radio or other public forum in his professional capacity or use such appearances for advertisement or engage in any appearance that might bring the legal profession into disrepute. For example, a ruling of the Law Society of Alberta indicates that a lawyer can appear in his personal and private capacity if the reason for his appearance is not related to his professional capacity. It was held in one case to be "conduct unbecoming" for a lawyer to carry on a regular radio broadcast, not for reason of the conducting of the broadcast itself, but for its particular style and type. In that case, the offender was reprimanded and ordered to cease the broadcasts. The decision gives the impression that if the lawyer had refused to comply, he would have been disbarred. Reference may be made to the case of *Merchant v. Law Society (Saskatchewan)*, [1972] 4 W.W.R. 663, 25 D.L.R. (3d) 708 (Sask. Q.B.), reversed [1973] 2 W.W.R. 109, 32 D.L.R. (3d) 178 (Sask. C.A.). Rules concerning advertising have been substantially relaxed in recent years. For example, in Alberta, ads have appeared in newsmagazines,[51] The Talking Yellow Pages,[52] regular listings in the Yellow Pages, television, billboards, etc. In Ontario, there are even bench ads at bus stops advertising lawyers and their services. Canadian law firms are even hiring professional marketers. In a recent book on marketing, it was stated as follows:

> In response to an increasingly competitive business environment, Canadian law firms are beginning to hire marketers! Clients are becoming more savvy and less loyal. Rather than return to the same firm or have that firm handle all their legal business, they are more likely to shop around for a better price and the best service. In order to keep clients and attract new ones, law firms are finding that they need to develop a market orientation.[53]

Nationally, an advertisement accompanying the August 1991 Eaton's bill was sent to all credit card holders offering the services of "Legal 'Safety Net' providing access to over 1700 law firms.

In examining the various governing statutes, most provinces use the words "professional misconduct" or "conduct unbecoming" a barrister or solicitor as the grounds for discipline. When the given provincial statute, however, contains only the expression "conduct unbecoming", then it appears that these words both encompass "conduct unbecoming" as well as "professional misconduct", as these two phrases are used in provinces containing the two-fold standard. Generally speaking, the term

---

[51] See, for example, Alberta Report, December 5, 1994.

[52] See 1994 Ed Tel Yellow Pages.

[53] E.J. McCarthy, S.J. Shapiro & W.D. Perreault Jr., *Basic Marketing: A Global-Managerial Approach*, 7th ed. (Burr Ridge, Illinois: Irwin, 1994). See also S. Noakes, "Learning the Marketing Ropes", The Financial Post, July 9, 1992, p. 16.

"professional misconduct" is concerned with indiscretions committed while exercising professional duties and the term "conduct unbecoming" relates to non-professional misconduct, which nonetheless harms the reputation of the legal profession. Reference should also be made to the new formulation in the Alberta Legal Profession Act where the test becomes one of conduct "incompatible with the best interests of the public" or which "tends to harm the standing of the legal profession". See the discussion appearing earlier in this chapter and an article reviewing the disciplinary role of the Law Society of Alberta in the Alberta Report, 9th May 1983.

However, the particular behaviour which falls under either or both of the above formulas is more difficult to define. Some assistance has been rendered by legal writers such as Mark M. Orkin, who in his treatise *Legal Ethics* has divided the disciplinary offenses into various categories. Also, the statute governing the legal profession in a province may contain provisions that specifically define what constitutes "conduct unbecoming". For example in the Legal Profession Act of Alberta, it is conduct unbecoming a barrister or solicitor to fail to co-operate with an investigating committee inquiring into a lawyer's conduct, to have been convicted of an indictable offence, and to fail to give an accounting to a client when directed to do so by the Secretary of the Discipline Committee. However, such conduct will not necessarily lead to disbarment. For example, whether the commission of a criminal offence gives rise to discipline depends on several factors. At common law, prima facie, conviction of a criminal offence was a ground for discipline. However, disbarment was not mandatory: the nature of the crime was usually considered. Orkin suggests that the test was whether the offence imported the notion of disgrace of character rendering a person unfit for an honourable profession. However, it is of interest to note that a recent amendment to the Legal Profession Act in Alberta states that conduct may be "unbecoming" whether or not the conduct is disgraceful or dishonourable. Therefore, in at least the province of Alberta, the statutory standard may be more rigid than Orkin's suggested common law standard. It would seem to be immaterial whether such conduct is committed in the course of a lawyer's private conduct or in his professional capacity. Obviously it is a more serious matter if such an offence is committed in the latter capacity. Reference may be made to the case of *Prescott v. Law Society (British Columbia),* [1971] 4 W.W.R. 433, 19 D.L.R. (3d) 446 (B.C. C.A.), wherein a lawyer was disbarred for committing an offence contrary to the Income Tax Act, R.S.C. 1952, c. 148. Although he did not attempt to evade the law, he was found guilty of gross negligence in keeping accounts. In this case, it was held to be immaterial that the particular offence was not committed within the lawyer's professional capacity. With respect to the nature of the crime, criminal offences involving fraud or dishonesty, by their very nature, generally lead to disciplinary action and often disbarment. Examples of such offences include bribery, forgery, perjury, making false affidavits, embezzlement, theft, obtaining money or goods by false pretenses, and several others. In addition, a conviction for obstructing justice would almost certainly be a ground for disbarment, whether committed in the course of a lawyer's professional or private capacity, since its very nature is such as to bring the legal profession into disrepute.

Conviction for an offence involving immoral conduct or moral turpitude would constitute conduct unbecoming but would probably not lead to the ultimate sanction of disbarment.

There is some behaviour often, but not necessarily, leading to conviction for a criminal offence involving fraud or dishonesty for which, it can be said with assurance, disciplinary action will take the form of disbarment. Such conduct includes a lawyer's misusing funds that he holds in trust for his clients, misappropriating clients' funds, failing to apply clients' funds as directed, obtaining money from clients for fictitious disbursements, and falsely stating that disbursements have been paid. A ruling of the Law Society of Alberta stating that failure to give a client an accounting when he demands it will constitute conduct unbecoming and a prescription in the Canadian Bar Association Code of Professional Conduct that a lawyer has a duty to keep his clients' property safe would indicate that even less serious such behaviour would nevertheless render a lawyer liable to severe disciplinary sanctions.

In addition to all of the foregoing, Orkin lists some specific types of conduct which are grounds for disbarment:

1. Making a false recital in a deed
2. Subornation of perjury in a witness
3. Attempted subornation of a jury
4. Assisting a client to obtain a fraudulent discharge in insolvency
5. Permitting a client to make a false affidavit
6. Accepting a transfer of property in fraud of transferor's creditors
7. Advising how improperly to defeat a garnishee order
8. Assisting a criminal to escape from the country
9. Obtaining the release of a prisoner by a bribe
10. Advising collusion in a divorce case (see *Dicks v. Dicks*, [1949] 2 W.W.R. 866 (B.C.))
11. Maintenance and champerty
12. Bribery
13. Compelling a client to sign an agreement giving the lawyer a share of property recovered on prosecution
14. Canvassing for business
15. Abusing position as commissioner for oath to obtain retainer
16. Acting as a solicitor while under suspension

17. Acting without a practising certificate

18. Holding out as a solicitor before admission to practice

19. Malicious conduct

20. Failing to supervise staff properly so that they were able to defraud the public

21. Employing a person of known bad character without supervision

22. Assisting a creditor to obtain an undue preference

23. Passing worthless cheques

24. Giving offensive or improper letters

25. Giving false references

26. Making untrue statements to procure a passport for another person

27. Permitting a client to suppress a will

28. Antedating deed to defraud creditors or income tax authorities or to avoid judgments

29. Forging a signature to a mortgage

30. Making a false income tax return

Professional responsibility, including professional ethics, is a vast and extremely important topic which must be studied in even more depth, in order to truly understand the role of the lawyer in our legal system.[54] Although the above discussion has included several references to the now classic text by Orkin, there are presently other publications which warrant the reader's attention. For a thorough and up-to-date study of professional conduct in the legal profession, see W.B. Cotter, *Professional Responsibility Instruction in Canada: A Coordinated Curriculum for Legal Education* (Montreal: Conceptcom, 1992); B.G. Smith, *Professional Conduct for Canadian Lawyers* (Toronto: Butterworths, 1989); and Stephen

---

[54] The public perception of lawyers is often not good. According to the Consumers Association of Canada lawyers head the list of professionals most frequently complained about. See the Edmonton Journal, 27th February 1980. The questions of competence, ethics, and, indeed, "caring" frequently arise. With respect to "caring", see the Financial Post, 20th June 1981. With respect to competence and ethics, see U.S. News & World Report, 1st December 1980 ("Lawyers Giving Public a Raw Deal"); the Toronto Star, 26th January 1981 ("Lawyers Who Stoop to Fraud Eroding Faith in the Profession"); the Financial Post, 6th June 1981 ("Lawyers Probe Origins of Legal Incompetence"); U.S. News & World Report, 11th May 1981 ("Why Lawyers are in the Doghouse"); Newsweek Magazine, 11th December 1981 ("Lawyers on Trial"); the Edmonton Journal, 3rd February 1979 ("Incompetent Alberta Lawyers May Face Action From Peers"); Harper's Magazine, October 1978 ("Ontario Moves to Stamp Out Lawyers' Errors"); the Toronto Star, 11th March 1979 ("Feel Your Lawyer's Blundered? Now, Finally, You Can Sue Him"); Time Magazine, 10th April 1978 ("Those #&X*!!! Lawyers"); U.S. News & World Report, 26th February 1979 ("Putting the Spotlight on Lawyers' Misdeeds"); and the Edmonton Journal, 29th January 1982 ("Critics Call Lawyers Greedy and Arrogant"). See also the Edmonton Journal, 10th August 1978 and 14th January 1982, where U.S. Chief Justice Warren Burger is very critical of recent law school graduates. See also the Edmonton Journal, 16th April 1979 and Time Magazine, 8th December 1980.

M. Grant and Linda R. Rothstein, *Lawyers' Professional Liability* (Toronto: Butterworths, 1989).[55]

For a greater understanding of the ethical requirements of the legal profession and of professional responsibility in general, the following sources might be helpful:[56]

---

[55] See also, Law, J.M. (ed.), *Professional Responsibility: Cases and Materials*, Faculty of Law, University of Alberta, 1994. On the question of "[w]hat clients really want from their lawyers", see The Law Society of Upper Canada, Errors and Omissions, January 1995.

[56] The following is a survey of some recent cases in connection with various aspects of the legal profession in Canada: *Royal Bank v. Bradley* (1988), 60 Alta. L.R. (2d) 347, 39 B.L.R. 265, 89 A.R. 121 (Q.B.); *Fraser & Co. v. Holden* (1988), 29 B.C.L.R. (2d) 31 (C.A.), reversing (1987), 14 B.C.L.R. (2d) 293 (S.C.); *Law Society of Man. v. Eadie*, (May 27, 1988), Doc. 100/88 (Man. C.A.), reversing (1988), 51 Man. R. (2d) 279 (C.A.); *Kimmerly v. Law Society of Yukon* (1987), 3 Y.R. 54 (S.C.); *Spring v. Law Society of Upper Can.*, (1987) 60 O.R. (2d) 699, 41 D.L.R. (4th) 374 (*sub nom. Re Spring and Law Society of Upper Can.*) (Div. Ct.), affirmed (1988), 63 O.R. (2d) 736 (Div. Ct.); *Crysdale v. Carter-Baron Drilling Services Partnership* (1988), 62 O.R. (2d) 693, 30 C.P.C. (2d) 191 (H.C.), leave to appeal to Ont. Div. Ct. refused (1988), 62 O.R. (2d) 693 at 696, 30 C.P.C. (2d) 191 at 192 (H.C.); *McAlpine & Hordo v. United Services Funds*, (April 26, 1988), Vancouver No. CA007185, *Bowles v. Johnston, Oliphant, Van Buekenhout & Deans*, [1988] 4 W.W.R. 242, 53 Man. R. (2d) 81 (Q.B.); *Wright v. Bryant* (1988), 26 B.C.L.R. (2d) 359 (S.C.); *Cady v. Hanson*, (1988), 26 B.C.L.R. (2d) 169, 51 D.L.R. (4th) 139 (C.A.); *Cady v. Hanson* (1988), 68 C.B.R. (N.S.) 201 (Ont. S.C.); *Button v. Law Society (Newfoundland)* (1988), 71 Nfld. & P.E.I.R. 39, 220 A.P.R. 39 (Nfld. C.A.); *Kolbe v. Kolybaba* (1988), 86 A.R. 1 (Q.B.); *Sutton v. Toronto (City)* (1988), 26 C.P.C. (2d) 18 (Ont Dist Ct.); *Landru v. Landru*, [1989] 3 W.W.R. 705, 19 R.F.L. (3d) 113, 58 D.L.R. (4th) 85, 73 Sask. R. 196 (C.A.); reversing (1988), 26 C.P.C. (2d) 175, 67 Sask. R. 229 (C.A.); *Tri-Crest Investment Corp. v. Davidson & Co.* (1988), 24 B.C.L.R. (2d) 248, 50 D.L.R. (4th) 81 (S.C.); *Commonwealth Construction Co. v. Defazio Bulldozing & Backhoe Ltd.* (1988), 25 B.C.L.R. (2d) 140 (S.C.); *Haunholter v. Law Society (Alberta)* (1988), 88 A.R. 313 (C.A.); *Chopra v. Law Society (Alberta)* (1988), 88 A.R. 312 (C.A.), leave to appeal to S.C.C. refused (1988), 91 A.R. 80n, 90 N.R. 319n (S.C.C.); *A. & E. Land Industries Ltd. v. Sask. Crop Insurance Corp.*, [1988] 3 W.W.R. 590 (Sask. Q.B.); *Aciers Valam Inc. v. Carrier* (1987), 28 C.L.R. 298, 86 N.B.R. (2d) 1, 219 A.P.R. 1 (Q.B.); *Frew v. Shrum, Liddle & Hebenton*, [1988] 3 W.W.R. 642, 23 B.C.L.R. (2d) 243 (S.C.); *Prousky v. Law Society of Upper Can.* (1987), 61 O.R. (2d) 37, 41 D.L.R. (4th) 565 (H.C.), affirmed (1987), 62 O.R. (2d) 224, 45 D.L.R. (4th) 640n (C.A.); *Kutilin v. Auerbach* (1988), 34 B.C.L.R. (2d) 23, 54 D.L.R. (4th) 552 (C.A.), leave to appeal to S.C.C. refused (1989), 101 N.R. 231n; *Tulick Estate v. Ostapowich* (1988), 62 Alta. L.R. (2d) 384, 91 A.R. 381 (Q.B.); *Saskatoon (City) v. Plaxton, Loewen & Weibe*, [1988] 6 W.W.R. 85, 30 C.P.C. (2d) 158, 70 Sask. R. 206 (Q.B.), reversed [1989] 2 W.W.R. 577, 33 C.P.C. (2d) 238, 73 Sask. R. 215 (C.A.); *Luchka v. Zens* (1988), 32 B.C.L.R. (2d) 345 (S.C.), reversed (1989), 37 B.C.L.R. (2d) 127, 36 C.P.C. (2d) 271 (C.A.); *Carlson v. Loraas Disposal Services Ltd.* (1988), 30 C.P.C. (2d) 181, 70 Sask. R. 161 (Q.B.); *Szarfer v. Chodos* (1988), 66 O.R. (2d) 350, 54 D.L.R. (4th) 383 (C.A.), affirming (1986), 54 O.R. (2d) 663, 36 C.C.L.T. 181, 27 D.L.R. (4th) 388 (H.C.); *Central & Eastern Trust Co. v. Rafuse*, [1986] 2 S.C.R. 147, 37 C.C.L.T. 117, 42 R.P.R. 161, 34 B.L.R. 187, 31 D.L.R. (4th) 481, 75 N.S.R. (2d) 109, 186 A.P.R. 109, 69 N.R. 321, (*sub nom. Central Trust Co. c. Cordon*) [1986] R.R.A. 527 (headnote only), varied (*sub nom. Central Trust Co. v. Rafuse*) [1988] 1 S.C.R. 1206, 44 C.C.L.T. xxxiv; *Coffin v. MacBeath* (1988), 29 C.P.C. (2d) 294, 71 Nfld. & P.E.I.R. 273, 220 A.P.R. 273 (Nfld. T.D.), reversed (1990), 81 Nfld. & P.E.I.R. 333, 255 A.P.R. 333, 43 C.P.C. (2d) 259 (Nfld. C.A.); *Quo Facta Legal Services v. Law Society of Upper Can.* (1988), 24 C.P.R. (3d) 286 (Ont. C.A.), leave to appeal to S.C.C. refused (1989), 24 C.P.R. (3d) 286n, 100 N.R. 240n, 36 O.A.C. 213n (S.C.C.); *Levine v. Abe Levine & Sons Ltd.* (*sub nom. Levine v. Levine (Abe) & Sons Ltd.*) (1988), 86 N.B.R. (2d) 322, 219 A.P.R. 322 (Q.B.); *Lucky Venture Holdings Ltd. v. Hogue* (1988), 56 Man. R. (2d) 172 (C.A.);

1. Smith, *Professional Conduct for Canadian Lawyers*
2. Orkin, *Legal Ethics*
3. Grant & Rothstein, *Lawyers' Professional Liability*
4. Arthurs, *Casebook on the Legal Profession*
5. Law Society of Upper Canada, *Professional Conduct Handbook*
6. Boulton, *A Guide to Conduct and Etiquette at the Bar* (U.K.)
7. Freedman, *Lawyers' Ethics in an Adversary System* (U.S.)
8. American Bar Association, *Code of Professional Responsibility and Commentary*, May 1981
9. American Bar Association, *Draft Model Rules of Professional Conduct*, May 1981
10. *American Lawyers Code of Conduct*, June 1980 (Discussion paper)
11. Laud, *Lectures on Professional Conduct and Etiquette* (U.K.)
12. Council of Law Society, *A Guide to Professional Conduct*, 1974 (U.K.)
13. Disney *et al., Lawyers* (Australia)
14. Pirsig & Kirwin, *Professional Responsibility* (U.S.)
15. Kaufman, *Problems in Professional Responsibility* (U.S.)
16. Hazard, *Ethics in the Practice of Law* (U.S.)
17. Galston, *Professional Responsibility of the Lawyer* (U.S.)

There are many recent articles on the issue of professional responsibility and legal ethics. Some selected Canadian articles are set out as follows: Arthurs, H.W., R. Weisman and F.H. Zemans, "Canadian Lawyers: A Peculiar Professionalism" in R. Abel and P. Lewis, eds., *Lawyers in Society*, vol. 1, Berkeley: University of California Press, 1988 at p. 123; Abella, R.S., "Women in the Legal Profession", (1990) 48 The Advocate 507; M. Fitz-James, "Our Law Societies Do Nothing to Regulate Basic Professional Competence: Arthurs", 14:10 The Lawyers Weekly (8 July

---

Junger v. Law Society of Upper Can. (1988), 65 O.R. (2d) 749, 34 Admin. L.R. 309, 53 D.L.R. (4th) 312 (Div. Ct.); *Lefebvre v. Gardiner* (1988), 27 B.C.L.R. (2d) 294 (S.C.); *Rusonik v. Law Society of Upper Can.* (1988), 28 O.A.C. 57 (Div. Ct.); *Bentler v. Wilfley* (1987), 79 A.R. 338 (Q.B), affirmed (1988), 91 A.R. 317 (C.A.); *Moore-Stewart v. Law Society (B.C.)*, [1989] 2 W.W.R. 543, 32 B.C.L.R. (2d) 273, 54 D.L.R. (4th) 482 (C.A.), leave to appeal to S.C.C. refused (1989), 100 N.R. 238n (S.C.C.); *Painchaud v. Painchaud* (1988), 69 Sask. R. 146 (Q.B.); *Davies v. Fiddes* (1989), 34 B.C.L.R. (2d) 137 (C.A.); *Elizabeth Fry Society of Sask. Inc. v. Saskatchewan (Legal Aid Comm.)*, [1989] 2 W.W.R. 168, 32 C.P.C. (2d) 62, 56 D.L.R. (4th) 95, 72 Sask. R. 1 (C.A.); *Volrich v. Law Society (B.C.)* (1988), 29 B.C.L.R. (2d) 392 (S.C.); *Gorrie v. Neilson*, [1989] 2 W.W.R. 437, 64 Alta. L.R. (2d) 24, *(sub nom. Gorrie v. Nielson (No. 2)* 92 A.R. 167 (C.A.); *Petrashuyk v. Law Society (Alta.)*, [1984] 2 W.W.R. 530, 29 Alta L.R. (2d) 251, 7 Admin. L.R. 37, 41 C.P.C. 279, 5 D.L.R. (4th) 592, 50 A.R. 386 (Q.B.), reversed [1985] 2 W.W.R. 549, 35 Alta. L.R. (2d) 259, 10 Admin. L.R. 117, 8 C.C.L.I. 27, 16 D.L.R. (4th) 22, 58 A.R. 94 (C.A.), reversed [1988] 2 S.C.R. 385, [1989] 4 W.W.R. 663, 66 Alta. L.R. (2d) 289, 33 Admin. L.R. 145, 34 C.C.L.I. 161, 53 D.L.R. (4th) 607, 91 A.R. 319, 88 N.R. 148; *R. v. Kopyto* (1987), 62 O.R. (2d) 449, 61 C.R. (3d) 209, 39 C.C.C. (3d) 1, 47 D.L.R. (4th) 213, 24 O.A.C. 81 (C.A.); *Law Society (Man.) v. Giesbrecht*, [1984] 1 W.W.R. 430, 30 R.P.R. 77, 39 C.P.C. 26, 2 D.L.R. (4th) 354, 24 Man. R. (2d) 228 (C.A.).

1994) 7; Hurlburt, W.H., "Incompetent Service and Professional Responsibility", (1980) 18 Alta L. Rev. 145; Dickson, The Hon. Mr. Justice B., "The Public Responsibilities of Lawyers", (1983) 13 Manitoba L.J. 175.[57]

For a recent discussion of one important aspect of professional concern, see Perell, P.M. *Conflicts of Interest in the Legal Profession*. Markham: Butterworths, 1995.

There is, of course, no mandatory retirement age for members of the legal profession, although there is provision in the enabling statutes governing the provincial law societies for resignation from the law societies. The danger that an unsuspecting public is without protection against a lawyer who has become mentally incapacitated, senile, ill, infirm[58] or addicted to alcohol or drugs is only partially allayed by the availability of an action in negligence for damages. Thus, some law societies in Canada are presently considering making such incapacity or infirmity a ground for disciplinary sanction.

THE MODERN LAWYER

Today's lawyer faces new challenges. The proliferation of laws has meant that he or she[59] is encouraged to specialize. The growing number of lawyers has created a highly competitive marketplace. For some this has led to unemployment.[60] Others have been prompted to try new methods of attracting clients: some now advertise the areas to which they have

---

[57] In addition to formal publications, there have been a number of recent conferences and seminars on these issues. For example, a meeting on "A New Look: A National Conference on the Legal Profession and Ethics" was held at the University of Calgary in June of 1994 and a course on "Regulation of Professionals and Disciplinary Hearings" was held in Vancouver in October of 1994.

[58] See discussion by G. Parker on "Disability as a Form of Incompetence" in *The Legal Profession and Quality of Service, supra*, note 34, at p. 505. Recently, in Manitoba, this problem has been addressed by the creation of both Standards and Discipline Committees of the Law Society of Manitoba. In the case of incompetence or infirmity, the matter would be dealt with by the Standards Committee with a view to assisting the lawyer through remedial or therapeutic measures, while in the case of traditional disciplinary concerns, the matter would be dealt with by the Discipline Committee. These changes followed the recommendations of the Law Society of Manitoba Report on Competency (otherwise known as the Matas report).

[59] A growing number of women are entering the legal profession. A decade ago, approximately forty per cent of the students in all first year law school classes were female. Now the figure is closer to fifty per cent. See The Globe & Mail, 15th May 1980, on "Women Lawyers".

[60] See the Canadian Bar Association, *Economic Survey of Canadian Law Firms* (1980). See also the Edmonton Journal, 17th November 1981 and the New York Times, 6th August 1978. See also "Nice work if you can get it" (1986), 10 Can. Lawyer 2:11; L. Osberg, "A note on incomes of lawyers" (1985), 40 Indust. Rel. 865; and The Globe & Mail, 8th March 1983.

restricted their practice;[61] others depict or describe their practices in unconventional ways;[62] some are practising in new locales, i.e., supermarkets or department stores; some are reaching out to different segments of the community through "storefront" practices.[63] To increase the range of legal services that can be offered, a large established Toronto law firm attempted to break new ground by opening a so-called "branch office" in Calgary. The Law Society of Alberta reacted by passing two rules disallowing this type of operation. The validity of the rules was challenged in the courts, culminating in the Supreme Court of Canada holding that the rules violated the Charter of Rights and Freedoms.[64]

This has resulted in the emergence of several interprovincial law firms who have branch offices in various cities throughout Canada. Akin to the development of interprovincial law firms is the recent spate of mergers in which smaller law firms have become absorbed by larger multi-urban and international firms. For a discussion of this phenomenon see Maclean's Magazine, 6th November 1989, and The Globe & Mail, 5th May 1990. Yet another development relates to the establishment of multi-disciplinary law firms, in which lawyers and non-lawyers (specializing in other disciplines) are partners. A sub-committee of the Professional Conduct Committee of the Law Society of Upper Canada has been created to look into the feasibility of such law firms. See Ontario Reports, 28th October 1989 (69 O.R. (2d) Pt. 5, "Notice to the Profession").

The "public image" of the profession could be improved upon.[65] The

---

[61] For Canadian commentary on advertising by lawyers, see the Vancouver Sun, 18th September 1979; the Calgary Herald, 19th December 1978; the Edmonton Journal, 6th February 1979, 5th September 1979 and the editorial of 4th June 1979; and The Globe & Mail, 15th May 1978. For a discussion of the American position on advertising by lawyers, see the New York Times, 26th November 1978 and 3rd August 1980, Time Magazine, 21st August 1978 and the Edmonton Journal, 14th December 1978.

[62] For example, Vancouver lawyer Jack James established "The Law Shoppe" — see the Edmonton Journal, 21st February 1980 and 3rd February 1981. An American lawyer founded a chain of legal service centres called the "Law People" — see the Edmonton Journal, 22nd May 1979. Another example is the "Dial-A-Law" service operated by the Calgary Legal Guidance Public Service Project sponsored by the Alberta Branch of the Canadian Bar Association and the Law Society of Alberta. See earlier discussion of the *Jabour* case and a description of Mr. Jabour's Neighbourhood Legal Clinic in Maclean's Magazine, 19th February 1979.

[63] See, for example, Hoffman, "Lawyers for the Poor: Why Not the Best?", in New York Magazine, 14th May 1979, and the articles in Newsweek Magazine 9th October 1978, 14th January 1980, and 6th April 1981.

[64] See *Black v. Law Society (Alta.)*, [1989] 1 S.C.R. 591, [1989] 4 W.W.R. 1, 66 Alta. L.R. (2d) 97, 37 Admin. L.R. 161, 38 C.R.R. 193, 58 D.L.R. (4th) 317, 96 A.R. 352, 93 N.R. 266; for a discussion of the background to this case, see the Financial Post, 20th March 1983. See also B. McDougall, "Merger Mania" (1988), 12 Can. Lawyer 5:6, and Maclean's Magazine, 6th November 1989.

[65] See the Toronto Star, 9th February 1982 ("Lawyers Worry About Future of Profession"). See the Edmonton Journal, 8th March 1990 regarding public distrust of lawyers. On "How

misbehaviour and incompetence of a few has severely affected the professional reputation of all members of the profession.[66] One by-product of this is that malpractice insurance rates have increased.[67] In Alberta, as a result of two very serious cases of defalcation, special levies have had to be assessed for two years in a row in order to restore the Law Society's Assurance Fund.

However, the modern lawyer continues to do well financially[68] (in some cases attracting considerable notoriety from such financial success[69]) and to maintain a highly visible profile.[70]

(As an aside, changes in the financing of legal services should be noted. One new development is the growth of prepaid legal service plans[71] which often form part of the benefits sought in collective bargaining.[72] Another older development, legal aid, began in the mid-1960's and is now established in every province.)[73]

The practice of law continues to be a satisfying profession,[74] but in view of the new challenges being faced it has become an increasingly stressful occupation.[75] A consortium of the Law Society of Upper Canada, the

---

to Challenge Your Lawyer's Bill'', see the Financial Post, 10th January 1981 and on the procedure to launch complaints against lawyers, see the Edmonton Journal, 31st January to 2nd February 1980. See the discussion of the public perception of the law in Chapter 13.

[66] See Today Magazine, 19th July 1980, and J. Anderson, ''How to Choose the Right Lawyer'', in Reader's Digest, December 1980. See also ''Know Your Lawyer'', a pamphlet prepared by the Law Society of Alberta and the Alberta Branch of the Canadian Bar Association.

[67] See the Edmonton Journal, 29th October 1979.

[68] See Canadian Bar Association, *Economic Survey of Canadian Law Firms, supra*, note 56. For a discussion of this report, see the Financial Post, 22nd November 1980.

[69] The counsel to the Krever Royal Commission on Confidentiality of Health Records billed the Ontario government more than $200,000 for his work over 15 months. This attracted some controversy. See the Toronto Star, 27th June 1979. See also Goulden, *The Million Dollar Lawyers* (New York: Putnam, 1979); Time Magazine, 27th July 1981; and the New York Times, 3rd August 1979.

[70] See M. Ryval, ''The Defender'', in Quest Magazine, 1981; ''The New High Rollers: Canada's Celebrity Lawyers'' in Maclean's Magazine, 17th September 1979; J. Battan, Lawyers (Toronto: MacMillan, 1979); and K. Auletta, ''Don't Mess with Roy Cohn: The Legal Executioner'', in Esquire Magazine, 5th December 1978.

[71] This is also briefly discussed in Chapter 12.

[72] See L. Wilson and C. Wydnzynski. ''Prepaid Legal Services: Legal Representation for the Canadian Middle Class'' (1978), 28 U.T.L.J. 25. See also The Globe & Mail, 5th May 1979 and 26th May 1980, Time Magazine, 4th September 1978 and the Financial Post, 11th November 1978, 10th February 1979, and 6th March 1982.

[73] See The Globe & Mail, 4th May 1978 and 18th October 1979; the Toronto Star, 3rd May 1978, and the Calgary Albertan, 16th August 1979.

[74] See, for example, The Globe & Mail Report on Lawyers, July 25, 1995.

[75] See S. Benson, ''Why I Quit Practicing Law'', Newsweek Magazine, November 4, 1991, p. 10 and C. Nicholls, ''Why I'm Returning to Law'', Canadian Lawyer, March 1994, p. 11. Also for an interesting discussion on lawyers and stress, see Maclean's Magazine, 29th January 1979.

Ontario Branch of the Canadian Bar Association and other groups have joined together to sponsor LINK — a professional counselling program for members of the Law Society experiencing personal stress.

For a discussion of other aspects of the professional life of the modern lawyer, readers should consult the extensive bibliography appended to this chapter.[76]

Some concluding remarks on the role of the lawyer will follow the discussion of the role of the judge.[77]

JUDGES

The role of the judge does not lend itself to simple definition. A consideration of the fundamental role that a judge plays within our legal system pertains, of course, to a judge exercising his power as judge. However, there is a related capacity arising out of the prestige and status of the judiciary in our system, and that is the judge acting in a special capacity off the bench. For example, judges are often appointed members of Royal Commissions of Inquiry, tribunals, and other such bodies. These commissions of inquiry usually deal with ad hoc matters of national or provincial importance. A discussion of judges serving in other capacities will be raised at a later point in this chapter.

The role of the judge depends, to some extent, upon the particular bench on which he or she sits. The courts in the various jurisdictions are all governed by different enabling statutes. These statutes set out the judge's power and the nature of the matters over which the judge has jurisdiction. Thus, the role of one judge may be somewhat different than that of another by virtue of the different enabling statutes. However, these differences are often minor and, they do not preclude a more generic description of the

---

[76] For a discussion of lawyers as lobbyists, see G. Gall (1977), 15 Alta L. Rev. 400; and see U.S. News & World Report, 10th March 1980 ("Washington Lawyers: Rise of the Power Brokers"); for a discussion of the large number of lawyers, the modern law student and professors, the work done at major law reviews, bar exams, recent hiring practices of major law firms, and recent new publications for lawyers, all in the context of the U.S. judiciary system see, respectively, the New York Times, 1st April 1979, 4th November 1979 and 13th May 1980, Time Magazine, 25th February 1980, Newsweek Magazine, 1st December 1980 and Time Magazine, 26th February 1979. For a discussion of the draft of the new American Bar Association Code of Professional Responsibilities, see the New York Times, 7th January 1980.

[77] See bibliography appended to this chapter on the "Role of the Lawyer" in Canada. For a comparative analysis, see, in respect of the United Kingdom, R. Hazell (ed.), *The Bar on Trial* (London: Quartet Books, 1978), and, in respect of the United States, F. Rodell, *Woe Unto You, Lawyers!* (New York: Berkeley, 1980) (originally published in 1939), and J.C. Goulden, *The Million Dollar Lawyers* (New York: G.P. Putnam's Sons, 1978). (The same author wrote *The Superlawyer*, published in 1972.) See also P. Marcotte, "Lawyers Not so Powerful in D.C." A.B.A. Journal, February 1989, p. 32.

judicial function in Canada.[78] (The constitutional basis for judicial authority in Canada, including the legal structural basis for the various enabling statutes under which our courts are established, is set out in Chapter 5.)

Generally speaking, the role of the judge[79] within the Canadian legal system may be defined as that of an arbiter in resolving particular disputes. Disputes of a factual nature are determined by trial judges; disputes relating to the interpretation of a point of law are determined by judges having appellate jurisdiction.

To take this definition one step further, the role of the judge as arbiter in resolving particular disputes is carried out objectively, on the basis of evidence adduced through the workings of the adversarial system.[80] The essential nature of the adversarial system is that the judge acts as the objective decision-maker in the face of opposing interests, with each interest arguing and articulating the merits of its position. In contrast, the inquisitorial, or continental European, judge takes carriage of the proceedings and is ultimately responsible for the ascertainment of truth within the court. The system in Canada is founded on the belief that through an adversarial contest the truth will eventually emerge. The European system on the other hand is premised on the belief that only through an activist role on the part of the judge will the truth be ascertained.

Any attempt at providing a more detailed description of the role of the judge in the Canadian legal system must take into account that judges themselves do not share the same belief as to their role.[81]

---

[78] See Peter H. Russell, *The Judiciary in Canada: The Third Branch of Government* (Toronto: McGraw-Hill Ryerson, 1987), for a comprehensive discussion of the judiciary in Canada.

[79] For a biographical sketch of certain judges, see, for example, Deslauriers, *La Cour Supérieure du Québec et ses juges 1849 — 1er janvier 1980* (Quebec: Imprimerie Provinciale Inc., 1980); F. Vaughan, "Emmett M. Hall: A Profile of the Judicial Temperament" (1977), 15 O.H.L.J. 306; R. St. G. Stubbs, "The First Juvenile Court Judge: Hon. T. Mayre Daly, R.C." (1979), 10 Man. L.J. 1; and C. Troulis, "Biographies of the Justices of the Supreme Court of Canada, 1875-1985", [1986] Sup. Ct. Conf. 389.

[80] For some further recent discussion on the role of the judge, see S. Fine, "Should Judges Make Own Inquiries", The Globe & Mail, February 10, 1995; The Alberta Report, December 5, 1994; R.S. Abella, "Public Policy and the Judicial Role", (1989), 34; T.W. Church, "A Consumer's Prospective on the Courts", Canadian Institute for the Administration of Justice, vol. v, No. 2, Spring 1995; Lord Devlin, *The Judge.* (Chicago: Univ. of Chicago Press, 1979) at p. 8; R. Hon. A. Lamer P.C., "Remarks to the Conference 'Open Justice'", Canadian Institute for the Administration of Justice, Ottawa, Canada, October 13, 1994; S. Bindman, "Seat of Judgment: Canada's Most Powerful Judges Toil in Virtual Anonymity", The Edmonton Journal, April 12, 1992.

[81] Reference may be made to two special editions of the Canadian Bar Review published in commemoration of the 100th anniversary of the establishment of the Supreme Court of Canada. These two editions appear in volume 53 of the Canadian Bar Review and are cited as (1975), 53 Can. Bar Rev. 459, and (1975), 53 Can. Bar Rev. 649. In addition, also celebrating

Consider the following extract of comments made by the former Chief Justice of the Quebec Superior Court concerning the role of the judge. [82]

Judges Should Be Legislators, Quebec Chief Justice Argues

A two-month-old controversy over how far judges can go in replacing the lawmakers surfaced again here yesterday in a meticulously documented speech by Chief Justice Jules Deschênes of the Quebec Superior Court.

Chief Justice Deschênes told a Chamber of Commerce meeting that on paper the legislative, executive and judicial sections of Government are distinct but in practice they overlap, and when the lawmakers don't pass laws that are in keeping with "changing social conditions" it is up to the judges to exercise their "legislative power" and change the law to suit the times.

Yesterday, Chief Justice Deschênes tried to explain to his audience of businessmen why judges should legislate at times.

He cited more than 40 cases in which courts changed the law or overruled provincial or federal laws they decided didn't apply any longer or were wrong.

These included:

The 1970 Drybones case in which the Supreme Court of Canada decided that the Indian Act section forbidding Indians' being drunk on reserves was inoperative because it didn't apply equally to all Canadians;

The 1959 Roncarelli case in which the Supreme Court said the Quebec Government had acted wrongly by revoking a man's license because he was a Jehovah's Witness;

The 1973 Manitoba Egg War case in which the court said a provincial law impeded interprovincial commerce.

He said there had been 1972 judicial interpretations of Canada's constitution since Confederation.

He said that judges have "opened new roads and widened perspectives on the law as they sought modern solutions compatible with changing conditions in our society."

Chief Justice Deschênes said provincial labor laws are undergoing a "mini-revolution" in the courts because of recent court decisions. "Jurisprudence has more surprises in store for the citizens of our country."

"The first role" of judges, he said, "is to apply the law as it exists and this is the task to which they put most of their effort. More often than not, there is no doubt in the law. . . However, sometimes the evolution of thinking or morals tends to create an imbalance between the law and the facts.

---

the Centenary of the Supreme Court of Canada, a special edition of the Alberta Law Review was published. That edition is cited as (1976), 14 Alta L. Rev. 1. A major study of the Supreme Court of Canada is contained in Paul Weiler's treatise entitled *In the Last Resort* (Toronto: Carswell, 1974). For a history of the Supreme Court of Canada see J.G. Snell and F. Vaughan, *The Supreme Court of Canada: History of the Institution* (Toronto: Osgoode Society, 1985). For suggested future changes to the Supreme Court of Canada see *Report of the Canadian Bar Association Committee on the Supreme Court of Canada* (Ottawa: Canadian Bar Association, 1987). For the little known information on ad hoc Supreme Court Justices, see R. Boult, "Ad Hoc Judges of the Supreme Court of Canada" (1978), 25 Chitty's L.J. 289. See the detailed description of the study conducted at the University of Alberta in 1976 appearing in the first edition in this book. Work has been done in respect of two studies conducted under the auspices of the Canadian Institute for the Administration of Justice, namely the "Study of the Alberta Judiciary" and research relating to the "Role of the Chief Justice and Chief Judge in Canada." See *Compendium of Information on the status and role of the chief justice in Canada* (Canadian Institute for the Administration of Justice, 1987).

[82] See The Toronto Globe & Mail, 30 October 1974. See also J. Deschênes, *A Passion for Justice* (Montreal: Wilson & Lafleur, 1984).

"That's when the courts must take on, with a reflected audacity, the heavy burden of adapting the law to the new social realities which show up."

He said that if a judge were there only to apply the law he would be reduced to a robot.

"The defenders of such a view would become its victims and soon be among its most virulent critics."

Consider also the following sample of the views expressed by some Alberta judges as to the role of the judge in the Canadian legal system:[83]

(1) As far as the legislative role of the judges is concerned. . .I emphatically state that the function of a judge is not that of the law maker. The problem with this whole area of course is one of connotation and semantics. There can be no question that in the day to day functioning of judges they will contribute considerably to the growth and development of law. It is also true that in our constitutional system there is a fair amount of overlapping between the functions of the executive, the legislature and the judiciary. It is important to recognize that the lines dividing the three branches of government are rather gray and broad, but I think it is equally important to emphasize the paramount function of each branch of government and that each should be vigilant in minimizing its interference with the others' responsibility.

Basically I am of the view that there should be as much certainty in the law as possible. In other words the citizen at any given time should know where he stands in his relationships with his fellow citizen and with the state. If laws are changed without notice then the position of the citizen is rendered uncertain. For that reason I feel that generally the law should not change except by the action of the legislature. The problem with laws being changed by judges is that the change occurs without notice to the public. Secondly, I feel that even in a democratic system as highly developed as our own the citizen has a rather limited opportunity to control the law. That opportunity is of course expressed by the fact that the legislature is accountable to the voter. There is no similar accountability between the judiciary and the public and it is therefore my view that the judiciary must be very careful to keep its law making role within the limits set by the existing rules of law. I therefore of course feel that the doctrine of stare decisis is a doctrine essential to the proper functioning of our judicial system. If that doctrine is taken away from the judicial system then each judge becomes a law unto himself and the citizen is no longer subject to the role of the law but is in danger of being subject to the rule of the man.

(2) The judge is to apply the law fairly as it is enacted. Without this, the law is unknown not only to the practising lawyer but to the judges and the public and jockeying for a particular judge would be a large part of the court work of barristers. No judge, applying the law as it is, becomes a robot, but at least he should know in fact what it is, and if he should err, the appeal courts will give guidance in their judgment.

(3) . . . should exercise an essentially interpretative process . . . one should apply the laws as enacted and be guided accordingly, and this does not mean that we necessarily agree to all of them.

(4) All human societies have one characteristic in common and that is that the struggle for power therein is an ongoing phenomenon. The great achievement of liberal democratic societies was that they domesticated that struggle and brought it within constitutional confines. In our system government power is diffused amongst the judicial, executive and legislative branches of government out of a wholesome recognition of the fact that no person and no group can be trusted with too much power. It is only by continuing to recognize such self-evident truths and by continuing to preserve such a division of power that individual liberty can be maintained.

It therefore follows that judges have no right to invade the legislative function. They

---

[83] This sample is taken from a 1976 study conducted at the University of Alberta. For more details concerning that study, see the first edition of this book.

cannot be trusted with absolute or excessive power any more than any other group in society. The judge's role is to interpret the law and not to make it. I realize of course that in the course of interpreting the law a judge may incidentally also be said to be making law on occasion. It is impossible to place the three government functions into watertight compartments. There is necessarily some overlapping but it is important that each branch of government recognize its limitations and not endeavour to assume the role of another.

(5) The notion that a judge should legislate in the real sense is a destructive one. [The courts would become] an oligarchy of dictators, imposing their ideas about the shape of society upon the ordinary citizen. [This would be a] gross abuse of judges' powers [and would result in] a lack of public respect for the impartiality of the courts . . . A judge who adopts an activist role respecting social questions becomes a protagonist, and loses his capacity as an arbiter. A judge, however, can adapt law to new realities as a proper judicial function. The courts must take cognizance of changes in conditions in applying the rules.

(6) I believe that as judges, we are an arm of government and in the execution of our duties we should not transgress the role of the legislator or the administrator. If the rule of law is to have any validity, legislating should be done by legislators and judges should restrict themselves to interpreting legislation and applying the common law, previous judicial interpretations and common sense to the facts before them for the purpose of reaching a decision. I believe that a judge can be innovative in his approach to the interpretation, and that in his interpretation he can reflect changing social values, but he should not go to the extent of usurping the function of the legislature. In summary, I feel that judges should exercise an essentially interpretive function.

(7) Lord Atkin said in *United Australia Ltd. v. Barclays Bank Ltd.,* [1941] A.C. at 29, [1940] 4 All E.R. 20, quoted approvingly by Milvain C.J.T.D. in *McGee v. Waldern and Cunningham,* [1971] 4 W.W.R. 684 at 693, 4 R.F.L. 17 (Alta.):

"When these ghosts of the past stand in the path of justice clanking their medieval chains the proper course for the Judge is to pass through them undeterred."

(8) My view is that it is not the judge's function to make laws. That is up to the legislatures and Parliament . . . The fact is, however, that the judge has frequently to interpret any given piece of legislation in the light of changed conditions and circumstances which may or may not have existed at the time the legislation was enacted, and to that extent a judge may be thought to be making the law . . . It is to be borne in mind that the very nature of the common law is that it is a growing thing, it has to adapt itself to changing times and to different environments, but I do not think a judge should consider himself as a lawmaker.

(9) I cannot agree, however, that judges should have the power to, in effect, determine the public pulse, and as a consequence of this determination override clear statutory provision. The judge must function within the framework of the law. Responsibility for determining when changes in law are appropriate must rest with the legislative authority.

(10) [A judge should stay out of the political and social arena for the reason that he doesn't have the] facility to canvass public opinion nor to properly assess it . . . [However, he should not be in an] ivory tower [impervious to social change].

(11) Certainly in some new areas where the law can be applied or extended logically to fit a new situation a judge is in fact "making" new law. But it is only really a logical extension of an existing principle to fit a new set of facts and not breaking new legislative ground.

(12) The role of the judge in our legal system is to formulate the law and to keep in pace with the times. That naturally involves formulating law which is in accordance with the needs of society today. In other words, what one might have thought fifty years ago on any subject might not be applicable at all today and if a judge were to apply the law in that sense we would soon have chaos, and to apply the law a

judge would be reduced to a robot. His function of course is to decide judicially
in the light of existing conditions which involves many changes from time to time,
and in my thinking a good judge must be in tune with the times . . . The law is
an amorphous body of principles and the judge's function is most important because
he must, in reaching his judgment, keep in mind the widened perspectives on the
law as Chief Justice Deschênes mentions, compatible with changing conditions in
our society.

(13) A judge's role is primarily to interpret and apply the law . . . I see no impropriety
in saying I don't like the law, so long as I apply it and enforce it (which it is my
duty to do). We recall that Mr. Justice Sissons of the Northwest Territories in one
case refused to enforce a law with which he did not agree. I would not be surprised
that in the long view, and in these fast-changing times, and with the prospect of
new young judges "tempered in the crucible of change", the old attitude of interpreting the law but not criticizing it will be "bent if not broken".

Shortly after the death of the late Chief Justice Laskin, an article in
the Toronto newspaper, The Globe & Mail, summarized the late Chief
Justice's view as to the role of the judge. A small excerpt from that article,
written by journalist Jeff Sallot, is set out as follows:

The "Laskin court" is not easily characterized, but a common thread seems to be a will-
ingness of judges to actively address political issues that in an earlier era would have been
considered beyond the Supreme Court's mandate. "It is too easy for judges to say that
if the law needs to be changed that is the responsibility of Parliament," Judge Laskin
told an interviewer shortly before he was elevated to the top spot on the court.

. . .

Judge Laskin was dubbed "Moses, the law-giver" by his law students at Osgoode Hall.
The "law-giver" tag was resurrected in recent years as the court moved into an era of
activist and creative interpretation of statutes.

Common-law traditionalists frequently criticized what they saw as the "Americanization"
of the Supreme Court. These traditionalists interpreted the law literally. But Judge Laskin
didn't think there should be any great difference in the roles of the Canadian court and
its U.S. counterpart. He liked the U.S. approach of creative interpretation.[84]

But whether the judge sees himself as lawmaker or law interpreter, it
is of paramount importance that he or she, for purposes of credibility and
public acceptance, ensure that the court is an arena where the interests of
justice are served by searching for the truth in an atmosphere of fairness,
dignity and decorum.[85]

There will be some discussions later in this chapter on legal and other
constraints imposed upon judges. Essentially, these constraints are imposed

---

[84] See The Globe & Mail, 28th March 1984.

[85] See Cecil, *The English Judge* (London: Arrow Books, 1979); and Lord Denning, *The Discipline of Law* (London: Butterworths, 1979). See also D. Gibson, "Judges as Legislators:
not whether but how" (1987), 25 Alta. L. Rev. 249; and J.D. Whyte, "Legality and Legitimacy:
the problem of Judicial Review of Legislation" (1987), 12 Queen's L.J. 1. For a further discussion of the Canadian judiciary as reported in the press, see the Edmonton Journal, 13th
December 1977, 16th November 1979, 15th August 1980, 14th July 1980, The Globe & Mail,
16th January 1980, 12th January 1981 and 29th June 1981 and the Alberta Report, 10th March
1986. See especially the Edmonton Journal, 24th January 1981 and the feature in the Toronto
Star, 10th February 1982, as part of its series on "Justice in the 80's". See also the Toronto
Star, 10th February 1982.

to ensure impartiality on the part of the judge, to promote public acceptance and credibility of our courts and the judicial system and most importantly, to guarantee that the search for truth will be conducted in a fair and dignified manner. Ultimately, if the judicial process operates successfully, the search for truth will become synonymous with the achievement of justice.

Because judges play such an important role in our legal system, it is necessary to examine how they are appointed and what conduct is expected of them during their tenure of office. Although the constitutional basis for the appointment of judges is discussed in Chapter 5 of this book, a brief review is set out below.

1. THE APPOINTMENT OF JUDGES

(a) Constitutional Basis

The relevant provisions of the Constitution Act of 1867 are set out below:

VII. JUDICATURE

96. The Governor General shall appoint the Judges of the Superior, District, and County Courts in each Province, except those of the Courts of Probate in Nova Scotia and New Brunswick.

97. Until the Laws relative to Property and Civil Rights in Ontario, Nova Scotia, and New Brunswick, and the Procedure of the Courts in those Provinces, are made uniform, the Judges of the Courts of those Provinces appointed by the Governor General shall be selected from the respective Bars of those Provinces.

98. The Judges of the Courts of Quebec shall be selected from the Bar of that Province.

99. (1) Subject to subsection (2) of this section, the judges of the superior courts shall hold office during good behaviour, but shall be removable by the Governor General on address of the Senate and House of Commons.

(2) A judge of a superior court, whether appointed before or after the coming into force of this section, shall cease to hold office upon attaining the age of seventy-five years, or upon the coming into force of this section if at that time he has already attained that age.

100. The Salaries, Allowances, and Pensions of the Judges of the Superior, District and County Courts (except the Courts of Probate in Nova Scotia and New Brunswick), and of the Admiralty Courts in Cases where the Judges thereof are for the Time being paid by Salary, shall be fixed and provided by the Parliament of Canada.

101. The Parliament of Canada may, notwithstanding anything in this Act, from Time to Time provide for the Constitution, Maintenance, and Organization of a General Court of Appeal for Canada, and for the Establishment of any additional Courts for the better Administration of the laws of Canada.

Exclusive Powers of Provincial Legislatures

92. . . .

4. The Establishment and Tenure of Provincial Offices and the Appointment and Payment of Provincial Officers.

14. The Administration of Justice in the Province, including the Constitution, Maintenance, and Organization of Provincial Courts, both of Civil and of Criminal Jurisdiction, and including Procedure in Civil Matters in those Courts.

It is important to realize that there is no provision per se in the Constitution Act of 1867 establishing a specific court in Canada. What the Constitution Act of 1867 does provide is as follows:

(i) Federal Courts and Tribunals

The Parliament of Canada is granted legislative competence to enact laws providing for the establishment of certain courts and tribunals under the provisions of s. 101 of the Constitution Act of 1867.

(ii) Provincial Courts and Tribunals

The various provincial legislatures are given authority to enact laws to provide for certain provincial courts and tribunals under the provisions of s. 92(14) of the Constitution Act of 1867. (This section must be read together with the exclusion of federal jurisdiction to do so in s. 91(27) of the Constitution Act of 1867.)

(iii) Provisions in the Constitution Act of 1867 Regarding the Appointment of Judges

There are three sets of provisions of the Constitution Act of 1867 regarding the appointment of judges. First, s. 101 gives Parliament the authority to enact laws establishing certain federal courts and tribunals and, by implication, also gives Parliament the authority to pass legislation respecting the appointment of judges for these courts, their salaries, tenure of office and removal from office.[86] Secondly, ss. 96 to 100 provide for the appointment of the judges of the superior, district and county courts in each province, and their salaries and pensions. And thirdly, s. 92(14) of the Constitution Act of 1867 authorizes by implication the appointment of judges at the provincial level to serve on provincial courts established under that section.

Thus, in Canada, the judiciary presides over three types of courts:

(1) Federal courts constituted under federal legislation enacted pursuant to s. 101 of the Constitution Act of 1867, with federally appointed judges.

(2) Provincial courts constituted by provincial legislation enacted pursuant to s. 92(14) of the Constitution Act of 1867, with federally appointed judges under the provisions of ss. 96 to 100 of the Constitution Act of 1867.

(3) Provincial courts constituted under provincial legislation enacted pursuant to s. 92(14) of the Constitution Act of 1867 with provincially appointed judges.

---

[86] The process of appointment of judges to the Supreme Court of Canada was about to be altered by the Meech Lake and Charlottetown Constitutional Accords. See the discussion at the beginning of Chapter 5.

(b) The Process of Appointment

Essentially, there are eleven, not one, processes of appointment. First, there is the single federal process of appointment of justices to the Supreme Court of Canada,[87] to courts of superior jurisdiction in the provinces, and to county and district courts in the provinces.[88] In addition, each of the ten provinces has its own process of appointment of provincial judges to the provincial courts.[89] As a result, there may be no uniformity in these processes.

The process of judicial appointment has always been surrounded with secrecy. This perpetuated the belief held by many that political considerations were paramount as factors in appointing judges. Many held (and indeed many still do hold) the view that to become a judge it is beneficial to have had a political affiliation with the party in power which is making the judicial appointment.[90] This is, of course, impossible to ascertain with any certainty. However, owing to recent public disclosures at the federal level, there is good reason to believe that if there ever was a political component in the appointment process, that component has now substantially been removed. These disclosures are as follows. First, in February 1976, at a conference sponsored jointly by the Canadian Institute for the Administration of Justice and the Annual Lecture Series of Osgoode Hall Law School of York University, an address was made to the conference by a Special Assistant to the Minister of Justice of Canada. This address, for the first time, put on public record previously undisclosed details concerning the process of appointment.[91] Secondly, in a feature article appearing in the Toronto Star, dated 17th April 1976, similar disclosures were made as to the federal process of appointment (including, in addition, a discus-

---

[87] Modifications in the appointment process with respect to this court were included in both of the ill-fated Meech Lake and Charlottetown Accords. The most recent suggestion for reform appears in M. Friedland, *A Place Apart: Judicial Independence and Accountability in Canada* (Ottawa: Canadian Judicial Council, 1995). Specifically, he suggests, at p. 267, as follows:

. . . [I]t is suggested that special nominating committees be established for each appointment to the Supreme Court of Canada. The committee could consist of nominees of the provinces from which the appointment will be made, nominees of legal groups, and nominees of the federal government. The committee would present a short ranked list of names to the government. If the government went outside the list, a public confirmation hearing (with the exception of personal matters) would be held by, perhaps, a joint House and Senate Committee.

[88] See also M. Friedland, *supra* at p. 267.

[89] The province of Ontario has implemented a practice of advertising for judicial positions when vacancies occur. A brief discussion of this practice follows at a later point in this chapter.

[90] See Simpson, J., *Spoils of Power: The Politics of Patronage* (Toronto: Collins, 1988).

[91] Proceedings of that conference were recently published in a treatise entitled *The Canadian Judiciary*, edited by Allen M. Linden (now Mr. Justice Linden) (Toronto: Osgoode Hall Law School, York University, 1976).

sion of the appointing process for provincially appointed judges in the province of Ontario). This article is set out, in part, as follows:

> Nearly every judge on the bench vividly remembers the day, while he was still practising law, that his secretary buzzed on his intercom to tell him the federal justice minister — or the provincial attorney-general — was calling him.
>
> Those first calls revolve around a single question: Would the lawyer accept appointments to, for example, the trial division of the Supreme Court? If he says yes, the minister thanks him and says he'll be in touch. He usually — but not always — will be.
>
> If the lawyer gets the second call, it will come any time from a week to a month later. This time, the minister tells him his appointment will be announced within a few days or, occasionally, within a few hours. He thanks the lawyer for agreeing to serve.
>
> Lawyers sometimes turn down the opportunity in the first phone call. They are seldom asked again . . .
>
> Picking the men and women to fill the vacancies involves a talent search that is both endless and increasingly meticulous.
>
> The pressures that make it this way include the law's growing complexity, the relentless expansion of caseloads and the belief of governments that appointing the best people is really the only way to restore the public's shrunken respect for the courts. One result of all this is that the bench is rarely used any more as a reward for faithful political cronies of dubious ability.
>
> Instead, the federal justice department — whose approach is roughly duplicated by the provinces — actively encourages lawyers, judges, members of Parliament, law school deans and private citizens to send in the names of lawyers they think would make good candidates.
>
> Sometimes, a lawyer who wants to be a judge will ask his colleagues to write the minister and propose his name. During one month in mid-1975, former justice minister Otto Lang got 69 letters on behalf of one lawyer. . . .
>
> It used to be regarded as bad form to be openly eager for the job but Ottawa recently passed the word that there would be nothing wrong with a lawyer writing in to say he'd take the post if it was offered.
>
> Every name seriously put forward is checked. Lawyers and judges across the nation are growing accustomed to phone calls from the Ottawa office of Ed Ratushny, special ministerial adviser on judicial appointments, asking about an individual's integrity, temperament, personal and work habits, professional competence and ability to get along with other people.
>
> Says Ratushny: "Assurances are given in relation to the absolute confidentiality of any comments which are made. Indeed, the comments, which are taken down by hand, are given to the minister in exactly the same form. They are not dictated or transcribed and no one other than the minister has access to them.
>
> "If specific problems are suggested, more detailed inquiries are made to determine whether they are confirmed or prove not to be substantial."
>
> The inquiries have to be exhaustive because the stated qualifications for selection are so general. About the only requirement for the provincial criminal bench is a law degree. The federal courts, however, are restricted to lawyers with at least 10 years in practice — which the government insists is the reason it hasn't picked more women, who began enroling in law schools in large numbers only within the last five or six years.
>
> Once candidates have been decided upon, the federal and provincial procedures differ.
>
> Ottawa submits the names to the Canadian Bar Association's national judiciary committee, which assesses them as either "well qualified," "qualified" or "not qualified." Neither Justice Minister Ron Basford nor his predecessor, Otto Lang, appointed anyone turned down by the organized bar.
>
> The Ontario attorney-general sends the name of his candidates to the Judicial Council,

whose seven members include chief Justice George Gale of Ontario and Chief Justice Willard Estey of the Ontario Supreme Court's trial division. Only one nominee rejected by the council ever made it to the bench — and that was more than six years ago.

Where do the successful appointees come from? Most are lawyers in private practice. In the four years he was federal justice minister, John Turner named 111 judges. Two were promoted from one bench to the next. Eleven others included a law professor, crown attorneys, an official from his own department, a member of Parliament and a lawyer who worked for Canadian National Railways.

Otto Lang, Turner's successor, named 161 federal judges and all but 22 were lawyers in private practice. The average age of the newcomers under both ministries was 48, but several were in their mid-30s.

Until Turner's appointment to the justice portfolio in 1968, only two women had ever reached the federal bench in Canada. Turner added three; Lang, five, and Justice Minister Ron Basford so far has picked two more.

When all the checks and reports and votes are in — and favourable — the candidate gets the second phone call. Between his acceptance and his swearing-in, he must unload his law practice by finding colleagues willing to take on his unfinished cases. He must resign his company directorships and other business connections . . .

At their installations, federal judges "do solemnly and sincerely promise and swear that I will duly and faithfully, and to the best of my skill and knowledge, execute the powers and trust reposed in me . . . so help me God."[92]

In the intervening years since the above disclosure, not a great deal has changed. Consider the following comments made by J. Richard Finlay in an article appearing in The Toronto Globe & Mail:

CAST OFF THE CLOAK OF SECRECY
JUDGES SHOULD BE PICKED IN PUBLIC

Citizens of the United States may differ over the suitability of Robert Bork to sit on their Supreme Court, but few question the process that has brought him into the public eye. It is in sharp contrast to the way the Supreme Court of Canada is selected, and the Meech Lake accord virtually assures it will stay that way.

In the United States, the president proposes nominees to the top court, but the Senate must decide on the appointment. And as the recent hearings revealed, it is an activity that both the country and the senators take very seriously. Unlike Canada, where judicial appointments are cloaked in secrecy, the U.S. system regards them as a public matter and allows for a full airing of views before the Senate will advise and consent. In the case of Judge Bork's nomination, for instance, the Senate judiciary committee's hearings were covered live and broadcast again in the evening.

For champions of democracy, it is an impressive exercise to observe. In this forum, senators and nominee alike expound upon their views of justice and fairness in an atmosphere that resonates with 200 years of constitutional history.

In Canada, no such similar exercise in democracy has ever been tolerated. Until recently, appointments to the top bench were made exclusively by the prime minister. The fact that so many judges have served well in their jobs has been more despite the system than because of it. As to what kinds of values, prejudices and opinions Supreme Court judges bring to their jobs, the Canadian system does not reveal nominees in advance. Indeed, Canadians never see a proposed judge — only the final product.

---

[92] For some earlier disclosures along similar lines see the remarks of Professor Ed Ratushny in "Le pouvoir judiciare en 1984" (1974), 5 Revue Generale De Droit 389, and the remarks of G.M. Stirling, Q.C., in "A Symposium on the Appointment, Discipline and Removal of Judges" (1973), 11 Alta. L. Rev. 279 at 285. See also an article by columnist Geoffrey Stevens appearing in The Globe & Mail, 16th March 1974.

In the past few years, prime ministers have made a practice of consulting the Canadian Bar Association for their evaluation of the "fitness" of top judicial candidates. Again, it is a process robed in elitism in which no wider vetting is permitted to intrude. Lawyers seem content to keep the ritual all in the family.

. . .

What is at stake in the way the country's highest judicial appointments are made involves more than an exercise in constitutional theory. With the adoption of the Charter of Rights and Freedoms, Canadians must look to the courts both to uphold and determine many of those rights. Judicial power in Canada has expanded considerably as a result. In a real sense, the Supreme Court has become the final arbiter of what a democracy's citizens hold most sacred — their rights to equality, fairness and freedom.

It should not be surprising, then, that Canadians may want to have some greater assurance of how those rights will be protected. Knowing more about the men and women who will be making those judicial decisions — before they don their robes of office — surely has become a right in itself.

. . .

Few things so typify the differences between the U.S. and Canadian versions of democracy than the way top judicial officials are selected. The heart of that difference is that, while U.S. citizens conduct themselves as the masters of their democratic system — including its judicial function, Canadians seem content to be treated as children not mature enough to be fully entrusted with theirs.

The U.S. process is rooted in a genuine system of checks and balances — between the president and Congress, and between the legislative and judiciary branches. Canada's, on the other hand, is based more on giving a blank cheque to those who prefer to cloak their use of power in a shroud of secrecy. . . .

It is time to take the selection of judicial candidates out of the solitary bureau of prime ministerial whim or patronage and turn it into a more open process of parliamentary review and conformation. To do otherwise is simply playing Russian roulette with the rights of too many Canadians who have nowhere to turn but the sanctuary of the Supreme Court.

. . .

The danger in Canada is . . . that, in a system devoid of any semblance of public scrutiny and open confirmation, Canadians are never afforded an opportunity to know about a nominee's record and views before he or she sits on the nation's highest bench. They simply wake up one day and learn about the appointment in the morning newspaper as a fait accompli.[93]

(c) Recent Changes in the Appointment Process

In 1984, there was a series of so-called patronage appointments to courts where judges are federally appointed. It was not as if patronage was something new. It has always been a factor in the appointment process. But the large number of these appointments, roughly co-incidental in time, caused a considerable controversy. As a result, two committees were struck. One was a special committee of the Canadian Bar Association[94] and the other was a special committee of the Canadian Association of Law Teachers. Working independently of each other, the two special committees conducted research and study into the matter and reported at about

---

[93] See The Globe & Mail, 22nd October 1987.
[94] See The Globe & Mail, 11th July 1984.

the same time. Interestingly, both committees made the same or similar kinds of recommendations.[95] Essentially, the two committees recommended the establishment of judicial nominating councils (akin to the so-called Missouri Plan in the United States). These new nominating councils would consist of members representing different facets of the legal profession and the public.[96]

As a result of these recommendations the then Minister of Justice in 1985 undertook a review of the appointments process. This eventually led to a new system of judicial appointments at the federal level.[97] The new appointments process does not alter the basic constitutional fact that under the Constitution Act of 1867, the prerogative of federal judicial appointments rests with the Minister of Justice of Canada. What it does alter is the means by which names of prospective appointees come to the Minister. The new process abolishes the C.B.A. Judicial Appointments Committee and replaces it with provincial and territorial committees mandated with the responsibility of screening names of prospective appointees. Each committee consists of a nominee of the provincial or territorial law society, a nominee of the provincial or territorial branch of the Canadian Bar Association, a puisne judge of one of the federally appointed courts, nominated by the Chief Justice, a nominee of the provincial Attorney General or territorial Minister of Justice, and a nominee of the federal Minister of Justice, the latter of whom must be a lay person.[98] A candidate for judicial office may be nominated by himself or others. Upon nomination, the candidate's name is forwarded to the appropriate committee for a determination as to whether the candidate is "qualified" or "not qualified". If it is determined that the candidate is "qualified", his name will be retained by the Commissioner for Federal Judicial Affairs for a two-year period, during which the candidate remains eligible for appointment by the Minister of Justice. This process was changed in 1991 and again

---

[95] See, for example, the C.B.A. Report on the Appointment of Judges in Canada.

[96] See Jacob S. Ziegel, "Federal Judicial Appointments in Canada: The Time is Ripe for Change" (1987), 37 U.T.L.J. 1. See also F.L. Morton (ed.), *Law, Politics and the Judicial Process in Canada* (previously titled, in earlier 1984 edition, *Law, Politics and the Judicial System in Canada*) (Calgary: University of Calgary Press, 1989), especially the chapter entitled "Judicial Recruitment and Selection"; Alberta Report, 9th September 1985; and the Financial Post, 18th August 1984.

[97] See "A New Judicial Appointments Process", Department of Justice of Canada, Ottawa 1988 and "Judicial Appointment: Information Guide", Commissioner for Federal Judicial Affairs, Ottawa, 1988. It is also noteworthy that similar initiatives have occurred at the provincial level. For example, the province of Ontario has established a new appointments process with respect to provincial court judges that is very similar to the federal model described in the above publications. See The Globe & Mail, 30th January 1987, 6th February 1988, 20th February 1988, 6th May 1988 and 16th December 1988. For a critical review of the new process, see also Law Times, 23rd-29th April 1990.

[98] See *A New Judicial Appointments Process* (Ottawa: Department of Justice of Canada, 1988).

in 1994. Professor Martin Friedland, in his work, *A Place Apart: Judicial Independence and Accountability in Canada*, discusses these changes.

> Several changes were made following a review of the procedures completed in 1991. The committees, instead of using the categories "qualified" and "not qualified", were now to use "recommended," "highly recommended," and "unable to recommend". Further, candidates would no longer be told their classification, although they would be notified of the date they were assessed. Committees would henceforth give to the Minister a précis of the candidate's qualities that caused them to make a positive recommendation. Another change was to ask those making nominations to the committees to give the Minister two or three names from which to choose . . . As was the case with federal elevations, provincial court judges would no longer be assessed by the committees.
>
> . . . [in 1994] the new Minister of Justice, Allan Rock, [announced] a number of modest changes . . . the C.B.A. [i.e., the Canadian Bar Association] had once again argued for the 1985 concept of a short list from which the Minister would choose . . . [Although this was not accepted, the Minister] did, however, publicly undertake not to appoint any person who had not been recommended by a committee. To cut down on the heavy workload of the committees in Ontario and Quebec and to increase the possibility for interviews, three regional committees were established in Ontario and two in Quebec.
>
> Another change was to increase the number of members of the committees from five to seven by giving the Minister the power to add two more persons, a lawyer and a lay person. . . . Decisions would be kept on file for three years, rather than two, as previously was the practice. The system, according to the Minister, would achieve greater visibility by publishing advertisements about the committees and by having committees produce annual reports. . . . The process would be improved by requiring more detailed information from applicants, establishing more detailed written guidelines to assist committee members, and encouraging the use of interviews. . . . There will be a one year "cooling-off" period for committee members, but not for members of Parliament, as had been recommended by the C.B.A.[99]

(d) Criteria for Appointment

Probably the most difficult question for the appointing authority is determining what qualifications should be sought in the potential judicial appointee. Anthony Lewis, a journalist, stated in an article appearing in the New York Times dated 20th October 1974 that "the character of any country's judges is one test of its civilization". In that article, entitled "What Makes a Good Judge", he compares the British and American methods of appointing judges. He makes reference to the American Bar Association's Committee on the Federal Judiciary and compares itsfunction with that of the Lord Chancellor who chooses High Court judges in England from approximately 2,000 practising barristers. The writer indicates, having regard to the American model, that

> in the last twenty years . . . [the American Bar Association Committee] has won for itself a weighty role in the Scrutinizing of Federal judicial appointments. The conservative history of the A.B.A. raised some doubts about that role, but on the whole the committee has satisfied most observers that it takes a non-ideological view of nominees based on a not their qualities. For example, the committee insists on trial experience for lawyers picked

---

[94] Friedland, *op. cit.*, p. 241.

as trial judges. But it might give warm approval to the choice of a law teacher for the Court of Appeals, where his reflective qualities would be more appropriate.

Again, referring to the American experience, the journalist makes reference to "a visionary model" of what constitutes a good judge. In particular, he refers to the views of Judge Learned Hand. Specifically, he states as follows:

Learned Hand, who sat as a district judge and then for decades as a revered member of the Court of Appeals for the Second Circuit, made the most ringing statement of the large view that a judge ought to bring to interpreting the Constitution. He should, Judge Hand said "have at least a bowing acquaintance with Acton and Maitland, with Thucydides, Gibbon and Carlyle, with Homer, Dante, Shakespeare and Milton, and Machiavelli, Montaigne and Rabelais, with Plato, Bacon, Hume and Kant . . . For in such matters everything turns upon the spirit in which he approaches the questions before him. The words he must construe are empty vessels into which he can pour nearly anything he will. Men do not gather figs off thistles, nor supple institutions from judges whose outlook is limited by parish or class."

That glorious statement, visionary even as to Supreme Court appointments, has to be read against other realities so far as lower Federal courts are concerned. Their judges simply must have the technical training, the legal interest and experience to get through enormous volumes of often highly complicated work.

Generally speaking, most people would regard honesty, fairness, patience and intelligence as the types of qualities that a judge should have. Age is also an important consideration. The appointing authority must balance the advantages and disadvantages of appointing a judge at a young age. At the provincial court level for example, the advantage is that the judge is more attuned to the problems faced by younger persons who represent most of the individuals who appear before him; on the other hand, remaining on the same bench for a number of years until the age of retirement may have a stultifying effect. A second disadvantage of an early appointment is the relative lack of experience up to the date of appointment. It is interesting to note that at the joint meeting of the Canadian Institute for the Administration of Justice and the Annual Lecture Series of Osgoode Hall Law School of York University held in February of 1976, the Special Assistant to the Minister of Justice of Canada indicated that at least in respect of federal appointments, one of the primary attributes sought in a prospective judge is the ability to listen. Undoubtedly, such an attribute includes more than the mere ability to hear evidence; in addition, it includes the patience to hear an argument through to its end and the intellectual capability to understand the complexities of a given position.

Consider the remarks of former Ontario Attorney General Ian Scott. He then stated:

Judicial decision-making is a subtle and critical exercise that requires of our judges a high sensitivity to the competing social interests increasingly at stake . . . Tomorrow's judges will require much more than technical expertise in the law — although that expertise will remain a prerequisite.[100]

The Government of Ontario (under Attorney General Ian Scott) actively sought applications for judicial appointments to the Provincial Court of Ontario. For example, consider the following advertisement that appeared in The Ontario Reports of October 28, 1994.

> The Judicial Appointments Advisory Committee advises the Attorney General of Ontario on the appointment of Judges to the Ontario Court (Provincial Division), and invites applications for a position in the Metropolitan Toronto Region — This position is primarily Family/YOA/Criminal law.

In addition to similar advertisements appearing from time to time, the Attorney General corresponded with every female lawyer in the province of at least ten years' practice experience encouraging applications for judicial appointments. For an interesting discussion on appointments to the Supreme Court of Canada see J.S. Ziegel, "Appointments to the Supreme Court of Canada", Constitutional Forum, Vol. 5, No. 1, Fall 1994.[101]

The issue of judicial accountability arises from time to time with the result that some politicians have suggested that Canada adopt, in part, a United States approach at the state court level. In particular, some have suggested that we elect some of our judges. For example, a private member's bill was introduced into the Alberta Legislature in the fall of 1995 requiring the election of Provincial Court judges and judges of the Court of Queen's Bench. Section 4(2) of Bill 221 provided that:

> (2) An election under this Act shall be conducted for the judicial district in which the vacancy in either the Provincial Court or the Court of Queen's Bench occurs and that judicial district shall consist of the electoral divisions falling within that judicial district.

Further, section 3(1) provided that:

> 3(1) Persons declared elected as justices under this Act shall have their names submitted by the Government of Alberta to the Minister of Justice for Canada as persons who may be appointed to the Court of Queen's Bench for the purpose of filling vacancies relating to the judicial district in which a justice is to be appointed.

Arguably, this Bill might be viewed as unconstitutional under the provision in section 96 of the Constitution Act, 1867 (although it merely nominates elected candidates to the Court of Queen's Bench) and might also be unconstitutional under the provision in section 11(d) of the Canadian Charter of Rights and Freedoms as it relates to the requirements of

---

[100] See The Globe & Mail, 6th February 1988.

[101] See also a recent editorial, "How to guarantee a strong judiciary", appearing in the Edmonton Journal, August 18, 1995.

an independent judiciary. The Bill[102] received only First Reading and subsequently died. Although the sentiment for an elected judiciary is marginally held, it did recently make it to the legislative floor of the Alberta Legislature. For a comprehensive and recent discussion of the appointment process, see M. Friedland, *A Place Apart: Judicial Independence and Accountability in Canada*, Ottawa: Canadian Judicial Council, 1995.

Unfortunately, no matter how carefully the process of appointment is conducted there will be members of the judiciary who will conduct themselves in less than an acceptable manner. One of the most important, but difficult, issues for resolution by the appropriate authorities is whether a judge ought to be removed from office or impeached.

2. REMOVAL OF JUDGES

(a) Retirement

Federally appointed judges may remain in office until the age of retirement. That age, for judges serving on the Supreme Court of Canada and the Federal Court of Canada, is seventy-five years, pursuant to provisions contained, respectively, in the Supreme Court Act, R.S.C. 1985, c. S-26, and the Federal Court Act, R.S.C. 1985, c. F-7.[103] For judges serving on courts of superior jurisdiction in the provinces, the age of compulsory retirement is seventy-five years, pursuant to s. 99(2) of the Constitution Act of 1867. Judges serving on the county or district court benches are compulsorily retired at the age of seventy-five years pursuant to s. 8 of the Judges Act, R.S.C. 1985, c. J-1.[104] Finally, judges serving on provincial court benches are compulsorily retired in accordance with the provisions contained in the enabling provincial statutes establishing those courts. Usually, these statutes provide for compulsory retirement at age seventy.

(b) Standards of "Good Behaviour"

Aside from mandatory retirement, the only other limitation on a judge's tenure of office is the requirement that he must conduct himself in such a manner as to constitute good behaviour. There is no test common to all courts as to what constitutes good behaviour and, therefore, it is necessary to consult the various enabling statutes. Judges of the Supreme Court

---

[102] 1995, Bill 221, Third Session, 23rd Legislature, 44 Elizabeth II, The Legislative Assembly of Alberta.

[103] Am. R.S.C. 1985, c. 16 (3rd Supp.), s. 7.

[104] Am. R.S.C. 1985, c. 16 (3rd Supp.), s. 1.

of Canada and the Federal Court of Canada, pursuant to the provisions contained, respectively, in the Supreme Court Act and the Federal Court Act, hold office during "good behaviour". Judges serving on courts of superior jurisdiction in the provinces, by virtue of the provision contained in s. 99(1) of the Constitution Act of 1867, also hold office during "good behaviour". This provision was derived from s. 7 of the Act of Settlement of 1701. Judges of the county or district courts, pursuant to the provision contained in s. 7 of the Judges Act, also hold office during "good behaviour".

In addition to the foregoing, reference should be made to ss. 58 to 71 of the Judges Act. These provisions, enacted in their original form in 1971, and now amended, establish and set out the mandate of the Canadian Judicial Council. The function of the Council is set out in s. 60:

60. (1) The objects of the Council are to promote efficiency and uniformity, and to improve the quality of judicial service, in superior and county courts and in the Tax Court of Canada.

   (2) In furtherance of its objects, the Council may

   (*a*) establish conferences of chief justices, associate chief justices, chief judges and associate chief judges;
   (*b*) establish seminars for the continuing education of judges;
   (*c*) make the inquiries and the investigation of complaints or allegations described in section 63; and
   (*d*) make the inquiries described in section 69.

More specifically, at the request of the Minister of Justice of Canada or the Attorney General of a province, the Council conducts inquiries, under the provision contained in s. 63, to determine whether a judge of a superior, district or county court, or of the Tax Court of Canada, should be removed from office. Under s. 65, the Council may recommend to the Minister of Justice of Canada that a judge should be removed from office. The particular grounds to support such a recommendation are set out in s. 65(2)[105] of the Act:

(2) Where, in the opinion of the Council, the judge in respect of whom an inquiry or investigation has been made, has become incapacitated or disabled from the due execution of his office by reason of

   (a) age or infirmity,
   (b) having been guilty of misconduct,
   (c) having failed in the due execution of his office, or
   (d) having been placed, by his conduct or otherwise, in a position incompatible with the due execution of his office,

the Council, in its report to the Minister under subsection (1), may recommend that the judge be removed from office.

---

[105] Am. R.S.C. 1985, c. 27 (2nd Supp.), s. 5.

The effect of this portion of the Judges Act is to provide some scope or definition as to what constitutes "good behaviour".[106] The provisions of s. 65(2) are probably not exhaustive in delimiting the bounds of what does not constitute "good behaviour", but they do provide at least some guidelines in applying this broadly worded standard. (Other grounds might include incompetence and non-judicial misbehaviour.) Moreover, the provisions of ss. 59-71 provide a mechanism for determining whether removal from office is warranted. Together, these provisions add greater precision to the removal procedure of federally appointed judges in Canada.

---

[106] An interesting issue arose recently as to whether 'no behaviour' is not good behaviour. A Justice of the Ontario Court of Justice, after suffering a stroke, could not perform his duties but refused to resign. According to the Canadian Press release dated February 11, 1994:

In a ruling released Friday, a committee set up by the [Canadian Judicial Council] . . . ruled it has jurisdiction to investigate an allegation that [a judge] cannot carry out his duties due to infirmity. The decision means the committee of three judges and two lawyers now will hear evidence on [Justice] Gratton's physical condition and capacity to be a judge.

. . . [Justice] Gratton challenged the judicial council's authority to investigate the case. He said only Parliament — not the judicial council — could remove federal judges from office and a judge could only be removed . . . for misbehavior and not incapacity due to infirmity. Gratton also said two lawyers should not be part of the committee.

The committee said Parliament has constitutional authority to allow the judicial council to be part of the process leading to the removal of a federal judge. It said judges can be removed from office because of incapacity due to physical or mental infirmity and that does not detract from judicial independence. And the inquiry committee said that since it is not a court, there is nothing wrong with lawyers sitting as members.

In a further Canadian Press story, also dated February 11, 1994, it was stated that:

Maintaining public confidence in the judiciary requires that incapacitated judges be removed from the bench, an inquiry committee of the Canadian Judicial Council has ruled. The committee decision, released Friday, said the judicial council has authority to continue an inquiry into whether an Ontario judge who had a stroke is fit to be on the bench.

. . .

"We are of the view that it is important for continued public confidence in the administration of justice that a person who holds the office of judge not be permanently incapable of fulfilling the office of judge," said the ruling.

. . .

The committee said Parliament has constitutional authority to allow the judicial council to be part of the process leading to the removal of a federal judge. And the inquiry committee said there is nothing wrong with lawyers sitting as members since it is not a court. The ruling may be appealed. [Justice] Gratton has already filed a court case challenging the judicial council's authority to investigate him.

. . . The inquiry committee will decide only if [Justice] Gratton is incapacitated. The full judicial council will then decide if it should recommend to the federal justice minister that he be removed from the bench. Parliament would have to make the final decision on whether to remove [Justice] Gratton.

This matter was subsequently considered in the Federal Court of Canada where it was held that ". . .a judge can only be removed for breach of good behaviour and that the failure to perform the functions of the office of judge by reason of permanent infirmity would constitute a breach of that condition of tenure". See *Gratton v. Canada (Judicial Council)*, 78 F.T.R. 214, [1994] 2 F.C. 769, 26 Admin. L.R. (2d) 120, 115 D.L.R. (4th) 81.

Finally, the standard of conduct expected of judges serving on provincial court benches is set out in the various provincial enabling statutes. In addition, a mechanism has been established in most provinces providing for an investigation, hearing, and other procedures before a removal is effected. It will therefore be necessary for the reader to refer to the various provincial enabling statutes in order to ascertain the specific details of the removal procedure in a given province. Consider, for example, the following commentary reported in The Globe & Mail, 26th February 1977:

> The Ontario Judicial Council is hindered in its task of hearing complaints against provincial judges because it is not empowered to discipline a jurist, Attorney-General Roy McMurtry said yesterday.
>
> The council, made up of Ontario's four senior jurists and the treasurer of the Law Society of Upper Canada, was created by the Provincial Courts Act in 1968. Under the statute, its proceedings are secret.
>
> Mr. McMurtry said if plans proceed to reorganize the administration of the courts, the council would receive the disciplinary powers. Reorganization plans set out by Mr. McMurtry in a draft document last fall would transfer formal control of the courts from his ministry to the judicial council.
>
> Under the existing setup, the council meets once a month to hear complaints against judges. Although it does not impose discipline, it can recommend action to the Attorney-General.

Consider further this additional commentary furnished some twelve years later on the operation of the Ontario Judicial Council as reported in The Globe & Mail, 4th March 1989:[107]

> Complaints about judicial misbehaviour tend to disappear without a trace, some legal observers familiar with the process say.
>
> They say these complaints . . . are scrutinized in the utmost secrecy by fellow judges and then usually consigned to oblivion.
>
> . . .
>
> "It is a classic case of self-regulation amounting to no regulation," Allan Hutchinson, a law professor at York University, said. "They sort of pull the wagons around in the circle when there is any problem."
>
> Many complaints about judges are based on a misunderstanding of the court process, while others involve out-of-character remarks by men and women under considerable strain.
>
> But as with other professions, legal observers say the judiciary has its share of alcoholics, burnouts, incompetents and judges with Messianic complexes.
>
> . . .
>
> They can escape for many years being reviewed by their peers, Mr. [Michael] Lomer [editor of the Criminal Lawyer's Association newsletter] said. "It is very hard for lawyers to speak out publicly about them. There is an understandable feeling that your clients may suffer."
>
> Moreover, speaking out seems to do no good, he said. "There is a widespread perception that judges who are not acting judicially do not get disciplined; that nothing ever happens."
>
> . . .

---

[107] See also Y. Begue and C. Goldstein, "How judges get into trouble" (1988), 12 Prov. Judges J. 2:8.

When complaints are made to a provincial judicial council or its federal counterpart, they are examined by a panel usually composed of senior judges (two of the nine members on the Ontario council are lay people). If they fall short of recommending a public judicial inquiry, the council's comments exonerating the judge are delivered privately to the parties. The public never finds out how the complaint is discharged.

Each province has a judicial council to discipline provincial court judges. The Canadian Judicial Council disciplines district, superior and appeal court judges, all of whom are appointed by the federal government.

When reviewing a complaint, the councils consider whether a judge's conduct was "incompatible with the execution" of his or her office.

The criteria used to make a finding of misconduct are far too vague, said Carl Baar, a Brock University professor who specializes in judicial administration.

Prof. Baar said that in the United States, judges have a much better idea what behaviour is expected of them because decisions of the council are public and widely circulated as a sort of jurisprudential precedent. This also helps the public recognize that misconduct actually gets dealt with.

Another flaw in Canada is that the councils lack flexibility in sanctioning a judge, Prof. Baar said. They are essentially limited to the options of two extremes — exonerating the judge or recommending dismissal.

Boris Krivy, executive officer to the Chief Justice of Ontario, said that in theory, Ontario's judicial council could recommend that a judge apologize to the complainant. "But there is no way, strictly speaking, to enforce it."

. . .

Proponents of the system say the mere experience of being scrutinized by a judicial council is unnerving for most judges and deters future misbehaviour. Some judges have even resigned simply because their exoneration, although delivered privately, was worded in a lukewarm manner.

. . .

While Ontario's judicial council publicizes no data, the federal body published three months ago a brief annual report for the first time. It showed that only one of the 47 complaints it scrutinized led to a judge being criticized.

. . .

The report from the federal judicial council noted that many complaints are filed by people who misunderstood a judge's comments or did not like the decision in their case.

"Judges must be independent, secure and relatively immune from subjectively applied supervision or discipline if they are expected to decide cases fearlessly and impartially," it said.

"The more easily judges can be removed from office or censured, the more they might be tempted to accommodate what they may perceive to be the wishes of the authorities or the public in their decisions."

Prof. Hutchinson said publicity about judicial council proceedings would also serve the useful purpose of "taking judges off their pedestal. It would show they are just a group of people who share the same prejudices other people have."

For an earlier discussion of the Ontario Council see The Globe & Mail, 30th December 1976.[108] Also, for a description of the British Columbia

---

[108] See Greene, "Judicial Independence and Professional Autonomy: A Discussion of Two Rationales for Judicial Involvement in Court Administration", a paper prepared for the Annual Meeting of the Canadian Political Science Association in Ottawa, June 9, 1982; and McCormick, "Judicial Councils for Provincial Judges in Canada: A Survey of the Experience of the Five Western Provinces", a paper delivered for the Annual Meeting of the Canadian Political Science Association in Montreal, June 1980.

Judicial Council see The Globe & Mail, 31st December 1976.[109]

For a comprehensive discussion of provincial judicial councils in connection with the appointment, discipline and removal, and education of provincial court judges, see Peter McCormick, "Judicial Councils For Provincial Judges in Canada" (1986), 6 Windsor Yearbook of Access to Justice 160.

Regarding the Canadian Judicial Council, see "Judging the Judges", Alberta Report, 1st January 1990, and the Edmonton Journal, 18th December 1989.[110]

In determining what constitutes "good behaviour" during which a judge may serve in office, it is interesting to note at the outset that no superior court judge in Canada has ever been removed under the provision contained in s. 99 of the Constitution Act of 1867. However, there have been four attempts at removal:

(1) 1868 — petition for removal of Mr. Justice Aime Lafontaine of the Quebec Superior Court. A select committee reported on the matter, but the report was not printed.

(2) 1874 — petition against Mr. Justice T.J.L. Loranger of the Supreme Court of Quebec. The matter went to a select committee in 1877 and after the inquiry, no further action was taken.

(3) 1874 — petition against Chief Justice E.B. Wood of Manitoba. There was a motion for appointment of a select committee, but before any action was taken, the Chief Justice died.

(4) 1966-67 — inquiry into the conduct of Mr. Justice Leo Landreville of the Supreme Court of Ontario by a Royal Commission consisting of Mr. Justice Ivan C. Rand, formerly of the Supreme Court of Canada. After considering the Rand report a joint committee recommended removal. However Mr. Justice Landreville resigned while Parliament was preparing for his removal by joint address.

County court judges, who also hold office during "good behaviour", are also removable for "misbehaviour, or for incapacity or inability to

---

[109] In one case, for example, a B.C. Provincial Court Judge was suspended after soliciting a prostitute but was reinstated after a period of convalescence in connection with a related alcohol abuse problem. See the Edmonton Journal, 11th November 1978. On the question of secrecy and the impeachment process, see the Edmonton Journal, 8th, 9th and 10th January 1981.

[110] As for a survey of how lawyers rated judges whom they practised in front of, see Michael G. Crawford, "Judging Judges" (1989), 13 Can. Lawyer 4:18.

perform [their] duties properly by reason of age or infirmity". Pursuant to these provisions, four county court judges have been removed:

(1) 1915 — His Honour Judge C.R. Fitch of the District Court of Rainy River, Ontario.

(2) 1928 — His Honour Judge H.F. Maulson of the County Court of the Northern Judicial District of Manitoba.[111]

(3) 1933 — His Honour Judge Lewis St. George Stubbs, Senior Judge of the County Court of the Eastern District of Manitoba. Judge Stubbs was removed for criticizing the actions of superior court judges, for publishing a pamphlet criticizing officers of the Crown, and for addressing an accused with defamatory language.

(4) 1933 — His Honour Judge L.H. Martell was removed for issuing dishonoured cheques and for drunkenness.

The review machinery of the Canadian Judicial Council was put into operation for the first time in respect of His Honour Judge William A. Sheppard, an Ontario County Court Judge. The judge was found in contempt of court for disobeying an order made in the course of a matrimonial dispute with his former wife. However, before the Canadian Judicial Council met to consider this matter, he resigned: see the Toronto Star, 11th December 1976, and The Globe & Mail, 29th January 1977.

Provincially, two Ontario magistrates were subject to removal for misbehaviour. In the first case, Magistrate Frederick Bannon was found guilty of such gross misbehaviour as to make himself totally unfit for his office. This finding arose out of an inquiry held by Mr. Justice Campbell Grant, a commissioner appointed for that purpose. Magistrate Bannon had discussed, with a criminal, cases pending before him, and aided the criminal by giving him information as to bail matters and as to which judges should try certain cases. The criminal then sold this information. Although the judge knew of the criminal's whereabouts when a warrant was out for his arrest he did not report it. He dealt with him in real estate and fraudulently obtained money for the criminal. Magistrate Bannon, however, resigned before the investigation took place.

---

[111] The first two removals were brought to the author's attention by Chief Judge Alan R. Philp (as he then was) of the Manitoba County Court. Chief Judge Philp (now Mr. Justice Philp of the Manitoba Court of Appeal) prepared a paper entitled "Judicial Conduct: Independence and Integrity — Discipline and Removal", for the County and District Court Annual Seminar sponsored by the Canadian Judicial Council, 1977, and revised in 1978. His assistance is greatly appreciated. See also the Research Project prepared by Kowalishin, "The Removal of Federally-Appointed Judges in Canada", C.I.A.J., 1975.

In the second case, Judge Lucien Kurata was found unfit for office in an inquiry held by Mr. Justice Donald Keith for attempting to solicit sexual gratification from a prostitute scheduled to appear before him and from a policewoman whom he believed to be a prostitute awaiting trial, and for falsely testifying as to these incidents.

A later case involves Ottawa Judge Harry Williams, who had invited a prostitute from an escort agency to visit him in his chambers. One of the key issues in this case was whether the hearing ordered by the Ontario Judicial Council and conducted by Mr. Justice Sydney Robins should be held in private or in public. Mr. Justice Robins recommended Judge Williams' removal from office, and this was effected by Act of the Ontario legislature.[112]

Subsequent to the above, there have been several cases of judges who, over the past decade, have attracted criticism and often formal review as a result of their conduct, sometimes on the bench and sometimes off the bench.

The R.E.A.L. Women of Canada organization recently lodged a complaint with the Canadian Judicial Council against a Supreme Court of Canada justice in respect of a speech she gave in which she said that some aspects of Canadian law are so biased in favour of men, they are "little short of ludicrous" and "cry out for change". The complaint was subsequently dismissed.[113] The same speech resulted in a feminist organization calling "for a national task force to examine sex discrimination in the Canadian legal system".[114] The R.E.A.L. Women organization also lodged

---

[112] See Government of Ontario, *Report of the Commission of Inquiry into the Conduct of Provincial Judge Harry J. Williams* (1978). This report also appears in (1978), 12 L.S.U.C. Gazette 161. See also The Globe & Mail, 16th December 1977.

[113] Madam Justice Bertha Wilson, "Will Women Judges Really Make a Difference?", Address to the Fourth Annual Barbara Betcherman Memorial Lecture, Osgoode Hall Law School, 8th February 1990. See also the Edmonton Journal, 9th, 14th and 15th February 1990 and 30th March 1990, The Globe & Mail, 10th February 1990 and 31st March 1990, and the Lawyers Weekly, Vol. 9, No. 39, 23rd February 1990.

[114] See the Edmonton Journal, 10th February 1990. Such a national task force was, in fact, established by the Canadian Bar Association. The "Task Force on Gender Equality in the Legal Profession", under its chair, the Honourable Bertha Wilson, a former Justice of the Supreme Court of Canada, was created in August of 1991 and released its report in August of 1993. The report, entitled "Touchstones for Change: Equality, Diversity and Accountability", dealt with such issues as the identification of different kinds of gender discrimination in the legal profession (direct, adverse effect (a kind of systemic discrimination) and multiple discrimination), barriers to entry into the legal profession, barriers to equality for women in the profession, generally, and more particularly, in private practice, government legal departments, private corporations and university faculties of law. The report also looked at gender equality on administrative tribunals, in the judiciary and in provincial law societies. The report also examined gender equality in terms of both substantive law and procedure. See M. Eberts, "Gender Issues in the Legal Profession: A Synopsis of the C.B.A.

a complaint with the Canadian Judicial Council in 1989 against the Chief Justice of the Supreme Court of Canada in respect of a meeting held between the Chief Justice and the Legal Education Action Fund, a group supporting challenges by women against discriminatory laws.[115]

The conduct of a British Columbia judge was referred to the Canadian Judicial Council after he referred to a 3-year-old victim of sexual interference as being "sexually aggressive". The Council concluded that the judge made an "unfortunate choice of words" which did not "constitute grounds for . . . formal investigation".[116]

A Manitoba Provincial Court Judge was found guilty of misconduct by the Manitoba Judicial Council as a result of his involvement in a ticket-fixing scandal.[117] Another Manitoba Provincial Court Judge resigned over the same scandal. Subsequently, he was criticized for showing disrespect for native persons "by stripping to his waist in front of them as he changed into his judicial robes" and by "[berating and chastising] some Indian defendants even before they had entered a plea".[118] A Nova Scotia Provincial Court Judge was removed by the provincial cabinet following a recommendation by the Nova Scotia Judicial Council. In this instance, " [t]he judge, who relied heavily on biblical guidance, had been known to advise women that they should be subservient even to abusive husbands."[119] An Ontario provincial court judge told a woman that "she was responsible for all the problems in her stormy marriage, including an assault at the hands of her husband. The judge at one point ordered her handcuffed and removed from his court."[120]

Gender Equality Task Force Report", a supplement with the Canadian Bar Review, Vol. 72, No. 3 — September 1993. The Law Society of Alberta also created a Women and the Legal Profession Committee. See, for example, the Law Society of Alberta, "Women and the Legal Profession in Alberta: Highlights of the Survey of Active Members", 1992. For a discussion of gender statistics and provincial law societies, See Canadian Lawyer, August/September 1993. For further commentary on women and the legal profession, see the Canadian Press report dated February 20, 1994, and the somewhat controversial Report to the Canadian Bar Association Mid-Winter Meeting of Council by the Canadian Judges Conference, February 1994. See also the remarks of Justice André Brossard of the Quebec Court of Appeal to a seminar of the Canadian Bar Association where he discusses

   . . . the idea of mandatory courses to "sensitize" judges about issues such as sexual assault. "If someone wants to train us in political correctness trends, then that . . . would be trying to influence our minds and our spirits and interfere directly with the judicative functions."

[115] For a review of both these complaints, see Alberta Report, 26th February 1990.

[116] See The Globe & Mail, 16th February 1990, and the Edmonton Journal, 16th February 1990.

[117] See The Globe & Mail, 22nd March 1989. See also The Globe & Mail, 27th June 1988 and 2nd March 1988.

[118] See The Globe & Mail, 8th February 1989.

[119] See The Globe & Mail, 6th March 1989. See also The Globe & Mail, 1st January 1987 and 4th December 1986.

[120] See The Globe & Mail, 28th February 1989 and 6th March 1989 and a subsequent story on 13th March 1989.

An Ontario Provincial Court Judge was removed from office following an inquiry into his conduct. In this case

> several complaints were made about the judge's involvement in a dispute with Windsor
> police over local parking bylaws.
>
> The judge maintained these bylaws were invalid and said he wanted police to stop ticket-
> ing his car. He threatened anyone who enforced the city's parking bylaw with contempt.[121]

Another Ontario Provincial Court Judge attracted criticism when he
ordered a spectator in his court to be handcuffed, removed and taken to
a holding cell for allegedly disrupting his court. She was strip-searched
and held for 90 minutes. According to witnesses, the woman was merely
trying to leave the court and was not making any noise.[122]

In yet another case, a senior Ontario Provincial Court Judge "took
the unusual step of appearing before a fellow provincial court judge on
behalf of a youth". According to some, the "action raises serious ethical
questions about the propriety of a judge appearing before a fellow judge
as a legal adviser".[123] An Ontario District Court Judge resigned as a head
of a public inquiry into the Niagara Regional Police Force as a result of
"extensive past dealings" with that police force.[124] Another Ontario
Provincial Court Judge was criticized for making the following remarks
about Sri Lankans during a criminal trial. He made this remark to the
accused:

> "You write back to Sri Lanka and get yourself a girl friend" he told the 25-year-old
> defendant at one point. "All she needs is a boat and she can come in."

He also stated to an interpreter:

> "First of all, you must repeat every word," he told the interpreter. "If he goes too fast,
> stop him. He has to know everything he is being charged with — otherwise you might
> both end up in a boat somewhere."[125]

An Ontario Provincial Court Judge was also the subject of an inquiry
because he

> maintained a friendship with a man he knew to be facing serious criminal charges, attacked
> an Ontario Provincial Police investigation and was involved in a drunken incident at
> a local bar.[126]

The conduct of a Provincial Court Judge was recently questioned when
he jailed a defence lawyer who objected to the adjournment of a case before

---

[121] See The Globe & Mail, 6th March 1989. See also The Globe & Mail, 13th May 1987.
[122] See The Globe & Mail, 6th March 1989.
[123] See The Globe & Mail, 10th December 1988.
[124] See The Globe & Mail, 20th February 1988.
[125] See The Globe & Mail, 9th January 1988.
[126] See The Globe & Mail, 18th March 1985 and 31st August 1984.

the judge. The lawyer apologized but the judge ignored the apology and insisted that the lawyer be confined.[127]

A Quebec Sessions Court Judge was the subject of an inquiry by the Quebec Judicial Council after thirteen complaints were lodged by "a group of Montreal lawyers who question[ed] the courtroom behaviour and objectivity" of the judge.[128]

A provincially appointed judge of the Court of Quebec was recently suspended by his Chief Justice for remarking during a trial that "rules are like women, they are meant to be violated." The matter was subsequently taken to the Quebec Judicial Council.[129]

A Manitoba Provincial Court Judge was criticized for remarks he made about women who wanted to have abortions. He had stated that they "should be given razor blades".[130]

Even Citizenship Court Judges have attracted some recent attention.[131]

There were two complaints to the Canadian Judicial Council arising out of the contentious issue of abortion. Both complaints concerned senior superior court justices in Manitoba and attracted considerable publicity. One of the judges had signed an anti-abortion petition. Both complaints, however, were dismissed by the Canadian Judicial Council.[132]

A judge in Quebec sentenced a man to 23 months in jail after the man was convicted of sodomizing his step-daughter. Apparently viewed as a mitigating factor, the judge noted that the man, by avoiding vaginal penetration, had spared his step-daughter's virginity. Although her judicial elevation was apparently imminent at the time of this case, the judge was subsequently appointed as Chief Judge of her court.[133]

A Justice of the Court of Queen's Bench of Manitoba, when asked by an abused spouse to drop charges against her husband, stated that the next time she calls the police, he hoped that the police would take their time in responding.[134]

---

[127] See The Globe & Mail, 10th May 1989.

[128] See The Globe & Mail, 21st February 1985.

[129] See The Globe & Mail, 15th February 1990.

[130] See The Globe & Mail, 23rd June 1983 and 21st May 1983.

[131] See The Globe & Mail, 19th January 1987, 13th January 1987, 12th January 1987 and 17th December 1986.

[132] See The Globe & Mail, 1st February 1990.

[133] See the Edmonton Journal, January 1994.

[134] Canadian Press, January 28, 1994.

A provincial court judge in Manitoba gave a suspended sentence to a man who was convicted of sexually assaulting four female relatives for reason that the man had just been curious. A public inquiry was held but the judge resigned before its conclusion.[135]

An Ontario Justice of the Peace admitted engaging in sexually suggestive conversations with a 21-year-old female high school student and a 21-year-old private investigator. He subsequently agreed the remarks were improper.[136]

A judge of the Court of Quebec commented after releasing a man who had threatened to kill his wife:

> If the gentleman assassinates the lady I won't lose any sleep over it and I won't die. Don't worry I won't suffer from a depression either, because it is not my responsibility.[137]

In a well-publicized case, an Ontario provincial court judge had kissed two female Crown prosecutors and improperly touched a court reporter at a Christmas party. It was recommended that he be removed from office.[138]

In respect of the possibility of mandatory judicial education programs on issues such as sexism and racism, an Alberta Court of Queen's Bench justice commented that "I think you'd get a better response if you didn't try to make the horse drink" while a Quebec Superior Court justice stated "We're not schoolchildren".[139]

A 17-year-old victim of an alleged sexual assault requested that she be allowed to testify in camera. Rather than comply with the request, a judge of the Court of Quebec freed the accused.[140]

A Manitoba Provincial Court judge told a female lawyer, who had requested an adjournment in a case for reason that she and the infant she was nursing were ill, that she ought to find a replacement who "is not trying to be a mother and a lawyer at the same time". Subsequently, in sentencing a man who had threatened to kill both himself and his girlfriend, the judge stated that " [t]here isn't any woman worth the trouble you got yourself into". The matter went before the Manitoba Judicial Council. The Council reprimanded the judge.[141]

---

[135] See Canadian Press, 9th January 1994.
[136] See The Globe & Mail, 21st December 1993.
[137] See The Globe & Mail, 13th December 1993.
[138] See The Globe & Mail, 26th December 1993.
[139] See The Globe & Mail, 15th September 1993.
[140] See The Globe & Mail, 26th August 1993.
[141] Canadian Press, 2nd September 1993.

An Alberta judge attracted media attention after he acquitted a man despite a plea of guilty to two charges of indecent assault against a young girl. A new trial was subsequently ordered.[142]

A Nova Scotia Provincial Court judge distributed a poster at the courthouse. The poster stated that "[a] high performance woman can turn into a bitch in seconds". The poster was intended as a spoof of an advertisement and the judge subsequently apologized.[143]

A judge in dealing with a request that a man accused of assaulting his wife should be allowed to spend Christmas with her, commented that "[i]f she's prepared to put up with these beatings, I don't see why I should worry about it". The Canadian Judicial Council considered the matter and concluded the judge made an "unfortunate remark".[144]

Finally, in the recent report of the so-called Donald Marshall inquiry, some Nova Scotia judges were seriously criticized. A Royal Commission was established to inquire into the reasons why Mr. Marshall was improperly convicted of murder in Nova Scotia and why he served over eleven years in prison before the matter was rectified. The report of the Commission contained many criticisms (and recommendations) related to various aspects of the justice system in that province. As a result of those criticisms, lawyers for Mr. Marshall

> have formally asked the Canadian Judicial Council to investigate the conduct of four Nova Scotia judges and the former chief justice of the province who appointed them to hear an appeal of Mr. Marshall's case in 1983.
>
> The request comes . . . after a royal commission's scathing indictment of the Court of Appeal panel that acquitted Mr. Marshall but said he was to blame for the original wrongful conviction.[145]

A similar suggestion for an investigation in this matter by the Canadian Judicial Council was made in the House of Commons in respect of two of the justices of the Nova Scotia Court of Appeal.[146] Subsequently, three of the five appellate court justices resigned in a one-month period during the investigation by the Canadian Judicial Council.

Even legitimate activities by judges have attracted unwarranted criticism. At the invitation of the Law Reform Commission of Canada, several distinguished judges provided advice to the Commission in respect of the reform of the criminal law. This, surprisingly, was criticized.[147]

---

[142] The Edmonton Journal, 9th January, 1993.

[143] Canadian Press, 15th December, 1993.

[144] Canadian Press, 3rd March, 1992.

[145] See the Edmonton Journal, 31st January 1990.

[146] See The Globe & Mail, 4th December 1986.

[147] See, for example, The Globe & Mail, 14th May 1983 and the Edmonton Journal, 17th May 1983.

For a thorough review of judicial conduct in the province of Quebec, See Rodolph Morisette, *Les Juges quand éclatent les mythes* (Montréal: VLB 1994).

Often, a judge will resign from office in anticipation of the invocation of the impeachment process. This occurred in Alberta with respect to a District Court Judge who suffered from kleptomania, in Ontario with respect to a County Court Judge for reasons not publicly advanced, and in British Columbia with respect to two superior court justices, one convicted for a second time of impaired driving,[148] and the other allegedly involved in a morals impropriety.

On occasion, the impeachment process is begun but does not lead to removal. The most dramatic recent example of this is the Canadian Judicial Council's investigation of Mr. Justice Thomas Berger prompted by certain remarks that he made relating to the political events surrounding the "patriation" of the "new" constitution. The Council concluded that the public expression of political views in the nature of those made by Mr. Justice Berger constituted an "indiscretion", but that they were not a "basis for a recommendation that he be removed from office". On the basis of this recommendation, no further action was taken.[149]

However, several months later, Mr. Justice Berger somewhat surprisingly tendered his resignation as a judge. Consider the following account of his resignation as reported in The Globe & Mail, 29th April 1983.

> Thomas Berger has resigned as a judge of the B.C. Supreme Court because of a disagreement with Bora Laskin, Chief Justice of the Supreme Court of Canada, over whether judges should ever speak out on political issues.
>
> Announcing he will leave the bench on August 27, Mr. Justice Berger said he could not accept the recent ruling by the Canadian Judicial Council and the Chief Justice that it was improper for judges to speak out on political issues or on their work on royal commissions.
>
> Judge Berger said he agrees that judges should not discuss their inquiries into alleged wrongful acts, but he said there are rare occasions when members of the bench should speak out on matters of public interest.
>
> Judge Berger was faulted by a fellow judge and excoriated by Prime Minister Pierre Trudeau last year for criticizing the constitutional accord reached in November, 1981, by nine premiers and the Federal Government. In speeches and in an article published by the Globe and Mail, the B.C. Judge had condemned the absence from the new Constitution and Charter of Rights of native rights guarantees and a veto for Quebec.
>
> The council, composed of the country's 27 Chief Justices, said last June that Judge Berger's comments had been indiscreet. Many interpreted the ruling, the first of its kind in Canadian history, as a reprimand.

---

[148] See the Edmonton Journal, 12th May 1981.

[149] See The Globe & Mail, 4th September 1982, and the Edmonton Journal, 3rd September 1982. See also the C.B.A. National, May 1983.

Chief Justice Laskin, head of the council, reinforced the ruling when he said in a rare public speech last September that judges do not have the right to speak out on political issues. He said judges must not only be impartial but must appear to be impartial.

"A judge has no freedom of speech to address political issues which have nothing to do with his judicial duty", the Chief Justice said.

In an obvious reference to the incident involving Judge Berger, he said that any judge who feels so strongly that he must speak out "is best advised to resign from the bench."

In his letter of resignation this week to federal Justice Minister Mark MacGuigan, Judge Berger said: "On rare occasions a judge may have an obligation to speak out on human rights and fundamental freedoms . . . this is in keeping with Canadian experience . . .

"I have conducted three royal commissions while on the bench. This is work in which Canadian judges have been engaged since Confederation. Chief Justice Laskin, in his speech to the Canadian Bar Association, . . . deprecated judges undertaking such tasks.

"Furthermore, he and the council take the view that, once the work of the commission is completed, a judge may not discuss its work in public.

"This is a sound rule in relation to inquiries into alleged wrongful acts. But . . . I and others (such as Mr. Justice Emmett Hall) have felt at liberty to discuss the work of our commissions, not in a partisan way but as a means of informing the bar, university audiences, and others about matters of public interest.

"I do not think that my concept of judge as public servant . . . entails any erosion of public confidence in the independence of the judiciary."

Consider also the reaction of key officials and others, as also reported in The Globe & Mail, of the same date:

Justice Minister Mark MacGuigan said yesterday he has no qualms about accepting the resignation of Mr. Justice Thomas Berger of the B.C. Supreme Court . . .

"In the light of the new Charter of Rights and Freedoms, I think it's especially important judges recognize (it is) much more important than ever before to avoid engaging themselves in controversial subjects which may well come before them on the bench," the minister said.

Mr. MacGuigan also said he was unhappy that Judge Berger made public his letter of resignation now although he plans to remain a judge until August 27. "This could engender a further controversy around a sitting judge."

Earlier, a leading human rights lawyer said the Government should refuse to accept the resignation of Judge Berger until there has been more debate on the propriety of judges speaking out on public issues.

"I would like to see Justice Minister MacGuigan request Mr. Justice Berger to defer that resignation until such time as there can be a parliamentary and public determination of what ought to be the ground rules for judges," Alan Borovoy, general counsel for the Canadian Civil Liberties Association, said in a telephone interview from Toronto.

Mr. Borovoy said he favors allowing judges, in certain circumstances, to speak out on public issues. The matter is so important and fundamental to society that Parliament and the public at large should help determine the rules for judges, rather than leave it to the Canadian Judicial Council, he said.

Conservative Senator Jacques Flynn, a former federal justice minister, said yesterday that judges should, on occasion, feel free to speak out on public issues, provided they are not being asked to render decisions on those questions.

Senator Flynn, now Opposition leader in the Senate, said that on a matter as important as the Constitution "as long as a judge doesn't have to render a judgment on a particular question . . . it seems to me that he would be entitled to comment.

". . . in this particular case, I would not have considered it out of place for a judge to express something like that". . .

Much has been written concerning Mr. Justice Berger's colourful career,[150] including the controversial review of his judicial status by the Canadian Judicial Council[151] and his subsequent resignation. In respect of the latter, see, for example, the editorial reactions of The Globe & Mail (29th April 1983) and the Edmonton Journal (30th April 1983).[152]

For important guides to judicial conduct (as drafted by senior, experienced members of the Canadian judiciary), see Canadian Judicial Council, *Commentaries on Judicial Conduct*, Cowansville: Les éditions Yvon Blais Inc., 1991; Wilson, Honourable J.O., *A Book for Judges*, Ottawa: Canadian Judicial Council, 198; and Fauteux, Right Honourable G., *Le livre du magistrat*, Ottawa: Canadian Judicial Council, 1980. In addition, moreover, the Canadian Judicial Council is presently developing a Code of Judicial Conduct. In this regard, it has sought the assistance of the Canadian Bar Association which, in turn, has created a special committee to assist the Council in the process. The Chief Justice of Canada, who also serves as Chair of the Canadian Judicial Council, has "noted that a Code could be of assistance to judges in their consideration of ethical and conduct dilemmas, and to the public in understanding better the role and responsibilities of judges".[153]

It was suggested by R. MacGregor Dawson in his treatise *The Government of Canada* that "good behaviour" includes all but "deliberate wrongdoing". He further suggests that "a judge may be stupid", often in error on the law, lazy and neglectful and somewhat biased, without threat of removal. He suggests that "bribery, gross partiality and criminal proclivities" are the only examples of misbehaviour. Nonetheless, the standards required of good behaviour seem to have been raised with the Landreville affair. Mr. Justice Landreville was found to be unfit for office in that:

(1) He failed to remove suspicion of impropriety in receiving 7,500 shares of stock without consideration;

(2) He showed gross contempt before the Securities Commission of Ontario in giving evidence; and

---

[150] See Carolyn Swayze, *Hard Choices: The Life of Tom Berger* (Vancouver: Douglas and McIntyre, 1987).

[151] The report of the Canadian Judicial Council in respect of the Berger matter is contained in F.L. Morton (ed.), *Law, Politics and the Judicial Process in Canada* (Calgary: University of Calgary Press, 1989). See also M. Felsky, "The Berger Affair and the Independence of the Judiciary" (1984), 42 U.T. Faculty L. Rev. 118, and J. Webber, "The Limits to Judges' free speech; a comment on the Report of the Committee of Investigation into the Conduct of the Hon. Mr. Justice Berger" (1984), 29 McGill L.J. 369.

[152] See also a subsequent editorial which refers to the Berger matter in The Globe & Mail, 3rd June 1986, and a letter to the editor in connection with that editorial, 12th June 1986. As well, see The Globe & Mail, 6th July 1983.

[153] See Canadian Bar Association, Touchstone, November, 1995.

(3) He failed to show his innocence surrounding the dealing of a franchise to supply natural gas to Sudbury.

It is important to note that the transaction took place before Mr. Justice Landreville was appointed to the bench and that it was recognized that Mr. Justice Landreville's conduct in exercising his judicial duties did not constitute misbehaviour. Mr. Justice Rand suggests that the test to be applied in considering a judge's behaviour is as follows:

> Would the conduct, fairly determined in the light of all circumstances, lead such persons to attribute such a defect of moral character that the discharge of the duties of the office thereafter would be suspect? Has it destroyed unquestioning confidence of uprightness, of moral integrity, of honesty in decision, the elements of public honour?[154]

Mr. Justice Rand also suggests other conduct which would not constitute good behaviour:

> Persistent neglect of duty, persistent incapacity arising from drink or similar causes, deliberate refusal to accept and apply unquestioned rules of law to the detriment of suitors; following a life of profligacy . . .[155]

Lastly, in order to better understand what constitutes "good behaviour", consider the following summary of cases of removal for reason of misbehaviour. These cases all arose in various non-Canadian jurisdictions.

English and Welsh

Many of the following cases are set out in Henry Cecil, *Tipping the Scales*, Hutchinson & Co., London, 1964, and Andrew Dewar Gibb, *Judicial Corruption in the U.K.*, W. Green & Son, Edinborough, 1957.

1. Two Lord Chancellors have been impeached:
   1620 — Lord Bacon, for accepting gifts from suitors.
   1725 — Lord Macclesfield, for appointing people to the office of Chancery Master in exchange for money, knowing such money came from suitors' funds paid into court.

2. 1865 — Lord Chancellor Westbury was investigated on charges of arranging the resignations of two legal officials so he could substitute his relatives. He subsequently resigned.

---

[154] Commission of Inquiry into the dealings of the Honourable Mr. Justice Leo A. Landreville with Northern Ontario Gas Limited, 1966. The Federal Court of Canada (Trial Division) a decade later criticized the proceedings of this Royal Commission. See *Landreville v. R., (No.2)*, [1977] 2 F.C. 726, 75 D.L.R. (3d) 380 (T.D.). See also The Globe & Mail report on this decision, 12th April 1977.

[155] *Ibid.*

After the enactment of the Act of Settlement of 1701 providing for security of tenure only during good behaviour, complaints have been made to Parliament against seventeen high court judges. Of these, nine were English, one was Welsh and seven were Irish.

3. 1721 — Baron Page, for alleged bribery of electors. This attempt at impeachment was narrowly defeated.

4. 1813, 1816 — Lord Ellenborough, for, on a first charge, writing down evidence not fair to the accused. It was held that this was not a ground for impeachment as it was not done deliberately. A second charge, for alleged "partiality, misrepresentation, injustice and oppression" was held to be not founded. During the trial it was often said there had to be not only evidence of misconduct but also evidence of a corrupt mind or improper motive. Moreover, the tendering of a personal opinion to a jury as to the guilt or innocence of an accused is not misconduct.

5. 1821 — Mr. Justice Best, for fining a man five times during the course of the trial. It was held not to be misconduct and was justified to stop blasphemy in court.

6. 1825-1826 — Mr. Kenrick (Welsh), on a first charge, for allegedly trying to have someone prosecuted for theft so the accused would forfeit his house and Mr. Kenrick could then buy it. It was held that the allegation was not proved, but it was also held that a judge's private conduct could provide grounds for removal. On a second charge, for refusing to grant a search warrant but issuing a note instead. He later demanded that the note be given back and had it forcibly taken. For this he was liable for damages. However, while such conduct was held to be discreditable it was not serious enough to require removal. It was also held that being obstinate and irritable is not enough for removal. In this case, the judge eventually resigned.

7. 1843 — Lord Abinger, for using the bench for purposes of making political speeches. The motion for removal was defeated as there was no evidence of badness of heart or corrupt intent.

8. 1867 — Lord Chief Baron Kelly, for allegedly pledging the truth of a statement for purposes of deceiving a committee. It was held to be completely unfounded.

9. 1906 — Mr. Justice Grantham, for allegedly deciding two identical cases in completely opposite ways for political reasons. In this case, it was held that there must be some moral defect. Although the judge's behaviour was discreditable, his conduct was not sufficient for removal.

10. 1924 — Mr. Justice McCardie, for speaking in court against the government's action on a particular issue. It was held that although judges should not speak on political matters, this conduct was not a moral delinquency justifying removal.

Irish

1. 1830 — Sir Jonah Barrington was removed for using court money for his own purposes.

2. Mr. Justice Fox resigned after he had called members of the jury names because he disagreed with their verdict.

3. Mr. Justice Johnson was found guilty of libelling high-ranking officials and he subsequently resigned.

Malaysia

An interesting case arose recently in connection with the removal of the Lord President of Malaysia's Supreme Court, Malaysia's most senior judge. The judge was removed from office after a royal tribunal determined that he "had undermined the Government". Five other judges of the Supreme Court were also suspended pending a tribunal's determination on charges of "gross misbehavior". Malaysia has a British-style judiciary.[156]

General

1. It is recognized that, at common law, an office held during good behaviour could be forfeited for: (a) misconduct in office; (b) neglect of duties; (c) the acceptance of an incompatible office; or (d) conviction for a serious crime. (See B. Shartel, "Federal Judges — Appointment, Supervision and Removal" (1929-30), 28 Mic. L. Rev. 870 at 901.)

2. (a) It is the opinion of some that misbehaviour does not include incapacity or incompetence. (See Webster, *The Judiciary: The Report of a Justice Sub-Committee*, Stevens & Sons, London, 1972, pp. 58-59, and Shartel, *supra*, at p. 904.)

   (b) Others believe incapacity by reason of health is misbehaviour. (See Cecil, *Tipping the Scales, supra*, at p. 144.)

3. To constitute misbehaviour, it appears there must be some element of moral blame which almost seems to be in the nature of a mens rea requirement (see Cecil, *Tipping the Scales, supra*, at p. 144).

---

[156] See The Globe & Mail, 8th August 1988.

United States

Generally, an analysis of the term "good behaviour" based on United States[157] authorities is not particularly helpful in understanding the term as it is used in Canada. The United States constitutional position is such that its federal judges hold office during good behaviour but are impeachable for treason, bribery, and other high crimes and misdemeanours. This has led some to believe that misbehaviour must be in the nature of treason, bribery, and other high crimes and misdemeanours. (See, for example, Preble Stolz, "Disciplining Federal Judges: Is Impeachment Hopeless?" (1969), 57 Cal. L. Rev. 659 at 663.) However, others have recognized certain distinctions in defining misbehaviour. For example, one suggestion is that misbehaviour includes insanity, disability (including senility), alcoholism, ignorance, sustained neglect of duty and conduct less serious than high crimes and misdemeanours. (See, for example, Raoul Berger, "Impeachment of Judges and Good Behaviour Tenure" (1970), 79 Yale L.J. 1475 at 1529.) Similarly, it is conceded that less than good behaviour could include misconduct off the bench although not amounting to the commission of a crime. (See P. Kurland, "The Appointment and Disappointment of Supreme Court Justices", [1972] Law and the Social Order 183 at 228.)[158]

On balance, however, it appears to be the general consensus that, as the term is used in the United States Constitution, it must amount to "misconduct in judicial capacity or abusing judicial power". (See, for example, Kurland, at p. 228, and John D. Feerick, "Impeaching Federal Judges: A Study of the Constitutional Provisions" (1970-71), 39 Fordham L. Rev. 1 at 57.)

The process of impeachment and removal in the United States involves,

---

[157] For a discussion of the controversies surrounding the prospective appointments of Robert Bork and Douglas Ginsburg to the Supreme Court of the United States, see The Globe & Mail, 1st October 1987 and 12th November 1987, and Robert Bork, "The Case Against Political Judging", National Review, 8th December 1989, p. 23. See also Alberta Report, 15th January 1990. For further discussion of the American judiciary, see, for example, The Globe & Mail, 9th August 1988 and 6th August 1988; Time Magazine, 15th August 1988; Newsweek Magazine, 12th February 1979, 25th June 1979, 15th June 1981, and 19th April 1982; Time Magazine, 11th December 1978, 22nd January 1979, the cover story of 20th August 1979, 5th May 1980 and 21st December 1981; U.S. News & World Report, 4th and 18th June 1979, 5th November 1979, 22nd December 1980, and 19th January 1981; Maclean's Magazine, 15th January 1979; and the New York Times, 15th May 1980, 10th August 1980, 27th July 1979, 7th May 1978, 26th November 1978, 5th May 1979 and 22nd April 1979. For some instances of judicial misfeasances in the U.S., see the Edmonton Sun, 12th June 1980, 29th January 1981, 3rd June 1980, and 12th May 1982. And for some "unbelievable" advice for U.S. judges, see the Edmonton Journal, 30th December 1980.

[158] See Stolz, *Judging Judges: The Investigation of Rose Bird and the California Supreme Court* (New York: The Free Press, 1981). For a more recent assessment of Judge Bird's career, see The Globe & Mail, 2nd January 1987.

essentially, two steps. First, the judge must be charged and impeached by simple majority before the House of Representatives. Then he is tried before the Senate, and if convicted by a two-thirds vote of the members of Senate, he is removed from office. This is not altogether dissimilar from the Canadian requirement for the removal of federally appointed judges by joint address of the House of Commons and the Senate.

Since 1796, fifty-six federal judges have been charged before the House of Representatives. Of these, thirty-four were charged with "treason, bribery or other high crimes and misdemeanours". Of the fifty-six only four were found guilty and removed by the Senate. However, during the course of the proceedings, twenty-two resigned.

The grounds for the removal of the four convicted judges are as follows:

(1) Blasphemy and drunkenness (Pickering — 1803).

(2) Treason for joining the Confederacy (Humphreys — 1862).

(3) Accepting bribes (Archibald — 1912).

(4) Accepting bribes, kickbacks, income tax evasion (Ritter — 1936).

In addition, four other judges were impeached but were acquitted by the Senate. The grounds upon which these judges were impeached are set out as follows:

(1) Being "tyrannical, overbearing and oppressive" (Chase — 1804).

(2) Abuse of contempt power (Peck — 1831).

(3) Defrauding the government and bribery (Swayne — 1904).

(4) Being influenced in judicial appointments (Louderbach — 1932).

Subsequent to the impeachment of Pickering in 1803, it is interesting to note that drunkenness alone has been considered as insufficient to justify removal. In addition, misconduct in court, such as being rude, tyrannical, and irritable, which does not amount to the commission of a crime, is not impeachable conduct. Nor may a judge's decisions be grounds for removal.

On only two occasions has a judge been charged in connection with private activities:

(1) Accepting a job as commissioner of major league baseball (Landis — 1921). In this case, the House refused to even report on the matter.

(2) Alleged conflict of interest by reason of writing publicly on political subjects (Douglas — 1970). It was held that there was no evidence to support this charge.

The most recent example of the invocation of the impeachment process in the United States relates to the conduct of Judge A.L. Hastings, a federal District Court judge. Judge Hastings is alleged to have committed some seventeen high crimes and misdemeanours, namely, conspiracy to accept a bribe, perjury and improper disclosure of confidential information. More specifically, he was accused of conspiring with an attorney to obtain money from convicted racketeers in exchange for a guarantee that they would not serve time. The House of Representatives voted 413-3 in favour of impeachment. Judge Hastings became the eleventh judge to be impeached by the House of Representatives in over 200 years. Subsequently, the U.S. Senate has voted 92-1 against the dismissal of the impeachment charges.[159]

Finally, other charges have included treason, bribery and financial irregularity, favouritism, practising law while on the bench, and appointing unqualified trustees and receivers.

(c) Conclusions

A student of the judiciary in Canada must be aware of some serious concerns.[160] It can be argued that the standard of "good behaviour" required of judges before the removal provisions become operative is not particularly stringent. That is, it takes a very dramatic malfeasance before the removal provisions are brought into force. Perhaps the removal provisions ought to be tightened, and indeed they were, to some extent, by the 1971 amendment to the Judges Act. Alternatively, one might argue that, owing to the Canadian experience to date and the dictates of tradition, the present system is quite satisfactory.

Although a judge must retire at age seventy-five, he may be quite capable of adjudicating beyond that age. By forced retirement his expertise and experience are lost. On the other hand it is possibly not too uncommon for some judges who become sick and infirm before the age of retirement to insist on maintaining their position.[161]

---

[159] See the New York Times, 17th March 1989, 10th August 1988 and 4th August 1988.

[160] For a somewhat critical evaluation of the Canadian judiciary, see Martin, "Criticising the Judges" (1982), 28 McGill L.J. 1.

[161] See, for example, the case of a senile judge who was suspended by the California Commission on Judicial Performance, reported in Newsweek Magazine, 24th January 1977. See also a report in the New York Times, 28th November 1976. It is interesting to note that there are new developments in easing burnout suffered by judges by providing them with a sabbatical program to return to school. See the Edmonton Journal, 22nd September 1989.

This, however, has probably been remedied, in respect of federally appointed judges, by the 1971 amendment to the Judges Act, discussed in some detail earlier. In addition, similar provisions are contained in provincial enabling statutes in respect of provincially appointed judges.

3. INDEPENDENCE OF THE JUDICIARY

The effect of such removal provisions is to provide the judiciary with security of tenure, and this in turn is directed at achieving an independent judiciary. In addition, there are special statutory constraints imposed on judges during their tenure of office (and, to a lesser extent, after their tenure of office) setting them apart from the average citizen or the average lawyer. These constraints have been established, essentially, for two purposes. The first is to ensure and provide for a special integrity on the part of the judiciary as an institution in society. The second is to bolster this integrity by providing for judicial independence, which is vital to the impartial and objective role that a judge must play. The judiciary must function as an independent arm of the body politic. While it is true that judges are appointed by politicians and are removable by politicians, the removal is intentionally made difficult so that a judge can objectively decide cases without fear of government retribution. Security of tenure is vital to the effective operation of the judiciary, particularly in respect of those cases in which government is either directly or indirectly concerned.

One corollary of the foregoing is that a judge, in deciding a case, should not be influenced by external sources. Indeed, a judge should not even be approached by an external source in connection with a case that he must decide. This rather fundamental principle was brought into the public eye early in 1976 in the so-called "judges affair", wherein a federal cabinet minister was alleged to have criticized a decision of a court conducting a trial under the Combines Investigation Act, R.S.C. 1970, c. C-23. In particular, the cabinet minister said, "I find this judgment completely unacceptable. I think it is a silly decision. I just cannot understand how a judge who is sane could give such a verdict. It is a complete shock and I find it a complete disgrace." As a result of these remarks, the cabinet minister was subsequently convicted of contempt and required to issue a "full, complete, and unreserved apology" to the court, serve a three-month probationary period, and pay costs of $500. On appeal, the requirement for an apology was dispensed with, the probationary period was annulled and the $500 in costs was converted to a $500 fine. In the course of these events, a second cabinet minister interceded on behalf of the cabinet minister convicted of contempt by telephoning the judge before whom the contempt citation was to be heard and making representations on behalf of the minister charged. This so-called "judges affair" created a substantial amount of public furor, including demands that the particular cabinet minister involved resign. It represents a recent instance where political intrusion upon an independent judiciary was not tolerated.[162] Whether the political imposition on the judiciary accomplished anything or even to what extent it constituted an imposition was irrelevant. The public debate reflected the notion that even the appearance of an imposition is contrary to the notion of an independent judiciary and is not permissible.

The independence of the judiciary is more than an ideal to be strived for, and it is more than merely a concept derived from history and tradition. The independence of the judiciary has a technical meaning defined in terms of the security of tenure provided for judges and the special constraints imposed upon judges. Constitutionally, our political system is based upon three branches of government — executive, legislative and judicial. Unlike the United States, there is some overlap in the executive and legislative branches of government in Canada; nonetheless, there is a rigid demarcation between the judicial and other branches of government. One could argue that, however, even this is not so since judges are appointed by the executive branch of government and are removable, at least in respect of federally appointed judges, by a joint address of the two federal legislative bodies. Furthermore, the governing statutes constituting the various courts are, of course, enacted by the legislative branch.

In the mid-1980s, some four Ontario Provincial Court Judges held, in four separate cases, that they had no jurisdiction to hear cases for reason that they lacked independence. The Canadian Charter of Rights and Freedoms provides in s. 11:

> Any person charged with an offence has the right . . .
>
> (d) to be presumed innocent until proven guilty according to law in a fair and public hearing by an independent and impartial tribunal . . .

Essentially, the argument advanced was that since a provincial court judge is appointed, paid, pensioned etc. by the Attorney General of a province and since in criminal cases one of the parties to a prosecution, the Crown Prosecutor, is also appointed, paid, pensioned etc. by the same Attorney General of the province, then it follows that the judge lacks independence. This argument was accepted by four provincial judges in the so-called "judges' revolt". On appeal to the Ontario Court of Appeal

---

[162] A similar situation arose in 1980 in British Columbia. For a full account, see the Vancouver Sun, 20th March 1980. Another example involves a federal cabinet minister phoning a provincial court judge on behalf of a man about to be sentenced by that judge. See the Edmonton Journal, 9th September 1978, and The Globe & Mail, 8th September 1979. In yet another example, an Ontario cabinet minister phoned an assistant crown attorney on behalf of a constituent. See The Globe & Mail, 9th November 1978, 9th and 16th December 1978; the Toronto Star, 10th September 1978; and the Edmonton Journal, 11th and 13th September 1978.

a panel of five judges rejected the argument. On a further appeal, the Supreme Court of Canada held that the provincial court judges did not lack independence. The court outlined the three major benchmarks of independence; namely, security of tenure, financial security and what the court described as "the institutional independence of the tribunal with respect to matters of administration bearing directly on the exercise of its judicial function". The court held that, with the exception of part-time judges who lack security of tenure, full-time provincial court judges were, in fact, independent. Accordingly, a hearing before them did not violate s. 11 of the Charter.[163]

As an aside, it is interesting to note that this is the same section of the Charter that is being used to advance some of the arguments in favour of the open court. While the media has recently advanced similar arguments under s. 2(*b*) of the Charter in connection with "freedom of the press", accused persons, particularly juveniles, have argued that s. 11(*d*) protects their right to an open hearing, without the attendant fetters on publication of the proceedings. In any event, returning to the issue of judicial independence and s. 11(*d*) of the Charter, the matter presumably will ultimately be decided by the highest court of the land. For a further description of this so-called "judges' revolt" in Ontario, see the Canadian Lawyer, April 1983.

In recent years, because of deficit and debt concerns, governments across Canada have 'rolled back' the wages and benefits of civil servants. In doing this, judges have not been excluded from these cutbacks. This has concerned judges for several reasons. For example, the inclusion of judges with 'other' civil servants has failed to recognize, in the view of many, that judges are not merely civil servants as part of the executive branch of government, but rather they constitute a separate and distinct third branch of government. They would argue that the judiciary, or the judicial branch of government, is independent of the executive branch and should not be 'lumped in' with civil servants for the purpose of wage cutbacks or, for that matter, any other purpose. As a result, it is not surprising that this has led in the 1990s to a series of "judges' revolts" in various provinces.

Alberta

A Calgary Youth Court judge "refused to attend court because of frustrations over the pay of provincial judges".[164] This subsequently attracted criticism from the province's Premier who stated:

---

[163] See *R. v. Valente (No.2)*, [1985] 2 S.C.R. 673, 49 C.R. (3d) 97, 37 M.V.R. 9, 23 C.C.C. (3d) 193, 24 D.L.R. (4th) 161, 19 C.R.R. 354, 14 O.A.C. 79, 64 N.R. 1.
[164] See Canadian Press, April 29, 1994.

I'm not going to get into how a judge conducts himself in the courtroom. That isn't the question we're addressing here. The question is should a public service employee — be he a judge or in any other position — expect to get paid for not working.

The Premier also suggested that the judge be fired if he did not return to work.[165] The underlying reasons behind the Calgary judge's objections were a five percent wage cutback combined with the termination of an understanding, a few years earlier, that the salaries of provincial court judges would be pegged as a fixed percentage of the salaries of their federally-appointed counterparts. In any event, another provincial court judge granted a defence request for an adjournment in a criminal case on the grounds that he lacked independence as a result of the Premier's remarks.[166] The argument, essentially, is based on the notional requirement that a judge should not be lumped together with civil servants and should not be subject to removal on the basis of dissatisfaction by the head of the executive branch of government. The legal framework for this notion is framed in the Supreme Court of Canada decision in the *Valente*[167] case. To reiterate, in that case the constitutional requirements of s. 11(*d*) of the Charter were reviewed and the indicia or benchmarks of independence were set out. As discussed earlier, these included both security of tenure and financial security.

The question whether the provincial court judge who granted the adjournment in the criminal trial mentioned above lacked independence and, generally, whether the Premier's comments and/or salary cutbacks constitute a lack of independence were then considered in a carefully considered and well-written judgment in the Court of Queen's Bench. In *R. v. Campbell* (1994), 25 Alta. L.R. (3d) 158, [1995] 2 W.W.R. 469, 160 A.R. 81 (Q.B.), affirmed 31 Alta. L.R. (3d) 190, [1995] 8 W.W.R. 747, 169 A.R. 178, 97 W.A.C. 178, (*sub nom. R. v. Wickman)* 100 C.C.C. (3d) 167 (C.A.) and *R. v. Wickman* (1995), 166 A.R. 310 (Prov. Ct.), the Alberta Court of Queen's Bench concluded, inter alia, that

[t]he . . . Order in Council reducing the judges' salaries by 5% violates the constitutional guarantee of financial security which the court holds is applicable to federally-appointed judges *and* to Provincial Court judges. The court held that the reduction cannot be supported as being part of an "overall economic measure" unless it is the result of a statutory provision applicable to all citizens, such as provincial income tax. Thus it is not constitutionally permissible to defend a reduction in judges' salaries on the basis that it is part of a measure applicable to all other persons who are paid from the public purse. The Order in Council [reducing judges' salaries] is held to be invalid. But the defence cannot succeed in obtaining an order staying proceedings, or an order of prohibition and certiorari, because, the Order in Council having been declared to be invalid, the

---

[165] See Canadian Press, May 3, 1994.

[166] See Canadian Press, May 3, 1994, May 5, 1994, May 6, 1994, May 18, 1994 and June 25, 1994.

[167] *Supra*, n. 156.

reduction in salaries no longer exists in law. So there is no longer a violation of financial security.

. . .

. . . there is a constitutional obligation to maintain the financial security of the judges by increasing their salaries to correspond with increases in the cost of living. However, the information placed before the court does not permit it to decide in these cases whether this obligation has not been met.

. . .

. . . certain remarks made by [the] Premier . . . did not constitute a direct attack on the independence of the Provincial Court.[168]

Prior to this decision, 69 of Alberta's 104 provincial judges launched a lawsuit against the provincial government alleging that:

. . .the province "has failed to maintain and impaired the independence of the provincial court" by imposing a five per cent wage cut and reducing their pension formula. "The public perception can be that we are not independent, that we are subject to the whims of an elected official" . . .

and further:

. . .wants the [C]ourt [of Queen's Bench] to reinstate a formula that paid the judges 80 per cent of the salaries of Court of Queen's Bench judges.

That case is ongoing, although the Court of Queen's Bench decision, discussed above, addresses some of the judges' concerns in their civil suit.[169]

After the former decision (by Mr. Justice McDonald)[170], the government launched an appeal of the decision and, for technical reasons relating to the available grounds of appeal, two of the three judges of the Alberta Court of Appeal held that the Crown had no right of appeal.[171]

As a result of the foregoing series of events, the Government of Alberta was required to restore the five percent salary reduction of the provincial court judges, an amount totalling $450,000.[172]

---

[168] Executive Summary of the Reasons for Judgment of the Honourable Mr. Justice D.C. McDonald. See also the case comment, Wayne Renke, "Invoking Independence: Judicial Independence as a No-cut Wage Guarantee" (1994) No.5, Centre for Constitutional Studies: Points of View 1.

[169] Canadian Press, August 3, 1994 and August 4, 1994.

[170] Note 160, *supra*.

[171] *R. v. Campbell*, *supra*. See the Edmonton Journal, June 30, 1995.

[172] This led to somewhat of a backlash by some with respect to their view of the judiciary. See Alberta Report, December 5, 1994. The cover contains the heading "So much for Democracy: Alberta's unelected judges show Ralph who's really in charge" and the cover story is entitled "Tyranny of the courts: A judge interprets the Charter to mean that Klein can't cut judges' wages". There is also a story entitled "A rising demand for elected judges". See discussion of Alberta Bill 221 at an earlier point in this chapter.

British Columbia

A provincial court judge in British Columbia launched a lawsuit alleging age discrimination and its consequential effect on his independence. In particular, the lawsuit alleges that the

> province discriminates by eliminating the judges' life insurance and long-term disability insurance at age 65, when they are appointed to sit as judges to age 70 [and that]. . . the government threatened the judges' independence when it enacted legislation removing their right to become supernumerary, or part-time judges, after they have served 20 years or reach age 60.
>
> . . . The lawsuit says the government ignored a recommendation in 1988 from a legislative committee when it denied insurance coverage to judges over age 64. And it says the government acted unconstitutionally in 1989 when, without consultation, it removed their right to supernumerary status.[173]

Manitoba

Provincial court judges in Manitoba objected to provincial Bill 22 requiring the courts (and all provincial government offices) to close for ten working days a year, with the attendant reduction of salary, as a provincial cost-saving measure. The judges threatened to sue the provinces in a constitutional challenge to the Bill alleging that, as part of their independence, judges have a right to control the setting of court days. The province, wishing to avoid suit, promised the judges a salary increase if they did not commence legal action challenging the Bill. This, in turn, led to an allegation by the judges that the government, by linking salary increases to the proposed legal action, i.e. linking salary to the judges' assertion of independence, is "inappropriate and unseemly".[174] The judges (through the Association of Provincial Court Judges) decided to proceed with the challenge to Bill 22.[175] The action was heard in the Court of Queen's Bench and the judges were partially successful. Given that Bill 22 was only a temporary measure and not a general overall economic measure, it was not held to be unconstitutional per se. Its application to the judges would only be permissible if there were a full restoration of salary for required days off at the expiration of this temporary measure. As the Court said, "on the expiry of the legislation [there must be] full retroactive reinstatement of all compensation that was suspended".[176] A summary of the reasons is set out by the trial judge:

> 1. Subsection 11(d) of the Charter expressly enunciates the overriding, established constitutional requirement for an independent and impartial tribunal. This requirement applies not only to Superior Court judges but also to judges of the Provincial Court.

---

[173] See Canadian Press, December 3, 1994.

[174] Canadian Press, July 4, 1994.

[175] Canadian Press, October 25, 1994.

[176] Canadian Press, November 25, 1994.

Once fixed, judicial salaries may not be reduced except as part of a general overall economic measure.

2. Bill 22 is not a general overall economic measure. It is a specific restraint measure applicable only to members of the Legislature, to civil servants and to various state supported operations. These subjects of Bill 22 are not protected by the constitutional imperative of an independent and impartial tribunal. The Bill, therefore, cannot operate to effect a reduction in judicial compensation already fixed.

3. However, read in a manner that is consistent with the Constitution, Bill 22 is effective to defer payment while the statute is in force. This determinate deferment is not a limitation of any rationally-defined constitutional right, provided that restoration is made following the expiry of the legislation.

In the circumstances, Bill 22 as I have construed it is not unconstitutional and the application of the Association is dismissed.[177]

Prince Edward Island

The province of Prince Edward Island imposed a seven and one-half percent reduction on the salary of its civil servants including, as in Alberta, its provincial court judges among those subject to the reduction. Again, similar to Alberta, a provincial court judge (the chief judge) refused to hear a case on the ground that the wage rollback amounted to an interference with his independence. The case was adjourned pending a ruling on the matter by the Prince Edward Island Supreme Court. The Chief Justice of the Supreme Court agreed with this assertion and held that the province had six months to exclude provincial court judges from the legislated wage rollbacks.[178] The court held

that the rollback legislation does affect judicial independence because it allows all civil servants — including provincial court judges — to negotiate with the government for a reduction in benefits instead of a wage rollback. And if judges entered negotiations, the public could reasonably believe that they might favour the government in rulings to gain ground in striking a salary deal.[179]

Following the decision, the provincial judges refused to hear cases and, effectively, the courts were shut down for a week [180] until the province "amended the law to exempt judges from negotiating to effect the wage cut with benefit reductions".[181]

---

[177] *Provincial Court Judges Assn. (Manitoba) v. Manitoba (Minister of Justice)* (1994), 30 C.P.C. (3d) 31, (*sub nom. Judges of the Provincial Court (Manitoba) v. Manitoba)* 98 Man. R. (2d) 67 (Q.B.), reversed [1995] 5 W.W.R. 641 *(sub nom. Manitoba Provincial Judges Assn. v. Manitoba (Minister of Justice))* 125 D.L.R. (4th) 149, 102 Man. R. (2d) 51, 93 W.A.C. 51 (C.A.).

[178] Canadian Press, September 22, 1994.

[179] Canadian Lawyer, April 1995, p. 5.

[180] Canadian Press, September 26, 1994 and September 27, 1994 and Canadian Lawyer, April 1995.

[181] Canadian Lawyer, April 1995.

The province then decided to refer the matter to the Prince Edward Island Court of Appeal (i.e., the Appeal Division of the Supreme Court of Prince Edward Island) and framed these questions for resolution:

1. Can the Legislature of the Province of Prince Edward Island make laws such that the remuneration of Judges of the Provincial Court may be decreased, increased, or otherwise adjusted, either:

   (a) as part of an overall public economic measure, or

   (b) in certain circumstances established by law?

2. If the answer to 1(a) or (b) is yes, then do the Judges of the Provincial Court of Prince Edward Island currently enjoy a basic or sufficient degree of financial security or remuneration such that they constitute an independent and impartial tribunal within the meaning of Section 11(d) of the Canadian Charter of Rights and Freedoms and such other sections as may be applicable?

The chief judge maintained that the questions posed to the Court of Appeal were too narrowly focused.[182] The Canadian Association of Provincial Court Judges also felt the case was now too narrow and decided not to intervene in the Court of Appeal.[183]

Meanwhile, the matter returned to the Prince Edward Island Supreme Court on the issue of the liability of the province to pay the legal fees of the judges in the earlier independence case. The province was held not to be liable. The chief provincial court judge then submitted his resignation as chief judge, though he remained on the bench.[184]

At the Court of Appeal, the two questions set out above were addressed. The answer to the first question was a 'qualified yes'. That is,

> the Legislature of Prince Edward Island does not have an unfettered right to deal with the salary and other benefits of Provincial Court judges. It does, however, have a limited constitutional authority to alter the salary and benefits of the judges of the Provincial Court and could reduce them as part of an overall public economic measure so long as in so doing: (1) it does not remove the basic degree of financial security which is an essential condition for their independence within the meaning of s-s. 11(d) of the Charter; and (2) there is no indication that the legislation amounts to arbitrary interference with the judiciary in the sense that it is being enacted for an improper or colourable purpose, or that it discriminates against judges vis-a-vis other citizens.

The answer to the second question was 'yes'. That is,

> in spite of the pay reduction effected by the Public Sector Pay Reduction Act, . . . [provincial court judges] still retain a sufficient standard of financial security to constitute

---

[182] Canadian Press, October 14, 1994.

[183] Canadian Press, November 29, 1994.

[184] Canadian Press, November 1, 1994.

an independent tribunal within the meaning of s-s. 11(d) of the Charter. . . . [the court has] reached that conclusion for the following reasons:

(1) the reduction is a coherent part of an overall public economic measure designed to meet a legitimate governmental objective;

(2) it is non-discriminatory in that it applies generally to all salaried public offices and indeed to virtually everyone who receives a pay cheque from the provincial government;

(3) the right of judges to their salaries remains established by law and therefore beyond arbitrary interference by government; and

(4) there is no hint that the Public Sector Pay Reduction Act was enacted for any improper or colourable purpose.[185]

After the Court of Appeal decision, the matter did not come to an end. The former chief judge again granted an indefinite adjournment in a criminal case permitting the defence lawyer an opportunity to again challenge the court's independence. The judge felt the Court of Appeal decision might not have adequately resolved the issue.[186]

Nova Scotia

After the decision of the Prince Edward Island Supreme Court was rendered (but before it was heard in the Appeal Division), the President of the Provincial Judges Association of Nova Scotia invited defence lawyers to challenge the independence of provincial courts in Nova Scotia.[187]

From the foregoing, one might consider whether some assertions of independence are constitutional issues in a labour context or whether they are merely labour disputes raising constitutional issues. In September of 1993, some judges in Quebec asserted that the requirement of paying parking fees at the courthouse was an interference with their independence. In fact, in litigating the matter, the judges were successful before the Quebec Superior Court. But cases like that raise the concern that there may be some instances when judges too readily invoke independence as a shield against unwarranted interferences. Arguably, this might affect their credibility in those more critical instances where their independence is seriously threatened.[188]

---

[185] See also, Canadian Press, December 16, 1994.

[186] Canadian Press, January 5, 1995 and Canadian Lawyer, April 1995.

[187] Canadian Press, September 26, 1994. For a brief discussion of salaries of federally-appointed judges, see the National, January 1990. For a comprehensive discussion of the same issue, see Friedland, M., *A Place Apart: Judicial Independence and Accountability in Canada, supra.*

[188] For some miscellaneous sources discussing independence, see Hon. Jules Deschênes, "Judicial Independence: A Challenge to the Executive" (1983), 7 Provincial Judges Journal 3; Centre for the Independence of Judges and Lawyers (C.I.J.L.) Bulletin, Special Issue — The Independence of Judges and Lawyers: A Compilation of International Standards. No. 25-6, April-October 1990, Canadian Judges Conference, Report to the Canadian Bar Association Report to the Mid-Winter Meeting of Council, February 1994; report of speech delivered to the Calgary Bar Association, Canadian Press, January 30, 1994.

Much has been written and said about the independence of the judiciary. Consider, for example, the following from Professor R. MacGregor Dawson's classic treatise on Canadian political science entitled *The Government of Canada* concerning the independence of the judiciary:

> The judge must be made independent of most of the restraints, checks, and punishments which are usually called into play against other public officials. He is thus protected against the operation of some of the most potent weapons which a democracy has at its command: he received almost complete protection against criticism; he is given civil and criminal immunity for acts committed in the discharge of his duties; he cannot be removed from office for any ordinary offence, but only for misbehaviour of a flagrant kind; and he can never be removed simply because his decisions happen to be disliked by the Cabinet, the Parliament, or the people. Such independence is unquestionably dangerous, and if this freedom and power were indiscriminately granted the results would certainly prove to be disastrous. The desired protection is found by picking with especial care the men who are to be entrusted with these responsibilities, and then paradoxically heaping more privileges upon them to stimulate their sense of moral responsibility which has been removed. The judge is placed in a position where he has nothing to lose by doing what is right and little to gain by doing what is wrong; and there is therefore every reason to hope that his best efforts will be devoted to the conscientious performance of his duty.
>
> The judge will thus usually begin with the twin assets of character and ability, and these become the foundation on which the indirect appeals are based. He is paid a substantial salary, which not only removes some of the obvious temptations, but frees him from financial distractions. The importance of his office is continually stressed; his own rectitude and sense of fairness are invariably assumed; the dignity of the court and the respect accorded his office are rarely, if ever, challenged; his social position is always assured. These efforts to accentuate the eminence of the office are made infinitely more effective by the fortunate habit which the legal profession has for the judiciary and its ingrained habit of regarding a seat on the Bench as the crown of a legal career. Thus some of the very men who build up the tradition may be induced to accept judgeships a few years later, influenced to a material degree by the tradition which they themselves have helped to create. Not the least important result of this prestige is its effect on the public, who have come to accept it — and with some justification — at its face value, and who see in judicial independence a greater promise of justice than could be obtained through the application of ordinary political sanctions.[189]

Consider also the following extract taken from a classic article on the independence of the judiciary written by Professor W. R. Lederman of Queen's University, a noted Canadian constitutional scholar. The author traces the historical basis of the independent judiciary, discusses the relevant sections of the Constitution Act of 1867 (ss. 96 to 101) and then concludes as follows:

> But, it may be asked, how is it that all these fine results follow from the conditions of judicial independence studied in this article? Many of these conditions are negative ones, making the judge irresponsible, or non-accountable, in office and preventing his removal except in the most extreme circumstances. As Dr. R. MacGregor Dawson shows [in the above extract], the answer is that the conditions of judicial independence, negative though most of them are, will stimulate any person of moral integrity to do his best. Given learning and ability as well as a conscience, this will be a very effective best. Political irresponsibility in these circumstances generates moral responsibility and conscientious effort. And

---

[189] 5th ed. (Toronto: University of Toronto Press, 1970).

thus, if care has been taken with the appointment in the first place, the conditions of judicial independence will justify themselves . . .

It is quite clear then that the success of our system of judicial independence rests upon the appointment of well-qualified persons to judicial office, and the question of how best to ensure this arises. The writer considers that responsibility and power in this respect should remain with the federal Cabinet, in particular with the Prime Minister and the Minister of Justice. They must answer eventually to the national Parliament for the quality of judicial appointments, and this is the proper constitutional reflection of the vital interest all citizens have in the proper administration of justice. No doubt official or voluntary association of the legal profession may play a valuable advisory role at times, but the real power of appointment should rest where it is now, at the highest level of political responsibility. Nevertheless, the professional contribution is a vital one, the impartiality and effectiveness of judges depending in important measure on the education, traditions, experience and autonomy of the legal profession from which they are drawn. Hence the main contribution that lawyers as a whole can make to the quality of the bench is to be true to their own standards as members of a learned profession.[190]

As mentioned above, the work of former Chief Justice Jules Deschênes, *Masters in Their Own House*, represents a definitive review of judicial independence in Canada. The work was commissioned by the Canadian Judicial Council and published in 1981.[191] In 1993, the Canadian Judicial Council commissioned Martin Friedland, a Professor and former Dean of the Faculty of Law at the University of Toronto, to undertake a comprehensive review of the issues canvassed by Chief Justice Deschênes in his earlier study. In the intervening years between Deschênes and Friedland, much has occurred. Most important, we now have an entrenched Charter of Rights in our Constitution with an independent judiciary provision in s. 11(d) of this Charter. We also have a number of judicial decisions exploring the meaning of independence in various contexts. Various courts have amalgamated or merged or have been eliminated. And, many of Chief Justice Deschênes' recommendations have been implemented.

---

[190] "The Independence of the Judiciary" (1956), 34 Can. Bar Rev. 1139 at 1178. See also the papers delivered to the meetings organized by the Canadian Judges Conference on Judge's Day at the Canadian Bar Association over the past few years. These included a paper by Professor B. Elman entitled "The Independence of the Judiciary" delivered in Calgary in 1979. Of great importance, see the definitive work, in the contemporary Canadian context, by Chief Justice Deschênes, *Masters in Their Own House* (Ottawa: Canadian Judicial Council,]981). This work is cited in *R. v. Valente*, supra, note 156. In addition, see W.R. Lederman, "Judicial Independence and the Court reforms in Canada for the 1990's" (1988), 12 Queen's L.J. 385; C.A. Kowosan, "The Independence of the Judiciary" (1987), 11 Prov. Judges J. 15; N.T. Nemetz, "The Independence of the Judiciary", in F.E. McArdle (ed.), Cambridge Lectures, 1985 (Montreal: Les Editions Yvon Blais, 1987), p. 335; N.T. Nemetz, "The Concept of the Independent Judiciary" (1986), 20 U.B.C.L. Rev. 285; and J. Smith, "Judicial Independence and Accountability: The Institutional Ethos", a paper prepared for the Ontario Law Reform Commission Conference on the Nomination of Persons for Judicial Appointment, 14th-15th September 1989, Kingston, Ontario (to be published by the Ontario Law Reform Commission). See the Financial Post, 7th November 1981. Work on this topic is now being conducted at the international level by the International Commission of Jurists, the International Bar Association, and other interested organizations. See, for example, the Chairman's Report at the 19th Biennial Conference, New Delhi, India, 17th-23rd October 1982.

[191] *Supra*, n. 190.

The Friedland report, entitled *A Place Apart: Judicial Independence and Accountability in Canada*, was published in May of 1995.[192] The report reviews the history of judicial independence in England, the United States and Canada, and examines the major constitutional (including Charter) cases. It discusses all aspects of judicial life — appointments and elevations, security of tenure, discipline, codes of conduct, judicial education and financial security. It raises the possibility of performance evaluations. The report discusses court administration as well as the role of the chief justice. Finally, the author makes a number of recommendations, some of which have attracted considerable discussion and some criticism. Some of the major recommendations are as follows:

1. The appointment of chief justices for limited term certain, preferably 7 years;

2. The establishment of special nominating committees for appointments to the Supreme Court of Canada. The committees would present a short ranked list of names to the government and if the government nominates a candidate from outside the list, there would be a U.S.-style confirmation proceeding.

3. A similar process for court of appeal appointments would be established, where it would be made public if a nominee was appointed from outside of the nominating committee's list, but a confirmation hearing would not be required.

4. The appointment of part-time judges (if constitutionally permissible) to provide an opportunity for the judge and others to determine if the part-time judge is suited to full-time judicial responsibilities.

5. A retirement age for federally-appointed judges of 70 years (as opposed to the present retirement age of 75 years).

6. With respect to the present Triennial Commission method of making remuneration recommendations for federally-appointed judges, the government would be required to respond to the commission's report by introducing legislation within a set time (whether or not the legislation reflects the commission's recommendation).

7. Some changes to the disciplinary process that "should enhance accountability and, at the same time, increase the public's confidence

---

[192] Friedland, M.L., *A Place Apart: Judicial Independence and Accountability in Canada* (Ottawa: Canadian Judicial Council, 1995).

in the judiciary and therefore encourage respect for judicial independence".[193]

8. The establishment of a code of conduct for the judiciary, perhaps modelled after the U.S. Federal Code.

9. Periodic performance evaluations of judges.[194]

10. The creation of a single Board of Judicial Management to administer the courts in all three levels of the provincial judiciary (i.e., the provincial court with provincially-appointed judges and the provincial superior trial and appeal courts with federally-appointed judges).

The report makes several other recommendations, but more importantly, its comprehensive discussion of the Canadian judiciary (and of the various contemporary issues confronting the judiciary) makes the Friedland report, like the Deschênes report before it, an important addition to Canadian legal literature.[195]

Internationally, there have been some significant developments in respect of the independence of the judiciary.[196] Certainly, one of the great movers for the establishment of international standards of justice has been the International Bar Association through its Committee on the Administration of Justice. For example, that committee's Project on Minimum Standards of Judicial Independence made a significant contribution in the 1980's. In addition, at the World Conference on the Independence of Justice, held in Montreal in 1983, a draft proposal for a Universal Declaration on the Independence of Justice (akin to the U.N. Universal

---

[193] See the Friedland report, *supra*.

[194] This recommendation has attracted considerable controversy. Judges generally maintain that they are now constantly being reviewed — by lawyers appearing before them, by bench and bar committees, by the media, by courts of appeal, by their peer group of fellow judges, by their chief justice and by academic analysis of their work. They further argue that periodic review would interfere with their independence, and suppress bold judicial initiatives, even if this is done subconsciously. They question the mechanics of a review process and suggest it might become a very subjective process. Others have argued that almost everyone in society is reviewed or scrutinized, whether it be in the form of student evaluations, broadcast ratings, or simply an annual job review. And the suggestion of periodic review is not really new — it has been studied by the Manitoba Law Reform Commission and has been considered in at least two other provinces, Ontario and Nova Scotia.

[195] For a summary of the Friedland recommendations, see Michèle Rivet, "The Friedland Report" (1995), Vol. v, No. 4, C.I.A.J. Bulletin 2. For other commentary on the Friedland report, see "Conduct code would inhibit free speech: Sopinka" The Lawyers Weekly, 15:17, September 8, 1995; "Top judge lukewarm to report cards for justices", The Edmonton Journal, August 20, 1995; "Code of conduct resisted", Edmonton Journal, August 23, 1995; and "U.S.-style scrutiny for a U.S.-style court", Alberta Report, September 11, 1995.

[196] Shimon Shetreet, "Judicial Independence: New Conceptual Dimensions and Contemporary Challenges", in Shimon Shetreet and Jules Deschenes (eds.), *Judging the World: Law and Politics in the World's Leading Courts* (Dordrecht: Martinus Nijhoff, 1985), p. 595.

Declaration of Human Rights) was adopted. During the 1980's, that draft proposal was slowly making its way through the various organs of the United Nations.[197] There is also considerable work being done by the International Commission of Jurists through its Centre for the Independence of Judges and Lawyers.[198]

Readers who wish to engage in further study of this vital topic may consult the bibliography of materials set out at the end of this chapter. We will now turn our attention to those special constraints imposed upon judges in order to promote and advance the integrity of the judiciary as a vital institution in society and to ensure the preservation of the concept of the independence of the judiciary.

(a) Special Standards in Public and Private Life

When a lawyer becomes a judge his whole world, that is, both his public and private life, changes. In public, he must always exercise the requisite dignity and decorum commensurate with his office. Nowhere is it written that a judge cannot write a letter to the editor of a newspaper taking a position in a political controversy. However, tradition dictates that this shall not be done. There are many other instances where tradition has imposed constraints on the public and private conduct of judges. These traditions, which are really no more than conventions of judicial behaviour, also dictate, to some extent, for example, how a judge spends his recreational hours, or where a judge eats. But perhaps, more accurately, these conventions dictate how a judge should not spend his recreational hours and what establishments he should not enter. Judges must exercise restraint in language and must never consume excessive liquor in public. The dictates of tradition require the greatest restraint, the greatest propriety and the greatest decorum from the members of our judiciary. We expect our judges to be almost superhuman in wisdom, in propriety, in decorum and in humanity. There is probably no other group in society which must fulfil this standard of public expectation and, at the same time, accept so many constraints.

Perhaps a better appreciation of the circumstances in which a new judge finds himself might be gained from a brief article which appeared in the New York Times dated 15th August 1976. That article, quoted in its entirety, is set out as follows:

ON TOP, A LONELY JUDGE

Supreme Court Justice Lewis F. Powell Jr. has provided, through an interview, an unusual glimpse of life at the judicial top. The necessity for judicial impartiality has forced

---

[197] See International Commission of Jurists, "Independence of Judges and Lawyers" (1989), 43 The Review 24.

[198] *Ibid.*

him to curtail many old friendships formed during almost 40 years in private practice. He also regrets the impact his position has had on the law careers of two of his children, both of whom resent, he says, being identified as the children of a Supreme Court Justice. But he still finds the work at the Court intellectually stimulating. "All of the negatives are out-weighed," he said, "by the feeling of privilege at the opportunity to be at the Court."

Indeed, Bora Laskin, the late Chief Justice of Canada, remarked "half facetiously" that "when you become a judge, you lose half of your freedom and when you become a chief justice, you almost lose the other half."

A judge is a public figure and, as a result, he is subject to the glare of publicity that public figures must inevitably face. For example, a County Court Judge in the province of Ontario was personally involved in a matrimonial dispute which involved a quarrel over a property settlement. Not every matrimonial dispute is reported on the front page of the local newspaper; this one was. Moreover, what might constitute folly or silly behaviour on the part of most persons becomes scandal if it involves a judge. Society has come to expect a very high standard of behaviour on the part of judges and that standard of behaviour is enforced through public scrutiny.

In addition, as discussed earlier, judges are limited in the extent to which they may make public remarks. First, a judge may not make any remarks in respect of any case which is "sub judice"; that is, he may not make any comments concerning an ongoing case, at least not before a decision has been rendered. This constraint applies equally to both the presiding judge and other judges as well. Secondly, where a judge makes certain comments in connection with a case which has already been decided, his remarks must be very tactfully expressed and within the bounds of propriety. Because of this requirement, most judges choose not to make any public remarks in connection with particular cases decided.

However, there do not seem to be any constraints on a judge against making remarks in an anecdotal manner concerning his experiences on the bench. In fact, if there were constraints of this nature, a tradition of many after-dinner speeches at bar association meetings would be lost.[199] Nor are there any constraints upon a judge in making public remarks concerning reform of the law and the administration of justice generally. However, it is very unwise and imprudent for a judge to extend his remarks into the political realm, suggesting, for example, that judicial reform and changes in the administration of justice would best be accomplished by the political action of a given party. In other words, a judge may say,

---

[199] For a humorous look at court proceedings, see two books by Peter V. MacDonald, Q.C., *Court Jesters* (Toronto: Stoddart, 1985), and *More Court Jesters* (Toronto: Stoddart, 1987).

for example, that the law concerning ownership of the matrimonial home upon dissolution of marriage ought to be changed by the legislature, but he ought not to remark that one party or another is more likely to implement this change. This whole issue, of course, came to the public's attention in respect of the Berger matter, discussed earlier.

(b) Special Legal Constraints Imposed on Judges

(i) Right to Vote

Under the various municipal, provincial and federal election Acts, certain judges are put into the same category as inmates in penitentiaries, inasmuch as they are all disenfranchised. In addition, as indicated above, in the course of a campaign for election, there is the additional constraint imposed upon a judge that he must be reserved and reticent in expressing his support for a particular candidate or a particular party or, for that matter, a particular ideology. In other words, he must effectively remain out of the campaign and out of politics. In summary, as a non-participant in the campaign and as a disenfranchised citizen, a judge can take no part in the electoral process.

This, however, is changing. First, in one case, two Federal Court judges successfully challenged the provision in the federal Elections Act disenfranchising them.[200] In addition, at the time of the writing, a commission was studying prospective changes to the Elections Act. It is anticipated that the new Act, irrespective of any judicial decisions, will no longer disenfranchise the federally appointed judiciary.

(ii) Law Society Membership

Certain judges must resign their membership in their respective provincial law societies upon appointment to the bench. If a judge happens to be a bencher of a law society, he must naturally, with his resignation from the law society, also resign as a bencher. Once he retires from the bench (and this, of course, refers to full retirement, including retirement from a supernumerary position), he must reapply to the law society for reinstatement before he can then engage in the practice of law.

(iii) Private Practice and Private Concerns

A newly appointed judge must immediately wind up the practice of law in which he was professionally engaged. The interim period from the time his appointment is confirmed until the time that he is officially sworn in as a member of the bench is usually reserved for this purpose. He may not, during this period, act for his clients, except to the extent necessary

---

[200] *Muldoon v. R.*, [1983] 3 F.C. 628, 21 F.T.R. 154 (*sub nom. Muldoon v. Canada*) (T.D.).

to ensure that their files are transferred to other lawyers. Furthermore, as a judge, he should not hear a case in which a former client is involved.

In winding up his former practice, the newly appointed judge must also terminate his partnership or his association with his former firm. Changes must be made in the nature of the relationship that he has with the lawyers with whom he was engaged in practice and with lawyers in general. Of course, long and meaningful relationships need not be terminated upon an appointment to the bench. However, there is at least some alteration in the nature of that relationship upon the appointment. It is difficult to define how this relationship is modified. Perhaps it might best be expressed as permitting a judge to maintain comity among his colleagues in the legal profession but to do so in a somewhat more reserved and distant posture than existed prior to his appointment.

Often, a lawyer is engaged in other private concerns which may or may not have arisen as a result of his membership in the legal profession. In any event, private business enterprises must be terminated upon appointment, corporate directorships must be resigned, and generally the new judge must sever all points of contact that may have existed between him and the business world. Indeed, ss. 55 and 56 of the federal Judges Act expressly provide that a judge must do so. Those sections are as follows:

55. No judge shall, either directly or indirectly, for himself or others, engage in any occupation or business other than his judicial duties, but every judge shall devote himself exclusively to those judicial duties.

56. (1) No judge shall act as commissioner, arbitrator, adjudicator, referee, conciliator or mediator on any commission or on any inquiry or other proceeding unless

(*a*) in the case of any matter within the legislative authority of Parliament, the judge is by an Act of Parliament of Canada expressly authorized so to act or the judge is thereunto appointed or so authorized by the Governor in Council; or (*b*) in the case of any matter within the legislative authority of the legislature of a province, the judge is by an Act of the legislature of the province expressly authorized so to act or the judge is thereunto appointed or so authorized by the lieutenant governor in council of the province.

(2) Subsection (1) does not apply to judges acting as arbitrators or assessors of compensation or damages under the *Railway Act* or any other public Act, whether of general or local application, of Canada or of a province, whereby a judge is required or authorized without authority from the Governor in Council or lieutenant governor in council to assess or ascertain compensation or damages.

In addition to all of the foregoing, some of the enabling statutes contain provisions requiring the judge to assume residence within a given municipality or within a particular radius of that municipality.

In short, the law imposes special constraints, legal and otherwise, upon judges in order to ensure the preservation of the integrity of our judiciary and to ensure that our courts always remain impartial and objective and, most important, independent institutions within our society.

(c) The Judge Serving in Other Capacities

Owing to the independence of the judiciary and the resulting freedom from influences from external sources, and owing to the status and prestige that members of the judiciary have in society, governments often turn to members of the judiciary to constitute Royal Commissions of Inquiry.[201] This, of course, presents some problems for the chief judge or chief justice of a particular bench: the docket of most courts is already overloaded and the services of every judge are needed. Notwithstanding this logistical problem, many judges serve in this special capacity. In recent years, for example, judges have served as chairmen of Royal Commissions of Inquiry in respect of such matters as the investigation into the management of one of our national airlines, an examination of the implications of pipeline construction on the integrity of northern life and environment, and the investigation into the causes of an airplane crash. In addition, in recent years, the tendency has been to appoint one-man commissions. This, of course, avoids the obvious problem of dissenting opinions.

Often, with many Royal Commissions of Inquiry, the reports of the commissioners do no more than gather dust after they have been submitted to government authorities. However, although this has not been documented, it appears that probably owing to the prestige and status afforded members of the judiciary, those Royal Commissions conducted by members of the judiciary are more often acted upon. No better example of this comes to mind than the McRuer Royal Commission of Inquiry into Civil Rights in the province of Ontario where, over a number of years, many recommendations have been enacted into law.

The number of Royal Commissions of Inquiry constituted and chaired by members of the judiciary is constantly increasing. For example, in the past decade, judges have served on royal commissions dealing, inter alia, with the following matters: the wrongful conviction of an accused and the administration of justice in the province of Nova Scotia, the administration of justice with respect to native persons in the provinces of Manitoba and Alberta, the collapse and loss of life in an offshore oil rig disaster, at least two instances of loss of life stemming from air disasters, the use of banned substances in amateur athletics, the murder of several babies at a major children's hospital, and the abuse of young male residents at an orphanage operated by a religious order.

---

[201] For a thorough reading about the conduct of a commission of inquiry, see Innis Christie, A. Paul Pross and John Yogis, *Commissions of Inquiry* (Toronto: Carswell, 1990).

(d) The Writing of Judgments

Judgment-writing has attracted considerable attention in recent years. For example, beginning in 1981 the Canadian Institute for the Administration of Justice embarked upon an annual programme on behalf of the Canadian Judicial Council on judgment-writing. Related issues have been voiced in recent years.[202]

(e) Personal Liability of Judges

Judges are exempt from civil liability for all acts done in their official capacity.[203] Essentially, this privilege provides an immunity for judges in respect of acts or omissions committed on the bench, and is usually directed at false imprisonment, defamation, and other like actions.[204] On the other hand, there is little jurisprudence suggesting the presence or lack thereof of a similar immunity in respect of criminal liability. Perhaps the closest indication that no such immunity exists is the case of *Slater v. Watts* (1911), 16 B.C.R. 36, 16 W.L.R. 234 (C.A.), where it was held that a justice of the peace was potentially liable for a civil action of assault for lashing a boy who came before him. The justice believed that the boy had attempted to entice his daughter.

Recently, Canadian and British courts have addressed the issue of judicial immunity. For example, the Supreme Court of Canada acknowledged the notion of absolute immunity from civil suit in respect of superior court judges.[205] The matter was further considered in a recent Supreme Court of Canada decision[206] relating to the so-called Donald Marshall inquiry. The commissioners inquiring into the wrongful conviction of Mr. Marshall attempted to compel the testimony, before the inquiry, of the five judges of the Nova Scotia Court of Appeal who had acquitted Mr. Marshall, but, in so doing, commented that essentially, he was the author of his own wrongful conviction. For this (and other reasons), the commissioners wanted to know

---

[202] See R. Koman, *Reasons for Judgment: A Handbook for Judges and Other Judicial Officers* (Toronto: Butterworths, 1980), and M. Taggart, "Should Canadian Lawyers be Legally Required to Give Reasoned Decisions in Civil Cases" (1983), 33 U.T.L.J. 1.

[203] See *Floyd v. Barker* (1607), 12 Co. Rep. 23, 77 E.R. 1305.

[204] There have been at least two recent attempts on the part of losing litigants to sue the presiding judges. One such litigant alleged that the members of the Alberta Court of Appeal who decided his case had been negligent. The Master had dismissed the claim on the basis that judicial negligence does not constitute a cause of action at common law. A similar attempt was made in Ontario a few years ago — see the Toronto Star, 26th December 1979.

[205] See *Morier v. Rivard*, [1985] 2 S.C.R. 716, 17 Admin. L.R. 230, 23 D.L.R. (4th) 1, 64 N.R. 46. See also the leading and influential British case, *Sirros v. Moore*, [1975] 1 Q.B. 118, [1974] 3 All E.R. 776 (C.A.).

[206] *MacKeigan v. Hickman* [1989] 2 S.C.R. 796, 72 C.R. (3d) 129, 50 C.C.C. (3d) 449, 99 N.R. 227n, 94 N.S.R. (2d) 1, 247 A.P.R. 1, 61 D.L.R. (4th) 688, 100 N.R. 81 (*sub nom. MacKeigan, J.A. v. Royal Comm.* (*Marshall Inquiry*) (S.C.C.).

the composition of the panel on the Marshall reference; the composition of the record before the panel on the reference; and the factors identified by the panel in support of their conclusion that a miscarriage of justice had occurred in the Marshall trial and conviction.[207]

This immunity from testifying, in terms of its rationale, is akin to the immunity from civil suit. The majority of the Supreme Court of Canada held that, like the immunity from civil suit, this was an absolute immunity.

For a thorough and excellent discussion of judicial and prosecutorial immunity, see J.M. Law, "A Tale of Two Immunities: Judicial and Prosecutorial Immunities in Canada" (1990), 28 Alta. L. Rev. 468.

For a recent discussion of judicial immunity from civil and criminal process, see Friedland, M.L. *A Place Apart: Judicial Independence and Accountability in Canada, op. cit.*, pp. 33-37. For some miscellaneous discussion of judicial life, see Kerans, Hon. Mr. Justice R.P., "Should Judges Have Study Leave?", Contact (Newsletter of the Joint National Committee on Legal Education) Fall, 1993 and Lamer, Rt. Hon. Chief Justice A., "The Criminal Law in a Changing Society: The Role of the Judge", Bulletin (National Judicial Institute), July, 1995. For an appraisal of the record of the present Sureme Court of Canada, see Beatty, D. "Order in the Supreme Court! Ad-hockery is running wild," The Globe & Mail, October 9, 1995.

In addition, readers may consult the following sources for further information on the question of judicial immunity.[208]

1. GENERAL SOURCES

Beatty, D. "Order in the Supreme Court! Ad-hockery is running wild", The Globe & Mail, October 9, 1995.

Brazier, M. "Judicial Immunity and the Independence of the Judiciary". [1976] Public Law 397.

Feldthusen, Bruce. "Judicial Immunity: In Search of an Appropriate Limiting Formula". (1980), 29 U.N.B.L.J. 73.

Gray, R.J. "Private Wrongs of Public Servants". (1959), 47 California L. Rev. 303. A good analysis of the Anglo-American jurisprudence concerning the civil liability of public officers from a historical, judicial, legislative and administrative viewpoint.

---

[207] J.M. Law, "A Tale of Two Immunities: Judicial and Prosecutorial Immunities in Canada" (1990), 28 Alta. L. Rev. 468.

[208] The author wishes to acknowledge the assistance of Professor John Law of the University of Alberta for providing these and other sources.

Halsbury's Laws of England. 4th ed. London: Butterworths, 1973. Vol. 1, paras. 206-210 and paras. 213-14, at pp. 197-203.

Jaffe, L. "Suits Against Governments and Officers — Damage Actions". (1963), 77 Harv. L. Rev. 209.

Jennings, Edward. "Tort Liability of Administrative Officers". (1936-37), 21 Minn. L. Rev. 263.

Kerans, Hon. Mr. Justice R.P., "Should Judges Have Study Leave?", Contact (Newsletter of the Joint National Committee on Legal Euca-tion) Fall, 1993.

Lamer, Rt. Hon. Chief Justice A., "The Criminal Law in a Changing Society: The Role of the Judge", Bulletin (National Judicial Institute), July, 1995.

Law, J.M. "A Tale of Two Immunities: Judicial and Prosecutorial Immunities in Canada". (1990), 28 Alta. L. Rev. 468.

Molot, Henry L. "Administrative Bodies, Economic Loss, and Tortious Liability". Chapter 12 of *Studies in Canadian Business Law*. Comprehensive analysis of characterization of function in public officer tort liability.

Rubinstein, A. *Jurisdiction and Illegality*. Oxford: Clarendon Press, 1965. Chapter VI.

Rubinstein, A. "Liability in Tort of Judicial Officers". (1963-64), 15 U.T.L.J. 317.

Sheridan, L.A. "The Protection of Justices" (1951), 14 Mod. L. Rev. 267.

Thompson, D. "Judicial Immunity and The Protection of Justices". (1958), 21 Mod. L. Rev. 517.

Wade, H.W.R. *Administrative Law*. 4th ed. Oxford: Clarendon Press, 1977. Pp. 640-43.

2. CASES

Bradley v. Fisher (1892), 80 U.S. at 649-50.

Foran v. Tatangello (1976), 14 O.R. (2d) 91, 73 D.L.R. (3d) 126 (H.C.).

Houlden v. Smith (1850), 14 Q.B. 841, 117 E.R. 323.

Lippé c. Charest (*sub nom. Lippé v. R.*) (1990), [1991] 2 S.C.R. 114, 61 C.C.C. (3d) 127.

Mackeigan v. Hickman, [1989] 2 S.C.R. 796, 72 C.R. (3d) 129, 41 Admin. L.R. 236, 99 N.R. 227n, 94 N.S.R. (2d) 1, 247 A.P.R. 1, 50 C.C.C. (3d) 449, 61 D.L.R. (4th) 688, 100 N.R. 81 (*sub nom. Mackeigan, J.A. v. Royal Comm. (Marshall Inquiry)*) (S.C.C.).

Morier v. Rivard, [1985] 2 S.C.R. 716, 23 D.L.R. (4th) 1, 64 N.R. 46, 17 Admin. L.R. 230.

Nelles v. Ontario, [1989] 2 S.C.R. 170, 69 O.R. (2d) 448n, 71 C.R. (3d)
   358, 49 C.C.L.T. 217, 35 O.A.C. 161, 37 C.P.C. (2d) 1, 98 N.R.
   321, 42 C.R.R. 1, 41 Admin. L.R. 1, 146 D.L.R. (3d) 322.

O'Connor v. Isaacs, [1956] 2 Q.B. 288, [1956] 2 All E.R. 417 (C.A.).

O'Connor v. Waldron, [1935] A.C. 76, [1935] 1 W.W.R. 1, 63 C.C.C.
   1, [1935] 1 D.L.R. 260 (P.C.).

Pierson v. Ray (1967), 87 S.C. 1213, 386 U.S. 547.

R. v. Celmaster , [1994] B.C.W.L.D. 591 (S.C.).

R. v. Valente, [1985] 2 S.C.R. 673, *(sub nom. R. v. Valente (No. 2))* 52
   O.R. (2d) 779 (headnote only), 37 M.V.R. 9 *(sub nom. Valente v.
   R.),* 49 C.R. (3d) 97, [1986] D.L.Q. 85 (headnote only), 64 N.R.
   1, 14 O.A.C. 79, 23 C.C.C. (3d) 193, 24 D.L.R. (4th) 161, 19 C.R.R.
   354.

Royal Aquarium & Summer & Winter Garden Society v. Parkinson, [1892]
   1 Q.B. 431 (C.A.).

Sirros v. Moore, [1975] Q.B. 118, [1974] 3 All E.R. 776 (C.A.).

The Marshalsea Case (1612), 10 Co. Rep. 68b, 77 E.R. 1027, 2 Brownl.
   125 (K.B.).

Unterreiner v. Wilson (1983), 41 O.R. (2d) 472, 146 D.L.R. (3d) 322
   (C.A.), affirming (1982), 40 O.R. (2d) 197, 24 C.C.L.T. 54, 142
   D.L.R. (3d) 588 (H.C.).

3. LEGISLATIVE PROVISIONS

See generally the Feldthusen article, *supra,* at pp. 88-91.[209]

Therefore, it appears that judges are exempt from civil liability for all
acts done in their official capacity but that this exemption probably does
not extend to the commission of any criminal acts. In any event, the best
protection against malfeasances on the part of judges in the course of exercising their official capacity lies in an invocation to the impeachment and
removal procedures. Realistically, impeachment and removal provide the
best method of remedying improper judicial conduct. In addition, the ultimate device in ensuring proper judicial conduct lies in the selection process. In short, the practice of preventive medicine, achieved through careful

---

[209] Although the common law provides the major source for judicial immunity, there are
statutory provisions conferring the same or similar protections, most often, with respect
to courts of inferior jurisdiction. See, for example, the Provincial Court Judges Act, S.A.
1981, c. P-20.1, s. 16(1), which confers a partial judicial immunity in respect of provincial
court judges in the province of Alberta.

refinement of the selection and appointment process, is far better than the surgical upheaval that comes with impeachment and removal.[210]

SUMMARY

Thus far, we have examined the basic foundation or substructure of the legal process in Canada. Upon that foundation, we have constructed a system which contains certain institutions. In this chapter, we have looked at the persons manning those institutions and, in particular, we have focused upon the two most important persons — the lawyer and the judge.

We are now left with a completed structure and need only to make it operational in order to correctly define the legal process in Canada. To illustrate by analogy, we have now manufactured the automobile and need only to discover the nature of the fuel that will make the vehicle operational.

With only a few remaining judges presiding to date at the provincial level without formal training in law, one can generally assume that all newly appointed judges were practising lawyers before appointment. Even this general conclusion is not without three qualifications. The first is the requirement respecting federally appointed judges that they have at least ten years' standing at the bar of any province prior to appointment. However, provincially appointed judges are not subject to this requirement. Therefore, although judges are appointed from the ranks of practising lawyers, their experience in practice will vary, depending upon the appointing authority. Secondly, and this is a fairly recent phenomenon, the federal government is appointing more academics to the bench, with practice limited, in some cases for example, to service on administrative tribunals or the conduct of arbitrations. The third point, and this too is a relatively recent phenomenon, relates to the frequency, in recent years, of vertical appointments from one bench to another. Previously, most judges, at all levels, were appointed directly from the practising bar and it was very rare to witness a vertical appointment from a lower bench to a higher one. Recently, however, this has become a fairly common practice.[211] These

---

[210] S. Fine, "Scales of justice tilt toward poser: Study of Supreme Court decisions says underdogs tend to lose", The Globe & Mail, November 6, 1993 (and the subsequent editorial "Court Favorites", The Globe & Mail, November 9, 1993); S. Fine, "Judge questions shielding of accused", The Globe & Mail, May 22, 1995; S. Fine, "Different styles on the bench", The Globe & Mail, October 25, 1993; and S. Fine, "Lamer judges critics severely", The Globe & Mail, October 14, 1994. See also Canadian Press, August 20, 1994. More recently, see " 'Judges' mandatory retirement upheld", The Globe & Mail, November 3, 1995.

[211] See, for example, The Globe & Mail, 31st March 1989. The article describes the impressive rise of a talented new Supreme Court of Canada judge who had received some five appointments, through the various judicial ranks, over an eight-year period.

qualifications aside, all newly appointed judges are persons trained and experienced in the law prior to appointment. And all lawyers, prior to engaging in the practice of the law and prior to formal training in the law, are, for the most part, ambitious young persons anxious to engage in a successful career.

There is no superhuman quality in those persons who eventually assume a judicial appointment; however, we do expect superhuman qualities in the members of the judiciary. We impose special legal and ethical constraints upon them and, at the same time, we expect them to resolve difficult disputes with the wisdom of Solomon.[212] In addition, we provide them with salaries considerably lower than those they were earning as practising members of the bar. In return, we offer them status, prestige and trust. Of these, the latter is most important. We trust them with resolving sometimes momentous issues and more often with adjudicating sensitive and emotional disputes. More important, however, we also trust them, as the ultimate arbiters, to ensure that a lawful and orderly process in resolving disputes and in determining truth replaces remedies of self-help on the streets. This same trust, to some extent, extends back to the practising lawyer. Every lawyer must not only articulate the interest of his clients to the best of his ability, but he must also act as an officer of the court, and this latter capacity provides him with a share of the trust that society reposes upon all members of the legal profession.

It is a vital feature of our liberal democratic society, in which the rule of law is supreme, that ultimate trust is placed in the legal profession to ensure that the resolution of disputes, and the search for truth, is conducted in a fair and just manner. Indeed, the imposition of this trust defines what is meant when one says that lawyers and judges occupy special positions in society. Moreover, so vital is this notion that the relationship of the legal profession, in general, and judges, in particular, to the rest of society defines an essential component of the social contract in modern society.

SELECTED BIBLIOGRAPHY

ROLE OF THE LAWYER

Abel, R.L. and P.S.C. Lewis. *Lawyers in Society*. Los Angeles: U of C Press, 1988.

Arnup, J.D. "Advocacy". (1979), 13 Gazette 27.

---

[212] See, for example, E. Didier, "Judicial Styles" (1990), 3 Bulletin of the Canadian Judicial Centre 1:6.

Arthurs, H.W., R. Weisman and F.H. Zemans. "Canadian Lawyers: A Peculiar Professionalism". In R. Abel and P. Lewis. (eds). *Lawyers in Society*, vol. 1. Berkeley: University of California Press, 1988, at p. 123.

Arthurs, H.W. "The Study of the Legal Profession in the Law School". (1970), 8 Osgoode Hall L.J. 183.

Arthurs, H.W. "Counsel, Clients and Community". (1973), 11 Osgoode Hall L.J. 437.

Arthurs, H.W., and P. Verge. "The Future of Legal Services". (1973), 51 Can. Bar Rev. 15.

Arthurs, H.W., A.M. Willms and L. Taman. "The Toronto Legal Profession: An Exploratory Survey". (1971), 21 U.T.L.J. 162.

Becker, C.A. "Professional Aristocracies and Social Change: Some Thoughts on the Profession of Law". (1974), 22 Chitty's L.J. 261.

Berlins, M. "Advocates of Incompetence". (1979), 13 Gazette 336.

Blakeney, A. "Should Lawyers Keep their Monopoly". (1973), 4 Can. Bar J. (N.S.) 2:23.

Bogart. "Immunity of Advocates From Suit". (1980), 29 U.N.B.L.J. 27.

Bork. "We Suddenly Feel that Law is Vulnerable". (1972), 6 Gazette 25.

Breitel. "Law and the Lawyers". (1981), 53 N.Y.S.B.J. 6.

Brossard. "Responsibilities of Lawyers". (1979), 13 Gazette 113.

Buchanan, D.W. "Additional Guidelines for Employment of Articling Students". (1977), 35 Advocate 250.

Canadian Bar Association. "To Practise from within: the roles, ethics, management, privileges and liabilities of corporate counsel". Ontario Continuing Legal Education, 1984.

Catzman, M.A. (1978), 56 Can. Bar Rev. 116 (case comment — *Banks v. Reid,* and *Gouzenko v. Harris*).

Christie, L.M. "The Nature of the Lawyers' Role in the Administrative Process". [1971] Lect. L.S.U.C. 1.

Cliche, R. "Lawyers in a Changing Society". (1977), 1 Can. Community Law J. 12.

Cohen, M. "Lawyers and Learning: The Professional and Intellectual Traditions". (1961), 7 McGill L.J. 181.

Cotter, W.B. *Professional Responsibility Instruction in Canada: A Coordinated Curriculum for Legal Education.* Montreal: Conceptcom, 1992.

Coutts, J.A. "The Public Profession of Law". (1963), 6 Can. Bar J. 101.

Cranor, C.F. "Legal Moralism Reconsidered". (1979), 89 Ethics 146, No. 2.

Crawford, M.G. "Too many Lawyers and many poorly trained". (1985), 12 Nat. (C.B.A.) 4:15.

Curran, B.A. "Surveying the Legal Needs of the Public: What the Public Wants and Expects in a Lawyer-Client Relationship". In D. Gibson and J.K. Baldwin (eds.). *Law in a Cynical Society? Opinion and Law in the 1980's.* Calgary: Carswell, 1985.

Davison. "Specialization . . . and Continuing Legal Education". (1980), 54 Aust. L.J. 575.

Dick, R.M. "Certification of Specialists". (1979), 37 Advocate 249.

Dickson, B. "Legal Education". (1986), 64 Can. Bar Rev. 374.

Dorsen, N. "The Role of the Lawyer in America's Ghetto Society". (1972), 6 Gazette 118.

Dussault, R. "La juriste dans la fonction publique québécoise". (1979), 39 R. du B. 30.

Erickson, P.G. "Legalistic and Traditional Role Expectations for Defence Counsel in Juvenile Court". (1975), 17 Can. J. of Criminology and Corrections 78.

Esau, A. "Specialization and the Legal Profession". (1979), 9 Man. L.J. 255.

Evershed, F.R. "Pursuing a Learned Art . . . In a Spirit of Public Service". (1962), 20 Advocate 5.

Farris, J.L. "A Look at Tomorrow". (1971), 2 Can. Bar J. (N.S.) 4:4.

Farris, J.L. "Let's Kill All the Lawyers". (1972), 3 Can. Bar J. (N.S.) 2:4.

Fera, N.M. "Negligence of Solicitors". (1977), 25 Chitty's L.J. 325.

Finkelstein, T., and R.J. Orr. "Lawyers as Businessmen See Them". (1967), 10 Can. Bar J. 243.

Finlay, J.R. "Conduct of Lawyers in the Litigious Process". (1979), Studies Civ. Proc. 15.

Finlayson, G.D. "The Legal Professional Under Attack". (1978), 12 Gazette 355.

Finlayson, G.D. "Self Government of the Legal Profession — Can it continue?" (1985), 4 Advocates' Soc. J. 1:11.

Fortier, L.Y. "The Changing Role of the Legal Profession". [1983] Cambridge Lect. 320.

Fortier, L.Y. "The Role of the Lawyer". In R.A. Abella and M.L. Rothman (eds.). *Justice Beyond Orwell.* Montreal: Les Editions Yvon Blais, 1985.

Freedman, M.H. "The Discipline and Judicial Committees". In C. Harvey (ed.). *The Law Society of Manitoba: 1877-1977*. Winnipeg: Peguis Publishers, 1977.

Fuke, J.M. "Can Tax advisers successfully serve two masters?" (1985), 118 C.A. Mag. 3:32.

Gauley, D.E. "A Lawyer and his Independence in Today's Society". (1966), 31 Sask. Bar Rev. 27.

Gill, P. "The Slice was Right when Air India Plaintiffs went Looking for Lawyers". (1986), 10 Can. Lawyer 2:6.

Gold, N. "Continuing Legal Education: A New Direction". (1975), 7 Ottawa L. Rev. 62.

Goodman, E.A."The Lawyer in Public Life". [1971] Pitblado Lect. 129.

Green, P.G. "The Pressure to Change". (1986), 10 Can. Lawyer 3:44.

Guile, R.H. "Lawyer's Lumps". (1980), 38 Advocate 477.

Haher, J.G., and B.H. Baumrin. "The moral obligations of Lawyers". (1988), 1 Can. J. of Jurisprudence 105.

Hall, E.M. "The Creative Role of the Lawyer". In *Beyond Socrates: Legal Education at Calgary. A Symposium*. Calgary: University of Calgary Faculty of Law, 1977.

Hall, E.M. "Lawyers and Canadian Criminal Law in the Seventies". (1971), 5 Gazette 24.

Hoffmann, P. *Career Handbook for Law Students 1993*. Toronto: Carswell, 1992.

Hogan. "The New Legal Scholarship: problems and prospects". (1986), 1 Can. J. of Law 35.

Honsberger, J. "Legal rules, ethical choices and professional conduct". (1987), 21 Gazette 113.

Horn, J.W. "If it ain't bust, don't fix it". (1985), 43 Advocate (Van.) 63.

Howland, W.G.C. "Old Fashioned Virtues and Legal Traditions". (1978), 12 Gazette 122.

Hunter, H.D.C. "The Law and Other Professions". (1972), 3 Can. Bar J. (N.S.) 9.

Hutchinson, A.C. "Articling", National, August/September, 1994.

Issalys, P. "The Professional Tribunal and the Conduct of Ethical Conduct Among Professions". (1978), 24 McGill L.J. 588.

Jarvis, K. "Debtors to the Profession". (1970), 4 Gazette 49.

Johnston, D.L. "Role of the Lawyer in our Society". (1979), 13 Gazette 119.

Killeen, G. "Your Future and the Future of Your Profession". (1978), 12 Gazette 213.

Klar, L. "Note on Barrister's Immunity from Suit". (1979), 7 C.C.L.T. 21.

Krever, R. "Professional Responsibility — Lawyers and Accountants". [1983] Lect. L.S.U.C. 445.

Kutak, R.J. "Coming: The New Model Rules of Professional Conduct". (1980), 66 A.B.A.J. 47.

LaForest, G.V. "Integrity in the Practice of Law". (1987), 21 Gazette 41.

Lang, O. "Lawyers in an Open Society". (1972), 3 Can. Bar J. (N.S.) 4:26.

Laskin, B. "The Interrelationship of a University Law School and the Legal Profession". (1970), 4 Gazette 210.

Laskin, B. "The Lawyer's Responsibility in the Supervision of the Legal Order". (1971), 5 Gazette 63.

Law, J.M. (ed.). *Professional Responsibility: Cases and Materials.* Faculty of Law, University of Alberta.

LeDain, G.E. "The Quest for Justice: The Role of the Profession". (1969), 19 U.N.B.L.J. 18.

Lederman, W.R. "Canadian Legal Education in the Second Half of the Twentieth Century". (1971), 21 U.T.L.J. 141.

Lewis, D.E. "The Lawyer's Image". (1964), 7 Can. Bar J. 210.

Linowitz, S.M. "The Law as a Human Profession". (1988), 22 Gazette 242.

Livesey, B. "The Tarnished Image". Canadian Lawyer, February 1995, p. 16.

Macdonald, R. St. J. *et al.* "The New Lawyer in a Transnational World". (1975), 25 U.T.L.J. 343.

MacIsaac, R.F. "The Age of Specialization". (1971), 2 Can. Bar J. (N.S.) 1:4.

Maloney, A. "Advocacy". (1978), 12 Gazette 144.

Maloney, A. "Role of the Independent Bar". [1979] Lect. L.S.U.C. 49.

Maloney, A. "The Role of the Lawyer in Society". (1979), 9 Man. L.J. 351.

Manes, R. and M. Silver. *Solicitor-Client Privilege in Canadian Law.* Markham: Butterworths, 1993.

Manning, H.W.B. "The Lawyer's Role and Other Disciplines". In *Estate Planning Seminar.* (Winnipeg: Can. Bar Assn., Manitoba Taxation Subsection, 1970).

Marshall, O.R. "Role of the Lawyer in Developing Societies". (1971), 4 Man. L.J. 392.

Martin, G.A. "The Role and Responsibility of the Defence Advocate". (1970), 12 Cr. L.Q. 376.

Martyn. "Informed Consent in the Practice of Law". (1980), 48 Geo. Wash. L. Rev. 307.

McCarthy, E.J., S.J. Shapiro and W.D. Perreault Jr. *Basic Marketing: A Global-Managerial Approach*, 7th ed. Burr Ridge, Illinois: Irwin, 1994.

McGillis, D. "Hanging Out Your Shingle". (1978), 2 Can. Lawyer 1:22.

McKelvy, E.N. "Challenge . . . Criticize . . . Question: An Address". (1973), 4 Can. Bar J. (N.S.) 4:1.

McMaster, R.J. "Law as a Profession". (1973), 31 Advocate 325.

McMurtry, R.R. "Administrative Advocacy — The Lawyer and Government". (1978), 12 Gazette 130.

McRae, D.M. "Pilot Project for the Certification of Specialists". (1977), 35 Advocate 481.

Megarry, R.E. "Problems of the Legal Profession". (1971), 5 Gazette 240.

Megarry, R.E. "Lawyers and the Public Today: Challenge and Antiphon". (1972), 5 Man. L.J. 1.

Meiselman. "Attorney Liability to Third Parties". (1981), 53 N.Y.S.B.J. 108.

Michener, D.R. "A Convocation Address". (1974), 8 Gazette 117.

Mignault, P.B. "The Law and the Legal Profession in the 21st Century". (1973), 5 Can. Bar Rev. 1.

Miller. "Advocate's Duty to Justice — Where Does it Belong?" (1981), 97 L.Q. Rev. 127.

Millman. "Counsellor Beware — Failure to Recognize Obvious Legal Trends". (1979), 27 Chitty's L.J. 279.

Minish, L. "The Contingent Fee: A Re-examination". (1979), 10 Man. L.J. 65.

Noakes, S. "Learning the Marketing Ropes". The Financial Post, July 9, 1992, p. 16.

O'Brien, B. "Role of the Legal Profession in Public Affairs". (1979), 13 Gazette 107.

O'Connor, S.D. "The Moral Role of the Lawyer". (1985), 19 Gazette 28.

O'Dea. "Lawyer-Client Relationship". (1980), 48 Geo. Wash. L. Rev. 693.

Ortved, W.N. "Why the Public Defender Won't Work". (1978), 12 Gazette 152.

Paisley, V. "Specialization, a challenge to the legal profession". (1984), 3 Advocates' Soc. J. 4:33.

Pattillo. "Reflections on the Law". (1970), 1 Can. Bar J. (N.S.) 4:7.

Pirie, A.J. "The Lawyer as Mediator: Professional Responsibility Problems, or Profession Problems?" (1985), 63 Can. Bar Rev. 378.

Pitch, H.D. "Poverty Law and the Private Law Firm: An Experiment in Judicature". (1974), 22 Chitty's L.J. 60.

Rachlin, T.H. "Criteria for Specialization". (1984), 3 Advocates' Soc. J. 1:27.

Radomski. "Actions Against Solicitors — Contract or Tort?" (1980), 2 Advocates' Q. 160.

Redmount. "Career Development and the Practice of Law". (1980), 5 J. Leg. Prof. 69.

Ribordy, F. "Legal Education and Information". Ottawa: Dept. of Justice, Communication & Public Affairs, 1986.

Robert, P. "Le secret professionnel . . .". (1979), 39 R. du B. 472.

Robins, S.L. "Our Profession and the Winds of Change". (1972), 6 Gazette 137.

Robins, S.L. "Our Profession on Trial". (1973), 7 Gazette 1.

Robinson, D. "Ethical Evolution: The Development of the Professional Conduct Handbook of the Law Society of Upper Canada". (1995), 29 No. 2, The Law Society of Upper Canada Gazette 162.

Rudyk, N. "Bringing Lawyers Closer to Legal Knowledge". (1987), 11 Can. Lawyer 3:19.

Ryan. "Acceptable Law in an Age of Dissent". (1971), 5 Gazette 73.

Saylor, G.M. " 'Ethical Dilemmas' Thoughts from Behind Closed Doors". Canadian Lawyer, Jan. 1995, p. 22.

Sgayias, D. "Liability of a Lawyer for Negligence in the Conduct of Litigation". (1978), 8 Man. L.J. 661.

Solomon. "Much pain, some shame: Calgary lawyers talk about life after the boom". (1984), 8 Can. Lawyer 3:31.

Sommers, R.J. "Liability of Solicitors When Recommending Settlement". (1978), 1 Advocates' Q. 361.

Stephenson. "A Self Governing Profession". (1984), 18 Gazette 200.

Stinton, H.P. "Errors and Omissions Insurance". (1977), 11 Gazette 249.

Syman. "The Priest and the Lawyer". (1973), 7 Gazette 272.

Taman and Zemans. "The Future of Legal Services". (1973), 5 Can. Bar Rev. 32.

Thom, S. "Independence of the Legal Profession". (1979), 13 Gazette 173.

Thurman. "Limits to the Adversary System". (1980), 5 J. Leg. Prof. 5.

Turner, J.N. "The Role of Crown Counsel in Canadian Prosecution". (1962), 40 Can. Bar Rev 439.

Turner, J.N. "Frontiers of Law and Lawyership". (1969), 12 Can. Bar J. 7.

Weiser. "Newspaperman Looks at Lawyers". (1972), 38 Man. Bar News 325.

Wilkins, R.K. "The person you're supposed to become: the politics of the law school experience". (1987), 45 U.T. Fac. L. Rev. 98.

Willis. "What I Like and What I Don't Like About Lawyers". (1970), 4 Gazette 52.

Wishart, A.A. "Law . . . The Great Profession". (1973), 7 Gazette 127.

Woodsworth, K.C. "Specialization". (1971), 29 Advocate 15.

Yarmolinsky, A. "The Role of the Lawyer in Today's City". (1970), 8 Osgoode Hall L.J. 393.

Yates, C.W. "The Lawyer in the Regulatory Process". (1980), 18 Alta. L. Rev. 70.

"About Our Colleagues in the Commonwealth". (1972), 6 Gazette 79.

"Assessment of Alternative Strategies for Increasing Access to Legal Services". (1980), 90 Yale L.J. 122.

"The Development of Law". (1962), 27 Sask. L. Rev. 26.

"Disbarred for 'Contemptible Conduct' ". Canadian Lawyer, January 1995, p. 6.

"Do You Really Want to be a Lawyer?" (1978), 32 Changing Times 45, No. 10.

"Law in the Space Age". (1962), 27 Sask. L. Rev. 10.

"Legal Imperatives". Canadian Lawyer, November 1993, p.15.

"Members have Role in Monitoring Unauthorized Practice". The Law Society of Upper Canada, The Adviser, October 1993.

"Mental or Physical Incapacity as a Bar to the Practice of Law". (1978), J. Leg. Profession 4:219.

"Parlor Legal Scholarship and Legal Education". (1985), 23 Osgoode Hall L.J. 653.

"Problems in Ethics and Advocacy: Panel Discussion". [1969] Lect. L.S.U.C. 279.

"Professionals Must Change". (1970), 4 Gazette 60.

"The Role of the Lawyer Today and How it is Changing". (1970), 9 Western Ont. L. Rev. 150.

"The Role of the Profession in the Future Environment". [1974] Lect. L.S.U.C. 339.

Selected Checklist of Materials on Specialization. (1979), 34 Record 441.

"Two Comments on A. Blakeney's Speech". (1973), 4 Can. Bar J. (N.S.) 2:27.

"The Unknown Experts: Legal specialists in Canada Today: Report of the Canadian Bar Association Special Committee on Specialization". Canadian Bar Foundation, 1983.

"The Wright Report and the Legal Profession". (1972), 6 Gazette 79.

"Women and the Law". (1992), 30 Alta. L. Rev. 3 (Special Issue).

ROLE OF THE JUDGE

Abella, R.S. "Public policy and Canada's judges: the impact of the Charter of Rights and Freedoms". (1986), 20 Gazette 217.

Abella, R.S. "Public Policy and the Judicial Role". (1989), 34 McGill Law Journal 1021.

Alpert, L., B.M. Atkins and R.C. Ziller. "Becoming a Judge: The Transition From Advocate to Arbiter". (1979), 62 Judicature 325.

"An Address of Welcome to Fauteux and Laskin". (1970), 4 Gazette 99.

Asselin, R. "Judicial Role Behaviour: A Critique and Reformulation". Ottawa: National Library of Canada (Canadian theses), 1987.

Bailey, F.L., with H. Aronson. *The Defence Never Rests* (New York: Stein and Day, 1971).

Batten, J. *In Court*. Toronto: MacMillan, 1982.

Batten, J. *Judges*. Toronto: MacMillan, 1986.

Batten, J. *Lawyers*. Toronto: MacMillan, 1980.

Beetz. "Le professeur de droit et le juge". (1979), 81 R. du N. 506.

Begue, Y., and C. Goldstein. "How Judges get into Trouble: What they need to know about developments in the law of judicial discipline (The A.B.A. Code of Judicial Conduct)". (1988), 12 Prov. Judges J. 2:8.

Berger, T. "A View from the Bench". (1974), 32 Advocate 1.

Bindman, S. "Seat of Judgment: Canada's Most Powerful Judges Toil in Virtual Anonymity". The Edmonton Journal, April 12, 1992.

Black. "Judicial Appointments — Time for a Change". [1978] N.Z.L.J. 41-42.

Black. "The Role of an Appellate Judge". [1980] N.Z.L.J. 377.

Blacksheild, A.R. "Five Types of Judicial Decisions". (1974), 12 Osgoode Hall L.J. 539.

Boughton, N. "The Hidden Danger of Judicial Burnout". (1988), 12 Can. Lawyer 3:28.

Boult, R. "Ad hoc Judges of the Supreme Court of Canada". (1978), 26 Chitty's L.J. 289.

Canadian Judges Conference. "Report to the Canadian Bar Association Report to the Mid-Winter Meeting of Council." February 1994.

Carter, R.J. "A Tribute to Mr. Justice G.A. Martin". (1988), 7 Advocates' Soc. J. 5:19.

Chayes. "Role of the Judge in Public Law Litigation". (1976), 89 Harv. L. Rev. 1281.

Centre for the Independence of Judges and Lawyers (C.I.J.L.) Bulletin, Special Issue. " The Independence of Judges and Lawyers: A Compilation of International Standards." No. 25-6, April-October 1990.

Church, T.W. "A Consumer's Prospective on the Courts". Canadian Institute for the Administration of Justice Newsletter. Vol. v, No. 2, Spring 1995.

"Code of Conduct resisted." Edmonton Journal, August 23, 1995.

Coffin, F. *The Ways of a Judge: Reflections from the Federal Appellate Bench.* Boston: Houghton, Mifflin Co., 1980.

Colvin, E. "The Executive and the Independence of the Judiciary". (1987), 11 Prov. Judges J. 229.

"Conduct code would inhibit free speech: Sopinka." The Lawyers Weekly, 15:17, September 8, 1995.

Coughlan, J.C. "Maxims and Suggestions for Criminal Trial Judges". (1972), 10 Alta. L. Rev. 347.

"Court Favorites." The Globe & Mail, May 22, 1995.

Davies, E. "The Role of the Judge in Contemporary Society". (1971), 5 Gazette 210.

Denning (Lord). *The Due Process of Law.* London: Butterworths, 1980.

Denning (Lord). *The Discipline of Law.* London: Butterworths, 1979.

De Grandpre, L.P. "From Realities to Abstractions". (1978), 9 R. Gen. 425.

Dershowitz, A.M. *The Best Defence.* New York: Random House, 1982.

Deschênes, J. "The Challenge from the Executive to the Independence of the Judiciary". [1984] Justice 277.

Deschênes, J. "Judicial Independence: A Challenge to the Executive." (1983), 7 Prov. Judges Journal 3.

Deschênes, J. "Justice et pouvoir". (1980), 11 R. Gen. 1:345.

Deschênes, J. *Maîtres Chez Eux.* Ottawa: Canadian Judicial Council, 1981.

Deschênes, J. *The Sword and the Scales (Les Plateux de la Balance).* Toronto: Butterworths, 1979.

Deschênes, J. "Toward an Independent Judiciary". [1984] Justice 239.

Deschênes, J., and C. Baar. "Administrative Independence: Concerns of the Canadian Judiciary". In F.L. Morton (ed.). *Law, Politics and the Judicial Process in Canada.* Calgary: University of Calgary Press, 1989.

Devlin, P. *The Judge*. Chicago: Univ. of Chicago Press, 1979.

Devlin (Lord). "Judges, Government and Politics". (1978), 41 Mod. L. Rev. 501.

Devlin (Lord). "Judges and Lawmakers". (1976), 39 Mod. L. Rev. 1.

Devitt. "Ten Commandments for the New Judge". (1979), 65 A.B.A.J. 574.

Dickson, The Hon. Mr. Justice B. "The Judiciary — Law Interpreters or Law-Makers". (1982), 12 Man. L.J. 1.

Dickson, B. "Role and Function". (1980), 14 Gazette 138.

Dickson, B. "The Rule of Law: Judicial Independence and Separation of Powers". (1985), 9 Prov. Judges J. 3:4.

Dion, L. "Du social, du politique et du judiciare — Pour l'autonomie du judiciare". (1978), 38 R. du B. 769.

Douglas, W.O. *The Autobiography of William O. Douglas: Go East Young Man*. New York: Random House, 1974.

Douglas, W.O. *The Autobiography of William O. Douglas: The Court Years: 1939-1975*. New York: Random House, 1980.

Eberts, M. "Gender Issues in the Legal Profession: A Synopsis of the C.B.A. Gender Equality Task Force Report." (1993), 72 Can. Bar Review 3.

Edwards, H.T. "Regulating Judicial Misconduct and Divining Good Behaviour For Federal Judges". (1989), 87 Mich. L. Rev. 765.

Esson, W.A. "The Judiciary and Freedom of Expression". (1985), 23 U.W.O.L. Rev. 159.

Estey, W.M. "The Changing Role of the Judiciary". [1983] Cambridge Lect. 329.

Feldthusen, B. "Judicial Immunity: In Search of an Appropriate Limiting Formula". (1980), 29 U.N.B. L.J. 73.

Felky, M. "The Berger Affair and the Independence of the Judiciary". (1984), 42 U.T. Fac. L. Rev. 118.

Fine, S. "Different styles on the bench". The Globe & Mail, October 14, 1994.

Fine, S. "Judge questions shielding of accused". The Globe & Mail, May 22, 1995,

Fine, S. "Scales of justice tilt toward poser: Study of Supreme Court decisions says underdogs tend to lose". The Globe & Mail, November 6, 1993.

Fine, S. "Should Judges Make own Inquiries". The Globe & Mail, February 10, 1995.

Finlayson, G. "The Judiciary in Canada — Essentials of Independence". (1986), 5 Advocates' Soc. J. 3.

Fitzpatrick, C.T. "Misconduct and Disability of Federal Judges: The Unreported Informal Responses". (1988), 71 Judicature 282.

Fango, V.E., and C.R. Ducat. "What Difference does Method of Judicial Selection Make?" (1979), 5 The Justice System J. 25.

Frank. *Courts on Trial*. Princeton: Princeton Univ. Press, 1949.

Franks, M.R., and R.R. Kenner. "A Proposal for a Saner Judiciary". (1977), 1 Leg. Med. Q. 264.

Friedland, M. *A Place Apart: Judicial Independence and Accountability in Canada*. Ottawa: Canadian Judicial Council, 1995.

Freedman, S. "Judges and the Law". (1962), 5 Can. Bar J. 208.

Gibson, D. "Judges as Legislators: Not Whether But How". (1987), 25 Alta. L. Rev. 249.

Gleeson. "Judging the Judges". (1979), 53 Aust. L.J. 338.

Glube. "The Role of the Judge". In R.A. Abella and M.L. Rothman (eds.). *Justice Beyond Orwell*. Montreal: Les Editions Yvon Blais, 1985. P. 481.

Griffith, J. *The Politics of the Judiciary*. Manchester: Manchester University Press, 1977.

Griffith, J. *The Politics of the Judiciary*. Glasgow: Wm. Collins Sons and Co. Ltd., 1977.

Hailsham (Lord). "Democracy and Judicial Independence". (1979), 28 U.N.B.L.J. 7.

Haines, E.L. "The Judge's Role in a Changing Society". (1976), 10 Gazette 103.

Hall, E.M. "Law Reform and the Judiciary's Role". (1972), 20 Chitty's L.J. 77.

Hansard, H. "Election versus Selection of Judges". (1967), 15 Chitty's L.J. 253.

Hansard, H. "Judicial Interference" (Editorial). (1970), 18 Chitty's L.J. 71.

Henderson, G.F. "The Independence of the Judiciary". (1980), 14 Gazette 236.

Higgins and Rubin. "Judicial Discretion". (1980), 9 J. Leg. Stud. 129.

Johnson, S.D. "Judge's Conduct: Judicial Ethics". (1979), Tex. Bar J. 42:211.

Joseph, G.S. "Advocate One Day — an Arbiter the Next". (1976), 24 Chitty's L.J. 187.

"Judges' mandatory retirement upheld." The Globe & Mail, November 3, 1995.

"Judicial Misconduct in California". (1983), 11 San Fernando Valley L. Rev. 43.

Kaminsky, M.I. "Available Compromises for Continued Judicial Selection Reform". (1979), 53 St. John's L. Rev. 466.

Kopstein, R.L. "The Thought of One Judge". In D. Gibson and J.K. Baldwin (eds.). *Law in a Cynical Society? Opinion and Law in the 1980s*. Calgary: Carswell, 1985.

Kritzer, H.M. "Federal judges and their political environments: the influence of public opinion". (1979), 23 Amer. J. of Political Science 194.

Kosowan, C.A. "The Independence of the Judiciary". (1987), 11 Prov. Judges J. 15.

Kroll, G.R. "Should There be a Right to Challenge Judges?" (1977), 35 Advocate 411.

La Forest, G.V. "Some Impressions on Judging". (1986), 35 U.N.B.L.J. 145.

Lamer P.C., Rt. Hon. A. "Remarks to the Conference 'Open Justice', Canadian Institute for the Administration of Justice, Ottawa, Canada, October 13, 1994.

Lang, O. "Judicial Appointments". (1974), 8 Gazette 121.

Laskin, B. "A Judge and His Constituencies". (1976), 7 Man. L.J. 1.

Laskin, B. "Judicial Integrity and the Supreme Court of Canada". (1978), 12 Gazette 116.

Laskin, B. "The Judge and Due Process". (1972), 1 Man. L.J. 235.

Laskin, B. "The Common Tie Between Judges and Law Teachers". (1972), 6 Gazette 147.

Laskin, B. "The Supreme Court of Canada". (1974), 8 Gazette 248.

Law Society of Alberta. "Women and the Legal Profession in Alberta: Highlights of the Survey of Active Members". 1992.

Le Clercq, F.S. "The Constitutional Policy that Judges be Learned in the Law (U.S.)". (1980), 47 Tenn. L. Rev. 689.

Lederman, W.R. "Democratic Parliaments, independent courts and the Canadian Charter of Rights and Freedoms". (1985), 11 Queen's L.J. 1.

Lederman, W.R. "Judicial Independence and the Court Reforms in Canada for the 1990s". (1988), 12 Queen's L.J. 385.

Linden, A. (ed.). *The Canadian Judiciary*. Toronto: Osgoode Hall Law School, 1976.

Markey, H.T. "Needed: A Judicial Welcome for Technology: Star Wars or Stare Decisis?" (1978), 50 N.Y.S.B.J. 380.

Martin, R. "An Open Legal System". (1985), 23 U.W.O.L. Rev. 169.

McCormick, P. "Judicial Councils for Provincial Judges in Canada." (1986), 6 Windsor Yearbook of Access to Justice 60.

McCormick, P. and I. Greene. *Judges and Judging*. Toronto: James Lorimer & Co., 1990.

Megarry, R.E. "Judges and the Public". [1983] Cambridge Lect. 60.

Megarry, R.E. "The Anatomy of Judicial Appointment: Change but Not Decay". (1985), 19 U.B.C.L. Rev. 113.

Morton, F.L. (ed.). *Law, Politics and the Judicial Process in Canada*. Calgary: University of Calgary Press, 1989.

Murphy, B. *The Brandeis/Frankfurter Connection: The Secret Political Activities of Two Supreme Court Judges*. New York: Oxford University Press, 1982.

Neely, R. *How Courts Govern America*. New Haven: Yale University Press, 1981.

Nemetz, N.T. "The Concept of the Independent Judiciary". (1986), 20 U.B.C. L. Rev. 285.

A New Judicial Appointments Process. Ottawa: Dept. of Justice Canada, 1988.

Perkins, C.E. "The Extra-judicial Role". (1979), 3 Prov. Judges J. 3:12.

Pigeon, L.P. "The Human Element in the Judicial Process". (1970), 8 Alta. L. Rev. 301.

Rivet, M. "The Friedland Report." (1995), Vol. v, No. 4, C.I.A.J. Bulletin 2.

Robins, S.L. "The Role of the Independent Judiciary". [1979] Lect. L.S.U.C. 23.

Robins, S.L. "Report of the Commission of Inquiry into the Conduct of Provincial Judge Harry J. Williams". (1978), 12 Gazette 161.

Russell. "Overcoming Legal Formalism: The Treatment of the Constitution, the Courts and Judicial Behaviour in Canadian Political Science". (1986), 1 Can. J. of Law 5.

Saltzburg, S.A. "Unnecessarily Expanding Role of the American Trial Judge". (1978), 64 Va. L. Rev. 1.

Schmeiser, D.A. "Common Sense and the Law". (1961), 26 Sask. Bar Rev. 101.

Schmitthoff, C.M. "Denning and the Contemporary Scene". (1974), 6 Man. L.J. 11.

Schwarzer, W.W. "Dealing with Incompetent Counsel — the Trial Judge's Role". (1980), 93 Harv. L. Rev. 633.

Shetreet, S. "Justice in Israel: A study of the Israeli Judiciary". Jerusalem: University of Jerusalem, 1993.

Silverman, H.W. "It's About Time: Study of the Judiciary". (1977), 25 Chitty's L.J. 19.

Silverman, H.W. "The Trial Judge: Pilot, Participant, or Umpire?" (1973), 11 Alta. L. Rev. 40.

Simpson, J. *Spoils of Power: The Politics of Patronage.* Toronto: Collins, 1988.

Slatter, R. "Quality of a Judge's Experience". (1979), 65 A.B.A.J. 933.

Slotnick, E.E. "Federal Judicial Selection". (1979), 62 Judicature 465.

Southin, M.F. "Lord Denning". (1970), 5 U.B.C. L. Rev. 1.

"Symposium on Appointment, Discipline and Removal of Judges". (1973), 11 Alta. L. Rev. 279.

"The Qualities of a Good Judge". (1962), 34 Man. Bar News 61.

Steel, J.B.B. "The Judge as Law Reformer". (1979), 3 Auckland Univ. L. Rev. 443.

Sturgess, G., and P. Chubb. *Judging the World: Law and Politics in the World's Leading Courts.* Sydney: Butterworths, 1988.

Swayze, C. *Hard Choices: The Life of Tom Berger.* Vancouver: Douglas & McIntyre, 1987.

"Symposium on judicial discipline and impeachment". (1987-88), 76 Kentucky L. J. 633.

Thom, S. "Judge and Company". (1974), 8 Gazette 237.

Tollefson, E.A. "The System of Judicial Appointments: A Collateral Issue". (1971), 21 U.T.L.J. 162.

"Top judge lukewarm to report cards for justices". The Edmonton Journal, August 20, 1995.

Tribe, L.H. "Trying California's Judges on Television: Open Government or Judicial Intimidation?" (1979), 65 A.B.A.J. 1175.

"U.S.-style scrutiny for a U.S.-style court". Alberta Report, September 11, 1995.

Vandor. "The Appointment of Judges in Canada". (1986), 7 Advocates' Q. 129.

Vaze, V. "Can Judges Be Law-makers?" (1978), 20 Journal of the Indian Law Institute 117.

Weiler, P. "Legal Values and Judicial Decision Making". (1970), 48 Can. Bar Rev. 1.

"Whither the Supreme Court of Canada?" (Editorial). (1973), 21 Chitty's L.J. 77.

Wilson, B. "Decision Making in the Supreme Court". (1986), 36 U.T.L.J. 227.

Wishman, S. *Confessions of a Criminal Lawyer*. New York: Times Books, 1981.

Woodward and Armstrong. *The Brethren: Inside the Supreme Court*. New York: Simon and Schuster, 1979.

LEGAL EDUCATION

Arthurs, H.W. "Paradoxes of Canadian Legal Education". (1977), 3 Dal. L.J. 639.

Barnes, J. "The Department of Law, Carleton Univ., Ottawa". (1977), 3 Dal. L.J. 814.

Campbell, S. "Toward an Improved Legal Education". (1978), 43 Sask. L. Rev. 81.

Consultative Group on Research and Education in Law. "Law and Learning". A Report to the Social Sciences and Humanities Research Council of Canada. Ottawa: April 1983.

Cooke, Dr. B.F., and J.P. Taylor. "Developing Personal Awareness and Examining Values: Inter-connected Dimensions of Supervision in Clinical Legal Education". (1978), 12 U.B.C.L. Rev. 276.

"Directory of Public Legal Education Services". (1973), 3 Can. Community L.J. 69.

Fraser, F.M. "The Faculty of Law at the University of Victoria". (1977), 3 Dal. L.J. 828.

Fraser, F.M. "Recent Development in Legal Education — the Victoria Experience". (1979), 13 U.B.C.L. Rev. 221.

Fraser, J. "Legal Research". (1980), 38 Advocate 373.

Foote, C. "On Completion of a Legal Education". (1978), 12 Gazette 377.

Gold, N. "Legal Education, Law and Justice: The Clinical Experience". (1979), 44 Sask. L. Rev. 97.

Janishce, H.N. "Law & Continuing Education: The Dalhousie Experience". (1977), 55 Can. Bar Rev. 57.

Johnston, D.L. "Report on Legal Education in the Maritimes — Why Not a National Study?" (1977), 11 Gazette 262.

Laskin, B. "The Interrelationship of a University Law School and the Legal Profession". (1970), 4 Gazette 210.

Lederman, W.R. "Canadian Legal Education in the Second Half of the Twentieth Century". (1971), 21 U.T.L.J. 141.

London, J.R. "Perspective on Legal Education and Admission to Practice in Manitoba". (1978), 8 Man. L.J. 553.

MacDonald, R.A. "Law Schools and Public Legal Education: The Community Law Programme at Windsor". (1979), 5 Dal. L.J. 779.

Macdonald. "Legal Education on the Threshold of the 1980's: Whatever Happened to the Great Ideas of the 60's". (1979), 44 Sask. L. Rev. 39.

Maczko, F. "The University of British Columbia Clinical Program". (1978), 36 Advocate 541.

Mazer, B.M. "Directory of Law-related Educational Activities — an Analysis". (1978), 2 Can. Community L.J. 74.

"Public Legal Education". (1979), 44 Sask. L. Rev. 123 at 131.

Trakman, L.E. "Canadian Law Schools". (1980), 6 Dal. L.J. 303.

Veitch, E. "The Vocation of our Era for Legal Education". (1979), 44 Sask. L. Rev. 21.

Woodsworth, K.C. "What's on in Continuing Legal Education?" (1978), 36 Advocate 35.

Zemans, F.H. "Articling: A Law School Perspective". (1988), 22 Gazette 382.

Chapter 10

THE DOCTRINES OF PRECEDENT AND STARE DECISIS

INTRODUCTION

The day-to-day role of the judge in the Canadian legal system might be described as falling somewhere along a spectrum, the poles of which reflect the two opposing perceptions of a judge's function: to exercise a "quasi-legislative" role in judicial decision-making or to exercise an essentially interpretative function. The former is often described as an activist role on the part of the judiciary, where judges resolve particular matters, not in isolation, but rather in the context of social, economic and other considerations, and render decisions in such a way as to permit the law to respond to changing social conditions. Although, of course, the legislative function in Canada resides, at the federal level, in the two houses of Parliament, and at the provincial level in the various provincial legislatures, this activist notion of the judicial function suggests that the law can and should be responsive to changing times, and that this responsiveness should be effected, not only by legislative enactments, but also by judicial decisions rendered in courts of law. Those who favour this view often point to the decisions of the eminent Lord Denning in the United Kingdom and to the decisions of the Supreme Court of the United States when it was led by Chief Justice Earl Warren as two modern examples of judges exercising the judicial function according to this model.

In contrast to this model of judicial activism is the view of many judges that their role is merely interpretative: to strictly apply the law to particular facts and decide cases accordingly. Under this model, a judge is bound by precedent cases and has no discretion to modify the law in response to changing social conditions and prevailing attitudes. This view of the judicial function has been referred to, at least in respect of constitutional cases in the United States, as a strict constructionist view of the judicial function.

It is important to realize that the above definitions of the judicial function represent the extreme poles of the spectrum. Undoubtedly, most judges view their role as falling somewhere between these extremes. As a general rule, the typical judge views his role as essentially an interpretative one, tempered, however, by the dictates of justice and fairness, together with the realization that the law, in order to gain public acceptance and credibility, must not be applied without reference to changing social conditions. However, there are limits to which a judge in deciding cases may respond to changing social conditions, limits which are defined by the dictates of certainty, predictability and consistency, and an appreciation as to where, in our system, the legislative function must properly reside.

However, to some extent, the "activist" model has been legitimized and, indeed, may become the norm as a result of the enactment of the Canadian Charter of Rights and Freedoms. The Charter clearly transfers power from Parliament and the legislatures to the constitution as the ultimate standard against which the content of all legislation must be measured. Indirectly, it is also a transfer of power from the legislative arm of government to the judiciary, for it is the judges who have the responsibility of interpreting the constitution. Since this represents somewhat of a departure from our tradition of Parliamentary supremacy, it becomes important that our judiciary come to accept its new role. This departure, however, is somewhat tempered by the presence of both s. 1 of the Charter, the so-called "limitations clause" and s. 33, the "notwithstanding" or "non obstante" clause. The latter permits Parliament or a legislature to make legislation immune from the application of the Charter for a certain period of time. In essence, it allows those legislative bodies to opt out of certain sections of the Charter in respect of its application to given pieces of legislation.

In assessing the model of judicial decision-making that is appropriate for a particular judge, one of the key factors is how he or she regards the doctrines of precedent and stare decisis. Are they rules of law, conventions or customs now enshrined within the law, judicial attitudes, or otherwise? The characterization of these doctrines is, of course, important in defining the scope of a judge's "law-making" role.

Accordingly, this chapter will focus upon these doctrines and, through reference to the writings of legal scholars and decisions rendered in particular cases and the results of a 1976 survey of judicial attitudes, attempt to characterize these two important doctrines. Although precedent and stare decisis will be defined separately, it is artificial to consider them apart from each other, as they both form an integral part of the judicial decision-making process.

Essentially, precedent is the doctrine that requires a judge, in resolving a particular case, to follow the decision in a previous case, where the fact situations in the two cases are similar. Of course, no fact situations are ever absolutely identical. A judge may avoid the theoretical constraints imposed upon him by the doctrine of precedent by utilizing a process called "distinguishing". This permits a judge to exercise some flexibility and perhaps even creativity. Nevertheless, there may be many past cases with similar fact situations dealing with the same particular legal problem which require a judge to decide which precedent case to follow. This is particularly important when, in dealing with the same set of facts, different judges have rendered different decisions in law. In order to resolve this problem, the doctrine of stare decisis requires that a judge of a particular court must follow the previous decision of the highest court within that particular provincial jurisdiction, although he may be persuaded to differing extents by co-ordinate and higher courts outside this provincial jurisdiction. Of course, all courts in Canada are bound by the highest court in the land, the Supreme Court of Canada.

THE OPERATION OF STARE DECISIS

The operation of the doctrine of stare decisis is best explained by reference to the English translation of the Latin phrase. "Stare decisis" literally translates as "to stand by decided matters". The phrase "stare decisis" is itself an abbreviation of the Latin phrase "stare decisis et non quieta movere" which translates as "to stand by decisions and not to disturb settled matters".

Basically, under the doctrine of stare decisis, the decision of a higher court within the same jurisdiction acts as binding authority on a lower court within that same jurisdiction. The decision of a court of another jurisdiction only acts as persuasive authority. The degree of persuasiveness is dependent upon various factors, including, first, the nature of the other jurisdiction. Is the other jurisdiction a Canadian one, and if so, is it one of the nine common law jurisdictions in Canada? If the other jurisdiction is non-domestic, is it a Commonwealth jurisdiction? In short, one must determine whether there is a common legal tradition between a given jurisdiction and a foreign jurisdiction in order to determine the degree of persuasiveness to be attached to decisions rendered in that foreign jurisdiction. Second, the degree of persuasiveness is dependent upon the level of court which decided the precedent case in the other jurisdiction. The decision of the highest court that has already dealt with the particular matter would be the most persuasive. Other factors include the date of the precedent case, on the assumption that the more recent the case, the more reliable it will be as authority for a given proposition, although this is not necessarily so. Also, on some occasions, the judge's reputation may affect the degree of persuasiveness of the authority.

There is another issue. Consider, for example, some recent prosecutions under Canada's hate propaganda law.

In *R. v. Keegstra*,[1] the Alberta Court of Appeal struck down s. 281.2(3)(*a*) of the Criminal Code, prohibiting the dissemination of hate literature, as being unconstitutional. In *R. v. Andrews*,[2] the Ontario Court of Appeal upheld the constitutionality of the same provision. In reaching its decision, the Ontario Court of Appeal had the benefit of the Alberta decision, but chose not to follow it, thus demonstrating that courts of coordinate jurisdiction in different provinces are not bound to follow each other, even in applying the national constitution to a federal statute. This has resulted in a situation whereby for a time there was one rule in Alberta and one in Ontario relating to the same issue, the constitutionality of s. 281.2(3)(*a*) of the Criminal Code. A court in a third province, faced with the same issue, could have been persuaded to follow one decision or the other, according to the factors outlined in the preceding paragraph, or could have chosen to follow neither decision and formulate its own rule. This example also serves to illustrate the importance of the Supreme Court of Canada as final arbiter of interjurisdictional differences of legal opinion, as clearly, in the criminal law at least, where national uniformity is considered desirable, it is undesirable to have opposing rules in different parts of the country. The Supreme Court of Canada heard the *Keegstra* and *Andrews* appeals in December 1989 and has not, at the time of writing, issued its judgments.

In order to explain in more detail the operation of the doctrine of stare decisis, there are five charts set out below which diagrammatically demonstrate how the doctrine operates, as it applies to each of the provincial courts in a given province and as it applies to the Supreme Court of Canada.

In examining each of the following five charts, note:

1. The degree of persuasiveness, described in the following charts, is in some cases speculative and will vary with the circumstances.

2. The binding or persuasive nature of past decisions and of collegial decisions of the same court within a given jurisdiction, as well as past and

[1] [1990] 3 S.C.R. 697, 72 Alta. L.R. (2d) 193, 1 C.R. (4th) 129, [1991] 2 W.W.R. 1, 114 N.R. 81, 61 C.C.C. (3d) 1, 3 C.R.R. (2d) 193, 117 N.R. 1.
[2] [1990] 3 S.C.R. 870, 75 O.R. (2d) 481, 1 C.R. (4th) 266, 61 C.C.C. (3d) 490, 3 C.R.R. (2d) 176, 77 D.L.R. (4th) 128, 117 N.R. 284, 47 O.A.C. 293.

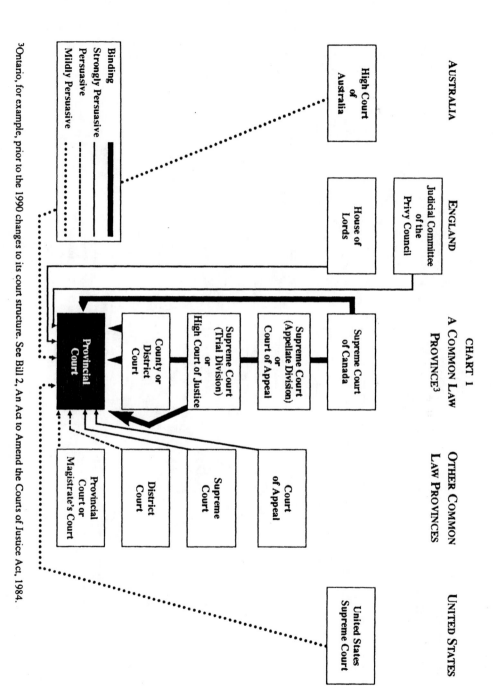

CHART 1

AUSTRALIA

ENGLAND

A COMMON LAW PROVINCE³

OTHER COMMON LAW PROVINCES

UNITED STATES

High Court of Australia

Judicial Committee of the Privy Council

House of Lords

Supreme Court of Canada

Supreme Court (Appellate Division) or Court of Appeal

Supreme Court (Trial Division) or High Court of Justice

County or District Court

Provincial Court

Court of Appeal

Supreme Court

District Court

Provincial Court or Magistrate's Court

United States Supreme Court

Binding
Strongly Persuasive
Persuasive
Mildly Persuasive

³Ontario, for example, prior to the 1990 changes to its court structure. See Bill 2, An Act to Amend the Courts of Justice Act, 1984.

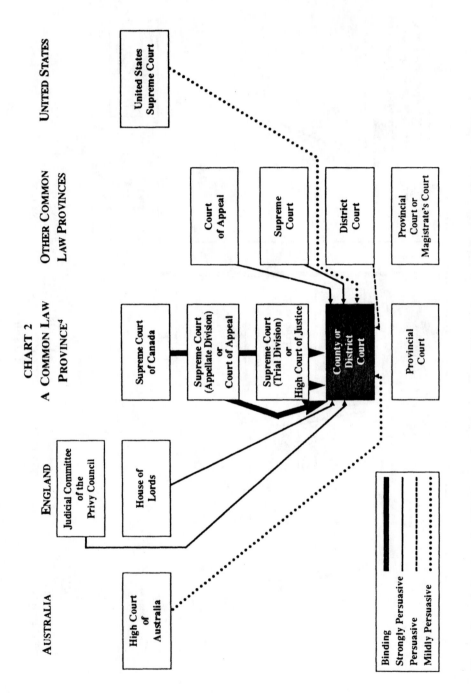

CHART 2
A COMMON LAW PROVINCE[4]

AUSTRALIA | ENGLAND | A COMMON LAW PROVINCE | OTHER COMMON LAW PROVINCES | UNITED STATES

High Court of Australia

Judicial Committee of the Privy Council

House of Lords

Supreme Court of Canada

Supreme Court (Appellate Division) or Court of Appeal

Supreme Court (Trial Division) or High Court of Justice

County or District Court

Provincial Court

Court of Appeal

Supreme Court

District Court

Provincial Court or Magistrate's Court

United States Supreme Court

Binding
Strongly Persuasive
Persuasive
Mildly Persuasive

[4]Ontario, for example, prior to the 1990 changes to its court structure. See Bill 2, An Act to Amend the Courts of Justice Act, 1984.

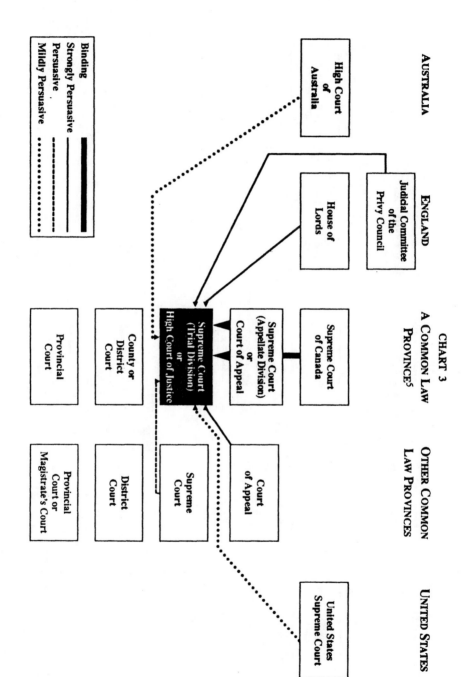

CHART 3

AUSTRALIA ENGLAND A COMMON LAW PROVINCES[5] OTHER COMMON LAW PROVINCES UNITED STATES

High Court of Australia

Judicial Committee of the Privy Council

House of Lords

Supreme Court (Trial Division) or High Court of Justice

Supreme Court (Appellate Division) or Court of Appeal

Supreme Court of Canada

County or District Court

Provincial Court

Court of Appeal

Supreme Court

District Court

Provincial Court or Magistrate's Court

United States Supreme Court

Binding
Strongly Persuasive
Persuasive
Mildly Persuasive

[5] Ontario, for example, prior to the 1990 changes to its court structure. See Bill 2, An Act to Amend the Courts of Justice Act, 1984.

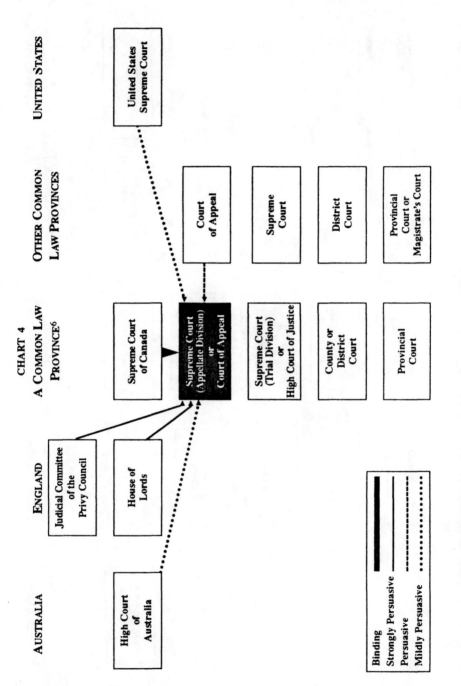

CHART 4

6Ontario, for example, prior to the 1990 changes to its court structure. See Bill 2, An Act to Amend the Courts of Justice Act, 1984.

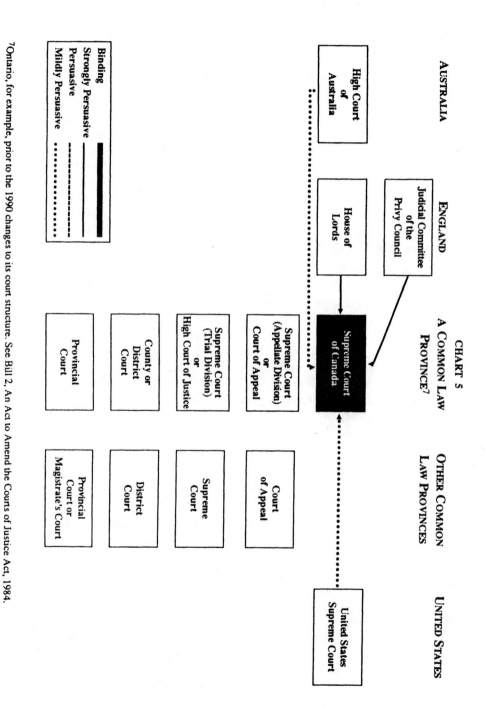

CHART 5

| AUSTRALIA | ENGLAND | A COMMON LAW PROVINCE[7] | OTHER COMMON LAW PROVINCES | UNITED STATES |

High Court of Australia

Judicial Committee of the Privy Council

House of Lords

Supreme Court of Canada

Supreme Court (Appellate Division) or Court of Appeal

Supreme Court (Trial Division) or High Court of Justice

County or District Court

Provincial Court

Court of Appeal

Supreme Court

District Court

Provincial Court or Magistrate's Court

United States Supreme Court

Binding
Strongly Persuasive
Persuasive
Mildly Persuasive

[7]Ontario, for example, prior to the 1990 changes to its court structure. See Bill 2, An Act to Amend the Courts of Justice Act, 1984.

collegial decisions of the Supreme Court of Canada, is not indicated in the following charts but is discussed elsewhere in this chapter.

A COMMENTARY ON THE OPERATION OF STARE DECISIS

This discussion will address four issues.[3] The first relates to the area of uncertainty as to whether the highest court within a given jurisdiction is bound by its past decisions. The second issue arises by virtue of an amendment to the Supreme Court Act in 1949, whereby all appeals to the Judicial Committee of the Privy Council in both civil and criminal matters were abolished. We are left with the residual question as to whether Canadian courts are bound by pre-1949 decisions of the Privy Council. The third issue concerns various aspects of the operation of the doctrine of stare decisis, and the fourth concerns the purposes, advantages and disadvantages of the doctrine of stare decisis.

Are the highest courts in the provinces and the Supreme Court of Canada bound by their own previous decisions? Can they reverse themselves in subsequent decisions? There is judicial authority in the following provinces supporting the proposition that the provincial court of appeal does have the power to overrule its previous decisions: Alberta, British Columbia,[4] Saskatchewan, Manitoba, New Brunswick, Prince Edward Island and Newfoundland. The Quebec Court of Appeal, however, in the tradition of the civil law system, has not committed itself to adhere to the doctrines of precedent and stare decisis and thus decisions of the highest court in that province are not binding, although they are, de facto, highly persuasive. The Ontario Court of Appeal has stated that it is bound by

---

[3] In the preparation of the second edition of this volume, the author is indebted to Dr. W. F. Bowker, the former Dean of Law at the University of Alberta and the Founding Director of the Alberta Institute of Law Research and Reform, who has taken an interest in this topic and who has kindly provided me with many cases, old and new, which serve to elucidate the many issues.

[4] See, for example, in B.C., *R. v. Jun*, [1938] 2 W.W.R. 274 (see corrigenda, p. iii), [1940] 2 W.W.R. 467, 54 B.C.R. 541, 73 C.C.C. 289, [1940] 2 D.L.R. 432 (*sub nom. Ex parte Yuen Yick Jun*) (C.A.); *Bell v. Klein (No. 1)*, 12 W.W.R. (N.S.) 272, [1954] 4 D.L.R. 273 (B.C. C.A.), reversed [1955] S.C.R. 309, [1955] 2 D.L.R. 513; and *R. v. Haas* (1962), 38 C.R. 154, 39 W.W.R. 224, 132 C.C.C. 362, 35 D.L.R. (2d) 172 (B.C. C.A.). The British Columbia Court of Appeal, however, has stated, in *Bell v. Cessna Aircraft Co.*, [1983] 6 W.W.R. 178, 46 B.C.L.R. 145, 36 C.P.C. 115, 149 D.L.R. (3d) 509 (C.A.), that a court of appeal is bound by its previous decisions unless it would be manifestly wrong or unjust not to overrule the earlier decision, and should do so only if a five-member court is sitting. See also the cases of *R. v. Armstrong* (1988), 45 C.C.C. (3d) 285 (B.C.C.A.) and *Betts v. Sanderson Estate*, [1989] 2 W.W.R. 113, 31 B.C.L.R. (2d) 1, 44 C.C.L.T. 97, 11 M.V.R. (2d) 146, 53 D.L.R. (4th) 675 (C.A.), leave to appeal to S.C.C. refused, 36 B.C.L.R. (2d) xxxvi (note), [1989] 3 W.W.R. lxx (note), 55 D.L.R. (4th) vii (note), 101 N.R. 232n (S.C.C.). In the latter case, three judges of the Court of Appeal felt they were bound by a previous decision of their court unless that decision was made per incuriam or was clearly wrongly decided.

its previous decisions, unless those decisions were decided per incuriam. The Nova Scotia Court of Appeal has been silent to date.

As to whether the Supreme Court of Canada is bound by its previous decisions, the leading case is *Stuart v. Bank of Montreal* (1909), 41 S.C.R. 516, which held that the Supreme Court of Canada is, in law, bound by its previous decisions. However, since that time, there has been strong suggestion that either the Supreme Court is not now bound by its previous decisions, or that in future, the Supreme Court will not likely regard itself as being bound by its previous decisions. This suggestion arises out of several developments. First, as indicated above, in 1949 the Supreme Court of Canada became the final court of appeal in all criminal and civil cases by virtue of an amendment to the Supreme Court Act abolishing all appeals to the Judicial Committee of the Privy Council. Secondly, in 1966 the House of Lords issued a Practice Statement to the effect that it was no longer bound by its previous decisions. This Practice Statement must certainly have had a strongly persuasive effect on the attitude of the Supreme Court of Canada. It is set out as follows:

> Their Lordships regard the use of precedent as an indispensable foundation upon which to decide what is the law and its application to individual cases. It provides at least some degree of certainty upon which individuals can rely in the conduct of their affairs, as well as a basis for orderly development of legal rules.
>
> Their Lordships nevertheless recognize that too rigid adherence to precedent may lead to injustice in a particular case and also unduly restrict the proper development of the law. They propose, therefore, to modify their present practice and, while treating former decisions of this House as normally binding, to depart from a previous decision when it appears right to do so.
>
> In this connection they will bear in mind the danger of disturbing retrospectively the basis on which contracts, settlements of property and fiscal arrangement have been entered into and also the special need for certainty as to the criminal law.
>
> This announcement is not intended to affect the use of precedent elsewhere than in this House.[5]

Thirdly, there have been several cases in which the Supreme Court of Canada has suggested, mostly in obiter, that a similar position will at some time be taken by the Supreme Court of Canada. For example, in the case of *R. v. George*, [1966] S.C.R. 267 at 278, 47 C.R. 382, [1966] 3 C.C.C. 137, 55 D.L.R. (2d) 386, Mr. Justice Cartwright (as he then was) stated in dissent as follows:

> I do not propose to enter on the question, which since 1949 has been raised from time to time by authors, whether this Court now that it has become the final Court of Appeal for Canada is, as in the case of the House of Lords, bound by its own previous decisions of law or whether as, in the case of the Judicial Committee or the Supreme Court of the United States, it is free under certain circumstances to reconsider them.

---

[5] Practice Statement (Judicial Precedent), [1966] 1 W.L.R. 1234.

Then, in the case of *Binus v. R.,* [1967] S.C.R. 594 at 601, 2 C.R.N.S. 118, [1968] 1 C.C.C. 227, Mr. Justice Cartwright expanded on his earlier remarks:

> I do not doubt the power of this Court to depart from a previous judgment of its own but, where the earlier decision has not been made *per incuriam*, and especially in cases in which Parliament or the Legislature is free to alter the law on the point decided, I think that such a departure should be made only for compelling reasons.

More recently, in the case of *Canada (Minister of Indian Affairs & Northern Development v. Ranville,* [1982] 2 S.C.R. 518, 139 D.L.R. (3d) 1, [1983] 1 C.N.L.R. 12, [1983] R.D.J. 16, 44 N.R. 616, Mr. Justice Ritchie reiterated Mr. Justice Cartwright's remarks from *Binus.* He stated, at p. 528, that

> the principle of *stare decisis* remains an important consideration in this Court even though it has announced its willingness to overturn a prior decision.

However, Mr. Justice Dickson also stated that, in the instant case,

> adherence to the *stare decisis* doctrine would generate more uncertainty than certainty.

In the case of *Harrison v. Carswell,* [1976] 2 S.C.R. 200, [1975] 6 W.W.R. 673, 25 C.C.C. (2d) 186, 62 D.L.R. (3d) 68, 75 C.L.L.C. 14,286, 5 N.R. 523, Chief Justice Laskin stated in dissent, and probably as obiter dictum, that an issue in the case was "whether this Court must pay mechanical deference to stare decisis". He then proceeded to expand on this issue and stated as follows at p. 683:

> This Court, above all others in this country, cannot be simply mechanistic about previous decisions, whatever be the respect it would pay to such decisions. What we would be doing here, if we were to say that *Regina v. Peters* (1971), 17 D.L.R. (3d) 128n (Can.)., because it was so recently decided, has concluded the present case for us, would be to take merely one side of a debatable issue and say that it concludes the debate without the need to hear the other side.
>
> I do not have to call upon pronouncements of members of this Court that we are free to depart from previous decisions in order to support the pressing need to examine the present case on its merits . . . But above all, this Court has not shown itself to be timorous in tackling important issues where it could be said, with some justification, that an important consideration was absent from an earlier judgment, even a recent one, upon which reliance was placed to foreclose examination of a similar issue in a subsequent case.

In this connection, the reader might consult a case comment related to the *Harrison* decision, written by Professors S. C. Coval and J. C. Smith of the University of British Columbia, entitled "The Supreme Court and a New Jurisprudence for Canada" (1975), 53 Can. Bar Rev. 819 at 825. In the comment the two authors make the following remarks:

> The Chief Justice focused his attention on "two areas of concern respecting the role of . . . the final Court in this country in both civil and criminal causes"; whether the Supreme Court of Canada "must pay mechanical deference to *stare decisis* and, second, whether this Court has a balancing role to play, without yielding place to the legislature". Chief Justice Laskin recognized the necessity for the law to deal with new and

changing social conditions. "The present case" he states, "involves a search for an appropriate legal framework for new social facts which show up the inaptness of an old doctrine developed upon a completely different social foundation." The Chief Justice found this framework in the balancing of interest doctrine which he applied in reaching the conclusion that the right to picket as a legitimate part of the collective bargaining process outweighed the interest of the property owner or occupier in preserving the right to choose who shall come onto his property after an invitation to enter has already been extended to the public at large.

Regardless of whether the Supreme Court of Canada makes any further dramatic pronouncements as to its ability to overrule its own previous decisions, the fact that it has done so on numerous occasions[6] probably indicates that it does not regard itself as being bound by its previous decisions.

Lower courts have also dealt with this matter. For example, in the case of *Nova, An Alberta Corp. v. Guelph Engineering Co.*,[7] the Alberta Court of Appeal held that it could overrule itself with respect to practice matters. The Court felt that since the Supreme Court of Canada seldom deals with practice matters and since each court should have control over its own practice, then it follows that it should overrule its past decisions in relation to practice. It could be that this pronouncement, however, is restricted to practice matters. In *Green v. British Columbia (A.G.)*,[8] a Justice of the British Columbia Supreme Court stated as follows:

I know of no rule of stare decisis which requires a judge to follow his own mistakes.[9]

The question as to whether Canadian courts are bound by pre-1949 decisions of the Privy Council has not, as yet, been conclusively answered. Discussion has centred on whether the Supreme Court of Canada, in particular, is bound by pre-1949 decisions of the Privy Council. Chief Justice Rinfret, in *Re Storgoff*, [1945] S.C.R. 526, 84 C.C.C. 1, [1945] 3

---

[6] See *R. v. Hill*, [1977] 1 S.C.R. 827, 23 C.C.C. (2d) 321, 58 D.L.R. (3d) 697, 6 N.R. 413; *Paquette v. R.*, [1977] 2 S.C.R. 189, 39 C.R.N.S. 257, 30 C.C.C. (2d) 417, 70 D.L.R. (3d) 129, 11 N.R. 451; *McNamara Construction (Western) Ltd. v. R.*, [1977] 2 S.C.R. 654, 75 D.L.R. (3d) 273, 13 N.R. 181 (*sub nom. Canada v. McNamara Const. (Western) Ltd.; Can. v. J. Stevenson & Associates*); and *R. v. Bell*, [1979] 2 S.C.R. 212, 9 M.P.L.R. 103, 10 O.M.B.R. 142, 98 D.L.R. (3d) 255, 26 N.R. 457. See also G. Bale, "Stare Decisis — The Supreme Court and Law Reform" (1978), 26 Chitty's L.J. 337, and "Casting Off the Mooring Ropes of Binding Precedent" (1980), 58 Can. Bar Rev. 255. By the mid-1980's, the Supreme Court of Canada had overruled itself on at least ten occasions.

[7] (1984), 30 Alta L.R. (2d) 183, 42 C.P.C. 194, [1984] 3 W.W.R. 314, 50 A.R. 199, 80 C.P.R. (2d) 93, 5 D.L.R. (4th) 755 (C.A.).

[8] (1986), 29 C.R.R. 35 (B.C. S.C.).

[9] This remark was referred to by the British Columbia Court of Appeal in *R.V.P. Enterprises Ltd. v. British Columbia (Minister of Consumer & Corporate Affairs)*, [1988] 4 W.W.R. 726, 32 Admin. L.R. 305, (*sub nom. R.V.P. Enterprises Ltd. v. British Columbia (A.G.)*), 25 B.C.L.R. (2d) 219, 50 D.L.R. (4th) 394, 41 C.R.R. 264 (C.A.), leave to appeal to S.C.C. refused [1988] 6 W.W.R. lxix (note), 32 Admin. L.R. 305n, 28 B.C.L.R. (2d) xxxi (note), 50 D.L.R. (4th) vii (note), 90 N.R. 319n (S.C.C.).

D.L.R. 673, suggested that the abolition of appeals to the Privy Council in criminal matters removed the binding character of previous Privy Council decisions in that field. The same argument could be applied to civil matters, as well, after all appeals were abolished in 1949. This was, however, a dissenting opinion and the rest of the court did not comment on the issue.

In *Negro v. Pietro's Bread Co.,* [1933] O.R. 112, [1933] 1 D.L.R. 490 (C.A.), it was held that Privy Council decisions were only binding if they arose on appeal from Canada and it was suggested in *Col. v. British Columbia (A.G.),* [1934] 2 W.W.R. 481, [1934] 3 D.L.R. 488 (B.C. C.A.), that Privy Council decisions were binding only if they arose on appeal from the same province. Professor Andrew Joanes, relying primarily on the *Negro* case, has concluded that the Supreme Court of Canada is bound by pre-1949 decisions of the Privy Council taken on appeal from Canada.[10] Joanes also suggests, however, that the intent of the Supreme Court Amendment Act, S.C. 1949 (2nd Sess.), c. 37, was that pre-1949 decisions should be considered as persuasive only. W. Friedmann also considers pre-1949 decisions of the Privy Council to be binding on the Supreme Court of Canada until it decides not to follow them.[11]

Another legal writer, G. R. B. Whitehead, agrees that there are no cases where the Supreme Court of Canada has not followed a Privy Council precedent, but he argues that the Supreme Court of Canada should not be bound as it has taken the place of the Privy Council and so should inherit the Privy Council's ability to overrule previous decisions.[12] The consensus in favour of the Supreme Court not being bound, therefore, seems to focus on whether the Supreme Court can overrule itself.

Notwithstanding the foregoing, in view of the changing attitudes suggested, for example, in *Harrison v. Carswell*, it is very doubtful that the Supreme Court of Canada would now feel bound by pre-1949 decisions of the Privy Council. The one exception, however, might be found in the area of constitutional law and even this is not certain.

This issue was considered by Professor Gordon Bale in his articles "Stare Decisis — The Supreme Court and Law Reform" (1978), 26 Chitty's L.J. 337, and "Casting Off the Mooring Ropes of Binding Precedent" (1980), 58 Can. Bar Rev. 255. See also *Reference re Agricultural*

---

[10] Andrew Joanes, "Stare Decisis in the Supreme Court of Canada" (1958), 36 Can. Bar Rev. 175.

[11] W. Friedmann, "Stare Decisis at Common Law and under the Civil Code of Quebec" (1953), 31 Can. Bar Rev. 723 at 731.

[12] G.R.B. Whitehead, "The Supreme Court of Canada and the Stare Decisis Doctrine" (1967), 15 Chitty's L.J. 146.

Products Marketing Act (Canada), [1978] 2 S.C.R. 1198, 84 D.L.R. (3d)
257, 19 N.R. 361; *A. V.G. Management Science Ltd. v. Barwell Development Ltd.*, [1979] 2 S.C.R. 43, [1979] 1 W.W.R. 330, 92 D.L.R. (3d) 289,
8 R.P.R. 1, 24 N.R. 554, and *MacDonald v. Vapor Canada Ltd.*, [1977]
2 S.C.R. 134, 22 C.P.R. (2d) 1, 7 N.R. 477, 66 D.L.R. (3d) 1. Finally,
see the Foreword to Volume 1 of the Supreme Court Law Review, where
Chief Justice Bora Laskin states as follows:

> When appeals to the Privy Council were abolished thirty years ago, the Supreme Court
> became not only the final appellate Court of Canada and for Canadians. It became the
> Court whose decisions could not be challenged or changed, unless it be by itself or by
> Parliament or Provincial Legislatures in other than constitutional cases. The Court,
> although long adhering to *stare decisis* in respect of its own decision and those by Privy
> Council, has over the past few years been more receptive to re-examination of such deci-
> sions and, indeed, has overruled some decisions of its own as well as a Privy Council
> decision on a Canadian constitutional issue. Thus, in *Hill v. The Queen (No. 2)*, [1977]
> 1 S.C.R. 827, the Court overruled *Goldhar v. The Queen*, [1960] S.C.R. 60; in *Regina
> v. Paquette*, [1977] 2 S.C.R. 189, the Court refused to follow *Dunbar v. The King*, [1936]
> 4 D.L.R. 737; in *McNamara Construction (Western) Ltd. v. The Queen,* [1977] 2 S.C.R.
> 654 the Court overruled *Farwell v. The Queen* (1893), 22 S.C.R. 553; and in *Reference
> re the Agricultural Products Marketing Act* (The Egg Marketing Reference), [1978] 2
> S.C.R. 1198, the Court overruled *Lower Mainland Dairy Products Sales Adjustment
> Committee v. Crystal Dairy Ltd.,* [1933] A.C. 178.

Other issues concerning the operation of the doctrine of stare decisis
are raised in the case law. For example, the question arises as to whether
a court is bound by a previous decision which was affirmed on appeal
by a tie vote. There are opposing views on this issue, however. It was held
in *R. v. Tenta*, 3 C.R.N.S. 263, 64 W.W.R. 7, [1968] 4 C.C.C. 237, 67
D.L.R. (2d) 536 (Alta. C.A.), that such a decision is binding on a lower
court.

Another issue that often seems to re-emerge relates to the question as
to whether a single judge is bound by a previous decision of another judge
of co-ordinate jurisdiction. Certainly, a County Court Judge in the province of Ontario, for example, is not bound by a decision of a County Court
Judge in the province of British Columbia. In *R. v. Wolf*, [1975] 2 S.C.R.
107, 27 C.R.N.S. 150, [1974] 6 W.W.R. 368, 17 C.C.C. (2d) 425, 47
D.L.R. (3d) 741, it was held, in reasons written by the Chief Justice, that
a provincial appellate court is not obliged, as a matter of law or of practice, to follow a decision of the appellate court of another province, unless
it is persuaded that it should do so on the merits of that decision or for
other independent reasons. Further, it was held that the only required
uniformity among provincial appellate courts is that which results from
universal conformity to decisions of the Supreme Court of Canada. In
S. v. S., [1974] 1 W.W.R. 671, 13 R.F.L. 265, 41 D.L.R. (3d) 621, it was
held by a justice of the Manitoba Queen's Bench that a decision of a court
in one province interpreting a federal statute is not binding on a court

of co-ordinate jurisdiction in another province. Nevertheless, such a decision should be followed, unless the judge is satisfied that the precedent
decision is wrong, in order to ensure that federal statutes are interpreted
uniformly throughout Canada.

In *Horne v. Horne Estate*,[13] it was held by the then High Court of
Ontario (Supreme Court of Ontario, Trial Division) "that a decision of
a court of co-ordinate jurisdiction ought to be followed in the absence
of strong reasons to the contrary". In *Meurer v. McKenzie* (1977), 73
D.L.R. (3d) 477, 2 C.P.C. 109 (S.C.), reversed on other grounds [1978]
1 W.W.R. 114, 4 B.C.L.R. 349, 81 D.L.R. (3d) 388 (C.A.), it was held
that a judge should follow a decision of a judge of a co-ordinate jurisdiction unless the validity of the prior decision has been affected by subsequent decisions, or it is shown that the judge in the earlier case made
his/her decision per incuriam, or that the earlier case was a nisi prius decision given without the opportunity to fully consult the authorities. But
the Trial Division of the Federal Court has held that in the absence of
a compelling reason or a distinguishable fact situation, the decision of
a court of co-ordinate jurisdiction is to be followed: see *Smith, Kline &
French Canada Ltd. v. Apotex Inc.* (1983), 71 C.P.R. (2d) 146 (Fed. T.D.),
reversed on other grounds (1984), 1 C.P.R. (3d) 256 (Fed. C.A.). See also
the case of *R. v. Kartna* (1979), 2 M.V.R. 259 (Ont. H.C.). In *Re Ellwood Robinson Ltd. and Ohio Dev. Co.* (1975), 7 O.R. (2d) 556, it was
held that an exception to the doctrine of stare decisis arises where a court
of co-ordinate jurisdiction has given its judgment per incuriam, that is,
without considering some aspects of the case which ought to have been
considered.

Essentially, the issue is one of "comity" among judges in the same jurisdiction. In *Wallace v. Wallace* (1976), 28 R.F.L. 335, 70 D.L.R. (3d) 375
(Sask. Q.B.), one judge was reluctant to give judgment contrary to another
judgment by a judge of the same court.[14] However, in *Ex parte Guenette*
(1975), 27 C.C.C. (2d) 279 (B.C. S.C.), a judge in a later case refused
to follow a judge of the same court in an earlier case where the judge in
the earlier case had not had the benefit of persuasive authorities brought
to his attention. In *Guenette*, it was held that where judges of the same
jurisdiction differ in their interpretation of the same statute, a judge does
not have to follow a previous interpretation if, for some valid reason, it
was improperly determined. Some other cases which considered similar
issues include: *Fickett v. Bignell*, [1977] 5 W.W.R. 599, 1 R.F.L. (2d) 269
(Co. Ct.), reversed [1979] 2 W.W.R. 379 (B.C. C.A.); *Re McLaughlin*

---

[13] (1986), 54 O.R. (2d) 510, 1 R.F.L. (3d) 335, 22 E.T.R. 272 (H.C.), affirmed on other
grounds (1987), 60 O.R. (2d) 1, 8 R.F.L. (3d) 195, 45 R.P.R. 223, 26 E.T.R. 233, 39 D.L.R.
(4th) 416, 21 O.A.C. 313 (C.A.).
[14] See also *R v. McLeod*, [1984] 3 W.W.R. 590 (B.C. S.C.).

(1977), 16 O.R. (2d) 375, 1 E.T.R. 181, 78 D.L.R. (3d) 275 (H.C.); *Metropolitan Trust Co. v. Latvala* (1979), 22 O.R. (2d) 680, 93 D.L.R. (3d) 688 (H.C.); *Mitrunen v. Anthes Equipment Ltd.*, [1984] 5 W.W.R. 639, 57 B.C.L.R. 287, 13 D.L.R. (4th) 597, affirmed [1985] 3 W.W.R. 445, 65 B.C.L.R. 291, 17 D.L.R. (4th) 567 (C.A.); *Indalex Division of Indal v. United Metal Fabricators Ltd.* (1986), 6 B.C.L.R. (2d) 243, 15 C.P.C. (2d) 19 (S.C.).[15]

The issue arises as to whether a lower court judge in one province is bound by the decisions of an appellate court in another province. In *R. v. Constable Transport Ltd.*, [1967] 1 O.R. 357, [1967] 2 C.C.C. 167, 60 D.L.R. (2d) 577 (Co. Ct.), a County Court Judge in the province of Ontario indicated that he felt he was bound by a prior decision of the Manitoba Court of Appeal and was not merely persuaded by it. In addition, similar views were expressed by a justice of the Supreme Court of British Columbia. In the latter case, *R. v. Simpson* (1968), 63 W.W.R. 606, 67 D.L.R. (2d) 585 (S.C.), the justice indicated that he was bound by a decision of another province's court of appeal "except in the most extraordinary circumstances". On the other hand, in *R. v. Beaney*, [1969] 2 O.R. 71, [1970] 1 C.C.C. 48, 4 D.L.R. (3d) 369 at 374-75 (Co. Ct.), a County Court Judge in Ontario indicated that he was not bound by an appellate court in another province. In addition, the judge made some controversial remarks concerning the operation of the doctrines of precedent and stare decisis. In particular, His Honour Judge Matheson made these comments:

> Thus, unless there is competent legislation imposing on the Courts a strict rule of *stare decisis*, whether one Court is bound to decide the *rationes decidendi* of the decisions of another Court cannot be a matter of law but only of judicial attitudes and practical convenience. Just as Parliament cannot enact a law that Parliament cannot repeal, the Courts cannot be the author of a true law of *stare decisis*. A rule or law that imposes a legal obligation on a Court to follow and apply certain precedents must have its source outside that Court. This is exemplified by the ease with which the House of Lords abandoned the view — and it could therefore only have been a view, however long and jealously guarded — that it was bound by its own past decisions . . .
> There is no legislative rule of law in Ontario to the effect that any Court in this Province is bound by the decisions of extra-provincial Court, or, indeed, of any Courts . . . Within the hierarchy of appeals it would be futile for a lower Court Judge to render a decision which is inconsistent with the prior decisions of the Courts to which an immediate or ultimate appeal *from him* may be taken, for he will in all likelihood be reversed.

In *R. v. Maika* (1974), 27 C.R.N.S. 115, 17 C.C.C. (2d) 110 (C.A.), it was held that, in respect of criminal cases, the Court of Appeal of Ontario was bound by its previous decisions operating in favour of the subject. On the other hand, in *R. v. McInnis* (1973), 23 C.R.N.S. 152, 1 O.R. (2d) 1, 13 C.C.C. (2d) 471 (C.A.), it was held by the same court

---

[15] For a detailed discussion of these issues, see R. Flowers, "Stare Decisis in Courts of Co-ordinate Jurisdiction" (1985), 5 Advocates' Q. 464.

that it was not bound to follow its own decisions where a prior decision was given without consideration of an applicable authority of a statutory provision. Moreover, in criminal cases, that court is not bound by its previous decisions to the same extent as in civil cases. (This perhaps represents somewhat of a departure from the previous position held by the Ontario Court of Appeal.) In *General Brake & Clutch Service Ltd. v. W.A. Scott & Sons Ltd.,* [1975] W.W.R. 349 (Q.B.), reversed (1975), 59 D.L.R. (3d) 741 (C.A.), the Manitoba Court of Appeal held that it has the power to depart from its own previous decisions. In *R. v. Doyle* (1976), 6 Nfld. & P.E.I.R. 479 (*sub nom. Re Doyle*) (T.D.), it was held by a justice of the Newfoundland Trial Division that in matters of form and procedure, the trend by the courts is to place a higher value on justice than on conformity to established precedents. It has been said that the question of following precedent may be reduced to the issue of whether it is better to be wrong than to be consistent or vice versa.

Where a district court and a provincial court in a province have parallel jurisdiction in respect of some matters, while in other matters the district court has appellate jurisdiction, it has been held in *R. v. Cotterhill* (1977), 3 Alta. L.R. (2d) 37 (Dist. Ct.), that the district court's decisions in its appellate capacity were binding upon the provincial courts.

Various issues have arisen concerning the doctrine of stare decisis and the Supreme Court of Canada. When the Supreme Court of Canada states a principle of law, without reference to authorities, then the Court of Appeal from which the appeal to the Supreme Court has been launched is binding authority: see *R. v. DePagie,* [1976] 6 W.W.R. 1, 1 Alta. L.R. (2d) 30, 32 C.C.C. (2d) 89, 1 A.R. 602 (C.A.), leave to appeal to S.C.C. refused (1976), 32 C.C.C. (2d) 89n (S.C.C.). Where the Supreme Court of Canada decides a case on the basis of a decision of the English Court of Appeal which is subsequently overruled by the House of Lords, it has been held[16] that, notwithstanding the overruling by the House of Lords, a provincial superior court justice is nonetheless bound by the decision of the Supreme Court of Canada.

In *Re Ward* (1975), 20 R.F.L. 173, 9 O.R. (2d) 35, 59 D.L.R. (3d) 361 (Div. Ct.), it was held that a minority decision of the Supreme Court is not binding on a lower court.

Other cases which readers may wish to consult concerning the operation of stare decisis are as follows: *Betts v. Sanderson Estate,* [1989] 2

---

[16] See *Marvco Color Research Ltd. v. Harris* (1980), 27 O.R. (2d) 686, 11 R.P.R. 112, 107 D.L.R. (3d) 632, 36 N.R. 90 (H.C.), affirmed (1980), 30 O.R. (2d) 162, 115 D.L.R. (3d) 512 (C.A.), which was reversed on other grounds [1982] 2 S.C.R. 774, 20 B.L.R. 143, 26 R.P.R. 48, 141 D.L.R. (3d) 577, 45 N.R. 302.

W.W.R. 113, 31 B.C.L.R. (2d) 1, 44 C.C.L.T. 97, 11 M.V.R. (2d) 146, 53 D.L.R. (4th) 675 (C.A.) (re decisions of courts of the same or co-ordinate jurisdiction); *R. v. Morris* (1988), 85 N.S.R. (2d) 200, 216 A.P.R. 200 (Mag. Ct.) (re decisions of courts of superior jurisdiction); *R. v. Bachman* (1987), 78 A.R. 282 (C.A.), affirmed [1988] 1 S.C.R. 1094, 86 N.R. 359, 89 A.R. 199 (re general principles related to stare decisis); *R. v. Davis* (1976), 21 C.C.C. (2d) 507, 74 D.T.C. 6595 (B.C. S.C.); *R. v. Dawood*, 31 C.R.N.S. 382, [1976] 1 W.W.R. 262, 27 C.C.C. (2d) 300 (Alta. C.A.); *R. v. Dennis*, 28 C.R.N.S. 268, [1975] 2 W.W.R. 630, 22 C.C.C. (2d) 152, 56 D.L.R. (3d) 379 (B.C.); *R. v. Wray (No. 2)*, [1974] S.C.R. 565, 10 C.C.C. (2d) 215, 33 D.L.R. (3d) 750; *R. v. Mueller* (1975), 32 C.R.N.S. 188, 29 C.C.C. (2d) 243 (Ont. C.A.); *R. v. Robertson* (1975), 29 C.R.N.S. 141, 21 C.C.C. (2d) 385 (Ont. C.A.); *Nedco Ltd. v. Clark* (1973), 41 D.L.R. (3d) 565 (Sask. Q.B.), reversed [1973] 6 W.W.R. 425, 43 D.L.R. (3d) 714, 73 C.L.L.C. 14,192 (Sask. C.A.); *R. v. Santeramo* (1976), 36 C.R.N.S. 1, 32 C.C.C. (2d) 35 (C.A.), leave to appeal to S.C.C. granted (1976), 32 C.C.C. (2d) 35n (S.C.C.); *Woloszczak v. Onyszczak* (1976), 14 O.R. (2d) 732, 1 C.P.C. 129, 74 D.L.R. (3d) 554 (H.C.); *R. v. Ostridge* (1979), 22 Nfld. & P.E.I.R. 123, 58 A.P.R. 123, 2 M.V.R. 160 (P.E.I. S.C.); *Conder v. North Star Construction Co.* (1979), 17 B.C.L.R. 186, 12 R.P.R. 313, 106 D.L.R. (3d) 673 (S.C.); *R. v. Kennedy*, [1980] 4 W.W.R. 577, 6 M.V.R. 178 (Alta. Q.B.); *Sigurdson v. Reid* (1979), 32 C.B.R. (N.S.) 170, 17 B.C.L.R. 117 (S.C.), reversed (1980), 37 C.B.R. (N.S.) 146, 26 B.C.L.R. 336, 118 D.L.R. (3d) 555 (C.A.); *Re British Columbia (A.G.)*, [1980] 3 W.W.R. 193 (*sub nom. A.G.B.C. v. Diebolt*), 4 M.V.R. 167 (B.C. S.C.); *R. v. Barrett*, [1980] 4 W.W.R. 339, 15 C.R. (3d) 361, 54 C.C.C. (2d) 75, 31 A.R. 499 (C.A.); *R. v. Sellars*, [1980] 1 S.C.R. 527, 20 C.R. (3d) 381, 52 C.C.C. (2d) 345, 110 D.L.R. (3d) 629, 32 N.R. 70; *Weiss v. R.*, [1980] 5 W.W.R. 93, 19 B.C.L.R. 207, 108 D.L.R. (3d) 253 (S.C.).

Probably the best outline of the operation of the doctrine of stare decisis is the MacGuigan article, cited in the bibliography, although it should be read subject to the comments made in the more recent cases discussed above.

Essentially, the purposes and advantages of the doctrines of precedent and stare decisis are to provide in the law for:

1. certainty and predictability;

2. continuity and stability;

3. consistency; and

4. the possibility of growth: as new factual circumstances occur, this gives rise to new statements of principle.

It has also been suggested that a further advantage of these doctrines is that they contribute to the development of a case law that contains an abundance of detail as well as a practical character. Indeed, in *Woods Manufacturing Co. v. R.,* [1951] S.C.R. 504, 67 C.R.T.C. 87, [1951] 2 D.L.R. 465 at 475, Chief Justice Rinfret made these remarks:

> It is fundamental to the due administration of justice that the authority of decisions be scrupulously respected by all Courts upon which they are binding. Without this uniform and consistent adherence the administration of justice becomes disordered, the law becomes uncertain, and the confidence of the public in it undermined. Nothing is more important than that the law as pronounced, including the interpretation by this Court of the decisions of the Judicial Committee, should be accepted and applied as our tradition requires; and even at the risk of that fallibility to which all Judges are liable, we must maintain the complete integrity of relationship between the Courts. If the rules in question are to be accorded any further examination or review, it must come from this Court or from the Judicial Committee.

It is often said that a lawyer would not be capable of rendering advice to his clients if the law lacked the predictability and certainty which arise out of the operation of the doctrine of stare decisis. However, against the desirability for certainty must be balanced the dictates of justice and fairness. Jerome Frank in his treatise *Courts on Trial* made these remarks on this balance:

> For if actually and rigorously adopted, the precedent doctrine would mean this: No matter how absurd or unwise or unjust a legal rule, once announced by a court, may turn out to be, that court must not, cannot properly, change it, but must go on endlessly applying it until the legislature, by a statute, intervenes. As the legislature often does not intervene, the precedent doctrine, as avowed by some of the courts and generally praised by the lawyers, has led to severe criticism of the legal profession by many non-lawyers . . .

> In sum, the doctrine of *stare decisis* seems to mean that certainty outweighs justice: Let certainty be achieved though injustice be done and the heavens fall . . .

> Several arguments have been advanced in support of this harsh doctrine. (1) The first is an argument of justice. Justice, it is said, requires equality of treatment. It would be intolerable, so the argument goes, if the rule that applied when Mr. Wiseman sues Mr. Simple were not applied when the same question arises subsequently in a suit of Mr. Bold against Mr. Timid . . . Only so can caprice and subjectivity be precluded. Through following precedents, courts achieve uniformity, continuity, objectivity, and, thereby equality . . . (2) A more powerful argument for *stare decisis* rests on the need for stability. Only if rules are certain and stable, it is said, can men conduct their affairs with safety. This argument assumes that most men do conduct their affairs relying on certain legal rules . . . (3) Still another argument for *stare decisis* is that without it, the "beauty and symmetry" of the legal system would be destroyed . . . (4) Another argument, seldom openly expressed but not entirely without influence, was assigned by a famous English judge, Lord Ellenborough. "If," he said, "this rule were to be changed, a lawyer who was well stored with these rules would be not better than any other man without them." . . . (5) Still another argument is the convenience of the judges . . . For a settled system is easier for judges to operate than a set of variable and mutable rules . . .

> The precedent system, as I have thus far described it, seems to cause much injustice and to impede desirable social change. Yet its bark is worse than its bite. It does not really bite when a court follows a precedent which it considers just or wise; or when the judge-made rule it accepts is of neutral kind. Neither just or unjust, wise nor unwise; or when a court consults and heeds its own or other judges' earlier opinions because those

opinions contain sagacious solutions of difficult problems . . . The precedent system really bites viciously only when a court, regarding a precedent as undesirable, nevertheless refuses to deviate from it.

Two further interesting commentaries along similar lines are: E.M. Hall, "Law Reform and the Judiciary's Role" (1972), 10 Osgoode Hall L. J. 399; and S. Freedman, "Continuity and Change — A Task of Reconciliation" (1973), 8 U.B.C.L. Rev. 209. The authors of these two articles are, respectively, a former Justice of the Supreme Court of Canada and a former Chief Justice of the province of Manitoba. In addition, other comments have been made by distinguished members of the judiciary in connection with the doctrines of precedent and stare decisis. Chief Justice Laskin once remarked:

It is worth remembering that for a final court consistency in decisions is merely a convenience and not a necessity. No one expects the Supreme Court to break out in a rash of reversals of previous decisions, even if it should formally dissociate itself from stare decisis . . . In my view, such dissociation, whether formally expressed or not, is imperative if the court is to develop a personality of its own.

In addition, the late eminent Mr. Justice Holmes of the Supreme Court of the United States also commented:

It is revolting to have no better reason for a rule of law than that it was so laid down in the time of Henry IV. It is still more revolting if the grounds upon which it was laid down have vanished long ago, and the rule simply persists from blind imitation of the past.

There are certain disadvantages arising out of the operation of the doctrines of precedent and stare decisis:

1. Rigidity and inflexibility in the law;

2. The danger of illogical distinctions; and

3. The vast magnitude and complexity of detail in the common law.

DEPARTURE FROM THEORY: THE PROCESS OF DISTINGUISHING

In order to overcome the rigidity and inflexibility inherent in a system which operates under the doctrines of precedent and stare decisis, and in order to resolve the issue as to whether justice or certainty is paramount in the event that the two are inconsistent in a particular case, the courts have utilized various devices. One such device is the process of distinguishing. Basically, distinguishing is the way by which judges can avoid the binding or persuasive nature of precedent decisions. To do so, a judge examines the material facts of the precedent case to which he must conform and the material facts of the instant case. If he finds that the precedent case has a material fact or facts absent in the instant case, or alternatively, the instant case contains a material fact or facts absent in the precedent case, he will then be in the position to deny the necessity of following the precedent case. Distinguishing cases on the basis of differences in their material facts is a somewhat subjective process in that the judge must render an opinion as to the materiality of the facts contained in both the precedent and instant cases, and sometimes to satisfy the dictates of justice and fairness in the particular case before him, a judge will make illogical distinctions. While this may serve the interests of justice in respect of the instant case, it is questionable whether illogical reasoning on the part of judges, in the long run, serves the interests of justice.

The process of distinguishing is not, however, the only way in which a judge can avoid the hardships imposed upon him under the operation of stare decisis. In addition, for example, he can characterize objectionable judicial opinions as obiter dicta; that is, he can reinterpret a precedent case so that what appears, perhaps, at first glance, to be the ratio decidendi is held to be a mere obiter comment. The ratio decidendi is the "part of the case that is said to possess authority" containing "the rule of law upon which the decision is founded".[17] On the other hand, an obiter dictum is any statement of law made by a judge that is part of a case but which does not contain the particular rule of law upon which that case is decided. A future judge, of course, is not bound by an obiter dictum, as the doctrine of stare decisis is not applicable to it[18] and it merely has persuasive force at best. Very significantly, a recent ruling from the Supreme Court of Canada, however, indicates that this is not true of obiter statements from the Supreme Court of Canada. In *R. v. Sellars*, [1980] 1 S.C.R. 527, 20 C.R. (3d) 381, 52 C.C.C. (2d) 345, 110 D.L.R. (3d) 629, 32 N.R. 70, the Court stated that even obiter dicta emanating from that court are binding on lower courts.[19]

Sometimes, there is an issue as to whether a statement is obiter dictum or part of the ratio decidendi. In *Ciba-Geigy Canada Ltd. v. Apotex Inc.*[20], the Ontario Court of Appeal reviewed the judgment of an earlier case and determined that certain statements in that earlier case were carefully

---

[17] G. Williams, *Learning the Law*, 11th ed. (1982), p. 67.

[18] See, e.g., *R. v. Pollock*, [1982] 1 F.C. 710, [1981] C.T.C. 389, 81 D.T.C. 5293 (Fed. T.D.), affirmed [1984] C.T.C. 353, 84 D.T.C. 6370 (Fed. C.A.); see also *R. v. Miller* (1982), 39 O.R. (2d) 41, 29 C.P.C. 159, 29 C.R. (3d) 153, 70 C.C.C. (2d) 129, 141 D.L.R. (3d) 330 (C.A.), affirmed [1985] 2 S.C.R. 613, 52 O.R. (2d) 585, 49 C.R. (3d) 1, 16 Admin. L.R. 184, 23 C.C.C. (3d) 97, 24 D.L.R. (4th) 9, 14 O.A.C. 33, 63 N.R. 321.

[19] See also A. Peltomaa, "Obiter Dictum of the Supreme Court of Canada: Does it Bind Lower Courts?" (1982), 60 Can. Bar Rev. 823.

[20] (1991), 75 O.R. (2d) 589, 32 C.P.R. (3d) 555, 45 O.A.C. 356 (C.A.), reversed [1992] 3 S.C.R. 120, 44 C.P.R. (3d) 289, 95 D.L.R. (4th) 385, 143 N.R. 241, 58 O.A.C. 321.

considered and intended to authoritatively declare the law. As such, those earlier statements were not obiter dicta.

A judge can also refuse to follow a precedent case on the basis that it was decided per incuriam, that is, he may conclude that the precedent case was decided through inadvertence. For example, he may take the position that the judge in the precedent case inadvertently did not take an important authority into consideration in rendering his decision.

Where a precedent decision is arrived at by various concurring reasons, the judge can pick and choose which reasons for judgment in the precedent case he wishes to follow. For example, often a panel of three judges will constitute the majority in a precedent decision. While all three might reach the same conclusion, they may each do so for different reasons. In examining the precedent case, a judge in an instant case can decide which reasons for judgment he wishes to follow and ignore the others.

Finally, the boldest (and probably intellectually the most honest) way in which a judge can avoid any injustice or rigidity imposed upon him under the operation of stare decisis is to take the position that a precedent case was wrongly decided and then simply ignore it.

JUDICIAL PERCEPTION OF THE DOCTRINES OF PRECEDENT AND STARE DECISIS

One way of determining how the doctrines of precedent and stare decisis operate is to ask sitting members of the judiciary how they regard these doctrines. Accordingly, a study, sponsored and financed by the Canadian Institute for the Administration of Justice, was conducted in the summer of 1976 at the University of Alberta. (This research is briefly mentioned in the previous chapter.)

Set out below are some of the comments received in response to this specific question posed to all judges of the province of Alberta:

Should judges, in applying the law, exercise a quasi-legislative role, as suggested by Chief Justice Deschênes [in an attached newspaper extract], in judicial decisionmaking, or alternatively, should judges exercise an essentially interpretative function? In this connection, I am also interested in your views as to the nature of the doctrines of precedent and stare decisis . . . how would you characterize these doctrines? Are they rules of law, conventions or customs now enshrined within the law, judicial attitudes, or otherwise?

1. . . .[precedents must be interpreted] in light of changing social conditions and values.

2. . . .[precedent and stare decisis can be characterized as] rules of law . . .[and] are needed to prevent judges from imposing their personal whims and philosophies upon society under the guise of pronouncive law.

3. Some judges are revolutionary in their thoughts and attitudes and in the law-making

role of the judge, he must have some regard to precedent and should follow certainly the higher courts which are his guidelines until overruled or changed.

4. Stare decisis has become such an integral part of our law that, in my opinion, it is now a rule of law and should continue to be such . . . The doctrines of precedent and stare decisis are a fundamental part of our system of law. [There are three purposes for them: (1) they provide a basis from which lawyers can advise clients; (2) they avoid additional costs of appeals and unnecessary litigation; and (3) there is a danger that different parts of the same jurisdiction and different jurisdictions would otherwise apply different principles of law in Canada.]

5. Turning to the doctrines of precedent and stare decisis, I remember that someone once said: "I would rather be right than consistent." But precedent and stare decisis are necessary if there is to be certainty and consistency in law. Lord Reid points out in the borstal boys case that the trend is regarding the law of negligence as depending upon principle so that, when a new point emerges, one should ask not whether it is covered by authority, but whether recognized principles apply to it. The system of common law is based on precedent and on the rule that lower courts follow the rulings of appellate courts. This is necessary, but this does not mean that an appellate court cannot, for good reason, reverse itself at some future time. These, in my opinion, are rules of law.

6. [Stare decisis is, at present, a rule of law. Trial judges] are appreciative of and feel bound by decisions of other courts. [When they disagree with a superior court, it is because there is] an inclination to stretch and look for answers which meet the "justice" of the situation. [Appeal courts should not allow the law to shift too drastically and also should not have the ability to reverse themselves. The Supreme Court of Canada has, in some cases, the ability to reverse itself.]

7. [Precedent and stare decisis are subject to the process of distinguishing. They are binding rules of law.] By seeking out and finding distinctions we would of course be fulfilling a good deal more than a merely interpretative function, merely applying the law.

8. [The doctrines of precedent and stare decisis are important for certainty. An alternative would not be rule of law, but rule of man. Each judge would become a law unto himself.] As far as the legislative role of the judges is concerned . . . I emphatically state that the function of a judge is not that of the law-maker. The problem with this whole area, of course, is one of connotation and semantics. There can be no question that in the day-to-day functioning of judges they will contribute considerably to the growth and development of law. It is also true that in our constitutional system there is a fair amount of overlapping between the functions of the executive, the legislature and the judiciary. It is important to recognize that the lines dividing the three branches of government are rather grey and broad, but I think it is equally important to emphasize the paramount function of each branch of government and that each should be vigilant in minimizing its interference with the other's responsibility.

Basically, I am of the view that there should be as much certainty in the law as possible. In other words, the citizen at any given time should know where he stands in his relationships with his fellow citizen and with the state. If laws are changed without notice then the position of the citizen is rendered uncertain. For that reason I feel that generally the law should not change except by the action of the legislature. The problem with laws being changed by judges is that the change occurs without notice to the public. Secondly, I feel that even in a democratic system as highly developed as our own, the citizen has a rather limited opportunity to control the law. That opportunity is, of course, expressed by the fact that the legislature is accountable to the voter. There is no similar accountability between the judiciary and the public and it is therefore my view that the judiciary must be very careful to keep its law-making role within the limits set by the existing rules of law. I therefore, of course, feel that the doctrine of stare decisis is a doctrine essential to the proper functioning of our judicial system. If that doctrine is taken away from the judicial system, then each judge becomes a law unto himself and the citizen is no longer subject to the rule of the law but is in danger of being subject to the rule of the man . . .

9. The doctrines of precedent and stare decisis are essential to the administration of law . . . [If] some precedent or stare decisis philosophy [is not in tune with new social realities, it is the legislature, not the courts, which has the burden of adapting the law to the new realities].

10. [Precedent and stare decisis] play an important role in our courts . . . While a judge is not necessarily bound by a precedent, he is by stare decisis, i.e., a judge other than a peer.

11. Stare decisis is not a form of concrete; forever immutable . . .[The doctrine of stare decisis is the] embodiment of the desire that the law should be stable and known . . . [But it must be applied in moderation, otherwise it], when pushed to doctrinaire limits, becomes utter nonsense.

12. [Precedent is a rule of law and is binding.]

13. [The doctrines of precedent and stare decisis are hard and fast legal rules but there is always room for the device of distinguishing.]

14. I would characterize doctrines of precedent and stare decisis as conventions or customs enshrined within the law.

15. I . . . see stare decisis as tantamount to a rule of law. The force of precedent must of course, vary from place and time, and in the absence of detailed legislative enunciation, must serve as an informative guide other than where stare decisis is in effect . . . [Both precedent and stare decisis provide for] consistency in application of the law.

16. Stare decisis is clearly a rule of law, but like our institutions it arises from custom; viz, it is enshrined because it is accepted and recognized by the populace at large . . . [A] court of last resort, [on occasion, may apply social policy to past decisions but this should not apply to provincial courts of appeal in respect of Supreme Court of Canada decisions for this would result in significant variations of law between the provinces].

17. [The role of stare decisis will probably be relaxed here as the legislature tends to lag behind social change. The House of Lords declaration in 1966 that it is not binding on itself will be a contributing factor. Also, this latitude will be particularly applicable to certain fields of law], those with social overtones [such as pornography].

18. [The quality or nature of a doctrine is irrelevant to how one labels it. Stare decisis is] useful.

In examining the above comments, it is important to realize that any conclusions reached arising out of these comments are subject to various drawbacks related to the unempirical nature of the 1976 study. The study was in the nature of a descriptive portrayal of the views of those members of the judiciary who responded to the questions posed. The survey solicited views from judges at all levels of the Alberta judiciary. In any event, set out below are some conclusions which might be reached from a study of the responses received.

First, some judges hold the view that they must slavishly adhere to the doctrines of precedent and stare decisis. Although the number of judges who subscribe to that view without qualification is small, it does represent a certain hardcore component within the Canadian judiciary. Most judges, however, strongly believe in a strict adherence to the doctrines of precedent and stare decisis but recognize that, as one judge aptly put it, "[adherence to stare decisis] when pushed to doctrinaire limits becomes utter nonsense''. Judges gave various reasons for their belief that they must follow the doctrines of precedent and stare decisis. The most common reasons advanced were those related to the notion that there must be certainty, predictability and consistency in the law. One judge, however, suggested another advantage of adherence to the doctrines in that the certainty and predictability that prevails does, in turn, avoid additional costs of appeal and unnecessary litigation.

Secondly, while most judges did subscribe to the view that their primary judicial function is to interpret the law as it presently exists, they also suggested in their responses that in the exercise of this primary function there exists room for some judicial flexibility and creativity in order to satisfy the dictates of justice and to permit the law to be responsive to changing social conditions. In order to temper the results that would follow a strict adherence to precedent and stare decisis, most judges agreed that a resort to the process of distinguishing was the best way to inject this flexibility into the judicial function.

Thirdly, many judges expressed a sensitivity as to where the true legislative function lies. It was not uncommon for a judge to delineate the constitutional boundaries of the judicial and the legislative functions. While there might be some judges who wish to assume a "quasi-legislative" function, most chose to reserve any legislative function to the legislative bodies and to reserve to themselves a purely interpretative function. As a result, one could conclude that while the members of the judiciary appreciate the constitutional limitations on their function, nonetheless, there are some judges who proceed to utilize the doctrines of precedent and stare decisis, together with the process of distinguishing, to play an essentially "quasi-legislative" role under the guise of a purely interpretative one. The extent to which judges exercise this quasi-legislative role depends upon the extent to which an individual judge employs the process of distinguishing and other devices which give rise to judicial flexibility and creativity. This, of course, reflects the great dilemma faced by judges and the immense difficulties in sorting out the various expectations which underlie the judicial function.

As to the difficult question of categorizing the doctrines of precedent and stare decisis, there were some judges who thought it was unimportant to make such a categorization. These judges felt that it was sufficient to conclude that the doctrines of precedent and stare decisis were "useful" or "essential to the administration of justice" or "play an important part" (in our legal system) or were an "embodiment of the desire that the law should be stable". One judge described attempts at categorization "to be of limited use, much like the signs on the highway, they help, but you could get there without them". Indeed, it is possible that precise definition might have a negative effect; if precedent and stare decisis were strictly categorized, it might not be possible to employ a device to circumvent them.

The question posed to the judges suggested that the doctrines of precedent and stare decisis might be regarded as, perhaps, rules of law, judicial attitudes, customs or conventions enshrined within the law, or otherwise. Most judges adopted one or another of these various suggested sources of the doctrines. Some, however, advanced alternatives. For example, one judge suggested that the doctrine of stare decisis was a "matter that has been determined by judicial decision". Another judge defined the doctrines in terms of their function. He suggested that, in effect, they imposed constraints in order to prevent judges from imposing their personal whims and personal philosophies. No judges, however, were as bold as Judge Matheson of the County Court in the case of *R. v. Beaney, supra,* who expressed the view (discussed earlier in this chapter) that unless there existed a statute of the legislature imposing an obligation upon a judge to follow a previous case, the doctrine of stare decisis was essentially no more than a matter of judicial attitudes and practical convenience. Although Judge Matheson may ultimately be proven correct, this strong a statement did not appear among the responses received in the survey conducted.

Yet another conclusion that might be reached is that there exists, as there existed with respect to the judicial perception as to the role of the judge, no unanimity in judicial perceptions of the doctrines of precedent and stare decisis, although there emerges a majority view. Probably the dictates of custom and convention, together with an element of judicial comity, demand universal acceptance of these doctrines. At the very least, if this conclusion is correct, it indicates how important the notion of convention is in defining an important source of law in the Canadian legal system.

As indicated earlier, the research conducted at the University of Alberta during the summer of 1976 related only to the members of the judiciary in the province of Alberta. The results from the Alberta survey are only suggestive of certain conclusions and, while many of these conclusions are probably universally accurate, unfortunately they are derived from only a small local sample. Perhaps, at some future time, a nationwide survey of this nature might be conducted. Only then will a truly representative picture emerge as to judicial perceptions of the doctrines of precedent and stare decisis, and of the role of the judge in the Canadian legal system. In the meantime, the University of Alberta project represented a first and unprecedented step in examining the fundamental attitudes of the judiciary in conducting its day-to-day responsibilities as an essential arm of the Canadian body politic.

SELECTED BIBLIOGRAPHY
ON THE
DOCTRINES OF PRECEDENT AND STARE DECISIS

TEXTS AND TREATISES

Cross, R. *Precedent in English Law*. 4th ed. Oxford: Clarendon Press, 1991.

Frank, J. *Courts on Trial*. Princeton: Princeton University Press, 1949.

Frank, J. *Law and the Modern Mind*. Gloucester: P. Smith, 1970.

Friedmann, W. *Legal Theory*. 5th ed. London: Stevens, 1967.

Goldberg, A.J. *Equal Justice*. Evanston, Ill.: Northwestern University Press, 1971.

Goldstein, L. *Precedent in Law*. Oxford: Clarendon Press, 1987.

Jaffe, L.L. *English and American Judges as Lawmakers*. Oxford: Clarendon Press, 1969.

Llewellyn, K.N. *The Common Law Tradition: Deciding Appeals*. Boston: Little Brown, 1960.

McWhinney, E. *Supreme Courts and Judicial Law-Making: Constitutional Tribunals and Constitutional Review*. Boston: Dordrecht, 1986.

Montrose, J.L. *Precedent in English Law and Other Essays*. Shannon: Irish University Press, 1968.

Murphy, J.D., and R. Rueter. *Stare Decisis in Commonwealth Appellate Courts*. Toronto: Butterworths, 1981.

Phillips, O.H. *A First Book of English Law*. 7th ed. London: Sweet & Maxwell, 1977.

Pound, R. *Law Finding Through Experience and Reason*. Athens: University of Georgia Press, 1960.

Rudd, G.R. *The English Legal System*. London: Butterworths, 1962.

Stone, J. *Precedent in Law: Dynamics of Common-Law Growth*. Sydney: Butterworths, 1985.

Zander, M. *The Law-Making Process*. 3rd ed. London: Weidenfeld and Nicolson, 1989.

ARTICLES

Abraham, K.S. "Three Fallacies of Interpretation: A Comment on Precedent and Judicial Decision". (1982), 98 L.Q. Rev. 29.

Allen, C.C. "Importance of Following Precedent in the Development of Law and the Administration of Justice". (1970), 26 Mo. Bar J. 190.

Ashman, A. "Courts . . . Establishing Precedent". (1982), 68 A.B.A.J. 206.

Bale, C.G. "Casting Off the Mooring Ropes of Binding Precedent". (1980), 58 Can. Bar Rev. 255.

Bale, C.G. "The Quiet Revolution". (1966), 14 Chitty's L.J. 329.

Bale, C.G. "*Stare Decisis* — The Supreme Court and Law Reform". (1978), 26 Chitty's L.J. 337.

Barr, B. *et al.* "Legalese and the Myth of Case Precedents". (1985), 64 Mich. Bar J. 1136.

Bentil, J.K. "Court of Appeal's Adherence to its Jurisprudence". (1974), 34 New L.J. 733.

Bernier, N. "L'autorité du précédent judiciaire à la Cour d'appel du Québec". (1971), 6 Thémis 535.

Birmingham, R.L. "Neutrality of Adhering to Precedent". [1971] Duke L.J. 541.

Birnbaum, H.F. "Stare Decisis versus Judicial Activism: Nothing Succeeds Like Success". (1968), 54 A.B.A.J. 482.

Blume, L.E., and L. Rubinfeld. "The Dynamics of the Legal Process". (1982), 11 J. Leg. Stud. 405.

Boulanger, J. "Le précédent judiciaire dans le droit privé français contemporain". (1961), 21 R. du B. 65.

Bratz, D.C. "Stare Decisis in Lower Courts: Predicting the Demise of Supreme Court Precedent". (1984), 60 Wash. L. Rev. 87.

Brazier, R. "Overruling House of Lords Criminal Cases". [1973] Crim. L.R. 98.

Calder, B. "Stare Decisis and the Supreme Court of Canada". (1961), 1 Western Ont. L. Rev. 36.

Canton, E.M.C. "The House of Lords and Precedent: A New Departure". (1987), 137 New L.J. 491.

Cardozo, B. "Adherence to Precedent. The Subconscious Element in the Judicial Process". In *The Nature of the Judicial Process*. New Haven: Yale University Press, 1932.

Carson, C.R. "The Influence of U.S. Intellectual Property Law Precedents in Canadian Courts". (1987), 3 Can. Intell. Prop. Rev. 371.

Coval, S.C., and J.C. Smith. "The Supreme Court and a New Jurisprudence for Canada — *Harrison v. Carswell*". (1975), 53 Can. Bar Rev. 819.

Cross, R. "Ratio Decidendi and Obiter Dictum". In *Precedent in English Law*. 2nd ed. Oxford: Clarendon Press, 1968.

Cross, R. "Recent Developments in the Practice of Precedent — The Triumph of Common Sense". (1969), 43 Aust. L.J. 3.

Cross, R. "Stare Decisis in Contemporary England". (1966), 82 L.Q. Rev. 203.

Curtis, C.F. *"Stare decisis* at Common Law in Canada". (1978), 12 U.B.C.L. Rev. 1.

Deutsch, J.G. "Precedents and Adjudication". 83 Yale L.J. 153.

Deutsch, J.G., and M.H. Hoeflich. "Legal Duty and Judicial Style: The Meaning of Precedent". (1981), 25 St. Louis U.L.J. 87.

Dickson, B. "The Judiciary — Law Interpreters or Law-Makers?" (1982), 12 Man. L.J. 1.

Dobbyn, J.F. "Prospective Limitation of Constitutional Decisions on Criminal Cases". (1971), 36 Mod. L. Rev. 301.

Downey, P.J. "Certainty and Stare Decisis". (1986), 3 N.Z.L.J. 137.

Downey, P.J. "On Certainty". (1986), 1 N.Z.L.J. 181.

Dworkin, G. "Stare Decisis in the House of Lords". (1962), 25 Mod. L. Rev. 163.

Evans, P.J. "On Case Law Reasoning". (1985), 85 Jurid. Rev. 118.

Evans, P.J. "Status of Rules of Precedent". (1982), 41 Camb. L.J. 162.

Fairchild, T.E. "Limitation of New Judge-Made Laws to Prospective Effect Only: 'Prospective Overruling' or 'Sunbursting'". (1967), 51 Marq. L. Rev. 254.

Finch, J.D. "Stare Decisis and Changing Standards in English Law". (1973), 51 Can. Bar Rev. 523.

Finkelstein, N. "The Relevance of Pre-Charter Case Law for Post-Charter Adjudication". (1982), 4 Sup. Ct. L. Rev. 267.

Flowers, R. "Stare Decisis in Courts of Co-ordinate Jurisdiction". (1985), 5 Advocates' Q. 464.

Frank, J. "Illusory Precedents: The Future of Judicial Somnambulism". In *Law and the Modern Mind.* 1970, p. 159.

Fraser (Lord) of Tullybelton. "The Role of the Court of Last Resort in the United Kingdom". In *The Supreme Court of Canada: Proceedings of the October 1985 Conference.* Cowansville, Quebec: Les Editions Yvon Blais, 1986, p. 281.

Freedman, S. "Continuity and Change — A Task of Reconciliation". (1973), 8 U.B.C.L. Rev. 209.

Friedland, M.L. "Prospective and Retrospective Judicial Lawmaking". (1974), 24 U.T.L.J. 170.

Friedmann, W. "Stare Decisis at Common Law and under the Civil Code of Quebec". (1953), 31 Can. Bar Rev. 721.

Friedmann, W.G. "Precedent and Legal Development". In *Legal Theory.* 5th ed. London: Stevens, 1967, p. 463.

Geddes, R.S. "Authority of Privy Council Decisions in Australian Courts". (1978), 9 Fed. L. Rev. 427.

Gibson, D. "Judges as Legislators: Not Whether but How". (1986/87), 25 Alta. L. Rev. 249.

Gibson, D. "*Stare Decisis* and the Action *Per Quod Servitium Amisit* — Refusing to Follow the Leader". (1980), 13 C.C.L.T. 309.

Gilbert, G.S. "Stare Decisis — Value of Obiter Dictum — Supreme Court of Canada". (1982), 60 Can. Bar Rev. 373.

Goldstein, L. "Some Problems About Precedent". (1984), 43 Cambridge L.J. 88.

Good, I.J., and G. Tullock. "Judicial Errors and a Proposal for Reform". (1984), 13 J. Leg. Stud. 289.

Hall, E.M. "Law Reform and the Judiciary's Role". (1972), 10 Osgoode Hall L.J. 399.

Hare, F.H. "Stare Decisis". (1970), 31 Ala. Law 273.

Heiner, R.A. "Imperfect Decisions and the Law: On the Evolution of Legal Precedent and Rules". (1986), 15 J. Leg. Stud. 227.

Hiller, J.A. "The Law — Creative Role of Appellate Courts in the Commonwealth". (1978), 27 Int. and Comp. L.Q. 85.

Hirsch, W.Z. "Reducing Law's Uncertainty and Complexity". (1974), 21 U.C.L.A. L. Rev. 1233.

Hubbard, H.A. "Le processus judiciaire du 'common law' ". (1968), 28 R. du B. 1.

Jackson, P. "Precedent and the Liberty of the Subject". (1985), 101 L.Q. Rev. 323.

Jackson, P. "The Divisional Court: The Survival of Binding Precedent". (1985), 101 L.Q. Rev. 484.

Joanes, A. "Stare Decisis in the Supreme Court of Canada". (1958), 36 Can. Bar Rev. 175.

Jones, P. "Stare Decisis — Sovereignty — Cows and Changing Circumstances". (1960), 18 U.T. Fac. L. Rev. 163.

Judges, D.P. "Keeping the faith?: the lower courts' dubious interpretation of Lynch v. Donnelly (104 S. Ct. 1355) and Stare Decisis". (1989), 24 Land and Water L. Rev. 167.

Kavanagh, P.B. "Stare Decisis in the House of Lords". (1973), 5 N.Z.U.L. Rev. 323.

Kennedy, G.D. "Case and Comment". (1955), 33 Can. Bar Rev. 340.

Kennedy, G.D. "Case and Comment". (1959), 27 Can. Bar Rev. 465.

Kelman, M. "Force of Precedent in the Lower Courts". (1967/68), 14 Wayne L. Rev. 3.

Kidd, C.J.F. "*Stare decisis* in intermediate appellate courts : Practice in the English Court of Appeal, the Australian State Full Courts and the New Zealand Court of Appeal". (1978), 52 Aust. L.J. 274.

Knapman, L. *et al.* "Overruling Previous Decisions of Divisional Court". [1985] Crim. L.R. 792.

Knifton, M.N. "Overruling Supreme Court Precedents: Anticipatory Action by United States Courts of Appeal". (1982), 51 Fordham L. Rev. 53.

Lambert, D., "Ratio decidendi and obiter dicta". (1993), 51 Advocate (Van.) 689.

Landes, W.M., and R.A. Posner. "Legal Precedent: A Theoretical and Empirical Analysis". (1976), 19 Journal of Law and Economics 249.

Lang, A.G. "Is There A Ratio Decidendi?" (1974), 48 Aust. L.J. 146.

Langbein, J.H. "Modern Jurisprudence in the House of Lords: The Passing of the London Tramways". (1968), 53 Cornell L.R. 807.

Lapres, D. "Stare Decisis — Binding Effect of Decisions of House of Lords on Lower Courts". (1974), 52 Can. Bar Rev. 128.

Lawlor, R.C. "Axioms of Fact Polarization and Fact Ranking — Their Role in Stare Decisis". (1969), 14 U.T.L. Rev. 703.

Leach, W.B. "Revisionism in the House of Lords: The Bastion of Rigid Stare Decisis Falls". (1967), 80 Harvard L. Rev. 197.

L'Heureux-Dubé, C., "By reason of authority or authority of reason". (1993), 27 U.B.C.L. Rev. 1.

Llewellyn, K.N. "The Two-Faced Doctrine". In *The Bramblebush*. New York: Oceana, 1930, p. 66.

Lyon, J.N. "Drybones and Stare Decisis". (1971), 17 McGill L.J. 594.

Lyons, D. "Formal Justice and Judicial Precedent". (1985), 38 Vand. L. Rev. 495.

MacGuigan, M.R. "Precedent and Policy in the Supreme Court". (1967), 45 Can. Bar Rev. 627.

MacIntyre, J.M. "The Use of American Cases in Canadian Courts". (1966), 2 U.B.C.L. Rev. 478.

Maltz, E.M. "The Concept of Precedent in Choice of Law Theory". (1986), 51 Mo. L. Rev. 191.

Maltz, E.M. "The Nature of Precedent". (1988), 66 N.C.L. Rev. 367.

Marshall, H.H. "Binding Effect of Decisions of the Judicial Committee of the Privy Council". (1968), 17 Int. and Comp. L.Q. 743.

Mitchell, C.M. "The Role of Courts in Public Policy-Making: A Personal View". (1975), 33 U.T. Fac. L. Rev. 1.

Moran, T.J. "Stare Decisis in an Era of Judicial Activism: One State's Answer". (1969), U. Tel. L. Rev. 51.

Murphy, C.F. "Legal Quality of Judicial Decisions". (1969), 7 Duquesne L. Rev. 365.

Mykkeltvedt, R. "Ratio Decidendi or Obiter Dicta?: The Supreme Court and Modes of Precedent Transformation". (1981), 15 Ga. L. Rev. 311.

Nelson, S.B. "Canadian Use of American Precedent under the new Charter of Rights and Freedoms". (1986), 3 Can.-Am. L.J. 161.

Nicol, A.G.L. "Prospective Overruling: A New Device for English Courts?" (1976), 39 Mod. L. Rev. 542.

Noland, J.D. "Stare Decisis and the Overruling of Constitutional Decisions in the Warren Years." [1969] Val. U.L. Rev. 401.

Oliphant, H. "A Return to Stare Decisis". (1928), 14 A.B.A.J. 71.

Orchard, G.F. *"Stare Decisis* in the Court of Appeal". [1980] N.Z.L.J. 380.

Peltomaa, A. "Obiter Dictum of the Supreme Court of Canada: Does it Bind Lower Courts?" (1982), 60 Can. Bar Rev. 823.

Perry, S.R. "Judicial Obligation, Precedent and Common Law". (1987), 7 Oxford J. Leg. Stud. 215.

Post, G.G. "Stare Decisis: The Use of Precedents". (1984), Law and Pol. 190.

Prott, L.V. "Refusing to Follow Precedents: Rebellious Lower Courts and the Fading Comity Doctrine". (1977), 51 Aust. L.J. 288.

Prott, L.V. "When Will a Superior Court Overrule its own Decision?" (1978), 52 Aust. L.J. 304.

Quigley, T. "A Shorn Beard". (1987), 10 Dal. L.J. 3:167.

Raphael, R.H. "Stare Decisis in the Ontario Court of Appeal: *Delta Acceptance v. Redman*". (1969), 27 U.T. Fac. L. Rev. 112.

Rickett, C.E.F. "Precedent in the Court of Appeal". (1980), 43 Mod. L. Rev. 136.

Rippon, P.H. "Doctrine of Precedent". (1983), 133 New L.J. 874.

Rogers, C.S. "Perspectives or Prospective Overruling". (1967/68), 36 U.M.K.C. L. Rev. 35.

Rudden, B. "Courts and Codes in England, France and Soviet Russia". (1973/74), 48 Tul. L. Rev. 1010.

St. John, E. "Lords Break from Precedent: An Australian View". (1967), 16 Int. and Comp. L.Q. 808.

Schaeffer, W.V. "Control of 'Sunbursts': Techniques of Prospective Overruling". (1967), 42 N.Y.U. L. Rev. 631.

Schaeffer, W.V. "New Ways of Precedent". (1967), 2 Man. L.J. 255.

Schaeffer, W.V. "Precedent and Policy". (1966), 34 U. Chic. L. Rev. 3.

Schmidhauser, J.R. "Stare Decisis, Dissent and the Background of the Justices of the Supreme Court of the United States". (1962), 14 U.T.L.J. 194.

Schmitthoff, C.M. "Should Precedents be Binding?" (1982), J. Bus. L. 290.

Schreuer, C.H. "Authority of International Judicial Practice in Domestic Courts". (1974), 23 Int. and Comp. L.Q. 681.

Seligson, R.A., and J.S. Warnlof. "Use of Unreported Cases in California". (1972), 24 Hastings L.J. 37.

Shapiro, M. "Toward a Theory of Stare Decisis". (1972), 1 J. Leg. Stud. 125.

Silverman, H.W. "Panacea for a Judgment". (1971), 9 Alta. L. Rev. 397.

Simmons, C.G. "Arbitral Stare Decisis: An Unheralded but Important Doctrine in Canadian Arbitral Jurisprudence". (1986), 11 Queen's L.J. 347.

Sobeloff, J. "Tax Effect of State Court Decisions". (1967/68), 21 Tax Lawyer 507.

Starke, J.G. "Conflicting Decisions of Courts of First Instance — Whether Earlier or Later Decision Should be Followed by Another Court of First Instance". (1985), 59 Aust. L.J. 236.

Stevens, J.P. "The Life Span of a Judge-Made Rule". (1983), 58 N.Y.U.L. Rev. 1.

Stone, J. "1966 and All That! Losing the Chains of Precedent". (1969), 69 Colum. L. Rev. 1162.

Stone, J. "The Lords at the Crossroads — When to 'Depart' and How!" (1972), 46 Aust. L.J. 483.

Stone, J. "On The Liberation of Appellate Judges: How Not To Do It!" (1972), 35 Mod. L. Rev. 449.

Stone, J. "The Ratio of the Ratio Decidendi". (1969), 22 Mod. L. Rev. 597.

Stone, J. "A Court of Appeal in Search of Itself: Thoughts on Judges' Liberation". (1971), 71 Colum. L. Rev. 1420.

Summers, R.S. "Two Types of Substantive Reasons: The Core of a Theory of Common Law Justification". (1978), 63 Cornell L. Rev. 707 at 730-35.

Taggart, M. "The Binding Effect of Decisions of the Privy Council (New Zealand)". (1984), 11 N.Z.U.L. Rev. 66.

Tancelin, M. "Exemple d'application de régle du précédent et d'interprétation stricte du droit statutaire". (1980), 40 R. du B. 364.

Traynor, R.J. "Quo Vadis, Prospective Overruling: A Question of Judicial Responsibility". (1977), 28 Hastings L.J. 533.

Trope, R.L. "Double Standard in Stare Decisis: Should Stare Decisis be Less Applicable in Constitutional Cases than in Statutory Cases?" (1986), 20 J. Bev. Hills Bar Assoc. 85.

Tur, R.H.S. "Varieties of overruling and judicial law-making: prospective overruling in a comparative perspective". (1978), 23 Juridical Rev. 33.

Weaver, G.M. "The Precedential Value of Unpublished Judicial Opinions". (1988), 39 Mercer L. Rev. 477.

Weiler, P.C. "Legal Values and Judicial Decision-Making". (1970), 48 Can. Bar Rev. 1.

Weinrib, A.S. "Property, Precedent and Public Policy". (1985), 35 U.T.L.J. 542.

Weinrib, A.S. "Precedents, Statutes and Legal Reasoning". (1984), Law and Pol. 185.

Wesley-Smith, P. "*Per incuriam* doctrine". (1980), 15 J. Soc. Pub. T.L. 58.

Whitehead, G.R.B. "The Supreme Court of Canada and the Stare Decisis Doctrine". (1967), 15 Chitty's L.J. 146.

Williams, H.R., and R.M. Myers. "Stare Decisis and the Pooling of Non-Executive Interests in Oil and Gas". 46 Mer. L. Rev. 1013.

Williams, J. "Stare Decisis and the Doctrine of the Incorporation of Customary International Law". (1983), 34 N. Ir. Leg. Q. 166.

Willock, I.D. "Judges at Work: Making Law and Keeping to the Law". (1982), Jurid. Rev. 237.

Wright, C.A. "Precedents". (1942), 4 U.T.L.J. 247.

Zellick, G. "Precedent in the Court of Appeal, Criminal Division". [1974] Crim. L.R. 222.

Practice Statement (Judicial Precedent). [1966] 1 W.L.R. 1 234.

CASES

A.V.G. Management Science Ltd. v. Barwell Developments Ltd., [1979] 2 S.C.R. 43, [1979] 1 W.W.R. 330, 92 D.L.R. (3d) 289, 8 R.P.R. 1, 24 N.R. 554.

Banque Canadienne nationale v. Gingras, [1977] 2 S.C.R. 554, 1 B.L.R. 149, 15 N.R. 598, 76 D.L.R. (3d) 91.

Bell v. Cessna Aircraft Co., [1983] 6 W.W.R. 178, 46 B.C.L.R. 145, 36 C.P.C. 115, 149 D.L.R. (3d) 509 (C.A.).

Betts v. Sanderson Estate (1988), [1989] 2 W.W.R. 113, 31 B.C.L.R. (2d) 1, 44 C.C.L.T. 97, 11 M.V.R. (2d) 146, 53 D.L.R. (4th) 675 (C.A.), leave to appeal to S.C.C. refused 36 B.C.L.R. (2d) xxxvi (note), [1989] 3 W.W.R. lxx (note), 55 D.L.R. (4th) vii (note), 101 N.R. 232n (S.C.C.).

British Columbia (A.G.), Re, [1980] 3 W.W.R. 193 (*sub nom. A.G. B.C. v. Diebolt*), 4 M.V.R. 167 (B.C. S.C.).

Canada (Minister of Indian Affairs & Northern Developments) v. Ranville, [1982] 2 S.C.R. 518, 139 D.L.R. (3d) 1, [1983] 1 C.N.L.R. 12, [1983] R.D.J. 16, 44 N.R. 616.

Ciba-Geigy Canada Ltd. v. Apotex Inc. (1991), 75 O.R. (2d) 589, 32 C.P.R. (3d) 555, 45 O.A.C. 356 (C.A.), reversed [1992] 3 S.C.R. 120, 44 C.P.R. (3d) 289, 95 D.L.R. (4th) 385, 143 N.R. 241, 50 O.A.C. 321.

Conder v. North Star Construction Co. (1979), 17 B.C.L.R. 186, 12 R.P.R. 313, 106 D.L.R. (3d) 673 (S.C.).

Dywidag Systems International Canada Ltd. v. Zutphen Brothers Construction Ltd. (1987), 17 C.P.C. (2d) 149, 35 D.L.R. (4th) 433, 29 C.R.R. 6, 76 N.S.R. (2d) 398, 189 A.P.R. 398 (C.A.), reversed [1990] 1 S.C.R. 705, 40 C.L.R. 1, 41 C.P.C. (2d) 18, 68 D.L.R. (4th) 147, 106 N.R. 11, 97 N.S.R. (2d) 181, 258 A.P.R. 181, 46 C.R.R. 259.

Ellwood Robinson Ltd. v. Ohio Development Co. (1975), 7 O.R. (2d) 556 (Dist. Ct.).

Ex parte Guenette (1975), 27 C.C.C. (2d) 279 (B.C. S.C.).

Fickett v. Bignell, [1977] 5 W.W.R. 599, 1 R.F.L. (2d) 269 (B.C. Co. Ct.), reversed [1979] 2 W.W.R. 379 (B.C. C.A.).

General Brake & Clutch Service Ltd. v. W.A. Scott & Sons Ltd., [1975] W.W.R. 349 (Man. Q.B.), reversed (1975), 59 D.L.R. (3d) 741 (C.A.).

Green v. British Columbia (A.G.) (1986), 29 C.R.R. 35 (B.C. S.C.).

Harrison v. Carswell, [1976] 2 S.C.R. 200, [1975] 6 W.W.R. 673, 25 C.C.C. (2d) 186, 62 D.L.R. (3d) 68, 75 C.L.L.C. 14,286, 5 N.R. 523.

Horne v. Horne Estate (1986), 54 O.R. (2d) 510 (*sub nom. Horne v. Evans*), 1 R.F.L. (3d) 335, 22 E.T.R. 272 (H.C.), affirmed (1987), 60 O.R. (2d) 1, 8 R.F.L. (3d) 195, 45 R.P.R. 223, 26 E.T.R. 233, 39 D.L.R. (4th) 416, 21 O.A.C. 313 (C.A.).

Indalex Division of Indal v. United Metal Fabricators Ltd. (1986), 6 B.C.L.R. (2d) 243, 15 C.P.C. (2d) 19 (S.C.).

MacDonald v. Vapor Canada Ltd., [1977] 2 S.C.R. 134, 22 C.P.R. (2d) 1, 7 N.R. 477, 66 D.L.R. (3d) 1.

Marvco Color Research Ltd. v. Harris (1980), 27 O.R. (2d) 686, 11 R.P.R. 112, 107 D.L.R. (3d) 632, 36 N.R. 90 (H.C.), affirmed (1980), 30 O.R. (2d) 162, 115 D.L.R. (3d) 512 (C.A.), reversed [1982] 2 S.C.R. 774, 20 B.L.R. 143, 26 R.P.R. 48, 141 D.L.R. (3d) 577, 45 N.R. 302.

May v. Minister of Natural Revenue, [1985] 2 C.T.C. 2407, 85 D.T.C. 690 (T.C.C.).

McLaughlin, Re (1977), 16 O.R. (2d) 375, 1 E.T.R. 181, 78 D.L.R. (3d) 275 (H.C.).

Metropolitan Trust Co. v. Latvala (1979), 22 O.R. (2d) 680, 93 D.L.R. (3d) 688 (H.C.).

Meurer v. McKenzie (1977), 73 D.L.R. (3d) 477, 2 C.P.C. 109 (B.C. S.C.), reversed on other grounds [1978] 1 W.W.R. 114, 4 B.C.L.R. 349, 81 D.L.R. (3d) 388 (C.A.).

Mitrunen v. Anthes Equipment Ltd., [1984] 5 W.W.R. 639, 57 B.C.L.R. 287, 13 D.L.R. (4th) 597 (S.C.), affirmed [1985] 3 W.W.R. 445, 65 B.C.L.R. 291, 17 D.L.R. (4th) 567 (C.A.).

Morrow v. R. (1984), 54 B.C.L.R. 182 (Co. Ct.).

Nova, An Alberta Corp. v. Guelph Engineering Co., [1983] 6 W.W.R. 501, 27 Alta. L.R. (2d) 268, 38 C.P.C. 42, 78 C.P.R. (2d) 229, 48 A.R. 241 (Q.B.), affirmed [1984] 3 W.W.R. 314, 30 Alta. L.R. (2d) 183, 5 D.L.R. (4th) 755, 50 A.R. 199, 80 C.P.R. (2d) 93, 42 C.P.C. 194 (C.A.).

P.(U.) v. P.(W.), [1980] 3 W.W.R. 263, 15 R.F.L. (2d) 301, 25 A.R. 412 (Fam. Ct.).

R. v. Andrews, [1990] 3 S.C.R. 870, 75 O.R. (2d) 481n, 1 C.R. (4th) 266, 61 C.C.C. (3d) 490, 3 C.R.R. (2d) 176, 77 D.L.R. (4th) 128, 117 N.R. 284, 47 O.A.C. 293.

R. v. Armstrong (1988), 45 C.C.C. (3d) 285 (B.C. C.A.).

R. v. Bachman (1987), 78 A.R. 282 (C.A.), affirmed [1988] 1 S.C.R. 1094, 86 N.R. 359, 89 A.R. 199.

R. v. Barrett, [1980] 4 W.W.R. 339, 15 C.R. (3d) 361, 54 C.C.C. (2d) 75, 21 A.R. 499 (C.A.).

R. v. Bell, [1979] 2 S.C.R. 212, 9 M.P.L.R. 103, 10 O.M.B.R. 142, 98 D.L.R. (3d) 255, 26 N.R. 457.

R. v. Cotterhill (1977), 3 Alta. L.R. (2d) 37 (Dist. Ct.).

R. v. Davis (1976), 21 C.C.C. (2d) 507, 74 D.T.C. 6595 (B.C. S.C.).

R. v. Dawood, 31 C.R.N.S. 382, [1976] 1 W.W.R. 262, 27 C.C.C. (2d) 300 (Alta. C.A.).

R. v. Dennis, 28 C.R.N.S. 268, [1975] 2 W.W.R. 630, 22 C.C.C. (2d) 152, 56 D.L.R. (3d) 379 (B.C.).

R. v. DePagie, [1976] 6 W.W.R. 1, 1 Alta. L.R. (2d) 30, 32 C.C.C. (2d) 89, 1 A.R. 602 (C.A.), leave to appeal to S.C.C. refused (1976), 32 C.C.C. (2d) 89n (S.C.C.).

R. v. Doyle (1976), 6 Nfld. & P.E.I.R. 479 (*sub nom. Re Doyle*) (T.D.).

R. v. Hill, [1977] 1 S.C.R. 827, 23 C.C.C. (2d) 321, 58 D.L.R. (3d) 697, 6 N.R. 413.

R. v. Ingram (1981), 14 M.V.R. 60, 12 Sask. R. 242 (Q.B.).

R. v. Jun, [1940] 2 W.W.R. 274, [1940] 2 W.W.R. 467, 54 B.C.R. 541, 73 C.C.C. 289, [1940] 2 D.L.R. 432 (*sub nom. Ex parte Yuen Yick Jun*) (C.A.).

R. v. Kartna (1979), 2 M.V.R. 259 (Ont. H.C.).

R. v. Keegstra, [1990] 3 S.C.R. 697, 77 Alta. L.R. (2d) 193, 1 C.R. (4th) 129, [1991] 2 W.W.R. 1, 114 N.R. 81, 61 C.C.C. (3d) 1, 3 C.R.R. (2d) 193, 117 N.R. 1.

R. v. Kennedy, [1980] 4 W.W.R. 577, 6 M.V.R. 178 (Alta. Q.B.).

R. v. Maika (1974), 27 C.R.N.S. 115, 17 C.C.C. (2d) 110 (C.A.).

R. v. McKibbon (1981), 34 O.R. (2d) 185, 61 C.C.C. (2d) 126 (H.C.), affirmed (1981), 35 O.R. (2d) 124, 64 C.C.C. (2d) 441 (C.A.), affirmed [1984] 1 S.C.R. 131, 38 C.R. (3d) 305, 10 C.C.C. (3d) 193, 52 N.R. 81, 6 D.L.R. (4th) 1, 3 O.A.C. 85.

R. v. McLeod, [1984] 3 W.W.R. 590 (B.C. S.C.).

R. v. McNamara Construction (Western) Ltd., [1977] 2 S.C.R. 654, 75 D.L.R. (3d) 273, 13 N.R. 181 (*sub nom. Canada v. McNamara Const. (Western) Ltd; Canada v. J. Stevenson & Associates).*

R. v. Menzies (1987), 56 C.R. (3d) 284, 49 M.V.R. 10, 28 C.R.R. 114, 21 O.A.C. 308 (C.A.).

R. v. Miller (1982), 39 O.R. (2d) 41, 29 C.P.C. 159, 29 C.R. (3d) 153, 70 C.C.C. (2d) 129, 141 D.L.R. (3d) 330 (C.A.), affirmed [1985] 2 S.C.R. 613, 52 O.R. (2d) 585, 49 C.R. (3d) 1, 16 Admin. L.R. 184, 23 C.C.C. (3d) 97, 24 D.L.R. (4th) 9, 14 O.A.C. 33, 63 N.R. 321.

R. v. Morris (1988), 85 N.S.R. (2d) 200, 216 A.P.R. 200 (Mag. Ct.).

R. v. Mueller (1975), 32 C.R.N.S. 188, 29 C.C.C. (2d) 243 (Ont. C.A.).

R. v. Ostridge (1979), 22 Nfld. & P.E.I.R. 123, 58 A.P.R. 123, 2 M.V.R. 160 (P.E.I. S.C.).

R. v. Pacific Press, [1977] 5 W.W.R. 507, 38 C.R.N.S. 295, 37 C.C.C. (2d) 487 (B.C. S.C.).

R. v. Paquette, [1977] 2 S.C.R. 189, 39 C.R.N.S. 257, 30 C.C.C. (2d) 417, 70 D.L.R. (3d) 129, 11 N.R. 451.

R. v. Pollock, [1982] 1 F.C. 710, [1981] C.T.C. 389, 81 D.T.C. 5293 (Fed T.D.), affirmed [1984] C.T.C. 353, 84 D.T.C. 6370 (Fed. C.A.).

R. v. Robertson (1975), 29 C.R.N.S. 141, 21 C.C.C. (2d) 385 (Ont. C.A.).

R. v. Santeramo (1976), 36 C.R.N.S. 1, 32 C.C.C. (2d) 35 (C.A.), leave to appeal to S.C.C. granted (1976) 32 C.C.C. (2d) 35n (S.C.C.).

R. v. Sellars, [1980] 1 S.C.R. 527, 20 C.R. (3d) 381, 52 C.C.C. (2d) 345, 110 D.L.R. (3d) 629, 32 N.R. 70.

R. v. Weiss, [1980] 5 W.W.R. 93, 19 B.C.L.R. 207, 108 D.L.R. (3d) 253 (S.C.).

R. v. Wolf, [1975] 2 S.C.R. 107, 27 C.R.N.S. 150, [1974] 6 W.W.R. 368, 17 C.C.C. (2d) 425, 47 D.L.R. (3d) 741, 2 N.R. 415.

R. v. Wray (No. 2), [1974] S.C.R. 565, 10 C.C.C. (2d) 215, 33 D.L.R. (3d) 750.

R.V.P. Enterprises Ltd. v. British Columbia (Minister of Consumer & Corporate Affairs), [1988] 4 W.W.R. 726, 32 Admin. L.R. 305, (*sub nom. R.V.P. Enterprises Ltd. v. British Columbia (A.G.)*) 25 B.C.L.R. (2d) 219, 50 D.L.R. (4th) 394, 41 C.R.R. 264 (C.A.), leave to appeal to S.C.C. refused [1988] 6 W.W.R. lxix (note), 32 Admin. L.R. 305n, 28 B.C.L.R. (2d) xxxi (note), 50 D.L.R. (4th) vii (note), 90 N.R. 319n (S.C.C.).

Reference re Agricultural Products Marketing Act (Canada), [1978] 2 S.C.R. 1198, 84 D.L.R. (3d) 257, 19 N.R. 361.

S. v. S., [1974] 1 W.W.R. 671, 13 R.F.L. 265, 41 D.L.R. (3d) 621.

Sigurdson v. Reid (1979), 32 C.B.R. (N.S.) 170, 17 B.C.L.R. 117 (S.C.), reversed (1980), 37 C.B.R. (N.S.) 146, 26 B.C.L.R. 336, 118 D.L.R. (3d) 555 (C.A.).

Smith, Kline & French Canada Ltd. v. Apotex Inc. (1983), 71 C.P.R. (2d) 146 (T.D.), reversed on other grounds (1984), 1 C.P.R. (3d) 256 (Fed. C.A.).

Ward, Re (1975), 20 R.F.L. 173, 9 O.R. (2d) 35, 59 D.L.R. (3d) 361 (Div. Ct.).

Wallace v. Wallace (1976), 28 R.F.L. 335, 70 D.L.R. (3d) 375 (Sask. Q.B.).

Woloszczuk v. Onyszczak (1976), 14 O.R. (2d) 732, 1 C.P.C. 129, 74 D.L.R. (3d) 554 (H.C.).

Chapter 11

THE RULES AND PRINCIPLES OF STATUTORY INTERPRETATION

In recent years, many old and settled principles at common law have been replaced or modified through legislative enactment at all levels of government. This phenomenon has been brought about both by principal legislation by Parliament and the various provincial legislatures and by regulations, ordinances, by-laws, statutory instruments and Orders in Council enacted by inferior legislative bodies. The result has been a proliferation of enactments dealing with all aspects of modern life, business, and relations between persons.

In addition, in the past quarter century the state of man's knowledge has rapidly increased. This has resulted in the development of complex modern technology in all fields in the natural and applied sciences. Similarly, in the social sciences, and particularly in the area of economics, man has devised new ways of looking at problems in society and new approaches in devising solutions to those problems. Society in the computer age is a matrix of complex institutions, riddled with complex problems. The law must reflect and respond to these complexities. The result is that much recent legislation has had to be expressed in complex language, and the first problem that the reader of the law faces is comprehending the language contained in many recent statutes.

THE PROBLEM OF COMPLEXITY

For example, the following provisions of the Income Tax Act, S.C. 1970-71-72, c. 63, constitute only one part of one section of the Act. In reading the section, the reader might consider the simple question of what the section is saying:

66(1) A principal-business corporation may deduct, in computing its income for a taxation year, the lesser of

(a) the aggregate of such of its Canadian exploration and development expenses as were incurred by it before the end of the taxation year, to the extent that they were not deductible in computing income for a previous taxation year, and

(b) of that aggregate, an amount equal to its income for the taxation year if no deduction were allowed under this subsection, subsection 66.1(2) or section 65, minus the deductions allowed for the year by sections 112 and 113.

(2) A corporation (other than a principal-business corporation the principal business of which is described in subparagraph (15)(h)(i) or (ii)), whose principal business is production or marketing of sodium chloride or potash or whose business includes manufacturing products the manufacturing of which involves processing sodium chloride or potash, may deduct, in computing its income for a taxation year, the drilling and exploration expenses incurred by it in the year and before May 7, 1974 on or in respect of exploring or drilling for halite or sylvite.

(3) A taxpayer other than a principal-business corporation may deduct, in computing his income for a taxation year, the aggregate of his Canadian exploration and development expenses to the extent that they were not deducted in computing his income for a preceding taxation year.

If the reader finds the above language complex, consider the language of s. 66(3) before it was amended several times[1] and as it was originally enacted in S.C. 1970-71-72, c. 63:

(3) A taxpayer who is an individual or a corporation other than a principal-business corporation may deduct, in computing his income for a taxation year, the lesser of

(a) the aggregate of such of his Canadian exploration and development expenses as were incurred by him before the end of the taxation year to the extent they were not deductible in computing his income for a previous taxation year, and

(b) of that aggregate, the greater of

(i) such amount as the taxpayer may claim, not exceeding 20% of the aggregate determined under paragraph (a), and

(ii) the amount, if any, by which the aggregate of

(A) such part of his income for the taxation year as may reasonably be regarded as attributable to the production of petroleum or natural gas from wells in Canada or to the production of minerals from mines in Canada,

(B) his income for the taxation year from royalties in respect of an oil or gas well in Canada or a mine in Canada,

(C) the amount, if any, included in computing his income for the year by virtue of paragraph 59(3.2)(b) or (c), and

(D) the aggregate of amounts included in computing his income for the year by virtue of any of paragraphs 59(2)(a), (c) and (d) and subsection 59(2.1)

exceeds

(E) the aggregate of amounts deducted in computing his income for the year under subsection 64(1) in respect of property described in paragraph 59(1.2)(b), or under subsection 64(1.1) or (1.2), if no deductions were allowed under this subsection, subsection 66.1(3) or section 65.

exceeds

---

[1] These provisions were eventually re-enacted by S.C. 1985, c. 45, s. 28(1). The replacement provision clearly reflects a move toward more simplified statutory language. Nonetheless, its language is still somewhat complex. For another example of the trend toward more simplified statutory language, see the reference in Chapter 7 to the newer terminology in respect of the law of wills and estates.

(iii) the amount of any deduction allowed by the *Income Tax Application Rules, 1971* in respect of this subparagraph in computing his income for the year.

Consider also the complexity of language in the next subsection as it presently reads:

(4) A taxpayer who is resident throughout a taxation year in Canada may deduct, in computing his income for that taxation year, the lesser of

(*a*) the aggregate of such of his foreign exploration and development expenses as were incurred by him before the end of the taxation year to the extent they were not deductible in computing his income for a previous taxation year, and

(*b*) of that aggregate, the greater of,

(i) such amount as the taxpayer may claim not exceeding 10% of the aggregate determined under paragraph (*a*), and

(ii) the aggregate of

(A) such part of his income for the taxation year as may reasonably be regarded as attributable to the production of petroleum or natural gas from natural accumulations thereof outside Canada or from oil or gas wells outside Canada or to the production of minerals from mines outside Canada,

(B) his income for the taxation year from royalties in respect of a natural accumulation of petroleum or natural gas outside Canada, an oil or gas well outside Canada or a mine outside Canada, and

(C) the aggregate of amounts each of which is an amount, in respect of a foreign resource property that has been disposed of by him, equal to the amount, if any, by which

(I) the amount included in computing his income for the year by virtue of section 59 in respect of the disposition of the property,

exceeds

(II) the amount deducted under section 64 in respect of the property in computing his income for the year,

if no deduction were allowed under this subsection, subsection 66(1) or (3), 66.1(2) or (3) or section 65.

If the reader has mastered an understanding of the above provisions, perhaps he might consult the regulations to the Anti-Inflation Act, S.C. 1974-75-76, c. 75, which were at least equal in complexity to the above provisions.

The late Dr. Max Wyman, a former President of the University of Alberta, a former Chairman of the Alberta Human Rights Commission and a member of the Board of Review investigating Provincial Courts in the province of Alberta, has made certain observations on the Canadian legal system. Since he is a lay person, his observations contain a certain objectivity which arises out of a first exposure to our legal system. In an addendum to the Board of Review's formal report in May of 1975 he made these remarks concerning "the language of the law":

The law belongs to the people who have chosen to be governed by that law. It is not the private domain of the bar, the bench, and the police. For this reason, it seems to me to be axiomatic that the law should be written in the language of the people, not the archaic, stilted and sometimes meaningless language that is now being used. This does not mean that each person should be capable of being his or her own lawyer. Far from it. The complexity of our society will ensure that highly-trained legal personnel will have important roles to play in the years to come. Nevertheless, reasonably educated people should be able, if interested, to read and understand the laws they are expected to obey. Those who are in difficulty with the law should be able, with legal help, to understand the nature of their difficulties, the alternatives that are open to them, and to make a reasoned choice from among those alternatives.

At the present time, it is extremely doubtful that even highly educated people can understand the language in which the law is written. In some extreme cases, even members of the legal profession have difficulty in providing an unequivocal interpretation of some laws.

In Gulliver's Travels, Jonathan Swift made many a pungent and ironical comment about the laws and customs of eighteenth century England. Gulliver describes in some detail the laws of Brobdignag, one of which dealt with the language of the law:

> No law of that country must exceed in words the number of letters in their alphabet, which consists only in two and twenty. But indeed few of them extend even to that length. They are expressed in the most plain and simple terms, wherein those people are not mercurial enough to discover above one interpretation. And to write a comment upon any law is a capital crime. As to the decision of civil causes, or proceedings against criminals, their precedents are so few, that they have little reason to boast of any extraordinary skill in either.

The laws of Canada might improve considerably if we were to follow the simplicity of the laws that were urged to govern the land of the giants. Even then, over two hundred years ago, Swift was not enamoured with the reliance that English law placed on precedents.[2]

These comments suggest that legislative draftsmen in Canada are not accomplished in performing their trade. On the contrary, however, legal drafting in Canada is an art which has been acknowledged and appreciated throughout the common law world. Canadian draftsmen are often sought by emerging nations in the Third World to draft their basic constitutions as well as the provisions of their regular statutes. Also, there is a substantial and important division of the Department of Justice of Canada in Ottawa concerned solely with the drafting of legislation. In addition, several law schools in Canada now provide courses in legal drafting, and Canadian texts have been published dealing with the related concerns of legal writing and legal drafting. So the problem lies not in a lack of Canadian expertise in drafting, but rather in the fact that complex laws couched in complex statutory language must be used in order to resolve contem-

---

[2] The move for plain language in legal writing, generally, and specifically in contracts and statutes has attracted considerable attention. There has been much written on the topic. See, for example, the following sources kindly provided to the author by Christine Mowat, a proponent for plain language in the law: Asprey, M.M., *Plain Language for Lawyers*, Sydney: The Federation Press, 1991; Mellinkoff, D., *Legal Writing: Sense and Nonsense*, St. Paul: West Publishing Co., 1982; Mowat, C., "A plain language writer considers consideration", LawNow, April/May, 1995; Mowat, C., "Buddhists, Running, and Plain Language in Calgary, Part One and Part Two", Michigan Bar Journal, July 1994, pp. 696-697, and August 1994, pp. 828-31; Wydick, R.C., *Plain English for Lawyers*, 3rd ed., Durham: Carolina Academic Press, 1994. See also Dick, R.C., Q.C., *Legal Drafting in Plain Language*, 3rd ed., Scarborough: Carswell, 1995. Continuing legal education agencies have also promoted this movement. For example, the Legal Education Society of Alberta sponsored a seminar in November of 1994 on the topic of "Clear Legal Writing: A Contemporary Approach".

porary matters. In addition, historically, we in the common law world are relatively inexperienced in drafting laws, while the civil or Napoleonic codes of Europe date back to the early Roman codification for their origins. Nations employing a civil or Napoleonic code thus share a much vaster experience in reducing propositions to statutory language, an experience spanning several centuries.

THE PROBLEM OF AMBIGUITY:
DETERMINING LEGISLATIVE INTENT

The major problem in dealing with statutes is the ambiguity often found in statutory language. Sometimes, of course, the ambiguity is intentional. More likely, however, it is totally unintentional. Often a statute must be applied in an area, or in connection with a fact situation, not within the contemplation of the drafter of the statute. In order to assist a judge in interpreting such provisions, various rules of statutory interpretation have been developed. In addition, courts have recognized and are receptive to the use of various aids in interpretation. Also, the entire interpretative process is conducted in the context of various presumptions recognized in law which serve as a guide to the judge in interpreting statutes.

The interpretation of ambiguous statutory provisions is a somewhat subjective process. A judge may select a particular rule of statutory interpretation or use a particular aid to interpretation and decide not to be receptive to an alternative rule or aid in interpretation. Nonetheless, that subjective exercise must be conducted in the context of an objective search for legislative intention. As one writer put it:

> In many modern cases, the principle that courts are bound to follow "legislative intention" has been taken to mean that in determining the effect of a statute in cases of interpretative doubt, the judge should decide in such a way as will advance the general objectives which, in his judgment, the legislators sought to attain by enactment of the legislation . . . Thus the principle that doubtful questions should be resolved in accordance with "legislative intention" requires, in this signification of "intention" that the judge interpret the statute not in the light of his own personal notions of justice and expediency, but in the light of the legislative conceptions of justice and expediency which underlie the policy of the enactment.[3]

It is important to realize that the process of interpreting ambiguous statutes represents, a significant part of the judicial function, especially at the appellate levels; that is, judges spend a large part of their time in interpreting ambiguous statutes. That is why an understanding of the process by which they conduct this exercise is necessary.

---

[3] H.W. Jones, "Statutory Doubts and Legislative Intention" (1940), 40 Colum. L. Rev. 157.

1. RULES OF CONSTRUCTION

The fundamental rule in interpreting ambiguous statutes is that a judge must ascertain the intent of the legislature in enacting the statute. Legislative intent is one of the many fictions throughout the law that serves a useful purpose. Another example of a legal fiction arises in the law of negligence, where in order to determine whether a defendant has breached a standard of care, we resort to an objective test: whether the defendant has conducted himself in accordance with the standard expected of a "reasonable man". In reality, of course, there is no such person who is reasonable in all circumstances and in all situations. Likewise, in reality there is no such single or, for that matter, collective legislative intent in any legislative body. There are opposition parties who do not share the same political views as the government in respect of a given piece of legislation; there are backbenchers of the governing party who do not share the views of the government in respect of a particular piece of legislation but do not complain owing to the dictates of party discipline; there may even have been dissent within the cabinet in discussions preceding the introduction of a piece of legislation. However, notwithstanding its somewhat artificial nature, the notion of legislative intent must be regarded as another one of those legal fictions which serve a useful purpose.

In order to determine the intent of the legislature in enacting a given ambiguous statute, a judge may resort to one of the three major canons of construction. First, the 'literal' or 'plain meaning' rule requires that if the precise words used are plain and unambiguous, the judge is bound to construe them in their ordinary sense,[4] even though such a construction might lead to an absurdity or a manifest injustice. The corollary of the above is that any legislative omissions or errors are not to be inferred. Secondly, the 'golden' rule requires that, in interpreting an ambiguous statute, the grammatical and ordinary sense of the words is to be adhered to, unless that would lead to some absurdity or some repugnance or inconsistency with the rest of the instrument, in which case the grammatical and ordinary sense of the words may be modified only so far as to avoid that absurdity and inconsistency.[5] Finally, the 'mischief' rule requires that, in interpreting an ambiguous statute, the judge must consider four things: First, what was the common law before the making of the Act? Secondly,

---

[4] See, for example, *R. v. Moore* (1985), 67 N.S.R. (2d) 241, 155 A.P.R. 241 (C.A.), where a trial judge was held to have erred in implying qualifications to an unambiguous statute.

[5] See, for example, the recent case of *Krieg v. Saskatchewan* (1993), 112 Sask. R. 225 (Q.B.). See also, *R. v. Wilson* (1978), 6 B.C.L.R. 231 (S.C.); *R. v. Boylan*, [1979] 3 W.W.R. 435, 8 C.R. (3d) 36, 46 C.C.C. (2d) 415, 3 Sask. R. 157 (C.A.); and *Pfeil v. Simcoe & Erie General Insurance Co.*, [1984] 5 W.W.R. 756, 8 C.C.L.I. 112, [1985] I.L.R. 1-1852, 35 Sask. R. 277 (Q.B.), affirmed [1986] 2 W.W.R. 710, 24 D.L.R. (4th) 752, [1986] I.L.R. 1-2055, 45 Sask. L.R. 241 (C.A.).

what was the mischief and defect for which the common law did not provide? Thirdly, what remedy did the legislature resolve upon to cure the mischief and defect? Finally, what was the true reason for the remedy? After entertaining those four questions, the judge must then construe the legislation so as to suppress the mischief and advance the remedy. The above definitions of the three canons of construction are taken from various early cases but they have been restated many times in various forms.

A statute may be enacted for one of two reasons: to codify the existing common law, or to remedy a defect present within the existing common law. Some statutes, called interpretation statutes, are enacted solely for the purpose of providing guidelines for interpreting other statutes enacted within the same jurisdiction. Many of these interpretation statutes contain provisions deeming these other statutes of the same jurisdiction to be remedial in nature. As a result, this seems to invite the application of the mischief rule in interpreting an ambiguous provision, although as indicated earlier judges may select the particular canon of construction that they prefer in the circumstances and interpret the ambiguous provisions in accordance with that canon of construction.

In addition to these three canons of construction, there are three more or less grammatical rules of construction. These rules, usually expressed in Latin, are as follows. First, the 'noscitur a sociis' rule is that a general word following a group of specific words takes its meaning from those specific words. Similarly, if an ambiguous general word is followed by specific words, the ambiguous word takes its meaning from those words that follow it. For example, in one case it was held that the word "interest" in the phrase "interest, annuities, or other annual payments" means annual interest.

The second grammatical rule of construction is the 'ejusdem generis'[6] rule. It is very similar to the previous one and, in fact, some writers have suggested that they both are the same. This rule is that a general phrase (rather than a general word as in the previous rule) takes its meaning from

---

[6] Some recent examples of the application of this rule may be found in *Westfall v. Eedy* (1991), 6 O.R. (3d) 422, 7 M.P.L.R. (2d) 226 (Gen. Div.); *Riddell v. Vancouver (City)* (1984), 5 C.C.E.L. 55 (B.C. S.C.), affirmed (1985), 11 C.C.E.L. 288 (B.C. C.A.); *Warren v. Chapman*, [1984] 5 W.W.R. 454, 5 C.H.R.R. D/2226, 11 D.L.R. (4th) 474, 29 Man. R. (2d) 172, affirmed [1985] 4 W.W.R. 75, 6 C.H.R.R. D/2777 (*sub nom. Warren v. Manitoba (Human Rights Comm.)*), 17 D.L.R. (4th) 261, 31 Man. R. (2d) 231 (C.A.). See also, *Francouer v. Prince Albert Community Clinic* (1986), 52 Sask. R. 221 (Q.B.); and *Schecter v. Bluestein*, [1982] C.A. 397, 36 C.R. (3d) 46, 70 C.C.C. (3d) 336, 142 D.L.R. (3d) 71 (*sub nom. Bluestein v. R.*) (C.A. Qué.); *Tiedemann v. Basiuk* (1977), 4 Alta. L.R. (2d) 12, 7 C.P.C. 192, 5 A.R. 435 (T.D.); *Bell v. North Vancouver School District No. 44* (1979), 16 B.C.L.R. 94 (S.C.); *Frehlick v. McLenehan*, [1980] I.L.R. 1-1270, 114 D.L.R. (3d) 310, 3 Sask. R. 340 (C.A.); and *R. v. Twoyoungmen*, [1979] 5 W.W.R. 712, 3 M.V.R. 186, [1979] 3 C.N.L.R. 85, 16 A.R. 413, 101 D.L.R. (3d) 598, 48 C.C.C. (2d) 550 (C.A.).

the specific words that precede it. For example, if a statute contained a provision to the effect that "no dogs, cats or other animals may wander in public places without being controlled by means of a leash," under this rule the general phrase "or other animals" would take its meaning from the preceding specific words, with the result that it would probably be interpreted to mean a domesticated animal, rather than, for example, wild game.[7]

The third grammatical rule of construction is the 'expressio unius, exclusio alterius' rule.[8] Under this rule, the express mention or inclusion of one word or phrase implies the exclusion of another word or phrase. A good example of this rule was set out by John Willis in an article entitled "Statute Interpretation in a Nutshell" (1938), 16 Can. Bar Rev. 1 at 8 as follows:

> If I have living in my house my wife, my children, two old aunts and my mother, and a friend says "Bring the family to our picnic, Sunday", what does he mean by "family"? — my wife and children only, or my whole ménage? If he adds, "your mother comes under that heading, you know", by specially mentioning my mother he shews, it may be said, that he was using "family" in the narrow sense of "wife and children": result, the aunts are not invited — *expressio unius, exclusio alterius,* the express mention of one person or thing implies the exclusion of other persons or things of the same class not mentioned.

Willis then concludes, as many others have concluded, that this rule of construction is unreliable and is very rarely applied by a court.[9]

2. AIDS TO STATUTORY INTERPRETATION

In addition to all of the foregoing rules of construction, there are various aids available to assist a judge in determining the legislative intent behind the enactment of an ambiguous statutory provision. Again, there is an element of subjectivity in that a judge may choose to use one aid and ignore another. While some aids are clearly inadmissible in evidence others may be admitted depending upon the receptivity of the individual judge.

---

[7] See *Saskatchewan (Human Rights Comm.) v. Engineering Students' Society (sub nom. Saskatchewan (Human Rights Comm.) v. Waldo)* (1984), 5 C.N.R.R. D/2074 (Sask. Bd. of Inquiry), reversed (1986), 7 C.N.R.R. D/3443 (Sask. Q.B.), affirmed (1989), 10 C.H.R.R. D/5636, 56 D.L.R. (4th) 604, 72 Sask. R. 161 (C.A.), leave to appeal to S.C.C. refused (1989), 102 N.R. 320n, 103 N.R. 212n (S.C.C.).

[8] See *LeBlanc Estate v. Bank of Montreal* (1988), [1989] 1 W.W.R. 49, 54 D.L.R. (4th) 89, 69 Sask. R. 81 (C.A.); and, *Texaco Can. Resources Ltd. v. Alta. (Assessment Appeal Bd.)* (1987), 53 Alta. L.R. (2d) 369, 85 A.R. 218 (Q.B.), reversed (1988), 64 Alta. L.R. (2d) 37, 41 M.P.L.R. 37, 93 A.R. 81 (C.A.).

[9] See *R. v. Baig* (1979), 23 O.R. (2d) 730 (Dist. Ct.). However, see also *Crease v. Metropolitan Toronto (Municipality) Commissioners of Police* (1976), 11 O.R. (2d) 459, 66 D.L.R. (3d) 403 (County Ct.) in which the rule was applied.

The following is a list of aids in interpreting ambiguous statutory provisions. Some of these aids are intrinsic to the statute containing the ambiguous provisions, while others are purely extrinsic in nature.

(a) Interpretation Statutes

There are in Canada interpretation statutes at the federal level and in every province as well. The federal Interpretation Act applies to all federal statutes and the various provincial Interpretation Acts apply to all statutes within a given provincial jurisdiction. The Supreme Court of Canada, in *Skapinker v. Law Society of Upper Canada*,[10] however, has held that neither the federal nor provincial interpretation statutes are binding in a Charter case. They do, however, have persuasive effect.

These statutes contain some general rules in interpreting statutes. Some of the typical rules are to the effect that a preamble to a statute shall be read as part of a statute, while any marginal notes explaining the purport of a given section are not to be read as part of the statute; that any words importing male persons in any statute include female persons; and that any words in the singular include the plural and any words in the plural include the singular.

In addition to these general rules, specific words are defined for purposes of all statutes within the given jurisdiction governed by the particular interpretation statute. For example, the federal Interpretation Act defines such words as "holiday", "radio-communication", and "standard time" for the purposes of all federal statutes.

(b) Definition Sections

Many statutes contain sections defining specific words used in the particular statute. Some statutes, like the Criminal Code of Canada, have a substantial definition section at the beginning of the Act. In addition, the Criminal Code is divided into various parts and there is a definition section at the beginning of each part. Moreover, on occasion, there are definition provisions at the beginning of some sections.

(c) Context

In determining legislative intent, a legitimate exercise is to examine the context in which an ambiguous provision is found, i.e., to examine other sections of the same statute.

---

[10] [1984] 1 S.C.R. 357, 20 Admin. L.R. 1 (*sub nom. Law Society of Upper Can. v. Skapinker*), 8 C.R.R. 193, 11 C.C.C. (3d) 481, 9 D.L.R. (4th) 161, 3 O.A.C. 321, 53 N.R. 169, reversing (1983), 40 O.R. (2d) 481 (*sub nom. Re Skapinker*), 3 C.R.R. 211, 3 C.C.C. (3d) 213, 145 D.L.R. (3d) 502 (C.A.), which reversed (1982), 38 O.R. (2d) 116, 68 C.C.C. (2d) 300, 137 D.L.R. (3d) 666 (H.C.).

(d) Other Statutes

A judge may resort to an examination of other statutes in order to determine the intent of the legislature in enacting an ambiguous provision in an instant statute.[10] However, in doing so he must remain within the bounds of two constraints. First, any other statute must have the same or similar subject matter to that contained in the instant statute. Secondly, the other statute must, presumably, have been enacted by the same legislative body as that which passed the instant statute. Unless they were both enacted by the same legislative body, it would be artificial to use the other statute in entertaining questions related to legislative intent. Although the notion of legislative intent is a legal fiction, the courts must treat that fiction with logical consistency.

(e) Legislative History

In Canada, a judge may make only limited use of the legislative history of a statute containing an ambiguous provision. Such use is confined to examining any amendments made to the statute, the prior existence of any predecessor statutes now repealed, and like matters. A judge may not examine any of the legislative debates contained in Hansard nor any speeches given by, for example, the minister responsible for the bill, nor any proceedings or reports of a parliamentary committee, nor any other extrinsic aid of that nature.[11] Similarly, a judge may not consult the transcript of a royal commission of inquiry, even though that royal commission recommended the very enactment of the ambiguous statute. The foregoing are general rules arising out of judicial custom and convention, so it is not surprising to find exceptions to these rules: for example, in *Re Ombudsman Act* (1970), 72 W.W.R. 176, 10 D.L.R. (3d) 47 (Alta.), the report of the Clement Commission (investigating whether there existed a need for the establishment of an ombudsman in the province of Alberta) was admitted in a subsequent challenge to the jurisdiction of that office.[12]

The theory behind this rule is that a statute is an embodiment of all the components of its legislative history; the final enactment is deemed

---

[10] See *Goulbourn (Township) v. Ottawa-Carleton*, [1980] 1 S.C.R. 496, 10 O.M.B.R. 491, 12 O.M.B.R. 126, 101 D.L.R. (3d) 1, 29 N.R. 267; and *R. v. Croft* (1979), 35 N.S.R. (2d) 344, 62 A.P.R. 344 (C.A.).

[11] See W.H. Charles, "Extrinsic Evidence and Statutory Interpretation: Judicial Discretion in Context" (1983), 7 Dal. L.J. 7, for a thorough discussion of the rule's treatment by American, Canadian and U.K. courts, and, by the same author, "Should the rules relating to the admissibility of Extrinsic Evidence be relaxed?", a paper prepared for the Canadian Institute for the Administration of Justice, National Seminar, 21st to 27th August 1987.

[12] See also *C.U.P.E., Local 963 v. New Brunswick Liquor Corp.* (1978), 21 N.B.R. (2d) 441, 37 A.P.R. 441 (C.A.), reversed [1979] 2 S.C.R. 227, 25 N.B.R. (2d) 237, 79 C.L.L.C. 14,209, 97 D.L.R. (3d) 417, 51 A.P.R. 237, 26 N.R. 341.

to include, through the plain meaning of its words, the sum total of all the debates, committee reports and other constituent elements of its legislative history.[14] In contrast, in the United States, all elements of legislative history, including debates in Congress and other legislative bodies, reports of congressional committees, etc., are admitted in determining legislative intent.[15]

There is a body of opinion which holds that the American experience has gone too far. For example, in an article entitled "The Rule Against the Use of Legislative History: 'Canon of Construction or Counsel of Caution?'" (1952), 30 Can. Bar Rev. 769 at 788, the author D.G. Kilgour states:

> . . .If legislative history was freely admitted and indiscriminately used, there would be a tendency to give it an exaggerated place. In the United States its free admission has led to the quip that "only when legislative history is doubtful do you go to the statute".

Notwithstanding the danger posed by fully adopting the American position, there is some suggestion that Canada will, at the very least, shift direction towards the United States rule, at least in respect of constitutional cases. Professor Barry Strayer wrote in his 1968 treatise on *Judicial Review of Legislation in Canada* that in the course of constitutional adjudication it is necessary to adduce evidence in respect of both "legislative" facts and "adjudicative" facts. In respect of the former, he argues for the admissibility in court of such evidence as statements by members of legislative bodies, reports of royal commissions and parliamentary committees and like matters. In this desire to adopt, at least in part, the American position, Canada does not stand alone. For example, para. 54

---

[14] For a discussion of the American position, see F.R. Dickerson's article, "Statutory Interpretation: Dipping into Legislative History" (1983), 11 Hofstra L. Rev. 1125.

[15] See, however, the following Canadian cases where legislative/parliamentary debates and other documents of that nature have been admitted in order to determine or clarify the intent of a legislative body in enacting a statute: *R. v. Stevenson* (1980), 19 C.R. (3d) 74, 57 C.C.C. (2d) 526 (Ont. C.A.); *Atlific (Nfld.) Ltd. v. Hotel Buildings Ltd.* (1993), 106 Nfld. & P.E.I.R. 330, 334 A.P.R. 330 (Nfld. T.D.), reversed on other grounds (1994), 120 Nfld. & P.E.I.R. 91, 373 A.P.R. 91 (Nfld. C.A.), leave to appeal to S.C.C. refused (January 26, 1995), Doc. 24313 (S.C.C.); *Quebec (Attorney-General) v. Eastmain Band (sub nom. Eastmain Band v. Canada (Federal Administrator))*, [1992] 3 F.C. 800 (*sub nom. Eastmain Band v. James Bay and Northern Quebec (Agreement Administrator))* 98 D.L.R. (4th) 206, (*sub nom. Eastmain Indian Band v. Robinson)* 148 N.R. 116 (Fed. C.A.); *Churchill Falls (Labrador) Corp. v. Newfoundland (A.G.)*, [1984] 1 S.C.R. 297, 8 D.L.R. (4th) 1, 47 Nfld. & P.E.I.R. 125, 139 A.P.R. 125, 53 N.R. 268 (Nfld. C.A.); *R. v. Mitchell* (1983), 42 O.R. (2d) 481, 35 C.R. (3d) 225 (*sub nom. Mitchell v. A.G. Ont.)*, 6 C.C.C. (3d) 193, 150 D.L.R. (3d) 449, 7 C.R.R. 153 (H.C.); *R. v. Giftcraft Ltd.* (1984), 13 C.C.C. (3d) 192 (Ont. H.C.); *Reference re s. 94(2) of Motor Vehicle Act (B.C.)*, [1985] 2 S.C.R. 486, [1986] 1 W.W.R. 481 (*sub nom. Reference re Constitutional Question Act (B.C.))*, 69 B.C.L.R. 145, 36 M.V.R. 240, 48 C.R. (3d) 289, 23 C.C.C. (3d) 289, 24 D.L.R. (4th) 536, 18 C.R.R. 30, 63 N.R. 266; *Xerox Canada Inc. v. Neary* (1984), 43 C.P.C. 274, 47 O.R. (2d) 776 (Prov. Ct.); *Lor-Wes Contracting Ltd. v. R.*, [1986] 1 F.C. 346, [1985] 2 C.T.C. 79, 85 D.T.C. 5310, 60 N.R. 321 (*sub nom. Lor-Wes Contracting Ltd. v. M.N.R.)* (C.A.).

of the Report of the Law Commission and the Scottish Law Commission on the Interpretation of Statutes states, in part:

> If the intention of Parliament is not to be treated as a mere figure of speech, it can hardly be denied in principle that proceedings in Parliament may be relevant to ascertain that intention.

Clearly, in light of recent cases, the rule in Canada respecting the use of legislative history is becoming more relaxed, generally,[16] and clearly, the rule may be of little importance when applied to contemporary constitutional (especially Charter) cases. For a thoughtful and enlightening analysis of the rule against legislative history, including its history and its anticipated future, see Bale, G. "Parliamentary Debates and Statutory Interpretation: Switching on the Light or Rummaging in the Ashcans of the Legislative Process", (1995), 74 Can. Bar Rev. 1. For another recent commentary, see Bennion, F., "Law and Texts and Legislative History." (1994), 4 C.I.A.J. 4, Newsletter 3.

(f) Treatises and Dictionaries

Some treatises have been written by learned authors on the process of statutory interpretation. Generally speaking, judges are receptive to an invocation of these treatises in order to verify a rule or principle of statutory interpretation. The two most influential such treatises are *Craies on Statute Law*, 7th ed. (1971), and *Maxwell on Interpretation of Statutes,* 12th ed. (1969). For recent Canadian works, see Dukelow, D.A. and B. Nuse. *Pocket Dictionary of Canadian Law*, (2nd ed) Scarborough: Carswell, 1995 and Yogis, J.A. *Canadian Law Dictionary* (3rd ed.). Hauppauge, N.Y.: Barron's Educational Series, Inc., 1995.

In attempting to define particular words and phrases reference may be made to definitions from well respected general dictionaries.[17] If, however, the word or phrase is legalistic in nature, judges will be receptive to definitions provided in law dictionaries.

(g) Text of the Statute in the Other Official Language

This aid in interpretation applies in Canada, to statutes which in their official text are published in both of our official languages, English and French. More particularly, it applies to Canadian, New Brunswick, and Manitoba statutes. As an aid in determining the legislative intent in enacting any of those statutes, it is perfectly legitimate to resort to an examina-

---

[16] See note 14, *supra.*

[17] See, for example, *Ontario New Home Warranty Program v. Crown Trust Co.* (1984), 7 C.L.R. 196, 32 R.P.R. 214, 50 O.R. (2d) 588 (Co. Ct.) affirmed (1985), 50 O.R. (2d) 593 (C.A.); *SKF Canada Ltd. v. Deputy Minister of National Revenue (Customs & Excise)* (1983), 10 C.E.R. 6, 47 N.R. 61 (Fed. C.A.); and *Alberta Treasury Branches v. Alberta* (1984), 32 Alta. L.R. (2d) 306, 50 C.R. 70 (Q.B.).

tion of the official text of the statute in both official languages. (See the case of *Pfizer Co. v. Deputy Minister of National Revenue (Customs & Excise)*, [1977] 1 S.C.R. 456, 24 C.P.R. (2d) 195, 68 D.L.R. (3d) 9, 6 N.R. 440.) Where the French and English versions of the Criminal Code conflict, the court usually prefers the interpretation more favourable to the accused. (See *R. v. McIntosh*, [1984] 4 W.W.R. 734, 28 Man. R. (2d) 81, 13 C.C.C. (3d) 130 (C.A.); but see *R. v. Voisine* (1984), 57 N.B.R. (2d) 38, 148 A.P.R. 38 (Q.B.).) Sometimes, a word or phrase might appear to be ambiguous, having regard only to the English text, for example, but an examination of that word or phrase in the French text might provide clarity as to the legislative intention and therefore avoid the ambiguity.[18]

(h) Miscellaneous Aids in Interpretation

The above list of aids in interpretation is not meant to be exhaustive. Indeed, from time to time, courts are receptive to aids not referred to above. For example, there is case authority to the effect that a court will examine international conventions and treaties in interpreting an ambiguous provision in a domestic statute.

Reference was made earlier to the admissibility of the preamble and the inadmissibility of marginal notes. There remain two similar matters to consider. First, the question arises as to the admissibility of various headings within a statute as aids in interpretation. Unless there is a statutory provision to the contrary (such as that which exists in the province of Ontario to the effect that such headings are not part of a statute), the common law position applies, which is that headings within a statute may be characterized as preambles and, as such, are admissible in determining legislative intent. A more difficult question relates to the title of a statute. Most statutes contain two titles, a long one and a short one. The law appears to be that both those titles form an integral part of the statute, but the long title is more reliable as an aid in interpretation.

3. PRESUMPTIONS IN STATUTORY INTERPRETATION

Following is a list of various presumptions regarding statutory interpretation which have arisen through pronouncements made in various cases and through the operation of custom and convention at common law. In

---

[18] See, for example, *Nima v. McInnis* (1988), 32 B.C.L.R. (2d) 197, [1989] 2 W.W.R. 634, 45 C.C.C. (3d) 419, 18 C.E.R. 81, 2 T.C.T. 4026 (S.C.); *R. v. O'Donnell*, [1979] 1 W.W.R. 385, 45 C.C.C. (2d) 208 (B.C. C.A.). See also M. Beaupré, *Interpreting Bilingual Legislation*, 2nd ed. (Toronto: Carswell, 1986); *Cardinal v. R.*, [1980] 1 F.C. 149, [1979] 1 C.N.L.R. 32, 97 D.L.R. (3d) 402 (T.D.), affirmed (*sub nom. Cardinal v. Canada*) [1980] 2 F.C. 400, 109 D.L.R. (3d) 366, 32 N.R. 209 (C.A.), which was affirmed on other grounds [1982] 1 S.C.R. 508, [1982] 3 W.W.R. 673, 133 D.L.R. (3d) 513, 41 N.R. 300, [1982] 3 C.N.L.R. 3.

examining these, the reader must bear in mind that some are archaic and therefore of little use to the modern judge.

(a) Presumption in Criminal or Penal Statutes

The presumption is that statutes of this nature are to be construed strictly and in favour of the accused. For a detailed discussion of this presumption, see S. Kloepfer, "The Status of Strict Construction in Canadian Criminal Law" (1983), 15 Ottawa L. Rev. 553. See also *R. v. Abbas,* [1984] 2 S.C.R. 526, 42 C.R. (3d) 243, 15 C.C.C. (3d) 513, 14 D.L.R. (4th) 449, 55 N.R. 224, reversing (1982), 68 C.C.C. (3d) 330, 6 O.A.C. 192 (C.A.).

(b) Presumption in Taxation Statutes

The presumption in respect of statutes of this nature is that they must be construed strictly, the charging sections in favour of the taxpayer and the exemption sections in favour of the government. In addition, there are many special rules of construction which apply uniquely to taxation statutes and which expand upon the above presumption.

(c) Presumption Against Alteration of the Law

This presumption, often expressed as a presumption against fundamental change, imports the notion that statutory enactments are presumed not to alter the common law. Such a notion is based upon the presumption that the legislative body knows the law; therefore, in the absence of an express provision in a given statute altering the existing common law, it is presumed that that statute is confirmatory of the common law.

However, this presumption is rebuttable by express language contained in the statute.[19] Moreover, this presumption is probably very unreliable in any case, in view of the provision contained, for example, in the federal Interpretation Act,[20] to the effect that all statutes are deemed to be remedial in nature.

(d) Presumption Against Strict Criminal Liability

Unless a provision expressly creates a strict liability offence, it is presumed that every criminal offence contains a mens rea component (i.e., a mental or intentional component of some nature) which must be proved beyond a reasonable doubt.

---

[19] See *Coles v. Roach* (1980), 25 Nfld. & P.E.I.R. 172, 112 D.L.R. (3d) 101, 68 A.P.R. 172 (P.E.I. S.C.); see also *Greater Niagara Transit Commission v. Matson* (1977), 16 O.R. (2d) 351, 78 D.L.R. (3d) 265 (H.C.).

[20] R.S.C. 1985, c. I-21, s. 12.

(e) Presumption Against Retroactivity

One of the best statements of this presumption is set out in *Maxwell on Interpretation of Statutes:*[21]

> . . . upon the presumption that the legislature does not intend what is unjust rests the leaning against giving certain statutes a retrospective operation. They are construed as operating only in cases or on facts which come into existence after the statutes were passed unless a retrospective effect is clearly intended. It is a fundamental rule of . . . law that no statute shall be construed to have a retrospective operation unless such a construction appears very clearly in the terms of the Act, or arises by necessary and distinct implication.

The author then cites R.S. Wright J. in the case of *Re Athlumney*, [1895-99] All E.R. Rep. 329, [1898] 2 Q.B. 547 at 551-52:

> Perhaps no rule of construction is more firmly established than this — that a retrospective operation is not to be given to a statute so as to impair an existing right or obligation, otherwise than as regards matter of procedure, unless that effect cannot be avoided without doing violence to the language of the enactment. If the enactment is expressed in language which is fairly capable of either interpretation, it ought to be construed as prospective only.[22]

(f) Presumption Against Ousting the Jurisdiction of the Courts

This presumption is so firmly entrenched in the law that in the area of judicial review by courts of superior jurisdiction of administrative decisions, a statutory privative clause, with few exceptions, will not prevent a superior court from exercising this review jurisdiction. In other words, even if an enabling statute establishing an administrative tribunal contains a provision to the effect that any decision of that tribunal is not subject to judicial review by courts of superior jurisdiction, notwithstanding such a clause, courts of superior jurisdiction, with few exceptions, will be receptive to the process of judicial review. This will be discussed further in the next chapter, which contains an introduction to administrative law.

(g) Presumption of Crown Immunity

This is a two-fold presumption. First, it is presumed that at common law, the Crown enjoys tortious immunity. This principle was discussed in the Supreme Court of Canada and in the Ontario Court of Appeal in the case of *Nelles v. Ontario*, [1989] 2 S.C.R. 170, 69 O.R. (2d) 448n, 71 C.R. (3d) 358, 41 Admin. L.R. 1, 49 C.C.L.T. 217, 37 C.P.C. (2d) 1, 60 D.L.R. (4th) 609, 98 N.R. 321, 35 O.A.C. 161, 42 C.R.R. 1, reversing

---

[21] P. St. J. Langan, *Maxwell on Interpretation of Statutes, 12th ed.* (London: Sweet & Maxwell, 1969), at p. 215.

[22] See also *Peel (Regional Municipality) v. Viking Houses*, [1977] 2 S.C.R. 1134, 104 D.L.R. (3d) 1, 29 N.R. 244, 49 C.C.C. (2d) 103, affirming (1977), 16 O.R. (2d) 765, 36 C.C.C. (2d) 337 (C.A.), affirming (1977), 16 O.R. (2d) 632, 36 C.C.C. (2d) 337 (H.C.).

in part (1985), 51 O.R. (2d) 513, 46 C.R. (3d) 289, 13 Admin. L.R. 213, 10 O.A.C. 161, *(sub nom. Nelles v. R.)* 16 C.R.R. 320, 21 D.L.R. (4th) 103, 32 C.C.L.T. 291, 1 C.P.C. (2d) 113 (C.A.). This case affirms the principle of tortious immunity in the Crown unless it can be established that the Crown acted in bad faith or with malice. Historically, this immunity arises out of the prerogative vested in the Crown. However, with the enactment of various Crown liability statutes in most jurisdictions, tortious immunity has now been lost. Secondly, this presumption also extends to statutory law, with the effect that no statute can bind the Crown in right of the Dominion or in right of a province unless that statute expressly states otherwise.[23] It may be that the presumption of Crown immunity is more a matter of historical significance and is now a presumption of limited application.

(h) Miscellaneous Presumptions

In addition to the foregoing, there are some miscellaneous presumptions which might serve as aids in construction. For example, there is a presumption against surplusage which requires a court to consider each word in a statute, on the theory that a legislative body enacted each word of the statute with a particular purpose in mind. Secondly, there is the presumption referred to in the Latin phrase 'generalia specialibus non derogant,[24] to the effect that when two or more statutes of the same jurisdiction are applicable to a given factual situation, in the event of conflict between the various statutes, the more specific statute takes precedence over the general statute. In addition, there is the related presumption expressed in the Latin phrase 'leges posteriores priores contrarias abrogant' to the effect that when two or more statutes of the same jurisdiction are applicable to a given factual situation and both statutes are of equal specificity, if they conflict with each other the more recent statute takes precedence over the older one. However, there is a presumption against the implied repeal of the older statute; a judge must make every effort to reconcile the two, if possible. Finally there is the important presumption contained in the Latin phrase 'de minimis non curat lex' to

---

[23] See the following articles in The Lawyers Weekly: Patricia Chisholm, "Cautionary Tales for Actions Against Cabinet", 8th November 1985; Jeffery Miller, "Impairing the Courts' Authority and Dignity", 21st February, 1986; R. Haliechuk, "P.M. off the Hook for N.S. Libel Case Subpoena", 15th April 1986; Cristin Schmitz, "Bill of Rights used to Invalidate Crown Liability Section", 8th May 1987; Cristin Schmitz, "Cabinet Ministers' Contempt Liability 'common sense'?", 29th January 1988. See also *Just v. British Columbia*, [1989] 2 S.C.R. 1228, 41 Admin. L.R. 161, 1 C.C.L.T. (2d) 1, 18 M.V.R. (2d) 1, [1990] 1 W.W.R. 385, 41 B.C.L.R. (2d) 350, 64 D.L.R. (4th) 689, 103 N.R. 1, [1990] R.R.A. 140.

[24] See, for example, *Strachan v. Melfort (Town)* (1979), 102 D.L.R. (3d) 761 (Sask. Q.B.); see also *R. v. Wheeler*, [1979] 2 S.C.R. 650, 9 M.P.L.R. 161, 97 D.L.R. (3d) 605 *(sub nom. Re Wheeler)*, 25 N.B.R. (2d) 209, 51 A.P.R. 209, 26 N.R. 323.

the effect that the law does not concern itself with trifles, nor with trivial acts or omissions, nor with inconsequential breaches.

Some of the rules and principles of statutory interpretation find their source in judicial custom or convention. Some are statutory in nature, such as those arising out of provisions contained in the various interpretation statutes. Most, however, arise out of judicial pronouncements in early cases. There is no better example of this than the mischief rule, one of the three major canons of construction. That rule arose out of the decision in *Heydon's Case* (1584), 3 Co. Rep. 7a, 76 E.R. 637.

(i) Drafting Errors

On occasion, the courts have to deal with drafting errors on the part of our legislative bodies. Generally speaking, the role of the courts in these instances is to correct the drafting error in order to give effect to the intention of the legislating body. See *R. v. Flaman* (1978), 43 C.C.C. (2d) 241 (Sask. C.A.); *R. v. Findlay* (1977), 3 B.C.L.R. 321 (Prov. Ct.); and *R. v. Paul* (1978), 39 C.C.C. (2d) 129 (Ont. C.A.); see also *Ontario (Ombudsman) v. R. (sub nom. Ontario (Ombudsman) v. Ontario (Minister of Housing))* (1979), 26 O.R. (2d) 434, 103 D.L.R. (3d) 117 (H.C.), affirmed (1980), 30 O.R. (2d) 768, 117 D.L.R. (3d) 613 (C.A.), where it was held that a court may fill a gap in legislation so as to make it logically perfect and so as to give effect to the intent of the legislature.

Notwithstanding the somewhat dated sources of these various rules, they are being presently applied by our courts. In this connection, the reader will find in the bibliography set out at the end of this chapter many very recent cases which apply these old rules to new fact situations.

The whole question of ambiguity is best summed up by reference to certain remarks made by the late Dr. Max Wyman in his addendum to the Report of the Alberta Board of Review. In that addendum, referred to earlier, Dr. Wyman makes these comments:

> Some of the words of a language must always remain undefined. This does not mean, however, that such words are devoid of meaning. It does imply that the meaning conjured up in the minds of people might be different for different people. Since those who legislate must use a language to communicate their thoughts to those who adjudicate, it is certain that in some instances the message that is sent will be different from the message that is received. This is a defect of all systems of law, and it cannot be avoided. It does not mean, however, that a society must condone vague and carelessly worded laws. Quite the opposite. Recognizing the existence of defects of this type, those who write the law must strive for clarity and precision, knowing full well that perfect clarity and absolute precision can never be obtained.

When one considers the time and energy committed by judges and lawyers to the exercise of statutory (and contractual[25]) interpretation, it is easy to recognize the importance of the various rules and principles outlined above as well as the related jurisprudence.[26] The next chapter is concerned with administrative law. As it turns out, so many aspects of administrative law depend upon the application of these same rules and principles of statutory interpretation.

As an exercise in applying the various rules and principles of statutory interpretation, consider the six problems set out below in the appendix to this chapter.

APPENDIX

PROBLEM ONE

ACME Foods Ltd., a company incorporated under the laws of the province of Manitoba, was engaged in the business of processing and packing instant coffee. In 1970, in the course of its business, the company decided to bolster sales by initiating a promotion in which the company placed on each jar of coffee a label containing the words "10 cents off regular price."

The finished product was then distributed through a local distributor to various retail outlets. In purchasing the coffee from the manufacturer, the distributor obtained a 10 cents reduction in the purchase price per jar and in turn passed on the reduction to the various retailers. The retailers then sold the coffee at a price of 10 cents less than the regular price which existed at the time that the promotion began.

The "cents off" promotion continued for some eighteen months, at which time many consumers complained that the reduced price had by that time become the regular price, and, as such, the price after eighteen months should be a further 10 cents off the now reduced regular price. As a result, various consumers complained to the Combines Investigation Branch of the Department of Consumer and Corporate Affairs. The Branch conducted an investigation, after which ACME Foods Ltd. was prosecuted for misleading advertising under the provisions of the Combines Investigation Act, R.S.C. 1970, c. C-23.

---

[25] In the interpretation of an ambiguous provision in a contract, judges and lawyers employ, essentially, the same rules and principles that apply to the process of statutory interpretation.

[26] In fact, recently, a number of judicial/legal organizations have dealt with issues related to statutory interpretations at national/regional meetings. For example, the National Judicial Institute/Institut national de la magistrature, a body mandated with the responsibility of conducting continuing education programs for judges, has sponsored two programs of this nature — in October of 1994 in Winnipeg and in February of 1995 in Ottawa.

At that time, the relevant provisions of the said Act were as follows (the Combines Investigation Act has since been substantially amended, but these amendments should be ignored for the purpose of this problem):

> 37.(1) Every one who publishes or causes to be published an *advertisement* containing a statement that purports to be a statement of fact but that is untrue, deceptive or misleading or is intentionally so worded or arranged that it is deceptive or misleading, is guilty of an indictable offence and is liable to imprisonment for five years, if the advertisement is published
>
>> (a) to promote, directly or indirectly, the sale or disposal of property or any interest therein, or
>>
>> (b) to promote a business or a commercial interest.

The various elements that must be established in order to support a conviction were as follows. First, the accused company must have caused to be published an advertisement. Secondly, the advertisement must have contained a statement which purported to be a statement of fact. Thirdly, the statement must have been untrue, deceptive or misleading. And fourthly, the advertisement must have been published to promote the sale of coffee. Assume that there was sufficient evidence to commit the accused company to trial providing the court could establish that a label on a coffee jar constitutes an "advertisement" under the provisions of the Act set out above.

Counsel for the accused argued that a label is merely a "representation" and not an "advertisement." In support of this argument, he cited the provisions of s. 36 of the same Act. Essentially, s. 36 prohibited a similar and related offence to that contained in s. 37. However, s. 36 referred specifically to the making of a *representation* to the public. The argument by counsel was simply that Parliament, in using the term "representation" in s. 36, had intended a wider scope than that encompassed in s. 37, which refers only to "advertising," that is, a distinction must be made between representations generally and advertising, and Parliament had made this very distinction in using different terminology in the two sections. Counsel then concluded that while a coffee jar label may constitute a representation, it does not constitute an advertisement as required under s. 37.

Counsel for the Crown, however, cited the definition of advertisement contained in the Food and Drugs Act, R.S.C. 1970, c. F-27, s. 2, which states that an advertisement *"includes any representation* by any means whatever for the purpose of promoting directly or indirectly the sale or disposal of any food, drug, cosmetic or device."

Counsel for the Crown then made reference to the Report of the Standing Committee of the House of Commons on Finance, Trade, and Economic Affairs, which report was released prior to the enactment of s. 37. That report stated in part as follows:

The Committee feels that stronger measures are necessary in order to protect the consumer. As a result, all representations to the public, in whatever form, from manufacturers, distributors and retailers alike, should be fair and honest.

There appeared to be no decided cases which could be argued in order to support one side or the other as to whether a coffee jar label does in law constitute an advertisement. Accordingly, the judge must rely upon the above arguments of counsel as well as upon the generally accepted rules and principles of statutory interpretation. How would the judge likely rule on the narrow question as to whether a coffee jar label constitutes an advertisement?

PROBLEM TWO

In response to a City of Toronto by-law imposing certain restrictions on dog owners requiring control of dogs in public areas, the local Canine Association suggested that it was only fair that the same controls be imposed upon cat owners as well.

As a result, in response to a successful lobbying effort, the Municipal Council of the City of Toronto enacted a cat by-law.

Essentially, that law placed the same restrictions on cats as those placed on dogs in the previous by-law and, in particular, required that cats must remain on leashes while in public places.

Shortly after the enactment of the by-law, the owner of a game farm situated around Toronto (the site of an African Big Game Safari) was seen walking along the Toronto lake front accompanied by his pet cheetah. The cheetah was not on a leash. An enthusiastic young police officer, in his first week on the job, upon seeing the game farm owner and his pet cheetah and assuming that a cheetah is, biologically, a member of the cat family, immediately summonsed the owner and charged him under the provision in the cat by-law prohibiting the walking of cats in public areas without a leash.

At the trial of this matter, a dispute in law arose as to what constitutes a "cat" for the purpose of the by-law. Counsel for the Crown pointed to the definition of "cat" in the introductory section of the by-law.

That definition stated as follows: "cat includes all species of animals possessing feline characteristics."

Reference was then made to the Webster's New International Dictionary in respect of three definitions:

1. "Cat" was defined as "a carnivorous mammal (felis catus) which has long been kept by man in a domestic state."

2. "Cheetah" was defined as "an animal of the cat family."

3. "Feline" was defined as "catlike, of or pertaining to the genus Felis or family Felidae."

In addition to the foregoing, reference was made to the debate in Municipal Council which preceded the enactment of the by-law. In particular, the speeches of several aldermen were cited, including the following remark:

> I agree with the proponents of this by-law. It is about time that we took measures to ensure that these little pests are kept out of the garbage cans of Toronto.

Counsel for the accused emphasized that the wording "little pests" was suggestive that the intent of the by-law was directed at small, domestic cats and not at large game, such as a cheetah.

In addition, counsel for the accused also made reference to the provisions contained in the preamble of the cat by-law. In particular, he cited the following provisions in the preamble:

> In recognition of the requirement of sanitation and the danger to health if standards are not maintained, and in recognition of the harmful effect of unsupervised domesticated cats upon sanitation standards, it is hereby enacted . . .

In addition, counsel for the accused cited the definition of "dog" in the dog by-law. In particular, "dog" was defined as follows:

> "Dog" includes all species of animals possessing canine characteristics, but excludes animals possessing those characteristics which are not normally domesticated.

Counsel for the accused argued that the latter phraseology in the above definition should have been, but unfortunately was not, contained in the definition of "cat" in the cat by-law; however, counsel for the Crown suggested it was specifically left out in order that the cat by-law control not only domesticated animals but undomesticated animals as well, such as cheetahs.

Assume that the rules and principles of statutory interpretation apply, as they do in interpreting municipal by-laws, in the same way as in interpreting any other statutory enactment. In applying the three major canons of construction, how would the judge rule in this case? Also, would the judge be receptive to any or all of the above arguments of counsel?

PROBLEM THREE

Assume that the Benchers of the Law Society of Alberta were required to make a determination as to whether two lawyers were guilty of conduct unbecoming a barrister and solicitor.

The particular provision which defines "conduct unbecoming a barrister and solicitor" is set out in Pt. 3 of the Legal Profession Act, R.S.A. 1980, c. L-9, s. 47 [re-en. 1981, c. 53, s. 20]. More specifically, s. 47 of the said Act provides as follows:

47 (1) Except as otherwise provided in this Part, the question of whether the conduct of a member or student-at-law is conduct deserving of sanction shall be determined by the Benchers or, on appeal, by the Court of Appeal.

(2) Any act or conduct of a member or a student-at-law that

(a) is incompatible with the best interests of the public or the members of the Society, or

(b) tends to harm the standing of the legal profession generally,

is conduct deserving of sanction within the meaning of this Part, whether or not that act or conduct is disgraceful or dishonourable and whether or not that act or conduct relates to the practice of law.

(3) Without restricting the generality of subsection (2), conduct deserving of sanction includes incompetently carrying on the practice of law and incompetently carrying out duties or obligations undertaken by a member or a student-at-law in his capacity as a member or student-at-law.

It was alleged that lawyer A was guilty under s. 47(2) of the Act set out above by virtue of a conviction under s. 36(1)(*a*) of the Criminal Code, R.S.C. 1985, c. C-46. The relevant provisions of the Criminal Code are set out as follows:

361. (1) A false pretence is a representation of a matter of fact either present or past, made by words or otherwise, that is known by the person who makes it to be false and that is made with a fraudulent intent to induce the person to whom it is made to act on it.

(2) Exaggerated commendation or depreciation of the quality of anything is not a false pretence unless it is carried to such an extent that it amounts to a fraudulent misrepresentation of fact.

(3) For the purposes of subsection (2) it is a question of fact whether commendation or depreciation amounts to a fraudulent misrepresentation of fact.

362. (1) Every one commits an offence who

(*a*) by a false pretence, whether directly or through the medium of a contract obtained by a false pretence, obtains anything in respect of which the offence of theft may be committed or causes it to be delivered to another person . . .

(2) Every one who commits an offence under paragraph (1)(a)

(*a*) is guilty of an indictable offence and is liable to a term of imprisonment not exceeding ten years, where the property obtained is a testamentary instrument or where the value of what is obtained exceeds one thousand dollars; or

(*b*) is guilty

(i) of an indictable offence and is liable to imprisonment for a term not exceeding two years, or

(ii) of an offence punishable on summary conviction,

where the value of what is obtained does not exceed one thousand dollars.

It was further alleged that lawyer B was also guilty under s. 47(2) of the Legal Profession Act by virtue of a conviction under s. 175(1)(*a*)(i) of the Criminal Code. This conviction arose out of lawyer B's public display of excitement immediately after the Edmonton Eskimos won the Grey Cup. Section 175 of the Criminal Code is set out as follows:

175. (1) Every one who
 (a) not being in a dwelling-house causes a disturbance in or near a public place,
  (i) by fighting, screaming, shouting, swearing, singing or using insulting or obscene language,
  (ii) by being drunk, or
  (iii) by impeding or molesting other persons,
 (b) openly exposes or exhibits an indecent exhibition in a public place,
 (c) loiters in a public place and in any way obstructs persons who are there, or
 (d) disturbs the peace and quiet of the occupants of a dwelling-house by discharging firearms or by other disorderly conduct in a public place or who, not being an occupant of a dwelling-house comprised in a particular building or structure, disturbs the peace and quiet of the occupants of a dwelling-house comprised in the building or structure by discharging firearms or by other disorderly conduct in any part of a building or structure to which, at the time of such conduct, the occupants of two or more dwelling-houses comprised in the building or structure have access as of right or by invitation, express or implied,
is guilty of an offence punishable on summary conviction.

In applying each of the three major canons of construction and any other rules and principles of statutory interpretation that might be appropriate, what is likely to be the decision of the benchers on the narrow question as to whether the behaviour of each of the two lawyers amounts to "conduct unbecoming a barrister and solicitor" as defined in s. 47(2) of the Legal Profession Act?

PROBLEM FOUR

A person was charged that he fraudulently and without colour of right used a telecommunication facility contrary to s. 326(1)(b) of the Criminal Code. The accused had obtained access to data contained in a university computer. He did this through the use of a remote terminal connected to the central computer by electric wires.

The wires and the electrical signals which flowed through them provided the means by which data was transmitted between the various terminals and the central unit. The accused's defence was that the above system does not constitute a telecommunication facility within the meaning of the Criminal Code.

The Criminal Code defines a telecommunication facility as follows:

326 (2) In this section and in section 327, "telecommunication" means any transmission, emission or reception of signs, signals, writing, images, sounds or intelligence of any nature by wire, radio, visual, electronic or other electro-magnetic system.

See *R. v. McLaughlin*, [1980] 2 S.C.R. 331, [1981] 1 W.W.R. 298, 18 C.R. (3d) 339, 53 C.C.C. (2d) 417, 113 D.L.R. (3d) 386, 32 N.R. 350, 23 A.R. 530.

PROBLEM FIVE

The reader might also consider the intriguing question as to whether God is a person. See the facts and the decision on *R. v. Davie*, [1981] 2 W.W.R. 513, 17 C.R. (3d) 72, 54 C.C.C. (2d) 216 (B.C. C.A.), which concerned itself with this very issue. See also the case comment, Meehan's "Candid Confessions" (1981), 59 Can. Bar Rev. 817, which discussed the above decision.

PROBLEM SIX

There has been a marked increase in the use of in-line skates or roller blades. This has given rise to a concern related to their regulation. Essentially, the issue arises as to whether in-line skates are to be categorized as recreational equipment or as a mode of transportation. The definition of "vehicle" is set out in s. 1(1) of the Ontario Highway Traffic Act, R.S.O. 1990, c. H-8:

> "Vehicle" includes a motor vehicle, trailer, traction engine, farm tractor, road-building machine, bicycle and any vehicle drawn, propelled or driven by any kind of power, including muscular power, but does not include a motorized snow vehicle or a street car.

Is a person using in-line skates considered to be a vehicle under the Highway Traffic Act?[27]

SELECTED BIBLIOGRAPHY ON THE RULES AND PRINCIPLES OF STATUTORY INTERPRETATION

TEXTS AND TREATISES

Aarnio, A. *The Rational as Reasonable: A Treatise on Legal Justification*. Boston: Dordrecht, 1987.

Allen, C.K. *Law in the Making*. 4th ed. Oxford: Clarendon Press, 1946.

Anson, W.R. *Law and Custom of the Constitution*. New York: Johnson Reprint Corp., 1970.

Asprey, M.M., *Plain Language for Lawyers*, Sydney: The Federation Press, 1991.

---

[27] See "Vehicle or Toy? Cities are Debating Whether the Hottest Thing on Wheels Should be Kept Off the Streets", *The Globe & Mail*, May 7, 1994. This article, in part, states as follows:

> . . .Municipal officials across the country are debating the true nature — and future — of the in-line skate: Is it merely a boot with wheels, or a potentially dangerous muscle powered vehicle? . . . The confusion . . . arises from the fact that the Ontario Highway Traffic Act defines a vehicle as something on wheels that is propelled by a source of power, including muscle power. In-line skaters, or bladers (from Rollerblade, the most popular brand of skate), would appear to fall into that category, but in Toronto those charged under the Act have always had their cases thrown out of court . . .

Beaupré, M. *Interpreting Bilingual Legislation*. 2nd ed. Toronto: Carswell, 1986.

Beaupré, M. *Interprétation de la législation bilingue*. Montréal: Wilson & Lafleur, 1986.

Bennion, F.A.R. *Bennion on Statute Law*. 3rd ed. London: Longman Group, 1990.

Bennion, F.A.R. *Statutory Interpretation*. 2nd ed. London: Butterworths, 1992.

Brewer, S. *Ends, Means & Meaning in Legal Interpretation*. Toronto: Faculty of Law, University of Toronto, 1994.

Clifford, F.A. *History of Private Bill Legislation*. London: Cass, 1968.

Côté, P.-A. *Interprétation des lois*. 2e ed. Montréal: Les Editions Yvon Blais, 1990.

Côté, P.-A. *The Interpretation of Legislation in Canada*. 2nd ed. Montreal: Les Editions Yvon Blais, 1991.

Cross, R. *Statutory Interpretation*. 2nd ed. London: Butterworths, 1987.

Dick, R.C., Q.C., *Legal Drafting in Plain Language*, 3rd ed. Scarborough: Carswell, 1995.

Driedger, E.A. *The Composition of Legislation, Legislative Forms and Precedents*, 2nd ed. Ottawa: Department of Justice, 1976.

Dworkin, G.D. *Odger's Construction of Deeds and Statutes*. 5th ed. London: Sweet & Maxwell, 1965.

Dukelow, D.A. and B. Nuse. *Pocket Dictionary of Canadian Law*, (2nd ed.) Scarborough: Carswell, 1995.

Edgar, S.G.G. *Craies on Statute Law*. 7th ed. London: Sweet & Maxwell, 1971.

Evans, J. *Statutory Interpretation: Problems of Communication*. Auckland: Oxford University Press, 1988.

Hurst, J.W. *Dealing with Statutes*. New York: Columbia, 1982.

Kiralfy, A.K.R. *The English Legal System*. 8th ed. London: Sweet & Maxwell, 1990.

Langan, P. St.J. *Maxwell on Interpretation of Statutes*. 12th ed. London: Sweet & Maxwell, 1969.

MacAdam, A.I., and T.M. Smith. *Statutes*. Sydney: Butterworths, 1989.

MacCormick, N. and R.S. Summers (ed.). *Interpreting Statutes: A Comparative Study*. Dartmouth: Aldershot, Hartts, 1991.

Marmor, A. *Interpretation and Legal Theory*. Oxford: Clarendon Press, 1992.

McLean, M.K. *The Thesaurus of Provincial Statutory Terminology*. Ottawa: Canada Law Information Council, 1986.

Mellinkoff, D., *Legal Writing: Sense and Nonsense*, St. Paul: West Publishing Co., 1982.

Mowat, C., "A plain language writer considers consideration, LawNow, April/May, 1995.

Pearce, D.C. & R.S. Geddes. *Statutory Interpretation in Australia*. 3rd ed. Sydney: Butterworths, 1988.

Phillips, O.H. *A First Book of English Law*. 7th ed. London: Sweet & Maxwell, 1977.

Pigeon, Louis Phillippe. *Redaction et interprétation des lois/Drafting and Interpreting Legislation*. Toronto: Carswell, 1988.

Singer, N.J. *Statutes and Statutory Construction*. 5th ed. Deerfield: Clar, Boardman Callaghan, 1992.

Statsky, W.P. *Legislative Analysis and Drafting*. 2nd ed. New York: West Publishing, 1984.

Stone, M. *Focusing the Law: What Legal Interpretation is Not*. Toronto: Faculty of Law, University of Toronto, 1994.

Sullivan, R. *Driedger on The Construction of Statutes*. 3rd ed. Toronto: Butterworths, 1994.

Twining, W.L. *How to Do Things with Rules: A Primer of Interpretation*. 3rd ed. London: Weidenfeld & Nicholson, 1991.

Walker, R.J., & R. Ward. *Walker and Walker's English Legal System*. 7th ed. London: Butterworths, 1994.

Wilberforce, E. *On Statute Law*. London: Stevens, 1881.

Wilson, G. *Cases and Materials on the English Legal System*. 3rd ed. London: Sweet & Maxwell, 1973.

Yogis, J.A. *Canadian Law Dictionary* (3rd ed.), Hauppauge, N.Y.: Barron's Educational Series, Inc., 1995.

ARTICLES

Canada

Bale, G. "Parliamentary Debates and Statutory Interpretation: Switching on the Light or Rummaging in the Ashcans of the Legislative Process". (1995), 74 Can. Bar Rev. 1.

Barbe, R.P. "Les définitions contenues dans les actes législatifs et réglementaire". (1983), R. du B. 1105.

Barry, L.D. "Law, Policy and Statutory Interpretation under a Constitutionally Entrenched Canadian Charter of Rights and Freedoms". (1982), 60 Can. Bar Rev. 237.

Beaupré, R.M. "Le bilinguisme législatif en Ontario de certain aspects de l'interprétation des lois". (1984), 18 Gazette 309.

Bisson, A.-F. "Effect de codification et interprétation". (1986), 17 R.G.D. 359.

Bisson, A.-F. "L'interaction des techniques de redaction et des techniques d'interprétation des lois". (1980), 21 Cahiers 511.

Boulois, J. "L'interprétation du droit écrit par le juge: rapport de synthèse". (1978), 13 R.J.T. 85.

Boyd, N. "Sentencing Canadian Narcotic Offenders: Some Dilemmas in Judicial Interpretation of Legislative Intent". (1984), 48 Sask. L. Rev. 353.

Butler, A.S. "A Presumption of Statutory Conformity with the Charter". (1993), 19 Queen's L.J. 209.

Carignan, P. "De l'exegèse et de la création dans l'interprétation judiciaire des lois constitutionnelles". (1986), 20 R.J.T. 27.

Caron, M. "L'utilisation du droit international aux fins d'interprétation et d'application de la Charte des droits et libertés de la personne du Québec". (1984), 1 R.Q.D.I. 307.

Charles, W.H. "Extrinsic Evidence and Statutory Interpretation: Judicial Discretion in Context". (1983), 7 Dal. L.J. 7.

Christian, T.J. "The Limited Operation of the Limitations Clause". (1987), 25 Alta. L. Rev. 264.

Corn, G. "Rules of Statutory Interpretation". (1985), 1 Can. Curr. Tax 95.

Corry, J.A. "Administrative Law; Interpretation of Statutes". (1939), 1 U.T.L.J. 286.

Corry, J.A. "The Use of Legislative History in the Interpretation of Statutes". (1954), 32 Can. Bar Rev. 624.

Côté, F.B. "Du language législatif au Canada ou de la difficulté de parler le même language avec des mots différents". (1986), 46 R. du B. 302.

Côté, L. "Retrospectivity, Acquired Rights, Existing Rights and Section 35 of the Federal Interpretation Act". (1984), 15 R.D.U.S. 113.

Côté, P.-A. "L'interprétation de la loi par le législateur". (1980/81), 15 R.J.T. 29; (1982), Etudes Cardinal 21.

Côté, P.-A. "La préasance de la Charte canadienne des droits et libertés". (1984), 18 R.J.T. 105.

Côté, P.-A. "Les règles d'interprétation des lois: des guides et des arguments". (1978), 13 R.J.T. 275.

Couzin, R. "What Does it Say in French?" (1985), 33 Can. Tax J. 300.

Cross, G. "On Legislation". (1982), 40 Advocate 437.

Cumbrae-Stewart, F.D. "Meant to Mean: A Note on the Problems of Extrinsic Aids to Statutory Construction". (1983), 13 U. Queensl. L.J. 3.

Davis, K.C. "Legislative History and the Wheat Board Case". (1953),

31 Can. Bar Rev. 1. (See also, on this article, the letter from Milner (1953), 31 Can. Bar Rev. 228.)

de l'Etoile, J. et M. Saint-Pierre. "La définition statutaire de l'expression 'disposition des biens' et son interprétation jurisprudentielle". (1984), 6 R.P.F.S. 325.

Deschênes, J. "Quelques observations sur la langue des tribunaux". (1984), Justice 111.

Driedger, E.A. "A New Approach to Statutory Interpretation". (1951), 29 Can. Bar Rev. 838.

Driedger, E.A. "Are Statutes Written for Men Only?" (1979), 22 McGill L.J. 666.

Driedger, E.A. "Statutes: The Mischievous Literal Golden Rule". (1981), 59 Can. Bar Rev. 780.

Driedger, E.A. "Statutory Drafting and Interpretation: Canadian Common Law". (1971), 9 Co. I. Dr. Comp. 71.

Elliot, R. "Interpreting the Charter — Use of the Earlier Versions as an Aid". [1982] U.B.C. L. Rev. Charter Ed. 11.

Friedmann, W. "Statute Law and Its Interpretation in the Modern State". (1948), 26 Can. Bar Rev. 1277.

Gautron, A. "French/English Discrepancies in the Canadian Charter of Rights and Freedoms". (1982), 12 Man. L.J. 220.

Gibson, D. "Interpretation of the Canadian Charter of Rights and Freedoms: Some General Considerations". [1982] Can. Charter 25.

Gibson, D. "L'interprétation de la Charte canadienne des droits et libertés: considérations générales". [1982] Charte Can. 29.

Gochnauer, M. "Statutory Interpretation — A Plea for Linguistic Sanity". (1984), 62 Can. Bar Rev. 211.

Hasson, R. A. "The Apparent Futility of Attempting to Reform the Common Law by Statute". (1991), 13 Advocates' Q. 107.

Hopkins, E.R. "The Literal Canon and the Golden Rule". (1937), 15 Can. Bar Rev. 689.

Horton, S.B. "The Manitoba Language Rights Reference and the Doctrine of Mandatory and Directory Provisions". (1987), 10 Dal. L.J. 3:195.

Jodoin, A. "L'interprétation par le juge des lois pénales". (1978), 13 R.J.T. 49.

Hutchinson, A.C. "Of Judges, Democracy and Business Driving". (1992), 26 L. Soc. Gaz. 26.

Johnson, P.E. "Legislative Drafting Practices and Other Factors Affecting the Clarity of Canada's Laws". (1991), 12 Statute L. Rev. 1.

Kernochan, J.M. "Statutory Interpretation: An Outline of Method". (1976), 3 Dal. L.J. 333.

Keyes, J. M. "Perils of the Unknown — Fair Notice and the Promulgation of Legislation". (1993), 24 Ottawa L. Rev. 579.

Kilgour, D.G. "The Rule Against the Use of Legislative History: 'Canon of Construction or Counsel of Caution?' " (1952), 30 Can. Bar Rev. 769. (See also, on this article, the letters from MacQuarrie (1952), 30 Can. Bar Rev. 1087; Milner (1953), 31 Can. Bar Rev. 228.)

Kloepfer, S. "The Status of Strict Construction in Canadian Criminal Law". (1983), 15 Ottawa L. Rev. 553.

Krauss, M. "L'interprétation des lois, histoire législative, 'La queue qui révue le chien' ". (1980), 58 Can. Bar Rev. 756.

Krauss, M. "Nihilisme et interprétation des lois". (1986), 20 R.J.T. 125.

Krishna, V. "The Demise of the Strict Interpretation Rule". (1986), 1 Can. Curr. Tax 135.

Krishna, V. "Use of Extrinsic Evidence in Determining the 'Object and Spirit' of Tax Legislation". (1985), 1 Can. Curr. Tax C117.

Krongold, S. "Writing Laws: Making Them Easier to Understand". (1992), 24 Ottawa L. Rev. 495.

Langlois, R. "L'application des règles d'interprétation constitutionnelle". (1987), 28 Cahiers 207.

Laskin, B. "Interpretation of Statutes — Industrial Standards Act Ontario". (1937), 15 Can. Bar Rev. 660.

Lauzière, L. "Le sens ordinaire des mots comme règle d'interprétation". (1987), 28 Cahiers 367.

Lawrence. J.W. "The Identification and Interpretation of Revised Statutes". (1982), 40 Advocate 323.

Leblanc, L., et R. Tremblay. "L'interprétation des lois; chroniques". (1982), 42 R. du B. 680.

Lemieux, V. "L'analyse structurale des lois". (1982), 15 Can. J. Pol. Sc. 67.

Lyman, S. "The Absurdity and Repugnancy of the Plain Meaning Rule of Interpretation". (1969), 3 Man. L.J. 253.

Lysyk, K.M. "Definition and Enforcement of Charter Equality Rights". (1986), Balance 215.

MacDonald, V.C. "Constitutional Interpretation and Extrinsic Evidence". (1939), 17 Can. Bar Rev. 77.

MacIntosh, D.A. "The Vagueness Doctrine and Overbreadth: A Comment of *Canada v. Pharmaceutical Society (N.S.)*". (1992), 2 N.J.C.L. 242.

Mallory, J.L. "Parliamentary Scrutiny of Statutory Instruments in Canada: A Proposal". (1970), 4 Ottawa L.J. 296.

Master, M.K. "Difficulties of Judicial Interpretation of Legislative Draftsmanship". (1971), 2 R.F.L. 1.

McDonnell, T.E. "Statutory Interpretation, 'Acceptable' Tax Planning, Courts Role in Filling in the Gaps in Tax Legislation". (1981), 29 Can. Tax J. 188.

McGregor, G. "Literal or Liberal? Trends in the Interpretation of Income Tax Law". (1954), 32 Can. Bar Rev. 281.

McGregor, G. "Interpretation of Taxing Statutes, Whither Canada?" (1968), 16 Can. Tax J. 122.

Meiklem, I.C. "Legislative Expression and Transformational Generative Grammar". (1970), 5 U.B.C.L. Rev. 57.

Nepveu, R. "Interprétation des lois; chroniques". (1983), 43 R. du B. 107.

Nova Scotia Commissioners and Alberta Commissioners. "Report and Comments on Sections 9, 10 and 11 of the Uniform Interpretation Act (Revised 1973)". [1975] Unif. L. Conf. 218.

Pescatore, P., et autres. "L'interprétation des lois et conventions plurilingues dans la Communauté européène". (1985), 25 Cahiers 989.

Pigeon, L.P. "La rédaction bilingue des lois fédérales". (1982), 13 R.G.D. 177.

Presby, S.S. "Interpretivism Naturalized: Dworkin's Minimalist Metaphysics". (1994), 47 Can. J. Law & Jur. 303.

Rémillard, G. "L'interprétation par le juge des règles écrites en droit constitutionnel au Canada". (1978), 13 R.J.T. 59.

Requadt, S.G. "Worlds Apart on Words Apart: Re-Examining the Doctrine of Shifting Purpose in Statutory Interpretation". (1993), 51 U.T.Fac.L. Rev. 331.

Roach, K. "The Problems of Public Choice: The Case of Short Limitation Periods". (1993), 31 Osgoode Hall L.J. 721.

Sanagan, G.D. "The Construction of Taxing Statutes". (1940), 18 Can. Bar Rev. 43.

Scott, S.A. "Neither Fish nor Fowl but Good Yellow Margarine: *M.F.F. Equities v. The Queen:* Statutory Interpretation and the Man of Common Understanding". (1972), 18 McGill L.J. 145.

Smith, J.A.C. "Statutory Drafting and Interpretation: Comparative Summing Up". (1971), 9 Col. I. Dr. Comp. 155.

Smith, J.A.C. "The Interpretation of Statutes". (1970), 4 Man. L.J. 212.

Thomas, R.B. "New Light on Statutory Interpretation". (1992), 40 Can. Tax J. 387.

Todd, E.C.E. "Statutory Interpretation: Literal versus Context". (1956), 34 Can. Bar Rev. 458.

Tucker, E. "The Gospel of Statutory Rules Requiring Liberal Interpretation According to St. Peter's". (1985), 35 U.T.L.J. 113.

Uniform Interpretation Act. [1984] Unif. L. Conf. 123.

Uniform Law Conference of Canada. "Bilingual Drafting in a Common Law Jurisdiction in Canada". [1986] Unif. L. Conf. 81.

Uniform Law Conference of Canada. "La version française des lois uniforms". [1981] Unif. L. Conf. 105.

Uniform Law Conference of Canada. "The Interpretation Act". [1967] Unif. L. Conf. 123.

Uniform Law Conference of Canada. "The Report of the Alberta Commissioners, the Interpretation Act and the Statutes Act". [1971] Unif. L. Conf. 25.

Uniform Law Conference of Canada. "The Report of the Manitoba Commissioners, Interpretation Act". [1966] Unif. L. Conf. 66.

Uniform Law Conference of Canada. "Sex and Gender in Legislative Drafting and Sexist Language in Legislation". [1986] Unif. L. Conf. 90.

Waluchow, W.J. "The Forces of Law". (1990), 3 Can. J. Law & Jur. 51.

Willis, J. "Statute Interpretation in a Nutshell". (1938), 16 Can. Bar Rev. 1.

Wilson, B. "The making of a constitution: approaches to judicial interpretation" (Of the Canadian Charter of Rights and Freedoms). Constitution Act 1982 (Canada). P.L. 1988, Aut. 370. Legal Journals Index, Vol. 3, No. 12, December 1988.

Wilson, J.D. "Criminal Law — Obscenity — Interpretation of Criminal Statutes". (1986), 64 Can. Bar Rev. 740.

Wood, J.C.E. "Statutory Interpretation: Tupper and the Queen". (1968), 6 Osgoode Hall L.J. 92.

Zalm, J.B. "Language and the Law: Towards a Linguistic Understanding". (1977), 25 Chitty's L.J. 109.

United Kingdom, Australia and New Zealand

Baker, J.H. "Statutory Interpretation and Parliamentary Intention". (1993), 52 Cambridge L.J. 353.

Barwick, G. "Divining the Legislative Intent". (1961), 35 Aust. L.J. 197.

Bates, T.M., St.J. N. "Parliamentary Material and Statutory Construction: Aspects of the Practical Application of *Pepper v. Hart*". (1993), 14 Stat. L. Rev. 46.

Bell, J. "Bennion's Statutory Interpretation". (1986), 6 Oxford J. Leg. Stud. 288.

Bennion, F.A.R. "Hansard — Help or Hindrance? A Draftsman's View of *Pepper v. Hart*". (1993), 14 Stat. L. Rev. 149.

Bennion, F. "If It's Not Broken Don't Fix It: A Review of New Zealand Law Commission's Proposals on the Format of Legislation". (1994), 15 Stat. L. Rev. 164.

Bennion, F. "The Science of Interpretation". (1980), 130 New L.J. 493.

Bennion, F. "Statutory Drafting and Interpretation: England". (1971), 9 Co. I. Dr. Comp. 115.

Bramwell, R. "Interpreting Consolidation Act: The Influence of History". (1992), Brit. Tax Rev. 69.

Brazil, P. "Legislative History and the Sure and True Interpretation of Statutes in General and the Constitution in Particular". (1961), 4 U. Queensl. L.J. 1.

Brazil, P. "Reform of statutory interpretation — the Australian experience of use of extrinsic materials: with a postscript on simpler drafting". (1988), 62 Aust. L.J. 503.

Brett, P. "The Theory of Interpreting Statutes". (1956), 2 U. Queensl. L.J. 99.

Bryson, J. "Statutory Interpretation: An Australian Judicial Perspective". (1992), 13 Stat. L. Rev. 187.

Burrows, J.F. "Statutory Interpretation in New Zealand". (1984), 11 N.Z.U.L. Rev. 1.

Burrows, J.F. "The Problem of Time in Statutory Interpretation". [1978] N.Z.L.J. 253.

Corns, C.T. "Purposive Construction of Legislation and Judicial Autonomy". (1984), 58 Law Inst. J. 391.

Crabbe, V.C.R.A.C. "Custom and the Statute Law: A Case Study". (1990), 11 Stat. L. Rev. 90.

Evans, J. "Some Fine Points of Statutory Interpretation and a Constitutional Upheaval". (1983), 10 N.Z.U.L. Rev. 278.

Fiocc, J.G. "Current Approaches to Statutory Interpretation". [1980] N.Z.L.J. 53.

Garner, J.F. "Within the Meaning of the Act (Interpretation of Statutes)". (1994), 138 Sol. J. 374.

Ghosh, I.J. "The Construction of Fiscal Legislation". (1994), Brit. Tax Rev. 126.

Girvin, S.D. "Hansard and the Interpretation of Statutes". (1993), 22 Anglo-Am. L. Rev. 425.

Gleeson, A.M. "Clarity or Fairness: Which is More Important?" (1990), 12 Syd. L. Rev. 305.

Goodrich, P. "Oedipus Lex: Slips in Interpretation and Law". (1993), 13 Legal Stud. 381.

Halpin, A. "New Rights for Old?" (1994), 53 Cambridge L.J. 573.

Harrison, W.N. "Methods of Statutory Interpretation in the House of Lords". (1955), 2 U. Queensl. L.J. 349.

Hart, G.L. "An Attempt at the Meaning of Statutes". (1956), 2 U. Queensl. L.J. 264.

Iles, W. "Legislative Drafting Practices in New Zealand". (1991), 12 Stat. L. Rev. 16.

Jamieson, N.J. "How Many Acts Make a Bill?" (1984), 2 Canterbury L. Rev. 230.

Kurzon, D. "Clarity and Word Order in Legislation". (1985), 5 Oxford J. Leg. Stud. 269.

MacLeod, I. "The Use of Hansard in Statutory Interpretation". (1992), 156 Loc. Gov. Rev. 102.

Marcrossan, J.M. "Judicial Interpretation". (1984), 58 Aust. L.J. 547.

Marshall, R.S. & R.S. Summer. "The Argument for Ordinary Meaning in Statutory Interpretation". (1992), 43 N. Ir. Legal Q. Ann. 213.

Mayhew, P. "Can Legislation Ever Be Simple, Clear and Certain?" (1990), 11 Stat. L. Rev. 1.

Mayo, H. "The Interpretation of Statutes". (1955), 29 Aust. L.J. 204 (followed by a discussion of the article on pp. 215-23).

Miers, D.R. "Barking Up the Wrong Tree: Determining the Intention of Parliament". (1992), 13 Stat. L. Rev. 50.

Miers, D.R. "Taking Perks and Interpreting Statutes: *Pepper v. Hart*". (1993), 56 Mod. L. Rev. 695.

Montrose, J.L. "Judicial Implementation of Legislative Policy". (1957), 3 U. Queensl. L.J. 139.

Rensen, T. "British Statutory Interpretation in the Light of Community and Other International Obligations". (1993), 14 Stat. L. Rev. 186.

Renton (Lord). "Interpretation of Statutes". (1982), 9 J. Legis. 252.

Samuels, A. "The Impact of Article 177 Rulings on English Law: Problems of Construction and Interpretation". (1993), 14 Statute L. Rev. 111.

Sampford, C. "Fundamental Legislative Principles: Their Meaning and Rationale". (1994), 24 Queensland L. Soc. J. 531.

Scutt, J.A. "Statutory Interpretation and Recourse to Extrinsic Aids". (1984), 58 Aust. L.J. 483.

Slapper, G. "Statutory Interpretation: A New Departure". (1993), 14 Bus. L. Rev. 56.

Snell, J. "Trouble in Oiled Waters: Statutory Interpretation". (1976), 39 Mod. L. Rev. 402.

Stark, J.G. "Interpretation of Statutes in Consonance with Equitable Principles". (1991), 65 Aust. L.J. 375.

Stark, J.G. "The High Court and Provisions in a Statute Prohibiting Contracting Out of the Statute". (1991), 65 Aust. L.J. 246.

Stark, J.G. "The High Court's New Approach to the Question Whether the Crown is Bound by a Statute". (1990), 64 Aust. L.J. 527.

Statute Law Society. "Report of the Committee appointed by the Society to Examine the Failing of the Present Statute Law System". London: Sweet & Maxwell, 1970.

Statute Law Society. Statute Law: The Key to Clarity: First Report of The Committee Appointed to Propose Solutions to the Deficiencies of the Statute Law System in the U.K." London: Sweet & Maxwell.

Street, L. "Judicial Law-Making — Some Reflections". (1982), 9 Sydney L. Rev. 535.

Styles, S.C. "The Rule of Parliament: Statutory Interpretation After *Pepper v. Hart*". (1994), 14 Oxford J. Legal Stud. 151.

The Law Commission and the Scottish Law Commission. *The Interpretation of Statutes*. London: H.M.S.O., 1969.

Todd, E.C.E. "Statutory Interpretation and the Influence of Standards". (1953), 2 U. West. Aust. Ann. L. Rev. 526.

Turnbull, I.M.L. "Clear Legislative Drafting: New Approaches in Australia". (1990), 11 Stat. L. Rev. 161.

Turner, A.L. "An Approach to Statutory Interpretation". (1950), 4 Res Judica 237.

Vranker, M. "Statutory Interpretation and Judicial Policy Making: Some Comparative Reflections". (1991), 12 Stat. L. Rev. 31.

Ward, D.A.S. "A Criticism of the Interpretation of Statutes in the New Zealand Courts". [1963] N.Z.L.J. 293.

White, P. "Hansard's Up!" (1992), 136 Sol. J. 1224.

Williams, G. "Meaning of Literal Interpretation". (1981), 131 New L.J. 1128.

Wilson, A. "Statutory Interpretation". (1987), 7 Leg. Stud. 62.

Wilson, W.A. "Trials and Try-Ons: Modes of Interpretation". (1992), 13 Stat. L. Rev. 1.

United States

Abrahamson, S.S. & R.L. Hughes. "Shall we Dance? Steps for Legislators and Judges in Statutory Interpretation". (1991), 75 Minn. L. Rev. 1045.

Aleinikoff, T.A. "Updating statutory interpretation". (1988), 87 Mich. L. Rev. 20.

Alexander, L. "Practical Reasons in Statutory Interpretation". (1993), 12 Law & Philosophy 319.

Ararjo, R.J. "The Use of Legislative History in Statutory Interpretation: A Recurring Question — Clarification or Confusion?" (1992), 16 Seton Hall Legis. J. 551.

Atiyah, P.S, "Common Law and Statute Law". (1985), 48 Mod. L. Rev. 1.

Bates, J.D.N. "The Impact of Directives on Statutory Interpretation: Using the Euro-Meaning?" [1986] Statute L. Rev. 174.

Benson, W. "Up a Statute with Gun and Camera: Isolating Linguistic and Logical Structures in the Analysis of Legislative Language". (1984), 8 Seton Hall Leg. J. 279.

Blatt, W.S. "The History of Statutory Interpretation: A Study in Form and Substance". (1985), 6 Cardozo L. Rev. 799.

Breyer, S.G. "On the Uses of Legislative History in Interpreting Statutes". (1992), 65 S. Cal. L. Rev. 845.

Burdney, J.J. "Congressional Commentary on Judicial Interpretations of Statutes: Idle Chatter or Telling Response?" (1993), Mich. L. Rev. 1.

Chibundu, M.O. "Structure and Structuralism in the Interpretation of Statutes". (1994), 62 U. Cin. L. Rev. 1439.

Cross, E.L. "The Views of a Statutes Draftsman: The Missing Link in the Statutory Interpretation Process". (1985), 26 N.H.B.J. 267.

Cunningham, C.D., *et al.* "Plain Meaning and Hard Cases". (1994), 103 Yale L.J. 1561.

Cuomo, M. M. "Constitutional Convention: An Instrument for Change". (1994), 211 N.Y. L. J. 51.

Dickerson, F.R. "Statutory Interpretation: Dipping into Legislative History". (1983), 11 Hofstra L. Rev. 1125.

Dickerson, R. "Statutes and Constitutions in an Age of Common Law". (1987), 48 U. Pitt. L. Rev. 773.

Dougherty, V.M. "Absurdity and the Limits of Literalism: Defining the Absurd Result Principle in Statutory Interpretation". (1994), 44 Am. U. L. Rev. 127.

Eagleson, R. "Plain English in the Statutes". (1985), 59 Law Inst. J. 673.

Easterbrook, F.H. "Text, History and Structure in Statutory Interpretation". (1994), 17 Harv. J. L. & Pub. Pol'y. 61.

Easterbrook, F.H. "The Role of Original Intent in Statutory Construction". (1988), 11 Harv. J.L. & Pol. 59.

Eskridge, W.N., Jr. "The Case of the Speluncean Explorers: Twentieth Century Statutory Interpretation in a Nutshell". (1993), 61 Geo. Wash. L. Rev. 1731.

Eskridge, W.N. "Dynamic Statutory Interpretation". (1987), 135 U. Pa. L. Rev. 1479.

Fagan, J. "The Legal Phoenix: The Plain Meaning Rule is Dead, Long Live the Rule". (1993), 29 Cal. W. L. Rev. 373.

Farber, D.A. "Revival of the Canons". (1992), 28 Trial 82.

Farber, D.A. "Statutory interpretation, legislative inaction, and civil rights". (1988), 87 Mich. L. Rev. 2.

Ferejohn, J.A. & B.R. Weingast. "A Positive Theory of Statutory Interpretation". (1992), 12 Int'l. Rev. L. & Econ. 263.

Frickey, P.P. "From the Big Sleep to the Big Heat: The Revival of Theory in Statutory Interpretation". (1992), 77 Minn. L. Rev. 241.

Frosini, V. "Law-Making and Legal Interpretation". (1993), 6 Ratio Juris. 118.

Grabow, J.C. "Congressional Silence and the Search for Legislative Intent: A Venture into 'Speculative Unrealities' ". (1984), 64 B.Y.U.L. Rev. 737.

Graham, B.L. "Supreme Court policy making in civil rights cases: a study of judicial discretion in statutory interpretation". (1988), 7 St. Louis U. Pub. L. Rev. 401.

Greenberger, S.R. "Civil Rights and the Politics of Statutory Interpretation". (1991), 62 U. Colo. L. Rev. 37.

Gudridge, P.O. "Legislation in Legal Imagination: Introductory Exercises". (1983), 37 U. Miami L. Rev. 493.

Harris, D.M. "The Politics of Statutory Construction". (1985), 65 B.Y.U.L. Rev. 745.

Hart and Sacks. "The Legal Process: Basic Problem in the Making and Application of Law". (Cambridge, Mass., tentative ed., 1958) (unpublished but available in certain libraries).

Hatch, O. "Legislative History: Tool of Construction or Destruction". (1988), 11 Harv. J.L. & Pol. 43.

Healy, P. "Proof and Policy: No Golden Threads". [1987] Crim. L. Rev. 355.

Hetzel, O.J. "Instilling Legislative Interpretation Skills in the Classroom and in the Courtroom". (1987), 48 U. Pitt. L. Rev. 663.

Hirrel, M. J. "The Solicitor General Cometh, Seeking Statutory Beheading". (1994), 16 Legal Times 22.

Holtsford, A.L., Jr. "Statutory Interpretation: Which Statute Applies When the Same Subject is Covered by More than One Statute". (1984), 7 Am. J. Trial Advoc. 425.

Hurst, D.J. "The Problem of the Elderly Statute". (1983), 3 Leg. Stud. 21.

Jackson, R.H. "The Meaning of Statutes: What Congress Says or What the Court Says". (1948), 34 A.B.A.J. 535.

Johnson, H.A. "Legislation — Procedure and Interpretation". (1984), 45 La. L. Rev. 341.

Jordan, W.S. III. "Legislative History and Statutory Interpretation: The Relevance of English Practice". (1994), 29 U.S.F.L. Rev. 1.

Karkkainen, B.C. " 'Plain Meaning': Justice Scalia's Jurisprudence of Strict Statutory Construction". (1994), 17 Harv. J. L. & Pub. Pol'y. 401.

Keeton, R.E. "Statutory Analogy, Purpose and Policy in Legal Reasoning: Live Lobsters and a Tiger Cub in the Park". (1993), 52 Md. L. Rev. 1192.

Kelch, T.G. "An Apology for Plain-Meaning Interpretation of the Bankruptcy Code". (1994), 10 Bankruptcy Dev. J. 289.

Kelsen, H. "On the Theory of Interpretation". (1990), 10 Legal Stud. 127.

Kovacic, C.S. "Remedying Underinclusive Statutes". (1986), 33 Wayne L. Rev. 39.

LaRue, L.H. "Statutory Interpretation: Lord Coke Revisited". (1987), 48 U. Pitt. L. Rev. 733.

Lloyd, H.A. "Plain Language Statutes: Plain Good Sense or Plain Nonsense?" (1986), 78 Law Libr. J. 683.

Liess, E.A. "Censoring Legislative History: Justice Scalia on the Use of Legislative History in Statutory Interpretation". (1993), 72 Neb. L. Rev. 568.

MacCormick, N. "Argumentation and Interpretation in Law". (1993), 6 Ratio Juris. 16.

Macey, J.R. "Promoting Public-Regarding Legislation Through Statutory Interpretation: An Interest Group Model". (1986), 86 Colum. L. Rev. 223.

Maltz, E.M. "Rhetoric and Reality in the Theory of Statutory Interpretation: Under-Enforcement, Overenforcement and the Problem of Legislative Supremacy". (1991), 71 B.U.L. Rev. 767.

Maltz, E.M. "Statutory interpretation and legislative power: the case for a modified intentionalist approach". (1988), 63 Tul. L. Rev. 1.

Martineau, R.J. "Craft and Technique, Not Canons and Grand Theories: A Neo-Realist View of Statutory Construction". (1993), 62 Geo. Wash. L. Rev. 1.

Mashaw, J.L. "Textualism, Constitutionalism and the Interpretation of Federal Statutes". (1991), 32 Wm. & Mary L. Rev. 827.

McCubbing, M.D., *et al.* "Legislative Intent: The Use of Positive Political Theory in Statutory Interpretation". (1994), 57 Law & Contemp. Prob. 3.

McLaughlin, G.T. and N.B. Cohen. "The Interplay of Statutes". (1992), 208 N.Y. L.J. 3.

Milles, J. "Rules, Facts and Hidden Narratives". (1992), 16 The Legal Stud. F. 63.

Meyer, B.S. "Some Thoughts on Statutory Interpretation with Special Emphasis on Jurisdiction". (1987), 115 Hofstra L. Rev. 167.

Mikva, A.J. "Reading and Writing Statutes". (1986), 28 S. Texas L.R. 181; (1987), 48 U. Pitt. L. Rev. 627.

Mowat, C., "A plain language writer considers consideration, LawNow, April/May, 1995.

Mowat, C., "Buddhists, Running, and Plain Language in Calgary, Part One and Part Two", Michigan Bar Journal, July 1994, pp. 696-697, and August 1994, pp. 828-31.

Nagle, J.C. "Severability". (1993), 72 N.C.L. Rev. 203.

Noyes, J.E. "Implied Rights of Action and the Use and Misuse of Precedent". (1987), 56 U. Cin. L. Rev. 145.

Oakes, J.L. " 'Plain Meaning', 'Original Intent', 'Administrative Deference': Judicial Abdication or Judicial Activism?" (1992), 47 Record of the Ass'n. of the Bar of the City of New York 772.

Perman, M.R. "Statutory Interpretation in California: Individual Testimony as an Extrinsic Aid". (1981), 15 U.S.F.L. Rev. 241.

Peters, D.M. "Finding Solutions to Problematic Law". (1995), 31 Ariz. Att. 18.

Phillips, J.J. "Truth and Fiction in the Judicial Handling of Statutes". (1984), 44 La. L. Rev. 1309.

Popkin, W.D. "Law-Making Responsibility and Statutory Interpretation". (1993), 68 Ind. L. J. 865.

Posner, R.A. "Legal Formalism, Legal Realism, and the Interpretation of Statutes and the Constitution". (1987), 37 Case W. Res. L. Rev. 179.

Quinn, R.W. "The Supreme Court's Use of Legislative History in Interpreting the Federal Securities Laws". (1994), Sec. Reg. L.J. 262.

Randolph, A.R. "Dictionaries, Plain Meaning and Context in Statutory Interpretation". (1994), 17 Harv. J. L. & Pub. Pol'y. 71.

Redish, M.H. & T.T. Chung, "Democratic Theory and the Legislative Process: Mourning the Death of Originalism in Statutory Interpretation". (1994), 68 Tul. L. Rev. 803.

Reynolds, W.L. "A Practical Guide to Statutory Interpretation Today" (1992), 94 W.Va. L. Rev. 927.

Rook, L. W. "Laying Down the Law: Canons for Drafting Complex Legislation". (1993), 72 Or. L. Rev. 663.

Romero, A.R. "Interpretative Directions in Statutes". (1994), 31 Harv. J. on Legis. 211.

Schachter, J.S. "Metademocracy: The Changing Structure of Legitimacy in Statutory Interpretation". (1995), 108 Harv. L. Rev. 593.

Schanck, P.C. "An essay on the role of legislative histories in statutory interpretation". (1988), 80 Law Libr. J. 391.

Schanck, P.C. "The Only Game in Town: Contemporary Interpretative Theory, Statutory Construction, Legislative Histories". (1990), 82 Law Libr. J. 419.

Schwartz, E.P., *et al.* "A Positive Theory of Legislative Intent". (1994), 57 Law & Contemp. Probs. 51.

Scutt, J.A. "Judicial Recourse to Extrinsic Materials: The Report of the Victorian Parliamentary Legal and Constitutional Committee". (1984), 58 Law Inst. J. 391.

Shapiro, D.L. "Continuity and Change in Statutory Interpretation". (1992), 67 N.Y.U.L. Rev. 921.

Shauer, F. "Statutory Construction and the Coordinating Function of Plain Meaning". (1990), Sup. Ct. Ann. Rev.

Slawson, W.D. "Legislative History and the Need to Bring Statutory Interpretation Under the Rule of Law". (1992), 44 Stan. L. Rev. 383.

Sneed, J.T. "The Art of Statutory Interpretation". (1983), 62 Tex. L. Rev. 665.

Snyder, F. "Researching Legislative Intent". (1982), 51 J. Kan. B.A. 93.

Steinhardt, R.G. "The Role of International Law as a Canon of Domestic Statutory Construction". (1990), 43 Vand. L. Rev. 1103.

Stevens, J.P. "The Shakespeare Canon of Statutory Construction". (1992), 140 U. Pa. L. Rev. 1373.

Summers, R.S. "The Comparative Statutory Interpretation Project". (1990), 17 Cornell L. F. 7.

Sutro, S.H. "Interpretation of Initiatives by Reference to Similar Statutes: Canons of Construction Do Not Adequately Measure Voter Intent". (1994), 34 Santa Clara L. Rev. 945.

Thomas, R. "Plain English and the Law". [1985] Statute L. Rev. 139.

Tribe, L.H. "Judicial Interpretation of Statutes: Three Axioms". (1988), 11 Harv. J.L. & Pol. 41.

Wilson, W.A. "Questions of Interpretation". [1987] Statute L. Rev. 142.

Wydick, R.C. *Plain English for Lawyers*, 3rd ed. Durham: Carolina Academic Press, 1994.

Zeppos, N.S. "Legislative History and the Interpretation of Statutes: Toward a Fact-Finding Model of Statutory Interpretation". (1990), 76 Va. L. Rev. 1295.

CASES

715341 Ontario Ltd. v. Minister of National Revenue (1993), N.R. 392 (Fed. C.A.), leave to appeal to S.C.C. refused (1994), 174 N.R. 319n (S.C.C.).

Acadian Pulp & Paper Ltd. v. New Brunswick (Minister of Municipal Affairs) (1973), 6 N.B.R. (2d) 755, 41 D.L.R. (3d) 589 (C.A.).

Ackland v. Yonge — Esplanade Enterprises Ltd. (1992), 10 O.R. (3d) 97, 27 R.P.R. (2d), 1, 95 D.L.R. (4th) 560, 58 O.A.C. 206 (Ont. C.A.), leave to appeal to S.C.C. refused (1993), 13 O.R. (3d) xvi (note), 63 O.A.C. 397n, 101 D.L.R. (4th) vii (note), 154 N.R. 320n (S.C.C.).

Administration de la Voie Maritime de Saint-Laurent v. Condiac Dev. Corp., [1987] C.A. 499.

Alberta v. Very, 27 Alta. L.R. (2d) 119, [1983] 6 W.W.R. 143, 29 R.P.R. 179, 149 D.L.R. (3d) 688, 47 A.R. 340 (Q.B.).

Alta. Government Telephones v. Bauer, [1975] W.W.D. 30 (Alta.).

Alberta Treasury Branches v. Alberta (1984), 32 Alta. L.R. (2d) 306, 50 A.R. 70 (Q.B.).

Associated Respiratory Services Inc. v. British Columbia (Purchasing Commission) (1994), 23 Admin. L.R. (2d) 183, 95 B.C.L.R. (2d) 357, 117 D.L.R. (4th) 353, 49 B.C.A.C. 221, 80 W.A.C. 221 (C.A.), leave to appeal to S.C.C. refused (1995), 5 B.C.L.R. (3d) xxxix (note), 29 Admin. L.R. (2d) 87n, 123 D.L.R. (4th) vii (note) (S.C.C.).

Athlumney, Re, [1895-99] All E.R. Rep. 329, [1898] 2 Q.B. 547 (Q.B.).

Atlantic Petfood Supply Inc. v. Adrice P. Cormier Ltd. (1977), 19 N.B.R. (2d) 602, 30 A.P.R. 602 (Q.B.), reversed (1978), (*sub nom. Atlantic Pet Food Supply Ltd., Re*) 22 N.B.R. (2d) 81, 39 A.P.R. 81 (C.A.).

Atlific (Nfld.) Ltd. v. Hotel Buildings Ltd. (1993), 334 A.P.R. 330 106 Nfld. & P.E.I.R. 330, (Nfld. T.D.), reversed (1994), 120 Nfld. & P.E.I.R. 91, 373 A.P.R. 91 (Nfld. C.A.), leave to appeal to S.C.C. refused (January 26, (1995), Doc. 24313 (S.C.C.).

Aves v. Nova Scotia (Public Utilities Board) (1973), 5 N.S.R. (2d) 370, 39 D.L.R. (3d) 266 (C.A.).

Badger v. R. (sub nom. Badger v. Canada) (1990), [1991] 1 F.C. 191, 38 F.T.R. 43, [1991] 2 C.N.L.R. 17 (1992), 146 N.R. 79, 57 F.T.R. 311 (T.D.), affirmed (C.A.).

Bains v. British Columbia (Superintendent of Insurance) (1973), 38 D.L.R. (3d) 756 (B.C. C.A.).

Barrett v. Winnipeg (City) (1891), 19 S.C.R. 374, reversed [1892] A.C. 445, 5 Cart. B.N.A. 32 (P.C.).

Barry v. Alberta (Securities Commission), [1989] 1 S.C.R. 301, *(sub nom. Brosseau v. Alberta (Securities Comm.))* 65 Alta. L.R. (2d) 97, 35 Admin, L.R. 1, [1989] 3 W.W.R. 456, 96 A.R. 241, 57 D.L.R (4th) 458, 93 N.R. 1.

B.C. Development Corporation v. Friedmann, Ombudsman of B.C., [1984] 2 S.C.R. 447, [1985] 1 W.W.R. 193 *(sub nom. B.C. Development Corp. v. Ombudsman (B.C.))*, 11 Admin. L.R. 113 *(sub nom. B.C. Development Corp.v Ombudsman (B.C.))*, 14 D.L.R. (4th) 129, 55 N.R. 298, affirming [1982] 5 W.W.R. 563, 38 B.C.L.R. 56, 139 D.L.R. (3d) 307 (C.A.), which reversed (1981), 34 B.C.L.R. 132, *(sub nom. Re B.C. Development Corp. v. Friedmann)*, 130 D.L.R. (3d) 565 (S.C.).

Bell v. Grand Trunk Railway Co. (1913), 48 S.C.R. 561, 16 C.R.C. 324, 15 D.L.R. 874.

Bell v. North Vancouver School District No. 44 (1979), 16 B.C.L.R. 94 (S.C.).

Bolling v. Canada (Public Service Staff Relations Board), [1978] 1 F.C. 85, 77 D.L.R. (3d) 318 (C.A.).

Brueckner v. Manitoba, [1973] 3 W.W.R. 214 (Man. Q.B.).

C.E. & V. Holdings v. British Columbia (Assessment Appeal Board), [1975] 4 W.W.R. 667 (B.C. S.C.).

Campbell Soup Co. v. Ontario (Farm Products Marketing Board) (1975), 10 O.R. (2d) 405, 63 D.L.R. (3d) 401 affirmed (1977), 16 O.R. (2d) 256, 77 D.L.R. (3d) 725 (C.A.).

Canada (A.-G.) v. Newfield Seed Ltd. (1989), 63 D.L.R. (4th) 644, 80 Sask. R. 134 (C.A.).

Canada (Chief Pensions Advocate) v. Canada (Minister of Veterans Affairs), [1989] 3 F.C. 249, 20 R.F.L. (3d) 199, 58 D.L.R. (4th) 164, 97 N.R. 151 (C.A.).

Canada (Director of Investigation & Research) v. Air Canada (1988), [1989] 2 F.C. 88, 33 Admin. L.R. 229, 23 C.P.R. (3d) 178, 54 D.L.R. (4th) 741, *(sub nom. American Airlines Inc. v. Canada (Competi-*

tion Trib.)) 89 N.R. 241 (C.A.), affirmed [1989] 1 S.C.R. 236, 26 C.P.R. (3d) 95, (*sub. nom. American Airlines Inc. v. Canada (Competition Trib.)*) 92 N.R. 320, 23 C.P.R. (3d) 178n.

Canada Indemnity Co. v. British Columbia (Attorney General), [1975] 3 W.W.R. 224 (B.C. S.C.).

Canada Life Assurance Co. v. Rieb, [1943] 1 W.W.R. 759 (Alta. T.D.).

Canadian Financial Co. v. O'Neill (1977), 26 N.B.R. (2d) 221, 55 A.P.R. 221 (Co. Ct.).

Canadian Pacific Ltd. & Canada (Canadian Transport Commission), [1979] 2 F.C. 808, 99 D.L.R. (3d) 52, 26 N.R. 482, affirmed [1980] 1 S.C.R 319, 33 N.R. 157.

Canbra Foods Ltd. v. Overwater, [1978] 1 W.W.R. 231, 84 D.L.R. (3d) 350, 7 A.R. 506 (C.A.), affirming (1976), 71 D.L.R. (3d) 603, (Alta. T.D.).

Candlish v. Saskatchewan (Minister of Social Services), [1978] 3 W.W.R. 515, 5 R.F.L. (2d) 166, 85 D.L.R. (3d) 716 (Sask. Q.B.).

Cardinal v. R., [1980] 1 F.C. 149, 97 D.L.R. (3d) 402, [1979] 1 C.N.L.R. 32 (T.D.), affirmed (*sub nom. Cardinal v. Canada*) [1980] 2 F.C. 400, 109 D.L.R. (3d) 366, 32 N.R. 209 (C.A.), which was affirmed [1982] 1 S.C.R. 508, [1982] 3 W.W.R. 673, 133 D.L.R. (3d) 513, 41 N.R. 300, [1982] 3 C.N.L.R. 3.

Carfrae Estates Ltd. v. Stavert (1976), 13 O.R. (2d) 537 (Div. Ct.).

Central Canada Potash Co. v. Saskatchewan, [1975] 5 W.W.R. 193, 57 D.L.R. (3d) 7 (Sask. Q.B.), reversed [1977] 1 W.W.R. 487 (C.A.), which was reversed in part [1979] 1 S.C.R. 42, [1978] 6 W.W.R. 400, 6 C.C.L.T. 265, 88 D.L.R. (3d) 609, 23 N.R. 481.

Century Aviation Services Ltd. v. British Columbia (Industrial Relations Board) (1976), 69 D.L.R. (3d) 176 (B.C. S.C.).

Chambre des notaires du Québec c. Haltrecht, [1992] R.J.Q. 947 (C.A.), leave to appeal to S.C.C. refused (*sub nom. Haltrecht v. Chambre des Notaires du Québec*) (1992), 145 N.R. 399n, (*sub nom. Haltrecht c. Chambre des notaires du Québec*) 56 Q.A.C. 104n (C.S.C.).

Churchill Falls (Labrador) Corp. v. Newfoundland (A.G.), [1984] S.C.R. 297, 8 D.L.R. (4th) 1, 47 Nfld. & P.E.I.R. 125, 139 A.P.R. 125, 53 N.R. 268, reversing (1982), 134 D.L.R. (3d) 288, 36 Nfld. & P.E.I.R. 273, 101 A.P.R. 273 (*sub nom. Re Upper Churchill Water Rights Reversion Act, 1980*) (Nfld. C.A.).

Coles v. Roach (1980), 25 Nfld. & P.E.I.R. 172, 112 D.L.R. (3d) 101, 68 A.P.R. 172 (P.E.I. S.C.).

Continental Finances Corp. v. Junico Ltd., [1978] 3 W.W.R. 759, 27 C.B.R. (N.S.) 65 (Man. Q.B.).

Cooligan v. British American Bank Note Co. (1979), 1 C.H.R.R. D/52 (Human Rights Trib.).

Cowieson v. Atkinson (1974), 52 D.L.R. (3d) 401 (Man. C.A.).

Crease v. Metropolitan Toronto (Municipality) Commissioners of Police (1976), 11 O.R. (2d) 459, 66 D.L.R. (3d) 403 (Co. Ct.).

C.U.P.E. Local 963 v. New Brunswick Liquor Corp. (1978), 21 N.B.R. (2d) 441, 37 A.P.R. 441 (C.A.), reversed [1979] 2 S.C.R. 227, 25 N.B.R. (2d) 237, 79 C.L.L.C. 14,209, 97 D.L.R. (3d) 417, 51 A.P.R. 237, 26 N.R. 341.

Drewery v. Century City Developments Ltd. (No. 2) (1975), 6 O.R. (2d) 299, 52 D.L.R. (3d) 523 (C.A.).

Dymond v. Stirling (1977), 21 Nfld. & P.E.I.R. 297, 56 A.P.R. 297 (Nfld. Dist. Ct.).

Excelsior Lumber Co. v. Ross (1914), 19 B.C.R. 289, 6 W.W.R. 367, 16 D.L.R. 593 (C.A.).

Francouer v. Prince Albert Community Clinic (1986), 52 Sask. R. 221 (Q.B.).

Frehlick v. McLenehan, [1980] I.L.R. 1-1270, 114 D.L.R. (3d) 310, 3 Sask. R. 340 (C.A.).

Garet v. Northwest Territories (Criminal Injuries Compensation Ordinances), [1975] 5 W.W.R. 36, 29 C.R.N.S. 391 (N.W.T. S.C.).

Goguen v. Shannon (1989), 97 N.B.R. (2D) 44, 50 C.C.C. (3d) 45, 245 A.P.R. 44, 3 T.C.T. 5053 (C.A.).

Good Electric Ltd. v. Thorne (1979), 24 Nfld. & P.E.I.R. 525, 107 D.L.R. (3d) 220, 65 A.P.R. 525 (P.E.I. S.C.).

Goulbourn (Township) v. Ottawa-Carlton (Regional Municipality), [1980] 1 S.C.R. 496, 10 O.M.B.R. 491, 12 O.M.B.R. 126, 101 D.L.R. (3d) 1, 29 N.R. 267.

Greater Niagara Transit Commission v. Matson (1977), 16 O.R. (2d) 351, 78 D.L.R. (3d) 265 (H.C.).

Greene v. D.R. Sutherland Ltd. (1982), 40 N.B.R. (2d) 27, 105 A.P.R. 27 (Q.B.).

Greenshields v. R., [1958] S.C.R. 216, [1959] C.T.C. 77, 17 D.L.R. (2d) 33.

Gustar v. Wadden, 91 B.C.L.R. (2d) 86, 26 C.P.C. (3d) 197, [1994] 7 W.W.R. 148, 72 W.A.C. 55, 45 B.C.A.C. 55 (C.A.).

Halifax Harbour Services Ltd. v. Maritime Telegraph & Telephone (1979), 38 N.S.R. (2d) 541, 69 A.P.R. 541 (T.D.), reversed (1980), 115 D.L.R. (3d) 335, 40 N.S.R. (2d) 448, 73 A.P.R. 448 (C.A.).

Harris v. Ontario (Ministry of Community & Social Services) (1975), 8 O.R. (2d) 721, 23 R.F.L. 383, 59 D.L.R. (3d) 169 (Div. Ct.).

Harvard Realty Ltd. v. Nova Scotia (Director of Assessment) (1979), 35 N.S.R. (2d) 60, 62 A.P.R. 60, 106 D.L.R. (3d) 739 (C.A.).

Hassard v. Toronto (City) (1908), 16 O.L.R. 500 (C.A.).

Hayes, Re, 25 Sask. L.R. 257, [1931] 1 W.W.R. 301, 12 C.B.R. 225 (K.B.).

Heare v. Insurance Corporation of British Columbia (1989), 34 B.C.L.R (2d) 324, 37 C.C.L.I. 293, [1989] I.L.R. 1-2450 (C.A.).

Heppner v. Alberta (Minister of Environment), 4 Alta. L.R. (2d) 139, 80 D.L.R. (3d) 112, 6 A.R. 154 (*sub nom. Heppner v. Alberta (Attorney General)*) (C.A.).

Heydon's Case (1584), 3 Co. Rep. 7a, 76 E.R. 637, Moore K.B. 128.

Hobby Ranches Ltd. v. R. (1978), 8 B.C.L.R. 247, 94 D.L.R. (3d) 529 (S.C.).

Hopper v. Foothills (Municipal District), [1975] 2 W.W.R. 337, 7 L.C.R. 97, affirmed [1976] 6 W.W.R. 610, 11 L.C.R. 215, 71 D.L.R. (3d) 374, 1 A.R. 129 (C.A.).

Houde v. Québec Catholic School Commission, [1978] 1 S.C.R. 937, 80 D.L.R. (3d) 542, 17 N.R. 451.

Hourie v. Petti, [1974] 5 W.W.R. 254, 15 R.F.L. 210, 45 D.L.R. (3d) 306 (Man. C.A.).

I.A.F.F., Local 209 v. Edmonton (City) (1979), 9 Alta. L.R. (2d) 119, 15 A.R. 594, 99 D.L.R. (3d) 109 (C.A.).

Imperial Investments Ltd. v. Saint John (City) (1993), (*sub. nom. Saint John (City) v. Imperial Investment Ltd.*) 140 N.B.R. (2d) 241, 17 M.P.L.R. (2d) 11, 358 A.P.R. 241, 106 D.L.R. (4th) 585 (C.A.).

Jurisdiction of a Province to Legislate Respecting Abstention from Labour on Sunday, Re (1905), 35 S.C.R. 581 (*sub. nom. Re Sunday Laws*).

Just v. British Columbia, [1989] 2 S.C.R. 1228, 41 Admin. L.R. 161, 1 C.C.L.T. (2d) 1, 18 M.V.R. (2d) 1, [1990] 1 W.W.R. 385, 41 B.C.L.R. (2d) 350, 64 D.L.R. (4th) 689, 103 N.R. 1, [1990] R.R.A. 140 (headnote only).

Juster v. R., [1974] C.T.C. 681, 74 D.T.C. 6540, [1974] 2 F.C. 398, 49 D.L.R. (3d) 256, 5 N.R. 219 (*sub nom. Juster v. M.N.R.*) (C.A.).

Krachan, Ex parte (1975), 24 C.C.C. (2d) 114 (Ont.).

Krieg v. Saskatchewan (1993), 112 Sask. R. 224 (Q.B.).

Kryworuchka v. Saskatchewan (Land Bank Commission), [1974] 5 W.W.R. 360 (Sask. Dist. Ct.).

Lamb, Re (1979), 25 O.R. (2d) 23 (Co. Ct.).

Lawson v. Wellesley Hospital (1975), 9 O.R. (2d) 677, 61 D.L.R. (3d) 445 (C.A.), affirmed [1978] 1 S.C.R. 893, 76 D.L.R. (3d) 688, 15 N.R. 271.

LeBlanc Estate v. Bank of Montreal (1988), [1989] 1 W.W.R. 49, 54 D.L.R. (4th) 89, 69 Sask. R. 81 (C.A.).

Logan v. New Brunswick School District No. 14 (1973), 6 N.B.R. (2d) 782, 40 D.L.R. (3d) 152 (C.A.).

Lor-Wes Contracting Ltd. v. R., [1986] 1 F.C. 346, [1985] 2 C.T.C. 79, 85 D.T.C. 5310, 60 N.R. 321 (*sub nom. Lor-Wes Contracting Ltd. v. M.N.R.*) (C.A.).

Lunney v. H.(M.), 33 Alta. L.R. (2d) 40, [1984] 5 W.W.R. 722, 14 C.C.C. (3d) 210 (*sub nom. M.H. and R.*), 56 A.R. 250 (Q.B.), additional reasons at 35 Alta. L.R. (2d) 246, [1985] 2 W.W.R. 444, 58 A.R. 231, 17 C.C.C. (3d) 443 (*sub nom. Re M.H. and R. (No. 2)*), 16 D.L.R. (4th) 542 (Q.B.), affirmed without written reasons (1985), 21 C.C.C. (3d) 384, 21 D.L.R. (4th) 767 (headnote only) (Alta. C.A.), leave to appeal to S.C.C. granted 63 A.R. 79n (*sub nom. M.H. v. Lunney*), 21 C.C.C. (3d) 384n, 21 D.L.R. (4th) 767n, 62 N.R. 322n (S.C.C.).

M.G.E.A. and Man., Re, [1978] 1 S.C.R. 1123, [1977] 6 W.W.R. 247, 79 D.L.R. (3d) 1, 17 N.R.506.

M. & M. Bulk Milk Service Ltd. v. Manitoba (Highway Transport Board), [1979] 6 W.W.R. 330, 102 D.L.R. (3d) 566 (Man. Q.B.).

M.R.T. Investments. Ltd. v. R., [1976] 1 F.C. 126, 75 D.T.C. 5224, [1975] C.T.C. 354 (T.D.), varied [1976] C.T.C. 294, 76 D.T.C. 6158, 12 N.R. 530 (C.A.).

MacKenzie v. British Columbia (Commissioner of Teachers' Pensions) (1992), 69 B.C.L.R. (2d) 227, 94 D.L.R. (4th) 532, 15 B.C.A.C. 69, 27 W.A.C. 69 (C.A.).

Mahon, Re (1975), 8 O.R. (2d) 511, 21 R.F.L. 362 (Div. Ct.).

Manitoba (Attorney General) v. Canada (National Energy Board), [1974] 2 F.C. 502, 48 D.L.R. (3d) 73 (T.D.).

Mathers v. Mathers (1992), 113 N.S.R. (2d) 284, 309 A.P.R. 284 (T.D.), additional reasons at (1992), 113 N.S.R. (2d) 284 at 310, 309 A.P.R. 284 at 310 (T.D.), (1993), 123 N.S.R. (2d) 14, 16 C.P.C. (3d) 16, 340 A.P.R. 14 (C.A.).

McIntyre Porcupine Mines Ltd. & Morgan (1921), 49 O.L.R. 214, 62 D.L.R. 619 (C.A.).

McLaren v. McLaren (1979) 24 O.R. (2d) 481, 8 R.F.L. (2d) 301, 100 D.L.R. (3d) 163 (C.A.).

McLean v. Pilon (1978), 7 B.C.L.R. 99 (S.C.).

McNeil v. Nova Scotia (Boardd of Censors), [1978] 2 S.C.R. 662, 84 D.L.R. (3d) 1, 25 N.S.R. (2d) 128, 36 A.P.R. 128, 19 N.R. 570, 44 C.C.C. (2d) 316.

Malczewski v. Sansai Securities Ltd., [1975] W.W.D. 35 (B.C.).

Manitoba Fisheries Ltd. v. R., [1976] 1 F.C. 8, 58 D.L.R. (3d) 119 (T.D.).

Manitoba Fisheries Ltd. v. R., [1978] 1 S.C.R. 101, [1978] 6 W.W.R. 496, 23 N.R. 159, 88 D.L.R. (3d) 462.

Marcotte v. Canada (Deputy Attorney General), [1976] 1 S.C.R. 108, 19 C.C.C. (2d) 257, 51 D.L.R. (3d) 259, 3 N.R. 613.

Menzel v. R., [1978] C.T.C. 351, [1978] 2 F.C. 776, 78 D.T.C. 6237, 22 N.R. 61 (Fed. C.A.).

Metropolitan Toronto & Region Conservation Authority v. Metropolitan Toronto (Municipality), [1973] 2 O.R. 531, 34 D.L.R. (3d) 483 (H.C.), reversed [1973] O.R. 1005, 39 D.L.R. (3d) 43 (C.A.).

Mobile Ad Ltd. v. Scarborough (Borough) (1974), 5 O.R. (2d) 303, 50 D.L.R. (3d) 191 (C.A.).

Montreal & Ottawa Railway v. Ottawa (City) (1903), 33 S.C.R. 376.

Morrison v. Minister of National Revenue, [1928] Ex. C.R. 75, [1928] 2 D.L.R. 759 (Exchequer Ct. of Can.).

National Trust Co. v. Larsen (1989), 6 R.P.R. (2d) 171, [1989] 6 W.W.R. 605, 61 D.L.R. (4th) 270, 77 Sask. R. 58 (C.A.).

Nelles v. Ontario, [1989] 2 S.C.R. 170, 69 O.R. (2d) 448n, 71 C.R. (3d) 358, 41 Admin. L.R. 1, 49 C.C.L.T. 217, 37 C.P.C. (2d) 1, 60 D.L.R. (4th) 609, 98 N.R. 321, 35 O.A.C. 161, 42 C.R.R. 1, reversing in part (1985), 51 O.R. (2d) 513, 46 C.R. (3d) 289, 13 Admin. L.R. 213, 10 O.A.C. 161, *(sub nom. Nelles v. R.)* 16 C.R.R. 320, 21 D.L.R. 103, 32 C.C.L.T. 291, 1 C.P.C. (2d) 113 (C.A.).

Neill v. Calgary Remand Centre (1990), 78 Alta. L.R. (2d) 1, 109 A.R. 231, [1991] 2 W.W.R. 352, *(sub nom. R. v. Neill)* 60 C.C.C. (3d) 26 (C.A.).

Nima v. McInnes (1988), 32 B.C.L.R. (2d) 197, [1989] 2 W.W.R. 634, 45 C.C.C. (3d) 419, 18 C.E.R. 81, 2 T.C.T. 4026 (S.C.).

Nitrochem Inc. v. Deputy Minister of National Revenue (Customs & Excise), [1984] C.T.C. 608, 8 C.E.R. 58, 53 N.R. 394 (Fed. C.A.).

Noah, Re (1961), 36 W.W.R. 577, 32 D.L.R. (2d) 185 (N.W.T.).

Northwestern Utilities Ltd. v. Edmonton (City), [1979] 1 S.C.R. 684, 7 Alta. L.R. (2d) 370, 88 D.L.R. (3d) 161, 12 A.R. 449, 23 N.R. 565.

Nova Scotia (Public Utilities Board) v. Nova Scotia Power Corp. (1976), 18 N.S.R. (2d) 692, 75 D.L.R. (3d) 72 (C.A.).

Ombudsman Act, Re (1970), 72 W.W.R. 176, 10 D.L.R. (3d) 47 (Alta. Q.B.).

Ombudsman Act, Re, [1974] 5 W.W.R. 176, 46 D.L.R. (3d) 452 *(sub nom. Re Ombudsman (Sask.))* (Sask.).

Ontario (Minister of Transport) v. Phoenix Assurance Co. (1975), 54 D.L.R. (3d) 768n, 5 N.R. 73 (S.C.C.).

Ontario (Ombudsman) v. Ontario (Minister of Housing) (1979), 26 O.R. (2d) 434, 103 D.L.R. (3d) 117 (H.C.), affirmed (1980), (*sub nom. Re Ombudsman of Ont. and R.*) 30 O.R. (2d) 768, 117 D.L.R. (3d) 613 (C.A.).

Ontario (Ombudsman) v. R. (sub nom. Ontario (Ombudsman) v. Ontario (Minister of Housing) (1979), 26 O.R. (2d) 434, 103 D.L.R. (3d) 117 (H.C.), affirmed (1980), 30 O.R. (2d) 768, 117 D.L.R. (3d) 613 (C.A.).

Ontario New Home Warranty Program v. Crown Trust Co. (1984), 50 O.R. (2d) 588, 7 C.L.R. 196, 32 R.P.R. 214 (Co. Ct.), affirmed (1985), 50 O.R. (2d) 593 (C.A.).

Ottawa-Carlton (Regional Municipality) v. Voyageur Colonial Ltd., (1975), 5 O.R. (2d) 601, 51 D.L.R. (3d) 161 (Dist. Ct.).

Oznaga v. Québec (Société d'exploitation des Loteries et courses), [1979] C.S. 186 (C.S.), reversed [1981] 2 S.C.R. 113, 40 N.R. 7.

Paramount Life Insurance Company v. Torgerson Development Corporation (Alberta) (1988), 48 R.P.R. 136, [1988] 3 W.W.R. 685 (*sub nom. Paramount Life Insurance v. Hilton*) 58 Alta. L.R. (2d) 13, 85 A.R. 253, (C.A.).

Peel (Regional Municipality) v. Viking Houses, [1979] 2 S.C.R. 1134, 104 D.L.R. (3d) 1, 29 N.R. 244, 49 C.C.C. (2d) 103, affirming (1977), 16 O.R. (2d) 765, 36 C.C.C. (2d) 337 (C.A.), affirmed (1977), 16 O.R. (2d) 632, 36 C.C.C. (2d) 337 (H.C.).

Petro-Canada Inc. v. Coquitlam Assessor, Area No. 12 (sub nom. Shell Canada v. Burnaby/New Westminste Assessor, Area No. 10) (1989), 64 D.L.R. (4th) 227 (B.C.C.A.), leave to appeal to S.C.C. refused (1990), (*sub nom. Shell Canada v. Burnaby/New Westminster Assessor, Area No. 10*) 68 D.L.R. (4th) vii (note), 107 N.R. 216 (S.C.C.).

Pfeil v. Simcoe & Erie General Insurance Co., [1984] 5 W.W.R. 756, 8 C.C.L.I. 112, [1985] I.L.R. 1-1852, 35 Sask. R. 277 (Q.B.), affirmed [1986] 2 W.W.R. 710, 24 D.L.R. (4th) 752, [1986] I.L.R.1-2055, 45 Sask. L.R. 241 (C.A.).

Pfizer Co. v. Deputy Minister of National Revenue (Customs & Excise), [1977] 1 S.C.R. 456, 24 C.P.R. (2d) 195, 68 D.L.R. (3d) 9, 6 N.R. 440.

Pic-N-Save Ltd., Re, [1973] 1 O.R. 809, 32 D.L.R. (3d) 431 (S.C.), affirmed on other grounds [1973] 3 O.R. 200, 19 C.B.R. (N.S.) 42, 36 D.L.R. (3d) 334 (C.A.).

Presbyterian Church v. R., [1976] 1 F.C. 632, 9 L.C.R. 301 (C.A.).

Price, Re (1973), 8 N.B.R. (2d) 620 (Q.B.).

Proc v. Ontario (Minister of Community & Social Services) (1974), 6 O.R. (2d) 624, 19 R.F.L. 82, 53 D.L.R. (3d) 512 (H.C.), affirmed (1974), 6 O.R. (2d) 624n, 53 D.L.R. (3d) 512n (C.A.).

Quebec (Attorney-General) v. Canada (National Energy Board) (sub nom. Re Hydro-Quebec), [1991] 2 C.N.L.R. 70 (N.E.B.), reversed in part, [1991] 3 F.C. 443, 7 C.E.L.R. (N.S.) 315, *(sub nom. Quebec (Procureur général) v. (office national de l'énérgie)* 132 N.R. 214, 83 D.L.R. (4th) 146 (C.A.), reversed [1994] 1 S.C.R. 159, 14 C.E.L.R. (N.S.) 1, [1994] 3 C.N.L.R. 49, 112 D.L.R. (4th) 129, 20 Admin. L.R. (2d) 79.

Quebec (Attorney-General) v. Eastmain Band (sub nom. Eastmain Band v. Canada (Federal Administrator)), [1992] 3 F.C. 800, *(sub nom. Eastmain Band v. James Bay & Northern Quebec Agreement Administrator))* 98 D.L.R. (4th) 206, *(sub nom. Eastmain Indian Band v. Robinson)* 148 N.R. 116 (Fed. C.A.).

R. v Abbas, [1984] 2 S.C.R. 526, 42 C.R. (3d) 243, 15 C.C.C. (3d) 513, 14 D.L.R. (4th) 449, 55 N.R. 224, reversing (1982), 68 C.C.C. (3d) 330, 6 O.A.C. 192 (C.A.).

R. v. Baig (1979), 23 O.R. (2d) 730 (Dist. Ct.).

R. v. Basaraba, [1975] 3 W.W.R. 481, 30 C.R.N.S. 358, 22 C.C.C. (2d) 335 (Man. C.A.).

R. v Bernier, [1978] C.S.P. 1095 (Que.).

R. v. Bilodeau, [1986] 1 S.C.R. 449, [1986] 3 W.W.R. 673 *(sub nom. Bilodeau v. Manitoba (A.G.))*, 25 C.C.C. (3d) 289, 27 D.L.R. (4th) 39, 67 N.R. 108.

R. v. Black & Decker Manufacturing Co., [1973] 2 O.R. 460, 10 C.P.R. (2d) 154, 11 C.C.C. (2d) 470, 34 D.L.R. (3d) 308 (C.A.), reversed [1975] 1 S.C.R. 411, 13 C.P.R. (2d) 97, 15 C.C.C. (2d) 193, 43 D.L.R. (3d) 393, 1 N.R. 299.

R. v. Boyce (1975), 7 O.R. (2d) 561, 28 C.R.N.S. 336, 23 C.C.C. (2d) 16 (C.A.).

R. v. Boylan, [1979] 3 W.W.R. 435, 8 C.R. (3d) 36, 46 C.C.C. (2d) 415, 3 Sask. R. 157 (C.A.), reversing (1978), 41 C.C.C. (2d) 497 (Sask. Q.B.).

R. v. Cadboro Bay Holdings Ltd., [1977] C.T.C. 184, 77 D.T.C. 5115 (Fed. T.D.).

R. v. Church of Scientology (1974), 4 O.R. (2d) 707, 18 C.C.C. (2d) 546.

R. v. Cook (1979), 25 N.B.R. (2d) 54, 51 A.P.R. 54 (C.A.).

R. v. Croft (1979), 35 N.S.R. (2d) 344, 62 A.P.R. 344 (C.A.).

R. v. Dagley (1979), 32 N.S.R. (2d) 421, 54 A.P.R. 421 (C.A.).

R. v. Davie, [1981] 2 W.W.R. 513, 17 C.R. (3d) 72, 54 C.C.C. (2d) 216 (B.C. C.A.).

R. v. Demeter (1975), 6 O.R. (2d) 83, 19 C.C.C. (2d) 321 (H.C.), affirmed (1975), 10 O.R. (2d) 321, 25 C.C.C. (2d) 417 (C.A.).

R. v. Donald B. Allen Ltd. (1975), 11 O.R. (2d) 271, 65 D.L.R. (3d) 599 (Dist Ct.).

R. v. Dubois, [1935] S.C.R. 378, [1935] 3 D.L.R. 209.

R. v. Dworkin Furs Ltd. (1976), 12 O.R. (2d) 460, 77 C.L.L.C. 14,071, 30 C.C.C. (2d) 452 (C.A.).

R. v. Dwyer, [1975] 4 W.W.R. 54, 23 C.C.C. (2d) 129 (*sub nom. Ex parte Dwyer*) (B.C. S.C.).

R. v. Eaton, [1973] 4 W.W.R. 101, 11 C.C.C. (2d) 80 (B.C.).

R. v. Faulkner (1977), 39 C.R.N.S. 331, 37 C.C.C. (2d) 26, 38 N.S.R. (2d) 329, 69 A.P.R. 329 (N.S. Co.Ct.).

R. v. Findlay (1977), 3 B.C.L.R. 321 (Prov. Ct.).

R. v. Flaman (1978), 43 C.C.C. (2d) 241 (Sask. C.A.).

R. v. Germain, [1995] 2 S.C.R. 241, 21 C.C.C. (3d) 289, 21 D.L.R. (4th) 296, 62 N.R. 87.

R. v. Giftcraft Ltd. (1984), 13 C.C.C. (3d) 192 (Ont. H.C.).

R. v. Goodbaum (1977), 1 C.R. (3d) 152, 38 C.C.C. (2d) 473 (Ont. C.A.).

R. v. Govedarov (1974), 3 O.R. (2d) 23, 25 C.R.N.S. 1, 16 C.C.C. (2d) 238 (C.A.), affirmed on other grounds (*sub nom. R. v. Popovic*) [1976] 2 S.C.R. 308, 32 C.R.N.S. 54, 25 C.C.C. (2d) 161, 62 D.L.R. (3d) 56, 7 N.R. 231.

R. v. "Gulf Aladdin", (The), [1977] 2 W.W.R. 677, 34 C.C.C. (2d) 460 (B.C. C.A.).

R. v. Jackson (1993), 46 M.V.R. (2d) 247, 80 C.C.C. (3d) 22, 104 Nfld. & P.E.I.R. 349, 329 A.P.R. 349 (Nfld. C.A.).

R. v. Johnston (1979), 52 C.C.C. (2d) 57, 20 A.R. 524 (Q.B.).

R. v. Kolot, [1973] 6 W.W.R. 527, 13 C.C.C. (2d) 417 (*sub nom. Ex parte Kolot*) (B.C. S.C.).

R. v. Krentz, [1976] 6 W.W.R. 527, 31 C.C.C. (2d) 450 (B.C. S.C.).

R. v. Langille (1992), 119 N.S.R. (2d) 79, 42 M.V.R. (2d) 116, 330 A.P.R. 79 (C.A.).

R. v. Laserich, [1977] 4 W.W.R. 703, 36 C.C.C. (2d) 285, 4 A.R. 148 (N.W.T. C.A.).

R. v. MacEachern (1985), 24 C.C.C. (3d) 439, 63 N.R. 59 (Ct. Martial App. Ct.).

R. v. McBurney, 19 E.T.R. 15, [1984] C.T.C. 466, 84 D.T.C. 6494 (T.D.), reversed 20 E.T.R., 283 (*sub nom. R. v. McBurney*, [1985] 2 C.T.C.

214, 85 D.T.C. 5433, 62 N.R. 104 (*sub nom. McBurney, v. M.N.R.*), leave to appeal to S.C.C. refused (1986), 65 N.R. 320n (S.C.C.).

R. v. McIntosh, [1984] 4 W.W.R. 734, 28 Man. R. (2d) 81, 13 C.C.C. (3d) 130 (C.A.).

R. v. McLaughlin, 12 C.R. (3d) 391, 51 C.C.C. (2d) 243, 19 A.R. 368 (C.A.), affirmed [1980] 2 S.C.R. 331, [1981] 1 W.W.R. 298, 18 C.R. (3d) 399, 53 C.C.C. (2d) 417, 113 D.L.R. (3d) 386, 23 A.R. 530, 32 N.R. 350.

R. v. McLeod, [1950] 2 W.W.R. 456, 10 C.R. 318, 97 C.C.C. 366 (B.C. C.A.).

R. v. Mallet (1975), 32 C.R.N.S. 73, 26 C.C.C. (2d) 457 (Que.).

R. v. Mansour, 25 Chitty's L.J. 284, 36 C.C.C. (2d) 493 (C.A.), affirmed [1979] 2 S.C.R. 916, 2 M.V.R. 1, 101 D.L.R. (3d) 545, 47 C.C.C. (2d) 129, 27 N.R. 476.

R. v. Maroney, [1975] 2 S.C.R. 306, 27 C.R.N.S. 185, 18 C.C.C. (2d) 257, 49 D.L.R. (3d) 481, 3 N.R. 209.

R. v. Miller, [1975] 6 W.W.R. 1, 33 C.R.N.S. 129, 24 C.C.C. (2d) 401, 63 D.L.R. (3d) 193 (B.C. C.A.), affirmed [1977] 2 S.C.R. 680, [1976] 5 W.W.R. 711, 38 C.R.N.S. 139, 31 C.C.C. (2d) 177, 70 D.L.R. (3d) 324, 11 N.R. 386.

R. v. Mitchell (1983), 42 O.R. (2d) 481, 35 C.R. (3d) 225, (*sub nom. Mitchell v A.G. Ont.*) 6 C.C.C. (3d) 193, 150 D.L.R. (3d) 449, [1984] S.C.R. 29 (H.C.).

R. v. Moore (1985), 67 N.S.R. (2d) 241, 155 A.P.R. 241 (C.A.).

R. v. Morgentaler (1985), 52 O.R. (2d) 353, 48 C.R. (3d) 1, 22 C.C.C. (3d) 353, 17 C.R.R. 223, 22 D.L.R. (4th) 641, 11 O.A.C. 81 (C.A.), reversed in part [1988] 1 S.C.R. 30, 63 O.R. (2d) 281n, 62 C.R. (3d) 1, 37 C.C.C. (3d) 449, 31 C.R.R. 1, 44 D.L.R. (4th) 385, 26 O.A.C. 1, 82 N.R. 1.

R. v. Morgentaler (No. 5), [1976] 1 S.C.R. 616, 30 C.R.N.S. 209, 20 C.C.C. (2d) 449, 53 D.L.R. (3d) 161, 4 N.R. 277.

R. v. Nabis, [1975] 2 S.C.R. 485, [1975] 6 W.W.R. 307, 18 C.C.C. (2d) 144, 48 D.L.R. (3d) 543, 2 N.R. 249.

R. v. Nielsen, [1974] 2 W.W.R. 379, 15 C.C.C. (2d) 224, 43 D.L.R. (3d) 634 (Y.T.)

R. v. O'Donnell, [1979] 1 W.W.R. 385, 45 C.C.C. (2d) 208 (B.C. C.A.).

R. v. Palomba, [1975] Que. C.A. 340, 32 C.R.N.S. 31, 24 C.C.C. (2d) 19 (C.A.).

R. v. Parkway Chrysler Plymouth Ltd. (1976), 32 C.C.C. (2d) 116, 28 C.P.R. (2d) 15 (Ont. C.A.).

R. v. Pasek, [1974] 3 W.W.R. 759 (Alta. T.D.)

R. v. Paul (1978), 39 C.C.C. (2d) 129 (C.A.), reversing (1977), 1 C.R. (3d) 173 (Ont. H.C.).

R. v. Prov. Treasurer of Alta. v. Can. Nor. Ry. and C.N.R., [1923] A.C. 714, [1923] 3 W.W.R. 547, [1923] 3 D.L.R. 719.

R. v. Raiche, [1975] W.W.D. 114, 24 C.C.C. (2d) 16 (Sask. Q.B.).

R. v. Rao (1984), 46 O.R. (2d) 80, 40 C.R. (3d) 1, 12 C.C.C. (3d) 97, 10 C.R.R. 275, 9 D.L.R. (4th) 542, 4 O.A.C. 162 (C.A.), leave to appeal to S.C.C refused (1984), 40 C.R. (3d) xxvi (note), 10 C.R.R. 275n, 57 N.R. 238n, 4 O.A.C. 241n.

R. v. Roche, [1983] 1 S.C.R. 491, [1983] 5 W.W.R. 289, 34 C.R. (3d) 14, 20 M.V.R. 97, 3 C.C.C. (3d) 193, 145 D.L.R. (3d) 565, 47 N.R. 217.

R. v. Rolland (1975), 31 C.R.N.S. 68, 27 C.C.C. (2d) 485 (Ont. C.A.).

R. v. Smith, [1980] 3 W.W.R. 591, 52 C.C.C. (2d) 290, 110 D.L.R. (3d) 636, 5 Man. R. (2d) 250 (Co. Ct.).

R. v. Sommerville, [1974] S.C.R. 387, [1973] 2 W.W.R. 65, 9 C.C.C. (2d) 493, 32 D.L.R. (3d) 207.

R. v. Stefaniuk, [1974] 4 W.W.R. 540 (Man.).

R. v. Stevenson (1980), 19 C.R. (3d) 74, 57 C.C.C. (2d) 526 (Ont. C.A.).

R. v. Tremblay, [1975] 3 W.W.R. 589, 23 C.C.C. (2d) 179, 58 D.L.R. (3d) 69 (Alta. C.A.).

R. v. Twoyoungmen, [1979] 5 W.W.R. 712, 3 M.V.R. 186, [1979] 3 C.N.L.R. 85, 16 A.R. 413, 101 D.L.R. (3d) 598, 48 C.C.C. (2d) 550 (C.A.).

R. v. Vasil, [1981] 1 S.C.R. 469, 20 C.R. (3d) 193, 58 C.C.C. (2d) 97, 121 D.L.R. (3d) 41, 35 N.R. 451.

R. v. Voisine (1984), 57 N.B.R. (2d) 38, 148 A.P.R. 38 (Q.B.).

R. v. Welsh (No. 6) (1977), 15 O.R. (2d) 1, 32 C.C.C. (2d) 363, 74 D.L.R. (3d) 748 (C.A.).

R. v. Wildsmith (1974), 16 C.C.C. (2d) 479 (N.S. C.A.).

R. v. Wilson (1978), 6 B.C.L.R. 231 (S.C.).

Reference re s. 94(2) of the Motor Vehicle Act (B.C.), [1985] 2 S.C.R.486, [1986] 1 W.W.R. 481 (*sub nom. Reference re Constitutional Question Act (B.C.)*), 69 B.C.L.R 145, 48 C.R. (3d) 289, 36 M.V.R. 240, 23 C.C.C. (3d) 289, 18 C.R.R. 30, 24 D.L.R. (4th) 536, 63 N.R. 266.

Royal Canadian Mounted Police Act (Canada), Re (1990),[1991] 1 F.C. 529, 123 N.R. 120, 41 F.T.R. 79n (C.A.), leave to appeal to S.C.C. refused (1991), 135 N.R. 319n (S.C.C.).

Riddell v. Vancouver (City) (1984), 5 C.C.E.L. 55 (B.C. S.C.), affirmed (1985), 11 C.C.E.L. 288 (B.C. C.A.).

Rocca Group Ltd. v. Muise (1979), 22 Nfld. P.E.I.R. 1, 102 D.L.R. (3d)
    529, 58 A.P.R. 1 (C.A.), refused leave to appeal (1979), 24 Nfld.
    & P.E.I.R. 90, 65 A.P.R. 90, 30 N.R. 613n, 102 D.L.R. (3d) 529n
    (S.C.C.).

*Rockcliffe Park Realty Ltd. v. Ontario (Director, Ministry of Environ-
    ment)*, (1975), 10 O.R. (2d) 1, 62 D.L.R. (3d) 17 (C.A.).

Royal Bank v. Riehl, [1978] 6 W.W.R. 481, 28 C.B.R. (N.S.) 211 (Alta.
    Dist. Ct.).

*SKF Canada Ltd. v. Deputy Minister of National Revenue (Customs &
    Excise)* (1983), 10 C.E.R. 6, 47 N.R. 61 (Fed. C.A.).

S.S. Marina Ltd. v. North Vancouver (City), [1976] 3 W.W.R. 284, 54
    D.L.R. (3d) 13 (B.C. C.A.).

St. Anne's Tower Corp. of Toronto v. Toronto (City) (1973), 1 O.R. (2d)
    717, 41 D.L.R. (3d) 481 (C.A.), reversed (1974), 5 O.R. (2d) 718,
    51 D.L.R. (3d) 374 (C.A.).

St. Peter's Evangelical Lutheran Church v. Ottawa (City), [1983] 2 S.C.R.
    616, 20 M.P.L.R. 121, 14 O.M.B.R. 257, 140 D.L.R. (3d) 577, 45
    N.R. 271.

Sale v. Wills, [1972] 1 W.W.R. 138, [1972] I.L.R. 1-453, 22 D.L.R. (3d)
    566 (Alta.).

Sam Richman Investments (London) Ltd. v. Riedel (1974), 6 O.R. (2d)
    335, 52 D.L.R. (3d) 655 (Div. Ct.).

Sanderson v. Russell (1979), 9 R.F.L. (2d) 81, 24 O.R. (2d) 429, 99 D.L.R.
    (3d) 713 (C.A.).

*Saskatchewan (Human Rights Comm.) v. Engineering Students' Society
    (sub nom. Saskatchewan (Human Rights Comm.) v. Waldo)* (1984),
    5 C.H.R.R. D/2074 (Sask. Bd. of Inquiry), reversed (1986), 7
    C.H.R.R. D/3443 (Sask. Q.B.), affirmed (1989), 10 C.H.R.R.
    D/5636, 56 D.L.R. (4th) 604, 72 Sask. R. 161 (C.A.), leave to appeal
    to S.C.C. refused (1989), 102 N.R. 320n, 103 N.R. 212n (S.C.C.).

Schecter v. Bluestein, [1982] C.A. 397, 36 C.R. (3d) 46, 70 C.C.C. (2d)
    336, 142 D.L.R. (3d) 71 *(sub nom Bluestein v. R.)* (C.A. Que.).

Schofield v. Glenn, 21 Sask. L.R. 494, [1927] 2 W.W.R. 727, [1927] 3
    D.L.R. 168 (C.A.), reversed [1928] S.C.R. 208, [1928] 2 D.L.R. 319.

Shannon v. Canada (Attorney General) (1992), [1993] 1 F.C. 331, 151 N.R.
    45 (C.A.).

Shell Canada Ltd. v. Canada (Director of Investigation & Research), [1975]
    F.C. 184, 29 C.R.N.S. 361, 18 C.P.R. (2d) 155, 22 C.C.C. (2d) 70,
    55 D.L.R. (3d) 713 *(sub nom. Canada (Director of Investigation &
    Research v. Shell Can. Ltd.)* (C.A.).

Silliker v. Newcastle (Town) (1974), 10 N.B.R. (2d) 118.

Skapinker v. Law Society of Upper Can., [1984] 1 S.C.R. 357, 8 C.R.R. 193, 11 C.C.C. (3d) 481 (*sub nom. Law Society of Upper Canada v. Skapinker*), 9 D.L.R. (4th) 161, 3 O.A.C. 321, 53 N.R. 169, 20 Admin. L.R. 1, reversing (1983), 40 O.R. 481 (*sub nom. Re Skapinker*), 3 C.R.R. 211, 3 C.C.C. (3d) 213, 145 D.L.R. (3d) 502 (C.A.), which reversed (1982), 38 O.R. (2d) 116, 68 C.C.C. (2d) 300, 137 D.L.R. (3d) 666 (H.C.).

Sous-Ministre du Revenu National (Douanes et Accise) c. Hydro-Quebec (1994), 172 N.R. 247 (Fed. C.A.).

Sparling c. Javelin International Ltée (1991), [1992] R.J.Q. 11, (*sub nom. Sparling c. Doyle*) 43 Q.A.C. 16 (C.A.), leave to appeal to S.C.C. refused (*sub nom. Sparling c. Doyle*) (1992), 53 Q.A.C. 169n (S.C.C.).

Stewart v. Kimberley (City) (1986), 70 B.C.L.R. 183 (C.A.).

Strachan v. Melfort (Town) (1979), 102 D.L.R. (3d) 761 (Sask. Q.B.).

Telegram Publishing Co. v. Zwelling (1973), 1 o.r. (2d) 592, 41 D.L.R. (3d) 176, 74 C.L.L.C. 12,210 (Dist. Ct.), reversed (1975), 11 O.R. (2d) 740, 67 D.L.R. (3d) 404, 76 C.L.L.C. 14,047 (C.A.).

Teperman & Sons Ltd. v. Toronto (City) (1974), 5 O.R. (2d) 507, 50 D.L.R. (3d) 675 (Div. Ct.), reversed (1975), 7 O.R. (2d) 553, 55 D.L.R. (3d) 653 (C.A.).

Ternette v. Canada (Solicitor General), [1984] 2 F.C. 486, [1984] 5 W.W.R. 612, 32 Alta L.R. (2d) 310, 9 Admin. L.R. 24, 10 D.L.R. (4th) 587 (T.D.).

Texaco Can. Resources Ltd. v. Alberta (Assessment Appeal Bd.) (1987), 53 Alta. L.R. (2d) 369, 85 A.R. 218 (Q.B.), reversed (1988), 64 Alta. L.R. (2d) 37, 41 M.P.L.R. 37, 93 A.R. 81 (C.A.).

Tiedmann v. Basiuk (1977), 4 Alta. L.R. (2d) 12, 7 C.P.C. 192, 5 A.R. 435 (T.D.).

Tony Murray Associates Co. v. Morris (1980), 26 Nfld. P.E.I.R. 31, 72 A.P.R. 31 (Nfld. T.D.).

Transco Mills Ltd. v. Louie (1975), 59 D.L.R. (3d) 665 (B.C. S.C.).

U.A., Local 488 v. Alberta (Industrial Relations Bd.), [1975] 2 W.W.R. 470, 75 C.L.L.C. 14,273, 49 D.L.R. (3d) 708 (Alta. C.A.).

Union Gas Ltd. v. Dawn (Township) (1977), 15. O.R. (2d) 722, 2 M.P.L.R. 23, 76 D.L.R. (3d) 613 (Div. Ct.).

United States v. Couche (1975), 31 C.R.N.S. 250, 26 C.C.C. (2d) 494, reversed [1976] 2 F.C. 336, 34 C.R.N.S. 340, 30 C.C.C. (2d) 443, 13 N.R. 49 (C.A.).

Victoria (City) v. Bishop of Vancouver Island, [1921] 2 A.C. 384, [1921] 3 W.W.R. 214, 59 D.L.R. 399 (P.C.).

Victoria School Trustees Bd. Dist. No. 61 v. C.U.P.E. (1976), 71 D.L.R. (3d) 139 (B.C. S.C).

Warren v. Chapman, [1984] 5 W.W.R. 454, 5 C.H.R.R. D/2226, 11 D.L.R. (4th) 474, 29 Man. R. (2d) 172 (Q.B.), affirmed [1985] 4 W.W.R. 75, 6 C.H.R.R. D/2777 (*sub nom. Warren v. Manitoba (Human Rights Comm.)*), 17 D.L.R. (4th) 261, 31 Man. R. (2d) 231 (C.A.).

Wasson v. New Brunswick (Minister of Finance) (1984), 56 N.B.R. (2d) 79, 146 A.P.R. 79 (Q.B.), affirmed (1985) 61 N.B.R. (2d) 37, 158 A.P.R. 37 (C.A.).

Western Mines Ltd. v. Childs (1974), 51 D.L.R. (3d) 145 (B.C.).

Westfall v. Eedy (1991), 6 O.R. (3d) 422, 7 M.P.L.R. (2d) 226 (Gen. Div.).

Wheeler, Re, [1979] 2 S.C.R. 650, 9 M.P.L.R. 161, 97 D.L.R. (3d) 605 (*sub nom. R. v. Wheeler*), 25 N.B.R. (2d) 209, 51 A.P.R. 209, 26 N.R. 323.

Worthington v. Robbins, 56 O.L.R. 285, [1925] 2 D.L.R. 80 (H.C.).

Xerox Canada Inc. v. Neary (1984), 43 C.P.C. 274, 47 O.R. (2d) 776 (Prov. Ct.).

Zavitz v. Brock (1974), 3 O.R. (2d) 583, 46 D.L.R. (3d) 203 (C.A.).

Zong v. Canada (Commissioner of Penitentiaries), [1975] F.C. 430, 22 C.C.C. (2d) 553 (T.D.), affirmed [1976] 1 F.C. 657, 29 C.C.C. (2d) 114, 10 N.R. 1 (C.A.).

Chapter 12

FAIRNESS AND NATURAL JUSTICE IN THE ADMINISTRATIVE PROCESS

INTRODUCTION

Administrative law is a division of what was earlier defined as "public law". An administrative body or tribunal conducts its affairs or renders its decisions in accordance with standards usually set out in the enabling statute which establishes the administrative body. Every administrative decision is presumably rendered, not in accordance with any benefit that might accrue to an interested party affected by the administrative decision, but rather in conformity to statutory or regulatory guidelines directed at serving the public interest. For example, assume an application is made by a private interest, such as a radio station, to the Canadian Radio-Television and Telecommunications Commission for a renewal of its licence to broadcast. Even though the renewal of the licence would primarily benefit a private business interest, the theory holds that the C.R.T.C. will render its decision on the basis of whether such a renewal is in accordance with public interest. In order to determine what constitutes public interest, the members of the commission must first look to any guidelines that might be suggested in the enabling statute, including, especially, those provisions establishing the commission and defining its jurisdiction. The administrative body may have to look at regulations passed pursuant to the enabling statute, for example by order in council, in order to determine those guidelines, or, in the absence of any written guidelines in the forms described above, the commission may itself have to be the judge as to what constitutes the public interest served by the regulatory jurisdiction of the particular administrative tribunal. In broadcasting, for example, such guidelines might include the broadcasting of a minimum number of hours of Canadian content. For the private interest to have its licence renewed, it must ensure that it conducts its private business in accordance with those particular guidelines.

THE IMPORTANCE OF ADMINISTRATIVE LAW

Probably no area of law has grown as significantly in recent years as administrative law. Not too many years ago, administrative law was rarely taught in the law schools, and was not considered to be an important branch of the law. However, since World War II and especially since the 1960's, there has been a proliferation of legislation at both the federal and provincial levels of government delegating authority to inferior tribunals composed of persons possessing expertise in particular areas to set policy and render decisions accordingly. In addition to reducing the workload of the primary legislative bodies, this development has theoretically created expert bodies which are better qualified to resolve the complex problems that arise in these particular areas. For example, the C.R.T.C. is better able and has more time than Parliament to deal with the technical questions which arise in the course of the various applications made before that body. Also, a commission is often given a budget sufficient to allow it to hire permanent staff and to pay outside consultants in order to assist the members of the commission in rendering appropriate decisions.

THE PROCESS OF DELEGATION

Under the doctrine of parliamentary sovereignty,[1] legislative (or policy-making) authority can be delegated by a sovereign legislative body. The Parliament of Canada and all of the provincial legislatures in Canada are constitutionally able to conduct this delegation process, subject to the following constraints. First, the delegation must relate to a matter within the sovereign jurisdiction of the particular legislative body, as set out in the Constitution Act of 1867; that is, a superior legislative body cannot delegate to any inferior tribunal powers which it does not itself possess.

The second constraint relates to what is referred to as "interdelegation". The basic rule concerning interdelegation is that Parliament may not delegate any of its powers under the Constitution Act of 1867 to any or all of the provincial legislatures, nor may a provincial legislature delegate any of its powers to Parliament.[2] However, as a result of two later cases,[3] it is now constitutionally permissible for Parliament to delegate any powers it possesses to an inferior body created by a provincial enactment. In other words, Parliament may delegate a matter within its legisla-

---

[1] See *Hodge v. R.* (1883), 9 App. Cas. 117, 3 Cart B.N.A. 144 (P.C.).

[2] This classic position was set out in *Nova Scotia (A.G.) v. Canada (A.G.)*, [1951] S.C.R. 31, [1950] 4 D.L.R. 369.

[3] *Prince Edward Island (Potato Marketing Bd.) v. H.B. Willis Inc.*, [1952] 2 S.C.R. 392, [1952] 4 D.L.R. 146, and *Coughlin v. Ontario (Highway Transport Bd.)*, [1968] S.C.R. 569, 68 D.L.R. (2d) 384.

tive jurisdiction to a subordinate tribunal created under a valid provincial law, but it may not delegate to the provincial legislature itself. The reverse is also true in respect of constitutionally permissible interdelegation between a provincial legislature and a subordinate agency created by federal statute.

This constitutionally permissible interdelegation, however,[4] is itself subject to certain constraints.[5] Although Parliament, for example, may delegate any of its exclusive powers to a subordinate agency created by a provincial statute, it must limit the delegation in order to avoid an abdication of jurisdiction. That is to say, Parliament cannot delegate all of its authority under a given enumerated head of the Constitution Act of 1867. Thus, if Parliament wishes to delegate its constitutional authority to enact legislation in the area of interprovincial trade in a given commodity to an inferior tribunal created by a provincial statute, it may do so, providing it does not delegate all of its authority over interprovincial trade to that body.

A second constraint on delegation is the doctrine delegatus non potest delegare (a delegate may not re-delegate). This rule is a general rule of administrative law that applies to any delegation from a superior legislative body in a given jurisdiction to an inferior body within that same jurisdiction. Thus, if a provincial legislature delegates rule-making authority to an inferior body created by the legislature, that inferior body cannot redelegate to a further inferior body unless: (1) the enabling statute expressly allows for a re-delegation; or (2) re-delegation is implied by the necessary intendment of the enabling statute. Thus, for example, when an enabling statute provides for a delegation of authority to a particular minister of the Crown to perform some act such as the issuing of licences, obviously, if the minister were to personally undertake that task, it alone would occupy his time day in and day out. Accordingly, it must be a necessary intendment of the enabling statute that the minister delegate that authority to appropriate persons, either on his staff or in the appropriate division of his department.

The inferior bodies to which authority is delegated are referred to as boards, commissions, tribunals, agencies, etc., and among the most common recipients of delegated authority are municipal councils. These bodies may already be in existence at the time the delegation is made or they may be newly created to receive such powers. The powers that they receive may include the power to formulate policy and to make rules or the power

---

[4] Often this is referred to as "administrative delegation".

[5] There is a significant interrelationship between constitutional and administrative law. In the U.K. for example, constitutional law consists, in a large part, of what Canadians regard as administrative law. In Canada, the two areas are highly intertwined.

to make decisions or both. The delegated authority, if in the nature of rule-making, may generically be described as the power to make statutory instruments. These statutory instruments may take the form of by-laws,[6] regulations, orders-in-council, ordinances, etc., the particular terminology depending upon the nature of the given delegate. For example, the provincial legislature commonly delegates authority to a municipality to make rules. In that context, the subordinate agency (i.e. the municipal council) is delegated authority to make rules (i.e. enact by-laws).

CLASSIFICATION OF ADMINISTRATIVE TRIBUNALS

Traditionally it was important to distinguish administrative tribunals in terms of their function because judicial review of administrative action and the application by our courts of the prerogative remedies for denial of the rules of natural justice were limited to only one category of administrative tribunals: those which exercised a judicial or quasi-judicial function. With the development of the doctrine of fairness the need for classification has been somewhat reduced. Nevertheless a study of this area of the law still requires some understanding of the traditional classification.[7]

First, those administrative tribunals which are delegated a rule-making authority exercise a "legislative" function. Those kinds of tribunals set policy and generally have a wide discretion. Therefore, the courts will intervene only where such a tribunal has exceeded its statutory jurisdiction, failed to perform its statutory duties or abused its powers.

Second, an administrative tribunal may exercise an "administrative" function. An administrative function is one in which the delegate renders decisions on the basis of the general policy set out in its enabling statute. In rendering such decisions, it has considerable discretion to set specific policy. An example of this kind of tribunal is the National Parole Board. A court may intervene in these proceedings for the same reasons that it may intervene in the case of legislative tribunals. However, it may also intervene where a decision has been made in breach of the doctrine of fairness.

The third kind of administrative tribunal exercises a ministerial or executive function which entails no exercise of discretion. For example, a body

---

[6] The Canadian Institute for the Administration of Justice recently sponsored a conference focussing on these kinds of delegated authority. This conference, entitled, "Regulation and By-laws: Real Laws in the Real World", was held in Ottawa in November of 1995.

[7] The confusion of terminology in the categorization of the various types of functions exercised by administrative tribunals is discussed in detail by the Honourable Mr. Justice J. C. McRuer in the now classic McRuer Report, arising out of the Royal Commission of Inquiry into Civil Right in the Province of Ontario. See, in particular, Report 1, vol. 1, c. 1 , in which Mr. Justice McRuer distinguishes among the various types of functions exercised by administrative tribunals and comments upon the confusing terminology in attempts at classification.

that issues automobile licences has no authority not to issue a licence where an applicant pays the appropriate fee, signs the appropriate documents and in every way meets all the requirements. These tribunals set no policy whatsoever and their exercise of authority can be reviewed for the same reasons as that of a legislative tribunal.

The fourth type of administrative tribunal exercises a "judicial" or a "quasi-judicial" function. These tribunals also set no policy and therefore render decisions on the basis of a pre-set policy. An example of a judicial tribunal is a provincial court. A provincial court judge, on the basis of evidence adduced, finds an accused guilty or innocent of an offence. The setting of policy as to what constitutes an offence is done by Parliament and is reflected in the provisions of the Criminal Code under which the provincial court judge operates. Theoretically, this kind of tribunal has very little discretion — if the evidence supports a conviction, there must be a conviction — although, in fact, there is considerable discretion in the sentencing process. However, even this exercise of discretion is done in accordance with pre-set policy as contained in the Criminal Code. The decisions of tribunals of this nature are the only ones that may be subjected to judicial review, strictly defined and quashed for non-compliance with the rules of natural justice.

The four kinds of administrative tribunals may be placed on a spectrum or a continuum of their roles in setting policy and exercising discretion. At one end, with a large policy-setting role and possessing a large amount of discretion, are the legislative tribunals. At the other end, with no policy-setting role and no discretion, are the ministerial or executive tribunals. The administrative and quasi-judicial tribunals fall in between.

It is important to realize that a given tribunal may exercise different kinds of functions at different times. For example, a municipal council normally exercises a legislative function, but on occasion a municipal council may be requested to render a decision which could substantially affect the applicant's rights. For this limited purpose, the municipal council will be exercising a quasi-judicial function.

A determination as to whether a given tribunal is judicial or quasijudicial in nature often presents difficulties for a court. As a result, from time to time the courts have enunciated various tests in order to distinguish a tribunal exercising this type of function from other tribunals. It is probably sufficient, although simplistic, to define a judicial or quasijudicial tribunal as one which exercises a function by which the tribunal has "the power to adjudicate upon matters involving consequences to individuals".[8]

---

[8] A. Gelinas. "Judicial Control of Administrative Action: Great Britain and Canada", [1963] Public Law 140 at 160.

The First McRuer Report offers similar definitions as to what constitutes a judicial or quasi-judicial administrative tribunal. It states that:

> [a] power is primarily "judicial" when the decision is to be arrived at in accordance with governing rules of law; in their application policy enters in only to the limited extent already discussed in connection with the exercise of judicial power. This type of decision will be referred to as a "judicial decision".[9]

In a brief comment Mr. Justice McRuer states that the obligation to act judicially constitutes a requirement "to follow . . . minimum standards of fair procedure".[10]

In addition, Professor H.W.R. Wade provides a definition of a "judicial" or "quasi-judicial" tribunal as follows:

> Is this administrative power one which deprives some individual of his rights or liberties, so that he must be given the elementary justice of a hearing before his rights are destroyed by administrative action?[11]

GROUNDS FOR JUDICIAL REVIEW OF ADMINISTRATIVE DECISION-MAKING[12]

When a sovereign legislative body, either Parliament or a provincial legislature, grants a subordinate tribunal authority to make regulations or render decisions, obviously the rights of individuals are affected by a decision of that tribunal. In order that such rights may be protected,

---

[9] First Report, vol. 1, c. 1, p. 28.

[10] *Ibid.*, p. 29.

[11] The Twilight of Natural Justice?" (1951), 67 L.Q. Rev. 103 at 108.

[12] In the following scheme, Mr. Justice McRuer sets out all the various grounds in defining the jurisdiction of the courts in quashing decisions of administrative tribunals. This list is set out in the First McRuer Report, vol. 1, p. 247. In respect of the fourth item confined in the following list, namely, the issue of bias, see the case of *Greenhut v. Scott*, [1975] 4 W.W.R. 645, 56 D.L.R. (3d) 634 (B.C.).
The following are grounds on which the courts have held decisions or actions by tribunals exercising judicial or administrative power to be invalid:

    (1) Unconstitutionality of the statute purporting to confer the power;

    (2) Invalidity of the appointment of the members of the tribunal;

    (3) Absence of preliminary matters of fact, law or mixed law and fact;

    (4) Bias or the absence of impartiality of members of the tribunal;

    (5) Failure to comply with the mandatory procedural requirements;

    (6) Exceeding scope or area of matters that may be decided: absence of collateral matters of fact, law or mixed law and fact:

    (7) Use of the power for an improper purpose, or the taking into account of extraneous or wrong considerations;

    (8) Failure to comply with the method required by the statute to make a decision;

    (9) Failure to comply with statutory requirements to render the decision legally effective;

    (10) Fraud of a party, misleading the tribunal; and

    (11) Any error of law on the face of the record of the proceedings before the tribunal, whether within its power or not, and an application in the nature of certiorari.

body of rules has developed at common law. A breach of these rules may cause the decision to be quashed by the courts.

1. CONFORMITY TO ENABLING STATUTE

Just as a sovereign legislative body may enact laws only within its constitutional jurisdiction, an administrative tribunal may enact rules or make decisions only within the bounds of the authority granted to it by its governing statute. If a tribunal exceeds these bounds, an individual whose rights are adversely affected by this may ask that a court of law adjudge that the board is not acting competently in accordance with its enabling statute. To use an extreme example, a provincial agricultural marketing board cannot issue drivers' licences. Such an action will be declared ultra vires, that is, outside the legal jurisdiction of the board, and thus be rendered null and void.

2. JURISDICTIONAL FACT DOCTRINE

The jurisdictional fact doctrine was described by Mr. Justice Roach in *Ontario (Labour Relations Bd.) v. Bradley* as follows:

> When an inferior Court or tribunal or body, which has to exercise the power of deciding facts, is first established by Act of Parliament, the legislature has to consider what powers it will give that tribunal or body. It may in effect say that, if a certain state of facts exists and is shewn to such tribunal or body before it proceeds to do certain things, it shall have jurisdiction to do such things, but not otherwise. There it is not for them conclusively to decide whether that state of facts exists, and, if they exercise the jurisdiction without its existence, what they do may be questioned, and it will be held that they have acted without jurisdiction. [13]

An example of the application of this doctrine may be found in the case of *Bell v. Ontario (Human Rights Commission)*. [14] The anti-discrimination provisions contained in the Ontario Human Rights Code [15] specifically limit the scope of the Act to cover only those instances of racial discrimination which arise from a denial of accommodation in self-contained dwellings. Upon an application for a writ of prohibition, a judge of the Trial Division of the Supreme Court of Ontario held that a board of inquiry had no jurisdiction to hear the matter unless and until the preliminary or jurisdictional fact, namely, that the facility was a self-contained dwelling, was present. Since, in this particular case, the facility was not a self-contained dwelling, the judge held that this ended the matter, and the board of inquiry had no jurisdiction to hear the matter further. Although this decision was overruled in the Appellate Division of the Supreme Court of Ontario, it

---

[13] [1957] O.R. 316 at 326, 8 D.L.R. (2d) 65, 57 C.L.L.C. 15,318 (C.A.).

[14] [1971] S.C.R. 756, 18 D.L.R. (3d) 1.

[15] S.O. 1961-62, c. 93 [see now S.O. 1981, c. 53].

was subsequently affirmed in the Supreme Court of Canada. This was, incidentally, the first and one of the few times the Supreme Court of Canada has heard a matter arising out of a provincial anti-discrimination statute.[16]

3. ABUSE OF POWER

If an administrative tribunal enacts subordinate legislation or conducts its affairs and renders its decisions in bad faith (in male fides or in the absence of bona fides), its decision and the subordinate legislation will be declared ultra vires the authority of the tribunal and, therefore, of no effect. This notion of bad faith encompasses the allied notions of dishonesty, fraud and malice.[17] In addition, the court will nullify a decision and subordinate legislation that have been made for "improper purposes", that is, improper having regard to the policy objectives establishing the tribunal.[18] In determining whether the tribunal has done something for an improper purpose, the court will entertain considerations relating to the intention of Parliament or the provincial legislature in enacting the particular legislation under which the tribunal was established. In addition, a court will attack the decision of an administrative tribunal, as constituting an abuse of power, if the decision is based upon irrelevant considerations.[19] This, however, is of narrow and limited application.

Finally, other kinds of abuses of power or, as it is alternatively expressed, abuses of discretion, include discrimination,[20] inadequate evidence or no evidence,[21] failure to consider relevant materials, fettering

---

[16] For a detailed discussion of the jurisdictional fact doctrine, particularly as it relates to the above case, see P.W. Hogg, "The Jurisdictional Fact Doctrine in the Supreme Court of Canada: *Bell v. Ontario Human Rights Commission*", (1971), 9 Osgoode Hall L.J. 203. And for a more general discussion of the doctrine, see J.E. Magnet, "Jurisdictional Fact, Constitutional Fact and the Presumption of Constitutionality" (1980), 11 Man. L.J. 21.

[17] See, *e.g., Roncarelli v. Duplessis*, [1959] S.C.R. 122, 16 D.L.R. (2d) 689.

[18] See the case of *Madoc (Township) v. Quinlan*, [1971] 3 O.R. 540 at 541, 21 D.L.R. (3d) 136. In that case, a judge of the trial division of the Supreme Court of Ontario held that the township of Madoc, as a subordinate agency of the provincial government having authority to enact bylaws, could not prohibit a rock music festival on the defendant's farm, under the guise of exercising its regulatory and licensing authority, "even if the vast majority of the inhabitants of the municipality wish that the holding of such a festival be prohibited. It is trite law that a municipal council cannot prohibit under the guise of regulation." See also *Roberts v. Hopwood*, [1925] A.C. 578 (H.L.).

[19] See *R. v. Smith & Rhuland Ltd.*, [1953] 2 S.C.R. 95, 107 C.C.C. 43, [1953] 3 D.L.R. 690, 53 C.L.L.C. 15,057.

[20] See *Arcade Amusements Inc. v. Montreal (City), (sub nom. Montreal (Ville) v. Arcade Amusements Inc.)*, [1985] 1 S.C.R. 368, 29 M.P.L.R. 220, 18 D.L.R. (4th) 161, 58 N.R. 339; and *Calgary (City) v. S.S. Kresge Co.* (1965), 51 W.W.R. 747 (Alta. S.C.).

[21] *See Control Data Canada Ltée v. Blanchard*, [1984] 2 S.C.R. 476, 14 Admin. L.R. 133, 84 C.L.L.C. 14,070, 14 D.L.R. (4th) 289, 55 N.R. 194.

discretion by contract,[22] fettering discretion by general policy formulation,[23] unreasonableness,[24] and uncertainty.[25]

4. RULES OF NATURAL JUSTICE

As indicated above, the requirement that an administrative tribunal adhere to the rules of natural justice is, strictly speaking, applicable only to those administrative tribunals which exercise a judicial or quasi-judicial function. If such a tribunal is not conducting its affairs in accordance with these rules, a court of superior jurisdiction of a province, in the case of a provincially constituted administrative tribunal, and the Federal Court, in the case of a federally constituted administrative tribunal, may entertain the process of judicial review and grant the appropriate remedy in order to withdraw the jurisdiction of the tribunal to hear a particular matter, or, if the matter has already been determined, to quash the decision of that tribunal.

There are two fundamental rules of natural justice, under which are subsumed many sub-rules. The two basic rules, expressed in Latin terminology, are the audi alteram partem (near the other side) rule and the nemo judex in causa sua debet esse (no one ought to be a judge in his own cause) rule.

The audi alteram partem rule dictates that both parties to a dispute must be heard. It requires that there must be a fair hearing[26] and that each party must receive notice of the hearing. See, recently, *T.W.U. v. Canada (Canadian Radio-Television & Telecommunications Commission)*, [1995] 2 S.C.R. 781, 183 N.R. 161, 125 D.L.R. (4th) 471. Moreover, during the course of the hearing each party must be allowed to rebut the evidence adduced, and to cross-examine witnesses.[27] Arguably, the audi alteram partem rule also includes a right to counsel, but the courts,

---

[22] *See Vancouver (City) v. Vancouver (Registrar Land Registration District)*, 15 W.W.R. 351, [1955] 2 D.L.R. 709 (B.C. C.A.).

[23] See *Leung v. Ontario (Criminal Injuries Compensation Bd.)* (1995), 24 O.R. (3d) 530, (*sub nom. So v. Criminal Injuries Compensation Bd. (Ont.)*) 82 O.A.C. 43 (Div. Ct.); *Wimpey Western Ltd. v. Alberta (Department of Environment, Director of Standards & Approvals)* (1983), 28 Alta. L.R. (2d) 193, 3 Admin. L.R. 247, 2 D.L.R. (4th) 309, 49 A.R. 360 (C.A.); and *Capital Cities Communication Inc. v. Canada (C.R.T.C.)*, [1978] 2 S.C.R. 141, 36 C.P.R. (2d) 1, 81 D.L.R. (3d) 609, 18 N.R. 181.

[24] *Associated Provincial Picture Houses Ltd. v. Wednesday Corp.* [1948] 1 K.B. 223, [1947] 2 All E.R. 680 (C.A.).

[25] *Red Hot Video Ltd. v. Vancouver (City)* (1985), 18 C.C.C. (3d) 153, 29 M.P.L.R. 211 (B.C. C.A.), reversing (1983), 48 B.C.L.R. 381, 24 M.P.L.R. 60, 5 D.L.R. (4th) 61 (C.A.).

[26] See *Blais v. Basford*, [1972] F.C. 151 (C.A.).

[27] In the First McRuer Report, vol. 1, p. 137, the Honourable Mr. Justice McRuer defines the audi alteram partem rule in terms of the following constituent elements:

    1. Notice of the intention to make a decision should be given to the party whose rights may be affected.

generally, have not extended the boundaries of the rule to include this right.

The nemo judex in causa sua debet esse rule requires the exclusion of all forms of bias from tribunal proceedings. If actual bias is proven or if there is a reasonable apprehension of bias the invocation of this rule of natural justice renders a tribunal's decision null and void.[28]

Although the requirement that a given tribunal conduct its affairs in accordance with natural justice applies only to judicial or quasi-judicial tribunals, recent case law suggests that, even if a tribunal's function is not categorized as judicial or quasi-judicial, the courts will treat bias as an abuse of power and nullify the decision.

5. DOCTRINE OF FAIRNESS

In the United Kingdom during the 1960's, the judicial creation of the doctrine of fairness was a major development in administrative law. A similar development occurred in Canada some time later. The breakthrough was the now landmark decision of the Supreme Court of Canada in the case of *Nicholson v. Haldimand-Norfolk (Regional Municipality) Commissioners of Police*,[29] followed by the equally important decision of the Supreme Court of Canada in *Martineau v. Matsqui Institution (No. 2)*.[30] As a result of these cases a court of superior jurisdiction may now

---

2. The party whose rights may be affected should be sufficiently informed of the allegations against his interest to enable him to make an adequate reply.
3. A genuine hearing should be held at which the party affected is made aware of the allegations made against him and is permitted to answer.
4. The party affected should be allowed the right to cross-examine the party giving evidence against his interest.
5. A reasonable request for adjournment to permit the party affected to properly prepare and present his case should be granted.
6. The tribunal making the decision should be constituted as it was when the evidence and argument were heard.

[28] See *R. v. Ontario (Labour Relations Board)*, [1963] 2 O.R. 239, 39 D.L.R. (2d) 113, 63 C.L.L.C. 15,478 (H.C.); *Alberta (Securities Commission) v. Albrecht* (1962), 38 W.W.R. 430, 36 D.L.R. (2d) 199 (Alta.); *Law Society of Upper Canada v. French*, [1975] 2 S.C.R. 767, 49 D.L.R. (3d) 1, 3 N.R. 410; *French v. Law Society of Upper Canada (No. 2)* (1975), 8 O.R. (2d) 193, 57 D.L.R. (3d) 481 (C.A.); *Ringrose v. College of Physicians & Surgeons (Alta.)*, [1977] 1 S.C.R. 814, [1976] 4 W.W.R. 712, 67 D.L.R. (3d) 559, 1 A.R. 1, 9 N.R. 383; *McArthur v. Foothills (Municipal District)* (1977), 4 Alta L.R. (2d) 222, 78 D.L.R. (3d) 359, 4 A.R. 30 (C.A.); *MacBain v. Canada (Canadian Human Rights Commission)*, [1985] 1 F.C. 856, 16 Admin. L.R. 109, 85 C.L.L.C. 17,023, 18 C.R.R. 165, 22 D.L.R. (4th) 119, 6 C.H.R.R. D/3064 (C.A.).

[29] [1979] 1 S.C.R.311, 78 C.L.L.C. 14,181, 88 D.L.R. (3d) 671, 23 N.R. 410.

[30] [1980] 1 S.C.R. 602, 13 C.R. (3d) 1 (Eng.), 15 C.R. (3d) 315 (Fr.), 50 C.C.C. (2d) 353, 106 D.L.R. (3d) 385, 30 N.R. 119. See also the following Supreme Court of Canada cases which deal with the issue of fairness by administrative tribunals: *Evans v. Canada (Public Services Commission)*, [1983] 1 S.C.R. 582, 1 Admin. L.R. 16, 146 D.L.R. (3d) 1, 83 C.L.L.C.

review decisions of inferior tribunals on the ground that they were made in a manner that was procedurally unfair. In the same way that conformity with the full range of natural justice requirements varies according to the extent to which a tribunal is required to act judicially, the requirements of procedural fairness vary from tribunal to tribunal. The doctrine of fairness is a part of the rules of natural justice. Indeed, it might be regarded as the core or central requirement of natural justice. As Mr. Justice Dickson (as he then was) Said in *Martineau, supra:*

> It is wrong, in my view, to regard natural justice and fairness as distinct and separate standards and to seek to define the procedural content of each. In *Nicholson, supra*, the Chief Justice spoke of a "notion of fairness involving something less than the procedural protection of the traditional natural justice". Fairness involved compliance with only some of the principles of natural justice. Professor de Smith, *Judicial Review of Administrative Action* (1973), 3rd ed., p. 208, expressed lucidly the concept of a duty to act fairly:
>
>> In general it means a duty to observe the rudiments of natural justice for a limited purpose in the exercise of functions that are not analytically judicial but administrative.
>
> The content of the principles of natural justice and fairness in application to the individual cases will vary according to the circumstances of each case, as recognized by Tucker, L.J., in *Russell v. Duke of Norfolk et al.,* [1949] 1 All E.R. 109 at p. 118.[31]

The importance of the doctrine of fairness is underscored by the declaration of the Supreme Court of Canada that it applies not only to judicial or quasi-judicial tribunals, but also to tribunals exercising an administrative function. To give meaningful effect to this declaration, the Supreme Court of Canada also held (in *Martineau*) that a writ of certiorari will lie to quash a decision of a tribunal exercising a judicial or quasi-judicial function or exercising a purely administrative function, for reason that the decision was made in a procedurally unfair manner. This development represents the first time that an order in the nature of certiorari has issued to quash a decision of a tribunal that was neither judicial nor quasi-judicial. However, it is restricted such that a writ of certiorari will only lie against tribunals exercising an administrative function for a breach of the doctrine of fairness.

Certiorari is still unavailable to quash decisions of tribunals exercising ministerial or legislative functions. This, coupled with the fact that the rules of natural justice (as they are traditionally known) still apply only to judicial or quasi-judicial tribunals, leaves the question of categorization or classification of function as an important issue.

Mr. Justice Dickson, in the *Martineau* case, summarizes this major development in the law as follows:

14,038, 47 N.R. 255, and *Beson v. Director of Child Welfare for Newfoundland*, [1982] 2 S.C.R. 716, 30 R.F.L. (2d) 438 (*sub nom. B.(D.) v. Newfoundland (Director of Child Welfare)*), 142 D.L.R. (3d) 20, 39 Nfld. & P.E.I.R. 246, 111 A.P.R. 246, 44 N.R. 602.
[31] 106 D.L.R. (3d) 385 at 411-412.

The authorities, in my view, support the following conclusions:

1. *Certiorari* is available as a general remedy for supervision of the machinery of Government decision-making. The order may go to any public body with power to decide any matter affecting the rights, interests, property, privileges, or liberty of any person. The basis for the broad reach of this remedy is the general duty of fairness resting on all public decision-makers.

2. A purely ministerial decision, on broad grounds of public policy, will typically afford the individual no procedural protection, and any attack upon such a decision will have to be founded upon abuse of discretion. Similarly, public bodies exercising legislative functions may not be amenable to judicial supervision. On the other hand, a function that approaches the judicial end of the spectrum will entail substantial procedural safeguards. Between the judicial decision and those which are discretionary and policy-oriented will be found myriad decision-making processes with a flexible gradation of procedural fairness through the administrative spectrum. That is what emerges from the decisions of this Court in *Nicholson, supra*. In these cases, an applicant may obtain *certiorari* to enforce a breach of the duty of procedural fairness.

3. . . . The fact that a decision-maker does not have a duty to act judicially, with observance of formal procedure which that characterization entails, does not mean that there may not be a duty to act fairly which involves importing something less than the full panoply of conventional natural justice rules. In general, Courts ought not to seek to distinguish between the two concepts, for the drawing of a distinction between a duty to act fairly, and a duty to act in accordance with the rules of natural justice, yields an unwieldy conceptual framework. The *Federal Court Act*, however, compels classification for review of federal decision-makers. . . .

8. In the final analysis, the simple question to be answered is this: Did the tribunal on the facts of the particular case act fairly toward the person claiming to be aggrieved? It seems to me that this is the underlying question which, the Court have sought to answer in all the cases dealing with natural justice and with fairness.[32]

For a good discussion of some of the earlier cases involving the application of the doctrine of fairness see D.P. Jones, "Administrative Fairness in Alberta" (1980), 18 Alta. L. Rev. 351. This article is expanded upon in a major paper delivered by the same author which appears in C.I.A.J., Judicial Review of Administrative Rulings (Montreal: La Révue du Barreau du Québec, 1983).

The reader should also bear in mind the important remarks of former Chief Justice Dickson quoted earlier concerning the relationship between the concepts of fairness and natural justice. It is clear that, in the intervening years, the notions of fairness and natural justice have significantly blended to the extent that the categorization of tribunals no longer requires a distinction to be made between judicial/quasi-judicial and administrative tribunals. This is also true of federal administrative tribunals following the 1990 amendment of the Federal Court Act. It still remains important, however, that a distinction be made at the provincial level between judicial/quasi-judicial and administrative tribunals, on one hand, and other tribunals exercising ministerial or legislative functions on the other, as only the former are subject to the blended concepts of fairness and natural justice.

---

[32] 106 D.L.R. (3d) 385 at 410-12.

The doctrine of fairness, or indeed the doctrine of fairness and the rules of natural justice, cannot be considered in isolation from the constitutional requirements of s. 7 (and other sections) of the Canadian Charter of Rights and Freedoms. Section 7 guarantees that "everyone has the right to life, liberty and security of the person and the right not to be deprived thereof except in accordance with the principles of fundamental justice". Predictably, the court, in interpreting the phrase "principles of fundamental justice", have looked to court decisions which have given meaning to the concepts of "fairness" and "natural justice" in administrative law. Likewise, in further defining these latter concepts, the courts have looked at decisions interpreting "fundamental justice" in s. 7 of the Charter.[33]

ERROR OF LAW ON THE FACE OF THE RECORD

Often an enabling statute requires a tribunal to keep a record of its proceedings and it is not uncommon for this to be done voluntarily even in the absence of such a statutory requirement. The major part of a record is the tribunal's reasons for its decisions. Tribunals, like courts, at common law, are not required to give reasons. There are some exceptions.[34] If there is an error of law on the face of this record, a court of superior jurisdiction has the inherent authority to grant the remedy of certiorari to quash the decision of a tribunal. Where tribunals do not maintain a record (or, more likely, the record contains no reasons), there can, of course, be no error of law on the face of the record, with the result that a court will not grant a writ of certiorari.

PROCEDURE FOR CHALLENGING DECISIONS OF ADMINISTRATIVE TRIBUNALS

1. WHEN THEY ARE ULTRA VIRES ENABLING LEGISLATION

The usual way in which a matter of this nature is litigated is by way of an action for declaration. The procedure will differ, of course, from province to province, depending upon the various rules of practice or rules

---

[33] See *Singh v. Canada (Minister of Employment & Immigration)*, [1985] 1 S.C.R. 177, 12 Admin. L.R. 137, 14 C.R.R. 13, 17 D.L.R. (4th) 422, 58 N.R. 1; and *Reference re s. 94(2) of the Motor Vehicles Act (B.C.)*, [1985] 2 S.C.R. 486, [1986] 1 W.W.R. 481 (*sub nom. Reference re Constitutional Question Act (B.C.)*), 69 B.C.L.R. 145, 36 M.V.R. 240, 48 C.R. (3d) 289, 23 C.C.C. (3d) 289, 24 D.L.R. (4th) 536, 18 C.R.R. 30, 63 N.R. 266.

[34] See, for example, the Alberta Administrative Procedures Act, R.S.A. 1980, c. A-2, wherein certain specified tribunals are required to give reasons for their decisions. Where a tribunal is required to provide reasons (and indeed, when reasons are provided whether required or not), they must be substantive and not just a recitation of the facts followed by a decision. They must sufficiently enable a court to determine the propriety of the tribunal's decision. See *Northwestern Utilities Ltd. v. Edmonton (City)*, [1979] 1 S.C.R. 684, 7 Alta. L.R. (2d) 370, 89 D.L.R. (3d) 161, 12 A.R. 449, 23 N.R. 565.

of court of the individual provinces. However, generally speaking, an action for declaration is commenced either by way of a statement of claim or by way of a notice of motion. A challenge of this nature is available to quash the decisions of all administrative tribunals, irrespective of the categorization of the particular function exercised by a given tribunal.

2. WHEN THEY CONSTITUTE AN ABUSE OF POWERS

Matters of this nature are brought before the courts in a variety of proceedings, depending upon the circumstances. An action for a declaration is available. Also an application for an injunction (again depending upon the particular rules of court of particular provinces) may be brought either by way of statement of claim or notice of motion, although before a court will entertain such an application the applicant must have the requisite locus standi. Because of this, in some circumstances, the appropriate action is a relator action brought by the Attorney General of the province at the instance of another person.

In addition, an action for damages, including both general and punitive damages, appears to be available where a tribunal exercises a public duty in bad faith, acting maliciously, and for an improper purpose. According to the Manitoba Court of Appeal,[35] it does not appear to be absolutely imperative that the action be made on the basis of a recognizable and actionable tort at common law.

Challenges on the basis of an abuse of power are available to quash the decisions of all administrative tribunals, irrespective of the categorization of their particular functions.

3. WHEN A JUDICIAL OR QUASI-JUDICIAL TRIBUNAL HAS BREACHED A RULE OF NATURAL JUSTICE

The process of judicial review, strictly defined, is available only with regard to those tribunals exercising a judicial or quasi-judicial function. For federally constituted tribunals, an application for judicial review is made to the Federal Court.[36] For provincially constituted tribunals, an application for judicial review is made to the courts of superior jurisdiction in the province. In particular, these applications are made to the trial division of the supreme court of a province or, in those provinces where the court possessing trial jurisdiction is constituted as a separate court, to that separate court.

---

[35] *Gershman v. Manitoba (Vegetable Producers' Marketing Bd.)*, [1976] 4 W.W.R. 406, 69 D.L.R. (3d) 114 (C.A.).

[36] In this connection, reference may be made to the particular provisions of the Federal Court Act, set out later in this chapter.

In making such an application, the applicant is asking the court to exercise its inherent jurisdiction to grant a prerogative remedy. There are various types of prerogative remedies, and the applicant will request the one which is appropriate in the particular circumstances.

The prerogative (or extraordinary) remedies are in the form of writs, known as prerogative writs, each having its own unique effect. For example, the granting of a writ of certiorari or, in some provinces, an order in the nature of certiorari, quashes the decision of an administrative tribunal, while the granting of a writ of prohibition prohibits an administrative tribunal from hearing the particular matter which is the subject of the application for judicial review.

A writ of mandamus compels a public official to perform an act which he has a statutory duty to perform, and it is not limited to persons or tribunals exercising a judicial or quasi-judicial function. A writ of quo warranto prevent the continued exercise of unlawful authority or power on the part of a public official, although this remedy is, in fact, of rare and limited application. Finally, there is the prerogative remedy of habeas corpus. If an application for a writ of habeas corpus is granted, it invalidates the unlawful incarceration of the subject. This, of course, is primarily applicable in the area of criminal law.

Generally speaking, and again this may vary from province to province, an application for a prerogative writ is commenced by way of notice of motion and, in some instances, by way of statement of claim.

Decisions of tribunals exercising a judicial or quasi-judicial function may also be challenged by way of an application for an injunction or by way of an action for declaration.

4. WHEN A JUDICIAL OR QUASI-JUDICIAL TRIBUNAL OR AN ADMINISTRATIVE TRIBUNAL HAS BREACHED THE DOCTRINE OF FAIRNESS

As indicated above, certiorari is now available to quash a decision of a judicial or quasi-judicial tribunal and of a purely administrative tribunal on the ground that the tribunal, in making its decision, did so in breach of the requirement of procedural fairness.

As indicated earlier, the notions of natural justice and fairness have, increasingly, become blended concepts in recent years. It seems well-established now that a categorization of function with respect to making a differentiation between judicial and quasi-judicial tribunals, on one hand, and administrative tribunals, on the other, is an exercize of the past. With the 1990 amendment to the Federal Court Act, categorization of function with respect to similar federal tribunals has lost its importance. However, it still remains an important issue to distinguish judicial, quasi-judicial and administrative tribunals from those exercising other kinds of functions.[37]

PRIVATIVE CLAUSES

One of the reasons underlying the increase in the number of administrative tribunals in recent years is the desirability of placing the authority to render decisions and to make subordinate legislation in the hands of those persons possessing a degree of expertise in the particular matter being regulated. In addition, neither Parliament nor a provincial legislature has the time to deal with all of the various regulatory and/or decision-making matters which presently fall into the hands of administrative tribunals.

In order to permit these tribunals to conduct their affairs in an expeditious and efficient manner, the conventional wisdom is that their decisions ought to be final and binding and not subject to interference by the courts. To promote this end, two legislative developments have occurred. First, there is a noticeable lack of provisions for appeal from the decisions rendered by administrative tribunals in many of the enabling statutes. Secondly, the enabling statutes often contain what are referred to as "privative clauses" which have the effect, at least in theory, of excluding from the jurisdiction of our courts the judicial review of decisions rendered by administrative tribunals. There are, however, various formulae of privative clauses, with each type of clause differing in the extent to which it excludes the jurisdiction of the court. Some only exclude the jurisdiction of the court to undertake judicial review, strictly defined, and are therefore directed at preventing the granting of certain prerogative remedies. Others are wider and attempt to exclude the jurisdiction of the courts in reviewing the decisions of administrative tribunals, in any respect and for any reason. Set out below is s. 110 of the Labour Relations Act, R.S.O. 1990, c. L.2, which is a typical privative clause:

> 110. No decision, order, direction, declaration or ruling of the Board shall be questioned or reviewed in any court, and no order shall be made or process entered, or proceedings taken in any court, whether by way of injunction, declaratory judgment, certiorari, mandamus, prohibition, quo warranto, or otherwise, to question, review, prohibit or restrain the Board or any of its proceedings.

Generally speaking, the courts have resented these attempts by Parliament and the provincial legislatures to exclude judicial review from their

---

[37] With respect to these developments, see The Honourable C.A. Fraser, "Searching For Fairness", a paper delivered at the 20/20 Anniversary Celebration, Faculty of Law, University of Alberta, September 1992. See also Jones, D.P., and A.S. de Villars. *Principles of Administrative Law.* (2nd ed.) Toronto: Carswell, 1994.

jurisdiction. Thus, through a process of statutory interpretation, the courts have largely ignored the privative clauses or have given little effect to them. In response, Parliament and the provincial legislatures have attempted to strengthen the effect of privative clauses by the use of wording which is directed at achieving an iron-clad exclusion of the court's jurisdiction in these matters. One example of a privative clause which has been successful in this regard is s. 5 of An Act to Amend the Succession Duty Act, S.B.C. 1970, c. 45, considered in *Minister of Finance v. Woodward*:

> ... and the determination of the Minister is final, conclusive, and binding on all persons and, notwithstanding section 43 or 44 or any other provision of this Act to the contrary, is not open to appeal, question, or review in any Court and any determination of the Minister made under this subsection is hereby ratified and confirmed and is binding on all persons.[38]

The desire on the part of Parliament and the provincial legislatures to exclude the jurisdiction of the courts continues to exist and, at the very least, it is predictable that the courts will continue to[39] do their best to avoid the application of this exclusion, wherever possible.[40]

CURIAL DEFERENCE VERSUS SUBSTITUTE DECISION-MAKING

Legislative bodies view their role in government as creating efficient ways and means (here, through the establishment of various agencies) of regulating societal affairs. Courts, on the other hand, view their role as supervising the work of the agencies created by our legislative bodies to ensure that there is no abuse of discretion nor procedural unfairness, for example.

When courts take the view that they must exercise restraint in this process and allow administrative agencies to enjoy greater independence with

---

[38] [1973] S.C.R. 120, [1972] 5 W.W.R. 581, 27 D.L.R. (3d) 608 at 612, [1972] C.T.C. 385.

[39] See *Crevier v. Quebec (A.G.)*, [1981] 2 S.C.R. 220, 127 D.L.R. (3d) 1, 38 N.R. 541, and *Quebec (A.G.) v. Farrah*, [1978] 2 S.C.R. 638, 86 D.L.R. (3d) 161, 21 N.R. 595. Also, for a discussion of private clauses, in the context of the "patently unreasonable" doctrine, see *C.U.P.E., Local 963 v. New Brunswick Liquor Corp.*, [1979] 2 S.C.R. 227, 79 C.L.L.C. 14,029, 25 N.B.R. (2d) 237, 51 A.P.R. 237, 26 N.R. 341; *A.U.P.E., Local 63 v. Alberta (Public Service Employees' Relations Board)*, [1982] 1 S.C.R. 923, [1983] 1 W.W.R. 593, 21 Alta. L.R. (2d) 104, 82 C.L.L.C. 14,203, 136 D.L.R. (3d) 1, 37 A.R. 281, 42 N.R. 559 (*sub nom. A.U.P.E., Local 63 v. Alta. Pub. Service Employees Rel. Bd.*); *Blanchard v. Control Data Canada Ltée*, [1984] 2 S.C.R 476, 14 Admin. L.R. 133, 84 C.L.L.C. 14,070, 14 D.L.R. (4th) 289, 55 N.R. 194; *Syndicat des employés de production du Québec et de l'Acadie v. Canada Labor Relations Board*, [1984] 2 S.C.R. 412, 14 Admin. L.R. 72, 84 C.L.L.C. 14,069, 14 D.L.R. (4th) 457, 55 N.R. 321 (*sub nom. C.B.C. v. Syndicat des Employés de Production du Qué. et de l'Acadie*). Arguably, these cases have strengthened the effect of private clauses.

[40] For a detailed discussion of various private clauses and the treatment they have been given by Canadian courts, see R. Carter, "The Private Clause in Canadian Administrative Law 1945-1985: A Doctrinal Examination" (1986), 64 Can. Bar Rev. 241.

out excessive interference by the courts, this is referred to as 'curial deference'. Some judges fall into the curial deference 'camp' while others maintain the view that courts ought to be aggressive in supervising the
decision-making of administrative agencies and, if necessary, intervene
and correct what they regard as defective decision-making. This latter
'camp' encompasses those that favour what is referred to as 'substitute
decision-making' by the courts. Probably, most judges fall in the middle,
and make their decisions on the basis of the facts of a particular case,
without an ideological underpinning in one direction or the other. But
there are definitely two distinct views of a court's role in dealing with
decision-making by administrative agencies. No where has this become
more pronounced than in recent cases concerned with the review of errors
of law on the face of the record.

There are, at a generic level, two kinds of defects preventing a tribunal
from performing the tasks assigned to it by an enabling statute. The first
kind is the so-called jurisdictional defect. This has the effect of preventing a tribunal from acquiring the authority to do its assigned task (for
example, an enabling statute requires a preliminary fact to exist before
a tribunal may perform its responsibility and that fact does not exist) or,
alternatively, this kind of defect has the effect of compelling a tribunal
to lose its authority to do its assigned task (for example, the tribunal has
acted procedurally in an unfair manner). The second kind of defect, again
at the generic level, is the so-called intrajurisdictional defect. In this case,
a tribunal has successfully acquired the authority to do its assigned task
and has not done anything defective to lose that authority.

Error of law on the face of the record is the only intrajurisdictional
defect.[41] This defect, like all others, is reviewable by a court and can be
remedied by what is referred to as the anomalous use of certiorari. But
that review is not normally permitted if there is a privative clause in the
enabling statute preventing review. However, even with a privative clause,
the courts have said they still can review an error of law if that error is
'patently unreasonable'. The courts have defined, in a general way, what
constitutes patent unreasonability.

The theory is that a patently unreasonable error of law, despite the presence of a privative clause, loses its characterization as an 'intrajurisdictional' error and is then regarded as a 'jurisdictional' error. Since the
Crevier[42] case, all jurisdictional errors may be reviewed by the courts, notwithstanding the presence of a privative clause. In this sense, the use of
the notion of patent reasonability is said to be in the nature of a sword,

---

[41] See earlier discussion of error of law on the face of the record.
[42] *Crevier v. Quebec (A.G.)*, [1981] 2 S.C.R. 220, 127 D.L.R. (3d) 1, 38 N.R. 541.

allowing courts to review errors if law, despite the presence of a privative clause. In short, it reflects a substitute decision-making point of view. To conclude that an error of law exists and to further conclude that the error is patently unreasonable is somewhat of a subjective process. Thus, it may be that some judges are taking this approach in order to substitute their own views, on the merits of particular cases, over the views of the administrative agencies mandated, at first instance, to make those decision. Theoretically, an administrative agency, in deciding a case, provided it does not commit either a jurisdictional or an intrajurisdictional error, is entitled to be wrong in its decision. Perhaps, substitute decision-making is no more than a corrective device to deal with judicially-perceived wrong decisions of administrative agencies in the overall interests of justice. On the other hand, some administrative decision-makers view this process as simply unwarranted interference.

Recently, there has emerged a new view of patent unreasonability. In the absence of a privative clause, where errors of law are normally reviewable, some judges will not review those errors unless they are patently unreasonable. Here, the notion of patent reasonability is serving as a shield preventing review of otherwise reviewable errors of law. This use of patent unreasonability is consistent with the ideology of non-interference or curial deference.

This issue is further complicated because the courts are now considering the expertise or degree of specialization of particular tribunals in measuring the extent to which the courts should intervene. The underlying rationale is that the courts ought to be more deferential and less interfering with respect to decision-making by a body consisting of specialized experts.

The use of patent unreasonability and the issue of curial deference is a complex, sometimes contradictory and rapidly changing part of administrative law. In essence, it underscores a larger issue of institutional territoriality where the courts and the legislatures (through their delegated authorities) endeavour to establish their respective niches in the landscape of the Canadian legal system.[43]

---

[43] See footnote 38, *supra*. See also the following recent cases on the issues discussed above: *Control Data Can. Ltée v. Blanchard*, [1984] 2 S.C.R. 476, 14 Admin. L.R. 133, 84 C.L.L.C. 14,070, 14 D.L.R. (4th) 289, 55 N.R. 194; *C.A.I.M.A.W., Local 14 v. (Cdn. Kenworth Co.*, [1989] 2 S.C.R. 983, 40 Admin. L.R. (2d) 1, 40 B.C.L.R. (2d) 1, (*sub nom. C.A.I.M.A.W. v. Paccar of Canada Ltd.*), [1989] 6 W.W.R. 673, (*sub nom. Paccar of Can. Ltd v. C.A.I.M.A.W., Local 14*) 89 C.L.L.C. 14,050, 62 D.L.R. (4th) 437, 102 N.R.1; *Canada (Attorney General) v. Mossop*, [1993] 1 S.C.R. 554, 13 Admin. L.R. (2d) 1, 46 C.C.E.L. 1, 93 C.L.L.C. 17,006, 17 C.H.R.R. D/349, 100 D.L.R. (4th) 658, 149 N.R. 1; *Canada (Attorney General) v. P.S.A.C.*, [1991] 1 S.C.R. 614, 48 Admin. L.R. 161, 91 C.L.L.C. 14,017, 80 D.L.R. (4th) 520, (*sub nom. Canada (Procureur général) v. A.F.P.C.*)

JUDICIAL REVIEW AND STATUTORY APPEAL

It is important to distinguish the appeal process from the judicial review process. The common law rule is that a right of appeal is statutory in nature; no right of appeal exists unless it is specifically provided for in a particular statute. In contrast (with the exception of some recent provincial enactments, especially those in the province of Ontario, as well as provisions contained in the Federal Court Act), the process of judicial review is conducted in accordance with an inherent jurisdiction vested in courts of superior jurisdiction to grant prerogative remedies. It should be noted that the existence of an appeal provision in an enabling statute may affect a court's exercise of its discretion in granting or not granting a prerogative remedy, depending upon whether the court feels the appeal provision is an adequate remedy.[44]

STATUTORY ENACTMENTS IN ADMINISTRATIVE LAW

Recently, statutes have been enacted to codify the process of judicial review. For federally constituted administrative tribunals, the enactment of the Federal Court Act represents a major and significant development in the law. For provincially constituted administrative tribunals, the enactment of a scheme of three Ontario statutes represents an important model of legislative reform in the area of administrative law. Following is a brief review of these enactments.

1. FEDERAL COURT ACT

Under the Federal Court Act,[45] enacted pursuant to Parliament's legislative authority under s. 101 of the Constitution Act of 1867, Parliament established a new court, called the Federal Court of Canada, replacing the former Exchequer Court of Canada. It was constituted in two divisions, a Trial Division and an Appeal Division (the latter may also be referred to as the Court of Appeal or the Federal Court of Appeal). The

---

123 N.R. 161; *C.U.P.E., Local 963 v. New Brunswick Liquor Corp.,* [1979] 2 S.C.R. 227, 25 N.B.R. (2d) 237, 51 A.P.R. 237, 79 C.L.L.C. 14,209, 97 D.L.R. (3d) 417, 26 N.R. 341; *National Corn Growers Assn. v. Canada (Canadian Import Tribuanl),* [1990] 2 S.C.R. 1324, 45 Admin. L.R. 161, 74 D.L.R. (4th) 449, 114 N.R. 81, *(sub nom. American Farm Bureau Federation v. Canadian Import Tribunal)* 3 T.C.T. 5303; *Syndicat national des employés de la comm. scolaire régionale de l'Outaouais v. Union des employés de service, Local 298 (sub nom. Union des employés de service, local 298 v. Bibeault)* [1988] 2 S.C.R. 1048, 35 Admin. L.R. 153, 89 C.L.L.C. 14,045, 95 N.R. 161, 24 Q.A.C. 244; *C.J.A., Local 579 v. Bradco Construction Ltd.,* [1993] 2 S.C.R. 316, 12 Admin. L.R. (2d) 165, 334 A.P.R. 140, 93 C.L.L.C. 14,033 102 D.L.R. (4th) 402, 106 Nfld. & P.E.I.R. 140, 153 N.R. 81.
[44] *Fooks v. Association of Architects (Alberta),* 21 Alta. L.R. (2d) 306, [1982] 6 W.W.R. 40, 38 A.R. 132, 139 D.L.R. (3d) 445 (Q.B.).
[45] R.S.C. 1970, c.10 (2nd Supp.) [now R.S.C. 1985, c.F-7].

Federal Court was granted exclusive original jurisdiction over certain matters and concurrent jurisdiction over other matters. One of its most important functions is a general supervisory role over the affairs of federal administrative tribunals.[46] In particular, under the provisions contained in s. 18 of the Act, the Trial Division has exclusive, original jurisdiction, over those tribunals falling within the scope of s. 2, to issue:

(a) an injunction,
(b) a writ of *certiorari*,
(c) a writ of prohibition,
(d) a writ of *mandamus*,
(e) a writ of *quo warranto*

or to grant declaratory relief . . . This jurisdiction extends, in addition to other proceedings designed to obtain equivalent relief such as actions against the Attorney General for a declaration.[47]

Notwithstanding these provisions, much of the jurisdiction assigned to the Trial Division was taken away and given to the Appeal Division by virtue of the provisions contained in the former s. 28 of the Act:

28.(1) Notwithstanding section 18 or the provisions of any other Act the Court of Appeal has jurisdiction to hear and determine an application to review and set aside a decision or order, other than a decision or order of an administrative nature not required by law to be made on a judicial or quasi-judicial basis, made by or in the course of proceedings before a federal board, commission or other tribunal, on the ground that the board, commission or tribunal

(a) failed to observe a principle of natural justice or otherwise acted beyond or refused to exercise its jurisdiction;

(b) erred in law in making in decision or order, whether or not the error appears on the face of the record; or

(c) based is decision or order on an erroneous finding of fact that it made in a perverse or capricious manner or without regard for the material before it.

Section 28(3) makes it clear that in the event that a given matter falls within s. 28, the Trial Division is deprived of jurisdiction over that matter.

---

[46] In the original s.2 of the Act, "federal board, commission or other tribunal" means "any body or person having, exercising or purporting to exercise jurisdiction or powers conferred by or under an Act of Parliament other than a superior, district or county court of a province or other body set up by provincial legislation": see W.R. Jackett, *The Federal Court of Canada: A Manual of Practice* (1971), p. 18.

[47] *Ibid.* It should be noted that the Federal Court Act does not give authority to the Federal Court to issue a writ of *habeas corpus*. Prior to the establishment of the Federal Court in 1971, all prerogative remedies were issued by provincial superior courts pursuant to their inherent jurisdiction to do so. When the Federal Court was created, this task was transfered, by statute, to judges of the Federal Court with respect to the review of the federal boards and tribunals. However, *habeas corpus* was left as a responsibility of provincial superior courts. The reason is that the Federal Court is essentially an itinerant court with judges travelling from city to city. Since *habeas corpus* is a remedy potentially available to those in the custody of others, it was thought that it would be more appropriate in terms of the availability of judges and timeliness, if the responsibility to issue the writ lay in the hands of resident local judges.

In this connection, one commentator made these observations:

By virtue of section 28 of the Act, the Court of Appeal has exclusive original jurisdiction in respect of all decisions of a "judicial or quasi-judicial" nature. What was previously a factor in certiorari, prohibition, and natural justice cases only, now becomes crucial in virtually every application for review, for on the issue of whether a function is of a judicial or administrative nature depends the questions of whether the matter is within the jurisdiction of the Court of Appeal of the Trial Division. Finally, the jurisdiction concept remains a place in the law, for, in section 28(1)(a), the Act allows review where an administrative authority has "acted beyond or refused to exercise its jurisdiction".[48]

In addition, consider the provisions contained in s. 29 of the Act:

29. Notwithstanding sections 18 and 28, where provision is expressly made by an Act of Parliament of Canada for an appeal as such to the Court, to the Supreme Court, to the Governor in Council or to the Treasury Board from a decision or order of a federal board, commission or other tribunal made by or in the course of proceedings before that board, commission or tribunal, that decision or order is not, to the extent that it may be so appealed, subject to review or to be restrained, prohibited, removed or otherwise dealt with, except to the extent and in the manner provided for in that Act.

Many commentators have described the effect of the above provisions as being confusing and unnecessarily complex.

Some reform proposals to address the above concerns were announced in 1983. However, nothing became of them. Finally, in September 1989, the federal Government introduced Bill C-38, a major amendment to the Federal Court Act under which many changes are made. The major change, however, relates to the s. 18 and s. 28 problems discussed above. Under the new legislation, the Trial Division of the Federal Court will have a general original jurisdiction to conduct judicial review of most federal tribunals, with the exception of several federal tribunals which are subject to the original supervisory jurisdiction of the Federal Court of Appeal. These boards are "courts of record" and any reviews of their decisions are to be conducted by the Appeal Division. Specifically, these tribunals are:

— the Tax Court of Canada
— the Canadian Radio-television and Telecommunications Commission;
— the Pension Appeals Board;
— the National Energy Board;
— the Competition Tribunal;

---

[48] D.J. Mullan, "The Federal Court Act: The Misguided Attempt at Administrative Law Reform" (1973), 23 U.T. L.J. 14. See also other articles contained in the selected bibliography at the end of this chapter.

— the Canada Labour Relations Board;
— the Immigration Appeal Division and the Convention Refugee Determination Division of the Immigration and Refugee Board;
— the Copyright Board;
— the National Transportation Agency
— the Public Service Staff Relations Board;
— the Board of Arbitration and [the] Review Tribunal established by the Canada Agricultural Products Act;
— the Canadian International Trade Tribunal; and
— umpires under the Unemployment Insurance Act[49]

Notwithstanding the exception, it should be emphasized that granting original supervisory jurisdiction over the vast majority of federal tribunals is a major (and positive) change. In addition, the application for relief is in the form of a general application for judicial review. The Act also sets out the nature of the relief or remedy that may be given. More particularly, the court may order a federal tribunal to:

— do any act or thing it has unlawfully failed or refused to do or has unreasonably delayed in doing; or
— declare invalid or unlawful, or
— quash, set aside, refer back, prohibit or restrain,

a decision, order. act or proceeding of a federal tribunal.[50]

Also, the Act specifically sets out the various grounds for which a remedy is available. These grounds are as follows.

The court may grant a remedy if the tribunal:

— acted without jurisdiction, acted beyond is jurisdiction, or refused to exercise its jurisdiction;
— failed to observe a principle of natural justice, procedural fairness or other procedure that it was required by law to observe;
— erred in law in making a decision or order, whether or not the error appears on the face of the record;
— based its decision or order on an erroneous finding of fact that it mad in a perverse or capricious manner, or without regard for the material before it;
— acted or failed to act, by reason of fraud or perjured evidence; or
— acted in any other way that was contrary to law.[51]

---

[49] S.C. 1990, c. 8. See also The Lawyers Weekly, 27th October 1989, at p. 22. This edition, generally contains an excellent discussion of the legislation.

[50] Federal Court Act, R.S.C. 1985, c. F-7, s. 18.1(3) [as amended by S.C. 1990, c. 8, s. 5].

[51] Federal Court Act, R.S.C. 1985, c. F-7, s. 18.1(4) [as amended by S.C. 1990, c. 8, s. 5].

Section 31 of the Act permits an appeal to the Supreme Court of Canada from the decisions of the Federal Court; however, leave to appeal must first be obtained from either the Federal Court of Appeal or from the Supreme Court of Canada itself.

2. PROVINCIAL ENACTMENTS

Administrative law reform at the provincial level has not occurred in a substantial way across Canada. One exception is the striking model of reform in the province of Ontario, following a somewhat interesting legislative history. In 1964, the Ontario government introduced legislation which granted wide-ranging investigatory powers to the then recently established Ontario Police Commission. That bill, referred to as the "Police Bill" or "Bill 99", caused a storm of publicity in the legislature, in the press, and in the public at large. As a result of that controversy, the legislation was dropped, the minister responsible for the legislation resigned, and the government appointed the former Chief Justice of the Trial Division of the Supreme Court of Ontario, the Honourable J.C. McRuer, to conduct a Royal Commission of Inquiry into Civil Rights in the Province of Ontario. As a result of this royal commission, the now classic McRuer Report was published, in which certain recommendations were made in connection with the reform of administrative law. Subsequently, these recommendations were adopted in the form of new Ontario legislation in the early 1970's. In particular, the Ontario legislature enacted the Statutory Powers Procedure Act, S.O. 1971, c. 47,[52] the Judicial Review Procedure Act, S.O. 1971, c. 48,[53] the Judicature Amendment Act, S.O. 1970, c. 97, and the Judicature Amendment Act, S.O. 1971, c. 57.[54]

The Statutory Powers Procedure Act sets out various procedures to which administrative tribunals must adhere in the course of conducting their affairs. Essentially, the Act is a codification of the rules of natural justice and dictates that administrative tribunals must conform to these requirements. It also requires that an administrative tribunal maintain a record of its proceedings. This remedies the defect at common law where an application for certiorari on the basis of an error of law on the face of the record must necessarily fail in the absence of a record.

---

[52] Now the Statutory Powers Procedure Act, R.S.O. 1990, c. S.22.

[53] Now the Judicial Review Procedure Act, R.S.O. 1990, c. J.1.

[54] Now the Courts of Justice Act, R.S.O. 1990, c. C.43. For a comprehensive review of the above legislative history, see W. Tarnopolsky, *The Canadian Bill of Rights* (Toronto: McClelland and Stewart, 1975). Although the reform of administrative law has been conducted in a substantial way only in the province of Ontario other provinces have enacted some statutory provisions in connection with administrative law. See, for example, the Judicial Review Procedure Act, R.S.B.C. 1979, c.209, and the Alberta Administrative Procedures Act, R.S.A. 1980, c.A-2.

Under the provisions of the Judicial Review Procedure Act, "judicial review through the prerogative remedies of prohibition, certiorari, mandamus, and the equitable remedies of a declaratory judgment and an injunction, are all replaced by one 'Application for Judicial Review'."[55]

And finally, under the two Judicature Amendment Acts referred to above, a new division was created in the Supreme Court of Ontario, namely, the Divisional Court, in order to specifically deal with the judicial review of administrative action. The judges of the Divisional Court are those appointed to the Trial Division of the Supreme Court and they share responsibilities in both of these divisions.

GROWTH OF GOVERNMENT BUREAUCRACY

The increase in the number of administrative tribunals has been matched by the growth in government bureaucracy. The public service, at all levels of government, has expanded to a considerable degree in the past few years. Many people feel that the bureaucracy has lost touch with the average citizen. Indeed, we have all experienced frustration in attempting to resolve a particular matter with a department of government assuming we have overcome the initial problem in attempting to locate the appropriate party with whom to deal. In order to mitigate these and other concerns, many provinces have enacted ombudsman legislation.

The institution of the ombudsman arose in Sweden and, in the modern era, developed significantly in New Zealand. Since that time, the institution has come to North America and, in 1967, following the recommendation of the Clement Commission, Alberta became the first province in Canada to have a legislative ombudsman. In recent years, virtually all other provinces have enacted similar ombudsman legislation. In addition, in 1976, the International Ombudsman Institute was established in Alberta as a resource centre and clearing house of materials of interest to ombudsmen around the world. The first international meeting of ombudsmen was held in Edmonton in 1976; the second was held in Jerusalem in 1980; the third was held in Stockholm in 1984; and the fourth took place in Australia in 1988.[56]

---

[55] Tarnopolsky, *ibid.*, p. 63. This Ontario model has been followed by British Columbia in its Judicial Review Procedure Act, R.S.B.C. 1979, c.209. A number of provinces have also amended their rules of court to incorporate the prerogative and equitable remedies into one all-inclusive "application for judicial review". See, for example, the 1987 changes to the Alberta Rules of Court, R.R. 753.01 to 753.19.

[56] See *British Columbia Development Corp. v. British Columbia (Ombudsman)*, [1984] 2 S.C.R. 447, [1985] 1 W.W.R. 193 (*sub nom. B.C. Dev. Corp. v. Friedmann, Ombudsman of B.C.*), 11 Admin. L.R. 113 (*sub nom B.C. Dev. Corp v. Ombudsman (B.C.)*), 14 D.L.R. (4th) 129, 55 N.R. 298, for a discussion of the ombudsman's powers and mandate.

Another aspect of concern in connection with government bureaucracy relates to the storage and usage of personal information contained in government data banks. Reference should be made to the privacy provisions contained in the Privacy Act,[57] so which address the issue of the individual's access to information concerning himself stored in government data banks. Reference might also be made to the protection of privacy provisions in the Criminal Code. It is interesting to note that the institution of the ombudsman has, thus far, developed only at the provincial level, whereas the protection of privacy, with some exceptions (for example, the Privacy Act, R.S.B.C. 1979, c. 336), has developed primarily at the federal level.

Akin to the foregoing developments is the enactment, at both the federal and provincial levels, but primarily at the federal level, of freedom of information statutes. Freedom of information legislation, generally speaking, is designed to give a citizen access to government information. It differs from federal privacy legislation in that the privacy provisions relate to an individual's access to and use of personal information in government data banks concerning himself, whereas freedom of information legislation relates not to personal information but to government information in the nature of "public business".[58] Both the privacy and freedom of information provisions were enacted by Parliament as part of a single access to government information package in 1982 and proclaimed into force in 1983. The privacy provisions are a strengthened version of an earlier enactment contained in the Canadian Human Rights Act. However, the freedom of information provisions are contained in a law which followed a somewhat checkered legislative history — among other things, private members' bills, a government "Green Paper", a bill introduced by the Conservative government, and the eventual enactment of the new package in 1982 by the Liberal government. Freedom of information is an area of law which has developed significantly in the United States, and, no doubt, will be of significant import, in future years, in Canada.[59]

CONCLUSION

The development of administrative law in recent years represents an important component of Canadian legal history. We have seen how the

---

[57] R.S.C. 1985, c.P-21. The Act was originally enacted as Pt. IV of the Canadian Human Rights Act, S.C. 1976-77, c.33.

[58] See the Access to Information Act, R.S.C. 1985, c.A-1.

[59] For a discussion of the current legislation, see D. Schneiderman, "The Access to Information Act: A Practical Review" (1987), 7 Advocates' Q. 474. In recent years, many provinces and municipalities throughout Canada have enacted similar legislation.

law has responded to the consequences of regulatory control over virtually all aspects of human affairs[60] and how the law strives, sometimes imperfectly, to ensure that under a regime of regulatory control there is, at the very least, a minimum standard of fairness and justice in the administrative process.

Administrative law is more than a single, substantive area of the law. It transcends all of the major divisions of the law. The direction that it takes in ensuring the achievement of justice and fairness in the administrative process may assist in providing an answer to the perplexing question as to adaptability of the law to changing social conditions.[61]

SELECTED BIBLIOGRAPHY OF TREATISES, ARTICLES AND OTHER MATERIALS ON ADMINISTRATIVE LAW

TEXTS AND TREATISES

Canada

Angus, W.H. *Cases and Materials on Administrative Law*. Toronto: York University, 1977.

Angus, W.H. *Federal Administrative Law*. Toronto: York University, 1980.

Arthurs, H.W. *Without the Law: Administrative Justice and Legal Pluralism in Nineteenth-Century England*. Toronto: University of Toronto Press, 1984.

Baum, D.J. *Cases and Materials on Administrative Law*. Toronto: Butterworths, 1987.

Bernier, I., and A. Lajoie. *Regulations, Crown Corporations and Administrative Tribunals*. Toronto: University of Toronto Press, 1985.

Blanche, P. *Droit administratif général: Introduction et pouvoir réglementaire*. Sherbrooke: Université de Sherbrooke, 1983.

---

[60] A report issued by the Ontario legislature's regulations committee in 1988 recommended "a complete overhaul of the regulatory process to provide wide prior consultation with people who would be affected by new regulations". See the The Globe & Mail, 27th June 1988. For some excellent summaries as to the extent of regulatory control over modem life, and, in particular, the growing use of the order-in-council (including its effect on civil liberties), see the Financial Post 23rd December 1978 and the editorial of 3rd November 1979; the Toronto Star, 7th January 1979 and The Globe & Mail, 3rd October 1981.

[61] This question is now more complicated in the sense that some governments are now privatizing former governmental functions. The legal issue that emerges relates to whether a privatized entity is beyond the reach of the courts in providing a remedy in the event of a defective action by the privatized agency. This question, in Alberta, for example, was underscored by the introduction, in 1994, of Bill 41, the Government Organization Act, and Bill 57, the Delegated Administration Act. The proposed laws attempted to facilitate government reorganization and allow for increased privatization.

Canadian Institute for the Administration of Justice. *Judicial Review of Administrative Rulings*. Montréal: La Révue du Barreau de Barreau de Québec, 1983.

Dussault, R. *Federal Administration Law: Cases and Materials*. Toronto: York University, 1984.

Dussault, R., and L. Borgeat. *Administrative Law: A Treatise*. Vol.1. 2nd ed. Toronto: Carswell, 1986.

Dussault, R., and L. Borgeat. *Administrative Law*. 2nd ed. Toronto: Carswell, 1990.

Evans, J.M., H.N. Janish and D.J. Mullan. *Administrative Law: Cases, Text and Materials*. 4th ed. Toronto: Edmond Montgomery, 1995.

Finkelstein, N.R., and B.M. Rogers. *Recent Developments in Administrative Law*. Toronto: Carswell, 1987.

Garant, P. *Aspects of Anglo-Canadian and Quebec Administrative Law*. Québec: Université Laval, 1979.

Garant, P. *Droit administratif*. 2e éd. Montréal: Les Editions Yvons Blais, 1985.

Garner, J.F., and B.L. Jones. *Garner's Administrative Law*. 6th ed. Toronto: Butterworths, 1985.

Griffith, J.A.G. *Principles of Administrative Law*. 5th ed. Toronto: Carswell, 1973.

Hogg, P.E., *Constitutional Law of Canada*, (3rd), Toronto: Carswell, 1992.

Jones, D.P. *Cases and Materials on Administrative Law*. 2nd ed. Edmonton: University of Alberta, 1987.

Jones, D.P., and A.S. de Villars. *Principles of Administrative Law*.(2nd ed.) Toronto: Carswell, 1994.

Kavanagh, J.A. *A Guide to Judicial Review*. 2nd ed. Toronto: Carswell, 1984.

Keyes, J.M. *Executive Legislation: Delegated Law Making by the Executive Branch*. Markham: Butterworths, 1993.

Law Society of Upper Canada. *Charter of Rights and Administrative Law 1983-84* (L.S.U.C. Bar Admission Course Material). Toronto: Carswell, 1983.

Law Society of Upper Canada. *Emerging Issues in Administrative Law*. Toronto: Osgoode Hall, 1983.

Law Society of Upper Canada. *Practice and Procedure before Administrative Tribunals*. Toronto: De Boo, 1953.

Lemieux, D. *Le Contrôl judiciaire de l'action gouvernementale*. Montréal: C.E.J., 1981.

McWhinney, E. *Judicial Review*. 4th ed. Toronto: University of Toronto Press, 1969.

Ouellette, Y., and G. Pépin. *Principles de contentieux administratif*. Montréal: Les Editions Yvon Blais, 1979.

Pépin, G. *Les tribunaux administratifs et la constitution*. Montréal: Université de Montréal, 1969.

Pue, W.W. *Natural Justice in Canadian Law*. Vancouver: Butterworths, 1981.

Reid, R.F., and D. Hillel. *Administrative Law and Practice*. 2nd ed. Toronto: Butterworths, 1978.

Strayer, B. *Judicial Review of Legislation in Canada*. Toronto: University of Toronto Press, 1968.

Strayer, B. *The Canadian Constitution and the Courts: The Function and Scope of Judicial Review*. 3rd ed. Toronto: Butterworths, 1988.

Great Britain

Aldous, G., and J. Alder. *Applications for Judicial Review: Law and Practice*. London: Butterworths, 1985.

Allen, C.K. *Law and Orders*. 3rd ed. London: Stevens, 1965.

Beatson, J. *Administrative Law: Cases and Materials*. Oxford: Clarendon Press, 1983.

Birkinshaw, P. *Grievances, Remedies and the State*. London: Sweet & Maxwell, 1985.

Borrie, G. *Elements of Public Law*. 2nd ed. London: Sweet & Maxwell, 1971.

Clarke, H.W. *Constitutional and Administrative Law*. London: Sweet & Maxwell, 1971.

Craig, P.P. *Administrative Law*. Sweet & Maxwell, 1983.

de Smith, S.A. *Constitutional and Administrative Law*. 5th ed. Harmondsworth: Penguin Education, 1985.

de Smith, S.A. *Judicial Review of Administrative Action*. 4th ed. London: Stevens & Carswell, 1980.

Emery, C.T., and B. Smyth. *Judicial Review: Legal Limits of Official Power*. London: Sweet & Maxwell, 1986.

Flick, G.A. *Natural Justice: Principles and Practical Application*. 2nd ed. Sydney: Butterworths, 1984.

Foulkes, D. *Administrative Law*. 6th ed. London: Butterworths, 1986.

Ganz, G. *Administrative Procedures*. London: Sweet & Maxwell, 1974.

Ganz, G. *Quasi-Legislation: Recent Developments in Secondary Legislation*. 2nd ed. London: Sweet & Maxwell, 1987.

Garner, J.F. *Garner's Administrative Law*. 6th ed. London: Butterworths, 1985.

Garrett, J. *Administrative Reform; The Next Step*. London: Fabian Society, 1973.

Gordon, R.J.F. *Judicial Review: Law and Procedure*. London: Sweet & Maxwell, 1985.

Griffith, J.A.G., and H. Street. *Principles of Administrative Law*. 5th ed. London: Pitman, 1973.

Hawke, N. *An Introduction to Administrative Law*. Oxford: E.S.C. Publishing Ltd., 1984.

Hotop, Stanley D. *Principles of Australian Administrative Law*. 6th ed. Sydney: Law Book Co., 1985.

Jackson, P. *Natural Justice*. London: Sweet & Maxwell, 1973.

Jennings, I. *The Law and the Constitution*. 5th ed. London: University of London Press, 1959.

Pearce, D.C. *Commonwealth Administrative Law*. Sydney: Butterworths, 1986.

Phillips, O.H. *Constitutional and Administrative Law*. 7th ed. London: Sweet & Maxwell, 1987.

Reid, R.F. *The Administrative Process*. London: Butterworths, 1971.

Schwartz, B., and H.W.R. Wade. *Legal Control of Government*. Oxford: Clarendon Press, 1972.

Thio, S.M. *Locus Standi and Judicial Review*. Singapore:Singapore University Press, 1971.

Wade, H.W.R. *Administrative Law*. 5th ed. Oxford: Clarendon Press, 1982.

Wade and Bradley. *Constitutional and Administrative Law*. 10th ed. London: Longman, 1985.

Wheare, K.C. *Maladministration and its Remedies*. London: Stevens, 1973.

Yardley, D.C. *Principles of Administrative Law*. London: Butterworths, 1981.

Yardley, D.C. *Source Book of English Administrative Law*. 2nd ed. London: Butterworths, 1970.

ARTICLES

Akehurst, C.M. "Statements of Reasons for Judicial and Administrative Decisions". (1970), 33 M.L.R. 154.

Alarie, J., et G. Boisvert. "Les critères de répartition des normes entre la loi et la règlement". (1980), 12 Cahiers 567.

Amyot, B. "De la notion de jurisdiction en droit administratif canadien". (1983), 24 Cahiers 605.

Angus, W.M.H. "The Individual and the Bureacracy: Judicial Review — Do We Need It?" (1974), 20 McGill L.J. 178.

Arthurs, H.W. "Jonah and the Whale: The Appearance, Disappearance and Reappearance of Administrative Law". (1980), 30 U.T.L.J. 225.

Arthurs, H.W. "Protection Against Judicial Review". (1983), 43 R. du B. 277.

Arthurs, H.W. "Recognizing Administrative Law". [1981] Admin. L. Conf. 2.

Arthurs, H.W. "Rethinking Administrative Law: A Slightly Dicey Business". (1979), 17 Osgoode Hall L.J. 1.

Arthurs, H.W. "The Three Faces of Justice — Bias in the Tripartite Tribunal". (1963), 28 Sask. Bar Rev. 147.

Atkey, R.G. "Freedom of Information: The Problems of Confidentiality in the Administrative Process". (1980), 18 U.W.O.L. Rev. 153.

Atkey, R.G. "The Statutory Powers Procedure Act, 1971". (1972), 10 Osgoode Hall L.J. 155.

Atkinson, W.J. "La discretion administrative et la mise en oeuvre d'un politique". (1978), 19 Cahiers 187.

Atkinson, W.J., et M.C. Lévesque. "Délégation de pouvoirs et délégation de signature: l'exercise par des Fonctionnaires des pouvoirs confiés à leur ministre". (1982), 42 R. du B. 327.

Barbe, R.P. "De certains aspects de la jurisdiction de la régie des services publics en matière de droit municipal". (1978), 19 Cahiers 447.

Beatson, J. "The Scope of Judicial Review for Error of Law". (1984), 4 Oxford J. of Leg. Stud. 22.

Belley, J.G. "La notion de protection du public dans la réforme du droit professional québecois: une analyse socio-politique". (1980), 21 Cahiers 673.

Blanche, P. "Les aspects procéduraux de la lutte administrative contre la discrimination, et la charte des droits et libertes de la personne". (1976), 17 Cahiers 875.

Bouchard, M. "Administrative Law Scholarship". (1985), 23 Osgoode Hall L.J. 411.

Bowman, B. "Judicial Review — No Evidence". (1984), 14 Man. L.J. 195.

Branson, C.O.D., and H.W.R. Wade. "The British Columbia Judicial Review Procedure Act: Procedural Means for Obtaining Judicial Review: Comments". [1981] Admin. L. Conf. 156.

Brown, D.J.M., "Privative Clauses" in N.R. Finkelstein and B.M. Rogers,

Recent Developments in Administrative Law, Toronto: Carswell, 1987.

Brown, L.N. "La nouvelle justice naturelle: l'administrateur équitable et raisonnable". (1980), 21 Cahiers 67.

Brown, L.N. "The Council on Tribunals; A Re-Assessment in its 20th Year". (1979), Aspects 1.

Bruni, M.J., and K.F. Miller. "Practice and Procedure Before the Energy Resources Conservation Board". (1982), 20 Alta. L. Rev. 79.

Bryden, P.L., "Canadian Administrative Law in Transition: 1963-1988" (1988-89) 23 UBCLR, 147.

Bryden, P.L., "Canadian Administrative Law: Where We've Been", (1991), 16 Queen's L.J.

Buckley, R.A. "Liability in Tort for Breach of Statutory Duties". (1984), 100 L.Q. Rev. 204.

Carter, R., "The Privative Clause in Canadian Administrative law, 1944-1985: A Doctrinal Examination" (1986), 64 Can. Bar. Rev., 241.

Castrilli, J., *et al.* "An Environmental Impact Assessment Statute for Ontario with Commentary". [1975] Environmental Management 319.

Cavalluzzo, P.J.J., "The Rise and Fall of Judicial Deference" in N.R. Finkelstein and B.M. Rogers, *Recent Developments in Administrative Law,* Toronto: Carswell, 1987.

Christian, T.J. "Section 7 and Administrative Law (Part 1)". (1987), 3 Admin. L.J. 25.

Christian, T.J. "Section 7 and Administrative Law (Part 2)". (1987), 3 Admin. L.J. 34.

Comtois, S. "On the Opportunity of Codifying Administrative Procedure (Practice Note)". (1987-88), C.J.A.L.P. 119.

Corry, J.A. "The Prospects for the Rule of Law". (1955), 21 Can. J. of Econ. and Pol. Sci. 405.

Coté, P.-A. "Droit civil et droit administratif au Québec". (1976), 17 Cahiers 825.

Couture, L.-A. "Introduction to Canadian Federal Administrative Law". (1972), 22 U.T.L.J. 47.

David, H. "Some Consequences of Procedural Error". (1983), 43 R. du B. 463.

Diplock (Lord). "Administrative Law: Judicial Review Reviewed". [1974] Camb. L.J. 233.

Doern, G.B. "Regulatory Process, Performance and Reform; Concluding Observations". (1978), Regulatory Process 1.

Doern, G.B. "The Regulatory Process in Canada". (1978), Regulatory Process 1.

Draft Report of the Institute of law Research and Reform, *Judicial Review of Administrative Action, Application for Judicial Review,* Edmonton, Alberta, March 1984.

Driedger, E.A. "Subordinate Legislation". (1969), 47 Can. Bar Rev. 1.

Dussault, R. "L'équilibre entre les pouvoirs judiciaire, législatif et éxecutif: rupture ou évolution?" (1979), 22 Can. Pub. Admin. 196.

Dussault, R. "Le rôle du juriste fonctionnaire dans l'aménagement des rélations entre l'administration et les citoyens". (1981), 24 Can. Pub. Admin. 8.

Dussault, R. "Relationship Between the Nature of the Acts of the Administration and Judicial Review: Quebec and Canada". (1967), 10 Can. Pub. Admin. 298.

Dussault, R., et M. Patenaude. "Le Contrôle judiciaire de l'administration vers une meilleure synthèse des valeurs de liberté individuelle et de justice sociale?" (1983), 43 R. du B. 163.

Dussault, R., et G. Pelletier. "Le professionnel fonctionnaire face aux mécanismes d'inspection professionnelle et de discipline institués par le Code des professions". (1977), 37 R. du B. 2.

Dyzenhaus, D., "CUPE's Spirit? Case Comment: *Domtar Inc. c Québec (Commission d'appel en matière de lésions professionnelles)"* (1994) 15 Admin. L.R. 73.

Edmond, P. "A Critical Evaluation of the Environmental Protection Laws in the Maritime Provinces (and more particularly the Nova Scotia Environmental Protection Act)". [1975] Environmental Management 258.

Elliott, R. "No Evidence — A Ground for Judicial Review in Canada?" (1972/73), 37 Sask. L. Rev. 48.

Emery, C.T., and B. Smythe. "Error of Law in Administrative Law". (1984), 100 L.Q. Rev. 612.

Estey, W.Z. "The Right to Know the Case Against You in Administrative Law". [1981] Cambridge Lect. 228.

Estey, W.Z. "Usefulness of the Administrative Process". [1971] Lect. L.S.U.C. 307.

Estrin, D. "The Legal and Administrative Management of Ontario's Air Resources 1973-74". [1975] Environmental Management 182.

Evans, J.M. "Developments in Administrative Law: The 1983-84 Term". (1985), 7 Sup. Ct. L. Rev. 1.

Evans, J.M. "Developments in Administrative Law: The 1984-85 Term". (1986), 8 Sup. Ct. L. Rev. 1.

Evans, J.M. "Developments in Administrative Law: The 1985-86 Term". (1987), 9 Sup. Ct. L. Rev. 1.

Evans, J.M. "Developments in Administrative Law: The 1988-89 Term". (1990), 1 Sup. Ct. L. Rev. (2d), 1.

Evans, J.M. "Judicial Review in Ontario: Recent Developments in the Remedies". (1977), 55 Can. Bar Rev. 148.

Evans, J.M. "Remedies in Administrative Law". [1981] Lect. L.S.U.C. 429.

Fairweather, G. "Procedural Fairness : a Challenge for the Canadian Human Rights Commission". (1985), 10 Queen's L.J. 430.

Fera, N.M. "Review of Administrative Decisions Under the Federal Court Act". (1971), 14 Can. Pub. Admin. 580.

Filion, M. "Le pouvoir discrétionnaire de l'administration exercé sous formes de normes administratives: Les directives". (1970), 20 Cahiers 855.

Flick, G.A. "Administrative Judicators and the Duty to Give Reasons — A Search for Criteria". [1978] Pitblado Lect. 16.

Flick, G.A. "L'abus de pouvoirs en droit administratif Canadien et québecois". (1978), 19 Cahiers 135.

Fraser, The Honourable Catherine A., Chief Justice of Alberta, *20/20 Anniversary Celebration*, University of Alberta, Faculty of Law, Address given September 18, 1992.

Gagnon, F.-M. "The Case of the Elusive Regulations". (1977), 1 Leg. Med. 247.

Garant, P. "Droit administratif: chroniques". (1982), 42 R. du B. 615, 813.

Garant, P. "La preuve devant les tribunaux administratifs et quasi-judiciaires". (1980), 21 Cahiers 825.

Garant, P. "Le protecteur de citoyen et le droit administratif". (1979), Aspects 26.

Garant, P., et S. Normand. "Le contrôle judiciare des erreurs de droit en présence d'une clause privative". (1982), 23 Cahiers 5.

Gauthier, M. "Le processus décisionnel de liberation conditionelle". (1981), 14 Criminologue 2:61.

Gélinas, A. "Judicial Control of Administrative Action: Great Britain and Canada". [1963] Pitblado Lect. 140.

Giles J. "Should There be Judicial Review When There is an Adequate Right of Appeal?" (1983), 43 R. du B. 497.

Glenn, J.M. "L'aménagement du territoire en droit public québecois". (1977), 23 McGill L.J. 242.

Gordon, D.M. "Jurisdictional Fact: An Answer". (1966), 82 L.Q. Rev. 515.

Gordon, D.M. "Quashing on Certiorari for Error of Law". (1951), 67 L.Q. Rev. 452.

Gordon, D.M. "The Relation of Facts to Jurisdiction". (1929), 45 L.Q. Rev. 459.

Grenier, R. "Contrôle administratif du pouvoir contractuel de l'administration municipale". (1982), 84 R. du B. 247.

Grey, J.H. "Can Fairness be Effective?" (1982), 27 McGill L.J. 360.

Grey, J.H. "Discretion in Administrative Law". (1979), 17 Osgoode Hall L.J. 107.

Grey, J.H. "The Duty to Act Fairly After Nicholson". (1980), 25 McGill L.J. 598.

Grey, J.H. "The Ideology of Administrative Law". (1983), 13 Man. L.J. 35.

Grey, J.H., and L.-M. Casgrain. "Jurisdiction, Fairness and Reasonableness". (1987), 10 Dal. L.J. 3:89.

Hendry, J. McL. "Some Problems in Canadian Administrative Law". (1967), 2 Ottawa L. Rev. 71.

Hogg, P.W. "Is Judicial Review of Administrative Action Guaranteed by the British North America Act?" (1976), 54 Can. Bar Rev. 716.

Hogg, P.W. "Judicial Review of Action by the Crown Representative". (1969), 43 Aust. L.J. 215.

Hogg, P.W. "The Jurisdictional Fact Doctrine in the Supreme Court of Canada: *Bell v. O.H.R.C.*". (1971), 9 Osgoode Hall L.J. 203.

Hogg, P.W. "The Supreme Court of Canada and Administrative Law: 1949-1971". (1973), 11 Osgoode Hall L.J. 187.

Holloway, I., "The Transformation of Canadian Administrative Law" (1993), 6 C.J.A.L.P. 295.

Issalys, P. "The Professions Tribunal and the Control of Ethical Conduct Among Professionals". (1978), 24 McGill L.J. 588; (1979), Aspects 222.

Janisch, H.N. "Administrative Tribunals in the 80's; Rights of Access by Groups and Individuals". (1981), 1 Windsor Yearbook of Access to Justice 303.

Janisch, H.N. "Beyond Jurisdiction: Judicial Review and the Charter of Rights". (1983), 43 R. du B. 401.

Janisch, H.N. "Bora Laskin and Administrative Law: An Unfinished Journey". (1987), 35 U.T.L.J. 557.

Janisch, H.N. "Independence of Administrative Tribunals: In Praise of 'Structural Heretics' ". (1987-88), 1 C.J.A.L.P. 1.

Janisch, H.N. "Policy Making in Regulation: Towards a New Definition of the Status of Independent Regulatory Agencies in Canada". (1979), 17 Osgoode Hall L.J. 46.

Janisch, H.N. "The Role of the Independent Regulatory Agencies in Canada". (1978), 27 U.N.B.L.J. 83.

Jones, D.P. "A Comment on 'Legitimate Expectations' and the Duty to Give Reasons in Administrative Law". (1987), 25 Alta. L. Rev. 512.

Jones, D.P. "A Note on the Relationship of Waiver and Estoppel to Jurisdictional Defects in Administrative Law". (1987), 25 Alta. L. Rev. 487.

Jones, D.P. "Administrative Fairness in Alberta". (1980), 18 Alta. L. Rev. 351.

Jones, D.P. "Administrative Progress in Alberta". (1980), 18 Alta. L. Rev. 357.

Jones, D.P. "Discretionary Refusal of Judicial Review in Administrative Law". (1981), 19 Alta. L. Rev. 483.

Jones, D.P. "Institutional Bias: The Applicability of the Nemo Judex Rule to Two-Tiered Decisions". (1977), 23 McGill L.J. 605.

Jones, D.P. "Natural Justice and Fairness in the Administrative Process". (1983), 43 R. du B. 441.

Jones, D.P., and A.S. de Villars. "Certiorari and the Correction of Intra-Jurisdictional Errors of Law". (1984), 22 Alta. L. Rev. 362.

Kaufman, D.S. "How Exclusive is 'exclusive'? An Examination of Section 18 of the Federal Court Act". (1985), 16 R.D.U.S. 435.

Kenniff, P. "Les récentes réformes législatives en droit municipal québecois: Bilan et perspective d'avenir". (1981), 12 R.D.U.S. 3.

Kenniff, P., and L. Giroux. "The Law Relating to the Protection and Quality of the Environment in Quebec". [1975] Environmental Management 213.

Kernaghan, K. "Political Control of Administrative Action: Accountability or Window Dressing?" (1976), 17 Cahiers 927.

Kerr, R.W. "Telephone Rate Regulation in New Brunswick and Rate Regulation Process". (1977), 26 U.N.B.L.J. 69.

Kushner, H.L. "Charter of Rights and Freedoms, s.11: Disciplinary Hearings Before Statutory Tribunals". (1984), 62 Can. Bar Rev. 638.

Kushner, H.L. "The Right to Reasons in Administrative Law". (1986), 24 Alta. L. Rev. 305.

La Forest, G.V. "Delegation of Legislative Power in Canada". (1975), 21 McGill L.J. 131.

Lafond, N. "La loi sur l'aménagement et l'urbanisme". (1981), 12 R.B.U.S. 43.

Lalonde, M. "Les règles vs. le citoyen: raport d'atélier". (1978), 38 R. du B. 496.

Lambert, J.L. "Administrative Law: Reform of the Public Law Remedies in England". (1978), 56 Can. Bar Rev. 668.

Lamer, A. "Administrative Tribunals — Future Prospects and Possibilities" (1992), 5 C.J.A.L.P. 107.

Law, J.M., "Tensions Within the Traditional Model of Control of Government" (1993), 6 C.J.A.L.P. 13.

Lawford, H.J. "Appeals Against Administrative Decisions: The Function of Judicial Review". (1962), 5 Can. Pub. Admin. 50.

Lemieux, D. "Le contrôle judiciaire comme technique de participation des citoyens aux choix énergétiques". (1983), 24 Cahiers 977.

Lemieux, D. "Les erreurs de droit dans l'exercice d'une compétence". (1982), 23 Cahiers 505.

Lemieux, P. "Les réactions de la doctrine à la création du droit par les juges en droit administratif". (1980), 21 Cahiers 277.

Lemieux, P. "Supervisory Judicial Control of Federal and Provincial Public Authorities in Quebec". (1979), 17 Osgoode Hall L.J. 133; (1979), Aspects 147.

Lévesque-Crevier, M.-C. "La motivation en droit administratif". (1980), 40 R. du B. 535.

Longtin, M.J., et M. Bouchard. "Vers une revision du processus et du cadre d'élaboration de la décision administrative au Québec". (1981), 22 Cahiers 159.

Loughlin, M. "Procedural Fairness: A Study of the Crisis in Administrative Law". (1978), 28 U.T.L.J. 215.

Lövgren, A.C. "Bad Faith as a Ground of Nullity in Canadian Public Law". (1984), 18 Gazette 277.

Lowery, J.B., and J.L. Smith. "Judicial Review of and Appeals from Conservation Board Orders". (1969), 7 Alta. L. Rev. 443.

Lucas, A.R. "Judicial Review of Crown Corporations". (1986-87), 25 Alta. L. Rev. 363.

Lucas, A.R., and S.K. McCallum. "Looking at Environmental Impact Assessment". [1975] Environmental Management 306.

MacCrimmon, M.R. "The British Columbia Judicial Review Procedure Act: Procedural Means for Obtaining Judicial Review". [1981] Admin. L. Conf. 98.

Macdonald, A. "In the Public Interest: Judicial Review of Local Government". (1983), 9 Queen's L.J. 62.

Macdonald, R.A. "A Bibliography of Legislation Relating to Administrative Law in Canadian Jurisdictions". (1979), 27 Chitty's L.J. 83.

Macdonald, R.A. "A Theory of Procedural Fairness". (1981), 1 Windsor Yearbook of Access to Justice 3.

Macdonald, R.A. "Absence of Jurisdiction: A Perspective". (1983), 43 R. du B. 307.

Macdonald, R.A. "Federal Judicial Review Under the Federal Court Act: When is a 'federal board, commission or other tribunal' not a 'federal board, commission or other tribunal'?" (1981), 6 Dal. L.J. 449.

Macdonald, R.A. "Judicial Review and Procedural Fairness in Administrative Law I". (1980), 25 McGill L.J. 520.

Macdonald R.A. "Judicial Review and Procedural Fairness in Administrative Law II". (1980), 26 McGill L.J. 1.

Macdonald R.A. "Reopenings, Rehearings and Reconsideration in Administrative Law". (1979), 17 Osgoode Hall L.J. 207.

Macdonald, R.A. "The Commissions of Inquiry in the Perspective of Administrative Law". (1980), 18 Alta. L. Rev. 366.

Macdonald, R.A. "The Limits of Procedural Fairness: Executive Action by the Governor-in-Council?" (1981-82), 46 Sask. L. Rev. 187.

Macdonald, R.A. "The Proposed Section 96B: An Ill-Conceived Reform Destined to Failure". (1985), 26 Cahiers 251.

Macdonald, R.A., and R. Janda. "Administrative Law I: Recent Developments in Canadian Law". (1984), 16 Ottawa L. Rev. 597.

Macdonald, R.A., and M. Paskell-Mede. "Annual Survey of Canadian Law: Administrative Law". (1981), 13 Ottawa L. Rev. 671.

MacDowell, R.O. "Law and Practice Before the Ontario Labour Relations Board". (1978), 1 Advocates ' Q. 198.

MacGuigan, M. "Legislative Review of Delegated Legislation". (1968), 46 Can. Bar Rev. 706.

MacKay, A.W. "Human Rights in Canadian Society: Mechanisms for Raising the Issues and Providing Redress". (1981), 4 Dal. L.J. 739.

MacLauchlan, H.W. "Developments in Administrative Law: The 1989-90 Term (1991), 2 S.C.L.R. (2d) 1.

MacLauchlan, H.W. "Developments in Administrative Law: The 1990-91 Term" (1992), 3 S.C.L.R. (2d) 1.

MacLauchlan, H.W. "Four Patterns of Change: Legalization, Democratization, Privatization and Regionalism" (1993), 6 C.J.A.L.P. 47.

MacLauchlan, H.W. "Judicial Review of Administrative Interpretations of Law: How Much Formalism Can We Reasonably Bear?" (1986), 36 U.T.L.J. 343.

MacLauchlan, H.W. "Some Problems with Judicial Review of Administrative Consistency". (1984), 8 Dal. L.J. 435.

Magnet, J.P. "Jurisdictional Fact, Constitutional Fact and the Presumption of Constitutionality". (1980), 11 Man. L.J. 21.

Manson, A. "Administrative Law Developments in the Prison and Parole Contexts". (1984), 5 Admin. L.R. 150.

Matas, D. "Validating Administrative Tribunals". (1984), 14 Man. L.J. 245.

McAllister, G.A. "Administrative Law". (1963), 6 Can. Bar J. 439.

McCallum, S.K., "Recent Developments in Canadian Administrative Law" (1992), 5 C.J.A.L.P. 51.

McDonald, P. "Contradictory Government Action: Estoppel of Statutory Authorities". (1979), 17 Osgoode Hall L.J. 160.

McRuer, J.C. "Control of Power". [1979] Lect. L.S.U.C. 1.

Mercer, P.P. "Administrative Law II: Recent Developments in Canadian Law". (1984), 16 Ottawa L. Rev. 597.

Mercer, P.P. "Administrative Regulation and the Right to Pursue the Gaining of a Livelihood: Paragraph 6(2)(b) of the Charter". (1986), 20 Admin. L.R. 131.

Millward, P.J. "Judicial Review of Administrative Authorities in Canada". (1961), 39 Can. Bar Rev. 351.

Mitchell, L. "The Relationship Between Government and Administration Tribunals". (1973), 39 Man. Bar News 52.

Mitchnick, M.G. "Some Aspects of Practice and Procedure before the Ontario Labour Relations Board". (1985), 6 Advocates' Q. 201.

Molot, H. "Administrative Discretion and Current Judicial Activism". (1979), 11 Ottawa L. Rev. 336.

Molot, H. "Administrative Law: Annual Survey of Canadian Law, Part 2". (1969), 3 Ottawa L. Rev. 465.

Molot, H. "The Self-Created Rule of Policy and Other Ways of Exercising Administrative Discretion". (1972), 18 McGill L.J. 310.

Morden, J.W. "Recent Developments in Administrative Law". [1967] Lect. L.S.U.C. 275.

Mullan, D. "Alternatives to Judicial Review of Administrative Action — the Commonwealth of Australia's Appeals Tribunal". (1983), 43 R. du B. 569.

Mullan, D. "Developments in Administrative Law: The 1978-79 Term". (1980), 1 Sup. Ct. L. Rev. 1.

Mullan, D. "Developments in Administrative Law: The 1979-80 Term". (1981), 2 Sup. Ct. L. Rev. 1.

Mullan, D. "Developments in Administrative Law: The 1980-81 Term". (1982), 3 Sup. Ct. L. Rev. 1.

Mullan, D. "Developments in Administrative Law: The 1981-82 Term". (1983), 5 Sup. Ct. L. Rev. 1.

Mullan, D. "Development in Administrative Law: The 1982-83 Term". (1984), 6 Sup. Ct. L. Rev. 1.

Mullan, D. "Fairness: The New Natural Justice". (1975), 25 U.T.L.J. 281.

Mullan, D.J. "The Future of Administrative Law" (1991), 16 Queen's L.J. 77.

Mullan, D. "Judicial Deference to Administrative Decision-Making in the Age of the Charter". (1985-86), 50 Sask. L. Rev. 2:203.

Mullan, D. "Judicial Restraints on Administrative Action: Effective or Illusory?" (1976), 17 Cahiers 913.

Mullan, D. "Natural Justice and Fairness, Substantive as Well as Procedural Standards for the Review of Administrative Decision Making?" (1982), 27 McGill L.J. 250.

Mullan, D. "Procedural Fairness: Nicholson and the Tasks Ahead". [1979] Admin. L. Conf. 219.

Mullan, D. "The Re-emergence of Jurisdictional Error" (1986), 14 Admin. L.R. 326.

Mullan, D. "Reform of Judicial Review of Administrative Action: The Ontario Way". (1974), 12 Osgoode Hall L.J. 125.

Mullan, D.J. "Judicial Deference to Administrative Decision-Making in the Age of the Charter" ('85-'86), 50 Sask. L.R. 203.

Mullan, D. "Standing: The Relevance of the Constitutional Cases to Administrative Law". [1983] Pitblado Lect. 172.

Mullan, D. "The Federal Court Act: A Misguided Attempt at Administrative Law Reform". (1973), 23 U.T.L.J. 14.

Mullan, D. "The Uncertain Constitutional Position of Canada's Administrative Tribunals". (1982), 14 Ottawa L. Rev. 239.

Mullan, D. "Tortious Liability of Public Officials; A Proposal for Evolution". [1981] Admin. L. Conf. 181.

Neilson, W.A.W. "Administrative Remedies: the Canadian Experience with Assurances of Voluntary Compliance in Provincial Trade Practices Legislation". (1981), 19 Osgoode Hall L.J. 153.

Neudorfer, A. "Cabinet Decisions and Judicial Review". (1985), 1 Admin. L.J. 30.

Norman, K. "*Certiorari* is Born Again: *Martineau v. Matsqui Institution Disciplinary Board*". (1980-81), 45 Sask. L. Rev. 157.

Ouellette, Y. "La Charte Canadienne et les tribunaux administratifs". (1984), 18 R.J.T. 295.

Ouellette, Y. "Les tribunaux administratifs et les réstrictions au contrôle judiciaire: un plaidoyer pour une autonomie contrôlée". (1983), 43 R. du B. 291.

Paquet, G. "The Regulatory Process and Economic Performance". (1978), Regulatory Process 34.

Patterson, G. "Practice and Procedure Before the Ontario Environmental Appeal Board". (1982), 3 Advocates' Q. 181.

Peiris, G.L. "Natural Justice and Degrees of Invalidity of Administrative Action". [1983] Pitblado Lect. 634.

Pépin, G. "Droit administratif: chroniques régulières". (1979), 39 R. du B. 121.

Pépin, G. "Droit administratif: chroniques régulières". (1981), 41 R. du B. 161.

Pépin, G. "Droit administratif: chroniques régulières." (1982), 42 R. du B. 269.

Pépin, G. "Droit administratif: chroniques régulières." (1983), 43 R. du B. 751.

Pépin, G. "L'Administration publique et le principe de l'égalité". (1984), 44 R. du B. 137.

Pépin, G. "Le pouvoir règlementaire et la Charte de la langue Française". (1978), 12 Thémis 107.

Pépin, G. "Les clauses privatives et contrôle des simples erreurs de droit". (1986), 45 R. du B. 439.

Pépin, G. "Les régies vs. le citoyen: explication du thème". (1978), 38 R. du B. 478.

Pépin, G. "L'indépendance judiciaire — l'article 11(d) de la Charte canadienne — une source d'inquietude particulièrement pour les juges des cours inféreures et une source d'interrogation pour les membres des tribunaux administratifs". (1986), 64 R. du B. 550.

Petraglia, P. "Confidential and Sufficient Information: Procedural Fairness". (1986), 2 Admin. L.J. 46.

Picher, M. "Adjudicator, Administrator or Advocate? The Role of the Labour Board in Judicial Review Proceedings". (1984), 62 Can. Bar Rev. 22.

Pigeon, L.-P. "Pourquoi un contrôle judiciaire des organismes administratifs?" (1983), 43 R. du B. 129.

Plunkett, T.J., and J. Lightbody. "Tribunals, Politics and Public Interest: The Edmonton Annexation Case". (1982), 8 Can. Pub. Policy 207.

Quinn, J., and M.J. Trebilcock. "Compensation, Transition Costs and Regulatory Change". (1982), 32 U.T.L.J. 117.

Rankin, M. "The Cabinet and the Agencies: Toward Accountability in British Columbia". (1985), 19 U.B.C.L. Rev. 26.

Ratushny, E. "What are Administrative Tribunals? The Pursuit of Uniformity in Diversity". (1987), 30 Can. Pub. Admin. 1.

Reid, R.F. "Administrative Law: Rights and Remedies". [1953] Spec. Lect. L.S.U.C. 1.

Richard, J.D. "The Judicialization of Administrative Tribunals?" (1993), 6 C.J.A.L.P. 113.

Richardson, G. "The Duty to Give Reasons: Potential and Practice". [1986] Pitblado Lect. 437.

Riddell, W.R. "Procedures before the Ontario Workmens Compensation Board". (1977), 1 Advocates' Q. 46.

Risk, R.C.B. "Lawyers, Courts, and the Rise of the Regulatory State". (1984), 9 Dal. L.J. 31.

Rivest, F. "Les politiques de régulation et la modelle d'Edelman: une analyse en fonction de la santé dans l'industrie de l'amiante". (1979), 22 Can. Pub. Admin. 290.

Robertson, J.R. "The Use of Official Notice by Administrative Tribunals". (1980), 6 Queen's L.J. 3.

Roman, A. "Governmental Control of Tribunals: Appeals, Directives, and Non-Statutory Mechanisms". (1985), 10 Queen's L.J. 476.

Roman, A. "Legal Constraints on Regulatory Tribunals: Vires, Natural Justice and Fairness". (1983), 9 Queen's L.J. 35.

Roman, A. "Regulatory Law and Procedure". (1978), Regulatory Process 68.

Roman, A. "The Possible Impact of the Canadian Charter of Rights and Freedoms on Administrative Law". (1985), 26 Cahiers 339.

Roman, A.J. "A Uniform Procedural Code: Pros and Cons" (1988), 1 C.J.A.L.P. 127.

Roman, A.J. "The Pendulum Swings Back, Case Comment *W.W. Lester (1978) Ltd. v. U.A., Local 740*" (1991), 40 Admin. L.R. 274.

Rousseau, G. "Le recours en cassation dans le contentieux municipal". (1980), 21 Cahiers 715.

Rutherford, G.S. "Legislative Review of Delegated Legislation". (1969), 47 Can. Bar Rev. 352.

Schachter, R.D. "Controlling the Ministers". (1978), 16 Alta. L. Rev. 388.

Schiller, T.D. "Paccar of Canada Ltd. Curial Deference for the 1990's?" (1990), 40 Admin. L.R. 290.

Schneiderman, D. "The Access to Information Act: A Practical Review". (1987), Advocates' Q. 474.

Scott, F.R. "Administrative Law 1923-1943". (1948), 26 Can. Bar Rev. 268.

Shibley, R.E. "The Personal Liability of Members of Municipal, Provincial and Federal Governments". (1985), 1 Admin. L.J. 56, 62.

Slayton, P. "Competitive Applications Before the Canadian Radio-Television and Telecommunications Commission". (1981), 59 Can. Bar Rev. 571.

Smillie, J.A. "Jurisdictional Review of Abuse of Discretionary Power". (1969), 47 Can. Bar Rev. 623.

Smith, B.E. "Practice and Procedures Before the Environmental Assessment Board". (1982), 3 Advocates' Q. 195.

Sproule, K. "The Uranium Mining Industry in Saskatchewan: Control Regulation and Related Constitutional Issues". (1979), 43 Sask. L. Rev. 65.

Stanley, D.C. "Res Judicata in Administrative Law". (1983), 32 U.N.B.L.J. 31.

Strayer, B.L. "Injunctions Against Crown Officers". (1964), 42 Can. Bar Rev. 1.

Taylor, M.R. "The Appearance of Justice: A Sober Second Look at Statutory Tribunals, Despotism and the Rule in *R. v. Sussex Justices*". [1981] Admin. L. Conf. 211.

Taylor, M.R. "The New Despotism — Fifty Years Later". (1979), 37 Advocate 417.

Thomas, P.G. "Administrative Law Reform: Legal vs. Political Controls on Administrative Discretion". (1984), 27 Can. Pub. Admin. 120.

Tokar, J.J. "Administrative Law: Codification of the Grounds of Judicial Review". (1984), 14 Man. L.J. 171.

Tokar, J.J. "Administrative Law: Locus Standi in Judicial Review Proceedings". (1984), 14 Man. L.J. 209.

Townsend, D.A., "The Growing Irrelevance of Judicial Review: Administrative Law and the Entrepreneurial Culture" (1993), 6 C.J.A.L.P. 79.

Trebilcock, M.J. "The Consumer Interest and Regulatory Reform". (1978), Regulatory Process 94.

Trudel, P., and R. Piotte. "Les réglementations infrastructures de télécommunications au Québec". (1978), 13 R.J.T. 139.

Wade, H.W.R. "Anglo-American Administrative Law: Some Reflections". (1965), 81 L.Q. Rev. 357.

Wade, H.W.R. "Some Anglo-Canadian Comparisons and Contrasts". [1981] Admin. L. Conf. 197.

Wade, H.W.R. "Unlawful Administrative Action: Void or Voidable?" (1967), 83 L.Q. Rev. 499; (1968), 84 L.Q. Rev. 95.

Wexler, S. "The Forms of Action and Administrative Law". [1981] Admin. L. Conf. 292.

Williams, D.G.T. "The Council on Tribunals: The First Twenty-Five Years". [1984] Pitblado Lect. 73.

Willis, J. "Administrative Law in Canada". (1939), 53 Harv. L. Rev. 251.

Willis, J. "Administrative Law in Canada". (1961), 39 Can. Bar Rev. 251.

Willis, J. "Canadian Administrative Law in Retrospect". (1974), 24 U.T.L.J. 225.

Willis, J. "Civil Right — A Fresh Viewpoint". (1965), 13 Chitty's L.J. 224.

Willis, J. "Three Approaches to Administrative Law". (1935), 1 U.T.L.J. 53.

Wilson, H.J. " 'Discretion' in the Analysis of Administrative Process". (1972), 10 Osgoode Hall L.J. 117.

Yalden, R. "Deference and Coherence in Administrative Law: Rethinking Statutory Interpretation" (1988), 46 U.T. Fac. L.R. 36.

Yardley, D.C.M. "The Grounds for Certiorari and Prohibition". (1959), 37 Can. Bar Rev. 294.

Yates, C.K. "The Lawyer in the Regulatory Process". (1980), 18 Alta. L. Rev. 70.

Young, A.H. and Macdonald, R.A. "Canadian Administrative Law on the Threshold of the 1990's" (1991), 16 Queen's L.J. 31.

Young, R.E. "Legitimate Expectations: Judicial Review of Administrative Policy Action". (1987), 3 Admin. L.J. 40.

Zimmerman, G.J. "Synergy and the Science Court: Scientific Method and the Adversarial System in Technology Assessment". (1980), 38 U.T. Fac. L. Rev. 170.

OTHER MATERIALS

Alberta Institute of Law Research and Reform. *Judicial Review of Administrative Action: Application for Judicial Review: Report No. 40.* Edmonton: Alberta Institute of Law Research and Reform, 1984.

Alberta, Legal Education Society of *Administrative Law: An Update.* Calgary: Legal Education Society of Alberta, 1984.

Alberta, Legal Education Society of. *Administrative Procedures* (Bar Admission Course Materials). Calgary: Legal Education Society of Alberta, 1983.

Alberta, Legislative Assembly of. *Report of Special Committee on Boards and Tribunals*. Alberta: Legislative Assembly, 1965.

Baum, D.J. (ed.). *Individual End of Bureaucracy*, 1974.

British Columbia. Continuing Legal Education Society of. *Appeals from Decisions of Administrative Tribunals*. Vancouver: Continuing Legal Education Society of British Columbia, 1981.

British Columbia, Continuing Legal Education Society of. *Judicial Review Procedure Act*. Vancouver: Continuing Legal Education Society of British Columbia, 1980.

British Columbia, Continuing Legal Education Society of. *Judicial Review Update*. (Audio Conference Materials). Vancouver: Continuing Legal Education Society of British Columbia, 1984.

British Columbia. Continuing Legal Education Society of. *Practice Before Administrative Tribunals*. Vancouver: Continuing Legal Education Society of British Columbia, 1980.

British Columbia, University of. *Administrative Law Conference, Proceedings, 1979*. Vancouver: University of British Columbia, 1981.

Canada, Law Reform Commission of. *Administrative Law — Commissions of Inquiry — A New Act: Working Paper No. 17*. Ottawa: Ministry of Supply and Services, 1977.

Canada, Law Reform Commission of. *Independent Administrative Agencies: Working Paper No. 25*. Ottawa: Law Reform Commission of Canada, 1980.

Canada, Law Reform Commission of. *Obtaining Reasons Before Applying for Judicial Scrutiny — Immigration Appeal Board: Report No. 18*. Ottawa: Law Reform Commission of Canada, 1982.

Canada, Law Reform Commission of. *Policy Implementation, Compliance and Administrative Law: Working Paper No. 51*. Ottawa: Law Reform Commission of Canada, 1986.

Canada, Law Reform Commission of. *The Legal Status of the Federal Reform Administration: Working Paper No. 40*. Ottawa: Law Reform Commission of Canada, 1985.

Canada, Law Reform Commission on Government Organization. *Report*. Ottawa: Ministry of Supply and Services, 1962-63.

Canada, Royal Commission on Government Organization. *Report*. Ottawa: Ministry of Supply and Services, 1962-63.

Canada, Special Committee on Statutory Instruments. *Report*. Ottawa: Ministry of Supply and Services, 1969.

Canadian Bar Association. *Administrative Law: Practice and Procedure Before Boards*. Toronto: Canadian Bar Association, 1983.

Canadian Institute for the Administration of Justice. *Judicial Review of Administrative Rulings* (1982 Annual Conference). Cowansville, P.Q." Les Editions Yvon Blais, 1983.

Frecker, J. *et al. Towards a Modern Federal Administrative Law*. Ottawa: Law Reform Commission of Canada, 1987.

Great Britain, Committee on Administrative Tribunals and Enquiries. *Report*. Great Britain, 1957.

Great Britain, Committee on Minister's Powers. *Report*. Great Britain, 1932.

Great Britain Law Commission. *Remedies in Administrative Law: Working Paper No. 40*. Great Britain: Great Britain Law Commission, 1971.

Janisch, H.N. (ed.). *Administrative Law Remedies*, 1973.

Janisch, H.N. (ed.). *Current Issues in Administrative Law,* 1974.

Law, J. "Damages in Administrative Law — An Old Remedy with New Potential" (prepared for the Administrative Law Seminar jointly sponsored by the University of Alberta Faculty of Law and the Legal Education Society of Alberta). Calgary: Legal Education Society of Alberta, 1984.

Law Society of Upper Canada. *Emerging Issues in Administrative Law and Administrative Practice*. Toronto: Law Society of Upper Canada, 1983.

Law Society of Upper Canada. *New Directions in Administrative Law* (phonotape). Toronto: Law Society of Upper Canada, n.d.

Leadbeater, *A Council on Administration*, Ottawa: Law Reform Commission of Canada, 1980.

Mildon, *Administrative Law*. Edmonton: Communities and the Legal Resource Centre, 1977.

Ontario, Committee on the Organization of the Government in Ontario. *Report*. Ontario, 1959.

Ontario Economic Council. *Government Regulation*. Toronto: Ontario Economic Council, 1978.

Ontario Regulatory Reform Program. *Achievements in Regulatory Reform in Ontario*. Toronto, 1982.

Ontario, Royal Commission of Inquiry Into Civil Rights. *Report*. Ontario, 1968.

Quebec, Barreau du. *Contentieux administratif*. (C.F.P.B.Q.). Cowansville, P.Q.: Les Editions Yvon Blais, 1983.

Scottish Law Conference. *Remedies in Administrative Law: Memorandum No. 14*. Scotland, 1970.

Slatter, F.F. *Parliament and Administrative Agencies.* Ottawa: Law Reform Commission of Canada, 1982.

Vandervort, L. *Political Control of Independent Administrative Agencies.* Ottawa: Law Reform Commission of Canada, n.d.

Winnipeg Law Reform Commission. *Report on Administrative Law: Report Nos. 56,69.* Winnipeg: Winnipeg Law Reform Commission, 1984-87.

SOME RECENT CASES

Ainsley Financial Corp. v. Ontario (Securities Commission) (1993), 14 O.R. (3d) 280, 17 Admin. L.R. (2d) 281, 10 B.L.R. (2d) 173, 106 D.L.R. (4th) 507, 1 C.C.L.S. 1, 16 O.S.C.B. 4077 (Gen. Div.), affirmed (1994), 21 O.R. (3d) 104, 28 Admin. L.R. (2d) 1, 121 D.L.R. (4th) 79, 77 O.A.C. 155, 6 C.C.L.S. 241, 18 O.S.C.B. 43 (C.A.).

Air Canada v. Davis (1994), 72 F.T.R. 283 (Fed. T.D.).

Alkali Lake Indian Band v. Westcoast Transmission Co., [1985] 3 W.W.R. 134, 11 Admin. L.R. 266 (C.A.).

Anisminic Ltd. v. Foreign Compensation Commission, [1969] 2 A.C. 147, [1969] 1 All E.R. 208 (H.L.).

Associated Provincial Picture Houses Ltd. v. Wednesday Corp., [1948] 1 K.B. 223, [1947] 2 All E.R. 680 (C.A.).

A.U.P.E., Local 63 v. Alberta (Public Service Employees Relations Bd.), [1982] 1 S.C.R. 923, [1983] 1 W.W.R. 593, 21 Alta. L.R. (2d) 104, 82 C.L.L.C. 14,203, 136 D.L.R. (3d) 1, 37 A.R. 281, 42 N.R. 559 (*sub nom. A.U.P.E., Local 63 v. Alta. Pub. Service Employees Rel. Bd.*).

Beaverbrook Ltd. v. Highway Traffic & Motor Transport Board, [1973] 4 W.W.R. 473 (Man. Q.B.).

Bell v. Ontario (Human Rights Commission), [1971] S.C.R. 756, 18 D.L.R. (3d) 1.

Blanco v. Rental Commission, [1980] 2 S.C.R. 827, 35 N.R. 585 (S.C.C.).

Bowen v. Edmonton (City) (No. 2), [1977] 6 W.W.R. 344, 3 M.P.L.R. 129, 4 C.C.L.T. 105, 80 D.L.R. (3d) 501, 8 A.R. 336 (T.D.).

British Columbia Development Corp. v. Friedmann, [1984] 2 S.C.R. 447, [1985] 1 W.W.R. 193 (*sub nom. B.C. Development Corp. v. Friedmann, Ombudsman of B.C.*), 11 Admin. L.R. 113 (*sub nom. B.C. Development Corp. v. Ombudsman (B.C.)*), 14 D.L.R. (4th) 129, 55 N.R. 298.

Council of Civil Service Unions v. Minister for Civil Service, [1984] 3 All E.R. 935, [1985] A.C. 374 (H.L.).

Crevier v. Quebec (A.G.), [1981] 2 S.C.R. 220, 127 D.L.R. (3d) 1, 38 N.R. 541.

Cuddy Chicks Ltd. v. Ontario (Labour Relations Board), [1991] 2 S.C.R. 5, 3 O.R. (3d) 128n, 50 Admin. L.R. 44, [1991] O.L.R.B. Rep. 790, 91 C.L.L.C. 14,024, 4 C.R.R. (2d) 1, 81 D.L.R. (4th) 121, 122 N.R. 361.

C.U.P.E., Local 963 v. New Brunswick Liquor Corp., [1979] 2 S.C.R. 227, 79 C.L.L.C. 14,209, 25 N.B.R. (2d) 237, 51 A.P.R. 237, 26 N.R. 341.

Dayco (Canada) Ltd. v. C.A.W., (*sub nom. Dayco (Canada) Ltd. v. CAW — Canada*) [1993] 2 S.C.R. 230, 13 O.R. (3d) 164n, 14 Admin. L.R. (2d) 1, (*sub nom. Dayco v. N.A.W.*) C.E.B. & P.G.R. 8141, (*sub nom. Dayco v. C.A.W.*) 93 C.L.L.C. 14,032, 102 D.L.R. (4th) 609, 152 N.R. 1, 63 O.A.C. 1.

Delanoy v. Canada (Public Service Commission), [1977] 1 F.C. 562, 13 N.R. 341 (C.A.).

Finlay v. Canada (Minister of Finance), [1986] 2 S.C.R. 607, 23 Admin. L.R. 197, 17 C.P.C. (2d) 289, [1987] 1 W.W.R. 603, 33 D.L.R. (4th) 321 (*sub nom. Canada (Minister of Finance v. Finlay)*), 8 C.H.R.R. D/3789, 71 N.R. 338.

Fooks v. Association of Architects (Alberta), 21 Alta. L.R. (2d) 306, [1982] 6 W.W.R. 40, 38 A.R. 132, 139 D.L.R. (3d) 445 (Q.B.).

Fraser v. Canada (Treasury Bd.), [1985] 2 S.C.R. 455 (*sub nom. Fraser v. P.S.S.R.B.*), 9 C.C.E.L. 233, 18 Admin. L.R. 72, 19 C.R.R. 152, 86 C.L.L.C. 14,003, 23 D.L.R. (3d) 122, 63 N.R. 161.

Gray, Re, 57 S.C.R. 150, [1918] 3 W.W.R. 111, 42 D.L.R. 1.

Harelkin v. University of Regina, [1979] 2 S.C.R. 561, [1979] 3 W.W.R. 676, 96 D.L.R. (3d) 14, 26 N.R. 364.

Heppner v. Alberta (Minister of Environment) (1977), 4 Alta. L.R. (2d) 139, 80 D.L.R. (3d) 112, 6 A.R. 154 (*sub nom. Heppner v. Alberta (A.G.)*).

Hodge v. R. (1883), 9 App. Cas. 117, 3 Cart. B.N.A. 144 (P.C.).

Homex Realty & Development Co. v. Wyoming (Village), [1980] 2 S.C.R. 1011, 13 M.P.L.R. 234, 116 D.L.R. (3d) 1, 33 N.R. 475.

Howard v. Stony Mountain Institution, [1984] 2 F.C. 642, 45 C.R. (3d) 242, 11 Admin. L.R. 63, 19 C.C.C. (3d) 195, 19 D.L.R. (4th) 502, 17 C.R.R. 5, 57 N.R. 280 (C.A.), appeal quashed [1987] 2 S.C.R. 687, 61 C.R. (3d) 387, 41 C.C.C. (3d) 287, 50 Man. R. (2d) 127n, 79 N.R. 350 (*sub nom. R. v. Howard*).

Hutfield v. Fort Saskatchewan General Hospital District 98 (1986), 49 Alta.
    L.R. (2d) 256, 24 Admin. L.R. 250, 74 A.R. 180 (Q.B.), affirmed
    (1988), 60 Alta. L.R. (2d) 165, 31 Admin. L.R. 311, 89 A.R. 274,
    52 D.L.R. (4th) 562 (C.A.).

Inuit Tapirisat of Canada v. Canada (A.G.), [1980] 2 S.C.R. 735, 115
    D.L.R. (3d) 1, 33 N.R. 304.

Joplin v. Vancouver (City) Commissioners of Police, [1983] 2 W.W.R.
    52, 42 B.C.L.R. 34, 2 C.C.C. (3d) 396 *(sub nom. Joplin v. Vancou-
    ver, Chief Constable)*, 144 D.L.R. (3d) 285, 4 C.R.R. 208 (S.C.),
    affirmed [1985] 4 W.W.R. 538, 61 B.C.L.R. 396, 10 Admin. L.R.
    204, 19 C.C.C. (3d) 331, 20 D.L.R. (4th) 314 (C.A.).

Just v. British Columbia, [1989] 2 S.C.R. 1228, 41 Admin. L.R. 161, 41
    B.C.L.R. (2d) 350, 18 M.V.R. (2d) 1, [1990] 1 W.W.R. 385, 1
    C.C.L.T. (2d) 1, 64 D.L.R. (4th) 689, 103 N.R. 1, [1990] R.R.A.
    140 (headnote only).

Kane v. University of B.C., [1980] 1 S.C.R. 1105, [1980] 3 W.W.R. 125,
    18 B.C.L.R. 124, 110 D.L.R. (3d) 311, 31 N.R. 214.

King v. University of Saskatchewan, [1969] S.C.R. 678, 68 W.W.R. 745,
    6 D.L.R. (3d) 120.

Klymchuk v. Cowan (1964), 47 W.W.R. 467, 45 D.L.R. (2d) 587 (Man.
    Q.B.).

Knight v. Indian Head School Division No. 19, [1990] 1 S.C.R. 653, 43
    Admin. L.R. 157, 30 C.C.E.L. 237, [1990] 3 W.W.R. 289, *(sub nom.
    Indian Head School Division No. 19, v. Knight)* 90 C.L.L.C. 14,010,
    69 D.L.R. (4th) 489, 106 N.R. 17, 83 Sask. R. 81.

Latham v. Canada (Solicitor General), [1984] 2 F.C. 734, 5 Admin. L.R.
    70, 39 C.R. (3d) 78, 112 C.C.C. (3d) 9, 9 D.L.R. (4th) 393, 10 C.R.R.
    120 (T.D.).

MacBain v. Canada (Canadian Human Rights Commission), [1985] 1 F.C.
    856, 16 Admin. L.R. 109, 85 C.L.L.C. 17,023, 18 C.R.R. 165, 6
    C.H.R.R. D/3064, 22 D.L.R. (4th) 119 (C.A.).

Martineau v. Matsqui Institution Inmate Disciplinary Bd., [1978] 1 S.C.R.
    118, 33 C.C.C. (2d) 366, 74 D.L.R. (3d) 1, 14 N.R. 285.

Martineau v. Matsqui Institution (No. 2), [1980] 1 S,C.R. 602, 13 C.R.
    (3d) 1 (Eng.), 15 C.R. (3d) 315 (Fr.), 50 C.C.C. (2d) 353, 106 D.L.R.
    (3d) 385, 30 N.R. 119, reversing [1978] 2 F.C. 637, 40 C.C.C. (2d)
    325, 22 N.R. 250 (C.A.), reversing [1978] 1 F.C. 312, 37 C.C.C.
    (2d) 58, 22 N.R. 250 at 255 (T.D.).

Metropolitan Life Insurance Co. v. I.U.O.E., Local 796, [1970] S.C.R.
    425, 70 C.L.L.C. 14,008, 11 D.L.R. (3d) 336.

Nat. Cablevision Ltd. v. La regie des services publics, [1975] C.A. 335
    (Que.).

National Corn Growers Assn. v. Canada (Canadian Import Tribunal), [1990] 2 S.C.R. 1324, 45 Admin. L.R. 161, 74 D.L.R. (4th) 449, 114 N.R. 81, 4 T.T.R. 267, (*sub nom. American Farm Bureau Federation v. Canadian Import Tribunal*) 3 T.C.T. 5303.

Newfoundland Telephone Co. v. Newfoundland (Board of Commissioners of Public Utilities), [1992] 1 S.C.R. 623, 4 Admin. L.R. (2d) 121, 301 A.P.R. 271, 89 D.L.R. (4th) 289, 95 Nfld & P.E.I.R. 271, 134 N.R. 241.

Nielsen v. Kamloops (City), [1984] 2 S.C.R. 2, [1984] 5 W.W.R. 1, 11 Admin. L.R. 1, 29 C.C.L.T. 97, 26 M.P.L.R. 81, 8 C.L.R. 1, 66 B.C.L.R. 273, 10 D.L.R. (4th) 641.

Nicholson v. Haldimand-Norfolk (Regional Municipality) Commissioners of Police, [1979] 1 S.C.R. 311, 78 C.L.L.C. 14,181, 88 D.L.R. (3d) 671, 23 N.R. 410.

North Vancouver (Municipality) v. Canada (National Harbours Board) (1978), 7 M.P.L.R. 151, 10 C.E.L.R. 31, 89 D.L.R. (3d) 704.

Old St. Boniface Residents Assn. Inc. v. Winnipeg (City), [1990] 3 S.C.R. 1170, 46 Admin. L.R. 161, 2 M.P.L.R. (2d) 217, [1991] 2 W.W.R. 145, 75 D.L.R. (4th) 385, 69 Man. R. (2d) 134, 116 N.R. 46.

Pearlman v. Law Society (Manitoba), [1991] 2 S.C.R. 869, 2 Admin. L.R. (2d) 185, (*sub nom. Pearlman v. Manitoba Law Society Judicial Committee*) [1991] 6 W.W.R. 289, 6 C.R.R. (2d) 259, 84 D.L.R. (4th) 105, 75 Man. R. (2d) 81, 130 N.R. 121, 6 W.A.C. 81.

Piggott Construction Ltd. v. United Brotherhood of Carpenters & Joiners of America, Local 1990 (1974), 39 D.L.R. (3d) 311 (Sask. C.A.).

Québec (Commission des affaires sociales) c. Tremblay, [1992] 1 S.C.R. 952, 3 Admin L.R. (2d) 173, 90 D.L.R. (4th) 609, (*sub nom. Tremblay c. Québec (Commission des affaires sociales)*) 136 N.R. 5, (*sub nom. Tremblay c. Commission des Affaires sociales*) 47 Q.A.C. 169.

R. v. Cadeddu (1982), 40 O.R. (2d) 128, (*sub nom. R. v. Nunery*) 32 C.R. (3d) 355, 4 C.C.C. (3d) 97, 146 D.L.R. (3d) 629, 3 C.R.R. 312 (H.C.), abated (because of death of respondent) (1983), 41 O.R. (2d) 481, 35 C.R. (3d) xxviii, 4 C.C.C. (3d) 112, 146 D.L.R. (3d) 653 (C.A.).

R. v. Metropolitan Police Commissioner, [1968] 2 Q.B. 118, [1968] 1 All E.R. 763 (C.A.).

R. v. Smith & Rhuland Ltd., [1953] 2 S.C.R. 95, [1953] 3 D.L.R. 690, 107 C.C.C. 43, 53 C.L.L.C. 15,057.

R. v. Tarrant (1984), 13 C.C.C. (3d) 219, 10 D.L.R. (4th) 751, 11 C.R.R. 368 (B.C. C.A.).

Red Hot Video v. Vancouver (City) (1983), 48 B.C.L.R. 381, 24 M.P.L.R. 60, 5 D.L.R. (4th) 61 (S.C.), reversed (1985), 18 C.C.C. (3d) 153, 29 M.P.L.R. 211 (C.A.).

Reference re Canada Assistance Plan (Canada), [1991] 2 S.C.R. 525, 1 Admin. L.R. (2d) 1, 58 B.C.L.R. (2d) 1, [1991] 6 W.W.R. 1, (*sub nom. Reference re Canada Assistance Plan (British Columbia)*) 83 D.L.R. (4th) 297, (*sub nom. Reference Re Constitutional Question Act (British Columbia)*) 127 N.R. 161, 1 B.C.A.C. 241, 1 W.A.C. 241.

Roncarelli v. Duplessis, [1959] S.C.R. 121, 16 D.L.R. (2d) 689.

Save Richmond Farmland Society v. Richmond (Township), [1990] 3 S.C.R. 1213, 46 Admin. L.R. 264, 52 B.C.L.R. (2d) 145, 2 M.P.L.R. (2d) 288, [1991] 2 W.W.R. 178, 75 D.L.R. (4th) 425, 116 N.R. 68.

Scivitarro v. British Columbia (Minister of Human Resources), [1982] 4 W.W.R. 632, 134 D.L.R. (3d) 521 (B.C. S.C.).

S.E.I.U., Local 333 v. Nipawin District Staff Nurses Assn., [1975] 1 S.C.R. 382, [1974] 1 W.W.R. 653, 73 C.L.L.C. 14,193, 41 D.L.R. (3d) 6.

Shalansky v. Regina Pasqua Hospital, [1983] 1 S.C.R. 303, 83 C.L.L.C. 14,026, 145 D.L.R. (3d) 413, 47 N.R. 76, 22 Sask. R. 153.

Shell Canada Products Ltd. v. Vancouver (City), [1994] 1 S.C.R. 231, 20 Admin. L.R. (2d) 202, 88 B.C.L.R. (2d) 145, 20 M.P.L.R. (2d) 1, [1994] 3 W.W.R. 609, 110 D.L.R. (4th) 1, 163 N.R. 81, 41 B.C.A.C. 81, 66 W.A.C. 81.

Singh v. Canada (Minister of Employment & Immigration), [1985] 1 S.C.R. 177, 12 Admin. L.R. 137, 14 C.R.R. 13, 17 D.L.R. (4th) 422, 58 N.R. 1.

Slaight Communications Inc. v. Davidson, [1989] 1 S.C.R. 1038, 26 C.C.E.L. 85, 89 C.L.L.C. 14,031, 40 C.R.R. 100, 59 D.L.R. (4th) 416, (*sub nom. Davidson v. Slaight Communications Inc.*) 93 N.R. 183.

Suncor Inc. v. McMurray Independent Oil Workers, Local 1, [1983] 1 W.W.R. 604, 23 Alta. L.R. (2d) 105, 142 D.L.R. (3d) 305, 42 A.R. 166 (C.A.).

Syndicat des employés de production du Québec et de l'Acadie v. Canada (Labour Relations Bd.), [1984] 2 S.C.R. 412, 14 Admin. L.R. 72, 84 C.L.L.C. 14,069, 14 D.L.R. (4th) 457, 55 N.R. 321 (*sub nom. C.B.C. v. Syndicat des Employés de Production de Qué. et de l'Acadie*).

Syndicat national des employés de la comm. scolaire regionale de l'Outaouais v. Union des employés de service, Local 298, (*sub nom. Union des employés de service, local 298 v. Bibeault*) [1988] 2 S.C.R. 1048, 35 Admin. L.R. 153, 89 C.L.L.C. 14,045, 95 N.R. 161, 24 Q.A.C. 244.

Tegon Developments Ltd. v. Edmonton (City) (1977), 5 Alta. L.R. (2d) 63, 81 D.L.R. (3d) 543, 8 A.R. 384 (T.D.), affirmed [1979] 1 S.C.R. 98, 121 D.L.R. (3d) 760, 24 N.R. 269.

Tetreault-Gadoury v. Canada (Employment & Immigration Commission), (*sub nom. Canada (Employment & Immigration Commission) v. Tétreault-Gadoury*) [1991] 2 S.C.R. 22, 50 Admin. L.R. 1, 36 C.C.E.L. 117, 91 C.L.L.C. 14,023, 4 C.R.R. (2d) 12, 81 D.L.R. (4th) 358.

University of Alberta v. Alberta (Human Rights Commission), [1992] 2 S.C.R. 1103, 4 Alta. L.R. (3d) 193, (*sub nom. Dickason v. University of Alberta*) [1992] 6 W.W.R. 385, 127 A.R. 241, 92 C.L.L.C. 17,033, 17 C.H.R.R. D/87, 11 C.R.R. (2d) 1, 95 D.L.R. (4th) 439, 141 N.R.1, 20 W.A.C. 241.

Vancouver (City) v. Vancouver (Registrar Land Registration District), 15 W.W.R. 351, [1955] 2 D.L.R. 709 (B.C.C.A.).

Vardy, Re (1976), 34 C.R.N.S. 349, 28 C.C.C. (2d) 164 (*sub nom. Vardy v. Scott*), 66 D.L.R. (3d) 531, 8 N.R. 91, 9 Nfld. & P.E.I.R. 245 (S.C.C.).

W.W. Lester (1978) Ltd. v. U.A., Local 740, [1990] 3 S.C.R. 644, 48 Admin. L.R. 1, 274 A.P.R. 15, (*sub nom. U.A., Local 740 v. W.W. Lester (1978) Ltd.*) 91 C.L.L.C. 14,002, 76 D.L.R. (4th) 389, 88 Nfld. &. P.E.I.R. 15, (*sub nom. Planet Development Corp. v. U.A., Local 740*) 123 N.R. 241.

Wilson v. Law Society (British Columbia), [1974] 5 W.W.R. 642, 47 D.L.R. (3d) 760 (B.C. S.C.).

Wimpey Western Ltd. v. Alberta (Department of Environment, Director of Standards & Approvals) (1983), 28 Alta. L.R. (2d) 193, 3 Admin. L.R. 247, 49 A.R. 360, 2 D.L.R. (4th) 309 (C.A.).

Zurich Insurance Co. v. Ontario (Human Rights Commission), [1992] 2 S.C.R. 321, 9 O.R. (3d) 224n, 12 C.C.L.I. (2d) 206, 39 M.V.R. (2d) 1, 16 C.H.R.R. D/255, 93 D.L.R. (4th) 346, (*sub nom. Ontario (Human Rights Commission) v. Zurich Insurance Co.*) [1992] I.L.R. 1-2848, 138 N.R. 1, 55 O.A.C. 81.

Chapter 13

NEW DIRECTIONS

INTRODUCTION

Generally speaking, the substantive law in each of the various divisions of law is always undergoing change. This change is effected either by way of the evolutionary process by which the common law develops through judicial pronouncements in recently decided cases, or by way of new statutory and/or regulatory enactments. Many new statutes are legislating in areas of human concern not previously covered by formal enactment. This is not to say that all of the substantive areas of the law are undergoing major revision. However, at the very least, one could readily argue that change is endemic to our legal system, if not a fundamental and central characteristic of that system.[1]

Aside from the substantive and procedural changes in the various divisions of the law, there have been some fundamental changes in the Canadian legal system as a whole. These developments have occurred to some extent because many persons are questioning the basic presumptions underlying our legal system. Modern thinkers are attempting to reevaluate the role of law in contemporary society and to seek devices permitting the law to adapt to changing social conditions. In addition, there are related questions being asked in connection with the reform of antiquated laws. The updating of these laws can take the form of simple reform on an ad hoc basis, or alternatively, it might take the form of a major revamping of a particular area of the law.

The law must respond to new problems. However, the manner in which

---

[1] The most dramatic example of this was the "patriation", in 1982, of our so-called "new constitution". What is particularly significant about that event is the incorporation in the new constitution of a domestic amending formula (actually, there is more than one formula the use of a particular one depending upon the nature of the proposed amendment). Therefore, in future, further constitutional changes will likely occur, as it is now easier to effect constitutional change without having the necessity to resort to a request to the U.K. Parliament to bring about the change.

the law responds to these problems often gives rise to considerable controversy. For example, two recent issues relate to the advisability of entering into a free trade agreement with the United States and the establishment of a national goods and services tax.

In these examples, the question, first, is whether a legislative response is the appropriate one in attempting to resolve complex economic issues. Given that there is a consensus that a legislative response is appropriate, then a second question relates to the form and substance of that response.

The process of law reform in Canada is perhaps made more difficult than in other sovereign nations owing to certain constitutional restraints. For example, there have been many recent developments in relation to the creation of a unified family court in Canada. Neither the federal government nor any province could entertain such a notion without regard to the serious constitutional constraints in conducting such a reform. Similarly, there are currently some proposals in connection with the creation of a single court of trial jurisdiction in criminal matters. Again, this can never happen unless there is federal/provincial co-operation. Moreover, in June of 1983, the Supreme Court of Canada held that it was unconstitutional to do so given the constraints flowing from s. 96 of the Constitution Act of 1867. Also, there are constitutional constraints on a province in enacting consumer protection legislation, owing to the prohibitions presently contained in the federal Competition Act, R.S.C. 1985, c. C-19 (2nd Supp.). In the event that there is an operational incompatibility between the provisions contained in the provincial consumer protection legislation and the Competition Act, the doctrine of federal paramountcy would apply. Constitutional constraints notwithstanding, the process of law reform in Canada has now become a well-developed and institutionalized component of the Canadian legal system.

In addition, there are other broad changes which will, in the long run, affect the form and structure of the existing legal system and the processes by which that system operates. These developments will, no doubt, play a major role in the evolution of our system and in its capability of adapting, not only to changing social conditions at present, but also to future realities.

TECHNOLOGY AND THE LAW

Not long ago, it could have been said that the law and modern technology had each grown to a level of substantial sophistication but their paths had never crossed. Consider, for example, the following editorial comment:

In many ways our courts still function as if electricity had never been discovered. When a trial is in progress, for example, a court reporter laboriously writes down the proceedings in shorthand, and then transcribes them at night. The result is delay and expense in preparing the transcript which are necessary for an appeal; and indeed the record of the witness' testimony may not be available if anyone wants to refer to it later at the same trial. Chief Justice Estey points out that a great deal of time and trouble could be saved by transcribing the testimony electronically.

And another use of electronics he suggested would be to take the testimony of witnesses living in distant places. Flying such a witness to Ontario and providing him with meals and lodging during the trial can be a heavy expense to the party who needs his evidence.

Why not have his evidence taken in his own home town before a TV camera, and show the video tape at the trial? The judge and jury could not only hear what the witness had to say, but listen to the tone of his voice and observe his behaviours under questioning just as if he were in court — and probably at a fraction of the cost of securing his physical presence.[2]

Now, however, much has changed. The advent of sophisticated computer and telecommunications technology has had a major effect on law office management and administration of justice in our courts. Consider, for example, the views of one American commentator:

The greatest impact of modern technology on law has been in the equipment of law offices and courts and the operational aspects related to equipment Legal "research" (which is the finding of case precedents and statutes, not of empirical data) can now be undertaken through two nationwide data retrieval systems, Lexis and Westlaw, each of which has full text computer storage permitting search inquiries and providing printouts in subscribers' offices through local terminals. Perhaps the most ubiquitous kind of equipment is the electronic photocopying machine, first popularized by Xerox, which has now made carbon paper virtually obsolete (to the immense relief, incidentally, of both secretaries and those who formerly were forced to read carbon copies). Also widespread in both law offices and judicial chambers were word processing systems, which permit lawyers and judges to change and correct a written text up to the moment of final printing (thereby reinforcing the legal propensity to do everything at the last moment). Law office accounting records of time and charges, and many court records, are now commonly maintained on computers. Documents are routinely transmitted from law office to law office and between law offices and clients by telex and telefax (long distance facsimile transmission by telephone connections). In large and complicated lawsuits, documentary evidence and other records are not infrequently indexed, stored and retrieved through computerized litigation support systems.

Telephone conferences between numerous parties in widely separated locations relating to legal problems and litigation are common. It is not uncommon for judges to hold hearings, hear arguments and make rulings on various procedural points by telephone conference calls when the lawyers involved are in different cities or taking depositions away from the seat of the court. By stipulation of the parties or order of the court, depositions may be taken by telephone or recorded by videotape. In a few jurisdictions, entire trials are now being conducted on an experimental basis through the use of previously recorded videotaped testimony. To conserve increasingly costly office space, old records are frequently stored on microfilm. Law books are now available on microfiche; and within a few years will surely be available on compact discs, one of which (less than five inches in diameter) can store the entire contents of a twenty-one volume encyclopedia. Although the general appearance of law offices is not much different today than it has

---

[2] The Toronto Star, 5th June 1975.

492 *The Canadian Legal System*

been, the change in the equipment utilized has been so dramatic that little of the equipment used a decade or two ago would have any utility in a modern law office.[3]

The above author does, however, admit that the impact of technology is only gradually penetrating the foundation of the legal system. As he states:

> In their impact on law, science and technology have changed, and are in the process of revolutionizing the equipment with which lawyers and judges work, and have increasingly provided data, or evidence, on a variety of specific questions. However, they have scarcely touched the foundations of the law, the logic and the thinking habits of lawyers and judges. Science and technology have partially redecorated the house of law, and have changed some of the furniture; but the structure and its foundations remain untouched.[4]

As indicated above, formalized programs of judicial education related to new technologies have been conducted in a substantial way over the past decade. These programs have largely been conducted under the auspices of such organizations as the Canadian Judicial Council, the National Judicial Institute, the Canadian Institute for the Administration of Justice and the Canadian Association of Provincial Court Judges. Often these programs are conducted in conjunction with continuing legal education agencies and university law schools. For example, the National Judicial Institute, the Legal Education Society of Alberta and the University of Alberta recently co-sponsored judicial education programs for judges on the use of computer technology.

One of the applications of computer technology to judging is the utilization of laptop computers by some trial judges in taking notes during the conduct of a trial. For judges that employ this method of note-taking, it has replaced the so-called 'judge's book', the handwritten record of proceedings recorded by a judge during the course of a trial.

---

[3] L. Loevinger, "Science, Technology and Law in Modern Society" (1985), 26 Jurimetrics J. of Law, Science and Technology 1.

[4] *Ibid.* Interestingly, some Canadian judges are now participating in computer literacy courses. One such pioneering course was offered in the Faculty of Law at the University of Alberta in communication with the Canadian Judicial Centre in February 1990. However, since that time, the number of similar courses has increased dramatically. For example, Mr Justice Fleury, Chairman of the Technology Committee of the Ontario Court of Justice (General Division), Chairman of the Computer Advisory Committee to the National Judicial Institute and a member of the Computer Advisory Committee of the Canadian Judicial Council recently stated that: "[j]udges are rapidly embracing computer technology. Hundreds of judges have taken computer instruction and become computer literate". See "Computer Technology Can Help *and* Hinder Efficient Conduct of Court Proceedings", June 18, 1993 Lawyers Weekly, p. 16. In the same article, Mr. Justice Guthrie, member of both the Superior Court on the Automation of Courtrooms and Judges' Chambers and Special Committee of the Quebec Ministry of Justice on the Automated Drafting and Distribution of Judgments, recently remarked that "courtroom use of computers can aid in obtaining an efficient and expeditious trial, but overreliance on computer technology has the potential disaster".

For lawyers, the use of computer technology has caused a major change in the practice of law. Again, there are courses to educate lawyers on the new technologies.[5] There are several kinds of software programs now available for lawyers to assist in the practise of law. Some relate to law office management [6]and some are specialized related to particular areas of the law, such as litigation, real estate, wills and estates and company law.[7]

As to ways in which lawyers use computers, consider the following data. A 1992 survey on the use of computers in the practice of law obtained the following data, in regards to the kinds of uses to which computers were applied:

Word Processing	92%
Accounting	78%
Legal Research	49%
Litigation Support	29%
Corporate Law	29%
Document Management	27%
Real Estate	24%
Document Assembly	22%
Family Law	21%[8]

One of the major uses of computerized technology for lawyers is in the area of legal research. There is a greater discussion of this elsewhere in this chapter. A recent phenomenon relates to lawyers' use of the internationally pervasive Internet. Consider, for example, the following articles on lawyers' use of the Internet: J. Sadler, "Finding the On-Ramp: "Gaining Access to the Electronic Highway" (1994), 19 Can. Law. Libr. 47; G. Medves, "Legal Reference Sources on the Internet" (1994), 19 Can. Law. Libr. 52 and S. Crysler, "Legal Research on the Internet" (1994), 6 Legal Res. Update.

The use of computers in legal education has dramatically increased. Some law schools have used computers to create the so-called 'electronic casebook'.[9]

---

[5] Similar to the courses for judges described above, in Alberta, for example, the Legal Education Society of Alberta, the Law Foundation of Alberta and the University of Alberta have co-sponsored courses for lawyers on the use of computers.

[6] Legal PRO, for example.

[7] Legal Link, for example.

[8] See Price Waterhouse survey in Lawyers Weekly, September 25, 1992 at p. 18.

[9] For example, the Faculty of Law at the University of Alberta has a formal "Electronic Casebook Project". Moreover, to support both the academic and non-academic staff in the conduct of teaching, research and other law school business, the same law school employs two full-time persons (one specializing in instructional technology, the other specializing in administrative computing network and application support) as well as others from time to time. The Faculty of Law at the University of Alberta also occupies a so-called 'web site' on the Internet.

As indicated above, one area of ongoing development is the application of computer technology to legal research. The entire question of electronic legal retrieval systems falls under the general heading of "jurimetrics". In Canada, there have already been some significant developments in the area of jurimetrics. For example, there exists a Jurimetrics Committee of the Canadian Bar Association. The objectives of that Committee are set out as follows:[10]

1. to provide information and advice to the Canadian Bar Executive on questions arising from the Jurimetrics area;

2. to provide exposure for the members of the Association to developments in the Jerimetrics area through presentations at such occasions as the annual meeting;

3. to encourage activities for projects in the Jurimetrics area where deemed appropriate;

4. to maintain close contact with similar organizations in other Bar Associations and with other appropriate groups such as the Computer Law Committee of the Canadian Law Information Council.[11]

Indeed, one of the projects of that Committee was the preparation of a commentary on a report on electronic legal retrieval systems prepared by Professor Philip Slayton for the federal Department of Communications. In that report, Professor Slayton reached the following conclusions:

1. Retrieval systems have been developed with little regard for how lawyers actually think, and to the extent they reflect those processes. They really do so accidentally.

2. Retrieval systems may impose certain alien logical structures on the verbal symbols of law, and thereby affect legal thought and ultimately substantive law.

3. Retrieval systems cannot operate by way of analogy, a key feature of legal thought.

4. Retrieval systems cannot be used satisfactorily to retrieve legal concepts.

5. Retrieval systems (unlike an ordinary library situation) do not allow for random conceptual searching, a creative process meeting a crucial need of both the practising lawyer and the judge.

6. Retrieval systems may accentuate existing social inequalities by providing superior legal information for large firms and government agencies, at the expense of small firms expense of small firms and solo practitioners who normally represent weak clients.

---

[10] The Law Society of Upper Canada established a computer-assisted legal research service in March of 1983, utilizing the "Quic/Law" computer for Canadian cases and statutes and the "Westlaw" system for U.S. materials.

[11] Special Committee on Jurimetrics, Canadian Bar Association, Report to 1974 Mid-winter Meeting, p.1. In the United States, the notion of jurimetrics extends back over a quarter of a century. The leading American periodical is the Jurimetrics Journal of Law, Science and Technology, jointly published by the American Bar Association Section of Science and Technology and the Center for the Study of Law, Science and Technology, Arizona State University College of Law. In 1986, the Jurimetrics Journal established its Annual Greyhound Research Awards program for publications related to law and science. An organization in Canada specifically concerned with technology and the law is the Canadian Society for the Advancement of Legal Technology. That organization, together with the Continuing Legal Education division of the Law Society of Upper Canada, sponsored a conference on "Technology for Lawyers '90" which was held in Toronto in April 1990. For a thorough bibliography on the topic of computers and the law, see M. Felsky (ed.), *The CLIC Bibliography of Computers and Law* 1983-86 (Ottawa Canadian Law Information Council, 1987).

7. Retrieval systems may seriously affect the stability of the doctrine of legal precedent by keeping the information out of the system and by encouraging through information overload rejection of information as the basis for legal thought.

8. Retrieval systems may destroy the ability of judges to make law by imposing a myriad of specific rules and by filling legal *lacunae*.[12]

The application of computer technology to legal research was originally embarked upon in 1968 by the Faculty of Law and the Computing Centre of the University of Montreal in a project known as DATUM. Similarly, in 1969, a joint project was undertaken by Queen's University and the federal Department of Justice known as Quic/Law. Through these pioneering efforts, the notion of computerized legal retrieval systems has advanced from mere concept to a substantial and operational reality. As one writer put it:

> The computer is now the most current source of information, and the legal profession is now not necessarily reliant on the "publishing process" for access to current cases.[13]

Computer retrieval systems have, in fact, developed into major commercial enterprises. In 1973, Quic/Law, mentioned above, evolved into QL Systems Limited and eventually contained a wide range of databases. In 1987, several databases were removed from QL Systems Ltd. and are now available through CAN/LAW. The result is that through QL and CAN/LAW, an individual is able to obtain access to a wide variety of legal literature. For example, he is able to search for reported cases, including Supreme Court of Canada cases handed down just days earlier, federal and provincial statutes, and even periodical literature. Through those systems, he is also able to obtain some access to some U.S. databases. Consider the following commentary:

Moving Towards the Total Electronic Law Library

We have evolved a long way in the past 20 years. The computer is providing the lawyer with efficient access to substantially more information. This is changing, and will continue to change, our whole approach to the storage. Retrieval, and use of legal and non-legal information.

The developments in the next 20 years will be rapid and revolutionary. More and more data will be accessible by computer. Optical character scanners will permit most printed copies to be "read" into the computer. More information will be created at source in machine-readable form CD-ROM technology (compact disks of read-only memory) will permit databases to be attached to powerful microcomputers. Software will encompass expert systems to guide the user through legal topics, retrieve relevant cases, and predict liability.

We are now confronted with the reality that we have too much information to deal with. The computer will become the only means to control the research and information function. Increasingly, this function will become integrated with the writing and

---

[12] *Ibid.*, Appendix 1. See also Appendix 2 for a selected bibliography on "Computer and the Law".

[13] D.S. Marshall, "The History of Computer-Assisted Legal Research in Canada", in J. Fraser (ed.), *Law Libraries in Canada: Essays to honour Diana Priestly* (Toronto: Carswell, 1988), p. 107.

communications function. How quickly this will happen depends on lawyers realizing that the use of microcomputers on their desktops is the only efficient way to integrate these functions and to more profitably practise law.[14]

The importance of computer-assisted legal research is such that some law school curricula now contain courses relating to computers and the law.

Some law schools go further. For example, the Faculty of Law at the University of Alberta has mandatory instruction on the use of computers for legal research as part of its first year curriculum. Moreover, in order to encourage the subsequent use of computers for legal research, the Faculty established a 'microlab' containing some twenty-one computer stations. In addition, one of the more substantial undertakings in Canada is the University of British Columbia Computers and the Law project. Initially, the project developed a database of sentencing decisions but now has expanded into other areas such as the development of "expert systems" databases. Virtually all law libraries contain terminals as part of a nation-wide computerized system.[15]

It has been suggested by Professor Slayton and others that computerized legal research might have the effect of favouring clients of large and established law firms, in that only those law firms will be able to afford the installation of a terminal in their offices. However, given that the price of computer systems has markedly declined in recent years, it is doubtful whether this is any longer a real concern.[16]

In the United States there are several computer systems to assist lawyers in the conduct of legal research. Two major systems are the Lexis System of Mead Data Central and the Westlaw System of West Publishing Company.[17]

The underlying object, of course, in developing computerized legal retrieval systems relates to the recent proliferation of statutory and regulatory enactments at all levels of government, as well as the massive number of cases decided and recorded in the case reports.[18] The obstacles, of course,

---

[14] *Ibid.*, p. 115. See also The Globe & Mail, 23rd October 1989, regarding law firms finally moving into computer technology.

[15] *Ibid.*

[16] See also *infra*, note 12.

[17] For further information see J.J. Galin, *Computers and the law; A Selected Bibliography* (Monticello: Vance Bibliographies, 1985).

[18] An alterative device directed at assisting lawyers in conducting legal research (and particularly directed at lawyers practising alone or in small groups) is the concept of a research service. Services of this nature originally began in the United States, and are developing in Canada. A description of this service is set out as follows in Time Magazine, 16th September 1974:

One way for the small firm to have a fighting chance, at reasonable rates, is to turn

relate to the high cost, as well as the restricted availability, at present, of such systems; however, it is also predictable that, as these systems become more widespread, the cost will fall.

In addition, it is likely that, for purposes of transcribing proceedings of court and administrative tribunals, electronic technology and modern science have much to contribute to the efficient operation of the Canadian legal system.[19] One example of this contribution may be found in the province of Ontario, where the registration of personal property security is conducted on a province-wide computerized basis: see the Personal Property Security Act, R.S.O. 1990, c. P.10.[20]

Some other developments relating to law and technology are as follows. There is now a Canadian Society for the Advancement of Legal Technology. The Society, for example, conducts annual conferences (in conjunction with the Law Society of Upper Canada) on the topic of Technology for Lawyers. Typically, an annual conference will deal with such topics as equipping the home office or the mobile office, confidentiality of electronic legal communications, automated legal aid billing, automated errors and omissions avoidance, marketing techniques, performance management, litigation budgets, etc.[21] The Law Society of Upper Canada also sponsored a recent day long session on Internet for Lawyers[22], as has the Legal

---

a research company manned by lawyers. There is now a handful of these in the U.S. doing legal spade work. The largest and most aggressive is The Research Group Inc., with offices in Cambridge, Mass., Ann Arbor, Mich., and Charlottesville, Va. — all cities with major university law libraries. The Group gears its services to smaller firms, which constitute an important market; about three-quarters of the private attorneys in the U.S. work in offices that have three lawyers or fewer.

The company will prepare basic analyses of statutes and precedents in question, draw up briefs, develop strategy or seek grounds for appeal. It claims to be competent in most legal specialties, from admiralty law to zoning. Relying solely on old-fashioned search and analysis, not computers. The Group charges its customers $17.50 an hour — a bargain compared with the average $40.00 that individual lawyers routinely charge for their own time. The difference can mean substantial savings for the client.

The staff that chums out this cut-rate research consists of 50 lawyers, most of them under 30, and some 150 third-year law student who work part-time.

[19] Indeed, U.S. Supreme Court justices now have and use computer keyboards in their respective offices to assist in the preparation of their opinions. See U.S. News & World Report, 30th October 1978. In the U.S., the American Bar Association Consortium for Professional Education and the A.B.A. Section of Science and Technology have produced a videotape on "Computer-Assisted Legal Research". For a recent discussion on the use of computers in the courtroom in the U.S., see C.J. Postell, "Computers in the Courtroom" (1985), 21 Trial 75. For a further discussion of technology and the Canadian legal system, see the Financial Post, 26th September 1979 and 1st August 1981.

[20] See also similar legislative schemes in other jurisdictions; namely, Alberta — S.A. 1988, c. P-4.05; British Columbia — S.B.C. 1989, c. 36; Manitoba — R.S.M. 1987 c. P35, C.C.S.M. c. P35; Saskatchewan — S.S. 1979-80, P-6.1; Yukon — R.S.Y. 1986, c. 130.

[21] See O.R., December 3, 1993, p. vi O.R., January 6, 1995, p. xiii and O.R., October 27, 1995, p. x.

[22] See O.R., January 6, 1995, p. xii.

Education Society of Alberta.[23] There are many courses and seminars for lawyers and judges in relation to computer technology and some of these are international in scope.[24]

Because of the high cost of computer equipment and the reticence (and time shortage) of some lawyers in taking advantage of the new technologies, various research services/organizations have been established. In fact, one has been established by the Law Society of Upper Canada, itself. [25] Moreover, the same Law Society has created a "Computer Education Facility" (CEF). The facility offers various courses, mostly in Toronto, but elsewhere as well.[26]

For a further discussion of lawyers and the new technology, see The Globe & Mail Report on Lawyers.[27]

The following is a brief bibliography of recent materials relating to the interaction of technology and the law.

"Admissibility and Technology (Canada)". (1989), 47 The Advocate 741.

"An Introduction to Canadian Legal Research". (1989), 81 Law Library J. 465.

Becker, J. "Computer Use by Lawyers to Mushroom in Next 10 Years", (1991), 11:24 Lawyers Weekly 14.

---

[23] See pamphlet "Internet for Lawyers: An Introduction". A Joint Program of the legal Education Society of Alberta and the Faculty of Law, University of Alberta.

[24] For example, in 1995, the City of Montreal hosted an international conference on computers and law; primarily organized by L'Association pour le développement de l'informatique, juridiques (ADY, France) with the co-operation of several agencies, including the Société québecoise d'information juridique (SOQUU).

[25] In fact, the Society provides two such services; namely, search — Law and Ontario Reports Database.

[26] The Law Society of Upper Canada is a leader in recognizing the importance of lawyer adaption to new technologies. In addition to the services and course delivery referred to above, consider the June, 1993 (vol. 2, No. 4) edition of the Adviser (a publication of the Society's Practice Advisory Service). That publication, under the title, "Ignoring law firm automation not an option", emphasized the importance of changing attitudes, outlined the value of computers to legal practitioners and provided some advice concerning the implementation of new technology. As mentioned earlier, The Law Society of Upper Canada and The Canadian Society for the Advancement of Legal Technology jointly sponsor, on an annual basis, a Technology for Lawyers conference. The most recent conference was titled, "Doing Law in '95 on the Computing SuperHighway". The Canadian Bar Association in Ontario (The Middlesex Law Association) recently held seminars on "The Computer and the Solicitor: Going On-Line Today: Business, Real Property and Estates." See O.R., October 27, 1985, p. xxi. In addition, the Canadian Bar Association has recently established a Civil System of Justice National Task Force and one of the issues addressed by that Task Force relates to "Technology and Modernization of the Civil Justice System".

[27] July 25, 1995. See also the editorial entitled "The Pluses and Minuses of Legal Technology", Canadian Lawyer, April, 1995.

Blackwell, G. "CD-ROMs Part 1: Do-It-Yourself". (1994), 18 Can. Lawyer 8:29.

Blackwell, G. "Focus on Computers". (1994), 18 Can. Lawyer 4:32.

Blackwell, G. "On-Line Research." (1994), 18 Can. Lawyer 7:28.

Blenkin, J.A.C. & R.T. Franson, *Searching Canadian Law Online: A Beginner's Guide* (Vancouver: Continuing Legal Education Society of British Columbia, 1991).

Brockhouse, G. "Focus on Computers". (1993), 17 Can. Lawyer 4:32.

Brooks, M.S. *Computerizing for Personal Productivity: A Guide for the High Performance Lawyer* (Toronto: Butterworths, 1989).

Chan, L. "A Survey of Computers in the Law Office: What's Happening, What's Next?". 12:20 September 25, 1991 at p. 18.

Chasse, K. "Computer Searching Will Become More Important than Manual Searching". (1991), 4 Legal Research Update No. 1,7.

Cohen, M.L. "Research in Changing World of Law and Technology". (1990), 13 Dalhousie L.J. 5.

Computers for Lawyers (Edmonton: Legal Education Society of Alberta, 1994).

Crysler, S. "Legal Research on the Internet". (1994), 6 Legal Research Update No. 1, 7.

Denton, V. "Online Legal Research Resources". (1994), 4 Can Corp Counsel 10.

"Down the Ringing Grooves of Change". (1988), 37 Buffalo L. Rev. 671.

Eisen, L.S. *Technology in Practice*, 2nd ed. (Toronto: Carswell, 1991).

Eisen, L.S. "Technology in the Law Office: How B.C. Measures Up". (1992), 50 Advocate 517.

Eisen, L.S. "Motivational Aspects of Lawyers Using Computers". (1992), 2 L.M.J. 9.

Electronic Legal Information: Exploring Access Issues (Ottawa: CLIC, 1991).

" 'Expert' Systems to Give Out Legal Advice in Law Firms of the Future?" 11:24 Lawyers Weekly, October 25, 1991, p. 24.

Fleury, C. *Distribution of Information: How to Select the Appropriate Technology* (Ottawa: Canada Communications Group, 1993).

Foti, K.E.H. *Access to Statutes: Opening the Doors of Justice* (Ottawa: Canadian Legal Information Centre, 1991).

Franson, R.T. *Electronic Distribution of Judgements* (Ottawa: Legal Information Centre, 1990).

Gertner, E. "Computerized Legal Data Bases: The Thrill is Gone". (1991), 4 Legal Research Update No. 1,4.

Gulej, J. "Can you Bring Your Laptop or Notebook Computer to Court?" 12:20 Lawyers Weekly, September 25, 1991, at p. 12.

Huculac, L.M. *Practicing Law With Computers* (Edmonton: Department of Justice, 1989).

Livingstone, S. & J. Morrison (ed.). *Law, Society and Change* (Dartmouth: Aldershot, Harts, 1990).

Lodge, J. *Computerized Litigation Support* (Sydney: The Federation Press, 1990).

Medves, G. "Legal Reference Sources on the Internet". (1994), 19 Can. Law Libr. 52.

Morgan, K. *The Law Library and the New Technologies: An Assessment* (Edmonton: Alberta Attorney-General, 1989).

"New Ontario Court Computer System Will Eliminate Wasted Time, Delay?" 11:02 Lawyers Weekly, May 10, 1991, p. 7.

Paliwala, Al. *Information Technology in Legal Education: A Resource Book* (Coventry: CTI Law Technology Centre, University of Warwick, 1991).

Peritt, H.H., Jr. *How to Practice Law With Computers*, 2nd ed. (New York: Practicing Law Institute, 1992).

"Profile of the online law firm". (1989), 75 A.B.A.J. 514(3).

Ray, R. "Computerized Law". (1993), 2 National No. 7, 28.

Sadler, J. "Finding the On-Ramp: Gaining Access to the Electronic Highway". (1994), 19 Can. Law Libr. 47.

Smith, S.B. "An Introduction to Legal Technology". (1993), 10 Solicitors J. No.1, 1.

Storozuk, M. *et al The Lawyer's Guide to the Online Galaxy: Legal Research and Communications Using Computers* (Edmonton: Legal Education Society of Alberta. 1991).

"The unfulfilled promise: use of computers by and for legislators". (1989), 9 Computer L.J. 73.

Vale, M. "Information Sources in Legal Research". (1993), 31 Alta. L.Rev. 334.

Wessel, Milton R. "What is law, science and technology anyway?" (1989), 29 Jurimetrics J. of law, Science and Technology 259.

"WESTLAW'S DISCourse: pilot program passes test — site trial". (1989), 81 Law Library J. 505.

Wright, B. "Paperless Contracts: Taming the Skeptics". (1991), 8 Bus. & L. 92.

THE LEGAL PROFESSION: PUBLIC IMAGE[28]
AND PUBLIC ACCOUNTABILITY

It is axiomatic and often said that the law belongs to all members of society, not only to lawyers and judges.[29] However, this notion has attracted little more than lip service until recently. Both the legal profession and members of the public at large have come to accept that we all share a proprietary interest in the law and in the legal process. As a result, courses in law for laypersons are now being taught in many institutions, and books and pamphlets designed for laypersons on particular areas of the law are being widely disseminated in order to educate members of the general public in respect of their rights and duties under the law. In fact, the teaching of law has now extended into the high schools, and courses in specialized areas of the law are being offered for members of the business community through university departments of extension or continuing education.

Some other instances of educational programs designed for the general public are as follows. First, an organization known as the "Toronto Community Law School" (and there are other similar organizations in major cities throughout Canada), has offered courses in the law of real estate transactions, income tax law, mental health law, small claims court procedure, consumer protection law, marriage and divorce law, criminal law, municipal law, and wills.

Similarly, law students at the University of Toronto established a few years ago what is referred to as "Lawline". Essentially, this service provides free legal advice in the areas of consumer law and landlord and tenant law, and it offers assistance to those persons engaged in disputes with

---

[28] For a detailed discussion of the issue of "Public Perceptions of the Administration of Justice", see the papers delivered at the annual conference of the Canadian Institute for the Administration of Justice held October 11-4, 1995 in Banff, Alberta. These papers include: Martinson, Judge D.J., "Some Thoughts on Public Perceptions of the Role of Judges in the Administration of Justice in Canada"; Sims, A.C.L., and A. de Villars Jones, "The Administration of Justice Response to Public Perception: An Administrative Lawyer's Perspective"; Gormley, J.K., "Public Perceptions of Parole"; Doob, A.N., "Criminal Justice Reform in a Hostile Climate"; Byfield, L., "Remarks on Public Perceptions about the Administration of Justice for the Canadian Institute for the Administration of Justice"; Baird, I.J.H., "Public Perceptions of Actors in the Justice System: A Defence Lawyer's View"; Martin, P., Q.C., "Sentencing — Principles, Pitfalls and Bill C-41"; Viau, L., "Victimes des ambitions royales"; Sirois, A., "De la décision en matière de jeunes contrevenants", and Michaud, P.A., Juge en chef, "L'Administration de la justice: La perception du public". See also, Fulford, R., "Considering the public perceptions of justice", The Globe & Mail, October 18, 1995; Saunders, D., "Revolt aimed at judges, laws nears Canada", The Globe & Mail, October 18, 1995; and Livesey, B., "The Tarnished Image: Why do lawyers have such a bad image?" Canadian Lawyer, February 1995, p. 16.

[29] For a greater public awareness, the Canadian Bar Association now annually conducts "Law Day", during which, in each province, the C.B.A. sets up panels and other information-disseminating formats for the general public. This includes, for example, open house at the court house in some provinces.

government agencies. This project is especially directed at those Toronto residents who cannot speak the English language. Similarly, the Law Society of Upper Canada, together with the Ontario Branch of the Canadian Bar Association, established a similar service called "Dial-a-Law": see Communique, 25th February 1983. Dial-a-Law originally operated on a 24-hour-a-day basis in conjunction with the Law Society's Lawyer Referral Service.

Generally speaking, there are an ever-increasing number of similar projects throughout Canada. These educational and assistance programs are to a large extent designed to assist those persons who cannot afford to retain the services of lawyers and who are not eligible to receive legal aid. In addition, many persons are simply eager to learn about various areas of the law. One can easily find in many bookstores "do-it-yourself" or "self-help" books on various areas of the law. There are, of course, some obvious dangers in assuming that one is able to attack a legal problem without the professional advice of a trained lawyer.[30] However, the popularity of these volumes is well established and suggests, at the very least, that there is a need for a wider dissemination of legal advice among the general public.

In summary, members of the public have demanded a greater understanding of the law.[31] People have come to realize that a knowledge of the law is consistent with responsible citizenship, and that an awareness of the law is vital in confronting the complex issues arising daily in business and in personal life.

It is likely that historians will look at the mid-1960'5 as marking the onset of what might be described as the "consumer era". One can, for example, point to Ralph Nader's work in the United States, the development of consumer protection associations throughout the North American continent and the enactment of consumer protection legislation at all levels of government. Consumerism has, in addition, spread to the professions. As a result, members of society regard themselves as consumers of professional services and in turn, the professions must now, of necessity, regard themselves as accountable to the consumers that they serve. Even

---

[30] See an interesting article entitled "When to Take the Law into Your Own Hand's", Money Magazine, March 1975, p.59.

[31] For a complete review of this subject see Friedland, *Access to the Law* (Toronto: Carswell/Methuen, 1975). One phenomenon relates to the establishment of interprovincial branch law offices. This may not be significant to the general public — it is a phenomenon having to do with the major, corporate-oriented law firms. In fact, it led to one of the first cases litigated under the mobility rights section of the Charter of Rights, *Black v. Law Soc. of Alta.,* [1989] 1 S.C.R. 591, [1989] 4 W.W.R. 1, 66 Alta. L.R. (2d) 97, 37 Admin. L.R. 161, 38 C.R.R. 193, 58 D.L.R. (4th) 317, 96 A.R. 352, 93 N.R. 266. For further information concerning the concept of interprovincial and international law firms, see the earlier discussions in Chapter 9. See also Clarry, "Inter-Provincial Law Firms" (1982), 16 L.S.U.C. Gazette 266.

though the profession of law is a self-governing profession, it is necessary that an element of accountability be included within the boundaries of self-government. This has led to lay representation on the governing bodies of some provincial law societies. For example, in Ontario there is provision for the appointment of four lay members to the governing body or "benchers" of the Law Society of Upper Canada. These four benchers serve, not only on the governing body of that law society, but also on many of the committees of the benchers. Some provincial law societies do not have lay benchers, but it is predictable that as consumerism develops further, the notion of lay representation in the decision-making process of provincial law societies will become widespread across Canada.

The public image of the legal profession is, unfortunately, not always a positive one.[32] A 1988 survey showed that "although lawyers are hated as a breed . . . they are surprisingly well-liked as individuals". That survey was conducted by Professor William Bogart of the University of Windsor and Professor Neil Vidmar of the University of Western Ontario. According to the study, people who "have dealt with individual lawyers . . . maintain a collective image of lawyers as evil people" but, because "they have been well-served", they liked their lawyers "as individuals".[33] In any event, the group image of lawyers is generally negative. There are many possible reasons for this. One can point to the two greatest impediments to access to the legal system — delay and cost. Because of the lack of expedition, some persons prefer to turn to alternative dispute resolving mechanisms.[34] However, within the formal legal system, there have been some significant developments recently that are aimed at achieving greater expedition in the resolution of cases. They are as follows:[35]

(a) The Pre-Trial

The pre-trial is a semi-formal hearing that is held in advance of the formal trial. The pre-trial occurs in both criminal and civil trials. It is mandated by the Criminal Code (for jury trials) and permitted in some other instances (for long trials, for example) by practice notes and rules of court, depending upon the province. In civil cases, the pre-trial is also mandated by practice notes and rules of court. The purpose of the pre-trial in criminal cases is to narrow or focus the issues that will emerge at trial. In a sense, it also is a form of discovery. The

---

[32] See, A. Fotheringham, Maclean's Magazine, December 6, 1994; K.E. Howie, "Lawyers Under Fire" (1991), 25 Gazette 164; and "Lawyer 'Arrogance' is Top Public Complaint: McLachlin" (1992), 11:48 Lawyers Weekly 6.

[33] See The Globe & Mail, 21st June 1988.

[34] This is discussed at length in Chapter 6.

[35] In addition to these devices, see the Arbitration Act, 1991, S.O. under which parties in a civil case can "design their own procedures or follow those outlined in the legislation": see the National, May, 1991.

purpose of the pre-trial in civil cases is the same, although it also serves the additional purpose of encouraging settlement. The judge who conducts the pre-trial is always different from the judge who conducts the actual trial.

(b) The Mini-Trial[36]

The mini-trial occurs in civil cases only. In effect, it is a non-binding, truncated version of the actual trial. It gives the lawyers and the parties an opportunity to assess their own case and the case of their opponents, again with a view to a possible settlement. As such, it affords a speedier and cost-efficient method of resolving a case, without having to go to a slow, expensive trial process. As with the pre-trial, the mini-trial is conducted by a judge other than the judge who might eventually conduct the actual trial.[37]

(c) Case Management

Case management is a process or system in which cases are streamlined. With the assistance of computers, judges take a managerial role in addition to their strict judicial responsibilities. Cases are rigidly scheduled with time lines drawn at the outset with respect to each stage of a given case. Although some U.S. courts have already taken this approach for about 20 years, Canadian courts have only adopted this system since 1990. In some provinces, case management has become an institutionalized feature of the civil court system [38]while in others it is still in an experimental stage through the conduct of various pilot projects.[39]

With respect to the cost of justice, there is a feeling shared by at least some consumers of legal services that lawyers are excessively compensated for the work that they do.[40] It flows from this that many persons are not able to afford the services of lawyers. One development which is directed at alleviating this concern is the growth of legal aid.

Legal aid is operated under differing authorities, varying from province to province. In some provinces, legal aid is run by the provincial govern-

---

[36] See Moore, The Hon. W.K., "Mini-Trials in Alberta". (1995), 34 Alta. L. Rev. 194.

[37] For an excellent discussion of the mini-trial in the province of Alberta, see the Edmonton Journal, July 17, 1995.

[38] The province of Alberta, for example.

[39] The province of Ontario, for example. See The Globe & Mail, February 28, 1995.

[40] Fee schedules have, in fact, been the subject of legal challenge. For example, in one case, two Ontario county law associations were prohibited by a court "from setting fee schedules or from even discussing the subject in committee for at least 10 years without prior approval by Ottawa". This arose as a result of a prosecution under the Competition Act. See the Montreal Gazette, 12th January 1988. For an interesting article on the setting of fees in the province of Ontario, see the Toronto Star, 19th October 1987.

ment while in others it is run either by the provincial law society or by the provincial law society in association with the provincial government. In yet other provinces, it is operated by special provincial societies mandated by statute for that purpose.[41]

The funding of legal aid also varies from province to province; it is funded in some provinces by direct government grants for that purpose and, in others, by provincial law foundations. Provincial law foundations receive their moneys from the interest earned on lawyers' trust accounts.

In general, legal aid is available only to those persons who are unable to afford to retain their own lawyers. The recipients of legal aid must first establish, to the satisfaction of the appropriate officials, that they are in need of financial assistance. Secondly, the particular matter for which they are seeking legal advice and assistance must be a matter covered by the particular legal aid plan. If these two preconditions are satisfied, the recipient will be granted a legal aid certificate and will then be able to pick the lawyer of his choice for the required advice. In some cases, legal aid may offer only partial assistance, depending upon the financial ability of the recipient to bear at least part of the costs of legal services rendered.

As the availability of and the conditions for the granting of legal aid vary from province to province, Canada's legal aid system has been described as a "patchwork quilt". For a recent review of that "quilt", see M. Kideckel, "Legal Aid: The State of the Union", (1988), 12 Can. Lawyer 14.

As stated above, only certain items are covered by a given legal aid plan. As a result, there are those who cannot afford a lawyer, yet cannot obtain legal aid for reason that the matter for which they are seeking assistance is not covered by the particular legal aid plan. A recent development directed at remedying this situation is the creation, at various law schools across Canada, of legal aid societies.[42] These organizations provide student legal

---

[41] For a more detailed discussion of legal aid, see, for example, D.L. Carlson, "The Legal Aid Lineup; Canada: Delivery in Dispute" (1993), 17 Can. Lawyer 3:19; M.J.Mossman, "Towards a Comprehensive Legal Aid Program in Canada: Exploring the Issues" (1993), 4 Windsor Rev. L. & Social Issues 1: J. Robarts, "The Ontario Legal Aid Plan" (1991), 25 Gazette 244; J. Middlemiss, "Legal Aid" (1994), 3 National No. 6, 22; *Solicitor and Client Fees — Legal Aid Society of Alberta*. Edmonton: The Society 1980, "Legal aid: A view from the 38th floor" (1987), 8 Quarterly (C.L.S.) 3; and "Legal Aid: A Fresh Approach to an old idea" (1987), 8 Quarterly (C.L.S.) 10.

[42] For a discussion of alternative legal service delivery systems, see T. Onyshko, "Secret Paper Shows Public Defender System Considered" (1991), 11: 31 Lawyers Weekly 9; "Report Urges Wide Changes to Legal Aid" (1992), 11:40 Lawyers Weekly 15; M. Blazer, "The Community Legal Clinic Movement in Ontario: Practice and Theory, Means and Ends" (1991), 7 J.L. & Social Pol'y 49; E. Blankenburg (ed.), *Innovations in the Legal Services* (Cambridge, Mass.: Oelgeshlager, Gunn and Hain, 1980), and G. Rivard, *Telephone Legal Information Services: Review and Current Issues* (Ottawa: Canadian Law Information Council, 1982).

services. In some law schools, student legal services are integrated into the curriculum as part of a clinical program. The first, and the largest of such organizations, is the Parkdale Community Legal Services, operated under the auspices of Osgoode Hall Law School of York University in Toronto. Consider the following remarks made by the director of Parkdale Community Legal Services:

> On March 14, 1975, the report of the Government-appointed Task Force on Legal Aid (the Osler Report) was published. It unanimously recommended a substantial expansion in the scope of legal aid and the adoption of new techniques of delivering legal aid services aimed at making these services truly accessible to all, including immigrants.
>
> The report points out that the total annual expenditure on legal aid by the province amounts to about half of the annual operating budget of one of the large community colleges — an expenditure, the report suggests, that is no longer an adequate reflection of the priority which the province ought to give to ensuring access of less fortunate members of other society to courts and tribunals . . .
>
> And the limitations in the success of the Ontario Legal Aid Plan in meeting the needs of the community for financially assisted legal services is not the fault of the Legal Aid Plan administrators or the Law Society, as public criticism tends to suggest.
>
> The administrators of the Ontario Legal Aid Plan have been remarkably successful in making free or financially assisted legal services available, having regard to limitations imposed by the legislation by which they are controlled. That legislation was modern when it was first proposed by the Law Society in 1965-66 but is inadequacies in the light of the growth in the need for assisted legal assistance since that time were apparent several years ago.
>
> This reluctance to pay the price for the handmaidens and machinery of law enforcement is particularly difficult to understand when one considers the extent to which this society has embraced law itself as the ultimate magic.
>
> We live in a society which is inundated with legislation-created law. To an extent never before envisaged in a democratic society, there is no social or economic activity, or indeed any aspect of our life, that is not shaped and coloured and in the end defined by legislation.
>
> There is, apparently, no social problem that cannot be solved by some carefully drafted legislation.
>
> The man who cannot afford legal assistance, whose legal rights in years gone by might fairly be said to have consisted mainly of defences — against the police, Crown, landlord — is now the beneficiary of innumerable legislated benefits and rights.
>
> He has pension benefits, medical benefits, hospital benefits, welfare benefits, workmen's compensation benefits, employment benefits and unemployment benefits. He has rights against his landlord and his used-car dealer. He has the right not to be discriminated against (the Human Rights Code, Employment Standards Act, Labor Relations Act, etc.), nor to be taken advantage of (credit and consumer protection legislation) and he has the right to insist that all of the tribunals and agencies administering those new benefits treat him fairly and with justice . . .
>
> And yet it is self-evident that rights and benefits that cannot be enforced are worse than useless. Robert F. Kennedy, speaking at the University of Chicago Law School in 1964 on the subject of poverty law, made the point that "University of Chicago Law School in 1964 unknown, unavailable right are no rights at all."
>
> It is apparent that known but unenforceable rights are worse than no rights at all. They are a trap and a delusion and a source of socially destructive bitterness and frustration.[43]

---

[43] These remarks were made by Professor S.R. Ellis, in an article contained in The Toronto Globe & Mail, 28th June 1975.

One outgrowth arising from the development of legal aid is the concept of duty counsel. Duty counsel, essentially, is a lawyer retained by legal aid for the purpose of representing persons appearing in court who are not otherwise represented by a lawyer. In the province of Ontario, duty counsel now provides representation in respect of involuntary admissions to mental facilities. Moreover, a former director of Ontario's legal aid plan was appointed in the early 1980's to head a team of full-time duty counsel to serve in the provincial courts at City Hall in Toronto. This appointment arose out of the deliberations of a committee of the Law Society of Upper Canada, which noted that the present system of duty counsel involved a lack of continuity and supervision among the lawyers acting as duty counsel, and suggested that many lawyers acting as duty counsel were inexperienced and rather uninterested in the area of criminal law. As a result, the concept of a permanent staff acting as duty counsel was initiated, on an experimental basis, on 1st April 1977.[44] The result of this experiment was that the services of duty counsel are now being administered in some jurisdictions by lawyers who, after a time, become professionally experienced in this area.[45] Accordingly, those persons not represented by their own lawyers will ultimately receive better service.[46] Some provinces, such as Saskatchewan, have adopted a public defender system. The province of Alberta has implemented a similar system, on a 3-year trial basis, with respect to juvenile proceedings. Whether staffed by a permanent staff or the private bar, the concept of duty counsel, as part of a legal aid plan, is now entrenched.[47]

An issue somewhat related to legal aid is that of prepaid legal insurance. This has not until recently been promoted in Canada to any considerable extent; however, there is a movement now in that direction. For example, the Quebec Branch of the Canadian Bar Association proposed, a few years ago, a prepaid legal insurance scheme for middle income earners; it was suggested at that time that an annual premium in the vicinity of $ 100 to $ 150 would be appropriate. The Bank of Nova Scotia and Allstate Insurance Co. Canada have recently established a legal insurance plan for the Bank's customers. Under the plan, legal advice is available on a 24 hour a day basis.[48] Another recent plan is that offered by Cana-

---

[44] See The Toronto Globe & Mail, 19th January 1977.

[45] This is akin to the development of what is known in the United States as the public defender system Saskatchewan is one province that has developed full-time duty counsel.

[46] A related phenomenon, in the United States, is the establishment of the so-called "public interest" law firms. These firms are primarily concerned with public issues. For example, in New York there is a women's rights law clinic. For further details on the development of those public-interest law firms, see the New York Times, 27th April 1980.

[47] "Hotline to Duty Counsel: Who Benefits?" (1994), 5 J.M.V.L. 309.

[48] See the Edmonton Journal, July 12, 1995.

dian Legal Shield Corporation in Ontario, British Columbia and Alberta.[49] The proponents of the proposed plan pointed to similar programs now in operation in some of the American states.[50] For a recent discussion of prepaid insurance programs, see T. Onyshko, "Ontario Considering Public Pre-Paid Legal Insurance" (1991), 11:21 Lawyers Weekly 3 and M. Cardwell, "Legal Insurance in Big Demand from Quebec Consumers" (1994), 13:48 Lawyers Weekly.

At the centre of issues such as legal aid and prepaid insurance is the fact that lawyers generally command a high fee for their services. This is not to say, of course, that the fee, in most circumstances, is unjustified. In fact, a lawyer usually performs a sophisticated service, having the ability to do so only after years of rigorous training and experience. Nonetheless, the high price of layering and the need for legal aid and prepaid insurance plans all suggest that there is a problem relating to the unavailability of legal services for many persons in society.[51] Even middle income earners are not hesitating to challenge the high price of legal services. For example, many clients are exercising their rights to tax their lawyers' bills before a taxing master or other appropriate official.[52] Lawyers, like all

---

[49] See the Edmonton Journal, May 23, 1995.

[50] As a result of a recent congressional amendment to the Taft-Hartley Act, both labour and management can now contribute to legal insurance funds. The result is, according to a former chief counsel of the House Special Subcommittee on Labor, "prepaid legal services will now be in the mainstream of collective bargaining", so that according to legal experts, in the next few years 70 per cent of all Americans and 50 per cent of all lawyers will be involved in group insurance plans: see Time Magazine, 23rd September 1974. See also W. Pfennigstorf and S.L. Kimball, *Research Contribution of The American Bar Foundation 1981, No. 2: A Proposed Act to Regulate Legal Expense Insurance* (Chicago: American Bar Foundation, 1981); *8th Annual Conference on Prepaid Legal Services Program and Materials* (Chicago: American Prepaid Legal Services Institute, 1980); "Prepaid Legal Services: The Blue Cross/Blue Shield of the Legal Profession" (1989), 3 Georgetown J. of Ethics 201; "Prepaid Legal Services' (1989), 30 Law Office Economics and Management 189. Again, for a further discussion of this issue, see Chapter 9, *supra*.

[51] One way of addressing the problem of availability appears to lie, in part, in placing law offices in commonly travelled public places. For example, in British Columbia, several operations, each designated as "The Law Office" are located at various Sears stores. Similarly, in Edmonton, at one time there was a law office located at the Hudson's Bay store.

[52] In addition, as a result of the enactment of comprehensive amendments to the Combines Investigation Act (now the Competition Act R.S.C. 1985, c. C-34) in 1975 (see S.C. 1974-75-76, c. 76), there is now new regulation of fee setting practices by local bar associations. Similarly, in the United States, in a recent decision of the Supreme Court of the United States, it was held that bar associations which set mandatory billing fees are subject to the provisions of the Sherman Anti-trust Act. For a description of the background of that decision, see Newsweek Magazine, 30th June 1975. On the issue of fees generally, see R.A. Aronson. *Attorney-Client Fee Arrangements: Regulation and Review* (Washington: Federal Judicial Centre, 1980); L.M. Fox, "Costs in Public Interest Litigation (Canada)" (1989), 10 Advocates 'Q. 385; "A Public Goods Approach to Calculating Reasonable Fees under Attorney Fee Shifting Statutes", [1989] Duke L.J. 438; "Yes: Commission to improve the availability of legal services — mandatory pro bono" (1989), 75 A.B.A.J. 52(1); and "Time and/or money: to buy out of their pro bono obligations?" (1989), 22 Clearinghouse Review 950.

professionals, have come to realize that clients are consumers of their services, and, in an age of 'consumer rights', they must respond to the needs of those who use their services.[53] Recently, legal aid programs have suffered from fiscal restraints. In some provinces, lawyers must pay surcharges to fund legal aid. In some jurisdictions, normal legal aid tariff fees must automatically be reduced by a certain percentage. In other provinces, the provincial law foundation must dedicate a portion of its revenue to fund legal aid.[54]

In Ontario, there is close to a crisis with legal aid. The legal aid plan is operating at a large deficit and the Law Society of Upper Canada (which administers the legal aid plan) must find ways of reducing or eliminating the deficit. In short, the Attorney-General "has invited the law society to to re-engineer the system to find the most effective management model".[55] Moreover, there is a risk that if the Law Society does not succeed, the government will assume the administration of the plan.[56] Many lawyers rely heavily on legal aid to earn their livelihood and therefore fear that cutbacks will seriously harm them and their low income clients.[57] Some lawyers have even considered "job action".[58] Following considerable debate and controversy, the Law Society decided to maintain the legal aid plan, but in order to satisfy the government's concern, it agreed "to drastically slash the number of people eligible for legal aid and to cut fees to lawyers". It also "defeated a proposal to hand over the staggering legal-aid plan to the province".[59] Earlier, the Law Society decided to launch an action against the Government of Ontario, arguing that the government had a "legal obligation to ensure payment within a reasonable time

---

[53] Lockeyer, "The Roles and Responsibilities of the Legal Profession in Further Access to Justice" (1992), 12 Windsor Y.B. Access Just. 356 and J.C. Major, "Lawyers' Obligation to Provide Legal Services" (1994), 28 Gazette 101.

[54] Law foundations are themselves funded by interest on lawyers' trust accounts. With this dedication of a portion of its revenue to legal aid and with lower interest rates generally, provincial law foundations are now less able to fund other projects that, in the past, would likely have received funding.

[55] See The Globe & Mail, August 28, 1995.

[56] *Supra.*

[57] *Supra*, fn. 55.

[58] *Supra*, n. 55. See also The Globe & Mail editorial, August 26, 1995. For a comprehensive examination of legal aid in the province of Ontario, see the Legal Aid Bulletin, published monthly by the Law Society of Upper Canada.

[59] See Makin, K. "Law Society keeps legal aid plan", The Globe & Mail, November 25, 1995. See also The Globe & Mail, November 23, 1995; Makin, K. "Funding woes put legal aid on trial", The Globe & Mail, November 14, 1995; Strigberger, M. "Legal aid, Ontario-style", The Edmonton Journal, November 14, 1995; October 30, 1995; The Edmonton Journal, October 29, 1995; The Globe & Mail, October 27, 1995; and The Globe & Mail, September 19, 1995.

for lawyers who have rendered accounts. . .''.[60] Moreover, a group of 82 lawyers asked the Ontario Court of Justice for a declaration "that the government and law society are breaching their statutory duties to properly fund the legal-aid plan.[61] These matters were scheduled to be heard by the Court in December of 1995.

There can be no doubt that the public perception of the legal profession includes the notion that lawyers are expensive. In a study conducted by the Contemporary Research Centre of Toronto, prepared for the Ontario Task Force on Legal Aid, it was discovered that three-quarters of the persons living in Ontario, over the age of sixteen, think that lawyers are too expensive.[62] Accordingly, if lawyers are to remedy this somewhat negative aspect of their professional image, an expansion of legal aid, the development of prepaid legal insurance schemes, and other measures will be necessary.

One other measure, often suggested, is the notion that fees would be lowered if lawyers were allowed to advertise their services.[63] There exists presently, across Canada, some dwindling ethical prohibitions against advertising by lawyers. The suggestion traditionally was, quite simply, that if lawyers were allowed to advertise freely, this would have the effect of lowering their fees through greater competition at the market place. Consider, for example, the following comments made by New York Times columnist William Safire:

> The services for which doctors and lawyers charge fees is a "market"; when medical or bar associations deny other qualified practitioners of the services entry to that market by means of advertising, that is a monopoly practice.
>
> Because the barriers set up by professional associations against advertising so obviously restrain trade, Joseph Sims. of the anti-trust division of the U.S. department of justice, recently suggested to the New York State Bar Association, that it consider modifying in canon of ethics: "Perhaps the rule should be worded so as to prohibit only that type of solicitation which is false, misleading, undignified or champertous." . . . The professions will one day be considering the how, and not the if, of advertising. Never, say never, such a flat statement is out of place in the field of anti-trust.[64]

---

[60] See The Law Society of Upper Canada Bencher's Bulletin, October 1995. See also Bencher's Bulletin, September 1995.

[61] See The Globe & Mail, November 23, 1995.

[62] Recently, the issue arose in several provinces as to whether law firms should be permitted to accept credit cards in payment of their professional fees. The question, essentially, relates to whether such a practice would be in the nature of unprofessional conduct. In this connection, there was no uniformity of opinion among the various provincial law societies.

[63] See J. Marlane, "Respicis, aspicis, prospicis: lawyer advertising on television" (1989), 12 Trial Diplomacy J. 151; T.L. Lee, *How to Market and Advertise Your Law Practice* (Aurora: Canada Law Book, 1987); M.J. Trebilcock and J. Yale, *Service Advertising in the Market for Legal Services* (Toronto: Professional Organizations Committee, Minister of Attorney General of Ontario, 1978); and Highlights of the Gallup Study of Attitudes to Lawyers and Lawyers' Advertising (Canadian Gallup Poll Ltd.. 1978).

[64] Edmonton Journal, 9th September 1974.

Michigan became the first state in the United States to permit lawyers to advertise their fees and other information concerning themselves. As a result of changes to Michigan's Code of Professional Responsibility, approved by the Michigan Supreme Court, lawyers were permitted to list fees and other information in the yellow pages of the local telephone directory. Also, as a result of a suit launched by the United States Justice Department against the American Bar Association, alleging that the American Bar Association's ban on advertising constituted a restraint of competition, many states altered the then existing rules banning advertising by lawyers. As a result of the above suit, the American Bar Association amended its Code of Ethics in order to allow for fee advertising in the yellow pages.[65] If one examines a typical wide-circulation U.S. newspaper, one sees in it many advertisements for lawyers. As a result of the *Jabour* case,[66] one sees the same phenomenon in Canada, although Canadian ads are still less flamboyant than those in U.S. newspapers. Although this is so, one does, in fact, see bench advertisements for law firms at bus stops in metropolitan Toronto. The *Jabour* case and advertising by lawyers generally is discussed in Chapter 9.

A LIFETIME OF EDUCATION

The process of legal education is discussed at some length in Chapter 9 but for our present purposes a brief review of some current developments is appropriate. One recent change in respect of the training of lawyers is that native and mature persons, owing to affirmative action programs in some law schools, now have a greater opportunity than ever before to enter the legal profession, and presumably with respect to native persons, to serve their own, previously unserviced, communities.[67] Also, it is encouraging to note the substantially greater number of women now

---

[65] See The Toronto Globe & Mail, 18th January 1977. See also V. Alboini, "A Lawyer's Limited Practice in Ontario — The Time for more Appropriate Recognition" (1976), 10 Law Society Gazette 154, and the reports appearing in the January and February 1977 editions of the National, published by the Canadian Bar Association. In addition see "Let Lawyers Advertise?", U.S. News & World Report, 28th February 1977.

[66] *Canada (A.G.) v. Law Society of (B.C.); Jabour v. Law Soc. of B.C.,* [1982] 2 S.C.R. 307, [1982] 5 W.W.R. 289, 37 B.C.L.R. 145, 19 B.L.R. 234, 137 D.L.R. (3d) 1, 66 C.P.R. (2d) 1, 43 N.R. 451.

[67] See M.D. Lepofsky, "Disabled Persons and Canadian Law Schools: The Right to the Equal Benefit of the Law School" (1991), 36 McGill L.J. 636; Special Advisory Committee to the Canadian Association of Law Teachers, "Equality in Legal Education: Sharing a Vision, Creating the Pathways" (1992), 17 Queen's L.J. 174; P.A. Monture, "Now that the Door is Open: First Nations and the Law School Experience" (1990), 15 Queen's L.J. 179; and B. Lively, "Learning Blocks: Aboriginals and Law School" (1994), 18 Can. Lawyer No. 9, 26; "Minorities and the legal profession" (1987), 12 Thurgood Marshall L. Rev. 299 and 359.

entering the legal profession. At present, approximately 50 per cent of the population of a typical law school class is female.

Another current phenomenon in legal education is the large number of persons desiring to enter the legal profession. This is reflected not only in the number of applications to all of the law schools across Canada, but also in the competitive job market, both in obtaining articles of clerkship following graduation from the law schools and in obtaining employment after being called to the bar.[68]

Consider, for example, the process in obtaining articles of clerkship. Over the years, law firms have begun to interview students earlier and earlier during the students' legal education, with the result that some law societies have attempted to regulate the process. These law societies have established so-called 'matching' services to alleviate this concern. However, from the students' point of view, many feel an obligation to study subject areas that make them more attractive to prospective employers, which, to some extent, has the effect of limiting their perspective. Consider the following initiative, described in a recent article, that attempts to address the above phenomena:

> The annual mating dance of the lawyers is under way — but the partners are changing.
>
> The ritual envelops Canadian law schools for one feverish week each year, as law students and law firms grapple for the best match of talents they can get.
>
> But one aspect of the mating ritual is increasingly troubling law schools, students and many law firms: The keen competition for talent has reached back from third-year to second-year students. Some firms even make overtures to first-year students.
>
> As a result students are being thrust into the world of litigation and commercial minutiae before they can get a taste of other areas of law.
>
> So this year, professors at the University of Toronto law school have persuaded 14 of Toronto's most prestigious law firms to help broaden the students' experience — by providing free legal research for public-interest groups.
>
> The firms will pay the way for the students of their choice to work with advocacy groups such as Amnesty International and the Aids Committee of Toronto.
>
> The professors behind the program said they hope it will spread to other law schools, permitting cash-strapped groups to benefit at the same time as it expands the horizons of future lawyers[69]

One result of the growing number of new lawyers is the number of law school graduates now engaging in various different capacities of legal work and indeed entering into other fields.[70] A lawyer can act as an advisor

---

[68] Peter Hoffman, in collaboration with the Placement Office of McGill University Faculty of Law, has prepared *Career Handbook for Law Students 1990* (Toronto: Carswell, 1990), to provide law student with information on the Bar Courses and Admissions programs in Canada and the U.S. and on obtaining articles of clerkship.

[69] The Globe & Mail, 17th February 1990. See also the Edmonton Journal, 19th February 1990.

[70] See Peter F. Hoffman, *Career Handbook for Law Students 1990* (Toronto: Carswell, 1990), and "Have Degree Will Travel", Time Magazine, 11th December 1989.

to the government, conduct legal research on behalf of the government, act as counsel to the government in litigation, or assist in the drafting of legislation. He may act as counsel for the corporation or work in a corporation's legal department or use his law degree as an adjunct to his business activities for a company. He may decide to enter the teaching or legal publishing professions; or he may combine a law career with another profession. For example, there are many persons in Canada who hold both law and medical degrees, and these persons often act as coroners or engage in advisory work for the government or for private industry in connection with medico-legal matters.

Also as a result of the increasing number of persons entering the legal profession, there is tremendous competition among graduates to obtain positions to serve their articles of clerkship. [71]Since the articling requirement is mandatory in order to be called to the bar and since, in some provinces (Alberta, for example), one is not eligible to enrol in the entire bar admission course unless one secures employment as an articling student, it becomes crucial for the new graduate to find an articling position. As a result, an increasing number of students take articling positions without pay in order to satisfy the above requirements.[72] Even if a new graduate successfully secures and completes articles of clerkship, there is no guarantee that a law firm will invite the new lawyer to stay on as an associate lawyer with the firm.[73] Many new lawyers are moving to smaller urban as well as rural communities to service previously underserviced areas. Some new lawyers are devoting a substantial portion of their practice to work under the various provincial legal aid plans. Others are entering into alternative modes of practice, such as "storefront" operations, and there is, for example, an organization known as the Law Union, which consists of several lawyers possessing a common ideology. Those lawyers are particularly interested in certain areas of the law, such as landlord and tenant and immigration law.

The training of lawyers itself is presently the subject of much change. Under existing curricula, many law schools offer such educational opportunities as clinical legal services, a wide range of optional courses, and opportunities for specialization in given areas of the law. In addition, there

---

[71] See Lynn Marchildon, "Articling job shortage requires creative approach", The Lawyers Weekly 15:17 (Sept. 5, 1995) p.10 and Howard Burshtein, "Stiff competition for fewer positions means little choice", The Lawyers Weekly, 15:17 (Sept. 8, 1995) p. 10.

[72] T. Onyshko, "Unpaid Jobs Help Ont. Grads Complete Articling Requirements" (1993) 13:20 Lawyers Weekly 3 and T. Onyshko, "Unpaid Articling Jobs are Unconscionable?" (1993) 13:21 Lawyers Weekly 2.

[73] See Jordan Furlong, "Not hired back? Take advantage of breathing space to evaluate options", The Lawyers Weekly, 15:17 (Sept. 8, 1995) p. 7.

have been other proposals for reform. For example, in Ontario, as a result of the report of the MacKinnon Committee,[74] there was considerable debate as to whether the requirement that law school graduates serve one year under articles of clerkship should be removed. However, the Committee's recommendation to dispense with the articling requirement was dropped. In addition, also in Ontario, a review was conducted by the Law Society of Upper Canada in connection with a substantial restructuring of the bar admission course in that province. That eventually led to a restructuring of Ontario's Bar Admission Course. As of the spring of 1990, students graduating from law school participate in a bar admission course consisting of three phases: one month of Law Society instruction prior to the commencement of articles, one year of articles of clerkship, and a further three months of Law Society instruction thereafter. These changes follow the recommendations of the Bar Admission Reform Sub-Committee (Spence Report) of the Legal Education Committee of the Law Society of Upper Canada. Other provinces also conducted similar reviews.[75] That program is now being reviewed. The Law Society of Upper Canada recently created a Bar Admission Course Review Subcommittee. The Subcommittee reported to a meeting of Convocation (i.e., the Benchers or directors of the Law Society sitting as a committee of the whole) on April 28, 1995 where the Report of the Subcommittee was approved "for the purpose of consultation with profession, law schools, students and other interested persons".[76] The Report makes the following recommendations:

1. It is recommended that the Law Society affirm its continuing obligation, enunciated in the Law Society Role Statement, to ensure that newly called lawyers attain a level of competence required to serve the public effectively.
2. It is recommended that the Law Society and the six Ontario law schools collaborate more effectively to enhance the continuum in legal education, and that to this end the Law Society and the law schools work together to develop and strengthen an ongoing effective partnership in legal education.
4. It is recommended that the Bar Admission Course continue teaching and testing lawyering skills.
5. It is recommended that the Bar Admission Course continue teaching and testing the "how-to" of lawyer practice, and in particular that it do so through a transactional approach to education.
6. It is recommended that the students be required to pass licensing examinations, skills assessments, and other tests of their entry-level lawyering competence, including their

---

[74] The Special Committee on Legal Education of the Law Society of Upper Canada. See also the Report of the Special Committee on Legal Education conducted by the Honourable Mr. Justice Roy J. Matas at the request of the Law Society of Manitoba and the Faculty of Law, University of Manitoba, 1979. See also the Report of the Task Force on Access to Professions and Trades in Ontario (Ontario Ministry of Citizenship, 1989).

[75] In addition, the National Committee on Legal Education commenced, in the Fall of 1989, a project styled "A coordinated curriculum — Teaching Professional Responsibility Across the Continuum of Legal Education".

[76] See Bar Admission Course Review Subcommittee Report, April 28, 1995, The Law Society of Upper Canada.

knowledge of substantive law and procedure in core subjects, but that the Bar Admission Course not focus on teaching substantive law and the procedure in the classroom.

7. It is recommended that the articling program be continued, as an important practical component in legal education.

8. It is recommended that a mandatory mentoring program be implemented for newly called lawyers.

9. It is recommended that a co-ordinated curriculum of continuing education courses be implemented to permit newly called lawyers to meet their particular needs, enhance their competence, and adapt to the rapidly changing practice of law.

10. It is recommended that the Law Society design and implement the model of Bar Admission Course described [at a later stage of the Report].

11. It is recommended that the Bar Admission Course Review Subcommittee carry on its work to further refine the proposed model of Bar Admission Course and deal with a number of significant issues.

The proposal for a new model for the Ontario bar admission course is summarized as follows[77]:

1. Teaching Term: 8 weeks

   (a) Professional Responsibility
   (b) Practice Management and Loss Prevention
   (c) Practice Skills
   (d) Solicitor Transaction
   (e) Barrister Transaction

2. Articling and Licensing Examination Term: 12 months

   (a) Articling
   (b) Licensing Examinations

3. Call and Post-Call

   (a) Call to the Bar
   (b) Mandatory two-year Mentoring Program
   (c) Continuing Legal Education[78]

The proposed implementation schedule for the new program is set out below:

1995-1996   Law school students advised of changes to the Bar Admission Course for purposes of law school course selection.

1996   Spence [i.e., existing] model continues: last offering of Phase 1, penultimate offering of Phase 3.

1997   Law school graduates begin new teaching program in May.
Final offering of Phase 3 in September-December.
Licensing examinations for new Course to begin.

---

[77] See *supra*, note 69; O.R., August 11, 1995, cover; and O.R., August 18, 1995, p. iv. Interestingly, the Law Society recently established a special bursary fund to assist lawyers who are unable to afford the cost of continuing legal education. Similarly, the Legal Education Society of Alberta has instituted a program of reduced registration fees for those unable to pay the cost of its programs.

[78] The Law Society of Upper Canada has established a Mandatory Continuing Legal Education Subcommittee. That Subcommittee is currently studying the advisability of establishing a program of mandatory continuing legal education. See *supra*, note 69 and O.R., Aug. 18, 1995, p. iv.

1998   Call to the Bar for first students in new Course.[79]

Some of the key issues the Subcommittee faced in making the new proposal related to whether the Bar Admission course teach substantive law as well as practical lawyering skills, what kind of examination system should be employed at each stage of the Bar Admission Course and what post-call to the bar requirements should exist.

Other jurisdictions have gone through a similar process. In Alberta, for example, a new re-designed bar admission course was established after the so-called Thrasher Report of 1992.[80] The Law Society of Alberta and the Legal Education Society of Alberta (which conducts and administers the bar admission course on behalf of the Law Society) have had to deal with similar issues as those facing the Ontario Subcommittee. Recently, the Legal Education Society has created a Bar Admission Course Advisory Committee as a first step in an upcoming review process in connection with the re-designed bar admission course.[81]

In addition, two provincial law societies, in Ontario and Alberta, have issued reports recommending the adoption of the notion of accredited specialization in certain areas of the law. For example, in Ontario, the initial proposal was as follows :

a plan allowing lawyers to advertise their competence in a specific field of law has been endorsed by the governing body of the Law Society of Upper Canada

It would be the first time such advertising has been allowed in Canada. To qualify, lawyers would be required to show that they have practised in a particular field of law for a set period of time — perhaps three to five years.

To maintain their accreditation, lawyers would be required to take a refresher course sponsored by the law society once every two years following accreditation.[82]

What has, in fact, evolved, in Ontario, is the establishment by the Law Society of Upper Canada of a Certification Program administered by a Certification Board. That Board is mandated to oversee the certification of specialists. At present, members of the Law Society may apply for certification in the fields of civil litigation, criminal litigation, or the combined areas of civil and criminal litigation. In order to be eligible for such a certification, members must fulfill the following requirements:

---

[79] *Supra*, note 69. It appears likely that the proposed schedule of implementation will be delayed.

[80] Legal Education Society of Alberta, Report of the Bar Admission Course Review Committee, June 1991.

[81] The Law Society in Nova Scotia is about to implement twelve mandatory, substantive entrance examinations as part of the bar admission course. While the course, like most bar admission courses in Canada, emphasizes skills training, these examinations are based upon the substance of the law and must be passed as an entrance requirement of the bar admission course.

[82] The Toronto Globe & Mail, 22nd February 1977.

In addition to full-time practice in Ontario for a minimum of seven years, applicants will be expected to establish that they have devoted a minimum of 50% of their professional time in recent years to the area of law in which certification is sought. They must satisfy the Specialty Committee to which application is made that they have acquired a thorough knowledge of the procedures and substantive law in their area of practice, that they participate in continuing legal education programs and that they are regarded by their peers as professionals who maintain a high standard of practice in their fields.

Once certified, members will be permitted to advertise themselves as specialists in their areas of practice.

Certificates of specialty, have currency for a period of five years after which they lapse and must be renewed upon further application. Applications for re-certification shall be governed by the same standards then applicable for the initial certification[83]

In addition, the number of areas of specialty is about to be expanded. Consider the following Notice to the Profession:

Standards for the certification of specialists in Family Law were approved by Convocation in October, 1989, and Family Law practitioners will be entitled to apply for certification in that specialty in the near future. Further details of the application process for Family Law will be published in the Ontario Reports in due course.

Finally, the Certification Board is planning to expand the program to include other areas of specialty. In particular, the Board is considering the establishment of Specialty Committees in the following areas of practice:

- Immigration Law
- Intellectual Property Law
- Bankruptcy and Insolvency Law
- Taxation Law
- Wills
- Estate Planning Law
- Worker's Compensation Law
- Administrative Law
- Labour Law
- Environmental Law
- Entertainment Law
- Real Estate Law
- Defamation Law[84]

The number of lawyers thus far in Ontario applying for certification as specialists originally was relatively small. However, in the years since the inception of the Specialist Certification Program, the number of specialists has significantly increased, especially in the area of civil litigation.

In Alberta the certification program is somewhat different. In that province, the initial certification program permitted a lawyer to designate "preferred areas of practice". Now, however, a lawyer may designate that his or her practice is "restricted to "no more than two areas of speciality, although any designation as a "specialist", as such, may not be used in any advertising. A lawyer may, however, advertise that his or her practice is restricted to designated areas. Moreover, if a lawyer does choose to designate his or her practice as "restricted to" no more than two areas of speciality, the lawyer is then not permitted to practice in any other areas. As in Ontario, very few lawyers in Alberta have availed themselves of this opportunity.

---

[83] 71 O.R. (2d) Pt. 1, p.xx, 23rd February 1990.
[84] *Ibid*.

Finally, irrespective of the mode of practice or the nature of work in which a lawyer is engaged, all lawyers must undertake continuing legal education throughout their professional lives. This is facilitated by attendance at seminars and conferences, the regular utilization of up-to-date publications, audio-visual aids, etc. Although continuing legal education is voluntary at present, it is becoming a mandatory requirement for continuing certification.[85]

ALTERNATIVE CAREERS FOR LAWYERS

The subject of 'Careers Open to Lawyers' was discussed in Chapter 9 and earlier in this chapter. The diverse opportunities available to those with legal training has always, to some extent, been the case. But now, with probably an oversupply of law graduates (necessitating some graduates to find novel means of using their training) together with dramatic changes in society, lawyers are finding new and different ways of utilizing their training. They are being assisted by so-called alternative career seminars. For example, the Law Society of Upper Canada (in Ontario) and the Women's Law Forum of the Faculty of Law at the University of Alberta have each conducted seminars of this nature.

Changes in the law and changes in society have each contributed to new opportunities for lawyers. For example, many lawyers have found their niche in the area of informational technology. Some have taken advantage of trade developments.[86] Some law firms now have full-time research departments with lawyers engaged solely in a research capacity. Some large law firms have a lawyer who is responsible for the continuing legal education of the other lawyers in the firm. That lawyer is usually designated as the firm's 'Director of Professional Development'. There are also many persons who engage in neither traditional nor innovative

---

[85] See earlier reference to the Law Society of Upper Canada Mandatory Continuing Legal Education Subcommittee. See also *Legal Education and Professional Development — An Educational Continuum Report of the Task Force on Law Schools and the Profession: Narrowing the Gap, 1992* (The MacCrate Report) and N. Gold, "Reconceiving Professional Competence" (1992), 10 *J. Prof. Legal Education* 135. On related issues, see A.A. Porro, Jr. *Sao Paulo Conference on the Law of the World — Report of the Committee on Cooperation with Lawyers on Continuing Legal Education of the World Association of Law Professors* (Washington: World Peace Through Law Centre, 1981); *Report of the Special Committee on Legal Education* (Toronto: The Law Society of Upper Canada, 1972); R.F. Devlin, "Legal Education 213; W.H. Hurlburt (ed.), *The Legal Profession and Quality of Service: Further Report and Proposals* (Edmonton: Federation of Law Societies of Canada, 1981); and F.-X Fibordy et al., *Access to Justice: Legal Education and Information Exploratory Study — Research Reports on Public Legal Education and Information, Report No. 2* (Ottawa: Department of Justice, Communications and Public Affairs, 1985).

[86] See, for example, A. Szweras, "NAFTA and the Legal Profession", Canadian Lawyer, January, 1995. Indeed, many law firms operate internationally, with many having offices in the Far East.

kinds of practice. They simply do other things.[87] Their jobs range from operating an airline to running a cookie franchise. Although they don't practice law in the traditional sense, their legal education probably played a significant role in contributing toward their subsequent success.

Lawyers have also had to adapt to changing economic and social circumstances. Law firms have to accommodate the needs, for example, of lawyers with young children through, for instance, job sharing and part-time employment arrangements. As mentioned earlier, some graduates have difficulty in seeking articles of clerkship. This may be a function of the oversupply of lawyers or the inability of some law firms, due to economic circumstances, to hire articling students. In an attempt to address these concerns, the Law Society of Upper Canada's Legal Education Committee recently announced various acceptable alternatives to the traditional 12 month articling period. For example, there is the possibility of 'joint articles' where a student works with one principal for a certain number of months and with another principal for the balance of the year. Or, it is possible that a student might work with one principal all year on a two day per week basis and another principal all year on a three day per week basis. There is also the possibility of 'part-time' articles where the equivalent of a 12 month period is spread, on a part-time basis, over a prolonged period of up to a maximum of three years. The Law Society also suggested the possibility of a greater number of non-traditional placements and the possibility of some persons of less than three years standing at the bar serving as principals to articling students.[88]

The legal system, like all facets of modern society, must accommodate the needs of those that it serves. In particular, our courts have to take into account the needs of those challenged by disability, age, etc. For an interesting discussion on "Advancing the case for elder justice", see The Globe & Mail, May 22, 1995.

LEGAL AGENTS

Because of the high cost of formal legal representation, some persons have turned to so-called 'legal agents' to provide the needed legal services. Legal agents ought to be distinguished from legal assistants. The term

---

[87] See J. Mucalov, "Alternatives ot Law Practice", National, August-September, 1995.

[88] See O.R., July 14, 1995, p. viii. Ironically, this suggestion from the Legal Education Committee comes at about the same time that another committee of the Law Society has recommended strengthening the bar admission requirements. In particular, as discussed earlier in this chapter, a subcommittee recommended a two-year mentor program following a lawyer's call to the bar. If both of the above changes occur, it might lead to the odd situation where a mentor guides and oversees the work of a lawyer who, at the same time, guides and oversees the work of an articling student.

paralegal[89] has traditionally meant what is now referred to as a legal assistant, although occasionally the term is used (incorrectly) to connote a legal agent. A legal assistant is usually formally trained, belongs to a parent organization (in Alberta, for example, the Alberta Association of Legal Assistants) and works in a law firm assisting the lawyer in the performance of legal services. The various law societies recognize the legitimacy of these support personnel.

On the other hand, a legal agent neither works with a lawyer nor within a law firm. The legal agent is an individual who performs services akin to some of the services provided by lawyers. The legal agent is limited as to the kinds of services that may be provided and if the agent exceeds these limits, the legal agent can be charged with practicing law without being authorized to do so under the enabling provincial statute. The question becomes one of determining what is a legal service that may be performed only by a lawyer and what is a legal service that may be performed by either a lawyer or a legal agent.[90] Some examples of services offered by legal agents, according to some of the advertisements appearing in the telephone directory (i.e., 'Yellow Pages') include traffic violations, pardons, family matters including uncontested divorces, incorporations, some criminal matters and civil claims.[91] Recent television advertisements suggest other services such as social service, unemployment insurance and workers' compensation board appeals, mediation, and matters under child welfare legislation. Obviously, there are some aspects of the above matters that may be performed by either lawyers or legal agents whereas other aspects of the same matters may only be performed by lawyers. In their advertisements, legal agents often emphasize the high cost and unaffordability of lawyers as a major incentive in seeking their services. Whether they are or are not considered legitimate in the eyes of the legal profession, and whether they, in fact, compete with or complement the services provided by lawyers, legal agents, nonetheless, represent a part, even if peripheral, of our legal system.[92]

---

[89] For detailed reference sources relating to the role of paraprofessionals in the legal system, including the work and training of paralegals, see fn 1 in Chapter 9.

[90] See *R. v. Laurie & Pointts Ltd.* (1987), 59 O.R. (2d) 161, 48 M.V.R. 189, 19 O.A.C. 81, 32 C.C.C. (3d) 549 (C.A.) and *Nixon v. Newfoundland (sub nom. Nixon v. R.)* (1993), 106 Nfld. & P.E.I.R. 91n, 334 A.P.R. 91n, 152 N.R. 240n, *(sub nom. Law Society (Newfoundland v. Nixon)* 99 D.L.R. (4th) vii (note) (S.C.C.). Several statutes actually refer to representation by agents. See, for example, sections 800 and 802 of the Criminal Code. In Alberta, see s. 74(i) of the Provincial Court Act (R.S.A. 1980, c. L-P-20), s. 103 of the Legal Profession Act (R.S.A. 1980, c. L-9) and s. 5.4 in part 1.1 of the Alberta Rules of Court.

[91] See 1995 EdTel Directory, pp.1096-1097.

[92] See the Edmonton Journal, May 23 1995 and June 12, 1995.

LAW REFORM

One of the most provocative and perplexing questions relates to the adaptability of the law in response to changing social conditions.[93] One of the ways that the law has responded to changing social conditions is the development of the concept of permanent law reform commissions at all levels of government. Virtually every province in Canada has a law reform commission, although not all provinces call them by that name. In addition, the Law Reform Commission of Canada, prior to its abolition in 1992, conducted work in respect of those matters which are, constitutionally, within federal jurisdiction. The elimination of the Law Reform Commission of Canada was effected as a result of expenditure reduction in the 1992 federal budget.[94] However, the Government of Canada has recently announced its intention to reinstate a new Law Reform Commission of Canada.[95] These law reform bodies, in the usual case, are mandated by statute[96] to conduct research, with a view to subsequent reform of the law, in those areas falling within their respective constitutional jurisdictions. After proposals for legislative reform are formulated, they are forwarded, in the first instance, to the Attorney General of the province or, in the case of the Law Reform Commission of Canada, to the Minister of Justice. Often, the proposals for reform are then referred to the whole of the cabinet for consideration, and ultimately, if approved, to the legislative body for enactment.

The usual manner in which a law reform commission operates is as follows. This description is, of course, an oversimplification of the process of law reform, and it obviously differs significantly from province to province. Upon the request of government (or, in respect of some law reform commissions, upon the request of members of the legal profession, members of the legislature, other interested parties or at their own instance), research is conducted in a particular area of the law. A project is usually led by a full-time member of the law reform body, although outside consultants and advisors are significantly utilized. The initial research usually gives rise to a research paper which is then refined and altered in form. This produces a working paper or a memorandum for discussion which

---

[93] See W. Friedmann, *Law in a Changing Society*, 2nd ed. (New York: Columbia University Press, 1972).

[94] C. Schmitz, "Lawyers Outraged by Law Reform Commission Abolition" (1992), 11:42 Lawyers Weekly 20.

[95] *Creating a New Law Reform Commission of Canada: A Consultation Paper* (Ottawa: Department of Justice Canada, 1994). In this regard, a bill was tabled in the House of Commons in October of 1995. See The Globe & Mail, October 6, 1995.

[96] In the case of the province of Alberta, however, the Institute of Law Research and Reform was established under an agreement between the University of Alberta, the Department of the Attorney General and the Law Society of Alberta.

essentially, is in the nature of a white paper for consideration and review by members of the public and the legal profession.

A final report is then prepared, reflecting the various submissions received in response to the working paper or memorandum for discussion.

When a given matter is finally referred to the cabinet, it is sometimes accompanied by draft legislation. The cabinet can act upon it, modify it or reject it.[97]

Generally speaking, at the provincial level, the reports of the various law reform commissions have led to considerable legislation. Unfortunately, however, at the federal level, there has been, to date, little legislative action taken in respect of the various recommendations made by the Law Reform Commission of Canada. The reason for this, probably, is that the federal proposals for reform are of a more controversial nature, whereas provincial proposals are usually of little controversy because they are in the nature of a modification of what might be referred to as "lawyer's law", i.e., those issues of law which are highly technical in nature.

There are various ancillary benefits arising out of the work conducted by law reform commissions, aside from their primary achievements in conducting a reform of the law. For example, the reports of the various law reform commissions represent an important contribution to the literature in the areas being researched. Often, these reports contain a comprehensive, well-researched and well-prepared review of the law in a particular area. This review is often of invaluable assistance to both teachers and students of the law, as well as to practising members of the legal profes-

---

[97] The Director of the Alberta Institute of Law Research and Reform describes the process of law reform in Alberta in this way:

> The process starts with research by the Institute staff or by consultants. It involves consultation with lawyers and other professionals, experts in various disciplines, and groups affected by a particular law.
>
> The Institute then considers the issues involved and issues a report, usually with draft legislation attached.
>
> It sends its reports to the Attorney General and to any other minister concerned with the subject matter. It also makes its reports public and sends them to those who express interest in them.
>
> It is, of course, for the government and the Legislature to decide whether or not to act upon the Institute's recommendations, but they have so far been receptive to them.
>
> The Institute chooses its own reform projects, though with due regard to the suggestions of the government and the Legislature. Its choices are governed by its capabilities, by the apparent need for reform, and by the desirability of maintaining a balance between reforms which primarily involve technical law and reforms which more clearly involve social policy.

See W.H. Hurlburt, "Institute of Law Research and Reform — A Report", [1978] Without Prejudice 10.

sion.[98] Secondly, various projects and experiments are conducted which, in themselves, are valuable. For example, in connection with a criminal law project conducted for the Law Reform Commission of Canada, the Borough of East York in the Municipality of Metropolitan Toronto altered the usual procedures followed in the course of criminal justice investigation. The normal policing practices were preempted in order to permit the employment of an alternative way of enforcement and remediation. These experimental projects conducted by law reform commissions often lead to the formulation of new concepts. For example, the concept of "diversion", in the area of criminal law, arose in part out of the above research and experimental work conducted by the Law Reform Commission of Canada. Accordingly, aside from the primary function of the reform of the law, there are many additional benefits that arise out of the process of law reform.[99]

The concept of a law reform commission is not unique to Canada. In fact, it is fairly widespread now throughout the whole of the common law world. Along these lines, for a definitive description and analysis of law reform commissions in the United Kingdom, Australia and Canada, see W.H. Hurlburt, *Law Reform Commissions in the United Kingdom, Australia and Canada* (Edmonton: Juriliber, 1986). Among other things, this work contains an excellent bibliography relating to law reform commissions in those jurisdictions.

Consider the following remarks delivered by Mr. Justice Patrick Hartt, a former chairman of the Law Reform Commission of Canada, to the Convocation of the Law Society of Upper Canada, held on 20th March 1975:

We decided to seek reform of the law through public persuasion rather than resort immediately to Parliamentary amendment. This decision was made with the confidence that the

---

[98] Two examples of this are as follows. First, a national publication of the Canadian Bar Association often contains excerpts from reports of the Law Reform Commission of Canada. It is hoped that this will arouse interest among the members of the profession and that, consequentially, there will be greater reaction, in the form of submissions, in response to the particular report set out. However, as an ancillary benefit, no doubt many lawyers use these excerpts for purposes of an up-to-date review of law in a particular area. Secondly, Dean Martin Freidland of the University of Toronto recently conducted research for the Law Reform Commission of Canada the result of which was later published in the form of a treatise entitled *Access to the Law*. That treatise represents a major contribution to the literature for it contains the results of his research, underscores the importance of access to the law for members of the public at large, and contains recommendations which, if adopted, might ultimately serve that end.

[99] For a more detailed review of the process of law reform see W.F. Bowkey, "Organized Law Reform in Alberta" (1969). 19 U.T.L.J. 376; Paul Thomas, "The Manitoba Law Reform Commission: A Critical Evaluation" (1975), 2 Dalhousie L.J. 417; and J.N. Lyon, "Law Reform Needs Reform" (1974), 12 Osgoode Hall L.J. 421. See also "Barristers and Solicitors: Prospects for the Lawyer as a Reformer" (1976), 15 U.W.O.L. Rev. 59.

concept of law could be redefined in a non-positive, value-laden way, and the citizens of Canada could be persuaded to actually participate in its reformulation.

This decision of the Commission has been criticized as being idealistic and unrealistic. It might well be expecting a lot, but in a pluralistic, truly democratic society, nothing less will suffice. In these turbulent times, the rule of law may be a very fragile thing, but we must never let ourselves forget that the alternatives to it are a series of profoundly unpleasant options. And if increased public involvement is the only way that a rule of law can be maintained, and in my opinion it is, then surely we would be very foolish indeed not to try. Otherwise, we shall have no choice but to live, or possibly die, with the consequences. What we are really talking about is a society in which the citizens are not simply joined collectively together by the threat of coercive state, but rather one in which they are united from within themselves, by agreement on core values and a shared desire to secure their common goals. This should be carried out within a supportive community that would develop an environment leaving everyone as free as possible to reach their maximum potential as human and spiritual beings, free for each to find his own centre.

As temporary members of a non-elected commission, it is certainly not our task to impose our views and values on the public. In the first instance, it is our responsibility to provide accurate, understandable information and clearly articulate realistic alternatives. By so doing, the public is reminded and made aware of the values which they actually hold, or "ought to hold" if they are to be consistent to a particular view of society. In addition, the implications of the holding of certain values become apparent.

But, in my personal opinion, the Commission ought to go further and actually assert what, in their opinion, are the values which should constitute the law's substance. Being only an advisory body, their views can, of course, be accepted or rejected. It then remains for the law to be brought into better alignment with the accepted values. In short, there is a role to be played in assisting the public to put morality back firmly into the centre of the law . . .

We must discover and develop new unifying principles capable of giving a general orientation to a fragmented society, and the law and its processes must be directed primarily to compatible goals of synthesis and reconciliation. No society or community can exist unless a significant number of people can agree upon, or at least tacitly accept a basic value structure.

Above all, we cannot look to legislative enactment alone to save us. Only laws rooted in popular sentiment can be enforced. Laws violating this sentiment merely arouse resentment. If our sentiments are superior, we will have superior laws. In the end, good men and women will support only those undertakings which they feel instinctively to be just. If our instincts are civilized, we will have civilized laws. Law reform cannot be better or worse than the society which generates it. In the end, I am satisfied we get what we really deserve.[100]

In addition, consider the following remarks on law reform, in general:

Reforming laws mean more than changing them; it means improving them. The two don't always go together. Cromwell's Parliament once passed an act outlawing Christmas — a change admittedly, but was it an improvement? Was the new law a true reflection of the social need?

. . . Alteration of law for alteration's sake was not enough: new laws must truly reflect society's needs and constitute some genuine progress. But how can we be sure of making real progress . . .

Before knowing where to go we must be quite clear where we stand; before knowing what alterations to make to our law, we need to understand all aspects of the legal situation — not only what the law prescribes but also what its purpose is, how it operates, which is the best way of altering it, and, last but not least, how far alteration will make

---

[100] Law Reform Through Consciousness-Raising" (1975), 9 Law Soc. Gazette 132.

any difference. This raises questions about the very nature of law reform itself, on which we have begun a fundamental jurisprudential investigation.

The usual coming of departure for law reformers has been the letter of the law. Sometime, indeed the actual working of the law can be the major problem. Laws suffering from what Bentham termed "overbulkiness", from ambiguity or from sheer obscurity impose too great a strain on courts and lawyers, but worse still, fail to provide satisfactory rules and guidelines for society.

Often, however, the letter of the law isn't the main problem. The rules, themselves, not just their wording, may need change. Official practice — the operation of the rules — may need to alter. The values which those rules enshrine may be untenable or no longer be the values of the society those rules serve. Or again, the rules themselves may be misunderstood.[101]

There are those, however, who are critical of the various reports issued by the Law Reform Commission of Canada, and indeed one critic, a former president of the Canadian Association of Police Chiefs, made these remarks:

[The Law Reform Commission of Canada has outlived its usefulness and should be dissolved immediately . . . the Commission's latest recommendation to abolish sentences of life imprisonment for those convicted of rape or manslaughter is intolerable.] The working paper reflect the thinking of an academic, social reformist without any real appreciation of the impact of such implementation . . . The law reform commission might do well to consider that there are also recidivists, too much crime and too many victims.[102]

Just as our courts and legislatures are institutions within the Canadian legal system, permanent law reform commissions have also become institutions within that system.[103] The process of institutionalized law reform represents a vital opportunity for the law to be adaptable to changing social conditions:

Law reform is like a never-ending relay race. As soon as one objectionable law is dealt with another takes its place. Just as the price of freedom is eternal vigilance, so the price of justice is eternal effort. The law reformer's race is never over. One lap complete, the next begins.[104]

One dramatic change in our law, in recent years, might be described as a move towards a liberalization in the law. Perhaps "liberalization" is the improper term; this development might be considered rather as a fundamental change in the relationship between the individual and the law.

On one hand, it can be argued that virtually every area of human affairs and human concern is controlled and regulated by law. On the other hand, there is current evidence to suggest that the law is abandoning certain areas

---

[101] Law Reform Commission of Canada, Third Annual Report, 1974.

[102] The Globe & Mail, 25th June 1975.

[103] See J.F. Handler. *Social Movements and the Legal System: A Theory of Law Reform and Social Change.* (New York: Academic Press, 1978); and "Is it time to reform the reforms?" (1989), 4 Notre Dame J. of Law, Ethics and Public Policy 63. See also W. Freidmann, *Law in a Changing Society*, 2nd ed. (New York: Columbia University Press, 1972).

[104] Law Reform Commission of Canada Fifth Annual Report, 1976.

in which it previously exercised control. For example, it is no longer an offence in Canada to attempt to commit suicide. As well, there are other amendments to the Criminal Code which implement the government's view as of 1968 "that the government has no place in the bedrooms of the nation".

The counter argument to this suggestion of "liberalization" is in the area of economic regulation, where it appears that the law has entered some fields which were previously unoccupied. One can easily point to several examples, such as the program of selective mandatory wage and price controls in the mid-1970's, the enactment of foreign investment review legislation, the recent and prospective comprehensive amendments to our anti-combines legislation, major revisions in our income tax law, and many others. In other words, one could argue that in the matter of economic regulation, the law has developed in such a way as to exercise an unprecedented domain over individual and corporate affairs.

This phenomenon, however, has abated somewhat as a result of the combined effects of deregulation and privatization and, arguably, it will continue to do so in future as a result of the Canada-U.S. Free Trade Agreement. On the other hand, in the area of personal morality, such as the matters raised above, as well as in connection with changes proposed by some in the areas of obscenity, abortion, possession and trafficking of "soft" drugs, etc., the law has abandoned this field to the dictates of individual morality. And where the law has not abandoned this field to individual morality, the courts, to a significant extent, are doing so through the application of the Canadian Charter of Rights and Freedoms.

The law, generally speaking, has drifted toward liberalization in a second sense. There are legislative developments which suggest that the law has become, essentially, more humanitarian. For example, virtually every province has anti-discrimination legislation and, since 1977, there has been federal legislation in the same field.[105] In addition, the Canadian Bill of Rights was enacted in 1960. Although in the past the Bill of Rights did not have a particularly significant impact, it is enjoying new life in the Charter era.[106] If any instrument suggests a drift toward "liberalization" in the "humanitarian" sense, it would have to be the Canadian Charter of Rights and Freedoms. Only future historians and lawyers will be able to judge, ultimately, what long range effect our entrenched constitutional Charter will have.[107] In addition, as indicated in the preceding chapter,

---

[105] See the Canadian Human Rights Act, R.S.C. 1985, c. H-6.

[106] See the discussion of the Canadian Bill of Rights set out in Chapter 5.

[107] Obviously, from the cases during the first thirteen years of its history, the Charter is having a major effect. See the discussion of the Canadian Charter of Rights and Freedoms set out in Chapter 5.

there is now federal (and some provincial) legislation providing for freedom of information and for privacy.[108] Virtually every province has a legislative ombudsman and there were proposals for a federal ombudsman.[109] One might also conclude that the abolition of capital punishment was consistent with this trend.

CONCLUSION

Broadly defined, the role of law is to ensure that the affairs of all persons in society are conducted in an orderly manner and in accordance with particular social objectives.[110] The role of lawyers, again broadly defined, is to ensure the effective, orderly regulation of the affairs of all persons in society and, at the same time, to ensure that such regulation is conducted in a manner consistent with the preservation of individual rights. It is always a balancing question, that is, one must always balance the protection of individual liberties against the preservation of the integrity of society as a whole, an integrity that flows from orderly regulation.

One interesting approach, in answer to the question as to the effectiveness of the law in achieving its social objectives, is contained in a recent treatise by Richard A. Posner, entitled *Economic Analysis of Law*,[111] in which the author conducts an analysis of the role of law in terms of economic principles, seeking to answer the fundamental question whether the law leads to economically correct solutions. He concludes, for example, in respect of the law of contracts, that the basic function of the law of contracts is to minimize breakdowns in the process of exchange. In addition, he observes that the economic function promoted in connection with negligence liability is not compensation for the victim, but rather deterrence of non-cost-justified accidents. Finally, in respect of the relationship between poverty and the criminal law, he states:

---

[108] See the Access to Information Act, R.S.C. 1985, c. A-1 and the Privacy Act, R.S.C. 1985, c. P-21. On the other hand, anti-discrimination legislation might be regarded as considering the opposite of a liberalizing effect. In this sense, anti-discrimination laws restrict the individual's freedom of choice (i.e., his freedom to discriminate), the exercise of which was previously permissible under the law.

[109] See D.C. Rowat, *The Ombudsman Plan — The Worldwide Spread of an Idea*, rev. 2nd ed. Lanham: University Press of America, 1985); and J.E. Richardson, *Having a Federal Ombudsman* (Edmonton: International Ombudsman Institute, 1986). See also R. Ivany (ed.), Special Anniversary Issue Commemorating Twenty Years of Ombudsmanship in Canada (1987), The Ombudsman Journal No. 7.

[110] An example of the articulation of a particular social objective may be found in the area of anti-competition law. Specifically, the 1969 Interim Report of the Economic Council of Canada promoted the specific social objective of achieving, by way of legislative reform, economic efficiency through the instrumentality of greater competition at the market place.

[111] 3rd ed. (Boston: Little Brown & Co., 1986).

Poverty imposes costs on the nonpoor that warrant, on strictly economic grounds and without regard to ethical or political considerations, incurring some costs to reduce it.

For example, poverty in the midst of a generally wealthy society is likely to increase the incidence of crime. One important cost of a criminal career, the forgone income of a legitimate alternative occupation, will be low for someone who has little earning capacity in legitimate occupations, while the proximity of wealth increases the expected return from crime, or stated another way, the cost of honesty.[112]

Another view advanced, on occasion, is that the lawyer has a role which might be described as that of a "social engineer". To some extent, the concept of social engineering is implicit in the lawyer's participation in the process of law reform, as well as the large participation of lawyers, generally, in the legislative process. Certainly, it is not illegitimate for a lawyer to regard himself as a social engineer; however that legitimacy is lost, no doubt, when a lawyer, in advancing a particular cause, behaves in a manner constituting unprofessional conduct.

Mark Green, a Washington lawyer and author of a treatise entitled *The Unseen Power of Washington Lawyers,* recently made these remarks:

It is an article of faith among lawyers, especially business lawyers, that they should zealously advocate their clients' cause without worrying about in moral unpopularity or social impact. "Any lawyer who surrenders this independence or shades this duty by trimming his professional course to fit the gusts of popular opinion in my judgment not only dishonours himself but disparages and degrades a great profession," wrote the venerable Wall Street attorney John W. Davis in 1924. "What is life worth, after all, if one has no philosophy of [one's] own to live by."

Admirers consider this soaring response the classic explanation of the lawyer's proper role. But others wonder exactly what philosophy it was that required Davis to devote his professional life to the House of Morgan.

A half century later, the law-for-hire ethic is still controversial. When, if ever, should a lawyer tell a client that a proposed argument or policy is unjust? Lawyers who answer that anything goes in legal combat overlook the fact that law is very much a public profession. Because lawyers are "officers of the court" licensed by the state and granted a monopoly of access to the judicial process, Louis Brandeis came to regard them as a kind of public utility, trustees of justice for us all. As he enjoyed saying, a lawyer should represent not merely his client, but the situation.[113]

Consider, in addition, the following remarks made by Dr. Max Wyman, in connection with the Canadian legal system:

Having said this, I am impelled to voice the deep concern I have about the vast ignorance that exists about the law and the legal process, an ignorance that exists both within and without the legal profession. It is almost unbelievable that the law and the legal process in Canada have no philosophical base, a base that should give purpose and scope to that law and to the legal process. It is inexcusable that there does not exist a definitive empirical base by means of which society can measure the effects that those laws have on the lives of people.

Our laws have grown like Topsy, without purpose, without scope, and without knowledge of their effect. With three-quarters of the twentieth century now passed into history, it is inexcusable that a twentieth century system of laws and a twentieth central system of legal procedures still remains to be written.

---

[112] *Ibid.*, p. 350.
[113] Newsweek Magazine, 16th June 1975,

My concern is heightened because of the high respect I have for the law and the legal process. That law and that legal process should be the mirror of civilization as it is now, or might be in the future, not of a civilization that existed hundreds of years ago. In Canada, that mirror has become distorted and opaque, and now reflects a grotesque image of civilization as it now has become.[114]

The role of law and lawyers in modern society is not the subject of universal agreement; rather it is the subject of considerable controversy. The law cannot, realistically, be regarded as the panacea of all the problems faced by contemporary society. However, it represents probably the best opportunity for members of society to collectively achieve desired social objectives. In turn, the legal system must be regarded as the structural framework in which the realization of this opportunity is brought about. It is the task of judges and lawyers to ensure that, within the framework, the law becomes an operational reality available to all persons that it governs, administered with its desired social objectives in mind.

It is not enough that modern legal thinkers simply devise new directions in our law. Any changes in our law and in our legal system must ultimately be designed to improve the quality of Canadian democracy. The test that must be applied in measuring the desirability of any new directions relates to the effects of those directions on the quality of democratic life and the preservation of individual freedom in a liberal, democratic society.

As indicated earlier, the law may be viewed as an opportunity to achieve international peace and progress, domestic tranquillity and major advancements in the quality of life. Moreover, the dictates of justice, fairness and equity demand that the Canadian legal system, in performing its functions, fulfil a promise. A judgment as to the success of Canadian law and the Canadian legal system, in fulfilling its promise and opportunity, is ultimately in the hands of future historians. It is incumbent upon lawyers, judges and members of society at large to ensure that our legal system does, indeed, fulfil its promise. In other words, as members of the legal profession in Canada or as members of the public at large, we jointly have the challenge, if not the shared responsibility, to mould the judgment of history. In short, to borrow the words of s. 1 of our Charter of Rights and Freedoms, we must preserve and protect the "free and

---

[114] Comments on the Criminal Law and the Legal Process, Alberta Board of Review, Provincial Courts (1975), p. 1. See also the following recent articles: Totenberg, "Behind the Marble, Beneath the Robes", New York Times Magazine, 16th March 1975; "America's Lawyers: 'A Sick Profession' " and "Why Courts are in Trouble", U.S. News & World Report, 25th March 1974 and 31st March 1975 respectively; and "Too Much Law", Newsweek Magazine, 10th January 1977. See also the following treatise: Auerbach, *Unequal Justice; Lawyers and Social Change in Modern America* (New York: Oxford University Press. 1975), and a review thereof in the New York Times Book Review, 25th January 1976.

democratic society'' that Canadians cherish. By the pursuit of innovative new directions, we can ensure that the Canadian legal system will continue to endure as a cornerstone of liberty and democracy in Canada.

INDEX